The Book of Acts
in the Setting
of Hellenistic History

The Book of Acts
in the Setting
of Hellenistic History

Colin J. Hemer

edited by Conrad H. Gempf

Eisenbrauns
Winona Lake, Indiana
1990

Published 1990 by Eisenbrauns, Winona Lake, Indiana, by special arrangement with J. C. B. Mohr (Paul Siebeck), D-7400 Tübingen. Originally published as volume 49 in the series Wissenschaftliche Untersuchungen zum Neuen Testament.

Reprinted 2015, in paperback
Paperback ISBN 978-1-57506-396-6

www.eisenbrauns.com

This book has been typeset on a standard Apple Macintosh Plus computer using the WriteNow word-processing program, and printed on the Tyndale House Apple Laser-Writer II using the Palatino font and the Tyndale House copies of Philip B. Payne's fonts for Greek and Hebrew in the final output.

Library of Congress Cataloging-in-Publication Data

Hemer, Colin J.
    The book of Acts in the setting of Hellenistic history / Colin J. Hemer ; edited by Conrad H. Gempf.
    p.   cm.
    Reprint. Originally published: Tübingen : J. C. B. Mohr, © 1989. (Wissenschaftliche Untersuchungen zum Neuen Testament ; 49)
    Includes bibliographical references and index.
    ISBN 0-931464-58-7
    1. Bible. N.T. Acts—History of contemporary events. I. Gempf, Conrad H. II. Title. III. Series: Wissenschaftliche Untersuchungen zum Neuen Testament ; 49.
BS2625.2.H415   1990
226'.6'067—dc20
                                              90-45799

The paper used in this publication meets the minimum requirements of the American National Standard for Information Sciences—Permanence of Paper for Printed Library Materials, ANSI Z39.48-1984.@™

Contents

Foreword

The question of the value of the Book of Acts as a source for the history of the early church has been discussed to such an extent that W.W. Gasque felt it right to organize his survey of modern study of Acts in terms of the answers given to this question. After a period when Luke's historical usefulness was given an extremely low rating in the dominant school represented by P. Vielhauer, E. Haenchen and H. Conzelmann, there appears to be some redressing of the balance away from this extreme assessment. In Germany a plea for a fresh look at Acts was made by M. Hengel in a brief but stimulating survey. More recently the question has been reopened by G. Lüdemann in an important effort to identify the traditions preserved in Acts and to assess their probable historical value. Presented, as it is, by a critical scholar who can be highly sceptical regarding certain aspects of Luke's work, Lüdeman's book is representative of a strand of scholarship which is more open to the possibility that Acts contains valuable historical information.

British scholarship has tended to be less concerned with the kind of traditio-historical analysis of the text practised on the Continent but stronger on the archaeological side. The pioneer work of W.M. Ramsay demonstrated clearly the value of examining Acts in the light of study of ancient geography, history and chronology, and, as is well known, Ramsay, who started as a sceptic regarding the historical value of Acts, came to describe the historical qualities of Luke in terms that might well be regarded as excessive. The same tradition of examining Acts from the angle of the Classical historian has continued with F.F. Bruce as its major exponent. And now we have the work of C.J. Hemer.

Colin Hemer is yet another example (like Bruce) of the Classicist turned New Testament scholar. He gave up a career in school-teaching to do research on the background to the messages to the seven churches in Revelation. His doctoral thesis (1969) was eventually published in 1986. The long delay was due to the development of Dr Hemer's interest in two related fields. The one was the study of Hellenistic Greek, and it led to his becoming deeply involved in the plans of Macquarie University to produce a new 'Moulton and Milligan' in which the fresh epigraphic and papyrological discoveries of the last sixty years or so would have been utilized to shed fresh light on the vocabulary of the New Testament. Sadly this project must now go ahead without the participation of one of its most enthusiastic protagonists. The other field was the historical background to Acts.

Over the years Dr Hemer produced a steady stream of meticulously researched essays on different aspects of the problem, and eventually conceived the plan of writing a fuller work which would be a fresh and rigorous re-examination of the kind of material presented by Ramsay. This in turn would form the preparatory material for a commentary on Acts which he was to co-author with Dr W.W. Gasque.

Early in 1987 Dr Hemer fell ill and he died in June of that year. Fortunately his work on Acts was well advanced, and it was immediately apparent that, though what had been completed lacked the author's final revision and some parts were in draft form, the manuscript was largely in a publishable form. The task of editing and completing the work was entrusted to Mr Conrad H. Gempf, and on behalf of Colin's many friends I should like to express our deep gratitude to him for his diligence and care in this labour of love.

Manifestly the work as here presented lacks the final touches that Dr Hemer would have added. It was judged appropriate not to attempt to interact with subsequent literature, although a number of references and an appendix have been added by the editor. The reader will spot some gaps in assessment of the earlier literature (there is, for example, no reference to A. Suhl's important work on chronology) which Dr Hemer would surely have remedied if he had been spared. There are also topics on which treatment was planned but there are insufficient hints in the author's meticulous notes as to how he would have tackled them.

Some readers may perhaps be tempted to dismiss the author's approach on two grounds. First, it may be argued that he ignores the whole question of *Traditionsgeschichte*, the attempt to penetrate behind the text to the sources and traditions which lay behind it. Hemer of course argues cautiously for authorship by Luke, the companion of Paul, and therefore he would have seen the whole question of sources differently from those who argue for non-Lukan authorship. What he does is to look at the text as we have it to see how it stands up historically. If it is not only plausible but has some probability attaching to it, this is good reason to claim a historical base for it.

Second, the whole approach may be dismissed as *apologetisch*. This, however, seems to be nothing more than a swear-word for condemning the work of anybody who defends a traditional position by suggesting that their work rests on bias rather than on an objective use of the evidence. One may well ask whether the attitude of anybody with a hypothesis to defend is any different; everybody looks for the evidence that supports their hypothesis and attempts to account for seemingly contrary evidence. If the hypothesis is an old one rather than a new one, one that is more in line with orthodox Christian thinking rather than with novel ideas, it is hard to see why it should be more liable to being dismissed in this way. What matters every time is surely the quality of the evidence and the argumentation, the absence of special pleading, and whether awkward counter-evidence and arguments are treated fairly. It is on that level that this work must be evaluated.

Dr Hemer's work involves some highly detailed discussion of specialist areas. It is not all written simply in defence of a thesis. There is much detail which he has unearthed which is interesting to specialists in itself and which he has not scrupled to include. Here is the mark of a genuine historian who writes not because he has an axe to grind but because the subject is fascinating for its own sake.

I. Howard Marshall

Preface

The death of Colin Hemer, research fellow at Tyndale House, Cambridge, in the spring of 1987 came as a blow and a shock to many of us who knew him and his work. It seemed especially sad in that he had spent years reading, learning, accumulating knowledge, and was just at the point of beginning to burst out with monograph after monograph applying this wealth of learning. Fortunately for us, most chapters of a first draft of his manuscript on History and the Book of Acts were complete.

The appearance of the manuscript was indicative of the mind behind it. Meticulous, clear, and densely packed, each of the nearly 400 narrow-ruled hand-written notebook pages contained twice the amount of material that the single-spaced typed versions could hold. Every 't' was crossed, every 'i' dotted; only very rarely was there a false start or a word crossed out.

Our process of preparing the manuscript for publication was straightforward. The staff at Tyndale House in Cambridge typed the manuscript onto computer disks. Each chapter would be edited for stylistic consistency and typographical errors. Once all the references were checked over, I would type-set the chapter and send it to readers for suggestions and comments, which would then be incorporated before printing a final camera-ready version of the chapter. It has been my aim to reduce the massive manuscript down and produce a book which sets forth Dr Hemer's views clearly, and which preserves at least some of the personality that made his writings and papers unique.

Dr Hemer's projections were for an even longer work, incorporating three more chapters than the present volume. Our Appendix 1 contains general material on speeches and miracles which were originally intended to be the subjects of separate chapters in their own right, chapters which were unfinished at the time of Dr Hemer's death.[1]

The Chapter 10 (the Conclusion) is the work of the editor, drawing together the threads of Dr Hemer's arguments in the book in the manner of an overview. Because of the importance of the recently published Aphrodisias inscription to some recent discussion on Acts, I have undertaken to compose the second appendix. This sets forth the place of that inscription in the context of the arguments in the book, consistent with the thought of Dr Hemer as expressed on related topics.[2] Other material added to the manuscript, usually notes of supplemental bibliography, are marked by the abbreviation [Ed.] whether the note stems from me or from other readers.

This book has been enhanced through the suggestions, comments and criticisms of Prof. Howard Marshall and Prof. F.F. Bruce, who read through the

---

1   Some extra material on particular speeches will be published in the form of articles in future volumes of the *Tyndale Bulletin*. With only 1 page of text extant, we have not attempted to reconstruct a chapter that was to have been titled 'Penultimate Problems', dealing with the purpose of Acts, among other topics.

2   Dr Hemer knew about the discovery of the inscription, but died before its publication.

entire book prior to publication. I am also grateful for the help of Mr David Deboys, the Tyndale House librarian, and Dr G.H.R. Horsley on the selections they read. Michael Howe and Carl Trueman joined me for the last two months of the project, checking the bibliographic references in chapters 6-9 and compiling all the indexes except the Subject Index. I am also indebted to Heather Richardson, Ruth Otway and Cathy Wegner for their work in typing the manuscript.

This book was prepared under the direction of the Tyndale House Council, and under the patient, watchful and encouraging guidance of Bruce Winter, the current warden of Tyndale House. Anyone who has worked for any length of time at Tyndale House in Cambridge knows what a idyllic place it is for doing research. Elements like the extensive New Testament collection of books and the comraderie at afternoon tea-time have, I am sure, influenced more than one scholar's ideas of the Paradise to come.

Others at Tyndale House have been of great help in a number of ways. I must at least mention Stan Toussaint, Marcy Massot, Peter Head, Stan Porter and Michael Thompson for their assistance. Thanks to Prof. Paul Wegner for unlocking the door every morning.

All students of Luke-Acts will be indebted to Colin Hemer for the scholarship which he has passed on through his book. As one who had already devoted several years of study to a more narrow topic in the book of Acts, I could not help but be awed by the depth and the breadth of Colin Hemer's knowledge and research. We might well say of Dr Hemer's work and life: '...though dead, he still speaks' (Hebrews 11:4).

Conrad H. Gempf

List of Principal Abbreviations

ABR	*Australian Biblical Review*
AJA	*American Journal of Archaelolgy*
AJP	*American Journal of Philology*
AJT	*American Journal of Theology*
Anc Soc	*Ancient Society*
ANRW	*Aufsteig und Niedergang der römischen Welt,* ed. H. Temporini
AS	*Anatolian Studies*
AthMitt	*Mitteilungen des deutschen archäologischen Instituts. Athenische Abteilung*
BA	*The Biblical Archaeologist*
BAGD	Bauer, Arndt, Gingrich and Danker, *A Greek-English Lexicon of the New Testament and Other Early Christian Literature*
BASOR	*Bulletin of the American School of Oriental Research*
BC	*Beginnings of Christianity,* ed. Foakes Jackson and Lake
BCH	*Bulletin de correspondance hellénique*
BGU	*Berliner greichische Urkunden (Aegyptische Urkunden aus den königlichen Museen zu Berlin)*
Bib Res	*Biblical Research*
BJRL	*Bulletin of the John Rylands Library, Manchester*
BMC	*Catalogue of Greek Coins in the British Museum*
BRD	W.M. Ramsay, *The Bearing of Recent Discoveries on the Trustworthiness of the New Testament*
BS	*Bibliotheca Sacra*
BT	*The Biblical Translator*
BZ	*Biblische Zeitschrift*
CAH	*Cambridge Ancient History*
CB	W.M. Ramsay, *Cities and Bishoprics of Phrygia,* 2 Vols.

CIG	Corpus Inscriptionum Graecarum
CIJ	Corpus Inscriptionum Iudaicarum
CIL	Corpus Inscriptionum Latinarum
CIS	Corpus Inscriptionum Semiticarum
CMRDM	Corpus Monumentorum Religionis Dei Menis
CP	Classical Philology
CR	Classical Review
CRAI	Comptes-rendus de l'Académie des Inscriptions et Belles-lettres
CRE	W.M. Ramsay, The Church in the Roman Empire before AD 170
CSP	W.M. Ramsay, The Cities of St. Paul
Dibelius, Studies	Martin Dibelius, Studies in the Acts of the Apostles
EB	Encylopedia Biblica, ed. T.K. Cheyne and J.S. Black
EBr	Encyclopedia Brittanica
EE	Ephemeris Epigraphica
ETL	Ephemeridum Theologicarum Lovaniensium
Expos	The Expositor
ExpT	Expository Times
FGH	Die Fragmente der greicheschen Historiker, ed. F. Jacoby
FTh	Faith and Thought
GPR	Die Griechischen Personennamen in Rom, ed. H. Solin
GGM	Geographici Graeci Minores, ed. C. Müller, 1855-61
HN	Historia Numina, ed. B.V. Head
HDB	A Dictionary of the Bible, ed. J. Hastings
HTR	Harvard Theological Review
HUCA	Hebrew Union College Annual
ICC	International Critical Commentary
I. Cret.	Inscriptiones Creticae, ed. M. Guarducci
IDB	Interpreter's Dictionary of the Bible
IEJ	Israel Exploration Journal
I. Eph.	Die Inschriften von Ephesus, ed. H. Wankel
IG	Inscriptiones Graecae
IGLS	Inscriptions Grecques et Latines de la Syrie
IGUR	Inscriptiones Graecae Urbis Romae

IGRR	*Inscriptiones Graecae ad Res Romanas pertinentes*
ILS	*Inscriptiones Latinae Selectae,* ed. H. Dessau
ISBE	*The International Standard Bible Encyclopedia,* ed. G.W. Bromiley
I. Smyrna	*Die Inschriften von Smyrna,* ed. K. Petzl
JBL	*Journal of Biblical Literature*
JEH	*Journal of Ecclesiatical History*
JHS	*Journal of Hellenic Studies*
JJS	*Journal of Jewish Studies*
JÖAI	*Jahreshefte des Österreichischen Archäolog. Instituts in Wien*
JRS	*Journal of Roman Studies*
JSNT	*Journal for the Study of the New Testament*
JTS	*Journal of Theological Studies*
Kremer, *Les Actes*	*Les Actes des Apôtres,* ed. Kremer
LSJ	*A Greek-English Lexicon,* ed. Liddell, Scott and Jones
MAMA	*Monumenta Asiae Minoris Antiqua*
MM	J.H. Moulton and G. Milligan, *The Vocabulary of the Greek New Testament Illustrated from Papyri and other Non-Literary Sources*
NBC	*New Bible Commentary*
New Docs.	*New Documents Illustrating Early Christianity*
NovT	*Novum Testamentum*
NTA	*New Testament Abstracts*
NTS	*New Testament Studies*
OGIS	*Orientis Graeci Inscriptiones Selectae,* ed. W. Dittenberger
Pauline Studies Bruce	*Pauline Studies: Essays Presented to F.F. Bruce* (ed. by Hagner and Harris) (Exeter: Paternoster, 1980)
PASA	*Papers of the American School at Athens*
PEQ	*Palestine Exploration Quarterly*
PIR	*Prosopographia Imperii Romani* ed. E. Groag, A. Stein, *et al.*
PTR	*Princeton Theological Review*
PW	A. Pauly, G. Wissowa and W. Kroll, *Real-Encyclopädie die klassischen Altertumswissenschaft*

RB	*Revue Biblique*
REG	*Revue des Études Grecques*
Rev Exp	*Review and Expositor*
RHR	*Revue de l'Historie des Religions*
RQ	*Restoration Quarterly*
RSRL	*Roman Society and Roman Law in the New Testament*, Sherwin-White
RTR	*Reformed Theological Review*
SB	*Sammelbuch greichischer Urkunden aus Aegypten*, ed. F. Preisigke *et al.*
SE	*Studia Evangelica*, ed. by F. Cross
SEG	*Supplementum Epigraphicum Graecum*
SERP	*Studies in the History and Art of the Eastern Provinces of the Roman Empire*, ed. W.M. Ramsay
SIG3	*Sylloge Inscriptionum Graecarum*, ed. W. Dittenberger, 3rd edition
SLA	*Studies in Luke-Acts*, ed. Keck and Martyn
SPTR	W.M. Ramsay, *St. Paul the Traveller and Roman Citizen*
TAM	*Tituli Asiae Minoris*, ed. E. Kalinka *et al.*
TAPA	*Transactions of the American Philological Association*
TB	*Tyndale Bulletin*
TDNT	*Theological Dictionary of the New Testament*
TLZ	*Theologische Literaturzeitung*
Textual Comm.	B. Metzger, *A Textual Commentary on the Greek New Testament*
UBS	*The Greek New Testament* (United Bible Societies)
ZNW	*Zeitschrift für die neutestamentliche Wissenschaft*
ZPE	*Zeitschrift für Papyrologie und Epigraphik*
ZTK	*Zeitschrift für Theologie und Kirche*

Chapter 1
Acts and Historicity

1. The Neglect of Historicity

Although there has been no lack of debate about the book of Acts, the question of its historicity has been strangely neglected. Indeed, opinion about the book of Acts has become polarized, and often between those who differ profoundly on the matter of historicity,[1] but this aspect of their disagreement is often implicit rather than explicit. It is integrated into differences of assumption and approach whose thrusts are aimed elsewhere. Many writers seem simply to assume that the question has been answered, one way or the other. Some even contend that the question is illegitimate, although again there is an answer implicit in such a contention.

A vast body of literature covers details within the range of our inquiry and deals with topics tangentially related to historicity, but few major works address the subject directly. The only two book-length studies in English are old discursive lecture-series, directed to a scholarly ambience very different from ours and much less deeply riven by confusing alternatives.[2] There is no focused or systematic treatment of the issues for our modern situation.[3]

---

1 Cf. W.C. van Unnik, 'Luke-Acts, a Storm Center in Contemporary Scholarship', *Studies in Luke-Acts*, ed. L.E. Keck and J.L. Martyn (Nashville: Abingdon Press, 1966), pp. 15-32.

2 J.S. Howson, *The Evidential Value of the Acts of the Apostles*, Bohlen Lectures 1880 (London: William Isbister, 1880); F.H. Chase, *The Credibility of the Book of The Acts of the Apostles, Hulsean Lectures 1900-01* (London and New York: Macmillan, 1902). There have of course been many commentaries and works on allied themes in which the issues have been raised. The most extensive and detailed of these studies are again old. The fullest sceptical treatment (from the classical Tübingen perspective) is in E. Zeller, *The Contents and Origin of the Acts of the Apostles, Critically Investigated*, tr. J. Dare, 2 vols. (London: Williams and Norgate, 1875-76). The only detailed study from a more conservative perspective is A. Wikenhauser, *Die Apostelgeschichte und ihr Geschichtswert* (Münster-Westfalen: Aschendorffsche Verlagsbuchhandlung, 1921).

3 [Ed.] G. Lüdemann's recent work *Das frühe Christentum nach den Traditionen der Apostelgeschichte* (Göttingen: Vandenhoeck & Ruprecht, 1987) was released only after Dr Hemer's untimely death.

There are, of course, some reasons for this neglect. One of them is so central to the modern approach that it seems an act of temerity to challenge it: the current all-pervasive interest in Lukan theology. While this interest is proper and important, it has been so emphasized that it has come to seem that the *only* correct way to study Acts is to focus on the writer and his theological grounds for altering (or preserving) tradition. Any approach that does not incorporate such redaction-critical concerns is made to look naïve and irrelevant. But complementary, and equally necessary, questions must be asked if we are to achieve a broadly balanced perspective on the whole range of the evidence.

A second reason, akin to the first, is the increasing specialization of modern scholarship. Again, proper in itself, this necessarily focuses attention upon the pressing current issues, narrows the field of debate, and may render inaccessible the insights of related disciplines. Lack of communication between specialists has become a major problem.

Thirdly, there is a lingering suspicion that the topic of historicity is peculiarly the preserve of a historicist pseudo-scholarship, often equated with a crude and simplistic abuse of archaeology for apologetic ends. If the polarization of opinion is in any measure due to a doctrinaire defensiveness or polemicism induced by anti-critical attitudes, people are understandably uneasy. This ghost ought to be laid to rest, and striving for fair and charitable scholarship will help to lay it. The issues raised by Acts are complex and many-faceted, and there is wide scope for seeking answers on their own merits. There is nothing inherently anti-critical about the question itself, though to ask it may be out of step with current trends. If the investigation is a rational and careful one, neither misunderstandings nor lack of communication nor the nature of the conclusions it yields should bias us against it. Yet the fact that such study is on a 'different wavelength'— one associated with a certain viewpoint— may have prejudiced scholars against considering the question.

A final reason for the neglect of our topic may well be the daunting complexity and delicacy of the task it poses. It is impossible to deal adequately with the theme without entanglement in many related New Testament debates and in the contributions of related disciplines, and without having to wade through many confusing cross-currents of opinion. But the temptation to provide either answer by over-simplifying the issues must be avoided.

2. Historicity and Scholarship

Ironically, this question *was* being tackled with Luke-Acts particularly in mind before certain historical circumstances side-tracked the discussion. Although this is not the place for a detailed account of *Actaforschung*,[4] an overview of the literature that touches on historicity and Acts will help to give direction to our discussion. The purpose of this section is merely to focus on a few points which seem to have been largely overlooked, but which are of immediate interest for our specific theme of historicity.

In the period approximately 1895-1915 there was a far-reaching, multi-faceted, high-level debate over the historicity of Acts.[5] It is interesting to note that in the Mattill bibliography of Acts[6] only six items out of sixty-eight listed as general studies on the theology of Acts are from this span of years. That proportion is representative of most other topics as well. Conversely, of a slightly smaller number of total entries on the historical value of Acts a clear *majority* belonged to those years.[7] Moreover, detailed discussions of closely related issues are a stronger feature of those years than general studies.

For the purposes of this limited discussion, we will exclude from consideration the important figure of J.B. Lightfoot, who died in 1889, at the outset of the years we have delineated. Indeed, the period 1895-1915 marks the climax of a preceding continuity. Lightfoot, as it happens, wrote relatively little specifically on Acts, and the appearance of Ramsay's *Church in the Roman Empire* at once dated him on a significant point and initiated a new and vigorous phase of debate by placing the South Galatian view on a firm basis and focusing on its implications for Acts.

Apart from Ramsay's series of books, these two decades were

---

[4] A task performed adequately from different perspectives by Haenchen, *Acts*, pp. 14-50 = *Apostelgeschichte*, 6th (15th) edn, pp. 13-47, and W.W. Gasque, *A History of the Criticism of the Acts of the Apostles* (Tübingen: J.C.B. Mohr, 1975).

[5] The period may even be delimited more precisely, i.e., by the publication of Ramsay's *Church in the Roman Empire* in 1893 and the outbreak of war in 1914, but the rounded half-decade limits have been chosen to allow time for publication and reaction.

[6] Mattill, *A Classified Bibliography of Literature on the Acts of the Apostles* (*New Testament Tools and Studies*, VII, ed. B.M. Metzger) (Leiden: Brill, 1966). More recent systematic bibliography will be found in G. Wagner, *An Exegetical Bibliography on the Acts of the Apostles* (Rüschlikon-Zürich: Baptist Theological Seminary, 1975) and *id.*, Second Series (1985).

[7] Mattill, pp. 189-93. Indeed, it would be possible to manipulate the data or extend the limits slightly, to produce an even more impressive contrast!

marked by some notable, and often neglected or undervalued, works. British scholarship, even in the preceding Victorian period, had produced influential studies, such as the monographs of James Smith[8] and W.K. Hobart,[9] the commentary in Alford's *Greek Testament*[10] and the comprehensive work of Conybeare and Howson,[11] as well as the magisterial contributions of Lightfoot. Most of these works are now decisively dated by the later progress of knowledge, though Smith has never been bettered,[12] and much of Lightfoot's achievement stands— except on the Galatian question, on which topic, paradoxically, he is still most often cited.[13] Ramsay then initiated a new phase, in which the fruits of pioneer exploration initiated a new understanding of Paul's Anatolian context in particular. One may choose to differ from Ramsay's views of the New Testament, but there is no doubt that in his own field he represents the beginning of modern knowledge, and those who disagree most strongly with him are no less indebted to him for the factual data which entered the debate through his discoveries. Ramsay's own views underwent progressive change during the two following decades: he understood this change as the gradual enlightenment of one blinded by preformed opinions;[14] he was working out the implications of the new knowledge in a context of keen debate.

The period 1895-1915 saw the appearance of the two crucial com-

---

[8] J. Smith, *The Voyage and Shipwreck of St. Paul* (London: Longmans, Green & Co., 3rd edn, 1866).

[9] W.K. Hobart, *The Medical Language of St. Luke* (Dublin: Hodges, Figgis and Co., and London: Longmans, Green & Co., 1882).

[10] H. Alford, 'The Acts of the Apostles', in *The Greek Testament*, 4 vols (London: Rivingtons and Cambridge: Deighton, Bell and Co., new edn, 1880-81), Vol. 2, Prolegomena pp. 1-31 and Commentary pp. 1-310).

[11] W.J. Conybeare and J.S. Howson, *The Life and Epistles of St Paul*, 2 vols. (London: Longman, Brown, Green and Longmans, 1853).

[12] [Ed.] Dr Hemer had not the chance to read and compare G. Kettenbach, *Das Logbuch des Lukas* (European University Studies, Series 23: Theology 276) (Frankfurt, Bern and New York: P. Lang, 1986). I am grateful to Mr Peter Head for drawing the book to my attention.

[13] It cannot be too strongly emphasized that Lightfoot's death antedated the new knowledge, and that those who hold the 'North Galatian' view today usually do so on grounds which contradict positions held in common by *both* sides of the earlier debate. This does not invalidate the 'North Galatian' interpretation, but it shows that Lightfoot's name ought not to be invoked without discrimination of his arguments and recognition that they are superseded. Cf. Hemer, 'The Adjective "Phrygia"', *JTS* n.s. 27 (1976), pp. 122-26, esp. p. 123; 'Phrygia: A Further Note', *JTS* n.s. 28 (1977), pp. 99-101.

[14] He expresses this perspective strikingly in a private letter to F.C. Burkitt, published in *EQ* 45 (1973), pp. 170-71.

mentaries of R.J. Knowling (1900)[15] and R.B. Rackham (1901),[16] respectively historical and theological in their emphases, and Rackham contributed also a classic defence of the early date of Acts.[17] Ramsay himself produced *St Paul the Traveller* (1895), *Cities and Bishoprics of Phrygia* (1895, 1897), *A Historical Commentary on St Paul's Epistle to the Galatians* (1899), *Pauline and Other Studies* (1906), *The Cities of St Paul* (1907), *Luke the Physician* (1908), *The Bearing of Recent Discovery on the Trustworthiness of the New Testament* (1915), to mention only books directly relevant to our theme.[18] The vigorous ensuing debate involved such British scholars as F.H. Chase, J.A. Cross, C.W. Emmett, M. Jones, F. Rendall, C. Anderson Scott, W.A. Shedd and W.T. Whitley,[19] and there was much interaction also with the contributions of such major figures as Harnack, Headlam[20] and Lightfoot. In America the major names were those of B.W. Bacon,[21] A.C. McGiffert[22] and C.C. Torrey.[23]

In Germany there were relatively few major studies of Acts in this period. The chief commentary was that by H.H. Wendt which appeared in successive editions in the Meyer series,[24] and Wendt addressed himself specifically to the question of historicity.[25] But the

15 R.J. Knowling, 'The Acts of the Apostles', *The Expositor's Greek Testament*, ed. W. Robertson Nicoll, Vol. 2 (London: Hodder & Stoughton, 1900), pp. 1-554.

16 R.B. Rackham, *The Acts of the Apostles. An Exposition* (London: Methuen, 5th edn, 1910 [1901]).

17 'The Acts of the Apostles. II A Plea for an Early Date', *JTS* 1 (1900), pp. 76-87.

18 I cite here only short titles, omitting some more popular or controversial works. All these books were published by Hodder and Stoughton, except *Cities and Bishoprics*, Vol. 1, Parts 1 and 2, by the Clarendon Press, Oxford, only these two separately bound 'Parts' ever being produced. Ramsay also wrote dozens of papers during this period, many of them being collected in some of the volumes mentioned here.

19 See Mattill, *Classified Bibliography*, for detailed references to the more important articles, chiefly in *Expos* and *ExpT*.

20 A.C. Headlam, 'Acts of the Apostles', *HDB* 1 (1900), pp. 25-35.

21 Bacon produced no large work on the subject, but see his book *The Story of St Paul* (London: Hodder & Stoughton, 1905), and for major articles see the bibliography in Mattill.

22 A.C. McGiffert, *A History of Christianity in the Apostolic Age* (Edinburgh: T. & T. Clark, 1897; revised edn, New York: Charles Scribner's Sons, 1903).

23 C.C. Torrey, *The Composition and Date of Acts* (Cambridge, MA: Harvard University Press, 1916).

24 H.H. Wendt, *Kritisch-exegetischer Kommentar über das Neue Testament von Dr. Heinr. Aug. Wilh. Meyer*, 8th- 9th eds. (Göttingen: Vandenhoeck & Ruprecht, 1880, 1888, 1888, 1889, 1913).

25 Wendt, 'The Historical Trustworthiness of the Book of Acts', *Hibbert*

figure of central interest for our present study was Harnack. Other of the major contributions of the time were incidental to our theme, as contained in more extensive New Testament Introductions (Zahn,[26] Jülicher[27]), or studies of particular issues (e.g. Blass).[28] Harnack however wrote three books within a few years which document a progressive shift of opinion.[29] In *Luke the Physician* he defended the traditional view of authorship while holding to a later date and remaining critical of the historical value of Acts. In the third of the series he strongly urges the early dating of Acts as well as traditional Lukan authorship.[30]

The case of Harnack is instructive, both as an instance of a progressive change of position induced by the influence of the British debate, and because his contribution to further discussion was abruptly truncated by the impact of the war. In the conclusion of his second volume (*Acts*, pp. 301-303) he acknowledges that his results closely approach those of Blass, Ramsay, (Bernhard) Weiss and Zahn, writers whom he censures for their prejudices in favour of miracles and the canon of the New Testament. While they are suspect as apologists, he as a historical critic is constrained to take similar ground.[31] In all three books he reacts freely to British scholarship, a point observed by his translator in his Preface (pp. vii-viii):

Journal 12 (1913-14), pp. 141-61.

[26] T. Zahn, *Einleitung in das Neue Testament* 2 vols. (Leipzig: A. Deichert, 2nd edn, 1900); ET *Introduction to the New Testament*, tr. Melancthon Williams Jacobus *et al.* from the 3rd German edn, 3 vols. (Edinburgh: T. & T. Clark, 1909).

[27] A. Jülicher, *Einleitung in das Neue Testament* (Tübingen and Leipzig: J.C.B. Mohr, 3rd edn 1901).

[28] F. Blass, *Acta Apostolorum, sive Lucae ad Theophilum liber alter, secundum formam quae videtur Romanam* (Leipzig: Teubner, 1896).

[29] A. von Harnack, *Luke the Physician. The Author of the Third Gospel and the Acts of the Apostles*, tr. J.R. Wilkinson (London: Williams & Norgate and New York: Putnam, 1911), from *Lukas der Arzt: Der Verfasser des dritten Evangeliums und der Apostelgeschichte* (Leipzig: Hinrichs, 1906); *The Acts of the Apostles* (London and New York, 1909), from *Die Apostelgeschichte* (Leipzig: Hinrichs, 1908); *The Date of the Acts and of the Synoptic Gospels* (London: Williams & Norgate and New York: Putnam, 1911), from *Neue Untersuchungen zur Apostelgeschichte und zur Abfassungszeit der synoptischen Evangelien* (Leipzig: Hinrichs, 1911).

[30] In an excursus at the end of the second book (*Acts*, pp. 290-97) Harnack sets out weighty reasons for both the early and the later dating, but chooses to leave the question open.

[31] Of Zahn he writes: 'Zahn cannot efface the impression that he conducts historical investigations like a counsel for the defence *à tout prix*' (p. 303).

that translator further confesses his own 'shock' at the views now propounded by the great German scholar and Harnack's 'reluctant yet complete conversion' to a position he had himself 'denounced ... as unscientific'. Yet despite all this it should be stressed that throughout these researches Harnack remained very critical, at times contemptuous, of Luke's 'inaccuracies and discrepancies',[32] a point which drew fire from Ramsay and others.[33] Otherwise his work had limited impact at the time, and the war marked a sharp discontinuity in the progress of scholarship.[34]

Some post-war perspectives on Harnack make this point clearly. James Stalker describes his change of mind as a 'revolution' in scholarship. Yet the great importance of his three books 'has failed to attract attention on account of the War'.[35] The large lives of Paul since published by Prof. David Smith and Prof. A.H. McNeile never refer to Harnack's views.[36] Stalker stresses that Harnack was only feeling his way in these books, though they were fruits of a slow growth over fifteen years, written under obligation to British scholars. It was no doubt largely due to Ramsay that he came to regard

---

[32] It is difficult to acquit Harnack here of an exaggerated hypercriticism. He offers a lengthy list of inaccuracies (*Acts* pp. 203-31), but most of the entries are bizarrely trivial: μέν without following δέ, shifts between direct and indirect speech, grammatical concord *ad sensum*, abrupt changes of subject or the unexplained introduction of new persons and topics, tautologies, *anacolutha*, awkwardnesses of narrative sequence, and the like. Few of the substantial historical difficulties are mentioned. It should be noted that Harnack's point is that these features are found alike in all the strands of source-material he isolates, and therefore belong to Luke's own style and indicate literary carelessness on his part.

[33] See esp. Ramsay in the title essay of *Luke the Physician and Other Studies in the History of Religion* (London: Hodder and Stoughton, 1908), pp. 3-68, in response to Harnack's first book. Cf. E.C. Selwyn, 'The Carefulness of Luke the Prophet', *Expos* 7th ser. 7 (1909), pp. 547-58.

[34] Among early discussions note J. Moffatt, 'Harnack on the Acts of the Apostles', *ExpT* 19 (1907-08), pp. 454-55; B.W. Bacon, 'Professor Harnack on the Lukan Narrative', *AJT* 13 (1909), pp. 59-76; C. Anderson Scott, 'Harnack on the Acts', *ExpT* 22 (1910-11), p. 567; M. Jones, 'Harnack on the Dates of the Acts and Synoptic Gospels', *Expos* 8th ser. 7 (1914), pp. 193-212. Moffatt's expectation that his 'sane, vigorous pages will help to dominate the criticism of Acts for years to come' (p. 455) was scarcely fulfilled.

[35] J. Stalker, 'A Revolution in New Testament Criticism', *Expos* 8th ser. 20 (1920), pp. 348-63, citing p. 348.

[36] D. Smith, *The Life and Letters of St Paul* (London: Hodder and Stoughton, 1919); A.H. McNeile, *St Paul. His Life, Letters and Christian Doctrine* (CUP, 1920). Neither book has an author index, but McNeile seems only to mention Harnack in a different connection.

Luke as a real and interesting human being, where even such as Wellhausen lived 'so long in a paper-world of editors and redactors as to have lost touch with the actual world' (p. 352). Stalker himself is confident that Ramsay's early dating of Galatians, a key point for the historicity of Acts, was slowly winning the assent of scholars. Harnack's contribution served to challenge the strength of the Tübingen assumptions which had influenced even Zahn, and opened the way for a more straightforward reconstruction of primitive Christian history.

In America J. Gresham Machen wrote in similar terms, stressing the astonishing 'return to tradition' among those known for their scepticism, among whom he names Harnack and Torrey, and seeing a similar tendency even in Wendt and McGiffert.[37] Harnack and others had 'introduced a dangerous antinomy into the imposing "liberal" reconstruction', to which late datings were integral. If their views were accepted, the objection to the New Testament account of Christian origins would be seen 'more and more clearly to be simply and solely an objection to the miraculous' (p. 593). Machen, too, sees the relation of Acts and Galatians as a central crux,[38] where the identification of the visit to Jerusalem in Gal. 2 with that of Acts 15 is problematic, and the difficulties in this area constitute a 'last stronghold of Tübingenism'; but this stronghold is not immune from attack. He considers the possibility of identifying Gal. 2 with Acts 11 rather than Acts 15, and dating Galatians early.

The First World War marked a definite break, and when work was resumed there was a shift of interest, and new initiatives came to the fore.[39] The rise of Form Criticism and Dibelius' development of the 'Style Criticism' of Acts in particular[40] superannuated not only Harnack's views but the debate in which he stood as protagonist.[41] From the new phase of mainstream German criticism his pre-war researches seemed an irrelevant aberration.[42] The war abruptly

---

[37] J.G. Machen, 'Recent Criticism of the Book of Acts', *PTR* 17 (1919), pp. 585-608.

[38] Cf. B.W. Bacon, 'Acts versus Galatians. The Crux of Apostolic History', *AJT* 11 (1907), pp. 454-74.

[39] Cf. G.D. Henderson, 'Adolf von Harnack', *ExpT* 41 (1929-30), pp. 487-91, referring on p. 488 to Harnack's attraction to British students 'until the gloomy years of the Great War turned our young divines somewhat vaguely to France and America for guidance'.

[40] M. Dibelius, 'Style Criticism of the Books of the Acts', *Studies*, pp. 1-25.

[41] For reaction to Harnack and others in this period cf. Gasque, *History of Criticism* pp. 160-63. There is perhaps a partial parallel in the supersession of the Jesus-debate of Wrede, Johannes Weiss and Albert Schweitzer by the post-war climate of criticism.

[42] Another remarkable instance of the discontinuity of this period is the

closed an era in some ways more vigorous than that which follows. Its debates were truncated unresolved, but perhaps fruitfully on the way to resolution, if we may believe some of the optimistic prognoses. In the event scholarship in the German and English-speaking countries took different, and separate, courses after the war.

The most impressive product in English of the new era was of course the five volumes of *The Beginnings of Christianity*. It is remarkable that a great synthesis of this type should have appeared at just the time it did (1920-1933). This synthesis departs in major respects from the thrust of the preceding debate, and shifts some of the questions on to ground different from its trend. It was clearly a valid and important function of this period to test the foundations, and Cadbury's work, for instance, in exposing the inadequacy of Hobart's *Medical Language* as proof of authorship is an admirable example of a type of scholarship constantly needed.[43] This is no place for a detailed evaluation of *Beginnings*. Inevitably, in a composite work of such scale, it is uneven, and it would not be fair to make generalized judgments on the strength of particular issues. Yet there are disquieting omissions and weaknesses on the historical side of the work.

For example, it is strange that the account in the Prolegomena of

often overlooked work of Edmundson on the church in Rome, G. Edmundson, *The Church in Rome in the First Century* (Bampton Lectures, 1913) (London: Longmans, Green, 1913). His book is of slight relevance to our present theme, and his central thesis is questionable, but the reaction to his work illustrates the neglect. His book represents a critical and historical reconstruction of real importance, of greater value than many works of greater fame and influence. Yet (perhaps alone among Bampton Lectures) it was never reviewed in *JTS* (nor in *JRS* and other major journals) and is little noticed until taken up in J.A.T. Robinson's *Redating the New Testament* (London: SCM, 1976) and F.F. Bruce in *Paul, Apostle of the Free Spirit* (Exeter: Paternoster, 1977). The reason for this neglect, as Robinson points out (p. 112), is quite simply the disruption caused by the outbreak of war. Cf. however also L.E. Browne, 'The Journeys of St Peter', *Expos* 8th ser. 9 (1915), pp. 242-53; Edmundson, 'The Journeys of St Peter. A Reply', *ibid.*, pp. 499-513; Browne, 'The Journeys of St Peter', *Expos* 8th ser. 10 (1915), pp. 148-54. Edmundson's name is not indexed in any of the volumes of *BC*, nor is it mentioned in Gerhard Schneider's recent 42-page bibliography of his commentary *Die Apostelgeschichte*, 2 vols. (Freiburg, Basel and Vienna: Herder, 1980) 1.11-52 (nor in the supplementary list in 2.11-16). It is also omitted from such recent studies as E.A. Judge and G.S.R. Thomas, 'The Origin of the Church at Rome: A New Solution?', *RTR* 25 (1966), pp. 81-94; and J.W. Wenham, 'Did Peter Go to Rome in A.D. 42?', *TB* 23 (1972), pp. 94-102.

[43] H.J. Cadbury, *The Style and Literary Method of Luke* (Cambridge, MA: Harvard University Press, 1920); cf. *BC* 2.349-55.

the Gentile world is limited to two essays: one on the Roman provincial system and one on life in the Roman Empire, a study largely devoted to cultural influences of Hellenism and to philosophical and religious movements.[44] It is not that these essays are in any way deficient for what they are, but it is clear that the world of Paul in Asia Minor was far removed from this impression of a Hellenistic-Roman cultural monolith seen through the perspective of political history and formal literature. For the cultural background of Paul we must inevitably wrestle with the thousands of inscriptional texts which testify, however imperfectly, to a changed, orientalized Hellenism, often thinly concealing very different conceptions. In the preceding period Ramsay and his peers were opening up this hidden world, and the debate was focused. The need for a closer, localized examination of specific settings was never really addressed.[45]

Another curious point is the treatment of the date of Acts in a brief addendum to a chapter of 'Subsidiary Points' (*BC* 2.358-59). The editors both formerly felt reasonably sure of the traditional authorship, but then inclined to think this only of the 'we-sections' and perhaps the narrative adhering to them. They leave the question of date open,[46] but surely this is a question of importance too fundamental to be handled so parenthetically. The kind of view we can hold of Acts as a whole, and of Christian origins at large, is so far implicit in alternative answers to these questions of date and authorship that it is difficult to disengage from them. Even when we give full weight to the preceding chapters by Emmet and Windisch which argue in broader terms respectively for and against the tradition,[47] this doubt persists. It must be noticed again that both these writers focus on the relationship of Acts with Galatians, Emmet defending the identification of Gal. 2 with Acts 11, and Windisch assuming its identification with Acts 15, and finding a central ground of scepticism in that identification. Emmet stands here in continuity with the tone

---

[44] H.T.F. Duckworth, 'The Roman Provincial System', *BC* 1.171-217; C.H. Moore, 'Life in the Roman Empire at the Beginning of the Christian Era', *ibid.* pp. 218-62.

[45] This is not to deny the massive learning adduced by the editors, for instance in the final volume of Additional Notes.

[46] Possibly anywhere from 60 to 150, probably between 70 and 115. If they had to choose, it might be 95-100, to leave room for the probability, as they see it, that Luke knew Josephus (*BC* 2.358-59). These are by no means unusual views, and this caution with which opinions are expressed on a controverted matter is commendable, the point is that these matters are seen as 'subsidiary'.

[47] C.W. Emmet, 'The Case for the Tradition. The Paul of Acts and the Paul of the Epistles', *BC* 2.265-97; H. Windisch, 'The Case against Tradition', *ibid.*, pp. 298-348.

of the pre-war debate where Windisch does not, and the editorial conclusion does not pick up this crux.

None of this is intended as a devaluation of the great achievement of *BC*. It is meant rather to illustrate the occasional dangers of giving definitive status to a work which is not exempt from the disabilities and limitations perhaps inherent in its time and circumstances. It reflects something of a division from pre-war scholarship and between English and German-speaking scholarship. It also stands between the strong classical background tradition of the older British work and the increasing availability of inscriptional texts later, between the critical application of limited materials to the task of exegesis by a Lightfoot and the frequent neglect of the fruits of more abundant later investigations by a later scholarship more specialized in its theological interests. It is sometimes necessary to return to Lightfoot or Hort or Ramsay for the starting-point of a debate which has been prematurely closed by a generalized reformulation in the post-1918 period and was never re-examined in the light of more recent work in areas such as Greek epigraphy.[48]

Without attempting to trace subsequent developments in detail, we might add a mere postscript to bring up to date some account of the tensions indicated here over the validity of historical study. The survey of scholarship in Haenchen's introduction is admirably learned. It is also, however, almost exclusively German in orientation. His entire account of British work is contained in a few lines. He names Samuel Davidson and W.R. Cassels as Baur's only followers in England; and J.B. Lightfoot as an opponent of the Tübingen theories, and he mentions Hobart as taken up by Harnack. The only British scholar whose own views he describes (in two lines) is the eighteenth century divine Edward Evanson, who denied the authenticity of Romans because it conflicted with Acts.[49] The difference of content between Haenchen and Gasque is remarkable, and their evaluations of the same scholars strongly opposed. Though Gasque

---

[48] A striking case is Lake's erroneous denial of a usage accepted by Lightfoot and Ramsay alike, and abundantly vindicated by the texts. See *JTS* n.s. 27 (1976), pp. 122-26; cf. *JTS* 28 (1977), pp. 99-101. Again the point is of immediate importance as having entered into the debate over the relationship of Acts with Galatians. Cf. the recurrence of a similar pattern elsewhere: *ExpT* 89 (1977-78), pp. 239-43, returning to Hort; *JSNT* 22 (1984), pp. 81-94, to Lightfoot, and *JTS* 26 (1975), pp. 100-111, to James Smith.

[49] For Hobart see Haenchen, *Acts*, p. 31 = *Apostelgeschichte* p. 29; for the others *Acts*, p. 22 (= p. 20). These references *in toto* occupy about *six lines* out of twenty pages devoted to the period. Haenchen's discussion of Harnack is almost all on his work as a source-critic of Acts.

takes full account of German work, he does not mention the scholar (Paul Wendland) whom Haenchen thinks to have produced perhaps the best thing written on Acts before 1914,[50] and Haenchen does not mention Ramsay, of whom Gasque thinks perhaps most highly.[51] Wide diversities of judgment are acceptable, of course, but it is a pity if the scholarly tradition of another nation is dismissed virtually unheard as though in essence radically uncritical. Without wishing to set British scholarship against German, we must insist once more on the legitimacy of taking up the threads of an interrupted argument against those who declare the question closed. In insisting afresh on historical study we want to be led by the *evidence*, and that has always seemed characteristic of the best scholarship.

The seminal contributions of Martin Dibelius,[52] Hans Conzelmann[53] and Ernst Haenchen,[54] which refocused attention on 'Luke the theologian' and either explicitly or implicitly promoted a historical scepticism have been partly countered on the exegetical and theological side, notably in the recent work of I. Howard

---

[50] Haenchen *Acts*, pp. 32-33 (= *Apostelgeschichte*, pp. 30-31), citing P. Wendland, 'Apostelgeschichten', *Die Urchristlichen Literaturformen*, 2nd and 3rd edn (Tübingen: J.C.B. Mohr, 2nd and 3rd edn [sic] 1912), pp. 314-42.

[51] Haenchen does of course mention (and contradict) Ramsay many times in his actual commentary. The neglect or disparagement of Ramsay in German scholarship has been commented on many times, e.g. Bruce, *Acts* p. viii; S. Neill, *The Interpretation of the New Testament 1861-1961* (London: OUP, 1964), p. 145 n. 2; W.W. Gasque, *Sir William M. Ramsay, Archaeologist and New Testament Scholar* (Grand Rapids: Baker Book House, 1966), p. 10, and elsewhere. For a reaction to this recurring criticism see W.G. Kümmel, *The New Testament. The History of the Investigation of its Problems*, tr. S. McL. Gilmour and H.C. Kee (London: SCM, 1973) from the 2nd German edn (1970), p. 438, n. 287: 'Ramsay's apologetic analysis of archaeology signifies no methodologically essential advance for New Testament research. Therefore Ramsay is missing from the second edition of this book as well ... One can regard this judgment of mine as in error, but it is beside the point to regard this as a characteristic example of German scholarship'. Kümmel's account of Ramsay may be thought to say more about Kümmel than about Ramsay.

[52] M. Dibelius, *Aufsätze zur Apostelgeschichte* (Göttingen: Vandenhoeck & Ruprecht, 1951); ET *Studies in the Acts of the Apostles*, tr. M. Ling and Paul Schubert (London: SCM, 1956).

[53] H. Conzelmann, *Die Mitte der Zeit* (Tübingen: J.C.B. Mohr, 1954); ET *The Theology of St Luke*, tr. G. Buswell (London: Faber and Faber, 1960); *Die Apostelgeschichte* (Tübingen: J.C.B. Mohr, 1963).

[54] E. Haenchen, *Die Apostelgeschichte*, 6th edn, = *Meyers Kritisch-exegetischer Kommentar* (Göttingen: Vandenhoeck & Ruprecht, 15th edn, 1968); ET *The Acts of the Apostles. A Commentary* tr. B. Noble *et al.* from the 5th/14th German edn (Oxford: Blackwell, 1971).

Marshall.[55] The historical question remains unsettled. The most thorough work is still that of F.F. Bruce,[56] which, however, antedates the debate provoked by Haenchen. Martin Hengel, in the Preface to his recent book on Acts, writes:

> Two things, above all, concern me. First, to question the radical histori-
> cal scepticism which is so widespread in a number of areas within
> German scholarship; this scepticism is often coupled with flights of
> imagination which suggest a retreat from any historical research worth
> taking seriously. Secondly, however, I am no less vigorously opposed
> to the primitive ostracism of historical— and that always means cri-
> tical— methods, without which neither historical nor theological
> understanding of the New Testament is possible. It is remarkable how
> closely the two extremes can converge in this "flight from history", no
> matter what the reasons for it may be.[57]

Hengel's book will provide much material for closer assessment in the course of our study.[58] The fact that it marks a vigorous reaction against prevailing trends in scholarship is not a fact to be simplistically abused to urge a more traditional viewpoint. Yet its appeal is profoundly salutary as a sharp corrective to an over-specialization which has too often discounted the balanced study of context.[59]

Hengel pursues his theme in his latest book:

> The destructive scepticism, a particular feature of the modern world,
> which works in a predominantly analytical way, often ultimately ends
> up, not by furthering real historical understanding but by making it
> impossible. It is striking here that in particular those authors who
> apply radical criticism to early Christian narrators like Mark or Luke
> and who shred up the two letters to the Corinthians into ten or more
> parts often invent facts of their own which have no basis whatever in
> the sources and indeed go directly against them. Despite the anxiety of
> fundamentalists we cannot and should not refrain from the consistent
> application of historical methods (using German jargon one can also

---

[55] I.H. Marshall, *Luke: Historian and Theologian* (Exeter: Paternoster, 1970); *The Acts of the Apostles. An Introduction and Commentary* (Leicester: IVP, 1980); See also *The Gospel of Luke: A Commentary on the Greek Text* (Grand Rapids: Eerdmans, 1978).

[56] F.F. Bruce, *The Acts of the Apostles* (London: Tyndale, 2nd edn 1952); *Commentary on the Book of the Acts* (Grand Rapids: Eerdmans, 1956).

[57] M. Hengel, *Acts and the History of Earliest Christianity* (London: SCM, 1979), tr. by J. Bowden from *Zur urchristlichen Geschichtsschreibung* (Stuttgart: Calwer Verlag, 1979), p. vii.

[58] Cf. my review of Hengel in *Themelios* n.s. 6.1 (Sept. 1980), pp. 26-27.

[59] Cf. Hengel's words: 'Unfortunately, theologians today increasingly lack historical knowledge and an interest in history, and above all are too ignorant of the legacy of the past, whether of the Old Testament and Judaism, or of Graeco-Roman antiquity' (*Acts*, p. viii).

call them "historical-critical" methods), but [from] the widespread combination of radical critical attitudes and extravagant (-critical) methods.60

He concludes,

We are concerned only with the truth, theological and historical. The truth is our sole obligation; we have to seek it and present it, and in the end it will prevail against all our conjectures, all our desires to be right, our imaginative constructions and our anxiety.61

3. *The Objections to an Attempt to Reopen the Question*

The preceding survey will serve for the moment as the barest background for meeting objections to the need for this study. (1) It may be objected that theological interpretation and not mere antiquarian interest should lie at the heart of *Actaforschung*, that the historical questions have been sufficiently settled, and modern study has moved beyond the need to be so preoccupied with them. (2) It may also be objected that the solution to the question of historicity, which, according to the first objection, has little significance in itself, is merely a matter of taking up a mediating position between Haenchen and Marshall. In other words, according to this view one must steer a middle course between studies which have said virtually everything that can be said.

In answer to the first objection, it is necessary to reaffirm the validity and great importance of our topic. The antithesis between theological interpretation and antiquarianism is falsely drawn; indeed, history and theology are closely bonded, and the nature of their relationship must be explored.

The solution, in reply to the second objection, is not likely to be an intermediate point as if between extremes that lie on the same linear scale,62 but involves the choice between radically different kinds of

---

60 Hengel, *Between Jesus and Paul. Studies in the Earliest History of Christianity* (London: SCM, 1983) tr. by J. Bowden from six articles published in German, p. xiv. I have cited these passages at some length, without omissions, as I wish to present the balance and context of Hengel's remarks fully.

61 *Ibid.*, p. xv.

62 For example, in the opening chapter of his book on Pauline chronology, Robert Jewett aims to steer a middle course between the harmonizer and the sceptic in his treatment of Acts. In the event he tends to be eclectic in using it. As a rule Jewett is sceptical where he suspects redactional manipulation by Luke or where the material conflicts with the evidence of the Epistles (e.g. pp. 21, 24). As one discerning reviewer puts it, 'There are times when the author seems to pick and choose the evidence in Acts which he terms reliable in order that later on it may fit into his theory'. R. Jewett, *Dating Paul's Life*

approach. Either may arguably be related to a conception of the weight of the evidence, where a mediating view will not necessarily cohere with either reading of the case.

This is not to advocate a simplistic confrontation. The alternatives may not be simple or monolithic: there may, and probably will, be many side issues, much need for qualification, many questions which are not predictably aligned with opposing stances. It may even be that the truth *is* found to lie significantly between poles of opinion, but if so it must be because the evidence points that way, not because there is necessarily a critical virtue in splitting the difference. When all such allowances are made, we may reasonably ask whether the narrative of Acts is essentially reliable or essentially unreliable, and expect to get an answer. We are not claiming to resolve all the problems from any one standpoint. The inquiry is overlaid with conflicts of presupposition and approach which may forbid a simply quantified solution. The answer is contained rather in working through a complex series of interrelated choices. Our concern is to invoke and apply the evidence openly available in the effort to resolve the deadlock, to find ground on which communication and discrimination become possible.

It is a recurring motif of contemporary scholarship to stress that the evidence of the Epistles is 'primary' for Paul, and that of Acts 'secondary'. Paul's own evidence is intrinsically 'superior'.[63] The trustworthiness of Acts is thus made the subject of a value judgment upon comparative, rather than internal, grounds. The use and the non-use of Acts as a source are treated like transitional or sceptical poles, where a partial, or eclectic, or qualified, or subordinate, use is made to seem the scholarly mean. The designation of Acts as 'secondary' is formally valid, but this does not answer the separate question of its trustworthiness as a source. Is Acts, 'secondary' as it is, trustworthy or not? 'Primary' sources themselves are not exempt from error either, and certainly not from *Tendenz*.[64] Until we re-examine the evidence specifically, the range of possible options remains open.

There may be a further objection made to attempts to re-open the question, and this attempt in particular, in that such a study is

---

(London: SCM, 1979) = *The Chronology of Paul's Life* (Philadelphia: Fortress Press, 1979), pp. 7-8. We have cited the review by E. Best in *SJT* 33 (1980), p. 488. See also the extended review by J.W. Drane in *JSNT* 9 (1980), pp. 70-75.

[63] Jewett's term, *Dating Paul's Life*, pp. 22-24 and *passim*. The distinction is characteristically developed in J. Knox, *Chapters in a Life of Paul* (London: A. & C. Black, 1954), and has become a commonplace.

[64] Obvious ancient examples, posing different kinds of critical problems are Caesar's *Gallic War* and *Civil War* and the *Res Gestae* of Augustus.

rendered *predictable* by the *presuppositions* of the author. Presupposition is a difficult and delicate topic. It is good to seek for a balanced historical study whose validity is not unnecessarily conditioned by presupposition. Yet none of us is free from presupposition, and it may be better for sound scholarship to allow for the fact than to pretend to a pseudo-objectivity belied in practice.

The impact of presupposition upon such a study as the present may be subtle and complex. It is deeply involved even in the concept of history itself. The word 'history' may be used in multiple senses, often covering hidden variations of understanding. First there is the obvious distinction between 'what actually happened' and the interpreted, selective account of what happened, between *Historie* and *Geschichte*.[65] Another tension is seen in the different practical conceptions of historical criticism and methods held by scholars in different disciplines. Thus theologians and ancient historians often display surprisingly diverse patterns of credulity and scepticism in their treatment of the Gospels or Acts. Both groups insist that they are practising historical criticism, but they ask different kinds of questions proceeding from a different presuppositional matrix in each discipline.[66] A third level of possible difference is in presuppositional confusions in the use of words in different languages. Thus Albert Schweitzer's use of the phrase 'the historical Jesus' strikes a British reader strangely, because it brings together the notions 'Jesus as he actually was' and 'a non-supernatural Jesus' in a unitary concept.[67] The British reader may accept the Enlightenment tradition of thought in which Schweitzer stands, but his or her normal use of the word 'historical' will not carry this implication, and there is thus the need to argue what has passed as axiomatic for the German.

This last tension leads us into the very sensitive matter of the supernatural in a narrative which purports to be historical. This is a topic on which presuppositions are quite important. Marshall has noted three main points of view on this problem: (1) categorical denial of the possibility of miraculous events; (2) the separation of

---

65 Cf. Marshall, *Luke* p. 21.

66 This difference is well seen by comparing reviews of the same books in journals of theology and of ancient history. For an example outside the sensitive NT area see the widely diverse brief reviews of the Otto Michel *Festschrift, Josephus-Studien*, ed. O. Betz *et al.*; by W. Horbury in *JTS* 28 (1977), pp. 136-38; C. Rogers in *JETS* 19 (1976), pp. 253-54; and T. Rajak in *JRS* 67 (1977), pp. 241-42. The last is especially instructive.

67 A. Schweitzer, *The Quest of the Historical Jesus. A Critical Study of its Progress from Reimarus to Wrede*, (ET London: A. & C. Black, 2nd edn, 1911), *passim*.

what a man believes *qua* believer from the rigorous naturalism required of him *qua* historian; (3) the attitude that history may take account at least of the possibility of supernatural events.[68] Quite clearly, the third option is a position from which the fundamental questions of debate remain open, and from which mind and heart are not divided by an unreasonable dichotomy. Presupposition in such a study as the present one may keep a relatively low profile. Much of the work in this study will be concerned with the presentation and assessment of details as a check upon conflicting hypotheses. The validity of such arguments will hinge more upon care, accuracy and fairness than upon extensive personal hypotheses, and we shall strive for the most objective evaluations possible in the awareness of the dangers of tendentiousness. Conversely, conviction is a stimulus to research. The issues are important, and it will not be enough to look for the means of proving a preconception. One can afford to consider all sides of the argument.

Yet the subject of presupposition remains a very delicate one. We must face the extreme complexity of its variations, its rooting in the varying approaches of different disciplines no less than the lingering sense of *parti pris* dividing opposite theological stances. One is sometimes made to feel that a scholar's views are predictable, because they accord with a personal approach exhibited elsewhere in his or her work. It is easy for a writer with a minority viewpoint to seem defensive and polemical, to indulge in special pleading which seeks standing by denial of the commoner trend. In the case of Acts, it is probably true to say that the minority position today is in line with the development of directions in criticism which have been normative in the longer perspective of the history of scholarship; further, that the trend away from them is *not* due to decisive progress, but to the truncating of an unresolved debate by a shift of interest. This minority view has a very respectable pedigree. It may need to win a hearing from an unsympathetic environment, but it has no need to be unwarrantably defensive. It may well argue that the opposite view is equally predictable, that it has so far shifted the balance of argument off-centre in one direction that a corrective must be no less predictable in the other.[69] And it is by no means clear that an appropriate degree of predictability is necessarily a scholarly vice in either party, if it interacts with the coherent reading of alternatives.

There is a related tension over what we really mean by historicity.

---

68 Marshall, *Luke*, pp. 28-32.

69 Cf. C.J. Hemer, *FTh* 108 (1981), p. 181, in review of Marshall's *Acts*. While a conservative is often labeled as 'predictably apologetic', the liberal is called 'consistently critical'.

As we have said, historicity and theological significance are sometimes made, in practice if not in theory, into mutually exclusive alternatives. But the question 'history or theology' is answerable in
various ways. The nature of historicity will be discussed in more
detail below. Here we may note simply that presupposition may be
involved in our expectations of an ostensibly historical narrative. It
is possible for instance to lay down unrealistically rigid pre-con-
ditions for acceptance of an account as historical. Some theological
writers make an exaggerated antithesis between 'pure history' and
interpretation.[70] But none of our sources, even for undisputed matters in more recent secular history, is 'pure history' in the sense
sometimes desired. The presuppositional factor necessarily exists in
our sources as in ourselves, and neither we nor our sources are necessarily the worse for that fact. That is integral to the essential task
of historical research. It ought to provoke caution, but not despair. It
is right to express uncertainty where appropriate, but *non liquet* is
not synonymous with *nego*. To be over-demanding of evidence is to
carry scepticism too far, and could issue in an irrationalism which if
applied logically rather than selectively could destroy the basis of
knowledge in areas far beyond our present concern.

There is quite simply a potential difference of expectation akin to
that of calling a cup 'half-full' or 'half-empty'. Conclusions may
easily become implicit in the questions asked. This strikes the reader
forcibly in Dibelius, whose questions, however acute, seem selective
and latently presuppositional.[71] Yet an alternative may as easily become open to the same objection, and communication is broken. In
any case we are not thinking of a simple division between Dibelius
and an unthinking traditionalism; the debate is multiform. There
seem to be two safeguards against the problem posed by presuppositionally preselected questions: (1) that we seek balance by addressing
a broader compendium of the facts of the subject, including those
commonplaces of critical introduction whose answers are often
taken for granted; (2) that we seek, and wrestle with the application
of, independently verifiable evidences, matters of context which we
cannot readily dispute but which may occasionally give a foothold

---

[70] For a recent example see J.K. Elliott, *Questioning Christian Origins* (London: SCM, 1982), pp. 2, 87, 94. He opposes the concepts of history and theology
many times (pp. 2, 4, 5, 14, 16, etc.). His skill in handling his texts does not
dispel the unease occasioned by the pervasiveness of his polarizations.

[71] Thus Dibelius' development of 'style criticism' arises directly from the difficulty of applying a strictly 'form-critical' analysis to the book of Acts, and
carries over the presuppositions and questions of form criticism ('Style Criticism of the Book of Acts', *Studies*, pp. 1-25).

for discrimination.

The profile of the question is still apt to be affected by the influence of presupposition on method. It is difficult to prove a negative. It is also difficult to establish a positive by the use of parallels unless their context, significance and application are very carefully controlled. If our aim is to look either for corroboration or for conflict of evidence, we shall probably find it too easy to find what we seek, at least to suit our own case. It can be easy to find what we are looking for. If however text and ostensible context interlock unobtrusively at a variety of levels and cast further light elsewhere, this complex of positive indications becomes increasingly suggestive. Conversely, an obstinate pattern of non-correlation would point increasingly to a negative conclusion. But we must avoid the simplistic conclusions often drawn on both sides upon inadequate grounds.

4. *The Importance of Historicity*

(a) Historicity and Our Knowledge of Paul

Can we in any degree use any of the evidence of Acts for our understanding of the 'historical Paul'? Many scholars will answer 'no', for the Epistles alone constitute our 'primary' evidence. From this perspective those who do use Acts may seem uncritical defenders of a traditional status quo, holding to a presuppositional view in the face of modern scholarship. We need somehow to take the tension out of this suggestion of *parti pris*. But the rejection of the evidence of Acts is arguably presuppositional itself. In either case presupposition may be influencing opinion, if not controlling it. And in either case the safeguard against the damaging effects of hidden or unconsidered presupposition is open scrutiny of the credentials of the evidence.

The present issue is the extent of the evidential base for our knowledge of Paul. The argument may run that caution dictates that we use only that which we can affirm by general consent to be authentically Pauline. We may personally wish to accept more, but we are not entitled to go beyond the minimal base in the 'primary' evidence. Such a method will give us what is undeniably Pauline, but if the base is too narrow it will not necessarily give us what is *typically* Pauline. If we want to know whether it is indisputably attested that Paul taught X, it will be our aim to demonstrate X's presence in the *Hauptbriefe*, for nearly all scholars accept their authenticity. But if we want to know whether X is characteristic of Pauline thought, we have to wrestle with the extent of our evidential base, to ask and attempt to answer the question of what is typically Pauline. Only when we have made some effort to settle that can we relate X to it without the danger of distortion.

There are not sufficient materials in a small number of letters to infer an adequate outline of the course of Paul's career. And without such an outline it is doubtful whether we have any stable frame of reference for the study of development in his thought. The study is at best hazardous, for our sources are occasional and unsystematic, giving little foothold to the attempt to establish in each a coherent pattern of Paul's thought. But if we are brought in danger of having to argue date from development and development from date, this may become a circle tenuously grounded anywhere. Yet we have in Acts what purports to be a framework. There may be many difficulties and dangers in using it, but we cannot avoid evaluating them. We must decide only after closer study whether and how to use Acts.

There are two essential alternatives involving different conceptions of the evidence and carrying different implications. If we are persuaded that Acts is essentially reliable, we shall probably feel justified in using its evidence, with whatever caution, at something near its face value. When we test our ground carefully, using Acts freely if critically, the question of possible correlation with the Epistles, with externally attested dates, positive or negative, is enhanced. It will at least be a live option to test whether the evidence of Acts and Epistles for Paul's life are broadly in accord. If, on the other hand, we are persuaded that the narrative of Acts has been heavily manipulated by the dictates of Lukan theology, we shall not be able to use it straightforwardly. If we refuse to use Acts, we can know relatively little of Paul. We have his occasional teaching and self-disclosures set in a contextual vacuum because we have no consensus about the authenticity, representativeness or developmental sequence of the documents. This implication may be disguised by the tendency to build over-elaborately on narrow foundations.

The operation of this danger may be seen in the work of Knox. In successive studies of Pauline chronology he refocused and developed his ground, but held to his basic principle of using only the primary evidence of the Epistles as basic sources.[72] The viability of his scheme hinges primarily on his unconvincing equation of the fourteen-year periods of Gal. 2:1 and 2 Cor. 12:2. This is the starting point of his earlier article, but in his book he virtually abandons it in the face of critical objections (p. 78 n), while elaborating the chronology it

---

[72] J. Knox, 'Fourteen Years Later: A Note on the Pauline Chronology', *Journal of Religion* 16 (1936), pp. 341-49; 'The Pauline Chronology', *JBL* 58 (1939), pp. 15-29; *Chapters in a Life of Paul* (1954).

prompted.[73] He has in fact to compound inferences from what seems to be no more than accidental coincidence in epistles of arguably different date and ostensibly referring to different periods of Paul's life, and is led by this to discount the apparent correlation of Acts with the independent evidence of the Gallio inscription.

The limitation of Acts is not so much that it is historically questionable as that Luke did not appreciate and understand Pauline thought, and preferred to impose his own redactional theology upon it. He does not tell us what we want to know. There is a somewhat similar, if more severe, problem with Socrates, for Xenophon did not understand Socratic thought and Plato redacted it into Platonic thought. Is the 'historical Socrates' unknowable? More important, is his thought irrecoverable? If we demand an inappropriate measure of objectivity and perception in our sources, perhaps yes; but if we will wrestle with their difficulties, no. There is actually an importance in the fact of different perceptions. We need to make the fullest examination of Plato, Xenophon and Aristophanes. The different impact Socrates made on these three is a datum of the problem. Even if we decide upon reflection to reject the portrait in *Clouds* we need to explain why Aristophanes got it wrong. Again, it is commonplace to draw attention to the importance of Qumran for understanding the variety in first century Judaism. It was inevitable, while the range of evidence was more limited, that scholars read the Pharisaic Judaism of the Gospels through spectacles tinted retrospectively by the Rabbis, and assumed that the resulting picture was more representative and monolithic than we now know it to have been.[74] We may be unsettled by this confusing dispersal of our focused picture, but we are better and less one-sidedly informed.

The evidence of Acts, then, must be heard and debated. We may decide that it is a bad source, but such a judgment ought to come at the end of the study, not at the beginning. If we decide it is good, we are offered the option of a larger, contextually-based understanding of Paul. While paying due regard to factors like redaction, we are committed to an alternative approach, and experimental methods, with the possibility of a radically different base for the knowledge of Paul. *If there is* a prospect of fruitful interlocking of Acts and Epistles in the first century context, this is crucial for determining the place of Paul in Christian origins.

---

[73] See esp. G. Ogg, 'A New Chronology of Saint Paul's Life' *ExpT* 64 (1952-53), pp. 120-23; cf. C.J. Hemer, 'Observations on Pauline Chronology', *Pauline Studies Bruce*, pp. 3-18, esp. pp. 9, 17n.

[74] Thus G.F. Moore, *Judaism in the First Centuries of the Christian Era*, 3 vols. (Cambridge, MA: Harvard University Press, 1927-1930).

(b) Historicity and Our Knowledge of Christian Origins

But yet more far-reaching options are implicit in the view we take of Acts. It is in some respects the book central to the historical problem of the entire New Testament.[75] It is widely agreed that the Third Gospel and Acts share common authorship, whatever be thought of the character and identity of the author. The importance of this point is usually stressed from the perspective of seeking a common Lukan theology. But it is equally crucial from the standpoint of the historical question. The Third Gospel is one of the Synoptics, and so one of our basic sources for the 'historical Jesus'— if we can in any degree accept its ostensible testimony. Acts purports, among much else, to give some outline of the 'historical Paul', and again we have the rudiments of a 'synoptic' problem, whether the ostensible outline can be related to the occasions of the Epistles. And the two parts together present a virtually continuous narrative with characters as central as Peter common to both. In the context of 'Lukan' studies it becomes relevant to explore the factor of a common style and method uniting two writings of evidently differing genre which present some diverse critical problems. It seems difficult, for instance, for G.A. Wells to combine the ideas of a non-historical Jesus and an historical Paul while admitting the common authorship of a consecutive narrative without a lapse of time between the events of the two parts.[76]

Luke-Acts then together provide a narrative ostensibly joining Jesus with Paul. The double work is unique in the New Testament in linking some of the events with Roman emperors and other persons and details known to secular history. The fact that some of the passages involved, notably the Nativity story, pose acute difficulties is not the point here. The apparent correlations exist, and therefore give a foothold to historical criticism. And here Acts, and the latter half of Acts in particular, is the key. There is a better prospect for historical criticism to work from Acts to Luke than from Luke to Acts. In particular, it may be easier to date Luke from Acts than Acts from Luke. From this significant viewpoint Acts is the best point of approach to the Synoptics-Acts-Paul complex of documents. I am not

---

[75] I develop here some of the ideas adumbrated in my paper 'Luke the Historian', *BJRL* 60 (1977-78), pp. 28-51.

[76] G.A. Wells, 'Can Luke Save Jesus?' *New Humanist* 93 (1977), pp. 108-10; 'Paul and Luke: Epistles and Acts: An Aspect of J.A.T. Robinson's *Redating the New Testament*', *Question* 11 (June 1978), pp. 80-105. Wells pays little regard to Acts in his books *The Jesus of the Early Christians* (London: Pemberton Books, 1971) and *Did Jesus Exist?* (London: Elek/Pemberton, 1975).

denying that this proposition is beset with formidable difficulties. Fundamental questions of source, genre, and redaction are immediately raised, and it will be part of our task to consider them.

If however our quest leads to acceptance of a considerable historical value in Acts, the consequences are far-reaching. If we set aside for the moment the pressure engendered by recent scholarly trends, we find that a surprisingly large number of the most eminent names in *Actaforschung* have maintained an early dating of the book and authorship by a companion of Paul, traditionally the physician Luke. These traditional views are not necessarily intimations of historicity, but they may tell strongly against some of the grounds on which historicity has often been denied. The supposition of extensive traditio-historical and redaction-historical developments requires some considerable lapse of time. The contrary supposition of a relatively early date straitens the conditions under which the resulting narrative has been produced. If the author were a contemporary, at least of the events at the end of Acts, writing to contemporaries, this places other constraints upon the kind of work he is likely to have written. None of this simplistically answers the historicity question, but it raises the need for alternative formulations. The hypothesis of an early date is commonly excluded by the insistence on a post-70 dating of the Third Gospel, based especially on the Lukan redaction of Luke 21:20-24. This complication too will be considered in its place below (See chapter 9 below). It will suffice here to note two ways in which this problem has been treated by those who persist in holding to a pre-70 date of Acts: either they think that Acts follows a proto-Luke and actually antedates the Third Gospel as we possess it, or they challenge the grounds on which a dogma is made of the post-70 date of Luke. Despite currently prevailing trends, there is a considerable, and often recent, literature in favour of both positions, and the latter is reinforced by an important article of C.H. Dodd, though he was not concerned to advocate an early dating of Luke-Acts.[77]

If anything on these lines poses even a viable option, we are confronted with the need to examine radical alternatives. Insofar as there is any approach to a consensus about a synthesis on Christian origins, based upon an often shifting 'critical orthodoxy', it often involves the assumption that many of the documents must be extensively reinterpreted to unravel the deleterious effects of redaction in the early church. We are not concerned to deny the subjective factor

---

[77] C.H. Dodd, 'The Fall of Jerusalem and the "Abomination of Desolation"', *JRS* 37 (1947), pp. 47-54, reprinted in his *More New Testament Studies* (Manchester University Press, 1968), pp. 69-83.

in a writer– to allow for that is one of the necessary tasks in assessing any historical source. But a synthesis largely dependent on a fundamental re-reading of many of its sources is liable to compound uncertainties. It even risks reflecting and intensifying dominant ideas in the mind of the critic, who may be tempted to harmonize the ancient evidence into a pattern dictated by one's own *Vorverständnis*. It is more difficult than we suppose to read the mind of an ancient writer from a different cultural context, unless at least we begin by taking straightforwardly what we are told at its ostensible face-value as a datum. If it proves impossible to make progress towards a coherent solution from a cautiously critical reading of the ostensible evidence, there will be time enough to experiment with more radical reconstruction. But if we are reduced to such straits, we should recognize the speculativeness of the exercise. It amounts to saying that we can really know with confidence relatively little of Paul or of Christian origins— or for that matter of Augustus or of Nero. An uneasy fluctuation between scepticism and speculation could be the death of the very critical rationality we value. It may be objected that we are already in this situation because the ostensible evidence cannot be reconciled, that Acts and Epistles conflict. But that is just the question at issue. Those who use a narrow evidential base and reject Acts have not argued their case so much as assumed it. And it is precisely our purpose to examine whether that assumption is correct.

Traditional and reconstructed accounts of Christian origins are not, on this view, extremes to be modified, but largely arise from alternative methods of treating the evidence. There is not necessarily a moderate and scholarly mean to be found somewhere between them, because it is not that kind of question.

The point ultimately at stake then in the debate we have outlined is the type of account we can give of the genesis of Christianity, a matter of the highest importance, even beyond the confines of technical theology. If the documents stand together at something near their traditional value, the consequences are profound. In any case the questions raised are fundamental for Christian theology, because the application of Christian theology to the modern world hinges upon our conception of the credentials and interpretation of the foundational documents and the nature of their relevance. Our subject necessarily involves a wide spectrum of New Testament debate.

(c) The Pastoral Dimension of the Historicity Question

There is a further tension between the different perspectives of scholarship and the laity. Our present discussion is directed exclusively to the scholarly issue, but to say that is not to disclaim concern with the pastoral dimension of the problem. Our theme is certainly important from the layperson's perspective, though the questions and difficulties in this sphere are different from those of the scholar. The objective of scholarly inquiry is the truth, and the truth can and must be responsibly communicable to different audiences. The level and content of the exposition will be conditioned by the audience, but that exposition must be representatively excerpted with integrity from a considered view of the truth of the total picture, in this case of a balanced overall view of Acts. From such a view the historical component is indispensable. It is specifically necessary to meet the naïve historical question of the layperson who wants to know 'if it really happened'. The kind of answer we give on that question is inseparable from the kind of theological teaching we can give about the book. Occasionally one sees a divorce between what people hold academically and what they preach. The preacher may indeed feel a deep tension here, and believe existentially more than can be justified intellectually. It is certainly right to exercise a proper academic caution. But if the two levels are at odds, there is a serious issue of truth at stake. Our teachings in different contexts ought to be of one piece, and none the less so if we are frank in both to confess what we do not know and what we cannot prove.

It may be objected that this opens the door to an opposite danger, that of making popular acceptability govern our notion of scholarly truth, to simplify and conform what is really exceedingly difficult, even to produce a facile and undisturbing apologetic which uses the profession of caution and ignorance to hide from the difficulties. The danger may be acknowledged: it is one more stimulus to the wish to strike a responsible balance, with the focus squarely upon seeking the truth. I am sometimes more impressed with a different phenomenon, with the layperson's frustration when the scholar will not answer a naïve question. This question may be badly formulated. It may be necessary to locate the substance of the difficulty rather than respond literalistically to the original wording. But often scholars are prone to think they ought not to have that difficulty, and transpose the lay query into the scholarly perspective, and give a sugared dose of unapplied scholarly thinking.

Perhaps we ought to be worried when the naïve question throws us, even after we have cleared up confusions of thought in its formulation. 'Is Acts historically trustworthy?' 'Does it matter if it is historically trustworthy?' These are naïve questions which may have far-reaching importance for the layperson who wants to know what theological belief they may reasonably accept. Their questions ought to be answered. They will probably respect a reasoned reply drawing on a scholarly background, and it will naturally be right to be fair about the limits of our expertise. They may not appreciate being forced on to alien ground, with perhaps a dismissive (and even suspect) general judgment on the matter that really troubles them.

It may seem improper to invoke this application in an academic study. But this is certainly an important factor in the significance of our theme. Scholarship should not lower its standards to accommodate itself to popular consumption. But it is concerned, whether it will or not, with issues of fundamental interest to a much wider spectrum of thinking people.

(d) Historicity as a Theological Crux

We have mentioned the antithesis often drawn between the importance of theological interpretation and the relative unimportance of 'antiquarian detail'. This contrast is sometimes so embedded in our way of thinking that it is hard to insist that it is misleading. Marshall has argued convincingly that history and theology go together, that Luke makes his case in part through the narrative of events.[78] The nature of that relationship clearly needs further study. For the present, we are concerned to stress the basic point that the relationship exists. The thing may be put simply by saying that it is integral to Luke's manner to argue 'This happened: therefore ...' While his preface contains some problems of interpretation, he ostensibly declares his purpose to be that Theophilus may know the ἀσφάλεια of the teachings in which he has been instructed from one who has followed the events ἀκριβῶς from the beginning.[79]

An important recent study by A.A. Trites examines the motif of 'witness' in the New Testament.[80] He finds Luke-Acts and John to lay great theological significance on bearing testimony. 'For both writers the significance of witness lies in its ability to induce faith' (p. 128). This point accords with the declared purpose of the Fourth Evangelist in John 20:31, another much debated passage. Trites insists upon the sustained juridical character of the Fourth Gospel. The 'signs' have evidential value: the details of John 19:34-35 provide evidence that Jesus was a real man and that he really died (p. 85).

---

[78] Marshall, *Luke: Historian and Theologian*, Chapter 2, esp. pp. 44-52.

[79] In this paraphrase of Luke 1:1 I take ἀκριβῶς with παρηκολουθηκότι, not with γράψαι.

[80] A.A. Trites, *The New Testament Concept of Witness* (SNTS Monograph No. 31) (CUP, 1977). Cf. e.g. Marshall, *Luke* pp. 41-44.

The Gospel presents a case in forensic terms. To call this a 'spiritual' Gospel does not mean that the 'spiritual' is necessarily to be opposed to the evidential. Indeed the Evangelist's own argument is focused upon the presentation of evidence.

Not that this concept of witness is a dominant principle of Lukan or of Johannine theology; we are only suggesting that it is an important element within the theological purpose of both writers. Other motifs of primary significance are present. But we are not justified in using them to overrule consideration of the expressed statements of the writers. It is sometimes assumed that those statements have to be reinterpreted, perhaps because 'historicism' is a modern notion alien to the ancient world, an assumption too often supported by over-simplified ideas of the nature of ancient historiography (See below ch. 3). There is no unequivocal proof that New Testament writers were influenced by ancient standards, but the existence of such standards serves to counter a denial which closes options unexamined. The argument in Luke (and in John) seems to run on these lines: 'This testimony assures you of the truth of the events we record, and therefore assures you also that your saving faith is reposed in reality and not in make-believe'. That is not a concept of faith congenial to an age pervaded with an existential pattern of thought, but it seems to be what they are saying. We are under no obligation to accept their argument. We may think it is a bad argument, perhaps because we cannot accept their testimony. If so, it seems more satisfactory to reject their case than to avoid the difficulty by re-mythologizing it into something more congenial to our cultural context. For Luke's argument at this level, history and theology seem to be bonded together.

The concept of Lukan theology may be understood in different ways. It is commonly identified through the attempt to isolate distinctive redactional emphases of the writer, a possibility facilitated in the Third Gospel by the availability of Synoptic parallels for comparison. It is entirely proper to pursue this study, but a danger arises if this becomes a technique built upon unexamined cumulative presuppositions, and so tending to override complementary controls in historical and contextual disciplines.

We may seek Lukan theology on a broader front, through the attempt to isolate Luke's purpose in writing. This is clearly a most important question, to which varied answers are on offer. It is difficult to find an answer which commands wide assent. Part of the trouble is doubtless that his purpose is not simple or monolithic. It is necessary to assess it in its relevance to the writer's situation, which is not easily agreed, and there is a danger of circular argument. If we place the book early, as by a companion of Paul, the pattern of viable options will differ from those preferred if the book is late. On this ground too we need independent criteria for breaking the deadlock between contrasting readings of Acts.

We may also wish to evaluate Luke's theology with regard to what he preserves, no less than what he redacts. If we see primitive Christianity as witnessing to a deposit of essentially unitary tradition, we may feel that what is characteristically Lukan falls within the natural variations of that unity, and represents his individual presentation of it. This immediately raises the immense issue of 'unity and diversity'.[81] We may reject many of Walter Bauer's arguments on the complexities of 'orthodoxy and heresy'[82] without thereby making a plain path for a simplistic alternative. To be specific, it is evident that the Paul of Acts is different from the Paul of the Epistles. Yet to be different is not necessarily the same as to be incompatible. One commonly sees, in other and less sensitive contexts, honest and independent accounts of people or events differ in surprising ways, especially when presented from diverse perspectives. Each may be incomplete; they may be complementary rather than contradictory. But, again, this principle must not be abused as a licence for harmonization. The most we can say is that the question should be kept open. The relevance of the historical crux must not be disallowed by premature cutting of many of the interwoven strands. If the theology of Luke bears significant reference to the primitive situation, if it was even developed in the context of common enterprise with Paul, its thrust may need to be differently pictured. He may still have disagreed with Paul or misunderstood him, but at least our category of interpretation will be considerably modified by whether we see him in the same context or in a later, unrelated, context. The historical context of Luke is important from this perspective also. Again the application of independent historical evidence may help to break the recurring danger of circular reasoning in support of any position.

---

[81] Cf. J.D.G. Dunn, *Unity and Diversity in the New Testament. An Inquiry into the Character of Earliest Christianity* (London: SCM, 1977).

[82] W. Bauer, *Orthodoxy and Heresy in Earliest Christianity*, ET ed. R.A. Kraft and G. Krodel (London: SCM, 1972), from *Rechtgläubigkeit und Ketzerei im ältesten Christentum* (Tübingen: J.C.B. Mohr, 2nd edn, 1934). Cf. the fullest reply in H.E.W. Turner, *The Pattern of Christian Truth. A Study in the Relations between Orthodoxy and Heresy in the Early Church* (Bampton Lectures, 1954) (London: A.R. Mowbray, 1954).

Conclusions

I cannot profess to have all the answers. I am merely asking whether Acts is essentially unreliable in what it narrates of Paul and the primitive church and insisting that we should not make the judgment based on easy extrapolation from the corroborations or difficulties of a few debated passages, unless they are shown to be central to the veracity of the book. Nor should we be prepared to have the question foreclosed by a scepticism which demands inappropriately rigid or literalistic criteria for the acceptance of authenticity or historicity. No doubt it is ultimately true that presupposition and conclusion are aligned in that judgment. (There is something to be said for not having a mind at odds with itself.) But the conclusion rests squarely upon the requirements of the evidence— and that evidence is in urgent need of review.

Some of the old scholarship was historically meticulous. The new work has (very naturally) become increasingly specialized, but has often lost the broader grasp of context. The new knowledge has often not been effectively applied. We have rested too securely on premature and dated critical syntheses, often dependent on the extensive rereading of evidence. The discontinuities of the war generation have broken the sequence of discussion without obviating the need for fundamental re-examination of the accumulation of hidden and suspect presuppositions. The question of Acts' relationship to the history which it purports to relate is too important and fundamental not to be re-opened.

Chapter 2
Preliminary Questions

1. The Unity of Luke-Acts

Before we begin to discuss the questions of genre or of the nature of historicity, it is necessary to decide upon the extent of the Lukan writings.[1] Are the Gospel and Acts from the same author? If the answer is positive, then problems of genre, literary and historical method, theological *Tendenz* and the like, need to be formulated in a way which recognizes this unity and is perhaps illumined by the recognition. To put it in the terms used of Paul in the last chapter, we want to know how wide a base we have for our study of Luke. We are concerned to focus upon Acts, but we must know whether we find our characteristic 'Luke' in Acts alone or in Luke-Acts together.

This question will not detain us long, for the unity of Luke-Acts is today so generally accepted as to seem a datum of the problem, and the onus does not lie upon us to establish a position which not many would care to deny. Yet there have been χωρίζοντες[2] and it is desirable at least to raise the options and be as sure as we may of our common ground before proceeding.

The two books are ostensibly bound together by the common dedication to Theophilus, the resumptive preface of Acts 1:1 evidently referring to the Gospel. The consensus of early tradition ascribes both to the same writer, whom it identifies, rightly or wrongly, with the physician Luke.[3] It is actually the arrangement of books in our New Testament, collecting the Gospels at the beginning, which has disguised this ostensible unity from the superficial reader.

The classic statement of the 'separatist' case is that of A.C.

[1] I am here using the name 'Luke' for convenience, as a term for the author whomever we may decide he was.

[2] The term traditionally used of those in antiquity who ascribed the Iliad and the Odyssey to different authors.

[3] Thus the anti-Marcionite Prologue to Luke (c. 160-180), the Muratorian Fragment (c. 170-200), Irenaeus, *Adv. Haer.* 3.1.1 with 3.14.1; Clem. Alex. *Strom.* 5.12; etc., See Bruce, *Acts*, p. 1. Cadbury, who sets out the patristic texts in full (*BC* 2.210-45), has championed the view that the tradition is based only on inference (pp. 250-64).

Clark,[4] followed more recently by A.W. Argyle.[5] Both writers focus upon the statistical argument for style. Clark points out that both Blass[6] and Hawkins[7] recognized major differences between Luke and Acts without rejecting common authorship. Clark himself was set on his track by his observation of the distribution of the particle τε in the New Testament. Although the figures here are rendered uncertain by the frequency of textual variants, on Clark's figures, τε occurs eight times in Luke's Gospel, and 158 times in Acts, and all eight in Luke are of the τε καί type, whereas Acts contains 99 of other types.[8] Numerous other examples are given by both Clark and Argyle. In syntax we may note particularly the Hebraic ἐγένετο ('it came to pass'), commonly followed in Acts by an infinitive, but in the Gospel by a finite verb, with or without a linking καί. These cases, and others, such as the relative prevalence of μέν, μὲν οὖν and σύν in Acts, may be used to suggest that Acts is markedly more literary, or classical in style than the Gospel.

The arguments of Clark and Argyle have been discussed by W.L. Knox[9] and B.E. Beck[10] respectively. Knox stresses the different influences of diverse sources and the variations even within Acts, where the source question is unclear. He shows that in the Gospel the writer is unpredictable in his stylistic adaptations from Mark. Beck takes up Argyle's objections to Knox, and discusses further Argyle's lists of contrasted synonyms, which include many which are not exactly synonymous, and are in any case to be judged in the context of the richness of synonyms in both writings. He concludes cautiously that these arguments against common authorship are indecisive.

Statistical arguments often appear impressive, but it is difficult to

---

4   A.C. Clark, *The Acts of the Apostles. A Critical Edition with Introduction and Notes on Selected Passages* (Oxford: Clarendon Press, 1933), pp. 393-408.

5   A.W. Argyle, 'The Greek of Luke and Acts', *NTS* 20 (1974), pp. 441-45.

6   I have not located the reference cited by Clark, p. 394, in which Blass describes the Luke of Acts as ἑλληνικώτερος.

7   Sir J.C. Hawkins, *Horae Synopticae, Contributions to the Study of the Synoptic Problem* (Oxford: Clarendon Press, 2nd edn, 1909), pp. 177-82. Hawkins thinks these differences point to a considerable lapse of time between the writing of the two parts, see esp. pp. 180-81.

8   Cf. the figures in J.B. Smith, *Greek-English Concordance to the New Testament* (Eastbourne: Kingsway, 1955): Luke 7; Acts 141; rest of the New Testament 61 (Rom. 18, Heb. 22).

9   W.L. Knox, *The Acts of the Apostles* (CUP, 1948), pp. 3-15, 100-109.

10   B.E. Beck, 'The Common Authorship of Luke and Acts', *NTS* 23 (1977), pp. 346-52.

decide upon the limits of variation compatible with common authorship. It is only too easy to discover from a concordance statistical
peculiarities which could fuel surprising hypotheses. It is probable
that this kind of argument requires lengthy samples and large numbers of occurrences before we are justified in resting too much confidence in it, and that other variables, like source and internal change
of subject or *Gattung*, may confuse the issue considerably.[11] The
extent to which the Third Gospel follows Mark, for instance, as well
as modifying it, is likely to produce linguistic phenomena which occasionally engender surprisingly different statistics. All this is not designed to discount disparities as great as that in the occurrence of τε,
but to suggest caution; the most apparently impressive variations
may be of less weight in any direction than they appear. If Acts, or at
least parts of Acts, is on average more literary than the Gospel on a
number of such (perhaps marginally significant) counts, that would
not be surprising in view of the differences in literary and narrative
form. It might even be used to support theories about Luke's adherence to traditional sources in the Gospel.[12]

The stylistic argument is in the end both two-edged and indecisive, for all its promise of statistical objectivity. The assurance of
common authorship rests more firmly on a combination of broader
considerations, within which are included the notable, if again indecisive, stylistic similarities of the two parts.[13] The ostensible evidence of the prefaces is reinforced by a number of general characteristics; Bruce mentions the catholic sympathies of both works, the
interest in Gentiles, the unusually prominent position given to women in both, and a common apologetic tendency.[14] This judgment

---

[11] Cf. L.F. Clark, *An Investigation of Some Applications of Quantitative
Methods to the Pauline Letters, with a View to the Question of Authority*
(unpublished Manchester M.A. dissertation, 1979), which discusses the statistical treatment of the Pastorals by A.Q. Morton, P.N. Harrison, and K. Grayston and G. Herdan in the light of technical statistics.

[12] Knox, pp. 6, 11 attributes Luke's lack of thoroughgoing stylistic revision of
Mark to haste or carelessness, but it may be noted how he is careful to reproduce his source with limited changes, for instance in transmitting the words
of Jesus. Knox argues that 'Clark's two test cases μέν and τε, if strictly applied,
would have the result of proving that Romans and Galatians do not come
from the pen of the same writer' (p. 10). But this counter-argument is without
weight, for the occurrences involved are too few to 'prove' anything.

[13] See Hawkins, *Horae Synopticae*, pp. 174-76.

[14] Bruce, *Acts*, p. 2. I defer at this stage the discussion of detailed correspon-
dences, as also of the problems of sequence, of the accounts of the Ascension,
and the like. The difficulties here are to be seen in the context of the admitted
overall unity, and are not sufficient in themselves to challenge it.

may be repeated on other fronts. Although we shall go into more detail later, in the interests of establishing the breadth of the indications of unity,[15] we might here mention also the apparent shared methods in the handling of sources in Luke and Acts and also the current studies of a common Lukan theology.

Ordinarily the common dedication would not prove identity of authorship, any more than the reference in 2 Pet. 3:1 proves identity of authorship in the Petrine epistles. But the issue of pseudonymity, raised here by Argyle (pp. 444-45), is at once undercut by the fact that both books are anonymous. So far from sheltering behind the name of an authoritative apostolic writer, the 'Luke' of both books is self-effacing. It is surely the only natural reading of the prefaces to suppose they indicate common authorship, and the onus lies upon the doubter to explain the case otherwise.

If we seem to have lingered unnecessarily over defending a near consensus, it is because a matter so foundational should not be taken for granted in a discipline where options can be so easily closed. We need a reasoned grounding for determining the extent of our Lukan base, no less than our Pauline base; the difference is only that here we can agree more easily.

2. *The Genre of Luke-Acts*

The question of genre is complex and elusive in its bearing on our subject. It may be helpful to begin with several general observations. (1) The first evident complication is the fact that Luke and Acts are themselves different in type, even when we grant their essential unity and continuity. The first writing is a 'Gospel', and it is keenly debated what kind of creature a 'Gospel' really is.[16] The second cannot be described under that head, but is not on that account the easier

---

15 This breadth is our safeguard against the danger of circularity, to use similarities to prove unity and then use the assumption of unity to give significance to similarities.

16 Cf. e.g. C.H. Talbert, *What is a Gospel? The Genre of the Canonical Gospels* (Philadelphia: Fortress Press, 1977). Talbert highlights the distinction between the view of the Gospels as biographies (cf. C.W. Votaw, 'The Gospels and Contemporary Biographies', *AJT* 19 [1915], pp. 45-73 and 217-49, reprinted as *The Gospels and Contemporary Biographies in the Greco-Roman World*, with introduction by J. Reumann [Philadelphia: Fortress Press, 1970]) and that which sees them as a unique phenomenon born of myth, cult and the cultural alienation of an eschatological moment (e.g. R. Bultmann, 'The Gospels (Form)', *Twentieth Century Theology in the Making*, ed. J. Pelikan (London: Collins, 1969) 1.86-92, and elsewhere). Talbert himself looks for a solution through a reclassification of ancient biography in terms of function.

to place under any alternative category. (2) The ultimate resolution of this question of genre may really be an academic irrelevance for our present purpose, provided only that we wrestle with its essentials so far as to satisfy ourselves that we are asking appropriate questions of our text. It is no good raising the question of historicity if we are dealing with avowed fairy-tale or fiction.[17] The answer may not be simple; a basically or partly historical narrative may prove to contain legend, embellishment or propaganda. But that will require a negative or qualified answer to the question. So far we are asking only whether the question is proper, and our basic choice divides on this point. (3) It is unclear to what extent any of the New Testament documents are self-conscious literature which make deliberate use of contemporary forms.[18] Contemporary Roman literature, in particular, was an aristocratic avocation pursued within the confines of a social and cultural élite, whereas the Christian movement seems to have been concerned from the outset with popular proclamation.[19] It is wholly probable that their writers, and especially one with the literary ability and aspiration of Luke, were influenced by their cultural environment and reflect its trends, but by no means certain how closely or consciously. (4) Akin to the previous observation is the need to stress the difficulty of the argument from literary parallels. The ancient world was a diverse cultural complex, which we know only in a piecemeal and occasionally fragmentary way dependent on the chance survival of sources. The continual temptation is to draw direct lines of comparison or influence between surviving pieces without knowing their place in the larger context. We can find almost whatever we seek, and we can see significance in what we find. In such a case the study of literary forms is a task to be pursued with special caution, with a care not to use categories which arise out of imposed, rather than inherent, classifications.[20] (5) In the face of the

---

[17] For an example of the fictional view held in conjunction with an early dating see E.R. Goodenough, 'The Perspective of Acts', *SLA*, pp. 51-59.

[18] Such traditional distinctions as those between 'literary' and 'non-literary', *Hochliteratur* and *Kleinliteratur*, 'epistle' and 'letter', are not quite in point here. A definitive answer to this kind of question would require a nuanced study of the writer's social and cultural context, for which our fragmentary materials are insufficient.

[19] See generally F.G. Kenyon, *Books and Readers in Ancient Greece and Rome* (Oxford: Clarendon Press, 2nd edn, 1951); for literary readings in first century Rome, p. 85. The focus upon proclamation through literature may help to explain the development of the papyrus codex in Christian circles long before it came to prevail among pagans (cf. Kenyon pp. 96-101).

[20] I am not concerned here to separate such elusive entities as 'form' and *Gattung:* Examples of the dangers of genre-criticism abound. In a somewhat

popularity of literary-critical studies today, a corrective, or at least complementary, approach should also be noted. A good writer may use, perhaps deliberately, literary forms. But he will make them his servants, not his masters. He ought ultimately to be judged by what he says, rather than by an over-preoccupation with the way he says it. If he is moved by an urgent mission, he will strive to express his meaning in the most effective style. But our focus is upon the matter, not the manner. The genre is important to our theme as it bears on content. We need at least to be satisfied that our text purports to recount a narrative of events rather than metaphor or fantasy.

These cautions should be stressed before we proceed to details. There are for instance evident parallels between the Lukan prefaces and those of the ancient historians, a feature stressed by Wikenhauser and others,[21] but a recent dissertation connects them more closely with the prefaces of technical and medical literature.[22] The latter point would be fully consistent with the tradition of 'Luke the physician'. It is also possible to adduce contemporary documents to illustrate the combination of the roles of historian and physician in the same person.[23] Yet this procedure would not be justified unless it

iconoclastic article, H.D. Jocelyn, 'Horace, Epistles 1', *Liverpool Classical Monthly* 4.7 (July 1979), pp. 145-46, denies that 'the Stoic-Cynic diatribe' ever existed, claiming that it was invented *ex nihilo* by H. Usener in 1887. Without going so far in scepticism, we may note that the term is understood differently by classical scholars and by theologians, and that the concrete form it often assumes in NT scholarship derives from the dissertation of R. Bultmann, *Der Stil der paulinischen Predigt und die kynisch-stoische Diatribe* (Göttingen: Vandenhoeck and Ruprecht, 1910), where its specific features are identified from a complex of overlapping resemblances derived piecemeal from a diverse assemblage of literature, Latin and Greek, prose and poetry, rhetoric, philosophy and satire. One may doubt whether the resulting concept of the 'diatribe' is more than an artificial composite. Many studies which find rigid forms are worth careful scrutiny. Such cautions apply to the articles of T.Y. Mullins on 'disclosure', 'topos' and the like ('Disclosure: A Literary Form in the New Testament', *NovT* 7 (1964-65), pp. 44-50; 'Topos as a New Testament Form', *JBL* 99 (1980), pp. 541-47; etc.), or to the detailed rhetorical criticism in H.D. Betz's Hermeneia commentary *Galatians* (Philadelphia: Fortress Press, 1979), pp. 14-25 and *passim*. All these cases raise the issue of the validity of the argument from parallels.

21 A. Wikenhauser, *Geschichtswert*, pp. 137-42; cf. Bruce, *Acts* p. 66.

22 Loveday C.A. Alexander, *Luke-Acts in its Contemporary Setting, with special reference to the prefaces (Luke 1:1-4 and Acts 1:1)*, unpublished D.Phil. thesis (Oxford, 1977), pp. 56f, cited by F.F. Bruce, 'The Acts of the Apostles To-Day', in *BJRL* 65 (1982-83), p. 49.

23 An inscription of Smyrna, on the tombstone of the physician Hermogenes (*CIG* 3311 = *IGRR* 4.1445), gives a select bibliography of his writings, which

could be subjected to strict controls. It is not a matter of seizing upon a series of attractive parallels as grist to the mill of supporting a case. If it were so, a literary case could be made on this ground as strongly as on any other. It would serve only, as do many such literary studies, to confirm the thinking of those already convinced by fitting a texture of related possibilities to a hypothesis already congenial. This gives no prospect of communication with those who, for better or worse reasons, construe the literary affinities differently. Let us say here, as with Hobart's arguments for medical style, that the style and genre of the books may be fully consistent with the possibilities of authorship by 'Luke the historian' or 'Luke the physician', or even both roles together, without *proving* such a conclusion. Proof is not in point here. Consistency with the possibility is as much as we may reasonably claim to show.

The remainder of this section may be seen as a preliminary and generalized consideration of some issues posed by literary study for the explanation of Acts with which we are principally concerned in this book. First is the matter of literary patterns, the 'architecture' of Luke-Acts. An obvious instance is the often observed parallelism in Acts between the narratives of Peter and of Paul as embodied in the structural parallels between Acts 1-12 and Acts 13–28.[24] The question is raised whether such patterns have been created by Luke through the assimilation of the irregularities of real events to a structural conformity of his own making. Rackham stresses the parallelism, but insists that it arises out of the facts (p. xlix); Cadbury argues that there may have been an unconscious tendency to stereotyping or assimilation (*Making*, p. 232).

That is however a simple and obvious instance of a tendency in scholarship which others have developed far more elaborately. The study of Robert Morgenthaler[25] finds the key to Luke's literary act in

included 77 medical works, along with a variety of historical books, especially on Smyrnean history, and the civic history of other cities also. For the man see *PW* 8.877-78, ('Hermogenes No. 23'); he is the victim of a scathing satirical epigram in the Greek Anthology (11.114). Cf. the physician of Rhodiapolis in Lycia (*IGRR* 3.733), a priest of Asclepius and Hygieia, who was in the first rank as a doctor and also a medical and philosophical writer and a poet ('the Homer of medical poetry'); also Lucian *de Hist. Conscrib.* 16, recording the claim οἰκεῖον εἶναι ἰατρῷ ἱστορίαν συγγράφειν.

[24] Thus e.g. Rackham, *Acts*, pp. xlvii-xlix; Cadbury, *The Making of Luke-Acts* (London: Macmillan, 1927), pp. 232-33; etc. See however P.H. Menoud, 'Le Plan des Actes des Apôtres', *NTS* 1 (1954-55), pp. 44-51 for a different division of Acts focusing on the Council of Jerusalem.

[25] R. Morgenthaler, *Die lukanische Geschichtsschreibung als Zeugnis. Gestalt und Gehalt der Kunst des Lukas*, 2 vols. (Zürich: Zwingli-Verlag, 1949).

the principle of 'duality' (*Zweigliedrichkeit*), exhibited at every level from the pairing of words to doublets and architectural parallelisms throughout the work. He sees the mainspring of this phenomenon in the Deuteronomic principle of testimony being established at the mouth of two or three witnesses (Deut. 10:15),[26] and so argues that Luke's material has been chosen to accord with canons of forensic evidence, offering, in effect, a literary defence of historicity. M.D. Goulder applies a 'typological' method to the study of Acts, finding a cyclical pattern and elaborate parallelisms, and taking a much more sceptical view of the historicity of the book.[27] Talbert finds two problems common to both, 1. neither stands in the main stream of work on Lukan theology and their theological positions are therefore deficient when seen from redaction-critical perspectives, and 2. neither works from a comparative literary stance using material from the wider Mediterranean world of Luke's time.[28]

Both those objections are problematical, the first because the 're-daction-critical perspective' itself is open to cautious reassessment, the second because, although it is right to be concerned with wider contextual study, the appeal to comparative literature may easily become another phase of the suspect procedure of 'proof through parallels'. In fact, Talbert's own work inspires the same doubts, *mutatis mutandis*, as the work both of Morgenthaler and of Goulder. All three find structural patterns, and proceed, upon differing perspectives and comparisons, to draw larger and more significant conclusions than can really be justified.[29]

This brief foray into studies of literary structure is linked to our present consideration of genre in so far as Talbert uses it in his comparative literary studies, especially in his comparison of Luke-Acts as a whole with Diogenes Laertius' *Lives of the Philosophers* (c. 3rd century AD). This comparison, developed further in Talbert's subsequent study of the genre of the Gospels in the light of a new, functional analysis of ancient biography, leads us to the consideration of Luke-Acts as biography. Since the time of Rudolf Bultmann and

---

[26] Morgenthaler 2.7-8. Cf. A.A. Trites, *The New Testament Concept of Witness* (CUP, 1977), pp. 133-35; W.W. Gasque, *History of Criticism*, pp. 266-68.

[27] M.D. Goulder, *Type and History in Acts* (London: SPCK, 1964).

[28] C.H. Talbert, *Literary Patterns, Theological Themes, and the Genre of Luke-Acts*, SBL Monographs 20 (Missoula, Mont.: Scholars Press, 1974), p. 3.

[29] It is interesting that Talbert is critical of the lack of interest in this aspect of Luke's literary artistry among the most influential recent Lukan scholars (Conzelmann and Haenchen) and calls for renewed study of formal patterns as a control on the subjectivity of redaction criticism (pp. 3-4). I am less sure than he of the efficacy of the remedy.

K.L. Schmidt,[30] the Gospels have often been seen as a unique genre, differing from biography, as cultic, mythical and world-denying; and as uninterested in human personality and development, though Bultmann makes a partial exception of Luke-Acts where history begins to compensate for the loss of the primitive, world-negating, eschatological consciousness.[31] After rejecting alternative attempts to relate the Gospels to Graeco-Roman or Jewish literary parallels Talbert offers a reclassification of ancient biography, first as didactic or non-didactic, and then distinguishing five functional types among the didactic.[32] Of these, he places Luke-Acts together in Type D, as distinct from all the other Gospels. This is the type modelled on Diogenes, in which the life of the founder of a philosophical school is followed by an account of his successors or disciples, indicating where the true tradition of his teaching is to be found. This enables Talbert to unite the double work Luke-Acts under a single category distinct from those to which the other Gospels are assigned, even if it is still a somewhat mixed example, whose first part includes the correction of misunderstanding of the founder, characteristic of Type B.[33]

We are not concerned here to pursue Talbert's argument for

[30] K.L. Schmidt, 'Die Stellung der Evangelien in der allgemeinen Literaturgeschichte', in *EYXAPIΣTHPION. Studien zur Religion und Literatur des Alten und Neuen Testaments* (Festschrift für Hermann Gunkel), ed. Hans Schmidt, Part 2 (Göttingen: Vandenhoeck and Ruprecht, 1923), pp. 50-134.

[31] Bultmann in *Twentieth Century Theology*, ed. Pelikan, 1.86-89. Following D.F. Strauss, he argues that the Gospels show no development of personality, as biography should. Yet this observation is equally true of most ancient biography, and highlights rather a difference between the ancient and modern focus of interest (cf. Talbert, *Gospel* pp. 2-3).

[32] He cites the older division by F. Leo, *Griechisch-römische Biographie nach ihrer litterarischen Form* (Leipzig: Teubner, 1901), which distinguished (1) the encomium, (2) the 'peripatetic', focussing on character through action to make a moral point and inspire invitation, and (3) the 'Alexandrian' or 'grammatical', concerned with chronology and a rudimentary weighing of evidence, as opposed to moral edification. Subsequent study added a category (4), the popular or romantic Life. If Talbert's 'non-didactic' be excepted, as roughly the counterpart of (3) above, his five types are: *A* a pattern to copy; *B* to dispel a false image and provide a true model; *C* to discredit by exposé; *D* to show the 'living voice' of the school, by joining the life of the founder to some account of his true successors; *E* to validate or interpret the subject's teaching. All are primarily applied to biographies of philosophy, D not, and E perhaps only exceptionally, being applicable to biographies of rulers (Talbert, *Gospel*, pp. 92-98).

[33] Talbert makes Mark and John Type B, Matthew Type E (Talbert, *Gospel*, pp. 134-35).

finding Bultmann's criteria (the mythical, the cultic and the world-denying, this last reinterpreted as an attitude of 'inclusive reinterpretation') in some Graeco-Roman biographies also, and so partly rehabilitating Bultmann's case upon biographical ground. The problem is more basic. The classification seems forced. The biographical form (in its widest sense) is surely a more fluid and adaptable entity; strict functional subdivisions seem inappropriate. We find the intimately linked Gospels are to be spread into what seem rather arbitrarily different categories, Matthew as type E, Mark as type B, Luke-Acts D, and John B again. This seems a heavy price to pay for uniting Luke-Acts in one apart. The three Synoptics, at least, cry out to be treated as the same type of composition, whereas Acts, if any of the group, is ostensibly a little different. Its literary and situational unity with the Third Gospel is a factor of the greatest interest and importance, and perhaps the more so because of this very difference of type. There are, on any view, analogies between both parts and various ancient biographies, but these analogies are fluid, and, unless substantiated in specific terms of chronology and influence, seem unlikely to justify significant conclusions in any direction. The study of ancient biography, as of ancient historiography below, may in its place have a specific and carefully delimited contribution to make to our study, but is not to be overplayed. In any case Diogenes Laertius wrote a couple of centuries later than the Gospels and Acts, and Talbert's evidence for the earlier existence of a type is tenuous.[34]

There are also many other analogies on the market: memoir, apologia, encomium, aretalogy,[35] 'false history',[36] novel or romance,[37] however these various types be severally defined; on the Jewish side,

---

[34] Talbert, *Gospel*, pp. 95-96, 110n. His secondary sources, E. Bikerman 'La chaine de la tradition Pharisienne', in *RB* 59 (1952), p. 49, and W.D. Davies in *Christian History and Interpretation: Studies Presented to John Knox*, ed. W.R. Farmer *et al.* (CUP, 1967), pp. 140-41, refer primarily to the care taken to establish lists of successors (*diadochoi*) in the schools. The only earlier example mentioned is fragmentary, cited only from a secondary source I have not been able to verify. He might have mentioned the inscription *CIG* 3311, cited above (p. 35, n. 23) in a different connection: the last of Hermogenes' books was a διαδοχή κατὰ χρόνους, probably a 'chronology'. But none of these substantiates the existence of a specific, identifiable genre which provides a comparative base for a significant interpretation of Luke-Acts.

[35] Thus especially M. Hadas and M. Smith, *Heroes and Gods. Spiritual Biographies in Antiquity* (London: Routledge and Kegan Paul, 1965).

[36] Cf. especially E. Gabba, 'True History and False History in Classical Antiquity', *JRS* 71 (1981), pp. 50-62.

[37] E.g. S.P. and M.J. Schierling, 'The Influence of the Ancient Romances on the Acts of the Apostles', *Classical Bulletin* (Chicago) 54 (1977-78), pp. 81-88.

we have midrash or lectionary as possibilities. Again, we are not concerned with detailed discussion of these alternatives, except as they bear on our basic theme of the legitimacy of the issue of historicity. The case of 'aretalogy' illustrates again a recurring difficulty. The term exists,[38] but there is no surviving work to which the name is explicitly applied as a genre title, and the concept is understood differently by classicists and by theologians.[39] In so far as such analogies pose doubts for our theme, their implications will be treated in the discussion of historiography below. But we shall persist in speaking of them as 'possible analogies', rather than as 'parallels', for analogies may exist between cases which are not organically related. Here the resemblances are apt to be fluid, and we need mainly to guard against serious category mistakes, like judging metaphor or poetry by prosaic standards of realism.

The question whether Luke-Acts, and for our purpose Acts in particular, can be fitted to a contemporary genre-type or is *sui generis* ought perhaps to be assessed on rather different ground. The question of the primitive Christian reaction to Greek culture is not a simple one. There is a difficult problem over the placing of Paul in his social and cultural context,[40] and a related difficulty confronts us in

---

[38] The only relevant cases I can trace are, strangely, in Biblical Greek, Sirach 36:19 (16) LXX and Ps. 29 (30): 6 Symmachus, in the sense of celebration of the goodness of God, though this or a similar word may occur in a variant reading of Strabo 17.1.17 = 801. The word ἀρεταλόγος as an occupational term is better attested, in inscriptions (SIG³ 1133. Delos, 1st BC; IG 11.4.1263), and *aretalogus* in Latin literature of a story-teller (Suet. *Aug.* 74.1— perhaps equivalent to *fabulator*, ibid. 78.1; Juvenal *Sat.* 15.16, with *mendax*).

[39] Contrast the definition by Hadas in Hadas and Smith, p. 60, with the inscriptional text published by Y. Grandjean, *Une nouvelle arétalogie d'Isis à Maronée* (Leiden: Brill, 1975). Grandjean draws attention in his introduction (pp. 1-8) to this difference of understanding. See also the discussion by G.H.R. Horsley in *New Docs 1*, No. 2, pp. 10-21, esp. 13. 'Aretalogy' in this sense is a formal hymn of praise for the good deeds of a god, not a biography of a wonder-working θεῖος ἀνήρ. A number of inscriptional documents of the type is preserved, though the name used for them is merely conventional, and they appear irrelevant to the kind of discussion which uses the term 'aretalogy' as a basis for making significant parallels between Luke and Philostratus. Grandjean draws attention to the ambiguity in the word ἀρετή, dating the occurrence of its secondary meaning 'miracle' from the 4th cent. BC (p. 1). Both meanings were current in the New Testament period, and the later has sometimes been seen in 2 Pet. 1:3 (e.g. NEB).

[40] See especially the programmatic study by E.A. Judge, 'St. Paul and Classical Society', *JAC* 15 (1972), pp. 19-36; cf. F.F. Bruce, 'The New Testament and Classical Studies', *NTS* 22 (1976), pp. 229-42. The work of R.F. Hock, 'Paul's Tentmaking and the Problem of his Social Class', *JBL* 97 (1978), pp. 555-64, and *The Social Context of Paul's Ministry. Tentmaking and Apostleship*

the case of Luke. The traditional Luke was the only Gentile among apostolic writers, and the possibility of Gentile origin may still be canvassed whether or not the tradition is accepted. There is currently much rethinking of traditional ideas of the relations of Judaism and Hellenism, tending to the breaking down of once accepted categories.[41] Again, how far are the New Testament writers, and our 'Luke' in particular, likely to have come under the specific influence of Greek literary education? It is difficult to place Luke or Paul in these terms within the indications of a measure of reaction against pagan educational principles in the primitive church.[42] Yet we have the specific quotations of Greek poetry in Acts 17:28, 1 Cor. 15:33 and Titus 1:12, and implicit allusions in places like Acts 17:31 and 21:39. We have the tradition that Luke was a doctor, and this tradition (apart from its truth) testifies at the very least to a measure of acceptance of that profession in the church. We are not concerned here to attempt to answer these questions, rather to suggest that in our consideration of Luke's cultural background they ought to be asked, to set the issue of genre in its context, even if we have still to confess how little we know.

A final note here concerns literary forms within Acts. The speeches are the obvious example, and we shall discuss them specifically in appendix 1. It is commonly said that as ancient historians felt free to invent speeches they thought appropriate to the occasion, Luke did likewise, and the speeches are therefore an obvious vehicle of Lukan theology. It will be seen that these axiomatic propositions embody

(Philadelphia: Fortress Press, 1980) represents an attempt to carry out this kind of programme, though some of Hock's conclusions are open to debate.

[41] For rethinking of the status of Diaspora Judaism cf. A.T. Kraabel, 'The Roman Diaspora: Six Questionable Assumptions', *JJS* 33 (1982), pp. 445-64, and other recent studies; for a test case which he sees as the catalyst for a new synthesis, see his 'Impact of the Discovery of the Sardis Synagogue', in G.M.A. Hanfmann, *Sardis from Prehistoric to Roman Times: Results of the Archaeological Exploration of Sardis 1958-1975* (Cambridge Mass: Harvard University Press, 1983), pp. 178-90, 284. His treatment of the 'god-fearers' will be discussed below. For the bearing of similar questions on the context of Christianity, cf. I.H. Marshall, 'Palestinian and Hellenistic Christianity: Some Critical Comments', *NTS* 19 (1972-73), pp. 271-87; S.K. Riegel, 'Jewish Christianity: Definitions and Terminology', *NTS* 24 (1978), pp. 410-15. See also M. Hengel, *Judaism and Hellenism. Studies in their Encounter in Palestine during the Early Hellenistic Period* (London: SCM, 1974), 2 vols., tr. by J. Bowden from the 2nd German edition of *Judentum und Hellenismus* (Tübingen: J.C.B. Mohr, 1973), with the criticisms cited by Kraabel, *JJS* 33 (1982), p. 448.

[42] Cf. E.A. Judge, 'The Reaction against Classical Education in the New Testament', *Journal of Christian Education* 77 (1983), pp. 7-14.

some of the very assumptions that we have been challenging. There is the doubt over the efficacy of argument from literary parallels; there is the doubt over this 'theology of the gaps', where theology and history are placed in exclusive antithesis; and there is a further doubt over the simplistic, and even inaccurate, notions involved of the practices of ancient historiography.

This matter of the speech-form is however one of some moment for our topic. The question whether the content of a reported speech represents what was actually said is in its way a question of historical reliability. If we decide to reply negatively, we may still want to excuse our writer by saying that he was working with literary canons which did not require him to meet our 20th century expectations, and we may thus need from our own perspective to qualify even a favourable view of him by recognizing where it is inappropriate to press him into the mould of our own historical standards. It amounts to saying that the speech-form is not to be judged as history, any more than poetry or metaphor is to be judged as history. Yet this line of defence leads us back into the same difficulty over literary parallels. Thucydides and Josephus, to take two obvious examples commonly invoked in connection with Acts, differ greatly between themselves in how they use and present speeches in their works. Not only from our 'horizon', but even from the ancient 'horizon', the question of historicity may indeed arise in the speeches. There may be difficult questions of interpretation of genre involved, but still we have to come to terms with the explanation of the content, apart from the form. We must evaluate Luke rather by his performance than by any literary *Vorverständnis*.

We may well conclude that we are not yet much further forward. One trouble is that we have many uniquely shaped keys on offer to open the lock. If some of their claims are accepted, it is at the cost of the high significance and exclusiveness of the claims. There are of course useful literary parallels. It is reasonable to consider the Gospels and Acts with reference to ancient biography or historiography. But the comparisons may be disappointingly fluid. Their significance is enhanced only as we can establish resemblances as reflecting organic relationship, conscious dependence, or the like. Acts (and its unique relationship with one of the Gospels) is not amenable to close comparisons. If we are moved on that account to treat it as in some aspects *sui generis*, we mean that differently from the way Bultmann meant it about the Gospels. It forces us to ask questions independently about the likelihood of Hellenistic literary influence upon Luke. In particular, we are committed to some discussion of ancient historiography because our subject concerns history. But the value of that study must be carefully demarcated, to clarify misconceptions, to formulate possibilities, to outline the profile of a likely cultural context without being too quick to dogmatize about Luke's relationship to it. Luke's historical reliability must in the end be judged by the detailed assessment of his performance. It is even possible that his performance may help to throw light conversely on his literary context and aims.

3. The Meaning of Historicity

It is possible to judge the work of an ancient writer from an unrealistic expectation by laying down criteria for acceptance which are too literalistically rigorous. It is thus important to outline the reasonable province and the proper limits of historical criticism. Some of these points may appear self-evident, but it will be helpful to guard against the pre-empting of the central issues by an atomized hyper-criticism.

First, there is an evident conceptual distinction between what is good history by ancient canons and what is good history by modern canons. We ought strictly to judge Luke by the standards of his own day, whether or not we conclude that he was consciously influenced by them or measured himself by them. We cannot at least expect him to write as a modern historian writes, and it would be anachronistic to use an inappropriately modern measure. Yet in another sense that is just what we want to do. We are concerned with crucial historical issues in our own perspective, and we are concerned practically to know what use we can make of him. We are not marking him on merit, to pass or fail him, as examiners mark the academic exercises of those who have not yet graduated to their own expertise. If he is good in his own class, but does not measure up to our need of him, we want to know that. We want to know the characteristics of his writing in some detail. The differences between ancient and modern concepts of historiography, and indeed between different ancient— and different modern— concepts, is all part of the intricacy we seek to unravel. And it would be a mistake to suppose the ancient standards are necessarily inferior. At least in some cases they were rigorously scientific and critical in their own way. Our modern methods might on occasion fall under the severe censure of ancients who grounded surprisingly rigorous practice upon a theoretical base we find unfamiliar. Some scholars still write as though critical standards were a modern invention, although the evidence of keen debate over historiographical theory is patent and extensive in the ancient sources.[43] The differences complicate our problem, but they do not engender the pessimism with which theologians sometimes regard ancient writings. The possibility is not excluded that an ancient writer may be deemed a good source across the diverse reasonable expectations of differing culture or theory, indeed that different cultural perspectives may themselves actually overlap more closely than we have recognized.[44]

We may approach our theme through the consideration of descriptive terms which may be used in common parlance of a historical writer, such terms as 'accurate', 'trustworthy' or 'reliable'. Without attaching special significance to these words, we may use them to illustrate what an elusive tangle of differing expectations may easily be masked by apparently simple language. 'Accuracy' is an ambiguous concept. It may suggest a mechanical exactitude of transcription, as opposed to copying-errors or unchecked references or misquotation from memory. But this is not a sense in which it is even appropriate to the central questions of our inquiry— though there are points of detail where this level of 'accuracy' may be in point. Generally however this will not be our main concern, for we meet Luke, demonstrably in the Gospel, as an editor of sources, there preserved or inferable. His material has at the least passed through his own mind and received something of the stamp of his own personality and style. It is no mere transcription of Mark or of Q.[45] There are many obvious questions to raise about his editing, order, selection, abbreviation, other sources, hindsight, apart from the common preoccupation with theological *Tendenz*. There is also the need to recognize the editorial significance of what he preserves. And in this complex operation it makes sense to speak of his 'accuracy'. Is he a writer who is careful or careless in his handling of these tasks? Has he a conscience about preserving or reconstructing 'what actually happened'? It may be objected that the very fact of editing removes him from the realm of historical 'accuracy' by removing him from its

---

[43] See Chapter 3 below, and cf. C.J. Hemer, 'Luke the Historian' *BJRL* 60 (1977-78), pp. 28-51, and especially the discussion of Polybius on pp. 30-32.

[44] The point is worth stressing in view of the tendency to the extreme separation of ancient and modern cultures exemplified in D.E. Nineham, *The Use and Abuse of the Bible* (London: Macmillan, 1976), and 'The Strangeness of the New Testament World', *Theology* 85 (1982), pp. 171-77 and 247-55. For a reply to Nineham's book see R.H. Preston, 'Need Dr. Nineham be so Negative?' *ExpT* 90 (1978-79), pp. 275-80.

[45] I use the term for convenience of the sayings-material common to Matthew and Luke and representing a body of source-material used by Luke, but without judgment on its status. My point is not necessarily dependent on any particular view of the Synoptic Problem.

first, transcriptional sense. This however would make it necessary to so regard all historical sources, except the baldest chronicles, for all are of their essence interpretative, and no discredit necessarily attaches to them on that account. It is for instance conceivable that an editor may reword his sources critically, and so improve his claim to historical 'accuracy' albeit of an interpretative transcription of a good source, or because of its critical editing of its sources, but the two cases are different, and may involve different assessments of 'accuracy', both in source and editor.

All that is obvious enough, and there is no need to labour the possible varieties of 'accuracy' and 'inaccuracy'. But when Harnack gives his twenty-three pages of 'instances of inaccuracy and discrepancy' in Acts,[46] we seem to be looking at phenomena of a much more exiguous kind. His point is that these flaws belong to the style of Luke himself, as they occur alike in all the six bodies of tradition he distinguishes. Thus there are awkward changes of subject (6:6b; 8:17; 16:10; 16:29; chosen from different strands, among many other examples), shifts between direct and indirect speech or between ὅτι and the infinitive (1:4; 7:7; 17:3; 27:10; different strands), prolepsis in narrative (4:1-3; 17:5; 28:1-2).[47] The list could be enormously extended. The objection is raised at 1:24; 4:19, 24ff., etc., that two or more persons are made to speak in unison. Yet, in reality, Harnack's objection is directed not so much at Luke as at the nature of human language. No normal speech or writing could bear the hypercritical analysis used here. There would be a serious category mistake in objecting to the truth of talk about 'sunrise' or 'sunset' on the ground that such language embodies an archaic notion of solar movement rooted in an 'untrue', pre-Copernican astronomy, or about 'disaster' or 'lunatic' because these words are rooted in an astrological world-view.[48] The metaphor in each case is dead, so dead that we never normally think of its strict or etymological meaning. In a similar way we report the substance of a conversation, perhaps even with an admixture of direct speech, without ever thinking of dividing up the dialogue parts of the participants. The issue here is not accuracy, but normal selectivity and abbreviation to suit the hearer and accord

---

[46] Harnack, *Acts*, pp. 203-25, with summary and conclusions, pp. 225-31.

[47] Harnack's argument depends on his source-critical theory. Apart from this we may observe that his phenomena are spread in every part of the book. For the difficulty of sustaining *oratio obliqua* in Hellenistic idiom cf. I.H. Marshall 'Luke xvi.8— Who Commended the Unjust Steward?' in *JTS* n.s. 19 (1968), pp. 618-19.

[48] With 'lunatic' cf. σεληνιάζεσθαι in Mt. 4:24; 17:15, where however the connection with popular aetiology may be much closer.

with the ordinary limits of human language, memory and patience.

The use of *constructiones ad sensum* and the like may be noted as a feature of Luke's style. But it is doubtful that it bears any significant relation to our question of 'accuracy'. His writing certainly does not display the self-conscious, pedantic purism of the subsequent literary Atticism, but that is not the issue at stake. One is driven back to search Harnack again for matters of more substance in his list. And, curiously, in the latter part of his list he frequently rejects inaccuracies which had been identified by Weiss, sometimes involving correction by conjectural emendation or interpolation theories which Harnack rejects. In the end it is bewildering. If this were the substance of the case for the prosecution, the charge must be dismissed. There is no case to answer, and our present study is superfluous. It is true that Harnack is looking for 'inaccuracy' on a narrow front; he does not for instance specify obvious problems like the death of Judas. But he certainly means to include historical inaccuracies, even if he seems so little able to find serious ones. Yet his work here might give too easy a passage, to acquit Luke by faint accusation. Our investigation is far from concluded, if only because Harnack is in this area an aberrant phenomenon from the mainstream of German scholarship since his day, and because Haenchen is made of much sterner stuff. Harnack serves here as a significant illustration of the problems inherent in unresolved differences of expectation.

Similar kinds of exploration might be made of words like 'reliable' and 'trustworthy', highlighting different facets of the qualities we seek in our source. We may ask 'reliable as what?' The question may be whether Luke is reliable as a historical source for Jesus and the primitive church, or as a witness to the concerns of the church in his own later day, whether reliable as an authority for details of travel or for primitive preaching. Is he 'trustworthy', in the sense that we are so favourably impressed with him where we can check him that we are inclined to take his word where we cannot? There is a question of the onus of proof to be explored.

Such considerations help to illustrate the complexity of the problem opened up by the attempt to reach a satisfactory understanding of the meaning of historicity. Therefore I have listed in conclusion not so much a definition as a tabulation of guidelines to what seem to be the reasonable expectations of historicity in a writing like Acts. Some of these points are provisional or anticipatory. Some will be discussed and justified more specifically in the chapter on ancient historiography; others may need to be modified in the course of later study. But these propositions are offered as setting the profile of the investigation.

(1) We cannot base far-reaching conclusions simplistically upon confirmatory or discrepant detail. We are concerned first to know the qualities of Acts in general and in principle. This is not inconsistent with developing a refined and qualified estimate, but such a judgment must be broadly based and well substantiated rather than derived from an atomized qualification of harmonizations or contradictions.

(2) It is then appropriate to ask whether Luke is habitually and in general a trustworthy source by the standards of his day, whether he exhibits accuracy or inaccuracy of mind, a general conscience for, or a general disregard of, historical fact. Again, the pattern may not be simple. He may prove inconsistent, or vary markedly according to his source. The answer may again have to be a refined one, broadly based on the assessment of his methods and performance.

(3) It is important to decide whether the narrative gives an essentially accurate chronological outline, but this does not involve the strictly chronological sequence of every detail. This is a subject for further study. There is for instance a wide difference between the principles of arrangement appropriate to an episodic or anecdotal narrative and those appropriate to a sequential narrative. Chronological arrangement is itself but one variety of arrangement, and sufficient attention must be paid to it in a historical account. But the natural complexity of events and the needs of explanatory recapitulation and anticipation preclude the rigid linearity of events which figures in some critical expectations. Yet explicit notes of time and the distinctness of ostensibly separate incidents are to be pressed. If for instance we are persuaded that the Jerusalem visits described in Acts 11 and Acts 15 are doublets of the same events or that one or both are seriously misplaced, such views are to be seen as strong points against historicity.

(4) Narratives are embodied in natural, phenomenological language, which is not to be judged by over-literal criteria. Though independent sources for the same incidents are not commonly available for Acts, it will not necessarily matter for historicity if such cases exhibit varying details and perspectives, provided the differences are not radically contradictory. Indeed, we should be concerned to force neither harmonization nor contradiction, if only because we stand in too distant an external position to possess a completeness of context on which such decisions are likely to depend. There may be places where we have enough information to attempt a positive fit. Otherwise we are wise to be cautious.

(5) The possibility of interlocking sources is however important,

notably in the larger relationship of Acts with Epistles, not in the narrow sense of harmonization, but in considering whether the different strands together contribute to the enlargement of a broadly consistent picture. If this is found to be a fruitful approach, this factor tells in favour of historicity, broadly conceived; if conversely the narrative is not historical, we should expect a lack of patterned correlation and illumination from the approach. But it remains difficult to reverse the latter proposition, to prove a negative verdict from negative evidence.

(6) Historicity is not necessarily at stake in the phenomena of incomplete or selective narrative. There is again a background in ancient theory, to which we must return. Omissions may need to be amenable to very different kinds of explanation: one of them may even be the lack of evidence meeting appropriate criteria; not mere ignorance, but belief or knowledge which falls short of a requisite selected standard of authentication. To suggest such a thing of Acts may seem to beg the question, but we are not asserting this, merely mentioning the possibility as one existing in ancient historiographical theory, even if neglected in modern simplistic assumptions about the ancient so-called 'pre-critical' method.

(7) It is an inescapable question of historicity whether or not the miracles happened. The issue is not always necessarily clear-cut. Luke is sometimes ambiguous in what he means us to interpret as miraculous, and we are not necessarily committed to his interpretations. But, apart from the occasional doubtful case, the acceptance or rejection of the miracles, or of individual miracles, is a matter whose crucial implications for historicity we cannot minimize. The fact that it is such a sensitive matter only reinforces the delicacy needed in unravelling the issues.

(8) It is also an essential question of historicity whether or not the substance of the speeches in Acts is authentic. It is crucial to note the distinction implied in the phrase 'the *substance* of the speeches', for even if we accept this, we shall say they are not transcriptions, but accounts rewritten in Luke's own style. The issue of historicity here lies between the view that they are Lukan summaries of events and that they are Lukan theological constructs independent of the substance of what was actually said on a historical occasion.

(9) An important issue is the assessment of precision and of approximation in the reporting of details. Neither lends itself to a simple evaluation. Inconsequential details may give scope for checking with external evidence, and are less amenable to the explanation from theological *Tendenz*, but some would see such specifics

as personal names as insertions created by the expansive tendencies of the laws of tradition. Approximation, too, even vagueness, is open to evident attack, but may also be due to the careful reserve of the writer who will not specify beyond the limits or credentials of his evidence. In fact both specificity and approximation may be used in opposite directions. A natural balance between inconsequential precision and reserve may be the expression of an accurate mind, but the probabilities must be carefully weighed before identifying this or a contrary pattern in the profile of the evidence.

(10) It should not need repeating that the presence of a theological motif is not necessarily a disproof of historicity. All sophisticated history is in its degree interpretative, and history and theology may not necessarily conflict, but run on parallel lines. The simplistic use of the argument against historicity on this score is a radical *non sequitur*, and while we recognize that reputable scholarship does not usually fall into such crudities, the danger is pervasive and often latent, and all the steps in the argument need to be established, and none the less when the position defended is deemed 'critical' rather than 'traditional'. It is a pity if the 'critical' position is less than rigorously presented because its popularity renders it less open to debate. The historical issue may where possible need to be settled apart from the theological.

(11) Our working view of historicity is thus descriptive and pragmatic rather than definitive, and involves bringing the preceding points into the modern perspective. Our real interest is to know what use we can make of Acts as a historical source for primitive Christianity. We need an estimate of its qualities, along the main lines of cleavage outlined above, and with due regard to its own cultural context, which will enable us to handle it critically, in the best and most open sense of that word.

4. *Approaches to the Question*

Although much has already been said (albeit in passing) about the present author's concepts of history and historical method,[49] a brief clearing of the methodological ground may be necessary, impelled rather by the awareness of some recent trends in New Testament study than by the essential needs of the case. I propose for the moment to label four conceivable types of approach to historicity: 1) the harmonistic, 2) the redactional, 3) the contextual, and 4) the sociological. They differ widely in status and acceptability, but they are

---

49 Furthermore, in the specific discussions of text and evidence which follow (where the strength of my case lies), the theory will be seen in practice.

not necessarily distinct and incompatible, and there may be at least a limited role for any of them, even if some like the harmonistic, need to be held within narrow bounds. There is an obvious tendency for the harmonistic to be congenial to the apologist,[50] and the redactional, while more sophisticated, may lend itself to the sceptic, especially if it be allowed to overshadow the debate so far as to preempt interaction and criticism from alternative stances. At best the redactional approach incorporates an inherent uncertainty, for it has to penetrate the mind and motives of a writer in an alien cultural context. That difficulty need not prompt the pessimism of a Nineham, but it does show the stronger focus upon the 'contextual' approach as a factor of basic importance. And the redactional approach suffers from the further disability that it claims to tell us directly not about the trustworthiness of the narrative, but about the theological concerns of the writer or his church in a later setting. To work back through 'style criticism' and 'tradition criticism' in Acts is a difficult and slippery task. There are few footholds to secure the missing sections of the argument.

There is then something of an impasse if historical criticism is treated as equivalent to a thoroughgoing application of tradition and redaction criticism.[51] It is important that the insights of these approaches are weighed, that the redactional factor is recognized, that the alternatives offered by redactional study are given their due attention as options, but also important that such redactional views are brought under constant scrutiny by the control of such external objectivity as we can attain through the meticulous and representative study of the context in its own terms. This too is admittedly difficult ground, for our knowledge of the context is often fragmentary. But we must not be content with redactional studies which ignore the contextual, for they seem to be ignoring a necessary control which must be allowed to strengthen or contest their argument. Nor should we be satisfied with conclusions reached on redactional grounds which subsequently adduce unrepresentative historical

---

[50] I use this word without the pejorative connotation it often seems to bear in scholarly study. It is an honourable office to be an apologist for a position of which one is firmly convinced, and the criticism is only applicable where an apologetic motive is permitted to cover a lowering of academic standards or integrity. If a conviction is well grounded, the best scholarship will in the long run be the best apologetic for it. In any case it is good to caution against overplaying harmonization as a method.

[51] For a balanced, broader discussion of 'historical criticism' see I.H. Marshall, 'Historical Criticism', in *New Testament Interpretation*, ed. I.H. Marshall (Exeter: Paternoster, 1977), pp. 126-38.

data, even of a sophisticated documentary kind, to confirm opinions based on different reasons.

But the purpose of this brief section is not to labour these familiar lines of debate, save as they highlight afresh the importance of the contextual approach. The study of context has in a sense received new impetus in recent years through the growth of the interest in the sociology of the New Testament.[52] The plea for context can now be made in a somewhat changed climate, where it may expect to meet a sympathetic hearing. But just for that reason, it is important that we discriminate between the qualities of distinct methods which may pass for one because they are sometimes concurrent, or because they ask similar questions and may reach similar answers. Our main pragmatic distinction may be characterized as a contrast between the 'contextual' and the 'sociological'. The difficulty for both is caused by the fragmentary nature of our knowledge of the ancient world.

This distinction, in broadest terms, that between the methods of the historian and of the sociologist, though it may be unfair to put it so simplistically. The 'historian' works inductively from the unique and particular, and the social historian in particular assesses how far his mass of data is representative of the social whole to which it belongs. The 'sociologist' (in our simplified sense) accommodates the particular to his theoretical understanding of what is representative.

There is a valid place in argument both for induction and for deduction. There is also a valid prospect of making progress in knowledge by a judicious combination of them, though this also easily engenders the dangers of spiral or even circular reasoning. But the 'sociological' approach may too easily proceed upon the assumption

---

52 The field was reopened by E.A. Judge, *The Social Pattern of Christian Groups in the First Century* (London: Tyndale, 1960); cf. among many later studies J.G. Gager, *Kingdom and Community: The Social World of Early Christianity* (Englewood Cliffs: Prentice-Hall, 1975); A.J. Malherbe, *Social Aspects of Early Christianity* (Baton Rouge and London: Louisiana State University Press, 1977); G. Theissen, *The First Followers of Jesus. A Sociological Analysis of the Earliest Christianity* (London: SCM, 1978), tr. by J. Bowden from *Soziologie der Jesusbewegung: Ein Beitrag zur Entstehungsgeschichte des Urchristentums* (Munich: Chr. Kaiser Verlag, 1977); published in America as *Sociology of Early Palestinian Christianity* (Philadelphia: Fortress Press, 1978); *The Social Setting of Pauline Christianity. Essays on Corinth*, tr. by J.H. Schütz from various German publications (Philadelphia: Fortress Press, 1982); R.F. Hock, *The Social Context of Paul's Ministry. Tentmaking and Apostleship* (Philadelphia: Fortress Press, 1980); W.A. Meeks, *The First Urban Christians. The Social World of the Apostle Paul* (New Haven and London: Yale University Press, 1983). The continuing influence of Adolf Deissmann's classic studies *Paul* and *Light from the Ancient East* should not be forgotten.

that the facts are known. E.A. Judge refers to what he terms the 'sociological fallacy', not the less real for its care to guard against the opposite error of judging the formation of Paul's world wholly through theological structures.[53] He cites B. Holmberg's assumption that the first stage of collecting the phenomena is done: 'There exists a considerable degree of consensus among scholars on the vast majority of details concerning philological and historical fact'.[54] But Judge is correct in thinking that it is precisely in this first stage that a radical weakness persists. Until the basic factual work is done thoroughly and representatively there is a danger inherent in importing social models which have been developed in the study of quite different cultures.[55] In the factual tradition derived from primary sources we are too prone to capitalize still on the legacy of Lightfoot (who is dated) and Ramsay (who is despised). We need to assess at first hand the new non-literary materials (especially in our case the inscriptions) with the rigour attained by the older scholarship.

There are then several points on which we must reassert the special importance of contextual historical study. (1) Without entering into detailed criticism of the 'sociological' approach, historical study is needed, often in a basic and traditional sense, as the methodological means of attaining a similar end. (2) There is an ongoing need,

[53] E.A. Judge, 'The Social Identity of the First Christians: A Question of Method in Religious History', *JRH* 11 (1980-81), pp. 201-17; citing pp. 209-12.

[54] B. Holmberg, *Paul and Power. The Structure of Authority in the Primitive Church as Reflected in the Pauline Epistles* (Lund: CWK Gleerup, 1978), p. 2, cited by Judge, 'Social Identity', p. 210. Cf. Holmberg's picture of the investigation as like that of an anthropologist collecting phenomena and organizing them into conceptual structures (*loc. cit.*).

[55] Cf. my review of J.H. Elliott, *A Home for the Homeless. A Sociological Exegesis of 1 Peter, Its Situation and Strategy*. (Philadelphia: Fortress Press, 1981), *JSNT* 24 (1985), pp. 120-23. While recognizing the vigour and learning of Elliott's work, I am disquieted that he has prematurely imposed a model upon a hypothetical setting which he has documented mostly from secondary sources, where the representative use of the inscriptions might give pause, or indeed point in other directions. Most recently E.A. Judge writes: 'Even if one accepts the assumptions of social determinism, the problem with this kind of explanation is that we simply do not know enough about the day-to-day workings of rank and status in the Roman world of the Caesars and St. Paul. The theories have usually been hammered out in the laboratory of a South-Seas-island anthropologist, and then transposed half-way around the world, and across two millennia, without adequate testing for applicability in the new setting: so powerful is the assumption of the indelible pattern of human social behaviour'. *Rank and Status in the World of the Caesars and St. Paul* (Christchurch NZ: University of Canterbury, 1982), p. 10. Judge's response is to insist on the importance of original documents, in this case the papyri.

beyond the necessary limits of our present topic, for the attainment of a detailed social profile of the context of primitive Christianity, analysed where possible by dates and individual cities, to illumine questions like the local strength of Judaism or local varieties of pagan religion or civic organization, and provide some framework for evaluating the Christian reaction. (3) We need study of the environment in its own terms, not merely as a means to an end of answering theological questions. There is also however a converse need, where the problems are posed by our Biblical texts themselves, and we are anxious to answer them. It is ultimately necessary to work from both ends, but with care against the pitfalls of method which may supervene if we try to take short cuts. (4) The concerns of our present study may sometimes afford to sit loose to the broader interest in sociology, or indeed social history, where we are preoccupied rather with the application of specific factual details. It is often through small and incidental points of fact that a text may be checked against its context, though we must be very careful about the conclusions drawn from such details. (5) All this leads to the crucial question whether the context to which these studies point us is the context of the historical Paul (or of the historical Jesus), or the context of Luke's church. If the latter be thought to be considerably removed in time from the former, the difference may be extremely significant, and carry appreciable implications for our study.

5. *The Textual Problem*

Our present undertaking is subject to a further dimension of tangled complexity in the factor of textual variation in Acts, where the so-called 'Western' tradition raises questions of definition, homogeneity, originality, source and tendency. In older studies its bearing on historicity was linked fairly directly to the question whether the 'Western' text as an entity was the 'original' text, or otherwise deserving of special respect. The newer stress is upon understanding the history of text-types, apart from a preoccupation with 'original' readings.[56] Our immediate difficulty is to demarcate the limits of our need to be involved in the textual question for the special purpose of our study.

Even when we start from the position that Codex Bezae is the most important witness to a type of text, uniquely longer and

---

[56] E.J. Epp, *The Theological Tendency of Codex Bezae Cantabrigiensis in Acts* (CUP, 1966), pp. 13-14. See also the useful survey article, F. Pack, 'The "Western" Text of Acts', *RQ* 4 (1960), pp. 220-34.

divergent in Acts, which may for convenience be loosely termed 'Western', we have not yet established the homogeneous identity of the type, or indeed of the manuscript. There are such complex possibilities of contamination in transmission that the pure 'Western' text may appear as an archetypal abstraction, a hypothetical entity to be inferred, rather than precisely reconstructed, from the broad and patterned attestation of its most characteristic peculiarities. Even when we assume the early existence and homogeneous identity of what amounts to being an alternative edition of Acts, its status remains problematic. Is it a secondary expansion of the 'Alexandrian' text,[57] or the 'original' from which the other has been abridged?[58] Are both ultimately to be traced to the same hand, as draft and finalized editions of the same work?[59] Is the Western text relatively free of any special point of view,[60] or is it marked by an overall anti-Jewish or other theological tendency which help significantly to explain its special character?[61]

We cannot attempt to pursue these questions at this stage, nor to prejudge the textual problem as a whole. It will suffice for the present to offer briefly some pragmatic guidelines for negotiating prospective pitfalls. (1) I shall work with the provisional assumption that the 'Alexandrian' text is in general to be preferred, and it would certainly be unwise to presuppose any minority positions. Yet such a general assumption will be open to modification or correction, and

[57] Thus B.F. Westcott and F.J.A. Hort, *The New Testament in the Original Greek*. (London: Macmillan, 2nd edn 1896), Introduction and Appendix volumes. Introduction, pp. 120-21, 172-75; J.H. Ropes in *BC* 3. ccxxiv-ccxxv; and many others. Westcott and Hort themselves protest strongly against the broader use of the term 'Alexandrian' for the type they prefer to call 'Neutral' (pp. 129-30), but their own word may seem to beg the question.

[58] A.C. Clark, *Acts*, Introduction, esp. pp. xxxi-xxxii.

[59] F. Blass, *Acta Apostolorum* (Leipzig: Teubner, 1896), Praefatio; followed by T. Zahn. *Einleitung* 2.339-60 = *Introduction* 3.8-41. Blass argued that the 'Western' text was the earlier draft.

[60] Thus Ropes, *BC* 3.ccxxxiii, though he acknowledges an emphasis on Gentile interests. Westcott and Hort, Introduction, pp. 282-84 had actually denied dogmatic alteration of texts as a factor in transmission, a view rejected from more recent scholarly perspectives.

[61] Among earlier essays in this direction we may note J. Rendel Harris, *Codex Bezae. A Study of the So-called Western Text of the New Testament. Texts and Studies* 2 (CUP, 1891), pp. 148-53 and 228-34, finding successively Montanist and Marcionite influences in individual Western readings. The most systematic study is now that of Epp, *Tendency*. In all these debates we must not forget the remarkable differences between the expanded character of the Western text of Acts and its less aberrant, even 'non-interpolated', features in the Gospels.

will be held loosely in the constant awareness of the complex variety of opinion. (2) Great caution must be used with regard to eclecticism in textual questions, not because eclecticism is necessarily wrong, but because it lends itself all too easily to the unconscious tendency to choose what is attractive for one's case. It may indeed be on almost any view that D preserves some significant original readings, or some accurate traditions independent of other texts, or the like. Such phenomena may certainly be noted, but we should refrain from using them to an end, except as they might help to a more coherent understanding of the nature of the Western text itself and its sources, but that in its turn is a question of such difficulty that it is wise to avoid any pretension to solve it parenthetically. (3) Conversely, the origin of the Western text is an important historical question in its own right, and any light we may gain on it could be a strand in the complex of historical authentication. But we must again stress the difficulty of expecting secure progress on this front. (4) The ultimate underlying reason for this reiterated caution is our belief that the Western text is not the 'original' text-form or edition of Acts. The nub of our question is not then raised by it directly. Yet, if not 'original', the fact remains that its roots go so near the original and form so much a single complex with it that they are difficult to disentangle. If for instance we accepted the now unfashionable option that the two editions were by the same author, and especially if he be identified with the traditional Luke, new questions would at once be posed. Did this author re-edit his own work from a later redactional perspective, or did he add good traditions discovered in the interval (if the 'Western' is later), or omit otiose or doubtfully accredited details (if the 'Alexandrian' is later)? Or did his redaction exhibit a mixture of phenomena? Even if this two-edition view of Blass and Zahn is now little accepted, it serves to illustrate the clinging intricacy of the case. Our safeguard is again to avoid any textual special pleading which might be turned to account in making a case.

We may in general accept the balance of probability that the longer text is more likely to be derived from the shorter by explanatory gloss and expansion than the shorter abbreviated from the longer. This balance is confirmed by the character of the distinctive western readings, which often read like inferential enlargements. It throws in clearer relief those few individual 'Western' readings which have been more widely received as likely to preserve authentic details. The assessment of these cases is difficult, for additional precision may be variously explained. J.H. Ropes, who is very cautious, offers three examples: καὶ μείναντες ἐν Τρωγυλλίῳ (before reaching

Miletus, Acts 20:15); καὶ Μύρα (following εἰς Πάταρα ,Acts 21:1); and δι' ἡμερῶν δεκάπεντε (for the time taken to traverse the sea of Cilicia and Pamphylia *en route* for Rome, Acts 27:5).[62] The first is the most widely attested, and is geographically appropriate, suggestive even of delay in negotiating the narrow strait between Trogyllium and Samos as a reason for not arriving earlier at Miletus. The mention of Myra is again geographically apt, if perhaps gratuitous or assimilated to the reference in 27:5. In that same verse the 'fifteen days' suits well enough the tempo of the belated autumn voyage against persistently adverse winds. Yet none of these readings is assured, and perhaps only the first has a strong claim.[63] M.J. Lagrange adds four more cases of this type which he believes could well be authentic: at Peter's escape from prison κατέβησαν τοὺς ἑπτὰ βαθμούς (12:10); Paul taught in the school of Tyrannus (Τυραννίου D) 'from the fifth hour to the tenth' (19:9); the crowd of demonstrators with Demetrius chanted δραμόντες εἰς τὸ ἄμφοδον (19:28); and the centurion 'delivered the prisoners to the captain of the guard' (στρατοπεδάρχῳ) (28:16).[64] Again, though the cases differ, and some again are attractive, perhaps none are original.[65] They are instructive for the task of trying to discriminate about the historical value of detail. Some of them might preserve accurate facts without belonging to the original text. 'The seven steps' look like a piece of gratuitous detail inserted by someone who supposed, rightly or wrongly, that he knew the place. It does not read like Luke– or Peter. It is an erratic boulder, an oddity which does not belong, however parenthetically. Inconsequential detail may authenticate when it is unstudied, but this looks both otiose and contrived. The other three cases all incorporate picturesque additions which may be appropriate and indeed true, without therefore being necessarily original.[66] The last has its claim

---

62 Ropes, p. ccxxxv.

63 None of these readings is accepted in B.M. Metzger, *A Textual Commentary on the Greek New Testament* (London and New York: United Bible Societies, 1971), the shorter versions being given preference on a probability rating respectively {C}, {C}, {B}. The relative magnitude of the textual problem in Acts is shown by the fact that Metzger devotes 245 pages to it, beside 258 for the four gospels and 263 for the rest of the NT, the number of pages of text in the UBS edition being respectively 113, 415 and 367.

64 M.J. Lagrange, *Introduction à l'étude du Nouveau Testament. II Critique textuelle* (Paris: Gabalda, 2nd edn, 1935), pp. 396-97.

65 Metzger assigns probability {B} to the shorter readings of 19:9 and 28:16. The other two additions do not rate even that degree of hesitation before rejection.

66 For the idea that Paul used a lecture-room during Tyrannus' siesta, cf. the epigram on the hours of the Roman day (Martial 4.8). The personal name

buttressed by its wider attestation in Byzantine manuscripts.

If these instances give a fair sampling, the results are somewhat negative. They do not suffice for trying to dismiss the problem, but do reinforce the reserve with which we propose to view Western readings. We may be constrained on occasion to include them in the necessary scope of debate, perhaps even as a secondary vehicle of authentic local colour, or the like, but we shall not build on them. And it is notable that these few cases which have commended themselves to recent scholarship are all matters of factual detail without theological import, and incur possible rejection upon straight grounds of textual criticism and historical verisimilitude or appropriateness. There is less disposition to find priority anywhere in the theology of D and its allies, where its apparent tendencies are aligned with its expansive and explicative relation to the shorter text in Acts.

6. *Sources for the Context*

It seems important to specify both the extent and the limitations of the collateral evidence. There is for instance a relative lack of secular Greek literature in the first century, a feature perhaps due in part to the growth of Atticism and its prevalence in the task of the period immediately following.[67] The principal names are Strabo and Dionysius of Halicarnassus at the turn of the Christian era, Dioscorides, Josephus and Philo the nearest contemporaries of Paul, and Dio Chrysostom, Epictetus and Plutarch overlapping the next century. It is remarkable that two of these are Jewish, and of acknowledged importance for the background of early Christianity, and also that all the others, save Plutarch, are of Anatolian birth, touching the land of Paul's origin and the focus of his travels in the Lukan narrative. The many other names preserved comprise epigrammatists in the Greek Anthology, or medical and historical writers known only from fragmentary citations. Josephus and Philo obviously stand apart, and the former is obviously of unique significance for our present study.

'Tyrannus', as against 'Tyrannius' in D, is attested in Ephesian inscriptions. ἄμφοδον may mean 'street', 'highway' (Hesychius ῥύμη, ἀγυιά, δίοδος), and has then been supposed to refer to the great avenue from the theatre to the harbour at Ephesus, surviving today as reconstructed by Arcadius (cf. Ramsay, *CRE* p. 153), but the word is usually employed in the papyri of a city 'quarter' or 'ward'. I defer discussion of the important Western reading at 11:28, which offers an anticipatory 'we-passage'.

[67] Cf. E.A. Judge, 'St. Paul and Classical Society', p. 31 for this point. This programmatic study of the context of Paul is of seminal importance, and of immediate relevance to the related, and perhaps even more difficult, problem of the context of Luke.

Otherwise, apart from a select few of higher literary pretension, the first century is notable as an era of technical writing.[68]

The surviving Latin literature of this time is at once much richer and different in its ethos and relevance. Of the great Augustans, Livy and Ovid lived into the Christian era. The century and its immediate aftermath were dominated by the great writers of 'Silver Latin', Lucan, Martial, Persius, Petronius, Pliny the Elder, Seneca, Quintilian, and Statius, followed by Juvenal, Pliny the Younger, Suetonius and Tacitus, among many lesser figures. More technical writing was represented by such as Celsus, Columella, Frontinus, Manilius and Scribonius Largus.[69] The higher Roman literature of this time was somewhat esoterically aristocratic, heavily influenced by the prevalence of rhetoric in education, so that its most brilliant practitioners often cultivated a bizarre individuality of allusive brevity, advised by the taste of a literary coterie and declaimed at public readings.[70] Viewed from this perspective Judaism and incipient Christianity were matters of small account, and when mentioned at all are treated with distaste and contempt.[71] But it needs to be emphasizing that this is a narrowly Roman viewpoint, remote from the everyday world of Luke and Paul within the exceedingly complex civilization of the day. There is even a 'Roman fallacy' which writes a context of

[68] I omit notice of writings of uncertain date and provenance like the *Library* of Apollodorus, which may belong to this century. The Letters of Apollonius of Tyana, if authentic, are contemporary, but the Philostratean literature is of the early 3rd century. We may compare this sparse array with a more diversified list of second century writers of Greek: Aelius Aristides, Appian, Arrian, Artemidorus of Daldis, Athenaeus, Galen, Lucian, Marcus Aurelius, Pausanias, Pollux, Polyaenus, Ptolemy, apart from the three major names above who overlapped from the first. The Asiatic provenance is strongly represented among these also. The impression that the first century is an epoch dominated by *Fachprosa* may be a misleading consequence of the pattern of survival: Judge pleads for someone to write the history of the lost Greek literature of this time, Judge, 'St. Paul and Classical Society', p. 31.

[69] The classification is of course arbitrary, for the elder Pliny was a pedantic polymath rather than a stylist, and is placed in the former list in deference to his fame, whereas Manilius wrote astronomical poetry, and Martial and Statius were near-contemporaries of the later group.

[70] This may be largely true even of many of the more apparently 'technical' writings. The knowledge displayed may be that of the well-read gentleman *littérateur*, not that of practical or clinical experience.

[71] The famous references to Christianity are in Tac. *Ann.* 15.44; Suet. *Claud.* 25.4 (probably) and *Nero* 16.2; Pliny *Ep.* 10.96, 97; also Tac. *Hist.* 5.2-5, 8-13, and note the pejorative remarks about Jews and Christians e.g. in Tac. *Hist.* 5.5; Quintilian *Inst. Or.* 3.7.21; Juv. 3.13-14; 6.157-60, 542-47; 14.96-106.

New Testament times out of imperial history and literature, perhaps rather baldly juxtaposed with a Jewish background written out of gleanings from Josephus, Qumran and the Rabbis, and a generalized view of Hellenistic culture. The context (or rather contexts) of Luke or of Paul need to be studied in much more specific and integrated terms.[72] The value of the Latin writers is less direct. They are historical sources: Tacitus in particular is indispensable for the larger political framework. But we need the means to gain a more closely focused picture, specifically for instance on the relevant cities of Asia Minor or Greece.

We have focused thus far on the contemporary century, combining as it happens literature strictly coeval with historical retrospect from near-contemporaries, notably Josephus and Tacitus. Writings earlier, concurrent or later have different kinds of relevance: we shall be concerned, for instance, to explore the previous course of historiography in order to discriminate among the possible concepts available to Luke from an understanding of the building of the cultural environment of his day; in the strictly contemporaneous we may catch an illuminating nuance or inflection; in the closely subsequent the nearest attempts at historical synthesis.[73]

But for the moment we aim to look more closely at the immediate environment of local and social context. The most extensive category of evidence here is that of the tens of thousands of inscriptions, of which the cities of Asia Minor are actually the most prolific source. The newly published corpus of the inscriptions of Ephesus contains more than 5000 texts from that city alone,[74] and Ephesus is but one of hundreds of cities in the land, if also perhaps the most richly documented of them all.[75] This is not the type of evidence we might have chosen, and we must recognize that any detailed study involves sifting through hundreds of monotonously similar epitaphs and dedications for what may seem small and marginal returns. Yet in the long run this task can scarcely be neglected, and historical criticism by dogmatism or by generalization is difficult to sustain without at least

---

72 Cf. Judge, 'St. Paul and Classical Society', pp. 24-25. His concern over the nature of the task is highlighted again in his review of F.F. Bruce, *New Testament History*, a book which he sees as the best of its kind, but which does not wholly silence his unease (*JRH* 7 [1972], pp. 163-65).

73 This reinforces the caution against the tendency to write a cultural history of literary forms out of the assumed significance of *later* parallels.

74 *Die Inschriften von Ephesos (Inschiften griechischen Städte aus Kleinasien* 11,1), ed. H. Wankel *et al.* (Bonn: Rudolf Habelt, 1979-81).

75 The topographical index to W.M. Calder and G.E. Bean, *A Classical Map of Asia Minor* (London: British Institute of Archaeology at Ankara, 1957) lists some 1600 names, of which the large majority are those of identified cities.

some first-hand acquaintance with the range, difficulty and limitations of this material. There is of course only a small proportion of the texts containing lexical, terminological or onomastic minutiae directly illustrative of Acts, and these have obvious relevance, though not as short cuts to instant apologetic. The larger value may be less tangible, to document the environment, if only in the fragmentary way permitted by the material. As with the papyri, we sometimes gain a vivid glimpse of the lives of unknown people, while major problems go unanswered. Yet there is a difference, for in the papyri we catch people informally, in the ephemeral concerns destined for the rubbish-heap, whereas the stone-cutter is engaged to make a record for posterity.

Inscriptions may be precisely dated, or approximate or possible datings may sometimes be inferred on various grounds.[76] Coins, which are a similar category of evidence, are also datable, and for a few favoured cities, like Ephesus and Tarsus, they may help to document the vicissitudes of their history over several centuries. The right to strike coins was a jealously guarded prerogative of civic independence. Coinage often sheds light on local history, occupations, and especially religious symbolism, of which we should otherwise be ignorant.[77]

A problem with both categories is that the picture they give, being fragmentary, may not be representative. It is a fair guess that it is heavily weighted towards the more literate and Hellenized values of cities where Anatolian or other oriental cultures existed. The coins for instance show a clear tendency to assimilate the emblems of native cult to the portrayal of Olympian deities and classical myth,[78]

---

[76] Examples are references to known persons or events, or to terms or titles introduced at known dates. For the Roman period the types of Romanized personal names are often of much circumstantial value, as where the *praenomen* and *nomen* of an enfranchising emperor provides a *terminus post quem* or the recurrence of the prenominal 'Aurelius' indicates a date soon after the *Constitutio Antoniniana* of AD 212. The use of letter-forms for dating is a specialist matter, and at best hazardous for this period, when the lapidary alphabet and its variants had long since matured, and a welter of stylistic revivals and crude inconsistencies coexists. For a valuable introduction see A.G. Woodhead, *The Study of Greek Inscriptions* (CUP, 1967), esp. ch. 5; note however that Woodhead's work is biased towards the Classical Attic, not the Hellenistic-Roman, period.

[77] See now R. Oster, 'Numismatic Windows into the Social World of Early Christianity. A Methodological Inquiry', *JBL* 101 (1982), pp. 195-223. For publication of the local coinage, city by city, see the *British Museum Catalogues*, whose volumes are organized geographically.

[78] Thus at Sardis, while some coins represent the familiar Greek story of the

and the inscriptions are (with rare and specialized exceptions) expressed in Greek (or occasionally Latin) in places where we know that indigenous languages survived.[79] There are questions of far-reaching import here, and the recurring debate over the social standing of Paul, Luke, and of the converts in the Pauline churches, is raised anew. Whether we side with Deissmann or with Judge on these questions,[80] we should probably agree that Paul and the early Christians generally probably had easiest access to the Hellenized stratum of the urban populations, and that the inscriptions are therefore likely to share a similar tendency. But this probability, too, must be held with due caution.

There is some prospect of building up a more rounded picture of the social life of an individual city by the synthesis of the evidence of epigraphy, numismatics, literary references, where available, with the aid of archaeology and topographical study. We shall not dwell further on these categories, except to notice the importance of topography (and of the use of topographical and geographical nomenclature in the texts) for the historical criticism of a narrative purporting to give detailed accounts of journeys. A city by city study with careful discrimination of historical development, in the hope of isolating and clarifying the specific New Testament environment out of strictly

rape of Persephone (*BMC Lydia*, Sardis No. 131, of Trajan; etc.), others preserve serpent-motifs and the like which are likely to reflect local cult assimilated to the Greek myth it most resembled (No. 89, Imperial, undated; No. 138, of Antoninus Pius).

[79] A Celtic dialect survived in ('North') Galatia in the time of Jerome, and Strabo speaks of four languages as spoken in his time in the city of Cibyra (Strabo 13.4.17 = 631: Pisidian, Solymian, Greek and Lydian), but the epigraphy is uniformly Greek. Phrygian is the main exception, but that is preserved almost exclusively in variants of a curse formula attached to inscriptions otherwise expressed in Greek, if sometimes of a strangely barbarous kind. For the Phrygian texts see *MAMA* Vols 1, 4, 6 *passim*, and O. Haas, *Die phrygischen Sprachdenkmäler*, Linguistique Balkanique X (Academie Bulgare des Sciences, 1966). For the brief undeciphered inscriptions from Sofular in Pisidia see C.J. Hemer, 'The Pisidian Texts. A Problem of Language and History', *Kadmos* 19 (1980), pp. 54-64, and literature cited there.

[80] A. Deissmann, *Paul. A Study in Social and Religious History* (London: Hodder and Stoughton, 1926), 2nd edn tr. W.E. Wilson; Judge, *Social Pattern*. Whereas Deissmann, under influence of the supposed parallel between Paul and the vernacular of the papyri, stressed his humble standing and manual labour, and saw Christianity as a lower-class movement, Judge has explained it as a movement prospering among the educated. He sees the complexity of social factors, notably in the distinction between 'rank' and 'status': 'Perhaps it is the discord between relatively high status in the home town and low rank in Roman eyes that explains the drive' (Judge, *Rank and Status*, p. 10).

contemporary sources, is an ideal we can scarcely attain, if only for lack of evidence. But it remains an ideal, and it is good to renew the plea in a work which must proceed upon available resources.[81]

---

[81] Among important existing studies of the NT cities of Asia Minor in particular see W.M. Ramsay, *Cities and Bishoprics of Phrygia I. The Lycos Valley and South-Western Phrygia* (Oxford: Clarendon, 1895); *The Letters to the Seven Churches of Asia*(London: Hodder and Stoughton, 1909); *The Cities of St. Paul* (London: Hodder and Stoughton, 1907) [Tarsus, Iconium, Pisidian Antioch, Derbe, Lystra]; G. Downey, *Ancient Antioch* (Princeton University Press, 1963); C.J. Cadoux, *Ancient Smyrna* (Oxford: Basil Blackwell, 1938) [incl. Pisidian Antioch, Lystra]. There are numerous shorter studies in journal and dictionary articles, and for some major sites a vast array of technical literature and archaeological publication. For the historical geography of a larger district cf. W. Leaf, *Strabo on the Troad* (CUP, 1923); J.M. Cook, *The Troad. An Archaeological and Topographical Study* (Oxford: Clarendon Press, 1973). For communications cf. now D. French, *Roman Roads and Milestones of Asia Minor* (London: British Institute of Archaeology at Ankara), of which the first fascicle, in English and Turkish, appeared in 1981. Most of these diverse studies are focused elsewhere than on the New Testament environment. The standing need is for detailed and applicable synthesis.

Chapter 3
Ancient Historiography

Preliminary: The Problem of 'Parallels'

This chapter contains comments on recent discussion of ancient historiography, sample trajectories through selected topics to illustrate the variety of ancient practice, and some assessment of the implications for Lukan studies from this perspective. A full study of the theme demands a much larger treatment, based on a much wider grasp of ancient sources and secondary literature than the present author can claim. While such a task needs in the long run to be undertaken, I suspect, and have previously argued in print,[1] that its immediate returns for the subject in hand are likely to be small. If one is studying the historicity of Luke, one should study him on his actual performance, where there are some fresh things to be said. The search for parallels is an attractive and often useful undertaking, but it is also fraught with danger.[2]

The question of Luke as historian has often, for example, prompted comparison with Josephus. In recent studies F.G. Downing has defended the view that Luke deserves some considerable respect as a historical source on the ground of his similarities with Josephus.[3] As we shall see below, the parallel may not be so close as Downing has suggested. A different approach appears in a valuable article by A.W. Mosley,[4] a broad survey of the standards of historical reporting in the ancient world. Mosley concludes cautiously that the best of the historians are trustworthy and that it is not unreasonable to ask whether the New Testament writers may be measured by similar standards. This study makes its basic point forcibly, but cannot, in its brief space, analyse all the divergent theory within

---

1 'Luke the Historian', *BJRL* 60 (1977-78), pp. 28-51, esp. pp. 29-34.

2 Cf. S. Sandmel, 'Parallelomania', *JBL* 81 (1962), pp. 1-13.

3 F.G. Downing, 'Redaction Criticism: Josephus' *Antiquities* and the Synoptic Gospels', *JSNT* 8 (1980), pp. 46-65 and 9 (1980), pp. 29-48; 'Ethical Pagan Theism and the Speeches in Acts', *NTS* 27 (1980-81), pp. 544-63; 'Common Ground with Paganism in Luke and in Josephus', *NTS* 28 (1982), pp. 546-59.

4 A.W. Mosley, 'Historical Reporting in the Ancient World', *NTS* 12 (1965-66), pp. 10-26.

ancient historiography: it gives what is probably too simplistic and optimistic a picture, for instance merely citing a view of Josephus as 'the Jewish Thucydides'.[5] The tendency is again to open the door to an unduly direct comparison of Luke with Josephus with an undifferentiated view of the context.

A salient point in the study of Josephus is his dependence on Dionysius of Halicarnassus. He never actually mentions Dionysius, but he evidently models his twenty-book Jewish Antiquities ('Ιου‐ δαϊκὴ Ἀρχαιολογία) closely and consciously upon the twenty books of Dionysius' Ῥωμαϊκὴ Ἀρχαιολογία.[6] Even apart from the titles and number of books striking resemblances of method have often been noticed.[7] Although it may appear different to Dionysius, Josephus' theological stance, later made more explicit in the work against Apion (*Ap.* 2.16.166-67; 2.22.190-92), is perhaps adapted to the sense of divine providence mingled with rationalistic explanation appropriate to his pagan readers,[8] a position consonant enough with the ethos of Dionysius. R.J.H. Shutt develops his sense of Josephus' dependence in much more specific terms, in a detailed and extended study of Dionysius' style and Josephus' imitative copying of it.[9] While we hesitate to build on indecisive stylistic parallels, his case here seems to rest largely upon the argument for the deliberate reminiscence marked by the recurring reproduction of rare words. There is every indication that we are dealing here, not with the ever-dangerous literary parallel, but with an explicit, derivative relationship.

There are of course several complicating factors. Dionysius is his

[5]   Mosley, p. 24, citing R.J.H. Shutt, *Studies in Josephus* (London: SPCK, 1961), p. 125, a valuable work whose assessment of its subject is often over-generous. A more representative, while still largely positive, view is that of H. St.J. Thackeray, *Josephus the Man and the Historian* (New York: Jewish Institute of Religion Press, 1929), esp. pp. 45-50.

[6]   Thackeray, *Josephus* p. 73, and in Loeb Josephus Vol. IV (London: Heinemann and New York: G.P. Putnam, 1930), *Antiquities*, Introduction, ix; cf. A. Momigliano, 'Greek Historiography', *History and Theory* (Middletown, Conn.) 17 (1978), pp. 1-28, citing pp. 16, 19, where he stresses the place of Josephus in relation to Dionysius in the line of Greek historiography; also Downing, *NTS* 27 (1980-81), pp. 544-45.

[7]   For example, in recounting from his sources events of doubtful authenticity or interpretation, especially where an appearance of the abnormal or supernatural is involved, Dionysius does not press his own opinion, but leaves his reader to judge for himself. His recurring formulae in such contexts are closely followed in Josephus. Cf. e.g. Jos. *Ant.* 1.3.9.108 with Dion. Hal. *Ant. Rom.* 1.48.1, and *passim*; Thackeray, *Josephus*, p. 57; Shutt, p. 99.

[8]   See Thackeray, *Josephus*, pp. 96-98.

[9]   Shutt, pp. 93-101.

model, not his source, and Josephus stands in a different kind of relationship with Nicolaus of Damascus, a major source, or indeed Polybius, an occasional secondary source, both of whom he names freely. The failure to acknowledge his model reads more strangely today than in antiquity, when authorities were commonly mentioned only when they conflicted, or were the subject of the author's criticism. Thus Polybius, a savage critic of his immediate predecessors and sources, mentions Thucydides only parenthetically (8.11.3), and contents himself with the occasional implicit claim to have emulated or even improved upon his ultimate model.[10] Again, the adaptation of Josephus' work to a Greek audience may have been much eased through his use of helpers versed in the Greek classics and perhaps responsible for specific instances of literary imitation.[11] His treatment of the Old Testament is another vast subject in itself.[12] He stands apart from the theocratic perspective of the older Biblical history, and his Biblical interpretation is suspect. Yet again he invites comparison with Dionysius in the attention he directs to the earliest traditions of the nation. Josephus needs also to be studied with relation to his sources and opponents, in particular the fragments of Nicolaus of Damascus and his own accounts of his bitter enemy Justus of Tiberias.[13]

The various considerations adduced for emphasizing the link between Dionysius and Josephus lead us to an important point, that both stand in a specifically rhetorical tradition of Greek historiography. But on any view Luke's work is not closely parallel

[10] See e.g. his more than Thucydidean insistence on truthfulness and improving didacticism (1.35.6-10; 2.56.11-12; etc.), his refinement of Thucydides' idea of causation (3.6-7), his more rigorous standards in the use of speeches (12.25a-b). M. Grant, *The Ancient Historians* (London: Weidenfeld and Nicholson, 1970), pp. 163, 390 is uncertain whether Polybius had actually read Thucydides systematically, as particular reminiscences could have come through intermediaries, but he accepts that Polybius was consciously affected by his approach.

[11] Josephus acknowledges his use of assistants on coming to Rome (χρησάμενός τισι πρὸς τὴν Ἑλληνίδα φωνὴν συνεργοῖς, *Ap.* 1.9.50), but Thackeray's elaborated theory of 'Sophoclean' and 'Thucydidean' assistants (*Josephus*, pp. 100-24; in Loeb Josephus IV, pp. xiv-xvii) has been criticized by Shutt in another careful study of style, pp. 59-78.

[12] See now H.W. Attridge, *The Interpretation of Biblical History in the 'Antiquitates Judaicae' of Flavius Josephus* (Missoula Mont: Scholars Press, 1976); S.J.D. Cohen, *Josephus in Galilee and Rome* (Leiden: Brill, 1979), pp. 35-42; T. Rajak, 'Justus of Tiberias', *Classical Quarterly* n.s. 23 (1973), pp. 345-68.

[13] Nicolaus: see F. Jacoby, *Die Fragmente der griechischen Historiker* IIA (Berlin: Weidemann, 1926), No. 90, pp. 324-430; Justus: Jos. *Vita* 9.34ff. and *passim*, esp. 65.357-67. Both were evidently also very Greek in style (cf. Jos. *Vita* 9.40).

with that of Dionysius. Those who are sceptical towards 'Luke the historian' are not likely to look for such a parallel; those who are amenable to the idea are likely to look for their parallels in directions other than Dionysius.[14] Although all agree, for instance, that neither the speeches of Josephus, Dionysius nor of Acts could realistically be delivered verbatim, the reasons are quite different, for the two former are unreal rhetorical exercises, whereas the last are too brief and too bald to carry the weight of their content to an audience. Once again, the student should be cautious about the significance and extent of the Luke-Josephus parallel, given the measure of disjunction between them within the complex development of ancient historiography.

1. *Literature about Ancient Historiography*

Although there is a large volume of work currently being produced about the ancient historians and their methods,[15] we shall confine ourselves mainly to some notice of the important sequence of articles by Guido Schepens of Louvain, especially as they touch on the concepts of source theory among ancient historians.[16] It is easy to develop the assumption that because the ancients cannot be measured to advantage by an imposed modern yardstick they had no standards of their own. In contrast to the common dogma that they had no notion of the 'modern' interest in factual truth 'for its own sake', it is clear that some of their keenest minds were exercised by the problems of source and critical method.[17] This is not of course to

---

[14] An exception is F. Lasserre, 'Prose grecque classicisante', *Le classicisme à Rome aux Iers siècles avant et après J.-C., Entretiens sur l'antiquité classique*, 25 Vandoeuvres-Genève: Fondation Hardt, 1979), pp. 135-37, which makes stylistic parallels between Dionysius, Josephus and Luke.

[15] E.g. A. Momigliano, *Essays in Ancient and Modern Historiography* (Oxford: Blackwell, 1977); *Historiographia Antiqua. Commentationes Lovanienses in Honorem W. Peremans Septuagenarii editae*, ed. T. Reckmans *et al.* (Louvain University, 1977). The annual volumes of *L'Année philologique* will reveal the scale and diversity of the periodical literature which needs to be considered in the long run.

[16] Especially 'Some Aspects of Source Theory in Greek Historiography' *Anc Soc* 6 (1975), pp. 257-74; on individual writers cf. 'Éphore sur la valeur de l'autopsie', *Anc Soc* 1 (1970), pp. 163-82; 'Arrian's View of his Task as Alexander-Historian', *Anc Soc* 2 (1971), pp. 254-68; 'The Bipartite and Tripartite Divisions of History in Polybius (XII 25e & 27)', *Anc Soc* 5 (1974), pp. 277-87; 'L'Idéal de l'information complète chez les historiens grecs', *Revue des études grecques* 88 (1975), pp. 81-93; 'Historiographical Problems in Ephorus', in Peremans *Festschrift*, pp. 95-118; 'Polybius on Timaeus' Account of Phalaris' Bull: A Case of δεισιδαιμονία', *Anc Soc* 9 (1978), pp. 117-48.

[17] Contrast C.S. Mann's comment 'that the discipline of historical investigation,

say that all were equally vigorous, or that their answers were the same as modern answers, or to prejudge the question whether Luke had any aspiration to their best standards. The interest of Schepens' work is the focus on the ancient historian's self-understanding, and his concept of his task. Schepens introduces us to the ancient cultural framework and shows it to be consistent with the possibility of a scholarship as rigorous in intent, if differently conceived. Lucian wrote an important treatise on the writing of history, and other lost works may have treated the theory,[18] but the subject is best studied empirically where theory is exemplified in the practice of a surviving writer. Polybius is a figure of special importance, an acerbic critic of his predecessors who professes exacting standards and largely attains them. I shall focus here on Schepens' programmatic essay on source-theory, which itself draws primarily on Polybius, and refer also to his more detailed studies of that writer.

To put it simply, there is almost a reversal of the roles of the subjective and objective in this concept of historiography, where written documents, including archives, are ranked *after* oral tradition and eyewitness reports. It is a disconcerting formulation. Earlier scholars, including men of the calibre of Wilamowitz, were often severely critical of Polybius' method, without understanding it in its own terms.[19] But Schepens adduces H. Strasburger's distinction (again surprising at first sight) between the *Primärforschung* of the ancients and the *Sekundärarbeit* of the modern scholar.[20] Herodotus in his account of Egypt (2.99) makes his own division: μέχρι μὲν τούτου ὄψις

and its attendant sifting of evidence, is a relatively modern discipline', in 'The Historicity of the Birth Narratives', in D.E. Nineham *et al.*, *Historicity and Chronology in the New Testament* (London: SPCK, 1965), pp. 46-47.

[18] Lucian, *de Historia Conscribenda*. This piece is largely a characteristically tongue-in-cheek assault upon pretension and extravagances, yet revealing of the attitudes of a sharp-witted contemporary critic. Schepens, *Anc Soc* 6 (1975), p. 257 refers to lost works by Theophrastus and Praxiphanes which may have dealt with methodology. For the use of Lucian's work with relation to Acts, see Hengel, *Acts*, esp. pp. 13-18, 21-22. For a less favourable view of Lucian see M.I. Finley: it is 'nothing but a concoction of the rules and maxims which had become the commonplaces of a rhetorical education, a shallow and essentially worthless potboiler'. M.I. Finley, 'Myth, Memory and History', *History and Theory* 4 (1964-65), p. 282.

[19] See U. von Wilamowitz-Moellendorff, *Greek Historical Writing* (Oxford: Clarendon Press, 1908), p. 15, a scathing dismissal of Polybius' work: 'as banal as Lucian's essay on the writing of history'— but made upon inappropriate criteria.

[20] H. Strasburger, *Die Wesensbestimmung der Geschichte durch die antike Geschichtsschreibung*, cited by Schepens from p. 12; now accessible in 2nd edition reprinted in *Sitzungsberichte der wissenschaftlichen Gesellschaft an der Johann Wolfgang von Goethe-Universität Frankfurt-am-Main* 5 (1966).

τε ἐμὴ καὶ γνώμη καὶ ἱστορίη ταῦτα λέγουσα ἐστί, before proceeding to record the oral tradition of the Egyptians (ἀκοή), where 'my own sight, judgment and inquiry' constitute the subject of the emphatic periphrastic verb: they are essentially 'to be understood as *active* faculties deployed by the historian in his inquiry'.[21] The focus of the theory is upon the researcher and his gathering and treatment of material rather than on the material itself, and this is the context for the great stress placed upon autopsy, participation, and then upon the critical examination of eyewitnesses. In Polybius' 'bipartite' distinction ὅρασις stands above ἀκοή (12.27.1), and written sources rank only as a secondary division of ἀκοή.[22] The ethical and intellectual qualities of the historian are involved in the choice of the discipline, hardship and expense of personal research over the soft option taken by such as Timaeus, sitting in his study comparing books. Elsewhere Polybius makes a related point through a different distinction. History, in its true sense,[23] has three parts, in rising order of importance: study, travel and political activity, as medicine has three parts, theory, dietetics and clinical practice. Timaeus is like the medical theorist whose rhetorical powers win him patients at peril to their lives.[24] The analogy may be faulty, but it illustrates Polybius' thinking.

Elsewhere (12.4c.3) Polybius gives pride of place in history to personal investigation (ἀνάκρισις), the term used in 12.27.3 of the interrogation of eyewitnesses, which there ranks as the most demanding kind of ἀκοή, neglected by Timaeus in favour of easier paths. This appears inconsistent with Polybius' preference for ὄψις, and one might wonder at first sight if he will criticize Timaeus whatever he

---

[21] Schepens, 'Source Theory', *Anc Soc* 6 (1975), p. 261; his italics. Γνώμη here appears to denote something like 'critical faculty', 'interpretative judgment', acting upon the data obtained through ὄψις and ἱστορίη. Herodotus is not concerned to deal with sources of historical information as such.

[22] Cf. Schepens, *Anc Soc* 5 (1974), pp. 277-87. The classic study of Polybius is F.W. Walbank, *A Historical Commentary on Polybius*, 3 vols. (Oxford: Clarendon Press, 1957-1979). Cf. recently B.A. Marshall, 'Polybius. An Introduction', *Classicism* (Sydney) 8 (1982), pp. 1-7. I have previously discussed Polybius and his bearing on Luke in *BJRL* 60 (1977-78), pp. 30-33. See also the review of Walbank by A.H. Macdonald, *JRS* 48 (1958), pp. 179-83.

[23] 'τῆς πραγματικῆς ἱστορίας' (Polybius 12.25e.1). The epithet, by which Polybius several times designates his work, is hard to render. It is not quite 'systematic' (W.R. Paton in Loeb), perhaps implicitly almost 'critical' or 'scientific' in handling political events, in the sense in which he separates his own work as a proved man of affairs from that of 'the armchair pretender'. Cf. ὁ τῆς πραγματικῆς ἱστορίας τρόπος (1.2.8), where Walbank (I. 42 *ad loc.*) says the phrase means little more than just 'history'.

[24] Polybius 12.25d-e.

does. But the difference is explicable, for autopsy is inevitably limited, as the individual eyewitness can never have seen everything at once. Oral investigation is *quantitatively* the more important as viewed heuristically, though autopsy is of superior *critical* value for the limited areas where it is available directly. The crucial distinction is that between direct and indirect information, where autopsy and its extension in oral inquiry are together opposed to written sources. This version is perhaps akin to the modern concern to evaluate the character of the material rather than the qualifications of the writer.

A third classification (Polybius 12.28a.6) is less clear, and complicated by textual problems, but Schepens shows from the context how Polybius intends once more to demonstrate from another angle the importance of αὐτουργία and αὐτοπάθεια. 'The inquirer contributes to the narrative as much as his informant': his suggestions guide the narrator's memory. The inexperienced man is not competent to question or understand: 'even if present he is in a sense not present'.[25] Experience is, from this point of view, μέγιστον and χαλε-πώτατον. In fact in various passages Polybius stresses three concerns: assembly of information, reliability of sources, and qualification of the historian. Ancient source theory actually draws attention to the subjective element in historical knowledge, but this 'in no way excludes any form of objective historical information ... It remains true that ancient, and particularly Greek, historiography is based on a scientific ideal not so much founded on the critical study of the transmitted sources, but on the historian's *immediate* contact with the *facts* themselves'.[26]

This brief survey permits interim conclusions at more than one level. The first, and simplest, is to stress afresh that at least some of the ancients were moved by a lively concern for historical accuracy. It is true that they viewed the personal factor in historiography differently, but that is not necessarily to be condemned, and we may even have something to learn from their insight into its positive, first-hand, rather than only its negative, tendentious, possibilities. The modern polarization between theological *Tendenz* and a hypothetical 'history for its own sake' is not realistic about the ordinary character of historical evidence. Facts do not come in sealed packets untouched by human hand: selection and interpretation, at however rudimentary stage, are inseparable from historical information, and it is none the worse for that.

Second, the question persists how Josephus, or Luke, relates to the

25 12.28a.8-10; Schepens, 'Source Theory', p. 271.
26 Schepens, 'Source Theory', p. 273; his italics.

kind of culture which produced these ideas. The answers are not so simple as they may be made to seem. Even if we continue to assume that we may compare them as historians, they may represent different currents in the tangled stream of ancient historiography. Both, however, ostensibly write about their own times and include events within their own experience. 'Ostensibly', for of course many would emphatically deny this of Luke, but this at least appears to be the claim of the 'we-passages' of Acts, and alternative viewpoints must explain them otherwise. These and other features recur through writers who otherwise seem to differ widely among themselves. One should not press *any* kind of literary parallel here. Writers must be judged on their actual performance. In the next section we shall consider some of the factors in which their diversity may be expressed.

2. *Topics Illustrating the Diversity of Ancient Historiographical Practice*

(a) *Scope and Scale*

Herodotus, Thucydides and Polybius, among others, claim, with variations, to be writing about events of importance close to their own times and experience.[27] All three, and others (notably including Josephus), were exiles and travellers who had seen both sides of the conflict they describe.[28] Polybius' statement may be seen as highly significant in the light of our preceding discussion: he begins his main period from the generation preceding his own, in part because he has been personally present at some of the events and has the testimony of eyewitnesses for the others (4.2.2).

There were however competing trends in historiography even before Polybius. Notable among them was the influence of Isocrates. One development of that influence is Ephorus' 'universal' history.[29] It is unfortunate that our knowledge of this significant writer depends on fragments and secondary comment.[30] He seems to stand at a parting of the ways, where a continuing stress on autopsy with participation is combined with a new desire for comprehensiveness,

[27] Herodotus, 1.1: his whole work, amidst its immense wealth of discursive information, is an artistic unity subordinated to his theme of the Persian Wars as the climax of the age-long struggle of Europe and Asia; Thuc. 1.1; Polybius 1.1.5-1.2.8; 1.4.5; etc.

[28] See *BJRL* 60 (1977-78) 31; cf. Momigliano, 'Greek Historiography', p. 9.

[29] See generally M. Grant, *The Ancient Historians*, and now esp. Schepens, *Anc Soc* 1 (1970), pp. 163-82 and in the Peremans *Festschrift*, pp. 95-118. The only full-length study is still G.L. Barber, *The Historian Ephorus* (CUP, 1935).

[30] For the fragments see Jacoby, *FGH* 'Ephoros von Kyme', IIA, No. 70, pp. 37-109.

even if signalled not so much by a universal, synoptic perspective as by the accumulation of separate themes, some inevitably derived from written sources. We can see here the impact of Isocrates' *pan-Hellenism*, even if Ephorus was less affected by Isocrates' tendency to stress rhetoric as the vehicle of teachings, and the consequent rhetorical glorification of the past (cf. e.g. Isocrates *Antidosis* 76-77).

Although it may be that the shift from primary to secondary research first appears in Ephorus, Polybius is relatively favourable in his judgment of him, and recognizes that he clearly distinguishes history from rhetoric.[31] One of the surviving fragments enunciates a principle of some importance: περὶ μὲν γὰρ τῶν καθ' ἡμᾶς γεγενη- μένων ... τοὺς ἀκριβέστατα λέγοντας πιστοτάτους ἡγούμεθα, περὶ δὲ τῶν παλαιῶν τοὺς οὕτω διεξιόντας ἀπιθανωτάτους εἶναι νομί- ζομεν, ὑπολαμβάνοντες οὔτε τὰς πράξεις ἀπάσας οὔτε τῶν λόγων τοὺς πλείστους εἰκὸς εἶναι μνημονεύεσθαι διὰ τοσούτων.[32] Pre- cision of detail inspires confidence in the record of contemporary events, but is suspect in the case of narratives of the remote past. Fur- ther, Diodorus gives an analysis of the difficulties of studying early times, which he may be repeating without acknowledgment from Ephorus, citing the lack of a contemporary written tradition, and the fact that history as a genre was a recent cultural achievement.[33]

Perhaps a principal reason for Polybius' relative approbation of Ephorus is the latter's aspiration to comprehensive 'universal' his- tory, as opposed to the disproportionate focus of the historical mono- graph which Polybius attacks elsewhere. Dionysius, on the other hand, under the influence of the rhetorical side of Isocratean influ- ence, is actually most verbose on the early period of Rome, and the scale of his work decreases later,[34] a reversal of Livy's more natural procedure as of Ephorus' principle. There is a tension between accuracy and scale, and comprehensiveness may be an unattainable ideal. The conscientious writer will sometimes be frustrated by the lack of evidence. The omission, the cautious summary, the vague or

---

31 Polybius 12.28a.2; cf. Schepens in Peremans *Festschrift*, p. 105.

32 Jacoby, IIA, No. 70, Frag. 9, p. 45.

33 Diodorus Siculus 1.9.2. The mention of Ephorus in a different connection in the immediate context further suggests this dependence. It may often be that Diodorus' value is due to his use of Ephorus. It is, however, a common practice to mention predecessors only when correcting or criticizing them.

34 Cf. E. Cary in Loeb Dionysius I (1968) pp. xix-xx. He observes for instance that the events leading to the exile of Coriolanus occupy 48 chapters, including 15 speeches, in Dionysius (7.20-67), but only half a chapter in Livy (2.34.7-12). The rest of his life is takes up 62 chapters in Dionysius (8.1-62), but only 6 in Livy (2.35-40).

qualified statement, are sometimes the mark of the careful historian who will be precise where he can. Dionysius' expansive treatment of the remote past is not much commendation of his method.

There was however a stated ideal of comprehensiveness among ancient historians. In another study, Schepens[35] considers the thesis of Luciano Canfora that this *pretesa di completezza* was no more than a fictional convention in Thucydides, deriving ultimately from a precritical etymological equating of 'seeing' with 'knowing' (root ιδ-).[36] Schepens argues that Thucydides is not exaggerating his claim to precision, and suggests rather that he is stressing the integral unity of autopsy with independent inquiry in achieving a balanced and complete perspective on events.[37]

Selection is in fact indispensable to intelligently written narrative, and the ancients do not deny this. One expression of this is in their choice of theme or period, and that may be governed by significance and by the availability of material. There may be an introductory summary of the preceding period, like Thucydides' *Pentekontaetia* or Josephus' account of the Herods and procurators in the opening books of the *Jewish War*. Again, selectivity may be influenced by cultural or traditional factors, as when the ancients stress political and military history at the expense of social and economic history, or conceive of their task in austerely moral terms, with a central interest on the impact of personalities upon events, though without focus on psychological development. There is also the selectivity governed by relevance and significance in arguing a case, and so inviting the danger of the subjective and the tendentious. Equally, selection may be controlled by patterns in the availability of evidence. Parts of a topic may be omitted or baldly summarized where clear documentation is deficient, or a chosen grouping of material may be excerpted from a larger body of less coherent and less focused information.

We return finally to Polybius' reiterated claim to be writing a 'universal' history. At the beginning of his period history became an 'organic whole' (σωματοειδής), and required a 'synoptic' approach (ὑπὸ μίαν σύνοψιν, 1.3.4; 1.4.2). None of his contemporaries had undertaken the task (1.4.2), and he is critical of those who write mere

---

[35] Schepens, *REG* 88 (1975), pp. 81-93.

[36] L. Canfora, *Totalità e selezione nella storiografia antica* (Bari: Laterza, 1972), esp. 15,49. Cf. Schepens *REG* 88 (1975), p. 85.

[37] τὰ δ' ἔργα τῶν πραχθέντων ἐν τῷ πολέμῳ οὐκ ἐκ τοῦ παρατυχόντος πυνθανόμενος ἠξίωσα γράφειν, οὐδ' ὡς ἐμοὶ ἐδόκει, ἀλλ' οἷς τε αὐτὸς παρῆν καὶ παρὰ τῶν ἄλλων ὅσον δυνατὸν ἀκριβείᾳ περὶ ἑκάστου ἐπεξελθών (Thuc. 1.22.2). Schepens stresses the correlative force of τε ... καί in this formulation (p. 88); cf. A.W. Gomme, *Historical Commentary on Thucydides* I (Oxford: Clarendon Press, 1945), p. 143.

monographs and therefore include the unimportant without discrimination and proportion (7.7.6-7).[38] He contrasts the severity and instructiveness of his own method with that of the mere antiquarian (9.1-2).[39] It is clear from this that Polybius' claim to comprehensiveness is consistent with selectivity; it is precisely his assertion of 'synoptic' study which requires the omission or subordination of the less significant.

This necessarily abbreviated survey may serve at least to highlight some of the themes in the complex of scope, scale and selectivity, the problems of demarcation of subject, of comprehensiveness, of partial information, of culturally-controlled interests, as well as of *Tendenz*. Additionally, it throws further light on the thinking which underlies the insistence on contemporary history written by participants.

(b) *Order and Arrangement*

The bearing of the sequence of a narrative on questions of historicity has entered so much into Gospel criticism that a special note on this theme also seems desirable. It is bound up, for instance, with the outworking of the form-critical approach to the Gospels, where the overthrow of Holtzmann's rigid concept of the primitiveness of the Markan framework led to a fragmentation of the Gospel *pericopae*. Even though redaction criticism has refocused attention upon their totality, it has done so from within cumulative presuppositions about the nature of the transmission of the tradition. On the assumption that the order in the Gospels is thematic rather than chronological, and therefore is theologically determined (with any incidental notes of time being added by an editor rather than being derived from sources), critics who insist over-rigidly on chronological order make a generalized attack on historicity which is not appropriate for ancient writing.

Of course the Gospel *pericopae* are to a greater or lesser extent arranged or rearranged. But that will be the case with *any* complex narrative, and historicity is not necessarily at stake in the fact. An ancient historical writing could be presented topically or annalistically. 'Annals', in the simplest form, could be built on the skeleton of a chronological table, fleshed out into narrative. A history of any

---

38 Cf. 2.37; 3.32; Grant, pp. 149-50.

39 It must be admitted that Polybius, for all his notable qualities, is ponderously didactic: 'His language has the flat and prosy verbosity of a government department. Unlike almost any other notable literary product of antiquity, it is actually improved by a good translation' (Grant, p. 156).

literary pretension could not stop short at so bald and unreflective a stage. Tacitus adopted a strict year-by-year method for his major work *Ab excessu divi Augusti*, and it has become universally known as the 'Annals'. Yet within each year events in Rome are followed by events in the provinces and external wars. There is in fact thematic arrangement within the years, and this holds good even though Tacitus conscientiously fragments the continuities into discrete annual instalments. 'Annals' turn out to be only a different pattern of arrangement. A complex narrative must in fact strike a clear balance between the chronological and the thematic. Chronology must be given sufficient attention if the narrative is to unfold clearly, but the actual resolution of the tension will vary according to subject, circumstance and choice. The tracing of complicated and intermeshed causes and effects sets a premium on clarity of arrangement, and may require a 'flashback' technique, however rudimentary, to give the minimal explanation of the antecedents. It may be a real test of literary skill to be clear to the reader, but the thing itself is evident and critically unimportant. The choice is not necessarily one between being chronological and being unhistorical, but may be between coherence and confusion.[40]

If, however, a narrative is episodic, woven for instance around the impact of a personality, it is not surprising if there is a much freer variation of order between versions. The factor of topical, and variable, arrangement is apparent in the Gospels, and equally in ancient biographers like Suetonius, Plutarch, or Tacitus in the *Agricola*– though it cannot be assumed on that ground that the genre of Gospels or Acts is necessarily to be related to any of them. There are different ways of telling a story. The traditional themes of Greek epic or tragedy presupposed that the hearer knew the outcome, and gave scope for an irony; Old Testament narrative is often prefaced by a summary not to be taken as antecedent to the unfolding of the circumstances.[41]

Some problems of sequence *are* problems. Some are not. Notes of time should be evaluated rather than discounted. To treat *pericopae*

---

[40] Dionysius of Halicarnassus, in his critical essay *Thucydides* (9ff.), appears in the surprising role of champion of truth and clarity against Thucydides' faults in presentation. The fault in his 'arrangement' (οἰκονομικόν) is that his division into summers and winters confuses and fragments events. Whatever we think of Dionysius' own practice, he is at least keenly sensitive to the difficulties of narrative as narrative, and stresses that a topical (or topographical) arrangement may sometimes be necessary to clarity of sequence. Lucian too is insistent on the importance of arrangement (*de Hist. Conscrib.* 50).

[41] On OT narrative see now R. Alter, *The Art of Biblical Narrative* (London and Sydney: George Allen and Unwin, 1981).

in isolation is to take them out of context. That may be at once a tautology and an eccentric remark, but the eccentricity harbours a cautionary truth. Where the context is temporally or logically sequential, the case differs from the merely topical and episodic. Acts has a stronger sequential thread than the Gospel of Luke, and we must recognize that. But we should not in either case make unnecessary difficulties for ourselves.

(c) *Speeches*

The inclusion of speeches in the Greek historians is another huge topic on which some brief comment is essential before coming in due course to the problem of the speeches in Acts.[42] It is by no means true that all ancient historians felt free to put fictitious speeches in the mouths of historical characters. There were wide variations of practice, and while some certainly did this, others are strong in their refusal to countenance such a proceeding. Should anyone defend Timaeus after Polybius' devastating exposure of his faults, there is a clinching argument: 'Timaeus *actually invents speeches*'. Polybius explodes with indignation against such an indefensible proceeding. It is 'the peculiar function of history' (τῆς ἱστορίας ἰδίωμα, 12.25b.1) to discover first of all what was actually spoken: Timaeus by his transgression here 'destroys the peculiar virtue of history' (ἀναιρεῖ τὸ τῆς ἱστορίας ἴδιον, 12.25b.4).[43]

We may consider the phenomenon of the use of sources for speeches. Again, Polybius is a test case, by whom we may hope to judge whether professions are merely conventional, or matched in practice. F.W. Walbank has discussed in some detail the thirty-seven or so speeches in the surviving text.[44] Polybius concedes that it is the part of politicians to say what the occasion demands, but it is not for historians to display their creative abilities, ἀλλὰ τὰ κατ' ἀλήθειαν ῥηθέντα καθ' ὅσον οἷόν τε πολυπραγμονήσαντας διασαφεῖν, καὶ τούτων τὰ καιριώτατα καὶ πραγματικώτατα (36.1.6-7). This is not to be interpreted rigidly, as a claim to verbatim accuracy; indeed, it implies selective editing. Walbank draws attention to the strange alternations between *oratio recta* and *oratio obliqua* in some Polybian

---

[42] Many inaccurate and over-simplified assumptions are current about the function of speeches in the ancient historians. See T.F. Glasson, 'The Speeches in Acts and Thucydides', *ExpT* 76 (1964-65), p. 165 and my discussion in *BJRL* 60 (1977-78), pp. 31-32.

[43] *BJRL* 60 (1977-78), p. 31.

[44] Walbank, *Historical Commentary*; also *Speeches in Greek Historians* (J.L. Myres Memorial Lecture) (Oxford: Blackwell, n.d. [c. 1965]).

speeches.[45] This may be merely a stylistic device to bridge between narrative and discourse. If so, it is still clearly an editorial feature, and an indication of Polybius' readiness to summarize what was said. When these facts are granted, the fact remains that Polybius' practice emerges well from Walbank's survey. Of the speeches at the Locris conference in the winter of 198 BC (18.1-10), Polybius' report 'has all the marks of being derived from a verbatim account of the meeting, and may be accepted as authentic'.[46] The elaborate pair of speeches in 9.28-39 is likewise adjudged to be authentic. Most of the speeches are by Greeks, where Polybius seems to have had access to Achaean records. The exceptions are largely contained in pairs of speeches, some of which are suspect on other grounds, like the pair before Zama (15.10-11), which may betray hindsight (and the improbability of knowing what Hannibal said to his troops). But even there Walbank thinks it probable that Polybius is using sources, but literary sources where the primary doubt attaches to the source. In fact the weaker passages in Polybian speeches are not characterized by rhetorical elaboration, but read like commonplaces in indirect speech, where he resorts to summarizing from poorer literary sources in default of Achaean or Roman records. When Polybius denounces Timaeus for inventing a speech of Hermocrates (12.25k.5-26.9), he was presumably well aware that it bore no resemblance to a prototype in Thucydides (4.59-64), though he makes no acknowledgment of Thucydides, and censures Timaeus' unconvincing rhetorical conceits.[47] The unstated implication may be that if you have a source like Thucydides it is inexcusable to manufacture what can have no claim to truth.

It may be, however, that Polybius is an exception. When we have the rare opportunity of comparing another historian (Tacitus) with the preserved original of one of his speeches, the historian does not emerge well from the encounter. Extensive, but discontinuous, fragments of Claudius' speech at Lugdunum (Lyon) are preserved epigraphically.[48] Tacitus' version (*Ann.* 11.24) is certainly briefer, but is cast in a different, characteristically abrupt, Tacitean style, and bears no detailed resemblance to the surviving parts of the original.

---

[45] *Speeches* pp. 7-8. The phrasing of Polybius 29.12.10 implies that even the τὰ κατ' ἀλήθειαν ῥηθέντα of 36.1.6-7 may not mean 'the actual words spoken'.

[46] *Hist. Comm.* I, p. 13.

[47] Gomme, Vol. 3, p. 523 *ad* Thuc. 4.59-64; cf. Walbank, *Hist. Comm.*, II, pp. 400-401.

[48] H. Dessau, *Inscriptiones Latinae Selectae* I (Berlin: Weidmann, 1892) 212, pp. 52-54; also accessible in E.M. Smallwood, *Documents Illustrating the Principates of Gaius, Claudius and Nero* (CUP, 1967), pp. 97-99, No. 369.

Dionysius again marks a strong contrast with Polybius. His own criticism of Thucydides is highly revealing. After praising Thucydides for his portrayals of horror and suffering, sometimes so successful ὥστε μηδεμίαν ὑπερβολὴν μήτε ἱστοριογράφοις μήτε ποιηταῖς καταλιπεῖν (*Thuc.* 15), Dionysius next comments on his treatment of speeches. Thucydides is said to have omitted them altogether in his final book at the instance of Cratippus (*Thuc.* 16),[49] and elsewhere to have included none where Dionysius thinks them essential. Much space in the criticism is devoted to the Funeral Speech of Pericles, as improperly placed in the Second Book, where its trivial occasion was unworthy of it (*Thuc.* 18). In Dionysius literary and rhetorical criteria are elevated above the historical conscience. Yet this is no sufficient basis for generalization, as contrary traditions co-existed in ancient historical writings.[50] Dionysius offers his own defence of speeches, and has his own way of using sources for them. He chooses 'to make his narrative accurate rather than brief' (ἀκριβεστέραν μᾶλλον ἢ βραχυτέραν, ποιήσασθαι τὴν διήγησιν), arguing that where others expend words on military details they neglect to report the speeches by which extraordinary events were brought to pass (7.66.3,5). From the Third Book the speeches occupy almost a third of his total text (Cary, Loeb I. xvi). They abound in phrases, sentences and whole passages imitating Demosthenes, Thucydides or Xenophon, and Cary (p. xviii) notes the imitation of the speech of Alcibiades (Thuc. 6.89-92) in that of Marcius in Dionysius 8.5-8.

Josephus clearly stands in a similar rhetorical tradition of history. Grant is severe on him in a number of places. Josephus' abuse of John of Gischala is borrowed from Sallust's attacks on Catiline (Grant, p. 248). Improbably pseudo-Jewish, monotheistic language is put in the mouth of the paragon Titus (p. 256). The visit of Alexander the Great to Jerusalem (*Ant.* 11.8.5.329ff.) and his honouring of the Jews and rejection of the claims of the Samaritans is all dismissed as fabrication (Grant, p. 263). In his two different accounts of Herod's exhortation to his troops after the earthquake of 31 BC (*BJ* 1.8.4.373ff. and *Ant.* 15.5.3.127ff.) Josephus offers two wholly dissimilar speeches, containing different echoes of Thucydides.[51] Again, he presses his own

---

49 It is often thought that the absence of speeches from Thucydides' Eighth Book is due rather to its unrevised state. Walbank (*Speeches*, p. 1) cites Cratippus and Trogus Pompeius as exceptions to the general rule that speeches were used in history.

50 See however H. Verdin, 'La fonction de l'histoire selon Denys d'Halicarnasse', *Anc Soc* 5 (1974), pp. 289-307 for a rather more positive evaluation of Dionysius. The article contains valuable bibliography and survey of discussion.

51 Cited by Cadbury, Foakes Jackson and Lake in *BC* 2.14. It may still be

viewpoint through an extraordinary two-thousand-word appeal by himself to the defenders of Jerusalem (*BJ* 5.9.3.362-4.420) which closely repeats some of the arguments he puts in the mouth of Agrippa II in an even longer speech at the outset of the war (*BJ* 2.16.4.345-401). This may also be seen in the comparison of 2.16.4.355-57 with 5.9.3.365, or in the argument that God was on the side of the Romans (2.16.4.390 with 5.9.3.369, 377-78).

There is in fact an important distinction between the two ways we find historians using their predecessors in their speeches. The use of literary reminiscence and allusion in the composition of a speech (as in Dionysius or Josephus) is quite different from the use of personal recollection and inquiry, or written sources, or possibly even an inscribed text (as in Thucydides or Polybius). The difference may be variously signalled: in the difference between relative brevity and the flagrantly rhetorical, in the difference between seeking sources and unanchored literary parallels. In the former case it is not surprising if there is much unevenness of style and scale, for the sources vary. Speeches may be detailed but condensed, or brief summaries where the evidence is more limited.

We are not yet ready to examine Luke in more detail, but it must be noted at this stage that the brief summaries in Acts bear no resemblance to the rhetorical compositions of Josephus. This is certainly not to say they are to be simply fitted into a 'Polybian' alternative. They must be assessed by appropriate critical criteria.[52] And their character is complicated here by the Luke-Acts relationship, where the 'Gospel' is of an apparently different genre, while sharing a close unity of method and continuity with its sequel. The Third Gospel too has its 'speeches' including substantial parable-discourses. We are so habituated to applying different kinds of critical approaches to the Synoptics and Acts that it may seem unwarranted to draw the Gospel into this kind of discussion. But there is a *prima facie* case for saying, whatever view one takes of the Synoptic Problem,[53] that the 'speeches', of Luke's Gospel in particular, are largely dependent on extant or inferable sources. There is editing; there is rearrangement–

---

questioned how far we attribute some of these features strictly to Josephus if we accept Thackeray's analysis of the large part played by 'Thucydidean' and 'Sophoclean' assistants (Loeb Josephus IV, *Ant*. Introduction, pp. xiv-xvi).

[52] Cf. *BJRL* 60 (1977-78), p. 50.

[53] I have generally assumed a conventional view of Markan priority, while recognizing that opinion has recently become much more fluid. The essential thesis of this study could be presented, perhaps even more strongly, *mutatis mutandis*, on a different model.

and that may hardly be surprising in an 'episodic' narrative– but the striking thing is the extent to which Luke uses sources almost verbatim. This poses many questions about historicity and about the speeches in Acts. It may be argued that the words of Jesus were unique. The caution against instant parallels with any kind of ancient historiography must here be repeated. But the preservation of the spoken word was not alien to the ancient world. The phenomenon merits further consideration.[54]

(d) Moral and Religious Stance

It is commonly understood that history was written in antiquity with a consciously didactic or ethical purpose, often stressed by the writer in his preface, and sometimes reiterated throughout the work. The highest conception of the historian's task is that he is pledged to the truth, and that the truth is 'useful'. The classic statement of Thucydides (1.22.4) that a true portrayal of events is useful for the guidance of those who may face similar circumstances in the future is widely echoed, as in Polybius 1.4.11 and Lucian, de Hist. Conscrib. 9.[55] The three writers cited certainly represent a sceptical strain in Greek thought detached from a morality rooted more directly in popular religion. They are no less moralists on that account; indeed, Polybius is so didactic and insistent on improving his reader's mind as to become tedious.

The earliest great Greek historian, Herodotus, stands nearer to the mainstream of older Greek thought. He announces his theme, with no self-conscious preface, and the digressive threads of his narrative gather slowly into the great climax. There is no overt moralizing, but the writer's world-view emerges in conceptions akin to those explored in contemporary Attic tragedy. Prosperity is precarious, and divine jealousy will square the account; sin and pride bring vengeance. Evil-doing and vaunted success may be closely connected in an inevitable process of ὕβρις, ἄτη and νέμεσις, of whose outworking

---

54 See Appendix 1 below.

55 Diodorus is also especially insistent on the utility of history (1.1.4 and passim); cf. C.H. Oldfather in Loeb Diodorus (1933) I.20. Polybius and Lucian both distinguish the τερπνόν from the χρήσιμον, and Lucian writes ἓν γὰρ ἔργον ἱστορίας καὶ τέλος, τὸ χρήσιμον, ὅπερ ἐκ τοῦ ἀληθοῦς μόνου συνάγεται (de Hist. Conscrib. 9). Again, it is the true historian's task to write 'about the important, essential, relevant and useful' (περὶ μεγάλων ἢ ἀναγκαίων ἢ οἰκείων ἢ χρησίμων, de Hist. Conscrib. 53). Cf. his praise of Thucydides for making truth the vehicle of usefulness (de Hist. Conscrib. 42). On Polybius see further also E.J. Tapp, 'Polybius' Conception of History', Prudentia 4 (1972), pp. 33-41.

Croesus and Xerxes are classic examples, no less than the mythical Prometheus or Oedipus.[56] In fact the story is told with great dramatic art, and the implicit moral theology is none the less real for the writer's urbane detachment as *raconteur*: 'I am obliged to tell what is said, but I am not at all obliged to believe it all, and that observation applies to all my book' (Hdt. 7.152).[57]

If the scepticism of Thucydides is more explicit, the moral effect of dramatic juxtaposition is no less apparent. The recital of the glories of Athens in the Funeral Oration (Thuc. 2.35-46) is followed immediately by the harrowing account of the onset of plague (2.47-54); the brutal aggression of Athens against Melos (5.84-116) by the disastrously over-ambitious Sicilian expedition (Book 6), and the immense hopes attached to this enterprise issue in catastrophe. His moral judgments are implicit.

We may then see two strong motifs variously exemplified in earlier Greek historiography as (1) political utility and instruction, and (2) the vindication of the moral order, as understood by the writer. To these we may add (3) the force of moral example, accounts of good men to be imitated and bad men to be repudiated, and (4) the patriotic idealization of the (Roman) state, characteristics which come increasingly to the fore in the Hellenistic and Roman periods. There is also the converse expression of the last in the bitter pessimism and nostalgia of Sallust and especially Tacitus.[58] It may seem hard to separate this last category from propaganda, except as there is an apparent difference between the fervent idealism of Livy and the detached and calculating self-justification of Caesar's political commentaries.

The third motif might be illustrated widely. Diodorus extols good men and censures the evil (11.46.1); more than others he insists that history should instruct in the good life.[59] Writers of 'universal histories' (κοιναὶ ἱστορίαι) deserve great gratitude; they are like 'ministers of divine providence' (ὥσπερ τινὲς ὑπουργοὶ τῆς θείας

---

[56] See the discussion and many examples cited in Grant, *Ancient Historians*, pp. 48-50 and notes.

[57] ἐγὼ δὲ ὀφείλω λέγειν τὰ λεγόμενα, πείθεσθαί γε μὲν οὐ παντάπασι ὀφείλω, καί μοι τοῦτο τὸ ἔπος ἐχέτω ἐς πάντα λόγον.

[58] We must recognize throughout this discussion the affinities of earlier historiography with both epic poetry and tragedy, and later the pervasive influence of rhetoric on history (cf. Cicero *de Oratore* 2.15.62-64, which sees truth as the first concern of history but calls for a worthy style; Quintilian *Inst. Or.* 10.1.31: *est enim [historia], proxima poetis, et quodammodo carmen solutum;* contrast Lucian, *de Hist. Conscrib.* 8).

[59] Cf. Oldfather in Loeb Diodorus I.20.

προνοίας, 1.1.3). Among the Romans too Livy announces his intention to choose examples to imitate in these decadent days (1. *praef*. 10-12). Tacitus regards it as 'the first duty of history that virtues shall not go unrecorded and that the terror of posterity and infamy shall attend evil words and deeds'.[60] The theme is strongly linked with the biographical interest which pervades history from the Hellenistic period and to which we will return below. At the cost of blurring the clear formal distinction made between history and biography we may adduce here Plutarch as an outstanding example of the moralizing tendency in a kindred field.[61] All his writings are marked by an ethical preoccupation. The recounting of virtues provokes in the reader a strong desire to emulate them (*Pericles* 1.4; etc.).

There is a constant stress on the importance of choosing noble and lofty themes for history (Dion. Hal. *Ant. Rom*. 1.2; etc). Both Polybius and Dionysius see profound significance in the rise of Rome to world power, but it remains for Livy to celebrate the ancient virtues of Rome. His prose epic is almost a counterpart of Vergil's *Aeneid*. Both are documents of the Augustan moral reformation. But Livy's nostalgia for a heroic past was the reverse side of the coin whose other face was denunciation of the present.[62] The ethical trend of Roman history had been set a generation earlier in the intense moralism of Sallust. The stability of the Republic had vanished with the fall of Carthage, and the commonwealth had been corrupted by the bitter strife of factions in a scramble for power (*Jugurtha* 41). The 'popular' party, no less than the senatorial, were at fault (*Jugurtha* 4.7-9; *Catiline* 38). Yet Sallust, exceptionally among the ancients, reflects bitter protest against social injustice.[63] His style and manner set a precedent for the yet more brilliant talents of Tacitus, whose experiences under Domitian impelled him to a devastating exposure of the origins of tyranny through mordant insinuation. Before the death of Augustus there were few alive who had known the Republic: *Igitur verso civitatis statu nihil usquam prisci et integri moris* (Tac. *Ann*. 1.4). Tacitus' various writings reiterate variations of the theme. His ethnographical study, the *Germania*, implicitly contrasts unspoiled virtue

---

[60] *Praecipuum munus annalium reor ne virtutes sileantur utque pravis dictis factisque ex posteritate et infamia metus sit* (*Ann*. 3.65).

[61] Plutarch himself stresses this distinction (*Alexander* 1.2), and proceeds to use the analogy of the painter found both in Polybius and in Lucian, *de Hist. Conscrib*. 13, though all three writers apply it quite differently. See below, p. 92.

[62] Cf. further L.W.A. Crawley, 'Rome's Good Old Days', *Prudentia* 3 (1971), pp. 24-38.

[63] Grant's citation of *Catiline* 20 comes from a speech placed in the mouth of the conspirator. Cf. however 21.1.

with the degenerate luxury of Rome, the *Agricola* is a biographical *encomium* of a noble man in evil times. Disaster is due to vice, where human character shapes events and not the reverse. It was Tacitus' misfortune to have to record an age when evil so far outweighed good (*Ann.* 4.32-33).[64]

It is not easy to separate the various moral motifs described above from the more specific 'theology' or world-view of the writers. There is in any case often a blending of contemporary popular theodicy with rationalizing elements, without regard for logical consistency. Herodotus, for instance, accepts oracles and signs from heaven more readily than miracles (Grant, p. 54), and refers to τὸ θεῖον as a divinity jealous of human prosperity,[65] and yet in his work 'narratives of divine management are commonly given at second hand, or as antecedents rather than causes' (Grant, p. 52). The Ionian 'Enlightenment' is discreetly at work upon what E.R. Dodds calls 'the Inherited Conglomerate'.[66] It is reasonable of the Thessalians to say the Peneus gorge was made by Poseidon: Herodotus thinks it was due to an earthquake, but people think Poseidon causes earthquakes, so one can put it that way if one so chooses (Hdt. 7.129).

In Thucydides the scepticism is more explicit, and the stress more directly upon a rigorous conception of causality. He recognizes religion as a historical phenomenon, a factor in the motivation of human actions, where the blood-guilt attached to Pericles' family (Thuc. 1.126-27), the mutilation of the Hermae and the religious scruples of Nicias were political or military facts in the circumstances of their day. Thucydides is severe on oracles (2.54); only one of the many in circulation happened to come true (5.26.3). Chance is a powerful factor in Thucydides. The chances of war are often stressed in the speeches (5.104; 6.23.3) and demonstrated in such a narrative as the Pylos-Sphacteria incident (4.3-41; see especially 4.12.3; 4.17.4-5; 4.29-30).[67] A similar view is found in Polybius: 'Causation ... is the

---

[64] Cf. Grant, pp. 279, 290-91.

[65] Twice described as φθονερός, in the classic cases of Solon and of Polycrates (1.32; 3.40) both however in direct speech, and so again with reference to τοῦ θείου ἡ προνοίη (3.108). J. Enoch Powell, *A Lexicon to Herodotus* (CUP, 1938) lists references to a monotheistic sense of ὁ θεός. Many of these however seem to denote an individual 'god'.

[66] E.R. Dodds, *The Greeks and the Irrational*, Sather Classical Lectures 25 (Berkeley: University of California Press, 1951) 179-80, quoting from a lecture by Gilbert Murray.

[67] Grant (p. 116) writes of Thucydides: 'In spite of his rejection of divine anger, he is not as consistently amoral as the truly impartial man would have to be'. This reads strangely. Thucydides is certainly a moralist in his way, and the issue

product of analysable events modified by a strong unpredictable element' (Grant, p. 158). One should never ignorantly attribute to the gods or to fortune what is the consequence of human action and foresight (Polybius 10.5.8). Yet τύχη is a powerful force, acting purposefully in a way amounting to the providential in the rise of Rome (1.4.1,5).[68]

The influence of popular religion and philosophy are strong through the Hellenistic and Roman periods. Under the progressive breakdown of the older beliefs and values, what Gilbert Murray called 'Failure of Nerve',[69] new cults and quests proliferated. Astrology and mystery religions flourished; Tyche was quasi-personified as a guardian goddess of cities or individuals, and the popular philosophical schools responded to the confusion of values. Historical compilers like Diodorus and Plutarch reflect a Stoic standpoint in their characteristically ethical interests. But in most writers of the period there is an inconsistency or ambivalence towards religion and the supernatural. Dionysius believes in Providence and records portents, but sometimes offers natural explanation and divine intervention as alternatives (*Ant. Rom.* 2.60-61, 68-69). He recounts myths and legends without necessarily embracing them.[70]

Similar remarks apply to the great Roman historians. The bizarre prodigies included periodically in both Livy and Tacitus are part of the annalistic tradition, but it is less clear whether our authors believed them.[71] Livy takes an essentially religious view of the institutions of early Rome. Grant calls attention to his phrase 'the benignity of the gods', and also to the prominence of the concept of Fate, especially in the supernatural sagas of his first decad (Grant, p. 242). Tacitus is a complex figure: he is contemptuous of the ignorant soldiers who thought a lunar eclipse was a sign from heaven (*Ann.* 1.28). He sees a mocking irony (*ludibria*) in human affairs (*Ann.* 3.18); prodigies, warnings and prophecies showed that the gods were eager to punish (*Hist.* 1.3); divine wrath and human madness collaborated on the rush to disaster (*Hist.* 2.38). A revealing passage is the

of 'impartiality' is not necessarily at stake in the fact. 'Amorality', no less than a moral stance of any other kind, is a definite presuppositional standpoint, and to that extent other than 'impartial'.

[68] See also G. Schepens, *Anc Soc* 9 (1978), pp. 117-48 for a most interesting discussion of Polybius' denunciation of a test-case of δεισιδαιμονία in Timaeus. The point of the criticism seems precisely to be that Timaeus invokes a morality backed by divine sanctions.

[69] G. Murray, *Five Stages of Greek Religion* (Oxford: Clarendon Press, 1925) Ch. 4.

[70] Cf. E. Cary in Loeb Dionysius I (1968), pp. xxiv-xxv.

[71] Grant, pp. 241, 303. He suggests that Livy saw prodigies as a sign of a disordered world. Note the implied scepticism at Livy 24.10.6.

account of Tiberius' testing of the astrologer Thrasyllus (*Ann*. 6.21), which provokes Tacitus to reveal his own questionings, a hesitant agnosticism between fate and accident, determinism and causation (6.22). The historian evidently accepts Thrasyllus' powers, where the modern reader sees rather the cleverness of a charlatan who must have exercised an unwarranted influence on the emperor.[72]

Throughout this literature the attitude to miracle fluctuates between acceptance and scepticism, but in either case it bears little significance to the matters at hand. If you can believe it happened thus, you may, but if so there is little more at stake than a provocative talking-point about an anecdote. Rationality does not necessarily exclude an interest in the marvellous or improbable. Secular writers use quasi-religious language. They may be more willing to ground morality in divine theodicy than to accept legend or myth. There is a mingling of acute criticism with popular inconsistency, and the marvellous as such is something of a gratuitous addition to be excluded by the more rigorously selective.

There is little yet to justify more than the most tentative remarks about the bearing of this survey on Biblical historiography. We have noted at least the existence of a critical interest in what happened and why, and of serious attempts to wrestle with philosophical and religious questions. But it is difficult to see any organic relationship between the elements of this cultural complex and the concerns either of Old Testament history or of Luke-Acts. The Old Testament historical books are distinctively theocentric. Omri, for example, was evidently an important figure, and his official chronicles (1 Kgs 16:27) would doubtless have thrown much light on his vigorous policies.[73] But for the Biblical historian his reign is summed up in the statement that 'he did evil in the sight of the Lord' (1 Kgs 16:25). The Biblical record presents a distinctive, divine perspective on events whose political and military significance might have been seen very differently. Yet the Lukan writings differ almost as markedly from this too. We may agree that Luke shares a theocentric (or Christocentric) base, and writes with an overriding theological purpose (however precisely we envisage it) to which the Greek historians offer no parallel. But his purpose is not ostensibly to reinterpret current

---

[72] See R.P. Oliver, 'Thrasyllus in Tacitus', *Illinois Classical Studies* 5 (1980), pp. 130–48.

[73] Cf. the evidence of the Moabite Stone (*Ancient Near Eastern Texts Relating to the Old Testament*, ed. J.B. Pritchard, Princeton University Press, 1950, p. 320; *Documents from Old Testament Times*, ed. D. Winton Thomas [London: Thomas Nelson and Sons Ltd., 1958], pp. 195-98). Israel was actually identified in Assyrian texts as 'Omri-land' (*ANET*, p. 284).

records in terms of that base. It is almost the reverse, to chronicle what really happened and thereby to show that the proclamation of divine events is rooted in a matter-of-fact reality which the reader can know to be true.[74] Luke is concerned not so much to vindicate God's working in history as to vindicate God's servants, and especially Paul, from within the acceptance of God's working. He meets conflict and opposition not with divine judgment, but with eirenical and ironical humour. We may grant he passes lightly over controversy— it is no part of his purpose to labour it. But the strength of his case seems to lie in his claim to give an accurate account. This runs quite counter to most current opinion about Acts, and most current opinion about the ancient context. But one point of contact with that context, if perhaps an indirect and incidental one, is precisely that Luke-Acts shares with some of the best minds of antiquity a concern for what actually happened, even if that concern arises out of a considerably different ethical and theological matrix. The difference is highlighted in the attitude to miracle. Miracle is integral to Luke's God-centred world and significant within it, even if also to be treated with a measure of reserve. It is an inseparable part of his concept of what happened, and we must cope with the difficulties which this factor poses for the modern mind. But for ancient secular history it was largely an excrescence, prompting a spectrum of attitudes, often varieties of inconsistent scepticism which might be paralleled today.

This section has inevitably been a brief treatment of a vast subject. It is little more than illustrative of the great complexity of the issues. Each theme may serve to raise afresh the recurring question of the nature of the first Christians' relation to their cultural environment, a question persistently difficult to answer, and deserving of more discriminating study on many points. Even though the specific links mentioned here may be tenuous and indirect, they help to militate against the common ideas that true historical interests did not exist, or that all ancients were credulous and uncritical. Our patronizing stance of cultural superiority is not warranted.

(e) *Bias*

Even a brief note on bias in antiquity must take account also of

---

74 Cf. Lk. 1:4. The point may stand even on differing views of the precise force of ἀσφάλεια. Cf. e.g. F.H. Colson, 'Notes on St. Luke's Preface', *JTS* 24 (1923), pp. 300-309; J.H. Ropes, 'St. Luke's Preface; ἀσφάλεια and παρακολουθεῖν', *JTS* 25 (1924), pp. 67-71; W.C. van Unnik, 'Remarks on the Purpose of Luke's Historical Writing (Luke I 1-4)', *Sparsa Collecta* I, *NovT* Supp 29 (Leiden: Brill, 1973), pp. 6-15.

shifting perspectives on the modern scene, especially the trends towards the integration of history as a discipline and also towards 'committed history'.[75] The usual separation of church history from secular history has its value in highlighting interests relevant to a specialized constituency, but can lead to an artificially segregated explanation of events, open to challenge by the concept of integration. The concept of 'committed history' questions the 'scientific' ideal of impartiality: if the historian himself is a creature of his time, his views of the past reflect the objectivities of his own context. It may be argued that traditional 'objectivity', preoccupied with supposedly hard facts, is itself only a covert and self-deceiving variety of subjectivity, and that conversely a sympathy with one's historical subject can give genuine insights which are otherwise denied. The way can be open, whether or not we approve, for the writing of diverse 'committed histories', whether Marxist, Christian, or other. And that could seem like a open acceptance of bias.[76]

These debates are salutary as they alert us to the difficulty, the reality of the personal factor in the most meticulous modern scholar. There are the dangers of false-objectivity on the one hand, and the positive claims of sympathetic insight on the other. It would be an extreme position to suggest that history is so far written in the historian's own image that no sufficient deposit of hard truth is left. The best course is to strike a balance in which historians are honest about their presuppositions and allow them to be present, even influential, in their thought, yet recognize the primacy of the documents, allowing the evidence to call those presuppositions into question.[77] There is in the last analysis enough 'hard' material there to make fruitful discussion and persuasion possible.

If then our modern house is in considerable disorder, without thereby becoming uninhabitable, we cannot pass comprehensive judgment on the ancients for not being exempt from the problems with which we are afflicted. It is precisely the historian's task to wrestle with the prepossessions of his sources, and none the less when those sources are themselves historiographers. The presence of

---

[75] See D.W. Bebbington, 'History for Theology and Mission', *FTh* 110 (1983), pp. 69-78, esp. pp. 71-73, in which the change in mood is described as being the result of the appearance of overtly Marxist interpretations of history on the one hand, and the rise of related disciplines such as sociology on the other.

[76] See D.W. Bebbington, 'History for Theology and Mission', pp. 69-78. For a classic Christian viewpoint see H. Butterfield, *Christianity and History* (London: Bell, 1949), notably his discussion of 'academic history', pp 19-22. Cf. also E.W. Ives, 'History and the Christian Faith', *FTh* 110 (1983), pp. 18-33.

[77] Cf. Bebbington, p. 74; Ives, pp. 32-33.

Tendenz in an ancient source does not invalidate that source; it merely requires the proper exercise of critical judgment upon it. No source is 'pure history' in the sense some theologians demand; all are to some extent interpretative and therefore open to the problem of bias. But they are not necessarily unusable for that reason.

There are many kinds and degrees of bias. An informal listing of some of the obvious varieties, progressing from the more blatant to the marginal, will show the range of the problem: (1) self-justification, (2) propaganda for a cause, (3) partiality for or against persons or institutions, whether through fear, favour or anger, (4) pious *encomium*, (5) an ethical, theological or philosophical understanding of the nature of history, (6) unconscious reproduction (or deliberate repudiation) of a cultural *Zeitgeist*, (7) personal temperament and background, (8) individuality of style and method.

Most of these things are not necessarily bad in themselves. The personal factor is ever present, and these or similar categories could probably be illustrated in the works of historians and scholars ancient or modern. All eight lend themselves to abuses, but even that fact need not induce despair. One modern scholar has written: 'The *Gallic War* is among the most potent works of propaganda ever written' (Grant, p. 190, on Caesar), but also 'it is usually extremely hard to fault him on facts' (Grant, p. 188). In fact Caesar possessed a remarkable gift to persuade through the apparently dispassionate presentation of a basically accurate story, yet his work remains of high historical worth.[78] Thus the speech of Ariovistus (*Bell. Gall.* 1.44), summarized in *oratio obliqua*, exemplifies Caesar's way of putting the strongest possible arguments in the mouths of his enemies (cf. Grant, p. 189), while yet implanting indirectly in the minds of his readers the idea that his military successes were being undermined by treachery in Rome. In the *Civil War* too we are given the impression of Caesar as the apostle of reconciliation, forced into a conflict he never wanted by a personal vendetta which left him no other defence (*Bell. Civ.* 1.4ff.).

It would be easy to cite examples whose bearing on historicity is diverse. Xenophon is careful to show his own conduct as correct (e.g. *Anab.* 4ff.) without showing Caesar's genius for self-justification, but where we can check his *Hellenica* against the papyrus fragments of the Oxyrhynchus historian he is open to criticism, less for bias than

---

78 See however the discussion of his works in Suet. *Div. Julius* 56, especially the opinion cited from Asinius Pollio that he was too credulous in accepting the accounts of others and gave a perverted account, whether deliberately or from forgetfulness. (56.4). To suggest carelessness underrates the remarkable, calculated skill of the writing.

because the latter is better informed.[79] Josephus, to whom we shall return below, is more blatant than either in his self-vindication. Yet he is also an important historical source, if used cautiously.[80] The more subtle forms of subjectivity are exemplified throughout ancient literature, not least in the cultural characteristics, the ethical and metaphysical interests, the focus on personalities, on military and political events. The most conscientious writers in any age are not exempt from the tendencies of their times, nor even from some partisanship within it. Thucydides, who can recount his own failure and exile without excuse (Thuc. 4.104-107; 5.26.5), and who was enabled by it to see both sides of the conflict impartially (5.26.5), cannot disguise his bitter contempt for Cleon (e.g. 4.28; 5.10.9; 5.16.1). Polybius, Dionysius and Livy are all in different ways moved by the phenomenon of the rise of Rome. But the most far-reaching problems in this area are posed by the major Roman figures, Sallust and especially Tacitus. Sallust's monographs are literary portraits of striking vividness and power, but highly suspect as historical sources, where for instance his chronology is sometimes distorted to suit the dramatic thrust of the narrative.[81] He makes an explicit claim to impartiality, his mind being 'free from hope, fear and partisanship'.[82] In the event his intensely moralistic view of history, and indeed his own previous record in public life, make this claim difficult to sustain. He uses a

---

[79] *The Oxyrhynchus Papyri* 5, ed. B.P. Grenfell and A.S. Hunt (London: Egypt Exploration Fund, 1908) 842, pp. 110-242. The unknown writer shows himself a historian of the first rank, and the work has been conjecturally attributed to either Theopompus or Cratippus, the latter suggestion being favoured by the lack of speeches in the twenty-one columns substantially preserved (cf n.46 above), though this writer is otherwise little more than a name. For his superiority to Xenophon see Grenfell and Hunt, pp. 124, 126, 141 (involving bias), 142. He is independent of Xenophon, and an important, previously unidentified, source for Diodorus. See I.A.F. Bruce, *An Historical Commentary on the Hellenica Oxyrhynchia* (CUP, 1967).

[80] Although in some aspects he is perhaps overrated through the failure to allow for his propensity for the rhetorical and exaggerated.

[81] Thus he antedates the beginning of Catiline's conspiracy to 64 BC (Sall. *Cat.* 17.1) rather than as following his electoral failure in that year (cf. J.C. Rolfe in Loeb Sallust (1921) p. xiii). Quintilian's judgment, comparing Sallust with Thucydides (*nec opponere Thucydidi Sallustium verear, Inst. Or.* 10.1.101) is overfavourable, and defensible only on literary, not on critical, grounds. Sallust's reputation, however, was founded more strongly on his lost *Histories* than on his extant monographs on Catiline and Jugurtha.

[82] *Mihi a spe, metu, partibus rei publicae animus liber erat* (Sall. *Cat.* 4.2). Note however his eulogy of Caesar and of Cato (*Cat.* 53.6-54.6) with his faint praise of Cicero (*Cat.* 22.3; 31.6; 43.1; 48.1, 8-9; 49.1), some of these references suggesting imputations which are not rebuffed.

study on one important conflict to indoctrinate the reader with his opinions of the whole sweep of Roman history.[83] In Sallust the personal factor makes for unreliable history, but the problem lies less in the personal factor, as such, than in his faulty treatment of the evidence which it has induced. Tacitus is the classic instance of the power of personal prejudice, despite his opening claim to write 'without anger or partiality, from whose motives I am far removed.'[84] He had first risen to high office under Domitian, at a time of fear and danger for the senatorial class to which he belonged, and wrote under the more liberal régime of Trajan, and projects back into his portrayals of Tiberius or Nero his sense of the origins of the suspicious and brutal tyranny he had experienced. His yearning for the supposed virtues of the old Republic may be unrealistic, but it inspired in him the bitter power to create indelible portraits which have stamped the early emperors as bizarre monsters upon the consciousness of posterity. As other sources for the period share a similar hostile tradition,[85] it has become a difficult problem whether the emperors were really as bad as they are painted. It is interesting to note that the *actions* of a Tiberius, as reported by Tacitus himself, are capable of a favourable construction: the damage is done in Tacitus' insinuations about their motivation. Lack of evidence only serves to prove Tiberius' ability to dissemble (e.g. *Ann.* 3.2). Tacitus goes to great length to deny an imputation that Tiberius had poisoned his own son Drusus, an idea we should never have entertained had it not been so insidiously planted (*Ann.* 4.10-11). The stages of Tiberius' self-revelation are finally unravelled in a concluding character-sketch (*Ann.* 6.51): he had had for instance 'an inscrutable and disingenuous period of hypocritical virtues'.[86] Yet in all this the bias can largely be separated out from the record of events, on which Tacitus is our principal authority. The difficulty of the process must not be underrated,

---

[83] E.g. Sall. *Cat.* 1-13 *passim; Jug.* 1-4; D.J. Stewart, 'Sallust and *Fortuna', History and Theory* 7 (1968), pp. 298-317, with discussions of the key Sallustian concepts of *fortuna, virtus* and *ingenium.*

[84] *Sine ira et studio, quorum causas procul habeo* (Tac. *Ann.* 1.1).

[85] Especially Suetonius, apparently the earliest writer of dispassionate biography, as opposed to *encomium.* His *Lives* are rich in dramatic anecdote, with little attempt at editing or consistent portrayal, but they are heir to a similar tradition. Among non-historical and non-political writers the savage satire of Juvenal and Martial's flattery of Domitian (renounced in 10.72 after the tyrant's death) enlarge the picture. The *Letters* of the younger Pliny occasionally reflect something of the same perils as those which occasioned the bitterness of his friend Tacitus (Pliny *Ep.* 3.11.3).

[86] *Occultum ac subdolum fingendis virtutibus* (*Ann.* 6.51).

but it is precisely the task of the historian to undertake it, and we need not be unduly pessimistic. Tacitus remains a most valuable and reliable source when critically evaluated, and our access to the 'historical Tiberius' or the 'historical Nero' would be minimal without him. He is in this respect far superior to Sallust, irrespective of the bias factor, because he is so much more reliable in his treatment of the 'hard' evidence.[87]

(f) *The Purpose and the Qualifications of the Historian*

Although this final heading overlaps some of the topics already considered, including selection, ethical stance and bias, it may be useful to restate our interim findings and prepare for the closer examination of Acts itself. Here then, is a tabulation, with occasional comment, of some of the conceptions of purpose and qualification which have emerged in our sampling of the ancient literature. **Purpose**: (1) to be politically useful; (2) to provide ethical instruction or example; (3) to record a subject of great intrinsic importance; (4) to enlarge the fame both of the subject and the author; (5) to present the subject in a style worthy of its greatness; (6) to create a work of literature, in the light of certain views of the kinship of history to epic poetry, tragedy or rhetoric; (7) to explain the writer's concept of his subject to his intended readership; (8) to present the truth 'as it actually happened'. **Qualifications**: (1) to have been an eyewitness participant; (2) to be a man of affairs, experienced in political and military matters; (3) to be a critically trained observer and interviewer; (4) to have seen both sides of a conflict, as an expatriate or exile; (5) to have travelled to the scenes of the events; (6) to have the ability to be impartial, as exempt from the direct operation of fear or favour; (7) to possess a literary style worthy of the subject.

These lists read strangely to the modern mind, even apart from the incompatibilities included together within them. Purposes (4) and (5), for instance, are variants of a literary motivation which seems to us misconceived. An illustration of (5), however, is the curious passage

---

[87] Discussion of this topic may be concluded with reference to the statement of Arrian (*Anab.* 1.1) that he follows Ptolemy son of Lagus and Aristobulus wherever they agree, as they are the best sources, for both were participants, and Ptolemy was actually a king. Mendacity would be dishonourable in a king. As moreover both wrote after Alexander's death, there was no ἀνάγκη or μισθός to induce falsification in their writing. It is perhaps a significant point about the ancient idea of bias that it could be categorized in these terms (cf. Sallust, Tacitus). Kings are not necessarily exempt from the temptation to a propagandist rewriting of history, even if directly mercenary or prudential motives are not operative on them.

in Arrian (*Anab.* 1.12): Alexander is less fortunate than Achilles in not yet having had his Homer.[88] Arrian is worthy of the theme. His name is not unknown. He can count himself a master in Greek literature if Alexander may be counted such in the profession of arms (1.12.5). Writer and subject depend on each other's renown. He refuses, like the writers satirized by Lucian, to boast of his credentials. Let his work speak for itself, alike in historical quality and style.[89]

Another point which deserves special notice is the last statement of purpose, the presentation of the truth, implicit in much of the best ancient historiography, however often denied. Lucian's words τοῦ δὴ συγγραφέως ἔργον ἕν, ὡς ἐπράχθη εἰπεῖν (*de Hist. Conscrib.* 39) are almost exactly the same as Ranke's *wie es eigentlich gewesen.*[90]

3. Biography as an Alternative Model for the Historiography of Luke

The ancients viewed biography as a genre distinct from history, with a separate course of development.[91] The earliest specimens are Xenophon's *Agesilaus* and Isocrates' *Evagoras*, both showing an ancestry in *encomium*, as Isocrates himself concedes.[92] The interest in the influence of personalities was already active in Greek literature, in such works as Plato's *Symposium* or Xenophon's *Memorabilia*. But Isocrates declares himself an innovator in a genre never previously attempted: περὶ δὲ τῶν τοιούτων οὐδεὶς πώποτ' αὐτῶν συγγράφειν ἐπεχείρησεν (*Evag.* 8).[93] Hellenistic biography is preserved only in

---

[88] Cf. also Sall. *Cat.* 8.2-5: the acts of the Athenians are celebrated even beyond their true glory because of the genius of their writers, while the Romans were 'men of action' and had never produced such writers among their ablest men.

[89] See Schepens, *Anc Soc* 2 (1971), pp. 254-68.

[90] It has however been pointed out that *eigentlich* usually meant 'essentially' rather than 'actually' in 19th century German usage (Bebbington, *Patterns in History* [Leicester: IVP, 1979], p. 107).

[91] See generally D.S. Stuart, *Epochs of Greek and Roman Biography* (Berkeley: University of California Press, 1928); A. Momigliano, *The Development of Greek Biography: Four Lectures* (Cambridge Mass: Harvard University Press, 1971). The classic work is F. Leo, *Die griechisch-römische Biographie nach ihrer literarischen Form* (Leipzig: Teubner, 1901). This however is organized by literary type, not in historical perspective, and begins with Suetonius. Biography is commonly a late development in a national literature, not least among the Greeks. Though the Greeks had 'a genius for commemoration', the Roman temperament was more addicted to chronicles (Stuart, pp. 6-7). See also A.J. Gossage on Plutarch and G.B. Townsend on Suetonius in *Latin Biography*, ed. T.A. Dorey (London: Routledge and Kegan Paul, 1967), pp. 45-77, 79-111.

[92] *Evag.* 8-11; Stuart, p. 19.

[93] Stuart, p. 92-94 questions the view accepted since Leo that Isocrates is

fragments of Satyrus' *Life of Euripides*[94] and Nicolaus of Damascus' *Augustus*.[95] The former has been considered the oldest pure biography, evidently a popular work, and remarkable in being written in a rudimentary dialogue form. The earliest surviving collection of biographies is that of the Roman Cornelius Nepos (1st cent. BC). The major names in the genre are Plutarch in Greek and Suetonius in Latin, both of whom wrote in the early 2nd cent. AD. Later exemplars of varieties of the genre are Philostratus and Diogenes Laertius in the 3rd cent. At the lowest level of biographical writing are the brief lives attached to manuscripts of ancient authors, which may be little more than a mixture of gossip and polemic with anecdotes based on fanciful influences from the writings, not least from literalistic construings of poetic metaphor.[96]

Polybius distinguishes the encomium sharply from history. His own encomiastic work on Philopoemen demanded 'a summary and heightened presentation of his achievements', whereas the history, 'impartial to praise and blame, seeks the strictly true account'.[97] Plutarch also makes the distinction: οὔτε γὰρ ἱστορίας γράφομεν, ἀλλὰ βίους (Plut. *Alexander* 1.2), and reinforces the point with another application of the recurring image of the painter: artists get their likenesses from the face and the expression of the eyes, and little from the other members, and likewise the biographer's portrait is an attempt to depict the features of the soul (1.3).[98]

It may be a more elusive task to delimit precisely the diagnostic characters of this distinction. It is rather that the two categories have a different pedigree, exemplified in broad, general differences of type, method and ethos, but without excluding much variability and even

justified in this claim.

[94] *P Oxy* 9 (1912) 1176, 2nd cent. AD papyrus of 2nd cent. BC writer.

[95] Jacoby, *FGH* II A No. 90, pp. 391-420, frags 125-30, early 1st cent. AD.

[96] See esp. J.A. Fairweather, 'Fiction in the Biographies of Ancient Writers', *Anc Soc* 5 (1974), pp. 231-75. Note her warning, 'The modern scholar has to be extremely cautious over applying to ancient literature a technique of literary criticism which can be most fruitful where modern authors are concerned: the detecting of psychological motivation for aspects of a man's writing in events which are known to have happened to him in the course of his life' (p. 239). The caution may apply no less, if for slightly different reasons, in the treatment of better sources from an ancient and imperfectly controlled context. On the general outline of the history of biography see further Momigliano, *Biography*, p. 8.

[97] ἀπήτει τὸν κεφαλαιώδη καὶ μετ' αὐξήσεως τῶν πράξεων ἀπολογισμόν, but history, κοινὸς ὢν ἐπαίνου καὶ ψόγου, ζητεῖ τὸν ἀληθῆ καὶ τὸν μετ' ἀποδείξεως καὶ τῶν ἑκάστοις παρεπομένων συλλογισμῶν (Polybius 10.21 [24].8).

[98] Lucian, *de Hist. Conscrib.* 13 scornfully likens the painter's idealization of his subject to the flattery which falsifies the truthfulness required of history.

overlap.[99] Many features are strongly evocative of just the same kind of cultural milieu, the strong ethical emphasis and purpose, the mixtures of popular religion, philosophical stance and partial rationalization, all elements clearly seen in Plutarch. But the biography is more likely to give an impressionistic portrait, less rigorous in its profession of detachment, chronology or critical treatment of sources, often anecdotal and topically arranged around the presentation of character. In Plutarch a character is presented as an example to be admired and imitated (Pericles), or occasionally to be shunned (Demetrius), or as a warning of flawed goodness (Cimon). A subject embodies a single master-virtue, the 'justice' of Aristides or the 'ambition' of Themistocles.[100] Plutarch, more than Suetonius, is basically chronological in outline, but singularly lacking in historical conscience where such conflicts with a greater priority: some unkind critics object to the possibility of a meeting between Solon and Croesus as anachronistic, but the story is so true to the characters of both men that he will not reject it for such slight cause as 'so-called canons of chronology' (χρονικοῖς τισι λεγομένοις κανόσιν, *Solon* 27.1).[101]

We have discussed the attempts of Talbert and others to find new light on Luke-Acts from literary parallels isolated by sub-divisions of the biographical genre (See above, pp. 37-39). We are here, however, considering biography as an alternative model for historiography. The Gospel at least is, on the face of it, a βίος. But from the perspective of our theme we need to measure Luke-Acts by a more exacting historical standard than that of Plutarch. The relevance of biography to this quest is largely negative. It is another kindred strand in the ancient cultural complex. It testifies to the existence of an anecdotal or encomiastic tradition of the interest in personality. Perhaps this recognition helps to reinforce from another angle the ancient consciousness of the distinctive rigour which their best practitioners required of history, as compared with biography. There are certainly parallels between Luke-Acts and features of history, biography and technical literature. But those parallels are neither exclusive nor subject to control. They are fluid, relevant to the general milieu, if perhaps partly in reaction against it and hard to place accurately within it.[102] Most of

---

99 Momigliano (*Biography*, pp. 1-2) stresses this further as an old and honoured distinction rarely questioned before the twentieth century, and still upheld vigorously by Eduard Meyer.

100 I am indebted in this account to Grant, pp. 314-24.

101 Cf. *BJRL* 60 (1977-78), p. 30.

102 There are many more variations and parallels within the complex of ancient biographical and kindred writing than may be covered in the present work. Lucian's *Alexander* and *Peregrinus* are bitter exposures of charlatans, Tacitus'

the New Testament is perhaps best seen as a popular literature, imperfectly representative of any defined literary type, and motivated by a dominant theological purpose scarcely paralleled in pagan writing.[103] If Luke is a partial exception, aspiring to a more formal style in addressing a man presumably of some literary education, his type is still somewhat free and mixed, a concisely effective vehicle for what he had to say, drawing on a flexible use of the style most natural to him. The uninitiated reader might have taken the Gospel at first sight for a biography, but soon have found it an unusual one, and then have been moved by the impact of the double work in directions other than the normal reactions to biography or history. It is my contention that one of the inevitable questions posed as a result of the document was whether it really happened. Ancient biography, no less than ancient historiography, may need to serve as a historical source. The question here is whether the work is a good source. And it needs to be measured by the stricter rather than the laxer measure. Rigorous concepts of history existed in Luke's world: Luke must be judged by his performance rather than on the slippery ground of parallels.

4. Luke and Josephus

We must return finally to the relationship raised at the beginning of this chapter. There are four levels at which the bearing of Josephus or Luke may need to be raised: (1) that there is a direct literary relationship between them, that one is dependent on the other; (2) that they are closely comparable as historians, treating overlapping events with similar principles and methods; (3) that they are not closely

Agricola is a pious tribute with the overtones of a moral and political tract, Josephus' *Vita* is a rare specimen of autobiography, and an evident self-vindication. Plutarch's idea of 'parallel lives' likewise may command informal parallels in the Roman and Smyrnean parallels of Hermogenes (*CIG* 3311) and the like, but these should not be used to enhance the significance of Peter-Paul or even Jesus-Paul parallels in Luke-Acts apart from rigorous study of date and dependence. All these features are naturally enough rooted in the general milieu.

[103] Partial exceptions may be found in some of the orations of Aelius Aristides in their bearing on Asclepius-cult or in Philostratus' *Life of Apollonius*, both much later, and the latter perhaps actually the product of a conscious reaction against Christianity. For discussion of the 'aretalogy' concept in this connection see above, and for criticism of the '*Theios Aner*' concept as applied to Apollonius see D.L. Tiede, *The Charismatic Figure as Miracle Worker* (Missoula Mont: SBL, 1972); C.H. Holladay, '*Theios Aner*' in Hellenistic Judaism (Missoula Mont: Scholars Press, 1977). For documentary attestation of an itinerant pagan dedicated to the service of his god see the letter of Zoilus of Aspendos (258/7 BC, Deissmann, *Light*, pp. 152-61).

comparable except as belonging to a broadly contemporary and re-lated milieu, which needs to be studied in itself if we are to reach a plausible account of their relative places in the social and cultural complex; (4) that in detail they offer independent, and sometimes contradictory, accounts of some of the same events.

The first point should not delay us here. I am not aware that any scholar has argued that Josephus is dependent on Luke, but the theory of Lukan dependence on Josephus has had in its day a certain vogue, and has been used as a major argument for the late dating of Luke-Acts.[104] But where the two writers touch, they often conflict. This scarcely favours the first hypothesis, unless we assume that Luke was singularly careless or prejudiced to contradict his source gratuitously. In other contexts scholars are wisely cautious to posit knowledge or dependence even where verbal resemblances exist.[105]

(3) and (4) are both relevant areas of exploration. The former expresses more nearly the nature of the relationship. It is beyond the scope of this study to analyse the common milieu in detail. I am reminded of a lecture by the ancient historian F.G.B. Millar, who undertook a comparative study on ground rather different from that of most New Testament scholarship. By-passing entirely the analysis of source and redaction in Luke which his audience expected, Millar, from his own familiarity with the Palestinian milieu shared by Josephus and the Lukan Jesus, affirmed Luke's closeness to the events, while remaining critical of Luke's veracity.[106]

Case (4) concerns such notable cruxes as the Nativity and census under Quirinius, the Theudas reference, the date of the succession of Festus, and the like, where the conflict of evidence poses concrete

---

104 The arguments prominent at the close of the last century, and associated particularly with the names of C. Clemen, M. Krenkel and P.W. Schmiedel, are forcibly rebutted by A. Plummer, *A Critical and Exegetical Commentary on the Gospel according to St. Luke* ICC (Edinburgh: T. & T. Clark, 4th edn, 1901) pp. xxix-xxx. The debate will claim further attention in chapter 9 below.

105 Note e.g. the caution displayed in finding specific knowledge of the New Testament in the earliest Apostolic Fathers. See e.g. D.A. Hagner, *The Use of the Old and New Testaments in Clement of Rome*, NovT Supp. xxxiv (Leiden: Brill, 1973). Plummer insists that 'Josephus must not be used both ways. If the resemblances are made to prove that Luke copied Josephus, then the discrepancies should not be employed to prove that Luke's statements are erroneous. If Luke had a correct narrative to guide him, why did he diverge from it only to make blunders? ... Moreover, where the statements of either can be tested, it is Luke who is commonly found to be accurate, whereas Josephus is often convicted of exaggeration and error' (pp. xxix-xxx).

106 Cf. *BJRL* 60 (1977-78), p. 50n. It is good again to stress the value of interaction between the different approaches of different disciplines.

historical problems. The instances found in Acts will of course be treated in their place as specific problems at the heart of our subject.

Concerning (2), we have seen that Luke and Josephus are not particularly close in aims and method, and actually reflect differing trends within ancient historiography. But this issue cannot be closed without some further consideration of recent discussion, especially the important contribution of F.G. Downing.[107]

Downing's examination of Josephus' handling both of the Old Testament text and of non-canonical material in the Epistle of Aristeas is of much interest. He concludes that Josephus is free in altering the wording of his sources, and that historian evidently does not think this at variance with his strong professions of accuracy. Further, Josephus seems to paraphrase for the sake of change, since most of these changes have no obvious motivation. There is no real *invention* of material, though he may variously rearrange, tidy, conflate or embellish his sources.[108] The second part of the study, which applies these findings to the purpose and method of Luke, is less successful. Downing claims that Luke is actually much closer verbally to his sources than Josephus, and points in at least one connection to his relative brevity.[109]

Although the bulk of Downing's detailed discussion is directed to the Gospel, and falls outside the scope of the present volume, his attempt to justify Luke on a Josephan model seems forced, and the further link with Dionysius accentuates rather than eases the problem. Downing's study amounts to being an interestingly documented study of some of the phenomena of redaction as such, and makes the important point that it involves more complex factors than *Tendenz*, even in a writer so evidently tendentious as Josephus. The resemblances between Luke and Josephus lack significant specificity.[110] The dissimilarities may cut more deeply. The differences which touch

---

[107] JSNT 8 (1980), pp. 46-65, 9 (1980), pp. 29-48; Cf. NTS 28 (1982), pp. 546-59.

[108] For *Aristeas* he follows the detailed study by A. Pelletier, *Flavius Josèphe, adapteur de la lettre d'Aristée* (Paris: Klincksieck, 1962), JSNT 8 (1980), pp. 48-49; for his use of the Biblical text, pp. 50-64.

[109] 'The extraordinary extent of verbal similarities' (JSNT 9 [1980], p. 33); for the brevity, noted in discussing the Lukan Preface, but equally evident elsewhere, see p. 31.

[110] 'Following Josephus' conventions' (JSNT 9 [1980], pp. 36, 41) makes the resemblances seem far more explicit than they really are. The passages discussed are either natural examples of 'editing' in a trivial sense applicable far more widely than this comparison, or parallels whose relevance may be considered forced, often prefaced by phrases like 'might have produced', 'would be entirely credible'.

directly on the historical question are the following:

(1) Josephus is attempting a comprehensive history of a people (*Ant.*) or period (*BJ*), whereas Luke's work is extremely narrow and selective in its focus.

(2) Where Josephus' major works are extended over many books, Luke has written two books tersely, though not incompatible with occasional repetition and duplication (e.g. Cornelius and the three versions of Paul's conversion).[111]

(3) The advocacy implicit in the two writers is different: Luke is on any view self-effacing, his purpose theological (even if its expression is through a historical record) whereas Josephus' record is intensely personal in areas where his own conduct had incurred criticism; he does not have a similarly evangelical motive.[112]

(4) The theological outlook of Josephus, on Downing's own view, is close to the 'ethical providential theism' of Dionysius (*NTS* 28 [1982], p. 547), but the further assimilation of Luke to this comparison (pp. 557-58) is difficult to sustain. Although both authors may be trying to communicate with a pagan readership, where Josephus may be prone to accommodate, Luke's theology, even as presented in Acts 17, may interact with pagan thinking, but is bold to counter it. These two headings involve a different resolution of the history-theology tension in the two writers.

(5) Josephus' writing is strongly marked by rhetoric, and stands (with Dionysius) in a distinctively rhetorical tradition within ancient historiography; Luke, while capable of sophisticated literary style in his preface, is never rhetorical.

(6) The speeches in Josephus are characteristic products of that rhetorical tendency; those of Acts are brief, and if we may adduce the 'speeches' of Jesus in the Third Gospel, their content is reproduced almost verbatim in part from a preserved source (Mark) or a closely inferable one (Q or equivalent).

(7) Josephus, while an invaluable witness to matters within his experience, is prone to sensationalize and exaggerate; Luke is restrained. Josephus dwells on the horrors of the famine in doomed Jerusalem (*BJ* 5.10.3.429-38) or the grotesque fates of refugees (*BJ*

---

111 It is perhaps a question for each part of his work how much could be packed into a single papyrus roll, yet without distorting his choice and the unhurried command of his material. Cf. Hengel, *Acts*, pp. 8-9.

112 Whatever the view taken of Downing's statement of the aim of both Josephus and Dionysius as to 'entertain high-minded pagans' (*NTS* 28 (1982), p. 558), his application of the same phrase to Luke reads strangely, even though for Josephus and Luke he qualifies it to imply that they did it by a parallel presentation of their respective groups. These parallels seem forced, as does the unqualified application to Josephus of the Lukan characteristics listed at *JSNT* 9 (1980), p. 32.

5.12.4.548-52), or a mother eating her child, a scene complete with speeches (*BJ* 6.3.3.199-4.213). This problem is especially apparent in the treatment of numbers. In Acts 4,000 men follow the Egyptian bandit into the desert, and in Josephus 30,000.[113] Josephus has 'not less than three million Jews' in an anti-Roman demonstration; can we accept such a figure?[114]

(8) The attitude to the miraculous is different in the two writers: In Josephus there is an ambivalence like that in pagan historiography. He rationalizes even Biblical narratives, often by omission or radical reinterpretation, yet he is not averse to heightening the providential action of God in dramatic natural events. He lists bizarre prodigies presaging the fall of Jerusalem (*BJ* 6.5.3.288-309), and turns at once to the providence of God as being on the Roman side (*BJ* 6.5.4.310-15). This is a far cry from Luke, for whom the miraculous is an inseparable part of God's dealing in vindication of Christ and in compassion to the needy, but not to be indulged in for its own sake. This of course does not make the miraculous less of a problem to the modern reader of Luke as opposed to Josephus, but the cases are considerably different.

The most telling apparent similarity is one which, ironically, the common trend of criticism would forbid the scholar to stress at face value, that Luke was, ostensibly, like Josephus, an eyewitness participant in some part of his narrative. Their professions of research and accuracy are couched in very similar terms. It is the historian's duty, according to Josephus, to know his facts ἀκριβῶς, 'either through having been in close touch with the events, or by inquiry from those who knew them' (ἢ παρηκολουθηκότα τοῖς γεγονόσιν ἢ παρὰ τῶν εἰδότων πυνθανόμενον, *Ap.* 1.10.53), a formulation closely recalling the evidential categories favoured by Polybius. Josephus was qualified to write the history of the war as 'a participant in many and an eyewitness in most of its events' (πολλῶν μὲν αὐτουργὸς πράξεων,

---

[113] Acts 21:38; Jos. *BJ* 2.13.5.261-63.

[114] οὐκ ἐλάττους τριακοσίων μυριάδων (*BJ* 2.14.3.280). Josephus' credit might be salvaged in particular cases by the assumption that there has been manuscript error in the transmission of numerals, but this will certainly not explain the habitual pattern. Note how his numbers grow from the *Jewish War* to the *Antiquities*: E.g. *BJ* 2.6.3.97 with *Ant.* 17.11.4.320 and *BJ* 2.6.3.100 with *Ant.* 17.11.5.323; see *BJRL* 60 (1977-78), p. 50. Cf. also '(Was it true) that a missile hit a pregnant woman and shot her child out of her body for a hundred yards? Did a stone used as a projectile really knock a man's head off and fling it like a pebble more than six times that distance?' (Grant, p. 258). The height of Mt. Tabor is given as ἐπὶ τριάκοντα σταδίους (*BJ* 4.1.55), nearly *four miles* or 20,000 ft., the actual elevation being 1843 ft., less than 10%.

πλείστων δ' αὐτόπτης γενόμενος, *Ap.* 1.10.55).[115] In his preface to
the *Jewish War* he condemns those who have written σοφιστικῶς
from hearsay (ἀκοῇ), and exhibit sometimes κατηγορία, sometimes ἐγ-
κώμιον, but τὸ ἀκριβές of history nowhere, from flattery of the
Romans or hatred of the Jews (*BJ* 1.1.1.1-2), vices from which Josephus evidently regards himself as exempt.

Josephus, then, makes strong professions of accuracy in terms
reminiscent of the best standards current in antiquity. While acknowledging his indispensable value to us, we may entertain grave doubts
whether he will stand the scrutiny of his own claims. Luke expresses
himself briefly and with restraint in similar terms, and our brief comparison above implies a *prima facie* impression that Luke acquits
himself very much better on some of the points where they differ.

We must refrain from pursuing here the great range of secondary
literature on historiography and studies of the significance of literary
parallels in particular. Thus S.J.D. Cohen has presented an interesting
case for supposing that Josephus saw himself as the Jeremiah of his
day, the true prophet who declared that the true vocation of Judaea
was in submission to the conqueror legitimated by God as the instrument of his judgment. The direct influence of a Biblical prototype is
plausible enough, whatever he thought of its influence on the psy-
chology of Josephus. But the further link with Polybius seems
tenuous, and the theological dimension of the supposed relationship
yet more so.[116]

Conclusions

The main interim conclusion of this chapter is somewhat negative,
that the question remains wide open. But it is a step forward to have
recognized that. Historiography is in any case a relevant part of the
context, and deserves exploring on that account alone. The key does
not lie in literary parallels, and we need to pursue complementary
approaches. Positively, weight should be given to several features
existing in ancient historiography which our study has thrown up,
not because Luke can be lightly presupposed to relate to them, but

---

115 Cf. Polybius 3.4.13: διὰ τὸ τῶν πλείστων μὴ μόνον αὐτόπτης, ἀλλ' ὧν μὲν
συνεργός, ὧν δὲ καὶ χειριστὴς γεγονέναι, and see the further parallels cited by
Wikenhauser, p. 139. The parallel use of the perfect participle of παρακολουθεῖν, is
also striking. Cf. also Polybius 3.32.2, where however the verb refers to the
reader's ability to 'follow clearly' Polybius' comprehensive narrative. Josephus'
criticism of Greek historiography (*Ap.* 1.2.6-5.27), and his defence of the credentials of the Hebrew scriptures, (*Ap.* 1.6.28-9.43) are of much interest.

116 S.J.D. Cohen, 'Josephus, Jeremiah, and Polybius', *History and Theory* 21
(1982), pp. 366-81.

because they raise the question whether he did, and forbid that question to be ruled out of court as inapplicable to the ancient world. The points in view are the following: (1) the existence of a distinctive and rigorous theory of historiography; (2) the stress on eyewitness participation; (3) the importance of interviewing eyewitnesses; (4) the limitation of coverage to material where the writer has privileged access to evidence of guaranteed quality; (5) the stress on travel to the scene of events; (6) the prospect then (and for us) of checking details with contemporary documents; (7) the occasional insistence on the use of sources for speeches; and (8) the vigour of the concept of 'truth' in history 'as it actually happened'.

Chapter 4
Types of Knowledge Displayed in Acts

In the preliminaries considered thus far, we have set the stage, clarified the issues, and insisted on the openness of the question. We are still confronted by the phenomenon of opinions so sharply polarized that it seems difficult to find ground for communication. Among older writers the spectrum ranges from judgments such as the following (on the Antioch passage): 'When we examine the whole contents of the narrative its historical value shrinks until it reaches the vanishing point. No single detail is possible',[1] or that the knowledge possessed by the writer (about the Apostolic Age) is 'significantly meagre',[2] to opinions which class Luke 'among the historians of the first rank'[3] or call his history 'unsurpassed in respect of its trustworthiness'.[4] He has even been ranked as 'the greatest of all historians'.[5] And the great Eduard Meyer wrote, 'Sein Werk, trotz des viel kleineren Umfangs, [erhält] doch denselben Charakter wie die der großen Historiker, eines Polybios, eines Livius und so vieler andrer'.[6] More recently the followers of Dibelius have urged a renewed scepticism. Haenchen writes, 'Luke was no professional historian and was not interested in writing a history of early Christianity, aside from the fact that in his time the concepts *history and early Christianity* were still nonexistent' (italics *sic*).[7] Vielhauer

---

1 C. von Weizsäcker, *The Apostolic Age of the Christian Church*, tr. J. Millar from the 2nd German edn (London and Edinburgh: Williams and Norgate, 1894), I.106, cited in part by A.T. Robertson, *Luke the Historian in the Light of Research* (Edinburgh: T. & T. Clark, 1920), p. 2, but without specifying that it applies to a particular passage and not the whole book.

2 Jülicher, *Introduction*, p. 434 ('von bezeichnender Dürftigkeit', *Einleitung*, p. 344). Jülicher is further critical of Baur's *Tendenzkritik*: 'The writer is wrongly credited with intentions where in reality all is explained by ignorance, by the incompleteness of his materials, and by his incapacity to carry himself back into the modes of thought even of a just-departed age' (p. 437).

3 Ramsay, *SPTR*, p. 4.

4 Ramsay, *Bearing*, p. 81.

5 Robertson, p. 43; cf. p. 41, where he cites a similar judgment by Ramsay.

6 E. Meyer, *Ursprung und Anfänge des Christentums*, (Stuttgart and Berlin: J.G. Cotta, 1924) I.2; cf. A.A.T. Ehrhardt, *The Acts of the Apostles. Ten Lectures* (Manchester University Press, 1969), p. 12.

7 Haenchen, *SLA*, p. 258. On the other hand, according to Haenchen, 'To him

speaks of the purpose of Acts as 'primarily to give the historical report', but regards Luke's concept of history as a continuous redemptive process, 'regardless of how far the result was from the examples
of antiquity and the claims of modern historiography'.[8] From this
perspective 'Ed. Meyer, who approaches Acts *with the presuppositions
of a historian of antiquity* [my italics] and treats it with the greatest
confidence, misunderstands the nature of its accounts and the way in
which they are connected'.[9] Yet the historical merits of Luke's work
have been strongly upheld in recent historical scholarship: Sherwin-
White has written, 'For Acts the confirmation of historicity is overwhelming ... Any attempt to reject its basic historicity even in matters
of detail must now appear absurd. Roman historians have long taken
it for granted'.[10] Sherwin-White criticizes trenchantly what he sees as
a hyper-critical tendency among theological scholars. While historians today often hold a higher opinion of Acts than do theologians,
the book also has its more cautious defenders among the theologians,
most recently in Marshall's words: 'There is a strong case for
regarding Acts as an essentially reliable account of what it reports'.[11]

The problem is that such diverse views, often hyperbolically expressed, give little firm common ground on which to proceed. Each
side may be tempted to subsist inviolate by ignoring or dismissing
the other, but such a proceeding offers little prospect of resolving the
real difficulties. There is a complex, and often hidden, disagreement
over presuppositions and methods. We should like to resolve the
impasse by insisting on the inductive, and perhaps relatively less presuppositional, approach of the historian, but such an aspiration immediately exposes a further conflict between diverse understandings
of the essence of historical method.

Our difficulty then is in the choice of starting-point for our specific
investigation of Acts. The only large-scale predecessor on our theme
is the admirably thorough study by Alfred Wikenhauser,[12] a German
Catholic work produced in the immediate aftermath of the First
World War, and so the more isolated both from the trends of contemporary German scholarship and from the Protestant scholarship of
the English-speaking world. Wikenhauser's work has never been

who knows how to read between the lines and to hear what is left unsaid, the
book of Acts gives rich information about what is commonly called "the post-
apostolic age"' (p. 261).

8   Vielhauer, *SLA*, p. 47.
9   Vielhauer, *SLA*, p. 50n.
10 Sherwin-White, *RSRL*, p. 189.
11 Marshall, *Acts*, p. 43.
12 Wikenhauser, *Die Apostelgeschichte und ihr Geschichtswert* (1921).

translated, and it has exercised much less influence than many books of far inferior merit. It treats its subject systematically in logical order, progressing from the examination of the purpose and composition of the book through successive categories of the internal and external evidence.

That is an admirably systematic plan of exposition, but our present situation prompts a rather different approach, in a sequence determined heuristically rather than logically. A central and tangible division of opinion concerns the value of the detail of Acts, and detail is open to the possibility of checking with external evidence. This approach is readily abused, being too often made the basis for a shallow apologetic, which proceeds from illustrative confirmations of a few details to large conclusions about the historicity of the book. This attitude virtually always involves facile jumps to congenial ends by omitting essential stages of the argument. A major theme of this chapter and the next will be to explore the values, and especially the limitations, of the approach, and to analyse the evidential significance of different categories of details. There is likely to be helpful material here, not for supporting simplistic conclusions, but for judging between the broadly conflicting interpretations of Acts. The implications must be carefully evaluated, however. The balance of argument may be difficult to strike. A negative is hard to prove, and might be indicated only by a persistent sparseness of unforced collateral evidence. Conversely, the mere confirmation of the accuracy of individual details proves little if these are merely incidental or reflect common knowledge. It is necessary to analyse our material in a degree sufficient to establish rough criteria of significance. Again, the interpretation and application of some of the crucial documents is hotly disputed, and it may seem that we have to engage in an intricate argument which looks like special pleading to establish a very simple correlation. Yet such intricacy is often inescapable in the delicate task of restoring and understanding texts whose resultant thrust is sufficiently clear and undisputed. In this first sampling we cannot aspire to wrestle with difficulties which must take their place later. Only examples are offered here, and we shall argue that these examples serve to make a *prima facie* case for the viability and plausibility of what is to follow. And to that end we shall focus on simple examples of diverse categories and tread more lightly on the more difficult questions without thereby discounting their force. If these samples tend most frequently to be drawn from the later chapters of Acts, that too is readily explicable, but I defer for the present factors of source-criticism and the like which may be involved. The subject-matter of those chapters lends itself more conveniently to our purpose.

The stress in the following tabulation of categories is upon the correlation of external, especially documentary, sources with inconsequential details in Acts, where the explanation from theological *Tendenz* is not naturally invoked. There is a traditional argument for historical veracity from 'undesigned coincidences'.[13] That is a debatable concept, but we present here an exploratory analysis of what may be seen as a more refined development of that type of approach.

A. Items of geographical detail and the like which may be assumed to have been generally known. It remains difficult to estimate the range of general knowledge to be expected of an ancient writer or an ancient reader. There may be some hints here, especially for the particular readership, in observing which terms or practices Luke finds it necessary to translate or explain. We shall note representative specimens of this category, but to do more adds nothing of substance to a cumulative argument and burdens it with otiose items which dissipate its impact.

B. More specialized details, which may still have been widely known to those who possessed relevant experience: titles of governors, army units, major routes, etc., which may have been accessible to those who travelled or were involved in administration, but perhaps not to those without such backgrounds. It is clearly hazardous to think in terms of ancient reference books, the more so as we have the means of estimating the shortcomings, for instance, of the geographical sections of Pliny's *Natural History*.

C. Specifics of local routes, boundaries, titles of city magistrates, and the like, which may not be closely controllable in date, but are unlikely to have been known except to a writer who had visited the districts.

It is clear that groups A to C are spread along a spectrum of increasing significance and that the diversions between the categories are fluid and arbitrary, but the more diversely the two latter may be documented, the stronger the indication that 'Luke' had at least travelled a wide range of the ground covered by the narrative.

D. The correlation of the dates of known kings and governors with the ostensible chronology of the Acts framework. The word 'ostensible' should be stressed here, for the issue of historicity lies between the ostensible and such reconstructed chronologies as that of J. Knox, which presuppose the erroneousness of Acts in this respect. The

---

13 I take the phrase from the old work of J.J. Blunt, *Undesigned Coincidences in the Writings both of the Old and New Testaments, an Argument of their Veracity* (London: John Murray, 5th edn, 1856).

'ostensible' chronology is of course itself an approximation overlying intricate inferences,[14] based partly on the very attempt to build the correlations into a pattern, but the implicit danger of circularity may be overcome if the pattern is real and capable of further extension. Put conversely, if Luke has produced a pattern of synchronisms, including more complex synchronisms between contemporary rulers, this is not easily explicable from a much later perspective, and may serve as an indicator to draw him close *in time* to the events.

E. Details appropriate to the date of Paul (or indeed to a hypothetical date of Luke in the early church), but not appropriate to the conditions of a date earlier or (especially) later. Indisputable examples of this class are probably hard to find, if only because of the difficulty of documenting the precise dates of changes and the fortuitous nature of finding such which lend themselves ready-made to our purpose. Partial or suggestive examples may be easier. Even where cases exist, however, we cannot automatically exclude the prospect of explaining them through the reproduction of earlier sources.

F. 'Undesigned coincidences' between Acts and the accepted Pauline Epistles. It may seem odd even to postulate these, when the contradictions of Acts and Epistles are of the common stuff of conventional criticism. But there is a tendency to compare by over-rigid criteria, so that many instances of supposed contradiction are as indecisive as the facile harmonizations of apologetic by special pleading. This category requires neither forced harmonization nor forced contradiction, but the natural fitting of independent pieces. It can remain difficult to handle, for some of the luminous examples are embodied in complex fragments of historical reconstruction, which lend themselves to wider debate.

G. Latent internal correlations within Acts. In view of the admitted redactional unity of the book, it is not likely that Luke will blatantly contradict himself within it, and probable rather that he will be broadly self-consistent, subject to minor anomalies of sequence, explanatory introductions and so on, such as might have been eliminated only by an exhaustively pedantic revision. We are not thinking here of such routine self-consistency, but of incidental details not stressed redactionally, whose correlation is implicit and belongs to the original situation.

H. Independently attested details which agree with the Alexandrian against the Western text (or the reverse), and may thus

---

14 Our working notion of the 'ostensible' chronology agrees closely with that tabulated in Bruce, *Acts*, p. 55-56, and differs markedly only in a few particulars from the variant approximations argued at length by G. Ogg, *The Chronology of the Life of Paul* (London: Epworth, 1968).

relate to stages in the textual tradition of Acts, where a secondary reading may refer to the conditions of a later period, and so provide an indirect approach to discrimination of time.

J. Matters of common geographical knowledge or the like, mentioned perhaps informally or allusively, with an unstudied accuracy which bespeaks familiarity. This is to be distinguished from categories A to C as focusing on the manner of allusion. It may be a subjective thing to judge, and this kind of refinement may be disputed. Yet familiarity with the evidence, especially of inscriptions, permits a more refined judgment, and while uncertainty and dissent should be frankly recognized, examples in this category may be stronger than their apparently slight character might suggest.

K. Differences in formulation within Acts as a possible indication of different categories of sources. We shall suggest for instance that the geographical terminology of the list of nations at Pentecost is differently formulated from the typical Lukan usage of the later chapters, where Luke has a fuller control of his sources.

L. Peculiarities in the selection of detail, such as the inclusion of details theologically unimportant, but explicable in other ways which may bear on the historical question.

M. As a particular case of the preceding, details whose 'immediacy' suggests the author's reproduction of recent experience and which are less readily explicable as the product of longer-term reflective editing and shaping.

N. Items reflecting culture or idiom which are suggestive of a first rather than a second century atmosphere. I acknowledge the imprecision and possible tenuousness of this type, and that its applications may be debatable and perhaps subjective. But the category is worth noting: there are, for instance, points of linguistic fashion which deserve more attention than they commonly receive.

P. Interrelated complexes in which two or more kinds of correlation are combined, or where related details each show separate correlations, so that the possibility arises of building a larger fragment of historical reconstruction from a jigsaw of interlocking units. This possibility is no stronger as an argument than is permitted by the value and accurate fitting of the pieces which compose it. Yet if there are valid examples of such complex correlations the fact of their presence may be more powerful than the individual categories.

Q. Cases where the progress of discovery and knowledge simply provides new background information of use to the commentator of whatever viewpoint, while not bearing significantly on the issue of historicity.

R. Precise details which lie within the range of contemporary possibilities, but whose particular accuracy we have no means of verifying one way or the other.

The examples will be tabulated according to these categories rather than given in sequence in the book. This involves many marginal decisions about classification, but displays the essential range of the evidence more plainly. Entries have been freely duplicated when appropriate, where a detail, perhaps as viewed from different perspectives, seemed significantly illustrative of more than one category. We have done this to emphasize the *categories* rather than the *details* as such. Our point in these chapters is the rich range of *types* of correlations that may be found, as well as the great number of cases in point. Cross-references have been included as well.

A. *Common Knowledge*

As stated above, we shall here list only a few representative examples of A and B, as these categories contribute little to the evaluation we are attempting to make.

The emperor's *title* 'Augustus' is rendered formally ὁ Σεβαστός in words attributed to a Roman official (Acts 25:21, 25), whereas 'Augustus' as the *name* bestowed on the first emperor is transliterated Αὔγουστος in Luke 2:1. This distinction may be illustrated *passim*.

General facts of navigation and corn-supply are exemplified by the voyage of an Alexandrian ship to the Italian port of Puteoli, following the institution of a state system of supply by Claudius, and allow illustration at many levels.

These are no more than interesting samples of a large body of trivia. It may be noted that Luke appears in general to be careful rather than careless in his rendering of commonplaces, and small points of terminology could be illustrated from the inscriptions almost endlessly, if it were worth the labour of collecting the references systematically. It is better to use space to cite cases which have more significance individually.

The limits of the category may be illustrated by noting where Luke thinks it necessary or unnecessary to explain terms to his reader. Thus points of Judaean topography or Semitic nomenclature are glossed or explained (Acts 1:12, 19, etc.), whereas basic Jewish institutions are not (1:12 again; 2:1; 4:1; etc.).

B. *Specialized Knowledge*

1:12, 19; 3:2, 11; etc. show knowledge of the topography of Jerusalem.

4:6 Annas is pictured as continuing to have great prestige and to bear the title high priest after his formal deposition by the Romans and the appointment of Caiaphas (cf. Lk. 3:2, Jos. *Ant.* 18.2.2.34-35; 20.9.1.198).[15]

12:4 gives detail on the organization of a military guard (cf. Vegetius, *de Re Milit.* 3.8).

13:7 shows correctly Cyprus as a proconsular (senatorial) province at this time, with the proconsul resident at Paphos.[16]

16:8 ff. acknowledges the part played by Troas in the system of communication (cf. Section C , pp. 112f.*ad* 16:11).

17:1 Amphipolis and Apollonia are known as stations (and presumably overnight stops) on the Egnatian Way from Philippi to Thessalonica.

27-28 contain many details in the geography and navigational details of the voyage to Rome, which will be noted more specifically under other headings.

These few examples illustrate the range of places and contexts in the narrative of which Luke possesses information. Even this type of evidence suggests some controls on the kind of person we conceive him to have been. It suggests that he was well travelled in the areas mentioned in the narrative or had access to special sources of information. Many more nuances might be classified under this head.

C. *Specific Local Knowledge*

We shall list examples exclusively from Acts 13-28, which are concerned with Paul's travels, and lend themselves to the supposition that Luke possessed intimate knowledge of local circumstances. It will be observed that the evidence is strongly represented in the 'we-passages', but extends beyond them. In some cases, specific local knowledge that has been claimed for the author of Acts by some scholars must be discounted because confirmatory evidence is not available, and we shall even see that there are cases where Luke's remarks are ostensibly at odds with existing historical knowledge (e.g.

---

[15] Cf. Wikenhauser, pp. 303-304.

[16] Cf. references to 'proconsuls' in *IGRR* 3.933, of Lapithus, AD 29; 971, of Curii, AD 52; 978, of Citium, time of Claudius. For metropolitan titles of Paphos, see *IGRR* 3.947.4-5, n.d.

the case of Theudas) and where the question of his reliability must be left open so far as historical argument is concerned.

13:4-5 A natural crossing between correctly named ports is indicated. Mt. Casius, which is south of Seleucia, is within sight of Cyprus.

13:7 The name of the proconsul cannot be confirmed, but the *family* of the Sergii Pauli is attested, though older arguments for their Christianity cannot be sustained, and it is doubtful if any reference to the man himself is preserved in the inscriptions mentioning them.[17]

13:13 The text names Perga, a river-port, and perhaps the direct destination of a ship crossing from Cyprus, whereas a coaster would have called only at the coastal harbour town of Attalia.[18]

13:14 'The Pisidian Antioch' may be more fully called ἡ 'Αντιόχεια ἡ πρὸς τῇ Πισιδίᾳ, as in Strabo 12.6.4 = 569. The Alexandrian reading is to be preferred to the Western (cf. H, p. 195); this Antioch was at this time in Phrygia, not Pisidia,[19] though it guarded the Pisidian frontier (see more fully the excursus below, pp. 228f.).[20]

---

17 For criticism of Ramsay's speculative reconstructions of the family history, see B. van Elderen, 'Some Archaeological Observations on Paul's First Missionary Journey', *Apostolic History and the Gospel (Festschrift* for F.F. Bruce), ed. W.W. Gasque and R.P. Martin (Exeter: Paternoster, 1970), pp. 151-61 (esp. pp. 151-56). The most significant of the possible epigraphical allusions is that which has been (conjecturally) restored as ... Κλαυδ]ίου Καίσαρος Σεβαστοῦ καὶ | [--- ἐπὶ Κ]οίν-του Σεργ | [ίου Παύλου ἀνθυπάτου ----] (*SEG* 20 [1964] 302.9-11; van Elderen, p. 155; of Cytheria, 1st AD). Mitford, however, now restores the emperor's name as Γ]αίου, not Κλαυδ]ίου, a fragmentary letter being read as Λ, not Δ, and the inscription placed under Caligula, not Claudius (*ANRW* 2.7.2 [1980], p. 1300, n. 54 and p. 1330, n. 195). If this reading is correct, it is fatal to the supposed identification. The family had a connection with Pisidian Antioch by virtue of the proximity of their estate to the *colonia*: see S. Mitchell, *ANRW* 2.7.2 (1980), p. 1074.

18 Cf. *SPTR*, p. 124; *CRE*, pp. 16, 19. For further details of these cities see G.E. Bean, *Turkey's Southern Shore* (London: Ernest Benn, 1968), esp. pp. 41-58.

19 Although S. Mitchell (*ANRW* II.7.2 [1980], pp. 1053-81) regards it as in Galatia: 'Antioch *by* Pisidia'.

20 The preferred reading is sometimes rejected, as (surprisingly) by Wikenhauser (p. 335), on the ground that Πισίδιος is unattested as an adjective. Ptol. *Geog.* 5.5.4-5 however, ascribes Antioch to Φρυγία Πισιδία, taken to mean 'Pisidian Phrygia', unless we read it as 'Phrygian Pisidia', an alternative which is open to the erroneous converse objection that an adjectival feminine Φρυγία is unattested also. This form is actually quite common— see on 16:6 below. It must be emphasized that the forms of ethnic adjectives are remarkably varied, and that many readily documented formations are unrecorded or misrecorded in the lexica. For the Phrygian character of the Antioch district (and of Iconium below) see W.M. Calder, 'The Boundary of Galatic Phrygia', in *MAMA* 7, pp. ix-xvi and the map on p. xliv, showing the actual survival of the Phrygian language to AD 250 in an area including both cities. Especially in these areas, there is a sharp demarcation between Phrygian and Pisidian or Lycaonian styles in monumental art and

14:6 The text implies that Iconium was not in Lycaonia, as has often been supposed on the strength of sources reflecting boundary changes and conditions of different date (cf. E, p. 178). Its ethnic inclusion in Phrygia, not Lycaonia, is confirmed by the geographical distribution of Neo-Phrygian texts, and could be illustrated extensively by onomastic study.[21]

14:6 The bizarrely heteroclitic declension of the name Lystra (acc. Λύστραν in Acts 14:6, 21; 16:1; dat. Λύστροις in Acts 14:8; 16:2; cf 2 Tim 3:11) is actually paralleled in Latin in the documents, though the point hinges on correct restoration: *Col ... Lustra consecravit* (*MAMA* 8.5, 1st AD); *a [Lus]tre[is] IV m* (*MAMA* 8.8, milestone, 3rd AD).[22]

14:11 The Lycaonian language is spoken in Lystra. The use of a native language is unusual in the cosmopolitan, Hellenized society in which Paul moved. Lystra, however, as a Roman colony in a less developed part of Anatolia, preserved a language otherwise attested in a gloss in Stephanus of Byzantium.[23]

in pottery, as well as in language, where Phrygian texts are separated by only a few miles from the undeciphered 'Pisidian' inscriptions of Sofular. See further J. Mellaart, 'Iron Age Pottery from Southern Anatolia', *Belleten* (Türk Tarih Kurumu) 19 (1955), pp. 115-36 (stressing the stability of this cultural frontier throughout the classical period; see p. 126); C.J. Hemer, 'The Pisidian Texts: A Problem of Language and History', *Kadmos* 19 (1980), pp. 54-64, and literature there cited.

21 See Excursus, pp. 228-230.

22 Perhaps an original plural was attracted into the singular in such cases as the former where the name stood in apposition with *colonia* in formal Roman designations. The distinction *Lystram/Lystris* is preserved in the Vulgate. I have not found the name in Greek texts here, which are mostly private and informal. If the point is correctly taken, it is a notable case of catching local usage in a detail. This is not a 'we-passage' but Luke ostensibly knew Timothy of Lystra as well as Paul. [(Ed.) This parallel is based on a reconstruction of the milestone text which must be in some doubt as a result of the re-reading by D.H. French in *Roman Roads and Milestones of Asia Minor, Fasc. 2, Interim Catalogue of Milestones* part 1 (B.A.R. S. 392(i); Oxford: B.A.R., 1988), p. 225, No. 628.]

23 Stephanus explains 'Derbe' as from δελβεία, said to be the Lycaonian word for 'juniper'. Among the native names of the Lystra district we may note Tas, Greios, Nalêmis, Kinnôs, Ouaka, Goulasis, Mouzouttos, Gous and Douthis, along with a few of Phrygian type (*MAMA* 8.33-98, *passim*). The Sofular texts, if the 'Pisidian' names in them are correctly demarcated, give such forms as Dôtari, Lir, Memoua, Eianis, Gpourôxa and Slpouroxa. Any attempt to identify Pisidian characteristics is complicated by the apparent existence of several distinct languages or dialects in the area, among which that of Sofular may be a minority speech quite unlike the others, perhaps more akin to features appearing in Lycaonia and Isauria than to the nomenclature of more southern Pisidia. The index to *TAM* 3 on the inscriptions of Termessus in southern Pisidia shows an astonishing abundance of Trokondas (130 entries) and of the theophoric names (Greek or in native variants) Hermaeus, Artemôn, Artemeis and Arteimas,

14:12 The striking collocation of gods Hellenized as Zeus and Hermes is paralleled epigraphically from Lystra itself and from its district.[24]

14:12 Barnabas and Paul are identified respectively with Zeus and Hermes, reflecting the native concept of the two gods (cf. note 24).

14:13 The 'priest' is in the best texts, whereas D has 'priests' (see H, pp. 195f. below).[25]

14:15-17 The character of the speech, with its 'natural theology', is at least appropriate to the occasion in the context of Anatolian religion, especially if the local forms of the divine father and mother are rightly understood as identified with the heavenly Zeus and Gê.[26]

14:25 The travellers return to the coasting port of Attalia to intercept a coasting vessel (cf. 13:13 above).

16:1 Derbe, then Lystra, is in fact the correct order of approach overland from the Cilician Gates.

16:2 Lystra and Iconium were relatively close, although belonging

---

together with an abundant recurrence of such native forms as Armasta, Kendeas, Korkainas, Molês, Nan(n)elis, Oa, Obrimotês, Oplês and Otaneis. Only the peculiar (and recurring) Kbêdasis recalls the difficult initial clusters 'gd-' and 'gp-' found at Sofular. The remarkable frequency of alternative names of the Σαῦλος ὁ καὶ Παῦλος type, of which dozens are recorded from Termessus alone, would repay study, and serve as indicators of the prevalence of mixed or alternative cultural identities. Cf. I. Kajanto *Supernomina. A Study in Latin Epigraphy* (Helsinki: Societas Scientiarum Fennica, 1966), which, however, deals almost exclusively with Latin examples from the Western provinces. See also G.H.R. Horsley, 'The use of a double name', in *New Docs* 1.89-96, No. 55. Horsley has also written a survey of the phenomenon for the forthcoming *Anchor Bible Dictionary*.

24 *MAMA* 8.1 (Lystra), as restored, is a dedication to a triad of deities (characteristic of the native Anatolian religion), Epêkoos ('he who hears prayer' = Zeus), Hermes, and a brief missing name, presumably the goddess, supplied as Gê. From Sedasa, 20m. south-southwest, come two inscriptions appearing to relate to the same cult, the first listing three priests with native (Isaurian) names and the second recording the dedication of a statue of Hermes Megistos with a sundial to Zeus (Helios). The Greek names are of course Hellenizations of local cult, where the sky-father, earth-mother and executive son are typical, and their epithets and attributes may be revealing of local feeling. These inscriptions are published and discussed by W.M. Calder, 'A Cult of the Homonades', *CR* 24 (1910), pp. 76-81, texts p. 77, and 'Zeus and Hermes at Lystra', *Expos* 7th ser. 10 (1910), pp. 1-6. Different Hellenizations were current in other places. Our point is that this grouping of Greek divine names is peculiarly characteristic of the Lystra district.

25 Cf. W.M. Calder, 'The "Priest" of Zeus at Lystra', *Expos* 7th ser. 10 (1910), pp. 148-55; 'Zeus and Hermes at Lystra', *Expos* 7th ser 10 (1910), pp. 1-6. He cites an inscription of the district which names three priests of Zeus. The Western reading is at least attractive here. There is no need for Haenchen's idea that its plurality shows the scene has 'grown' in the course of tradition (p. 427n).

26 Cf. note 24 above.

to different jurisdictions, whereas Derbe is now known to have been more distant than was supposed when it was wrongly placed at Zostra or Güdelisin.[27] It is thus natural that Timothy, if a native of Lystra, was known to these two churches rather than in Derbe.

16:6. 'The Phrygian and Galatian country' is a notoriously problematic phrase, which may be taken to denote 'Phrygia Galatica'. This view is rooted in specific geographical and epigraphical study; the denials rest upon demonstrable linguistic and geographical errors.[28]

16:8 The form of the name 'Troas' is given as current in the first century (cf. E, p. 179).

16:11 Troas is cited as a destination would open an assortment of possibilities and was a key point on the Roman system of communication. This, however, also poses difficulties which are rarely observed.[29] The delay and sudden sailing naturally related to change of

---

[27] Losta (= Zosta) by Sterrett, *The Wolfe Expedition to Asia Minor = PASA* 3 (1884-85) 22-23; Güdelisin by Ramsay, *JÖAI* 7 (1904), Beiblatt 75-77. For the site at Kerti Hüyük see now M.H. Ballance, 'The Site of Derbe: A New Inscription', *AS* 7(1957), pp. 147-51; 'Derbe and Faustinopolis', *AS* 14 (1964), pp. 139-45; cf. G. Ogg, 'Derbe', *NTS* 9 (1962-63), pp. 367-70.

[28] The huge literature goes back to the debate between W.M. Ramsay and F.H. Chase in *The Expositor* in 1893-94. Lightfoot and Ramsay agreed here in reading Φρυγίαν as an adjective, and in seeing the force of the common article as bracketing the two adjectives into an entity considered as a unit, whatever their precise relationship. The two men differed only in their geographical interpretation. Ramsay's 'South Galatian' interpretation was presented in 1893, after Lightfoot's death in 1889, and depended on pioneer exploration and documentation never available to Lightfoot. Moffatt and Lake later argued against Ramsay on grounds which contradicted Lightfoot on these points. Both denied the adjectival usage of Φρυγία, which is in fact abundantly documented in later Greek. See C.J. Hemer, 'The Adjective "Phrygia"', *JTS* n.s. 27 (1976), pp. 122-26; 'Phrygia: A Further Note', *JTS* n.s. 28 (1977), pp. 99-101. Moffatt denied that the linking καί could mean 'or', despite the earlier note of Ramsay entitled 'Καί Meaning "Or"', *CR* 12 (1898), pp. 337-41, which is severe on earlier denials, though on a different point. It is in any case unnecessary to press this, for this use of καί might correspond rather to various relationships now represented by a hyphen or an oblique stroke. We may observe for instance a fluctuation in the documents in the rendering of doubled Latin terms between the use of καί and asyndeton, as in the recurring πρεσβεύτης (καί) ἀντιστράτηγος (= *legatus pro praetore*) or in Βιθυνία (καί) πόντος. The fact that the term 'Phrygia Galatica' is never specifically attested is not a fatal objection, for our information is fragmentary, the overlap of ethnic Phrygia with provincial Galatia is now well documented, and the actual terms Φρυγία Ἀσιανή and 'Pontus Galaticus' are known, the latter frequently, as the designations of comparable or complementary overlaps.

[29] A major problem involves the uncertainties about the road-system in the hinterland of Troas and the fact that the principal known routes of the Troad connected the coastal cities. Conventional maps draw arbitrary straight lines of

adverse winds, as with Ignatius.

16:11 Samothrace was a conspicuous sailors' landmark, dominated by a 5000 foot mountain.

16:12 Philippi is correctly described as a Roman colony, as abundantly attested in its predominantly Latin epigraphy, with the explicit titles and magistracies of a colony, the grant having been made by Octavian after the battle in 42 BC. Its seaport is correctly named Nea Polis, properly rendered in the best manuscripts as two words (Νέαν Πόλιν).[30]

16:12 μερίς: the interpretation of this phrase is notoriously difficult in view of the divergences of manuscript readings, but in any case the 'division' of Macedonia to which Philippi belonged was designated by this distinctive word, and in fact it belonged to the 'first' of the four μερίδες, precisely suiting πρώτης μερίδος, if that emendation from some of the versions be accepted.[31]

---

route across the northern spurs of Mt. Ida. Troas was a nodal point of long-distance sea-routes, but not a likely point to strike the coast first from the interior. Was Troas a chosen destination, if Paul already had Rome in mind as an final objective? See the excellent discussion by W.P. Bowers, 'Paul's Route through Mysia. A Note on Acts XVI.8', *JTS* n.s. 30 (1979), pp. 507-11; cf. C.J. Hemer, 'Alexandria Troas', *TB* 26 (1975), pp. 79-112, see esp. pp. 101-102. It is remarkable that the Dibelius-Haenchen school, whose scepticism is keenly alert to theoretical improbabilities, fails to observe the existence of a specific, substantive historical problem.

30 A decree of Athens (Dimitsas, *Μακεδονία*, pp. 760-63, No. 976) gives the dative as Νέαι Πόληι [sic], line 36, and the ethnic title as Νεοπολῖται (οἱ παρὰ Θάσον), 410-409 BC. The early coins give the abbreviation ΝΕΟΠ (or variants) (*BMC Macedonia*, ed. R.S. Poole, Neapolis, Nos 14-35 *passim*, of c. 411-350 BC). Though some distribute these letters in a square, I take it on the analogy of similar contemporary lettering at Amphipolis and elsewhere that they are all to be read clockwise as Νεοπ. for Νεοπολιτῶν, not Νε.πο. for Νέα πόλις. In the Roman period relevant cases are the accusative Νέαν πόλιν (*IG* 3.1.128g, presumably of Neapolis = Naples) and genitive Νέας πόλεως (Dio 47.35.3, certainly of this city), beside the ethnic Νεαπολίτης (*IG* 3.2.2838, of Athens). E. Oberhummer, 'Neapolis', No. 11, in *PW* 16.2124 may not be strictly correct in positing a change from early Νεόπολις to Νέα πόλις, for the variants may all be explained by a shift of the ethnic from Νεοπολίτης to Νεαπολίτης. The catalogue lists no coins of the Roman period, when Neapolis was presumably subject to Philippi, and shows a like predominance of Latin (colonial) inscriptions. In Philippi itself Dimitsas gives only 7 inscriptions in Greek, beside some 40 in Latin. The peculiar pride of Philippi in its status, which has been seen as reflected in Luke's remark here, can be variously illustrated, by the coinage, for example, such as the 'Vic(toria) Aug(usti)' type of Augustus, with statue of Nike (*BMC Macedonia*, Philippi, No. 23), and those of Claudius depicting a statue-group of Julius Caesar crowning Augustus (Nos. 24-26).

31 The word μερίς, once condemned by Hort, is now well attested of

16:13 A small river, the Gangites, flows close to the walls of Philippi. It is also probable that the city, being a colony rather than a commercial centre, had relatively few Jews.

16:14 Lydia was from Thyatira, in Lydia, and it is possible that she is called by an ethnic cognomen, 'the Lydian woman' rather than by her proper name. The name 'Lydia' is attested both as a regular and as an alternative name (e.g. Νεωνὶς ἡ κ[α]ὶ Λυδία, *TAM* 3.661, Termessus, Pisidia) (see Excursus, p. 231).[32]

16:14 Thyatira as a centre of dyeing is attested in at least seven inscriptions of the city. Its purple dye came from the madder root rather than the marine *Murex*, and the use of this substance is attested in the district until the present century.[33] The close connection between the dyers of Thyatira and the Macedonian cities is paralleled

administrative districts in Egypt and elsewhere, e.g. *BGU* 975.6, of AD 45, cited by *MM*. The division of Macedonia is attested by Livy 45.18.6-7: *In quattuor regiones discribi Macedoniam, ut suum quaeque concilium haberet.* In the early days of the Roman province coins were issued by these divisions, with the legends ΜΑΚΕΔΟΝΩΝ ΠΡΩΤΗΣ/ΔΕΥΤΕΡΑΣ/ΤΕΤΑΡΤΗΣ preserving three of the four, with capitals respectively at Amphipolis, Thessalonica and Pelagonia (*BMC Macedonia*, 'Macedonia in Genere', Nos. 1-8, 9 and 10 respectively, of 158-146 BC). Among the various monograms on these coins is ME, clearest on No. 10. It is tempting to supply μερίδος as the specific feminine noun to be understood with the ordinals. Although subsequent coinage is either provincial or civic, there is no reason to think these divisions were abolished, indeed our passage at least appears to show the contrary.

The textual question is finely balanced, and merits a note here as it bears on the geographical purport of this verse. The UBS Committee only hesitantly preferred the conjecture πρώτης based on some Latin and other versions, but on no extant Greek manuscript, and assigned it only {D} probability ranking, and signalled their doubt by printing square brackets: πρώτη[ς] μερίδος τῆς ... This makes a correct statement that Philippi was a city of the first district, whereas πρώτη is difficult. The word was not a formal title of Philippi, nor was it capital of the district. Ramsay suggested taking it as a patristic claim of Luke for a city with which he was associated, asserting that it had overtaken Amphipolis in importance. It has also been understood as 'first' in order of approach, the seaport of Neapolis not then being reckoned. There might be point in calling attention to it as the first sphere of work in Macedonia (and in Europe), but this interpretation seems inappropriate here, as the phrase is apparently a parenthetical statement of the importance of Philippi, with verb ἐστιν, not a part of Paul's itinerary.

[32] See now *New Docs* 2.26-28, No. 3, with response in *New Docs* 3.54, No. 17. While the ethnic appellation might well suit a freedwoman who had been so called as a slave, the name is also now attested of women of apparently high social prestige. Good examples are Julia Lydia of Sardis (L. Robert, 'Documents d'Asie Mineure', *BCH* 102 [1978], p. 405, 1st AD) and Julia Lydia Laterane of Ephesus, 'high priestess and daughter of Asia' (*SEG* 28 [1978] 869, 1st-2nd AD).

[33] M. Clerc, *De Rebus Thyatirenorum* (Paris, 1896), p. 94, cf. *New Docs* 3.53-54.

in an interesting inscription of Thessalonica (*IG* 10.2.1.291). A Latin fragment of Philippi itself appears to contain 'pu]rpurari[us?' (*CIL* 3.664.1).

16:20-21 The passage gives an ironical treatment of the anti-Jewish feeling on the part of colonists proud of their Roman status.

16:22 The chief magistrates of the colony are here designated στρατηγοί, following the general term ἄρχοντες in v. 19. The use of the term for the *duoviri* of a colony is attested at Pisidian Antioch.[34] The flogging is appropriate to the ῥαβδοῦχοι (v. 35) = *lictores* attendant on colonial magistrates.

17:1 The mention of Amphipolis and of Apollonia should probably be taken to imply that these were the places where the travellers spent successive nights, dividing the journey to Thessalonica into three stages of about 30, 27 and 35 miles.

17:1 A synagogue at Thessalonica is attested by the Jewish inscription *CIJ* 693 (late 2nd AD or later).

17:5 In the free city of Thessalonica Paul is brought before the δῆμος.

17:6 The title of the board of magistrates in Thessalonica was 'politarchs', a term now abundantly attested from this and other Macedonian cities.[35]

17:10 Beroea is a suitable immediate refuge as a place off the major westward route, the Via Egnatia. Paul's movements, at least thus far,

---

34 J.R.S. Sterrett, *An Epigraphical Journey in Asia Minor* = *PASA* 2 (1883-1884) 96, where στρατηγία is used of the office. There is however a difficulty, despite e.g. Haenchen's reference to 'the exact title' (p. 496). The oft-repeated statement of Ramsay that στρατηγός here translates a courtesy title *praetor* ('On the Title of the Magistrates at Philippi [Acts XVI 19-22]', *JTS* 1 [1900], pp. 114-16) is questioned by F. Haverfield ('On the ΣΤΡΑΤΗΓΟΙ of Philippi', *JTS* 1 [1900], pp. 434-35), who points out that it can be a straightforward equivalent of the regular term *duovir, praetor* in this sense probably being restricted to early usage in the Western Empire. For the magistrates named at Philippi see *CIL* 3.633ff. and M. Dimitsas, ἡ Μακεδονία: *CIL* 3.633.1 = Dimitsas 934 (*aedile*); *CIL* 3.650 (*decurio and duumviri* conjoined, mid 1st AD), *CIL* 3.654 = 3.7335 (*aedile*), Dimitsas 957 (*decurio duumvir*), Dimitsas 961 (*decurio*), Dimitsas 962 = *CIL* 3.7342 (*duumvir quinquennalis*). These are characteristic colonial magistracies.

35 E. de W. Burton, 'The Politarchs', *AJT* 2 (1898), pp. 598-632, though still commonly cited, is now very dated. See now C. Schuler, 'The Macedonian Politarchs', *CP* 55 (1960), pp. 90-100; F. Gschnitzer, *PW* Supp. 13 (1973) col. 483-500; Horsley, *New Docs* 2.34-35, No. 5, who refers also to B. Helly, *Ancient Macedonia*, II.531-44, which I have not seen; this last arguing against the previous consensus that the Macedonian πολιτάρχαι were not a unique institution imposed by the Romans, but a pre-existing form essentially identical with the πολίαρχοι or πολίταρχοι attested in neighbouring Thessaly. [(Ed.) Horsley has collected all the documentary evidence and surveyed current knowledge of the *politarchs* in an article forthcoming in the *Anchor Bible Dictionary*.]

are consistent with the formation in his mind of a conscious strategy leading towards Rome,[36] but this move and the further journey to Athens (v. 15) are attributed to the agency of others.

17:14 The implication of sea-travel is at once the most convenient way of reaching Athens with the favouring 'Etesian' winds of the summer sailing-season and also removes Paul to a different jurisdiction remote from nearer land-routes where opponents might be expecting him. Luke does not here name a port of embarkation.

17:16 The abundance of images at Athens is abundantly attested in literature and in the remains. This may have been a matter of such general knowledge as scarcely to warrant special mention. Cf. δεισι-δαιμονεστέρους in v. 22 and other touches throughout the scene.[37]

17:17 Reference to the synagogue at Athens is illustrated by the occurrence of Jewish inscriptions there (*CIJ* 712-15). The point is slight, the texts look relatively late, and the fact not unexpected. A similar illustration may be offered for other Pauline cities such as Thessalonica (*CIJ* 693).

17:17 Philosophical debate in the Agora is again characteristic of Athenian life.

17:18 The mention of Stoic philosophers is particularly interesting, as the 'Stoa' (portico) from which they took their name was in the Athenian Agora, the Stoa Poikile, and this traditional meeting place is close to the Stoa Basileios, where the court of Areopagus transacted routine business. This northwest corner of the Agora was also close to a notable collocation of Hermae, apt to the adjective κατείδωλος.[38]

---

36 Cf. W.P. Bowers, 'Paul's Route through Mysia. A Note on Acts XVI.8', *JTS* n.s. 30 (1979), p. 511, and 'Paul and Religious Propaganda in the First Century', *NovT* 22 (1980), pp. 316-23, arguing at least for a deliberate, progressive and centripetal strategy. The attested timing further suits the interesting suggestion of F.F. Bruce that news of the expulsion of Jews from Rome reached Paul in Macedonia and contributed to deflecting him from his first purpose (*Paul, Apostle of the Free Spirit*, p. 235). This point depends on the dating of the expulsion to 49 (*pace* Lüdemann); cf. D, pp. 167f. *ad* 18:2.

37 Throughout this passage I am conscious of the judgment of A.D. Nock: '...brilliant as is the picture of Athens, it makes on me the impression of being based on literature, which was easy to find, rather than on personal observation' (review article of M. Dibelius, *Aufsätze zur Apostelgeschichte*, in *Gnomon* 25 [1953], pp. 497-506, citing p. 506; reprinted in A.D. Nock, *Essays on Religion and the Ancient World*, ed. Z. Stewart [Oxford: Clarendon Press, 1972] II.821-32, citing p. 381). Athens was of course a cultural centre whose characteristics were embodied in a great classical literature. I have tried to recognize this possibility frankly where it may apply. But in any case I doubt the feasibility of Nock's explanation. The most telling points are latent in the passage.

38 See Hemer, 'Paul and Athens: A Topographical Note', *NTS* 20 (1974), pp.

17:18 The Athenians call Paul a σπερμολόγος, which is a 'word of characteristically Athenian slang'.[39]

17:19 Ἄρειος πάγος: the two-word form, applied to the court, is regularly used in many inscriptions of the period. This hearing probably took place before the court in its meeting-place in the Agora, not on the actual hill so called.[40]

17:21 The comment on the Athenian character is again true to the literature, but is more likely to have been common knowledge.

17:23 Paul would have seen the Athenians' 'objects of worship' in profusion at the main approach to the Agora from the northwest.

17:23 Altars to 'unknown gods' are mentioned by Pausanias (1.1.4), and the background story is told by Diogenes Laertius (*Vita Philos.* 1.110; cf. Philostratus *Vita Ap. Ty.* 6.3.5, etc.). Much is sometimes made of the objection that the passages which speak explicitly of 'unknown' gods always do so in the plural, but these plurals, with the plural βωμοί, may be generalizing plurals, or Paul may have chosen to refer to a dedication to a particular god. Diogenes' phrase τῷ προσήκοντι θεῷ is singular, in any case.[41]

341-50. For the debate about whether the court met in the Agora or on the actual hill called Areopagus see n. 40 below. The combination of topographical hints suits the reconstruction here adopted and fits the placing of the whole scene in a narrowly circumscribed locality. For the significance of κατείδωλος and the abundance of 'Herms' in the area see R.E. Wycherley in *JTS* n.s. 19 (1968), pp. 619-20.

39 Ramsay, *SPTR*, p. 242. The word is used of a bird in Aristophanes *Birds* 232; Aristotle *Hist. Anim.* 8.3=592b; citations ap. Athenaeus *Deipn.* 8.344c, 9.388a; cf. 9.398d; of persons, Athenaeus *Deipn.* 3.85f.; Dion. Hal. *Ant. Rom.* 19.5.2; Demosthenes *de Corona* 127; of mischievous words, Plut. *Mor.* 456c.

40 The formal title of the court in the inscriptions of the Roman period is ἡ ἐξ Ἀρείου πάγου βουλή (*passim*, e.g. *IG* 3.1.706). In *IG* 3.1.781 a man is described informally and absolutely as 'of the hill of Ares', where the reference is evidently to the court, not the hill. See further n. 44 below. For the debate about the site see T.D. Barnes, 'An Apostle on Trial', *JTS* n.s. 20 (1969), pp. 407-19; W.G. Morrice, 'Where Did Paul Speak in Athens— on Mars' Hill or before the Court of Areopagus? (Acts 17:19)', *ExpT* 83 (1971-72), pp. 377-78; *NTS* 20 (1974), pp. 341-50. The problem is often confused by faulty formulation. It is often supposed, for instance, that there was room only for a few hearers on the rocky summit (Haenchen, *Acts*, p. 518 [cf. *Apostelgeschichte*, p. 456]), but I possess a photograph I took there myself of a gathering of many hundreds. Though I do not accept that location for the speech, it cannot be excluded simplistically by this supposition.

41 The inscription of Pergamum reading θεοῖς αγ[...] I Καπίτ[ων] I δᾳδοῦχο[ς] is indecisive (H. Hepding, *Ath Mitt* 35 [1910], pp. 454-57, of ?2nd AD). O. Kern, 'Das Demeterheiligtum von Pergamon und die orphischen Hymnen', *Hermes* 46 (1911), pp. 431-36 (esp. p. 434) proposed the restoration ἀγ[ιωτάτοι] as more probable than ἀγ[νώστοι]. See further Wikenhauser, p. 371; Lake, *BC* 5.240. Haenchen, *Acts*, p. 521n (cf. *Apostelgeschichte*, pp. 458-59n) puts the case against

17:24 The reference to temples made with hands (cf. 7:48, in Jerusalem) is here represented as uttered in a place dominated by the Parthenon and surrounded by other shrines of the finest classical art.

17.24ff. The content of this passage suits the view that we have a compressed summary of a dialogue with Stoic and Epicurean terms and ideas, so belonging naturally to the ostensible Pauline context (τὸ θεῖον, v. 29; οὐ ... προσδεόμενός τινος, v. 25, etc.).

17:28 'In him we live ...' These words are attributed to Epimenides the Cretan, who figures in Diogenes' story of the origin of the altars discussed above on 17:23. This also suggests a Pauline context, where Paul is interacting with the specific traditions of Athenian religion (cf. F, pp. 186f., P, pp. 215f.).[42]

17:28 The second citation is from the Stoic poet Aratus, of Soli in Cilicia, close to Paul's home in Tarsus. Again, we may see a Pauline context in Athens, and compare Paul's own citation of Greek literature in 1 Cor. 15:33 (cf. F, pp. 186-87).[43]

17:31 Judgment is entrusted to an appointed 'man' (ἀνδρί), used of Jesus to a pagan audience for whom Christological refinements would have been meaningless at this stage. This again is suitable to Paul at Athens rather than a deliberate Lukan theological construct.

17:32 The declaration of resurrection (ἀνάστασις) takes issue directly with the specific denial of ἀνάστασις in this sense in the religious classic of the archetypal trial of Orestes before this court of Areopagus, the words of Apollo as spokesman of divine wisdom (Aeschylus, *Eumen.* 647-48). The idea was alien also to both groups of philosophers, and the reaction to it is understandable in the

ἀγνώστοις strongly, but without meeting the arguments of Deissmann, *Paul*, pp. 288-91 against several alternative possibilities. Deissmann's photograph (Plate V, facing p. 286) shows that the foot of an upright stroke alone is preserved of the third letter of the word, a feature consonant with varied possibilities with I, N or Γ. The artistic symmetry of the lettering tells against the brevity of ἀγ[ίοις], but ἀγ[ιωτάτοις] or ἀγ[ιωτάταις] (of Demeter and Kore) may be slightly too long. Deissmann points out (*contra* Haenchen) that the stone was re-used for another dedication, and therefore less (not more) likely to have been dedicated to the principal deity of the sanctuary in the first place. Despite Deissmann, however, the case for ἀγ[νώστοις] is not established.

42 Apart from these altars, for which an alternative explanation is offered by Wycherley, *JTS* n.s. 19 (1968), pp. 620-21, there is a likely reference to the passage in the *Oresteia* which treats the actual foundation-legend of the court of Areopagus (17:32 below), and the double connection with the seer Epimenides. See further Lake, 'Your Own Poets', BC 5.246-51.

43 Cf. also Cleanthes, *Hymn to Zeus*, 4. If we are permitted to accept a larger Pauline base we may add Titus 1:12 (ascribed to the same Epimenides by Clement of Alexandria, *Strom.* 1.14), and from Acts the reference to Epimenides here, and the probable allusions to Aeschylus in 17:32 and to Euripides in 21:39.

Athenian context.

17:34 'Αρεοπαγίτης is the correct title for a member of the court (cf. "Αρειος πάγος above).[44]

18:2 This displays synchronism with probable date of Claudius' expulsion of Jews from Italy.[45]

18:3 Paul's trade, if understood as that of 'tentmaker', is interestingly appropriate to his Cilician origin, if indeed that played any significant part in his upbringing.[46]

18:4 A Corinthian synagogue is attested epigraphically.[47]

18:12 Gallio is said to be a proconsul, resident in Corinth as provincial capital. Achaia was governed by a proconsul from 27 BC to AD 15 and from AD 44 (cf. D, pp. 168-69, P, p. 214, §1). I have argued elsewhere that the incident belongs to the time of Gallio's arrival in the province in early summer 51, the only point in Paul's residence (autumn 50 - spring 52) when his opponents would be able to take advantage of a new and untried governor.[48]

18:13-14 The nature of the charge seems to involve the claim that Paul's preaching was not Judaism in the approved sense, and that he was therefore not to be accorded the privileges belonging to it as a

---

44 *Passim* in Athenian inscriptions of the Roman period: e.g. δόγματι 'Αρεοπαγιτῶ[ν] IG 3.1.704. Note the distinction between the two-word form ἡ ἐξ 'Αρείου πάγου βουλή (many times, e.g. IG 2² 3535, c. AD 57) and the one-word form 'Αρεοπαγ(ε)ιται.

45 See D, pp. 167-68 for the evidence regarding the date. Cf. also P, p. 214.

46 See now R.F. Hock, *The Social Context of Paul's Ministry: Tentmaking and Apostleship* (Philadelphia: Fortress, 1980); cf. his article 'Paul's Tentmaking and the Problem of his Social Class', *JBL* 97 (1978), pp. 555-64 (esp. p. 555n). Hock argues that σκηνοποιός denotes 'leather-worker' rather than literally 'tentmaker', but has not truly established his case against taking the word in its apparently straightforward sense. This view is based on some patristic and versional evidence, and was argued by Zahn. Hock's view on this point, central to his thesis, is rather loosely argued. On one page he discounts Paul's connection with Cilicia in rejecting the one (for he studied in Jerusalem) and affirms it in accepting the other alternative (p. 21).

47 Furnish writes: '... the inscription could be as late as the fourth century C.E.' (V.P. Furnish, *II Corinthians*, The Anchor Bible [Garden City: Doubleday, 1984], p. 21 and Plate VIb), although *CIJ* 718 lists it as from between the 1st cent. BC and the 2nd cent. AD.

48 *Pauline Studies Bruce*, p. 8. *Contra* the cautious consideration of other possibilities in K. Haacker, 'Die Gallio-Episode und die paulinische Chronologie', *BZ* n.s. 16 (1972), pp. 252-55, responding to B. Schwank, 'Die sogenante Brief an Gallio und die Datierung des 1 Thess.', *BZ* n.s. 15 (1971), pp. 265-66. Schwank follows Deissmann, *Paul*, pp. 280-83, from whom we differ in suggesting that the eighteen months of 18:11 comprehends the whole of Paul's stay, and not merely the period prior to the arrival of Gallio.

religio licita. Gallio's response amounted to the judgment that this was a dispute in Jewish theology, of which he took no cognizance.[49]

18:16f. The βῆμα, overlooking Corinth's *forum*, is shown today.[50]

18:21 The hasty departure from Ephesus in spring would suit the assumption, made explicit in the Western text, that Paul was anxious to reach Jerusalem for a feast, presumably Passover, in the limited time available after the opening of the sailing season (cf. H, p. 197).

18:23 The 'Galatian country and Phrygia' is a peculiarly difficult phrase, not the same as in 16:6. I am now inclined to think that 'the Galatian country' is here resumptive of 16:6, and refers generally to Paul's sphere of work in ('South') Galatia, and that 'Phrygia' (here, but not there, a noun) is appended loosely in the awareness that Phrygia extended into the province of Asia, beyond Galatia in any sense, and on Paul's present route towards Ephesus. Possibly Luke knew of Paul's preaching on this journey in Asian Phrygia, in e.g. Apamea Cibotus or Eumenea, major cities on or near the route implied by a likely geographical interpretation of 19:1 below.[51]

19:1 τὰ ἀνωτερικὰ μέρη are plausibly understood to refer to the traverse of the hill-road reaching Ephesus by the Cayster valley north of Mt. Messogis, and not by the Lycus and Maeander valleys, with which Paul may have been unacquainted (cf. F, p. 187; Col. 2:1).[52]

19:9 The name 'Tyrannus' is attested from Ephesus in first century inscriptions.[53]

---

[49] This in effect established a precedent in Paul's favour. Cf. Bruce, *Paul*, pp. 254-55.

[50] For this site and its identification see O. Broneer, 'Corinth: Center of St. Paul's Missionary Work in Greece', *BA* 14 (1951), pp. 78-96, esp. pp. 91-92. *Rostra*, the Latin equivalent of βῆμα, occurs on an inscription found in the vicinity, referring to this structure.

[51] Cf. Bean and Calder, *Classical Map*. The inscriptions depict both cities as notable centres of Diaspora Judaism and later of Christianity. See e.g. *CIJ* 761 (Eumenea), 773-74 (Apamea). The latter city is unique in its coins inscribed NΩE, and depicting Noah and the ark (*BMC Phrygia*, Phryg. Apam. No. 182, of Philip Senior). Both are in the region characterized by numerous discreetly Christian epitaphs of the 3rd century, embodying the expression actually called the 'Eumenean formula' (cf. W.M. Calder, 'The Eumeneian Formula', *Anatolian Studies Presented to William Hepburn Buckler*, ed. W.M. Calder and J. Keil [Manchester University Press, 1939], pp. 15-26). For further examples of the Eumenian formula see *New Docs* 1.136-37, No. 86; 3.136-39, No. 98; 4.159, No. 66.

[52] *BC* 4.236 *ad loc* and Lake in *BC* 5.240 take it of the 'hinterland', as resumptive of the disputed phrase in 18:23; and so Haenchen, pp. 552-53n. The interpretation followed here derives from Ramsay, *SPTR*, pp. 265-66, followed by Bruce, *Acts*, p. 353 *ad loc.*

[53] E.g. *I. Eph.* 20B.40, of AD 54-59; 1012.4, of AD 92-93. I possess a photograph I took of the latter in 1964; the name is inscribed on a column in the Prytaneum as

19:13 'Jewish exorcists': the part played by Jews in exploiting current superstitions is well attested in Asia Minor. The title 'high priest' presumably reflects Sceva's attempt to impress his clientele. Conversely, the names and spiritual power associated with the Jewish God are prominent in ancient magical documents.[54]

19:24 Silver shrines of Artemis: such images of the goddess in a niche, made of terracotta, are well known, if not in silver. The commentators seem to have overlooked the bilingual inscription of Tarentum: [Di]anae aidicolam votum dedit = Ἀρτάμιτι εὐχὰν ναίσκον ἀπέδωκε (IGRR 1.467). Neither aedicula nor ναίσκος seem to be noted in this sense by the lexica. This interpretation seems more likely than the suggestion of E.L. Hicks that ποιῶν ναούς reflects the title νεωποιός, held by members of the board of wardens of the temple.[55]

19:27 'The great goddess Artemis'; cf. vv. 28, 34: the formulations are illustrated from the inscriptions.[56]

19:29 The Ephesian theatre was the meeting-place of the city.[57]

19:31 The Asiarchs are naturally situated in Ephesus, and the friendship of some of them with Paul is interesting, and not merely to be dismissed as 'highly unlikely'.[58]

one of a list of Curetes. For reference to a 'lecture-hall' adjoining the Library of Celsus at Ephesus, designated by the unique word αὐδειτώριον, see *JÖAI* 7 (1904) Beiblatt 52 [(Ed.) Also found in *I. Eph.* 3009]; Hemer, *TB* 24 (1973), p. 128.

54 Examples are numerous both in the inscriptions and the papyri. Thus e.g. *IG* 14.859, a heathen plaque from Puteoli, with an invocation including Σαβαώθ, Σαβαώθ. ἅγιον ὄν[ο]μα Ἰαώ, Ἢλ, Μιχαήλ, Νεφθώ etc.; *IG* 14.2.2481, of Avennio (Avignon); etc. Among the papyri the 'Great Magical Papyrus' at Paris, partly reproduced in Deissmann, *LAE*, pp. 255-63, is a striking example. Though the text was written c. 300 AD, the Jewish influence on it probably belongs to a much earlier tradition. B.A. Mastin, 'Scaeva the Chief Priest', *JTS* n.s. 27 (1976), pp. 405-12 argues that the title 'high priest' is sufficiently explained if Scaeva were of a Jewish high-priestly family. There is certainly no need here for the scepticism of Haenchen (p. 564); the term may have been an impostor's stock-in-trade. Bruce, *Acts*, p. 358 points out that Luke did not have the use of quotation-marks or of 'sic' to show this; but he might well have written τοῦ λεγομένου ἀρχιερέως or the like in that case, however.

55 Hicks, 'Demetrius the Silversmith. An Ephesian Study', *Expos* 4th ser. 1 (1890), pp. 401-22, esp. pp. 418-19. [(Ed.) See however, Ramsay, *CRE*, pp. 113-34; and *New Docs* 4.8, No. 1.]

56 There are varied forms in the inscriptions, as here. The usual epithet is μεγίστη. For further discussion of the variants, and the alternation of ἡ θεά with θεός, as here, see n. 61 below.

57 *OGIS* 480.8-9, of AD 104; Sherwin-White, *RSRL*, p. 87. See now further *I. Eph.* 28.9-10 Lat., 19-20 Gk., 29.19-20 etc. Other attestations depend partly on restoration. The recurring phrase is ἵνα τιθῆνται κατ' ἐκκλησίαν ἐν τῷ θεάτρῳ.

58 Haenchen, p. 574n. [(Ed.) The most recent detailed study of the asiarchs is

19:33-34 The deflection of the move against Paul into an anti-Semitic channel accords with surviving evidence for such tensions in Ephesus, where Jews seem to have held citizenship and other special privileges guaranteed first by the Seleucids and maintained under the Romans.[59] Cf. the humorous comment in v. 32.

19:35 γραμματεύς: this is the correct title for the chief executive magistrate in Ephesus, and is attested *passim* in the inscriptions.

19:35 νεωκόρος: a title of honour commonly authorized by the Romans for major cities (including Ephesus) which possessed an official temple of the imperial cult. Used characteristically also in Ephesus of the cult of Artemis.[60]

19:35 The διοπετές was the archaic sacred image of the goddess, whether literally a meteorite or an ancient sculpture.

19:37 ἡ θεός was the formal designation of the goddess. The lexica are not specific about this usage in reference to Artemis, though it is abundantly attested in Roman Ephesus.[61]

R.A. Kearsley, *Asiarchs and arciereis of Asia: The Inscriptions of Ephesus* (diss. Macquarie University, 1987). Cf. *idem*, 'Asiarchs, *archeireis* and the *archiereiai* of Asia', *GRBS* 27 (1986), pp. 183-92; *idem*, in *New Docs* 4.46-55, No. 14. In a forthcoming article (*AS* 38 [1988]) Kearsley argues that there is epigraphic evidence which attests the asiarchy by the early 1st cent. AD.

[59] Seleucus Nicator is said to have granted citizenship to Jews in the cities which he founded, including those in Asia (Jos. *Ant.*12.3.1.119). The expression in *Ap.* 2.4.39 is ambiguous. The implication of *Ant.* 12.3.2.125-26 is that existing Jewish citizenship rights ought to be rescinded. Josephus cites decrees of Lentulus (*Ant.* 14.10.13.228-30, of 49 BC) and of Dolabella (*Ant.* 14.10.12.225-27, of 43 BC) in favour of Jewish privileges. The undated decree of the city in *Ant.* 14.10.25.263-64 concedes rights with patent reluctance under Roman pressure. There is no reason to doubt the essential authenticity of these documents, though some scholars are reluctant to accept the possibility of actual Jewish citizenship in a Gentile city. The point in the recurring debate over Jewish rights is that if these people claim to be citizens they must conform, and not claim also exceptional exemptions from the normal responsibilities of citizens. See my fuller discussion in *The Letters to the Seven Churches of Asia in their Local Setting* (Sheffield: JSOT Press, 1986), esp. pp. 37-39 and notes, and 136-37 and notes.

[60] See *I. Eph.* 300. This text gives the city's full titulature as [τῆς πρώτης καὶ μεγίστης μητροπ]όλεως τῆς Ἀσίας καὶ τ Ι [ρὶς νεωκόρων τῶν Σεβαστῶν, μόνω]ν ἀπα[σῶν] δὲ τῆς Ἀρτέμι[δο]ς Ι [Ἐφεσίων πόλεως ἡ βουλὴ καὶ ὁ νεωκό]ρος δῆμος (lines 5-7, of Septimius Severus). The restorations are well established by parallel formulations.

[61] BAGD cite the usage as 'Attic', but suggest it occurs 'later more rarely'. It appears many times however as the specific designation of Ephesian Artemis in the Salutaris document (AD 104), where the goddess is first introduced as τὴν μεγίστην θε Ι ὸν Ἄρτεμιν (*IBM* 481 = *I. Eph.* 27, lines 12-13), and resumptively throughout simply as ἡ θεός. θεά is also used in some places where she is named (*I. Eph.* 27, lines 224-25, 407 = *IBM* 481, lines 130-31, 278): τῆι γενεσίωι τῆς

19:38 The assizes: the term ἀγοραῖοι (ἡμέραι) reflects the Roman practice in Asia of holding courts under the proconsul in nine or more principal cities which served as district capitals. Ephesus was capital of one of the *conventus*, or assize-districts.[62]

19:38 If not merely a generalizing plural, ἀνθύπατοι may refer to the remarkable fact that *two* men were conjointly exercising the functions of proconsul temporarily after murdering their predecessor subsequent to Nero's accession in AD 54 (Tac. *Ann.* 13.1; Dio 61.6.4-5), a date which precisely suits the ostensible chronology of this passage (cf. D, p. 169). This view is severely criticized by Ramsay, however.[63]

19:39 The 'regular' assembly: the precise phrase is attested elsewhere (ἀγομένης ἐκκλησίας ἐννόμου, *SIG*[3] 852.20, of Thera, AD 149) and the concept is mentioned repeatedly in the Salutaris inscription of Ephesus itself.[64]

μεγίστης θεᾶς Ἀρ | [τέμιδος]; τὸ τῆς μεγίστης θεᾶς Ἀρτέμιδος ἱερόν, to be placed beside the recurring τῇ γενεσίῳ τῆς θεοῦ (*passim*, e.g. *I. Eph.* 27.535-36). So also commonly elsewhere, e.g. τῇ Ἐφεσίᾳ θεῷ (*I. Eph.* 3077.9; 3078.11).

62 Pliny *NH* 5.29.105 ff. appears to list nine of these jurisdictions, but in a confused and probably incomplete way: the Cibyratic (Laodicea), and those of Synnada, Apamea, Alabanda, Sardis, Ephesus (5.31.120), Smyrna Adramyttium and Pergamum. Cf. also Cic. *ad Fam.* 3.8.6. ἡ ἀγοραῖος (sc. ἡμέρα or σύνοδος) is used as the Greek rendering of the technical term *conventus* (Mason, *Greek Terms*, p. 19). Cf. e.g. τῇ μὲν | πρώτῃ ἐξαμήνῳ, ἐν ᾗ καὶ ἡ ἀγόραιος ἤχθη (*IGRR* 4.788.9-10, of Apamea in Asia— not Syria, as wrongly in Mason, 2nd AD; cf. *IGRR* 4.789, 790, of same city). See further V. Chapot, *La province romaine proconsulaire d'Asie* (Paris, Émile Bouillon, 1904), pp. 353-57.

63 Ramsay, *Expos* 6th ser. 2 (1900), pp. 334-35. Ramsay's criticisms are directed in part to an inadequate and inaccurate statement by H.M. Luckock. He is evidently right to reject the notion of an irregular tenure of power by the murderers, for constitutionally it would pass provisionally into the hands of the three deputies until a successor arrived, and an *eques* and a freedman were not qualified. But the chronological objection does not now apply, for since the Gallio inscription has helped to anchor this period of Paul's life, a date closely subsequent to the death of Claudius is suitable for this incident, and an interregnum between proconsuls coinciding with the change of emperor provides a plausible setting for the unrest in Ephesus attested both here and in the Corinthian correspondence. It thus remains plausible that the plural 'proconsuls', if generalizing, reflects the uncertainty of the time, or, if more specific, actually refers to the acting deputies. It is notable that Ramsay, often dismissed as an apologist, here (as not infrequently) appears as a trenchant critic of an inadequate traditionalism, where others have allowed faulty assumptions to pass. We may accept a probable setting for the passage in c. 54-55, and a slightly different formulation of the case meets the substance of Ramsay's objections.

64 κατὰ πᾶσαν νό | μιμον, *IBM* 481, lines 339-40 = *I. Eph.* 27 lines 468-69, of AD 104; cf. lines 165 = 229, [116, deficient =] 203, where wholly or partly restored.

19:40 These words reflect the preoccupation with civic privileges and the fear that sedition or irregularity could precipitate Roman intervention.

20:3 The change of plan occasioned by the plot may have induced Paul to travel overland to Macedonia rather than on an early ship for Passover in Jerusalem. In Troas he met representatives of various churches and reached Jerusalem for Pentecost (cf. F, pp. 188f.).

20:4 The form used as an ethnic designation, Βεροιαῖος, is precisely that attested on the local inscriptions (Dimitsas 52, imperial; 55, under Nerva; 58, early 1st AD). The form Βερεεύς is also found (*IG* 3.2.2395, of Athens, possibly referring, however, to a different Beroea).[65]

20:4 The ethnic Ἀσιανός, is again characteristic of the period. In *IGRR* 4.1756 (of Sardis, 2 BC) the 'Greeks in Asia' honour a Sardian citizen designated Ἀσιανός (lines 113, 116) with honours relating to the provincial *Koinon*. The ethnic title was the natural correlative of the province, and here designates two men, at least one of whom was an Ephesian (Acts 21:29), but both represent a wider district of which Ephesus was the centre.[66]

20:5 The beginning of a new 'we-passage' at Philippi, where the last ended, raises the possibility that the ostensible author joined the party as representative of that church, which is not otherwise mentioned (cf. G, p. 191).

20:6 It has been argued that the days of the week here permit a chronological argument which suits the year 57 for this journey, a date consonant with other circumstantial hints.[67]

20:7ff. Paul's determination to spend as long at Troas as his tight schedule will permit suits the specially strategic importance assigned

---

65 The coins attest ΒΕΡΑΙΩΝ (of Philip, dated AD 243-44), perhaps merely an abbreviation, beside the regular ΒΕΡΟΙΑΙΩΝ (e.g. on a coin dated AD 246). See Head, *HN*, pp. 241-43. On variation in ethnics see next note, and Excursus.

66 It is worth stressing this correlation in the face of the frequency of unjustified objections on points of this type. Both geographical names and their ethnics are flexible but patterned in their usage. As Ἀσιανός matches the current senses of Ἀσία and ἡ Ἰουδαία (γῆ) in the land of the Ἰουδαῖοι (21:10 below), so Γαλάτης may be an inhabitant of Γαλατία, whether correlative with it as ethnic unit, province or indeed as used of European 'Gaul' (see Excursus, pp. 241-43). Dozens of instances could be cited of persons with Greek names designated in Greek documents by such ostensibly 'barbarian', but in the Roman period probably more often 'provincial', ethnics as Ἄραψ, Καππάδοξ, Κίλιξ or Σύρος. See, e.g., *New Docs* 4.173, No. 87; 4.174, No. 90. Sometimes such a person is further identified as a citizen of a Greek city in the province. Thus if a Σύρος is further designated Ἀντιοχεύς, he is shown to belong to one of the greatest cosmopolitan Greek cities of the world.

67 Cf. D, pp. 169f., Chapter 6 below and *Pauline Studies Bruce*, pp. 10-11.

to this city.

20:13 Paul's staying behind at Troas and travelling overland to rejoin the ship's company at Assos is appropriate to local circumstances, where the ship had to negotiate an exposed coast and double Cape Lectum before reaching Assos.

20:14-15 The sequence of places mentioned in these verses is entirely correct and natural.[68]

20:16 The choice to by-pass Ephesus had presumably been made already in the choice of ship at Troas, where a faster coaster may have deliberately avoided entering the gulf of Ephesus, especially if the silting there was already causing delays. Paul too may have been acutely conscious that a visit to the church from a ship calling there would be likely to imperil his commitment to Jerusalem through personal entanglements there and the probable need for further trans-shipment.

20:17 Miletus was only some thirty miles distant from Ephesus by boat and road, and the summons is readily understood if the ship was scheduled to stay or delayed at Miletus for two or three days.

21:1 Patara (like Myra) was a port used by the Alexandrian corn-fleet. Both became important places of trans-shipment, and imperial granaries were built at these two ports under Hadrian.[69] It is notable that the city's name is correctly given as a neuter plural, as in the local epigraphy and elsewhere in literature.[70]

21:3 Eyewitness-like comments are given on the route passing across the open sea south of Cyprus, favoured no doubt by the persistent northwest winds (cf. M, p. 209 and below on Acts 27).

21:4 After the pressure of time early in the journey, the pace relaxes after a favourable voyage to Tyre.[71]

21:5 αἰγιαλός describes correctly the smooth beach at Tyre, as opposed to ἀκτή, used of a rocky shore.

21:8 The distance from Ptolemais (Akko) to Caesarea is about thirty miles, a suitable day's journey whether this stage was taken by

---

68 We do not attach much significance to the spelling Μιτυλήνη rather than the predominantly earlier Μυτιλήνη. The later form occurs as early as 303 BC and both continue in at least occasional use thereafter. The mention of Trogyllium in the Western text is also entirely appropriate, though the balance of textual evidence tells against its originality (cf. H, p. 198). See Metzger, *Textual Comm.*, p. 478, giving (C) rating to the committee's preference for the shorter text.

69 See on 27:5 below, and for the granary here *TAM* 2.397 = *CIL* 3.12129.

70 For an epigraphical reference, see *TAM* 2.905.VII H5. Among the literary examples are: Hdt. 1.182; Paus. 9.41.1; Diodorus 19.64.5; Lucian, *Philopseud.* 38; Appian, *Mithridatica*, 4.27; Arrian, *Anab.* 1.24.4. See further G.K. Sams, 'Investigations at Patara in Lycia, 1974', Archaeology 28 (1975), pp. 202-205.

71 Cf. *Pauline Studies Bruce*, p. 10.

sea or coastal road.

21:10 The curious usage of 'Judaea' here presumably reflects the Jewish perspective which associated the term with Jerusalem and district as the heart of Judaism, and excluded pagan Caesarea.[72]

21:16 The implication, made explicit in D, is perhaps that Mnason's home was not in Jerusalem, but an overnight stopping-place *en route*. The road distance from Caesarea to Jerusalem is scarcely less than sixty miles (cf. H, p. 198).[73]

21:24 Luke is aware of this characteristically Jewish act of piety, closely paralleled by the contemporary action of Agrippa I (Jos. *Ant.* 19.6.1.294).

21:28 The Gentiles were forbidden on pain of death to go beyond the Gentiles' Court of the Temple. Two examples of the well-known warning notice are extant (*CIJ* 1400).

21:31 There is a reference to the permanent stationing of a Roman cohort (τάγμα) at Antonia, with the specific responsibility of watching for and suppressing any disturbance at festival times is attested in Josephus (*BJ* 5.5.8.244).

21:35, 40 The flight of steps used by the guards is again explicitly described in Josephus (*BJ* 5.5.8.243). There is no reason to doubt the independence of the two writers here, or for that matter to attach undue significance to these points of contact.

21:38 On 'the Egyptian', cf. Jos. *BJ* 2.13.5.261-63; *Ant.* 20.8.6.169-71. The former passage clashes with Acts as giving the number of his followers as 30,000 not 4,000. We should be more ready to accept the smaller figure, especially as Josephus can be shown elsewhere to

72 Caesarea was officially the provincial capital, though geographically in the section called Samaria, rather than in Judaea in the narrower sense. After AD 70 the province was termed 'Syria Palaestina' (Head, *HN*, p. 802), and coins of Samaria (Sebaste), for instance, were inscribed ΣΕΒΑCΤΗΝΩΝ CΥΡΙΑC, and those of the new foundation of Neapolis (mod. Nablus) either ΦΛΑΟΥΙ. ΝΕΑΠΟΛ. ΣΑΜΑΡΕ. or ΦΛ. ΝΕΑC ΠΟΛΕΩC CΥΡΙΑC ΠΑΛΑΙCΤΙΝΗC (*HN*, p. 803). The statement in Blass-Debrunner-Funk, §261(4) that Ἰουδαία is an adjective and therefore requires the article ἡ Ἰουδαία (γῆ) cannot be sustained, for use of the article and the transition between adjective and substantive are much more flexible than their classifications allow. Cf. the excursus below, pp. 223, 243 for anarthrous Ἰουδαία, and the discussions of B.M. Metzger in *Apostolic History*, p. 133 and *Textual Comm.*, pp. 293-94 *ad loc*. Cf. also the post-70 coinage legend ΙΟΥΔΑΙΑΣ ΕΛΛ ωΚΥΙΑΣ (Head, *HN*, pp. 809-10).

73 See Bruce, *Acts*, pp. 389-90 *ad loc*. The point of introducing Mnason (and previously Philip's daughters) may have been partly as they were among Luke's important informants about the earliest days of the church. I incline to think however that the expansion reflects at least a plausible inference that Mnason was not actually Paul's host in Jerusalem but offered a stopping-place *en route*.

inflate numbers.[74]

21:39 The literary reminiscence of Euripides, *Ion* 8, is well calculated to impress the officer surprised at Paul's Greek education.

21:39 The claim to citizenship of a Greek city is unusual in a Jew, and possible only where a special constitution made a body of Jewish citizens possible. There are indications that the refoundation of Tarsus by Antiochus Epiphanes had created such a situation.[75]

22:1-16 The speech, delivered in Aramaic, stresses suitably those elements in Paul's background and experience which communicated with a Jewish audience in Jerusalem.

22:28 The tribune's *nomen*, Claudius (see 23:26) implies that he gained the citizenship under Claudius, when it was commonly bought for money, as indicated here. Dio says it became cheapened during the reign, and this accords with the possibility that a sarcastic edge should be seen in the tribune's remark, an implication made more explicit in the Western version.[76]

22:28 Paul's Tarsian citizenship evidently means that his family had been long settled in Tarsus and were presumably of standing there. It has been suggested that Pompey, Caesar, Antony and Augustus were all likely to have given Roman citizenship to some important Tarsians (*CSP*, p. 198), and an ancestor of Paul may have benefitted from such grant, but we have no means of knowing the circumstances. There are preserved many military *diplomata* authenticating

---

74 It is sometimes argued in Josephus' defence that the Greek numeral Δ (4000) could have been confused with Λ (30,000), whether in manuscript transmission or in Josephus' own transcription. In view however of his vagaries elsewhere I doubt the need to harmonize him with Luke.

75 See Ramsay, *CSP*, pp. 161ff. The implication that some Jews were known to have been citizens of Tarsus underlies the dilemma put to Titus by Apollonius of Tyana, according to Philostratus (*Vita Ap. Ty.* 6.34). The possibility of Jewish citizenship in a Greek city has sometimes been denied absolutely because of the religious difficulty. Thus W.W. Tarn and G.T. Griffith, *Hellenistic Civilisation* (London: Edward Arnold, 3rd edn, 1952), pp. 221-22 explain Paul's status as of 'isopolity', or 'potential citizenship', which could only be exercised practically at the cost of apostasy. V. Tcherikover, *Hellenistic Civilization and the Jews*, tr. S. Applebaum (Philadelphia and Jerusalem: Jewish Publication Society of America and Magnes Press, 1966), pp. 309-32 deals almost entirely with Alexandria, but is likewise sceptical about Jewish citizenship elsewhere, while recognizing varieties of status. Cf. E.M. Smallwood, *The Jews under Roman Rule* (Leiden: Brill, 1981), pp. 286-88. That such citizenship was possible on occasion is confirmed by the inscriptions of the synagogue at Sardis (L. Robert, *Nouvelles inscriptions de Sardes* [Paris: Librairie D'Amérique et D'Orient, 1964]: No. 14, p. 55, where a Jew is Σ]αρδιανὸ[ς βουλε]υτής; cf. Nos. 13, 16, 17). Sardis, like Tarsus, is likely to have owed this situation to a Seleucid constitution.

76 See Dio 60.17.5-7; Bruce, *Acts*, p. 407 and D, p. 170 below.

the discharged soldier's claim to citizenship, but it remains uncertain how a hereditary citizen could document his case.[77]

22:29 The tribune is impressed with Roman rather than Tarsian citizenship, and afraid of the consequences of having abused a Roman.

23:2 Ananias as high priest is correct for the ostensible date.

23:6ff. The prominence of the Sadducees as the focus of opposition stands apart from both the Gospel traditions of Jesus' controversies with the Pharisees and from the decline of the Sadducee party after 70, but fits what seem to have been the theological politics of this time.[78]

23:24 The governorship of Felix is correctly linked to the ostensible date. The term here used is the general word ἡγέμων, the formal Latin title of these governors of Judaea being *procurator* or *praefectus*.

23:31 Antipatris was the natural stopping-point on the way to Caesarea, whether reached via Lydda or by the hills through Gophna. The section from Antipatris to Caesarea is now documented.[79] In mainly Gentile country at a distance from Jerusalem the large guard ceased to be necessary.

23:34 Felix's acceptance of a case involving a man from Cilicia is significant, for this, like Judaea, was subject to the legate of Syria at this period.[80]

---

[77] For the registration of citizen births after the laws of AD 4 and AD 9 see Bruce, *Paul*, pp. 39-40, and the full discussion of citizenship in *RSRL*, pp. 146-62.

It is remarkable that Paul's full name is unknown to us. He must have possessed the characteristic Roman *tria nomina*, but these would not have been used in the Greek and Jewish contexts of his travels, and only as a formal and official Roman designation. If any of the speculations about his family are justified, it is possible that he was Cn. Pompeius Paulus, C. Julius Paulus or M. Antonius Paulus. See now C.J. Hemer, 'The Name of Paul', *TB* 36 (1985), pp. 179-83.

[78] Cf. I.H. Marshall in *Apostolic History and the Gospel*, ed. Gasque and Martin, pp. 96-98.

[79] See S. Dar and S. Applebaum, 'The Roman Road from Antipatris to Caesarea,' *PEQ*, 105 (1973), pp. 91-99. This branched from the direct route northwards through the inner Sharon plain at modern Qalansawa, thus avoiding most of the difficult, sandy oak-forest. Two milestones, one inscribed but undated, of perhaps 2nd-3rd AD, some stretches of the alignment, and pottery of Hellenistic as well as Roman date, have been found. It is unnecessary to follow Haenchen's hyper-literalistic requirements as a ground for supposing that Luke 'has only an inaccurate conception of the geography of Palestine' (p. 648). An attempt to measure on a map the Roman road distance from Jerusalem to Antipatris (via Lydda) gives c. 35 (English) miles, as compared with 37 (Marshall), 40 (Haenchen), 45 (Hanson). There is no need to insist that the infantry escort went all the way to Antipatris or that more mobile units returned thence without rest and provision.

[80] See *RSRL*, pp. 55-57; cf. E, p. 180.

24:1-9 Sherwin-White cites Mommsen's opinion of Paul's trial as 'an exemplary account of the provincial penal procedure *extra ordinem*'.[81] The details highlighted in the following items illustrate this judgment.[82]

24:1 (cf. 23:35) Felix awaits the arrival of private accusers from Jerusalem before the case comes to formal trial.

24:1 The accusers here employ an advocate, but no mention of an advocate is made in the appearance before Festus (25:7). In imperial *cognitiones* before Trajan, the parties appear with or without advocates as they please.[83]

24:3 (cf. 23:26) κράτιστος is the correct form of address to the procurator, as a man of equestrian rank.

24:5 The charges are what Cadbury terms 'constructive'.[84] Since Roman authorities would take no cognizance of Jewish religious controversy, the complaints are presented in terms which Felix could be induced to construe as political. Such a type of charge is said to be normal in this type of procedure.[85] The original charge and original accusers are tacitly dropped at this stage.[86]

24:10 Paul's statement that Felix had ruled this people for many years accords with his having ruled Samaria under Cumanus, and so having held office for eight or nine years altogether, a lengthy span for an imperial official, and sharply contrasted with the annual tenure of the senatorial proconsul (cf. D, p. 172).

24:14ff. Paul's defence stresses that the accusations are purely religious. He is a worshipper of the 'ancestral' God, and is called in question before the Sanhedrin about the resurrection, a matter on which he stands with the mainstream Pharisees.

24:19 It is a sharp tactic to bring up the absence of the original accusers, for Roman law was strong against accusers who abandoned

---

81 *RSRL*, p. 48.

82 There is an inevitable difficulty in communication here when Haenchen can write 'All our troubles are removed if, with Wendt, Bauernfeind and Dibelius, we resolutely interpret the speeches as Lucan compositions' (p. 657). His critical procedure throughout the scene does not consider the possibilities that the ostensible narrative could be assessed in terms of Roman practice.

83 Pliny *Ep.* 4.22 [without]; 6.31 [with]; cited in *RSRL*, p. 49.

84 *BC* 5.306; cf. *RSRL*, p. 50.

85 *RSRL*, pp. 14, 17-23, 51.

86 Sherwin-White, *RSRL*, p. 51, draws attention to a striking parallel with Claudius' letter to the Alexandrians, where the emperor threatens politically troublesome Jews κοινήν τ(ε)ινα τῆς οἰκουμένης νόσον ἐξεγείροντας (Smallwood, *Documents Gaius, Claudius and Nero*, No. 370, lines 99-100). He explains the parallel as a case of Acts using contemporary language, precisely the charge to bring against a Jew under Claudius or the early Nero.

their charges.[87] These details all argue specific familiarity with the procedures, and are naturally explained by Paul's situation rather than as editorial creations.

24:24 Felix's knowledge of 'the way' (24:22) may be related to his marriage to the Jewish Drusilla. For the circumstances (and approximate date) of this marriage see Jos. *Ant.* 20.7.2.141-43 (cf. D, p. 172).

24:27 The name 'Porcius Festus' agrees precisely with that given by Josephus (*Ant.* 20.8.9.182).

24:27 While we hesitate to use imputed motives as a factor in argument, it is worth noting that Felix needed to conciliate the Jews of Caesarea, who immediately went to Rome to accuse him.[88]

24:27 On the likely chronology,[89] these 'two years', interpreted as the duration of Paul's imprisonment, represent the period 57-59, and suit a change of procuratorial coinage to be related with some plausibility to the coming of Festus (cf. D, pp. 171, 173).[90]

25:5,6 Festus insists on acting in due form, appearing formally on his tribunal (βῆμα), and acts with the assistance of his *consilium* (συμβούλιον 25:12), so that his decision is shown to have legal effect.[91]

25:9-10 The suggestion of a trial in Jerusalem reveals that Festus is under pressure to conciliate Paul's opponents. The only damaging count for the Roman is political, but the alleged evidence for that is theological. The Jewish authorities have no jurisdiction anyhow in the only charge which concerns Festus.

25:11 The right of appeal for Roman citizens (*apellatio* and *provocatio* having become virtually identical under the Early Empire) would usually be used against a contrary verdict, but might be exercised at any earlier stage of the proceedings, as here, where the circumstances of the investigation were likely to be prejudicial and dangerous.[92]

---

[87] *Destitutio, RSRL*, p. 52.

[88] Jos. *Ant.* 20.8.9.182; cf. *RSRL*, pp. 53-54.

[89] This is subject to debate: see Chapter 6 below.

[90] Thus Cadbury, *The Book of Acts in History* (London: A. & C. Black, 1955), pp. 9-10. The series in question bears obv. LE KAICAPOC around palm-branch and rev. NERⲰNOC inside olive-wreath (*BMC Palestine*, Procurators under Nero, Nos. 1-28, with minor variations and imperfections). All this group is dated LE (ἔτος ε'), the fifth year of Nero extending from October 58 to October 59 and including the probable time of Festus' arrival in (early) summer 59. The procurators are never named on this coinage.

[91] Bruce, *Acts*, p. 430; *RSRL*, pp. 48-49.

[92] See Schürer-Vermes-Millar 1 [1973], p. 369, cf. Schürer 2.2.278, and literature cited. The difficulties outlined by Haenchen (*Acts*, pp. 667-70) are not substantial when the case is seen in legal terms with due regard for the complexity of the

25:13 The visit of Agrippa II, whose kingdom had been recently extended (in 56) to include part of Galilee, and his notorious sister-consort Bernice, sister also of Felix's wife Drusilla, is entirely timely and natural, the neighbouring king paying his respects to the new representative of Rome (cf. D, pp. 173-74).

25:18 The bewildered Festus, after his vindication of Roman justice, declares the charges, unrelated to any misdemeanours ὧν ἐγὼ ὑπενόουν, 'of which I could take cognizance', reflecting the legal formula *de quibus cognoscere volebam*.[93]

25:26 ὁ κύριος became a characteristic form of reference to the emperor from the time of Nero, here taking up the more formal preceding τὸν Σεβαστόν (25:25); cf. E, p. 180.

26:1ff. The literary characteristics of this speech show selection and exclusion which may be related to Paul's situation before Agrippa. The pious Jew Ananias, for instance, who figures prominently in the Jerusalem conversion speech of Acts 22, is not mentioned here. The general point is made here in the consciousness that others would strongly deny the appropriateness of the speech to Paul's, rather than Luke's, situation.[94]

---

forces at work. It is not, for instance, a problem that Luke does not associate Paul's appeal here with his Roman citizenship. His citizenship is known to the reader, and it was unnecessary to explain the connection in a time when it was a commonplace. Haenchen concedes (p. 669) that there is no adequate ground for suspicion that the appeal is unhistorical; rather it was a piece of authentic tradition to serve as a nucleus for the story. Its 'contradictions are immediately resolved if we consider the Lucan narrative no longer as a court minute but rather as a suspense-laden narrative created by the author'. But this 'solution' is more difficult than the purported problem. The most helpful discussion of the question of appeal in its bearing on Acts is *RSRL*, pp. 57-70. Many of the problems previously highlighted by Mommsen, Cadbury and others are met by the view of A.H.M. Jones that the right of appeal for citizens facing capital charges was absolute in cases *extra ordinem*, that is, outside the sphere of fixed, statutory offences and prescribed penalties, and that that distinction applied specifically in the Julio-Claudian period (cf. Jones, 'I Appeal Unto Caesar', *Studies in Roman Government and Law* [Oxford: Blackwell, 1960], pp. 53-65, esp. p. 57; and below pp. 180, 214). The work of Jones and Sherwin-White in this area suggests that much contained in the commentaries is seriously dated and erroneous.

93 *RSRL*, p. 50.

94 Haenchen's discussion, and his use of Auerbach, are unhelpfully simplistic. (p. 679). He supposes that realism in antiquity was appropriate only to middle or lower types of style intended as comedy or entertainment, but 'in Acts he sought to reach the heights of ancient historical writing', and could only show the significance of the scene by making Paul confront the great princes of his day. This argument needs to be questioned at several levels. (1) Auerbach's theory of the relation between 'realism' and levels of style in classical literature is itself based on a paradigmatic use of extremely contrasting literary styles (Petronius and

26:32 The innocent man could have been released if he had not appealed. The pluperfect here is significant as implying that this act of Paul had placed him in an irrevocable position. The compulsion was not so much strictly legal as political, a matter of the emperor's *auctoritas* in relation to his subordinates. Festus could scarcely venture publicly to short-circuit a case formally arrogated to Caesar's decision.[95]

27:1 The unit to which Julius belonged cannot be certainly identified, as the honorary title Σεβαστή = *Augusta* may have had multiple reference.[96]

Tacitus), and makes no allowance, for instance, for the complex diversity within ancient historiography (see Chapter 3 above). (2) Auerbach acknowledges a different, pre-classical paradigm, but again based on a questionably simplistic contrast between Homeric and Old Testament narratives, and stresses that the New Testament, and the Gospels in particular, provide an extreme counter example, a serious, unrhetorical, vernacular writing largely untouched by rules of style (*Mimesis*, tr. W.R. Trask, Princeton University Press, 1968, pp. 40-49). (3) There is a problem of definitions. 'Realism' might be 'fictional verisimilitude', as certainly in the case of Petronius' romance; it is not *simpliciter* the touchstone of historical reliability. Haenchen often requires inappropriate criteria of a historical narrative, completeness of logically presented circumstantial detail (which may not be available). But a narrative which fulfilled his conditions might well in fact be fictional, in the manner of Petronius or Defoe. (4) Haenchen makes a partial and unrepresentative use of Auerbach, who recognizes, albeit sometimes concessively, something of the diversity of the phenomena. Thus in Absalom's rebellion and David's last days 'the contradictions and crossing of motives ... have become so concrete that it is impossible to doubt the historicity of the information conveyed' (*Mimesis*, p. 20). Again, 'It was the story of Christ, with its ruthless mixture of everyday reality and the highest and most sublime tragedy, which had conquered the classical rule of styles' (*Mimesis*, p. 555). (5) Auerbach's treatment of ancient historiography is questionable at some points, where for instance he links the limits of 'antique realism' with limits of 'historical consciousness' (*Mimesis*, p. 40; cf. pp. 32-33, 38ff.). It is not necessarily 'rhetorical', and the lack of interest in, say, economic causation proves not an absence of historical consciousness but at most a different assessment of historical priorities.

95 *RSRL*, pp. 64-65.

96 The specific presence of a cohort with this title in the army of Syria/Judaea in the first century is attested in *ILS* 2683 = *CIL* 3.6687, found in Venice but attributed to Berytus (Beirut), giving the career of a prefect 'cohort(is) Aug. I' under Quirinius (after AD 6), and again in *IGRR* 3.1136 = *OGIS* 421, referring in fragmentary context to an ἔπα[ρχος—?] | σπείρης Αὐ[γούστης (from Eitha in Batanaea [Transjordan] under Herod Agrippa II).

Alternative possibilities are (1) that this was a colloquial name for a unit of imperial officer-couriers (the later *frumentarii*): thus Ramsay, *SPTR*, pp. 314-15, following Mommsen; (2) that this was one of the cohorts of 'Sebasteni', several times mentioned in Josephus, a force consisting of five cohorts (σπεῖραι) and one squadron of cavalry (ἴλη = *ala*) and forming a large part of Agrippa I's garrison

27:2 'Αδραμυττηνῷ: the name occurs in varied spellings, and Westcott and Hort read 'Αδραμυντηνῷ (AB 33 boh arm).[97] The ship was a coaster, presumably bound for its home port in Mysia. It would be natural for Julius to find a ship bound for Rome in one of the Lycian ports used by the Alexandrian corn-fleet.

27:4 This time, in contrast with the eastward voyage (21:3), they sailed in the lee of Cyprus, a course dictated by the prevailing west or northwest winds of summer in the Levant. Their coasting passage was assisted by local on-shore and off-shore breezes, and by the westerly trend of the currents along the south Anatolian coasts. Such considerations at least reflect experience of the climatic conditions of this voyage. The Western authorities again add 'fifteen days' as the duration of this voyage, a plausible time in adverse conditions, and suitable to the accumulating delays of the passing season but not to be favoured as original.[98]

27:5 The common article bonding 'Cilicia' and 'Pamphylia' here may be taken to reflect a unitary concept, of one sea-area bordering what we should term the south coast of Asia Minor. The point is slight, and may be insignificant, even accidental, but is apt to the instinctive nuance of an accurate mind writing from experience, if we

---

in Caesarea (Jos. *Ant.* 19.9.2.365-66), amounting altogether to some 3000 men (cf. Jos. *BJ* 2.3.4.52), and named from their having been recruited at Sebaste (Samaria): thus Schürer-Vermes-Millar 1.363-64 = Schürer 1.2.53. The difficulty here is that 'Augusta'/'Sebaste' is an honourable title, ostensibly quite different from the ethnic origin of the name of these cohorts; Schürer is driven to posit a hypothetical *cohors Augusta Sebastenorum* as one of the five. In any case his epigraphical examples of a *cohors* or *ala Sebastenorum* are of doubtful relevance: *ILS* 2738 = *CIL* 8.9358, *CIL* 8.9359, and *EE* 5 (1884), p. 469, No. 1000 = *ILS* 1436 are all perhaps much later, the two former not earlier than Hadrian, and all are of Caesarea in Mauretania, not of Caesarea in Palestine. The only case referring to a cohort (*CIL* 3.2916 = *CIL* 3.9984), mentioning *coh. I Sebastenorum*, is undated and from Iader (Zara) in Dalmatia. If any of these, or an example from Timgad in Numidia (*EE* 5 [1884], p. 390, No. 699, probably of M. Aurelius) refer to the same units, they imply that they were stationed in North Africa or Dalmatia at a very different date, and are of scant value for the Josephus passages, and less for Acts. Both alternative explanations are built on supposition, and it seems probable that Julius' unit was the one noticed in the text, especially if we may assume its presence in Palestine or Syria through the period from Quirinius to Agrippa II. But we need to recognize that our information is fragmentary.

97 So Bruce, *Acts*, p. 452 though he now prefers ⁻ ττ ⁻. Cf. *Adrymetion* (Pomponius Mela 1.18.91; ἐν 'Ατραμυ[τίωι]): A. Plassart, 'Les inscriptions de Delphes. La liste des théorodoques', *BCH* 45 (1921), pp. 1-85, 2nd BC, esp. p. 8, col. I D (a) 14.

98 Metzger, *Textual Comm.*, p. 497, probability {B}; cf. section H, p. 199 below. Lucian, *Navig.* 7 gives nine days as the duration of a voyage from Sidon to the Lycian coast (περιπεσόντας δεκάτῃ ἐπὶ Χελιδονέας).

admit that possibility.[99]

27:5 The spelling of the name 'Myra' varies in the manuscripts, and the UBS text prefers Μύρα (byz) against Μύρρα (B),[100] otherwise unattested. In either case the form is a neuter plural, as with Patara (21:1).

27:6 Myra, like Patara again, was a principal port for the Alexandrian corn-ships, and precisely the place where Julius would expect to find a ship sailing to Italy in the imperial service. Its official standing here is further illustrated by the Hadrianic granary.[101] Myra was also the first of these ports to be reached by a ship arriving from the east, as Patara had been previously from the reverse direction.

27:7 The slow passage to Cnidus was made in the face of the typical northwest wind (see Smith, *Voyage*, pp. 75-76). The expression may reflect mounting impatience and anxiety at continuing delays if the wind-force were greater than average, necessitating perhaps extensive tacking where they could not sail close enough into the wind.

27:7 They sailed in the lee of Crete. The assumption is often made that the normal course would have passed directly across the Aegean, north of Crete. Smith (pp. 75-76) is evidently right that this indirect route was forced on the ship by strong northwest winds, but this was in fact the normal direction, and the ship's response likewise normal. Luke's experience of the outward voyage had been direct and rapid before favouring winds. L. Casson seems now to have shown decisively how the return was dictated by weather conditions, and also the disparity in time between eastward and westward journeys.[102]

---

[99] Again, the treatment of the article with proper names seems to be misconceived in Blass-Debrunner-Funk, §261(6). Cf. n. 72 above.

[100] The possibilities of radical error are illustrated here by the early corruption 'Lystra' for 'Myra', presumably arising through dittography from the adjacent word Λυκίας, but betraying the kind of geographical absurdity from which Acts is so remarkably free (εἰς Λύστραν τῆς Λυκίας A; εἰς Λύστρα τῆς Λικύας ℵ). Such an instance sets in higher relief the notable accuracy of our access to geographical detail in the main text-types of Acts, when such obvious corruptions are set aside. I doubt the suggestion of Breusing that Λύστρα arose from Λίμυρα, supposedly a subsidiary alternative form of 'Myra'. Limyra was a distinct city (cf. e.g. *TAM* 2.905.XIX C, of Rhodiapolis, where the Λιμυρεῖς are listed with the other cities of the κοινόν of Lycia).

[101] *ILS* 5908 = *CIL* 3.6738, of Andriace, the post-emporium of Myra.

[102] Throughout this section see L. Casson, 'The Isis and Her Voyage', *TAPA* 81 (1950), pp. 43-56; 'Speed Under Sail of Ancient Ships', *TAPA* 82 (1951), pp. 136-48; *Ships and Seamanship in the Ancient World* (Princeton University Press, 1971); cf. B.S.J. Isserlin, 'The Isis and Her Voyage: Some Additional Remarks', *TAPA* 86 (1955), pp. 319-20; L. Casson, 'The Isis and Her Voyage: A Reply', *TAPA* 87

27:7 The passage southwest to Crete and the difficult rounding of its eastern cape again suit the conditions of a strong northwest wind. The name 'Salmone' is paralleled elsewhere in a slightly different form: Σαλμώνιον τῆς Κρήτης, ὅπερ ἐστὶ τὸ ἑῷον ἄκρον (Strabo 2.4.3 = 106). Pliny, *NH* 4.12.58, 60, 61, 71 gives the Latin as 'Samonium'. It has been suggested that this, like many names in Southern Crete, is of Phoenician origin, from a root cognate with Hebrew שלום, and aptly describing a refuge from exposure to the wind.[103] The Phoenician

(1956), pp. 239-40 ([Ed.] Now see also G. Kettenbach, *Das Logbuch des Lukas* [Frankfurt, Bern and New York: P. Lang, 1986]). Lucian's dialogue *Navigium* is a most valuable parallel. The ship 'Isis', identified explicitly as one of the Egyptian corn-ships (*Navig.* 1), had been first driven eastward before gales to Sidon, and then followed Paul's route north of Cyprus and along the south coast of Asia Minor to the dangerous reefs of the Chelidonian islands, a few miles east of Myra. A shift of wind to a point south of southwest prevented the usual run to the lee of Crete, and they attempted to cross the Aegean before it reverted to the normal northwest, but again met the adverse etesians and struggled to beat into Piraeus on the seventieth day after leaving Egypt, οὓς ἔδει τὴν Κρήτην δεξιὰν λαβόντας ὑπὲρ τὴν Μαλέαν πλεύσαντας ἤδη εἶναι ἐν Ἰταλίᾳ (*Navig.* 9). Casson stresses that this signifies sailing far south of Malea, not being compelled to round that perilous headland. The appearance of such a ship at Piraeus, or indeed in the Aegean, was exceptional.

Casson's studies of sailing speed and of voyage duration are most instructive. For ships dependent on sail the differences between eastward and westward passages are often enormous. A vessel travelling east could run before a favouring wind directly. The westward course was delayed by the necessity of beating into or tacking into adverse winds nearly all the way, and by the necessity of an indirect route to harness those winds and avoid lee shores. He calculates from surviving narratives an actual speed of 4-6 knots over open water with favouring winds, 3-4 knots when coasting or navigating islands, and 1 1/2 - 2 1/2 knots under adverse conditions. For some actual durations relevant to our present study, he estimates Naples to Alexandria 9-11 days, but Alexandria to Naples 50-70; Crete to Alexandria 3-4, Alexandria to Crete (via Myra) 11-14; Rhodes to Caesarea 3-4, Caesarea to Rhodes 10 (*TAPA* 82 [1951], pp. 145-46). It was actually an acclaimed feature of the imperial peace that 'we may travel at all hours, and sail *from east to west*' (πλεῖν ἀπ' ἀνατολῶν ἐπὶ δυσμάς, Epictetus (ed. Arrian), 3.13.9; cf. *TB* 26 [1975], p. 91).

Isserlin's objection that mediaeval galleys often passed north of Crete, although they relied mainly on sail, is met by Casson's rejoinder that the fact that they had oars available in emergency, and could also sail closer to the wind, made a crucial difference. The point is worth stressing, as the commentators have often assumed that the route north of Crete was normal, and have explained Acts 27 accordingly. In this respect the emergency course of the Isis is the exception. The words μὴ προσεῶντος ἡμᾶς τοῦ ἀνέμου (27:7) need not be given causal force to imply a change of plan. Bruce, *Acts*, p. 454 and Marshall, *Acts*, p. 405 incline to the route north of Crete, where Haenchen, p. 699 follows Casson, but unnecessarily reads a Lukan misconception into the narrative.

103 Bürchner, 'Salmone, No. 3', *PW* 2.1.1986-1987.

connection may again illustrate the unexpected maritime importance of this forbidding shore, and perhaps help to account for the extreme variety in the transcription of these names.[104]

27:8 The locations of 'Fair Havens' and the neighbouring site of Lasea are well attested, though obscure places unlikely to be known to any who had not made such a voyage. Καλοὶ Λιμένες, still known today by a demotic version of the same name, offered two contiguous roadsteads sheltered from the northwest winds, but open to half the compass, and so not an attractive winter harbour, though partly protected by offshore islets.[105] It was the last shelter before Cape Matala, after which the northward turn of the coast would have left the ship fully exposed to the northwest. There was evidently no significant settlement (and there are no remains today), and Luke names the πόλις, to whose territory the roadstead belonged, Lasea, whose discovery some 5 m. east of Fair Havens is described in Smith.[106] The assumption that this place was unknown to other ancient writers is due again to aberrant forms of its name.[107]

---

[104] Other renderings of the name include Σαμώνιον in Strabo 10.4.2 = 474; Σαμμώνιον ἄκρον (Ptol. *Geog.* 3.14.1,8); Σαμώνιον, *Stadiasmus Maris Magni,* 318, 319, 355 (ed. C. Müller, *Geographi Graeci Minores,* Paris: Firmin Didot, 1882, I.505, 514), of 1st BC/1st AD; *prom. Samonium* in Pomponius Mela 2.7.112 (early 1st AD); Σαλμωνίδος ἄχρι καρήνου, in Dionysius Periegiesis 110 (verse, probably early 2nd AD, *GGM* II.109); τῆς Σαλμωνίδος ἄκρης, in Schol. ad Dion. Perieg. 109 (*GGM* II.436); ὑπὲρ Σαλμωνίδος ἄκρης, in Apollonius Rhodius *Argon.* 4.1693 (verse, 3rd BC). The most precise navigational description is given in the *Stadiasmus:* ἀκρωτήριόν ἐστι τῆς Κρήτης ἀνέχον πρὸς βορρᾶν ἐπιπολύ· ἐστι δὲ ἱερὸν Ἀθηνᾶς· ἔχει ὕφορμον καὶ ὕδωρ· τὰ δὲ ἄλλα ἠφανισμένα (318, GGM, I.505). A number of votive graffiti are preserved from the temple (M. Guarducci, *I. Cret,* 3.7.1-27).

[105] Smith, pp. 84-85 and sketch facing p. 254.

[106] Smith, pp. 259-60, with sketch facing p. 260.

[107] The *Stadiasmus* describes the coast between the better-known city of Lebena and Matala thus: ἀπὸ Λεβήνας εἰς Ἀλὰς στάδιοι κʹ. Ἀπὸ Ἀλῶν εἰς Μάταλαν στάδιοι τʹ (322-23, GGM I.506-507). 'Halae' is taken here to be the same place as Lasaea, and Müller conjectures νʹ and πʹ to make the distances fit. I have not substantiated the supposed equivalence with 'Lasos or Alos' in Pliny *NH* 4.12.59, (*BC* 4.328; Bruce, p. 454-55; Haenchen, p. 699n.), for the critical apparatus in the Teubner edition of C. Mayhoff does not list 'Alos' among the variants, but the different corruptions 'Lappa' and 'Laspha', and in any case Pliny's 'Lasos' is among the *inland* cities of Crete, a position unsuitable to the other references, as to the ruins discovered on the shore. The problem is considerably complicated by the number of cities with more or less similar names in other parts of Crete: Lisses, Lyctus, Lato, Lappa, and their numerous overlapping variants which lend themselves to a compounding of confusion. Most of these however may be clearly identified, despite the divergences of the literary authorities and their

27:9 The 'Fast' was the Day of Atonement on 10th Tishri, which we suppose Paul to have observed at Fair Havens. In the year 59 this fell later than in adjacent years, about 5th October.[108] It is notable that the occasion is placed by recall of Paul's Jewish observance, and the fact that the Fast is mentioned rather than the beginning of the Feast of

transmission, and the same holds true of Lasaea. The clearest parallel with Acts is (significantly) in an inscription, a lengthy list of θεωροδόκοι, in effect consular representatives of Delphi in hundreds of cities of the Greek world, listed in geographical sequence (Plassart, 'Inscriptions', BCH 45 [1921], pp. 1-85). Col. IV, lines 7-10, names consecutively the men ἐν Γόρτυνι ... ἐν Λεβῆνι ... ἐν Λασσοίαι ... ἐν Φαίστωι, a group disposed clockwise in the angle southwest from Gortyn, between the plain of Mesará and the precipitous line of coast terminating in Cape Matala (Lithino). Allowing for varieties of transcription, complicated by the progress of itacism and the peculiarities of different Greek dialects within Crete, this is quite close to Acts, and constitutes a confirmation of the civic status of a place otherwise little known. The name is further attested, in the form 'Lisia' in Tab. Pent., as 16 miles from Cortina (Gortyn, Gortyna; K. Miller, Itineraria Romana [Stuttgart: Strecker and Schröder, 1916] col. 1610). Several brief inscriptions have been found at the actual site (I. Cret. 1.15. 1-5).

The only two cities of major importance on the eastern half of the south coast of Crete were Hierapytna and Lebena, the latter a centre of Asclepian cult and the principal port of Gortyn the Roman capital city. Inscriptions of the area occasionally reflect maritime interests or the development of travel facilities. A restoration of roads and footways was undertaken under Claudius in the Hierapytna district (I. Cret. 3.3.25-29). I have noted also the personal names Κατάπλους (I. Cret. 3.3.39, of Hierapytna), Εὔπλους (I. Cret. 3.9.1, E. Crete, of uncertain place) and possibly the fem. Εὐπλε(ί)a (I. Cret. 2.20.3, of Phoenix; cf. Acts 27:12). The goddess Hygieia, associated with Asclepius at Lebena, there bears the epithets Σωτείρα Συνοδοιπόρος (I. Cret. 1.17.26A, of Lebena, 2nd-3rd AD). The record there of an Asclepian miracle also involves the κυβερνήτης of a ship and mentions a κατάλυμα (presumably a lodging ashore), though the fragmentary context precludes clearer understanding (I. Cret. 1.17.10). These gleanings are slight in themselves, but gain interest from their collocation on this remote and largely precipitous shore less ostensibly attractive than the north coast save as developed through the exigencies of westward navigation.

Ptol. Geog. 3.17.4 does not mention Lasaea, but places Lebena precisely by latitude and longitude behind the headland Leon, close to the ruins of Lasaea, calling it Λεβήνα ἢ Λεία. There may be some further corruption or confusion here. While Ptolemy is in general an excellent authority, there is a distortion apparent in this district, especially with relation to the inland sites like Gortyn. For his method and its problems, cf. H.S. Cronin, 'Ptolemy's Map of Asia Minor: Method of Construction', Geographical Journal 25 (1905), pp. 429-41.

The principal variants here are λασαια LPS ς, λασσαια ℵ, λασεα B81, λαισσα ℵ*, αλασσα A 181 460 syhm, anchis h, t(h)alassa lat plerique. The first three are virtually identical in itacistic pronunciation; anchis is thought to have arisen from ἄγχι for ἐγγύς.

108 Bruce, Acts, p. 455.

Tabernacles on 15th Tishri suggests that that date had not yet arrived. A relatively late date for these lunar-based festivals in the year concerned is desirable in accounting for the lapse of time through the following winter (cf. D, p. 174, and G, p. 192).[109]

27:11 The principal persons responsible for the ship are designated the ναύκληρος (owner/master) and the κυβερνήτης (pilot), but both defer to the centurion as an imperial officer on a ship contracted to the state service. Paul may have been included in their consultation as a man of standing and experience who had won Julius' respect; he may have offered his advice more informally.[110]

[109] See W.P. Workman, 'A New Date-Indication in Acts', *ExpT* 11 (1899-1900), pp. 316-19. He stresses the force of καί before νηστείαν, as applying to a year when the Fast was later than the autumnal equinox, when sailing became dangerous, and so Luke stresses that *two* landmarks of autumn had passed, and this the later. The general force of his argument is convincing, though it might with advantage have been presented a little differently: (1) His focus on the equinox derives from Caesar, *Bell. Gall.* 4.36.2 and 5.23.5, passages referring to Caesar's British campaigns rather than the norms of Mediterranean navigation. Certainly Caesar would have desisted from campaigning and activity in unknown waters before the risk of winter storms, but the regularities of Mediterranean conditions in summer are not applicable, and it would have been better for Workman to base his point on Vegetius *de Re Milit.* 4.39, who says navigation is safe until 14th September, uncertain until 11th November, and then the seas are closed until 10th March. (2) While accepting the force of καί νηστείαν ('even the Fast was already past'), Workman's argument from comparative dating with the equinox seems a little forced: the reader would hardly have got the point unless primed with the Jewish chronology of that year. But the late incidence of the Fast does best suit the time-sequence of the succeeding winter, and does suit the placing of this scene in October 59 in concurrence with other indications.

[110] This simple statement overlies much dispute. I am content to leave my point at the general level of Luke's familiarity with the terminology and functions. Ramsay's picture of the centurion as superior officer taking the professional and other advice of an improvised *consilium* (*SPTR*, pp. 322-25) is illuminating in its portrayal of the essential 'otherness' of Roman practices and structures. Haenchen's criticisms (*Acts*, pp. 699n, 700) are not necessarily relevant here to the question of Luke's accurate knowledge, but they are not well judged in regard to Ramsay's understanding of ναύκληρος and κυβερνήτης, especially in the implication that the meaning of ναύκληρος had shifted from 'captain' to 'owner' since the Ptolemaic period. In the first edition of *SPTR*, to which I refer, Ramsay cites several passages in ancient literature and epigraphy in his discussion, but not the *later* comment of U. Wilcken in *Archiv für Papyrusforschung* 5 (1913), p. 298, to which Haenchen refers his view. Haenchen's proof-texts for the meaning 'owner' are themselves of early date (*OGIS* 140.7-9, of Ptolemy VIII; and 591.3 of Delos, early 1st BC), and *neither* of them proves his point. Both refer to guilds, the former τῶν | ἐν Ἀλεξανδρείαι πρεσβυτέρων ἐ | γδοχέων, the latter of ἐμπόρων καὶ ναυκλήρων καὶ ἐγδοχέων in Berytus (Beirut). The precise distinction of these terms, and the function of the last (*LSJ* ἐκδοχεύς = 'forwarding agent'), are not

27:12 'Fair Havens' was a poorly sheltered roadstead (cf. on 27:8 above).

27:12 'Phoenix' has been the centre of much debate.[111] Setting aside the possibility that Strabo 10.4.3 = 475 refers to a different place ('Phoenix of the Lampians') which if rightly placed has no harbour,[112] the site must be placed close to Cape Mouros, a rocky projection of the precipitous coast with a bay on either side, the eastern now occupied by the tiny fishing village of Loutro, the western larger and more open, now deserted, but still bearing the name Phineka. Ogilvie shows decisively that in ancient conditions the western bay was safer than it is now, and contained two recessed beaches on the western flank of the headland facing northwest and southwest respectively.[113]

settled here. ναύκληρος is not even mentioned in the former text. Conversely, there are many references to ναύκληροι. The fullest study is now Julie Vélissaropoulos, *Les naucléres grecs. Recherches sur les institutions maritimes en Grèce et dans l'Orient hellénisé* (Geneva: Droz and Paris: Minard, 1980), though this focuses on the pre-Roman period. See also Casson, *Ships and Seamanship*, pp. 314-16 for the view that the ναύκληρος was 'owner'/'charterer' who sailed with his ship, the hierarchy of officers on board a merchant ship being, according to Artemidorus (*Oneirocr.* 1.35; 2nd A D), ναύκληρος, κυβερνήτης, πρωπεύς, τοίχαρχος, πέρίνεως. Vélissaropoulos traces the long history of the ναυκληρία as an institution, and insists that it eludes modern definition (p. 48). Its importance, however, declined in the Hellenistic and Roman periods in the very fact of state intervention as 'partenaire privilégié', requisitioning private ships in the public service (p. 4). The ἐγδοχεῖς she defines as *entrepositaires*. (p. 108 n. 103). Cf. also the terminology used in inscriptions, e.g. *IG* 12.8.581A (ἀρχικερδέμπορος), 585 (ναύκληρος, προναύκληρος, κυβερνητής, Thasos).

The usage of both ναύκληρος and κυβερνήτης may be more flexible than is sometimes allowed. The former may, it seems, comprise the functions of owner, master and merchant-contractor, and indeed the term ναυκληροκυβερνήτης is found in the papyri (cf. Cic. *de Inventione* 2.51.154, *dominus navis, cum idem gubernator esset*). In a case such as the present, where the element of official Roman control over a regular contracted fleet is strong, it is possible that ν. and κ. reflect respectively the Latin terms *magister* and *gubernator*. For the special development and organization of the corn-supply service under Claudius, in response to the droughts and famines of his reign (cf. Acts 11:28), see Suet. *Claud.* 18-19. Cf. also the inscription of Phoenix cited below.

[111] The most valuable discussion is that of R.M. Ogilvie, 'Phoenix', *JTS* n.s. 9 (1958), pp. 308-14.

[112] See Ogilvie, pp. 308-309.

[113] Smith (3rd edn) includes testimonies to the harbour of the eastern bay of Loutro: 'it is the only secure harbour in all winds on the south coast of Crete' (pp. 91-92n). His identification however poses difficulty in understanding the phrase κατὰ λίβα καὶ κατὰ χῶρον, which despite his parallels, can only be naturally understood of the west-facing bay. To the range of evidence in Ogilvie we may add the details of latitude and longitude in Ptolemy, to which he refers only

27:12 The form χῶρος (northwest) is taken to be a ἅπαξ λεγόμενον, supposedly a faulty Greek transcription of Latin *caurus* or *corus*. The nomenclature of the winds is a notoriously complex and confused matter, with many duplicates and alternatives in both Greek and Latin. It is strange that the commentators have overlooked the twelve-point wind-rose inscription on a monumental base from Rome (*IGRR* 1.177 = *IG* 14.1308) which gives the Latin form *chorus*

implicitly (p. 311). Ptolemy (*Geog.* 3.17.3) reads from the west Ἑρμαία ἄκρα νγιβ' λδ [53 1/12° E, 34° N]. Φοινικοῦς λιμήν νγλ' λδ ς' [53 1/2° E, 34 1/6° N]. Φοῖνξ πόλις νγλιβ' λδ δ' [53 7/12°E, 34 1/4° N]. Hermaea is placed as a westward promontory, and the harbour of Phoenix is then placed 5 minutes south and 5 minutes west of the city. Ancient habitation covered most of the Cape Mouros peninsula behind Loutro, and the port was then clearly on its west side. The place is forbiddingly inhospitable by modern standards. I have seen recent photographs taken by Mr J.P. Stunt from the roadless and precipitous hinterland. Yet two ancient settlements, Aradena and Anopolis, both represented today by places preserving the ancient names, lay immediately behind the coastal heights, the latter a mere mile behind Loutro, and constituting the 'Upper City' with relation to Phoenix.

Ogilvie shows the former existence of two sheltered beaches on the west side, whose bearing gives precise point to the difficult phrase. There is then no need to regard λίψ and χῶρος here as a confused conflation of two nautical terms for 'west' (*BC* 5.343). The note on the winds in *BC* 5.338-44 is disappointing, especially in its neglect of the crucial epigraphical texts. I take the point that Luke got his information from sailors' speech, but it was much more precise information than the incomplete account of Lake and Cadbury can show. Ramsay (*SPTR*, p. 326) unnecessarily supposed that Luke got a false impression from sailors' description of the eastern bay, and never saw the place himself to correct that impression.

For the site of Phoenix see also *Stadiasmus* 328 (*GGM* I.507-508): ἀπὸ Ἀπολλωνίας εἰς Φοίνικα στάδιοι ρ' · πόλις ἐστιν· ἔχει λιμένα καὶ νῆσον. Ἀπὸ δὲ Κλαυδίας εἰς Φοίνικα στάδιοι τ' (for Claudia/Cauda see on 27:16 and p. 142, n. 117 below). The inscriptions are collected in *I. Cret.* 2.20.1-7, and a few fragments are also preserved from Anopolis and Aradena. The only text of any length from Phoenix (*I. Cret.* 2.20.7 = *CIL* 3.3, first published in Smith, p. 261) is of exceptional interest. It is a Latin dedication to Jupiter, to other gods, and to Trajan, by personnel of a wintering ship, the work being supervised by a *gubernator* from Alexandria, and the owner or master is also named, though the term *navicularius/nauclerus* is not used. Other remarkable parallels of terminology in this text will be noted on 28:11 below. It is an extraordinarily interesting illustration of several aspects of Paul's voyage, found precisely at the place where the responsible officers would have chosen to winter. It is remarkable that it is not noticed in the commentaries, perhaps because it is not mentioned in *SPTR*, nor in the usual reference works, save for a strangely erroneous entry appended to the new (1979) edition of *BAGD*.

The name 'Phoenix' points again to Phoenician influence on this coast, and reinforces again the sense of its unexpected maritime importance.

for the Greek λάπυξ (elsewhere *argestes, seiron,* etc.).[114] Luke could have taken the name from the speech of seamen, probably a Latin or hybrid patois (cf. εὑρακύλων for *euraquilo,* 27:14 below).

27:13 The south wind was ideal for reaching Phoenix, enabling them to cling to the coast to round Cape Matala, about 4 miles west, and then bear west-northwest across the bay of Mesará, some 34 miles to Phoenix (Smith, p. 97). There is a noted tendency of a south wind in these climes to back suddenly to a violent north-easter, the well-known *gregale.* This would have swept down upon them from the open plain of Mesará, just when they were in the open bay, beyond the shelter of Matala.

27:14 The reading εὑρακύλων p⁷⁴ א A B* (*euroaquilo* it^(ar,gig,s) vg) is to be preferred to εὑροκλύδων P^(mg) Ψ *al.* Despite the erroneous belief that the word is 'not found elsewhere and therefore suspect', it is an unsatisfactory hybrid neologism mixing Greek and Latin, north with southeast,[115] and attested epigraphically on the twelve-point wind-rose incised on a pavement at Thugga in proconsular Africa, which bears the wind-names in Latin only. Beginning from the north and reading clockwise, we have: *septentrio aquilo euroaquilo [vu]lturnus*

---

[114] See further G. Kaibel, 'Antike Windrosen', *Hermes* 20 (1885), pp. 579-624; D'Arcy Wentworth Thompson, 'The Greek Winds', *CR* 32 (1918), pp. 49-56. Lake and Cadbury are surely right in preferring the latter in the matter of the regular disposition of the ancient 12-point scheme in 30° divisions, but this is not the central point here. This arrangement could have been inferred from the epigraphical monuments, which they do not notice, esp. *CIL* 8.26652 (cited below); cf. *IG* 14.1308 here and *IG* 14.906. See my further discussions in 'Euraquilo and Melita', *JTS* n.s. 26 (1975), pp. 100-11, esp. pp. 102-103.

[115] For this objection see A. Acworth, 'Where Was St. Paul Shipwrecked? A Reexamination of the Evidence', *JTS* n.s. 24 (1973), pp. 190-93 (esp. p. 192). Acworth argues for the TR reading Εὑροκλύδων, interpreting this as a southeast wind, and reviving an old view that the Melita of Paul's shipwreck was not Malta but Mljet in the Adriatic. A similar case for Mljet has been presented independently by O.F.A. Meinardus, 'Melita Illyrica or Africana; An Examination of the Site of St. Paul's Shipwreck', *Ostkirchliche Studien* 23 (1974), pp. 21-36; cf. 'St. Paul Shipwrecked in Dalmatia', *BA* 39 (1976), pp. 145-47; 'Dalmatian and Catalonian Traditions about St. Paul's Journeys', *Ekklesiastikos Pharos* 61 (1979), pp. 221-30. I have responded to Acworth's arguments in the article cited above. Meinardus' work focuses rather on the local traditions of Mljet.

On Acworth's point here we may observe that in this complicated nomenclature of winds and nautical language there is much mutual interpenetration of Greek and Latin formation, translation and transliteration. Thus the aptly parallel hybrid *euroauster* (Isidoris, *Orig.* 13.11.6) occurs in Latin beside the pure 'Greek' *euronotus* (Pliny *N H* 2.46.120; Columella 11.2.42) and *eurus* and *aquilo* are never so far divergent as southeast and north in documents of the Roman period (see *JTS* n.s. 26 [1975], p. 103). The actual example cited from Thugga is in any case decisive against this sort of theoretical objection.

eurus etc. (*CIL* 8.26652). And although *vulturnus*, often elsewhere the Latin equivalent of *eurus*, is here interpolated, the compound lies between its components, in the position 30° north of east. There is also a partial parallel in Vegetius, *de Re.Milit.* 4.38, who gives *euroborus* in this position as the Latin (!) counterpart of *caecias*. As *boreas* equals *aquilo*, *euroborus* (*euroboreas*) should be exactly equivalent to *euraquilo*.[116] We conclude that *euraquilo* is an unusual, but logically formed, nautical term which a traveller is likely to have heard from sailors speaking a Latin or mixed jargon, and precisely apposite to the circumstances of Paul's voyage.

27:16 A square-rigged ancient ship, having no option but to be driven before a gale, finds transient shelter for completing necessary manoeuvres in the lee of the island of Cauda, which lay west-south-west of the likely point of impact of the storm beyond the protection of Cape Matala. The island is thus precisely placed, and correctly named, subject again to orthographic and declensional variants, both in the manuscripts and in other sources.[117]

27:16 The manoeuvres here described again relate to emergency measures necessary for the safety of the ship in its particular plight.

---

[116] *Euroborus* functions in Vegetius' scheme as the Latin equivalent of *caecias*. Pliny omits to give a Latin rendering of *caecias* (*NH* 2.46.120), and Seneca knew of no name for it in Latin (*Apud nos sine nomine est*, *Quaest.Nat.*5.16.4), and it is elsewhere confused with winds of different bearing. Thus *caecias* is (surprisingly) the cardinal east in Seneca, but north of east in Vegetius; yet in *I G* 14.1308 it is equated with *vulturnus*, though *vulturnus* in turn is placed by Aulus Gellius 2.22 even south of *eurus* and next to *notus* at the cardinal south. *Euraquilo* (*euroboreas*), for all its rarity, fills an acknowledged gap in the system of nomenclature in the position 30° north of east.

[117] καυδα Ｎcorr vg syp; κλαυδα Ｎ(A)81 vgcodd syh sah boh κλαυδην LPSς. The *Stadiasmus* has Κλαυδία at 300 stades from Phoenix (pp. 139-40, n. 113), and adds that the island possessed a city and a harbour. Ptolemy (*Geog.* 3.17.8) lists it as Κλαῦδος νῆσος among the islands off Crete, and also says it had a city, giving it a position on his reckoning at 52 1/2° E 34° N, a dislocation northwest, too near the west end of Crete. Pliny (*NH* 4.12.61) mentions an island Gaudos off Crete, but locates it off Hierapytna in the southeast, some 90 miles east of the true position of our island. Other versions of the name include Caudos (Pomponius Mela 2.7.114); Καῦδος (attributed to Strabo 17.3.22 = 838; a dubious reading); and Καυδώ (Suidas). The best criterion here is that of local documentary usage, the only examples of which are early and dialectal. There is extant from the island a dedication to Δί Καυδίοι (*I. Cret.* 2.7.1, of c. 3rd BC) and a treaty document from Gortyna (*I. Cret.* 4.184) refers to τοῖς τὰν Κα[ῦ]Ｉδον Ｆοικίονσι (lines 4-5), τὸνς Ｉ ἐν Καυδοῖ Ｆοικίοντανς (lines 8-9), etc. (early 2nd BC).

An original 'Caud-' may well have become corrupted or been deliberately changed to the imperial 'Claud-'. It is significant to contrast the incidental accuracy of a personal record in its implications for the location of the island with the vagaries of the literary geographers.

First, the ship's boat was hauled in. It was normal practice in less extreme weather to tow it behind the ship, but that became dangerous in a storm. σκάφη, itself a good Greek word, here probably reflects the use of its Latin borrowing *scapha* as a technical term for such a boat (Caesar *Bell. Gall.* 4.26.4, etc.) where later Greek usage preferred ἐφολκίς or ἐφόλκιον (Strabo, Plutarch, Philostratus, *et al.*).[118] The difficulty of bringing in the boat was no doubt due to its being waterlogged.[119]

27:17 There has been considerable debate over the precise manner of this procedure of 'undergirding the ship', but it is sufficiently clear that the point was to hold together and reinforce the hull against the battering of the waves across what must inevitably be a long traverse of open sea.[120]

27:17 The phrase χαλάσαντες τὸ σκεῦος is another that has been subject to varied interpretation. The best understanding is still probably that of Smith (pp. 110-11). All superfluous sail and rigging was taken down, and only a minimal storm-sail retained, as necessary to keep the ship steady. It is likely that Luke reports this action without a seaman's appreciation of its navigational importance.[121] Smith

---

[118] See Casson, *Ships*, pp. 248 n. 93, 399; cf. Acts 27:30.

[119] Smith, p. 106.

[120] See the discussion by Cadbury, 'Ὑποζώματα', *BC* 5.345-54. The question hinges partly on the meaning given to βοηθεῖαι. Assuming that the participle ὑποζωννύντες is not used in a merely general sense, of 'preparing (warships) for action' (Polybius 27.3.3), we may note four suggested views: (1) exterior cables transversely round the bottom of the hull; (2) exterior cables longitudinally round the hull from bow to stern on either side; (3) transverse interior braces across the hold; (4) lengthwise interior, a 'hogging truss'. While Cadbury inclines to (4), I prefer (1), the procedure known as 'frapping': the literal force of the verb inevitably suggests the passing of a brace underneath the hull, and this action seems feasible during a brief respite from the full force of the weather, whereas a lengthwise bracing in such conditions was scarcely practicable (Smith, pp. 106-108; Ramsay, *SPTR*, pp. 329). The βοηθεῖαι are then probably the ὑποζώματα, the cables carried on board for this purpose in emergency, their use here being expressed in the verb; they are not 'nautical expedients' in general, nor props to tighten an internal brace, nor need the word be emended to βοείαις, 'ropes of ox-hide' (S.A. Naber, 'Nautica', *Mnemosyne*, 23 [1895], pp. 267-69). Casson, *Ships*, p. 91 (and n. 74) argues for (2), citing J.S. Morrison and R.T. Williams, *Greek Oared Ships 900-322 BC* (CUP, 1968), pp. 294-98. This however remains indecisive, for their account is directed to the preparatory work done at the launching of oared warships for action, not to a storm-emergency on a sailing merchantman at sea, when different necessities and possibilities were operative.

[121] The word σκεῦος is of debated meaning here, and has been altered in syP and some miniscules into τὰ ἱστία or other reinterpretations, perhaps representing a Western tradition where D is deficient. The question may be put whether it is an

brings out the significance of laying the ship to on a starboard tack, with its right side pointed into the wind, to make as much leeway as possible northward of the natural line of drift, and so away from the Syrtis (below). To do this was a necessity of prudent seamanship, and the sequel shows it was managed with success.

27:17 A ship driven by a persistent east-northeast from this area was in danger of reaching a lee-shore on the coast of Cyrenaica, off which 'the Syrtis', an extensive zone of shallows and quicksands, formed a notorious navigational hazard and inspired an obsessional fear constantly mentioned in first-century literature.[122] Acworth's objection that σύρτις denotes, not this danger, but a sandbank between two entrances to the harbour of Phoenix, must be rejected.[123]

27:18-19 The ship was lightened. They began to jettison the cargo (cf. 27:38) and 'the spare gear',[124] presumably all that was not now essential to survival. Smith supposes the main-yard, an immense spar requiring the efforts of all to cast overboard.[125]

---

informal, a technical or a collective/comprehensive term. It is perhaps the last, like the Vulgate *vas*. There is record of a ship's officer entitled σκευοφύλαξ in a papyrus letter (*SB* 8.9780, of mid 3rd BC), which Casson (*Ships*, p. 400) renders 'guard of equipment and gear', cf. *LSJ*.

[122] Cf. e.g. Verg. *Aen.* 1.111, 146, etc.; Tibullus 3.4.91; Propertius 2.9.33, etc.; Horace *Odes* 1.22.5, etc.; Ovid *Metam.* 8.120; Strabo 17.3.20 = 835-36; Sen. *Hippol.* 569-70; Lucan, *Phars.* 1.367, 499, 686, etc. *passim*; Valerius Flaccus *Argon.* 7.86; Pliny *NH* 5.4.26; Silius Italicus *Pun.* 17.634.

[123] (1) 'Syrtis' is properly a geographical name, not a common noun for 'sandbank', which is θίς. (2) There is no evidence for the supposition that a sandbank at Phoenix caused a hazard. Though the shoreline is now evidently much changed in detail through seismic uplift, the approaches would have been deep, probably deeper than now (Ogilvie, pp. 312-13). (3) The application of σύρτις to a feature at Phoenix is open to the more fundamental objection that it is not even mentioned in the same context as Phoenix, but five verses later when the ship is already in the lee of Cauda. On a natural reading of the text, it is the fear of grounding on the Syrtis which prompted the manoeuvre off Cauda. But if the ship were already driven west of Cauda, it was already too far west to reach the Cretan coast as far east as Phoenix on any easterly wind. (4) The distance to the Syrtis is no problem, for the wind, if rightly interpreted here, would drive the ship straight towards it if they took no precaution.

The fear of the Syrtis is conversely decisive in support of the wind direction also (cf. *BC* 5.344). It blew 'down from' Crete (κατά + gen.), an offshore wind, not 'against' Crete, as Acworth argues, κατά commonly means 'against' in a metaphorical, not a literal, sense. See my full discussion and the parallels in *JTS* n.s. 26 (1975), pp. 104-105 and p. 104n. This wind was funneled down a lowland basin to strike them when bereft of shelter. It is not to be understood as coming off the mountains further west.

[124] Bruce, *Acts*, p. 460.

[125] Smith, p. 114. Wikenhauser (p. 418) renders σκεῦος in v. 17 as *Treibanker* (sea

27.20 Hope was progressively abandoned as the ship endured longer the buffeting of the waves. The focus of the anxiety was not so much the storm as the state of the ship, and the prospect of foundering at sea. The crisis of despair may have come among the crew when they realized they had probably missed Sicily and could never survive in the vain hope of reaching the Tunisian coast intact.[126]

27:21 Long abstinence from food is a feature plausibly seen to reflect personal experience. Among the contributory causes were probably the impossibility of cooking and damage to provisions and facilities.[127]

27:27 The fourteenth night: in a remarkable calculation, based inevitably on a compounding of estimates and probabilities, confirmed in the judgment of experienced Mediterranean navigators, Smith (pp. 122-26) concluded that at midnight on the fourteenth night the ship, after performing the necessary procedures here described, would have drifted to a point some $2^{1}/2$ miles from the entrance to St. Paul's Bay in Malta. This is of course coincidental, for he has to use arbitrary averages and approximations as the basis for rigid calculation. No doubt it is fortuitous that the errors have so closely cancelled out, but the possibility of showing so remarkable a fit, even in principle, is a striking confirmation of the narrative.[128]

27:27 Adria here evidently means the sea between Crete and Malta, bounded on the northwest by Sicily and the foot of Italy. The

---

anchor) to act as a brake on their drift, citing Plut. *de Garrulitate* 10 (*Mor.* 507a): νεὼς μὲν γὰρ ἁρπαγείσης ὑπὸ πνεύματος ἐπιλαμβάνονται σπείραις καὶ ἀγκύραις τὸ τάχος ἀμβλύνοντες, but notes that Balmer took it of the main yard, as not needed with a storm-sail. Here he renders σκεύη as *die Gesamtheit der Schiffsgeräte*. The crucial objection to the supposition that they dropped a sea-anchor is that their only hope in the open sea was now in a rapid landfall, even on a lee-shore, before the weakened ship foundered with all hands far from land. D.J. Clark, 'What Went Overboard First?' *BT* 26 (1975), pp. 144-46, makes the attractive suggestion of taking ἐκβολὴν ἐποιοῦντο as conative rather than inceptive, thus contrasting an implicitly unsuccessful (mechanical) manoeuvre with a manual unloading the next day (v. 19). This gives point to αὐτόχειρες without invoking the variant ἐρρίψαμεν. The first part of the supposed antithesis is not however explicit.

[126] Smith, pp. 114-15; *JTS* 26, pp. 107-108.

[127] Smith, pp. 115-17.

[128] The most serious error of principle in Smith's work consists in his treatment of the term *euraquilo* as denoting east-northeast in the modern, 16-point sense rather than E 30° N on the 12-point scheme. As however he estimates, on independent corroborating criteria, that the actual bearing of the wind was slightly north of east-northeast, actually east-northeast 1/4 N, or about E 28° N, the error is small enough in practice to be absorbed easily into the other imponderables.

sea now called the Adriatic was distinguished as the 'Adriatic Gulf' or 'Gulf of Adria'. Paul, like Josephus at almost the same date (*Vita* 3.15), voyaged across 'Adria', the sector of the open Mediterranean called 'Αδρίας in Ptolemy. Paul's days at sea in the storm were '*in*' Adria; he was driven across it and upon a shore at its farthest limit. Such was Malta.[129]

27:27 The sailors recognized that they were near shore. It is not explained how. Smith (pp. 119-22) has a most interesting passage here. If their landfall was indeed at the traditional St. Paul's Bay, which appears otherwise uniquely apt to the topographical indications of the story, he argues that a ship driven from the east must have passed within a quarter of a mile of the low rocky point of Koura, where the breakers are particularly violent in an easterly gale. They would have seen the breaking foam, but nothing of the shore or its configuration.[130]

---

[129] Acworth's argument here presupposes that 'Adria' means the 'Adriatic' in the modern sense. While it is only fair to recognize the elusiveness and variability in usage of this, as of many other geographical terms, there is strong and explicit evidence for the use of the word in the Roman period in the manner understood here. In Herodotus it is clearly the Adriatic; many later references are inconclusive or ambivalent. Strabo (5.1.3 = 211) likens the size and shape of 'Adria' to that of the main trunk of the adjacent peninsular section of Italy, and Polybius successively applies κόλπος and θάλαττα without appearing to make the same distinction as later in Ptolemy (Polybius 2.14.4 with 2.16.4). Ptol. *Geog.* distinguishes τὸ 'Αδριατικὸν πέλαγος (sometimes just 'Αδρίας, 3.4.1 with 3.4.4) from ὁ 'Αδριατικὸς κόλπος (or ὁ ῍Αδριος κόλπος). The 'sea' is the expanse limited explicitly by named places under the foot of Italy (3.1), by Sicily (3.4.1), by the Peloponnese (3.14.1), and by Crete (3.15.1). Crete, he says, 'is bordered on the west by the Adriatic Sea'. It is the whole sea south and west of Greece. Other references could doubtless be added. I have noted Suidas, 'Αρέθουσα (ed. G. Bernhardy 1.702); many other instances of the name are given in Wetstein 2.644-45.

[130] Other suggestions for recognizing land are open to objection. (a) The smells of land would certainly not be carried seaward in a gale blowing from the sea. (b) There is no question of a drift-anchor striking bottom, for this was twenty fathoms deep. In any case we have argued against the supposition that the ship used an anchor to retard their landfall with a breaking ship. (c) It seems less likely in the circumstances that they heard rather than saw the surf, amid the roar of the storm. The breaking of white foam was the *only* visual indication likely on such a night, and its exceptional violence about Koura was at once a plain sign and a source of renewed terror.

This whole scene is interpreted here as related to the traditional location at St. Paul's Bay, for which Smith makes a strong case, and the reality of this setting is implicit in Haenchen (pp. 707-708). I have not seen W. Burridge, *Seeking the Site of St. Paul's Shipwreck* (Malta: Progress Press, 1952), reviewed by J. C(assar) P(ullicino) in *Melita Historica* 1 (1952-55), p. 185. Burridge favours the neighbouring bay of Mellieha, where evidence survives of Roman wrecks; cf. D.H.

27:28 βολίσαντες is precisely the term used for taking soundings.[131] A number of ancient sounding leads have been recovered. They had a hollow on the underside, which was filled with tallow or grease to bring up adhering samples of the sea-bottom (Casson, *Ships*, p. 246).

27:28 The actual soundings offered here correspond closely, according to Smith, with the circumstances of approach to St. Paul's Bay. They would probably have been in near twenty fathoms of water at the point where they became aware of the point of Koura, and fifteen when they became aware of seas breaking on a precipitous shore ahead.[132] He suggests the interval was perhaps half an hour, corresponding to a suitable 3/4 mile of driving before the wind. These 'realistic' considerations militate against Conzelmann's treatment of the the number as 'literarisch',[133] for Luke would not have stood beside the man sounding.

27:29 Casting anchors from the stern was the right emergency action to take in the circumstances, though exceptional then as now. It prevented the immediate peril of letting the ship swing round broadside to the waves and of being smashed stern first on the rocks. It was all-important that the anchors should hold, and the ground in St. Paul's Bay is 'of extraordinary tenacity'.[134] Luke was not a seaman and appears to transmit the unusual necessity without technical understanding. Smith shows both that this was a necessary resource for ships of this kind forced on a lee-shore, and also cites a parallel from the *Antichità di Ercolano* illustrating how anchor-cables were attached to the stern.[135] The first object was to hold the ship from being dashed on the rocks, the second to await daylight in the hope of finding a place to run ashore bow first with some prospect of safety.

27:30 The episode of the sailors lowering the boat is not without

---

Trump, *Malta: An Archaeological Guide* (London: Faber, 1972), p. 145.

[131] This word has been treated as a ἅπαξ λεγόμενον. See however Casson, *Ships*, p. 390, for the rendering 'heave the lead', and MM's reference to Wetstein, *ad loc.*, who gives five references to Eustathius' commentaries on Homer, with the implication that this was a well-known term in older Greek, though, being a specialized term, it happens not to survive elsewhere in works preserved to us. Thus in discussing the word βόλος Eustathius writes ὅθεν καὶ ῥῆμα σπουδαῖον ἐν χρήσει τὸ βολίζειν, ἤγουν βάθος θαλάσσης μετρεῖν μολιβδίνη καθέτῳ ἢ τοιῷδε τινί (*ad Il.* 5.396, p. 427 ed. Bas. = Vol 2, p. 40 in the Leipzig edition [Weigel; 1825-30]). Cf. *ad Il.* 8.486, p. 615 = Leipzig 2.224; *ad Il.* 9.3, p. 624 = Leipzig 2.233; *ad Od.* 1.155, p. 39 = Leipzig *Od.* 1.40; *ad Od.* 1.424, p. 69 = Leipzig *Od.* 1.72. In Hdt. 2.5 a 'sounding lead' is καταπειρητηρίη.

[132] Smith, pp. 129-30 and chart facing p. 126.

[133] Conzelmann, p. 144.

[134] Smith, p. 130.

[135] Smith, pp. 131-32.

difficulty. There is no occasion for Haenchen's scepticism here. It was a natural instinct of the sailors to take a desperate chance to save their own lives at any cost to the rest. Haenchen notes that it was a necessary and legitimate proceeding to use the boat to attach an anchor to the bows in these circumstances, for the ship no longer had headway, and the anchor would not have taken hold if merely dropped vertically from the ship. It does not follow from the fact that their action could be given an innocent explanation that the narrative is wrong. Indeed, the command to fix bow anchors may precisely have provided occasion for their desperate betrayal. We may doubt Haenchen's confidence (*Acts*, p. 706) that if they remained on the ship there was no danger to their lives; the ship had taken such a battering that it might break up at any time, and desperate men would find it easier to risk death actively than wait passively. To insist here on Lukan redaction, evidently as glorifying Paul (Haenchen, *Acts*, p. 706n), begs the question whether the events, and Paul's part in them, are historically founded. If the events are better explained at nearer face value, Luke's hand may be seen rather in his preservation of the pertinent facts, without the professional seaman's perspective on them.[136]

27:31-32 The action of the soldiers in cutting away the boat is also open to debate. The safety of the whole party depended on having the skilled hands to work the ship, so it was essential to prevent the sailors' desertion. Whether the soldiers' action was a misunderstanding of Paul's advice which made escape more difficult, is less clear.[137] I take it that their case was more desperate than being able to wait to send the boat ashore after the storm, and that the captain's intention was to drive the ship bodily as high as possible up a shelving beach if such could be found at dawn. Whether tensions had polarized and exploded between soldiers and sailors is no more than fuel for speculation.[138]

---

[136] Thus I take it that he understood the need for stern-anchoring against the visually obvious peril of being dashed immediately on the rocks, but not necessarily the significance of other manoeuvres or the captain's calculations on the best prospect of bringing the ship ashore in safety. It is a more open question, not analysed by Luke, whether he intends us to see Paul here as possessing divinely inspired insight beyond a vigorous confidence in God's promise (17:24) and realism about human nature.

[137] Bruce, *Acts*, p. 464 *ad loc.*

[138] Paul's personality had evidently not made a transforming impact on the sailors and soldiers (cf. v. 42), as might have been supposed on Haenchen's picture of an unreal glorification of Paul. Part of the fascination of this narrative lies in his confrontation with the raw violence of passions and near break-down of discipline in men fighting for their lives, suddenly released from a controlled

27:33 Paul's advice to eat is meant to restore calm as well as to strengthen the crew for the tasks ahead. It is not without sense, since they can do nothing more than wait until daylight, but have meanwhile a precarious stability and the first glimmerings of light.[139]

27:37 The number of persons on board the ship: the larger figure of 276 is probably to be preferred to ὡς ἑβδομήκοντα (B sah).[140] This seems at first sight surprisingly large. Josephus (*Vita* 3.15) claims that there were 600 on board the ship on which he was shipwrecked in Adria— but we know that Josephus is prone to exaggerate numbers.[141] There is however considerable evidence of the size of larger ships in antiquity, and of the Alexandrian corn-freighters in particular. There is a valuable discussion in Casson, *Ships*, pp. 171-73. He argues that the imperial service preferred to use ships of at least 340 tons, and that giant freighters of perhaps 1300 tons plied between Alexandria and Rome (p. 172 n. 25). Lucian gives the actual dimensions of the 'Isis' (*Navig.* 5) as 120 x 30 x 29 cubits (180 x 45 x 43 1/2 ft), from which Casson infers a figure of 1228 tons on the basis of a keel length of 114 ft.[142] He finds no difficulty in Josephus' complement of 600, and suggests that Paul's 276 were on an off-season sailing, on a

and helpless resignation into a storm of conflicting emotions of hope and terror. Only the brevity and economy of the narrative deter the reader from undue speculation. We may limit comment to suggesting that the bald indications of a psychological realism are present, which derives from experience, not editing.

139 Cf. the tradition of Drake playing bowls on Plymouth Hoe, which seems to be attested at an early date. It has been suggested that the English fleet had to await the tide to put to sea, and the admiral's action was calculated to maintain morale through an enforced delay.

140 It has often been observed that the number 276, written COϛ after ΠΛΟΙΩ, could give rise, by a simple dittography, to πλοίῳ ὡς οϛ. ὡς before a numeral is indeed a characteristic Lukan usage, but is not appropriate here before an exact figure. Ropes (*BC* 3.247), Bruce (p. 466), Haenchen (p. 707n), Metzger (*Textual Comm.* pp. 499-500, probability (B)), and Marshall (p. 414) concur in preferring '276', though Lake and Cadbury (*BC* 4.336 *ad loc.*) incline to the B reading. Several other minor variants can be explained as having arisen from an original '276'. The observation of F.H. Colson, 'Triangular Numbers in the New Testament', *JTS* 16 (1915), pp. 67-76, that 276 is the 'triangular number' of 23 (p. 72), is the wrong kind of explanation, inappropriate and unhelpful here, and not to be invoked over the textual question.

141 Josephus' figure seems invariably to be quoted at face-value without raising the hypercritical redactional doubts which are reserved for Luke. Yet Josephus' unreliability in such matters can be demonstrated, and we should not be disposed to accept his testimony as certain merely because it offers a conveniently supportive large figure. It may indeed be right, or not far wrong, but I hesitate to build too simply on him.

142 Casson, *Ships*, pp. 186-89.

ship which could well have accommodated more.[143]

27:38 To lighten the ship becomes imperative at this stage. There had been a previous lightening of the ship at sea (v.18) when they had begun to sacrifice some part of the cargo, then apparently to prevent the ship being swamped in the storm, but now evidently in the hope of being able to run it as high as possible up a beach. Previously there had been need of ballast. Now everything has to go.[144]

27:39 At daylight they made out a creek with a sandy beach. Smith claimed to identify the place exactly from its proximity to a 'place of two seas' (τόπος διθάλασσος, v. 41), which apparently came into view close by only as they neared the coast, an apt description of the hidden channel separating the island of Salmonetta, which would have appeared hitherto a headland attached to the actual shore. According to Smith there were in his day two creeks on the west side of the lay along an otherwise rocky expanse, and though the one close to the 'meeting of two seas' had then no sandy beach, it was likely that this had been worn away by the sea. Its position suits admirably the probable line of approach of a ship now released again to run before an easterly wind, subject to careful steering and manoeuvre.

27:40 Smith (pp. 134, 138-39) explains the significance of the measures described here. When the ship was lightened, the objective selected, and all ready for the final dash to safety, these three actions,

---

143 The 'Isis' is said to have carried enough corn to feed all Attica for a year (*Navig.* 6). Casson (*Ships*, pp. 171-72 n. 23) cites epigraphic evidence from as early as the 3rd cent. BC, when a fragment of the port regulations of Thasos (*IG* 12 Supp. 348, emended *SEG* 17 [1960] 417) divided the harbour into two sections, one to take no ships of less than 300 talents (80 tons), the other nothing less than 500 talents (130 tons). He quotes from the jurist Scaevola (late 2nd AD) a regulation in *Dig.* 50.5.3 exempting from compulsory public burdens shipowners who have furnished the public service with a vessel of at least 50,000 *modii* (340 tons) or a number of vessels of 10,000 *modii* (68 tons). The calculations about the 'Isis' offered elsewhere are divergent, often vastly large. Casson shows that the length of keel is an essential factor, and he argues this from parallels which are likely to be closest in shape and function.

144 BC 4.337; Bruce, *Acts*, p. 466. The verb κουφίζω, here only in the New Testament, is widely used of 'lightening' a burden, literal or figurative, but in particular as a nautical term in contexts like the present. Cf. Polybius 20.5.11; Jonah 1:5 LXX. For σῖτον Naber (*Mnemosyne* 9 [1881], pp. 293-94) conjectured ἱστόν (mainmast) for he argues that the cargo had already been jettisoned at v. 18. But the imperfect tense there is inceptive, and a sufficient weight needed to be retained until their present straits dictated the total abandonment of the remainder. In any case the mast was capable of being lowered only on very small boats according to A. Breusing, *Die Nautik der Alten* (Bremen: Schünemann, 1886), p. 55, and it could scarcely be felled without critical damage to the breaking ship.

of cutting away the anchors, loosing the bands of the rudder and hoisting the foresail, performed simultaneously, put the ship immediately under control.[145]

27:41 The forepart of the ship stuck fast, but the stern began to be broken by the violence of the waves. Smith relates this to the local conditions.[146] The rocks of Malta disintegrate into very fine particles of sand and clay, which form mud in still water, but a tenacious clay where acted upon by surface water movements. So mud is found from below about three fathoms, which is about what a large ship would draw. Paul's ship was likely to have struck mud which quickly graduated into a shelving clay, where the forepart was held fast.[147]

---

[145] Anchoring from the stern was crucial here, for the ship was facing landward, and ready for the drive ashore. Several rare nautical terms are used here together. The rare word περιαιρεῖν is found both here and in 27:20 in different senses, and as a difficult variant in 28:13, where its sense is unclear, unless we may understand ἀγκύρας again, and take it of 'weighing anchor' from Syracuse. Smith (pp. 134, 138) takes it that they simply cut the cables, leaving the now-useless anchors embedded in the sea-bottom. The πηδάλιον was the 'steering-oar' (Latin *gubernaculum*), only the side-rudder being known in antiquity, but this being remarkably effective in controlling the movement of a great ship: cf. Lucian *Navig.* 6 (Casson, *Ships*, pp. 224, 397). A πηδάλιον would have been attached to each side of the stern by a ζευκτηρία, which Casson (*Ships*, pp. 228, 402) renders 'pennant-rope'. The ζευκτηρίαι served to lift the steering-oars when the ship was at anchor to prevent them banging about. This move instantly put the steering mechanism into operation. The third manoeuvre was the raising of the ἀρτέμων ('foresail', Casson, *Ships*, p. 390). Casson traces the history of this type of sail, as depicted in surviving art. The reference in this case is evidently to a small 'bowspritsail', slanting low over the bows, in order to be capable of being hoisted rapidly, and not give more canvas to the wind than could be controlled in the conditions for a shoreward run. This is the earliest occurrence of the word ἀρτέμων in Greek, though it is found in a different sense as a borrowing in Latin in Vitruvius 10.2.9 ('principal pulley', 'main block of a tackle', 1st BC). Its use is described in verse by Juvenal (*velo prora suo*, *Sat.* 12.697, and the scholiast glosses the passage with the actual use of the word *artemo*. It is also restored conjecturally (for *antenna*) in a passage of the elder Seneca (*Contr.* 7.1.2, early 1st AD), another case of a Greek word extant earlier as a Latin loan-word than in Greek.

[146] Smith, pp. 140-41.

[147] The reading ἐπέκειλαν (from ἐπικέλλω) is to be preferred to ἐπώκειλαν LPSs (from ἐποκέλλω). Both forms are rare, but the former is characteristic of poetry and is found in the Odyssey. In either case the meaning is 'run (the ship) ashore'. It has often been observed that this verb is conjoined with the only New Testament occurrence of classical ναῦς (for πλοῖον: 14 times in this narrative, 67 times in NT), and the phrase is paralleled for instance in Hom. *Od.* 9.148; cf. 9.546 with the simple verb κέλλω. It is not clear that this justifies our supposing that Luke knew his Homer, though such a literary background is not unlikely; this in itself may be no more than a traditional tag, even if deriving ultimately from Homer.

27:42 The ruthless action intended by the soldiers appears to reflect the severe liability on guards who permitted a prisoner to escape. Bruce cites Justinian's Code (9.4.4) for the ruling that the guard incurred the penalty which had awaited the prisoner.[148] It thus became a serious matter to guard those accused of capital offences. Cf. also 16:27, and the incident recounted in the closely contemporary Petronius, *Sat.* 112.

28:1 The identity of the island as Melita (Malta) seems to have been established only after landing. This is natural enough when they were cast at night on a low rocky shore some miles from any well-known harbour.

28:2 The significance of βάρβαροι here is that basic to the Graeco-Roman perspective, people unable to communicate in the cosmopolitan languages of the Empire. Punic inscriptions are preserved from Malta, and it is entirely probable that Maltese villagers may not have spoken languages known to the ship's company. It is tempting to see the word as reflecting a wholly unexpected difficulty that the party's first attempts to make contact and discover their whereabouts were frustrated by a language problem.[149]

---

[148] Bruce, *Acts*, p. 249 *ad* 12:19.

[149] The Semitic texts have been published in G.A. Cooke, *A Text-Book of North-Semitic Inscriptions* (Oxford: Clarendon Press [1903], pp. 102-107; H. Donner and W. Röllig. *Kanaanäische und aramäische Inschriften* (Wiesbaden: Harrassowitz, 1962), Band I, p. 14, Band II, pp. 76-79 (published in the same volume); *CIS* 1.1.122-32; A.M. Honeyman, 'Two Semitic Inscriptions from Malta', *PEQ* 93 (1961), pp. 151-53, of which the latter is Hebrew, a language unparalleled on Malta. Most of these texts, where datable at all, are earlier than our period. The most interesting of them is the Punic-Greek bilingual which gives examples of alternative names in a Tyrian family: Abdosir = Dionysius and Osirshamar = Sarapion in a dedication to Melkart, the Baal of Tyre, otherwise Heracles Archegetes (*CIG* 5753; *IG* 14.600; *CIS* 1.122; Cooke, pp. 102-103, No. 36; of 2nd BC). The early coinage of Malta, immediately following the Roman occupation in 218 BC, bears a Punic legend אנן ('nn), with a variety of types which show a strongly Egyptian character (Head, *HN*, new and enlarged edn, p. 883). A characteristic type is the mummy of Osiris with flail and sceptre, lying between Isis and Nephthys, each with wings crossed in front and wearing a solar disc and horns. Later types exhibit both Greek and Latin legends. On the coins of Gozo the characteristic type is of Astarte, but all are bronze of the 1st BC, inscribed ΓΑΥΛΙΤΩΝ. The island of Cossura (Pantelleria), 120m west-northwest, like Malta, combines Semitic legends with Egyptian character in its early issues. (Head, *HN*, pp. 882-83). The meanings of the Semitic words in both cases are unclear. They might be the names of local dynasts or magistrates.

The reading Μελίτη is to be preferred to Μελιτήνη (28:1) (B* *al*), which probably arose through dittography with ἡ νῆσος following (Metzger, *Textual Comm.*, p. 500, probability {B}). The identification of this Melita with Mljet in the Adriatic by Acworth and Meinardus is not to be accepted (see p. 141, n. 115).

28:2 The note of the persistent storm wind ending in cold and rain is again suitable to the *gregale,* and not for instance to warm winds of the 'Sirocco' type from a point nearer the southeast.[150]

28:3 There are now no poisonous snakes on Malta, though harmless species are found today. The snake episode is probably open to alternative explanations. It is likely that a noxious creature has disappeared or been exterminated since antiquity, given the fact that Malta is a small, densely inhabited island territory whose original forest cover has gone. Or else the scene, despite the use of the word ἔχιδνα may be taken to refer to a non-poisonous snake, possibly *Coronella austriaca,* which looks like a viper and fastens on its victim in the manner suggested by the description. In such a case the natives' reaction may be explained from popular belief that all snakes are poisonous, a notion shared at this date by the learned Pliny (*NH* 8.35.85), or from fear and superstition attached to them. Pliny again (*NH* 8.35.86) retails credulously the idea that snakes will brave every barrier to wreak vengeance on the killers of their mates. The snake as the agent of vengeance (v. 4) was a common idea. The nature of the people's expectation is not analysed. They expected something ἄτοπον, whether poisoning or divine visitation. They were impressed by Paul's fearless immunity to whatever powers, natural or supernatural, they supposed the snake to possess.[151]

28:4-6 The reactions of the local people reflect superstitions of the day, and are treated by Luke with an ironic humour.

28:7 The title πρῶτος (τῆς νήσου) is attested epigraphically. The clear instance is in *IGRR* 1.512 = *IG* 14.601.[152]

28:8 The case of fever may well have been that associated with this island, 'Malta fever', discovered in 1887 to be caused by an endemic

---

150 See *EBr* (1945) 14.738.

151 See *JTS* 26 (1975), pp. 109-10.

152 I have argued elsewhere ('First Person Narrative in Acts 27-28', *TB* 36 [1985], pp. 79-109, esp. p. 100) that the Latin inscription commonly cited in confirmation of the Greek (*CIL* 10.7495.1), and reading: ... munic]ipi Mel. primus omni[um. must be taken in its (mutilated) context, so far as that can be reconstructed. It seems likely to refer, not to *primus* as a title, but to the honoree as 'first' to perform various benefactions of the kinds fragmentarily listed in the subsequent lines (cf. formulations like πρῶτος καὶ μόνος, *IG* 14.737.5, Naples, 2nd AD; or μόνος καὶ πρῶτος, *IGRR* 4.1252, Thyatira, 3rd AD). The evidence for magistracies on Malta and Gozo may however be extended. One Latin text from Gaulos (Gozo) records titles closely similar to those of the πρῶτος of Malta, but lacking that title, which was presumably reserved for the chief magistrate of the principal island (*patronus municipii, flamen divi Hadriani, CIL* 10.7507.1-2). The two islands were under a Roman procurator (*proc. insularum Melit. et Gaul., CIL* 10.7494.1-2).

micro-organism *Micrococcus melitensis*, which infected the milk of the Maltese goats. The phrase πυρέτοις καὶ δυσεντερίῳ is apt to this undulant or enteric fever.[153]

28:11 To sail three months later was very early in the season. We have seen that the Day of Atonement in AD 59 was late (5th October; cf. 27:9). Even if the departure from Fair Havens were still somewhat delayed, the onset of *Euraquilo* and the drive past Cauda was a matter of hours, and if they reached Malta on the morning following the fourteenth night, the shipwreck can scarcely have been later than late October. Even if the days of hospitality and settling into winter-quarters are not included in the three months the departure can scarcely have been delayed beyond early February. This sequence is easier to accommodate to the winter 59-60, when the Fast was late, than to any of the neighbouring years, and this provides an additional confirmation of that year. According to Vegetius (*de Re Milit.* 4.39) the seas were closed until 10th March (*usque in diem sextum Iduum Martiarum maria clauduntur*), but Pliny says merely that spring opens the seas, and that at the beginning of spring (on 8th February) the west winds (*favonii*) soften the winter sky (*NH* 2.47.122). Where formerly pirates forced men in fear of their lives to attempt winter voyages, 'now avarice exercises the same compulsion' (*nunc idem hoc avaritia cogit*, *NH* 2.47.126). The crew of the 'Isopharia' put to sea at the earliest moment when they could expect favourable spring winds. It was important to them to take their cargo to Ostia in time to catch the spring sailing back to Alexandria and so avoid the loss entailed in falling behind schedule.[154]

28:12 The reason for three days' delay at Syracuse on a voyage of such urgency is unexplained, but is likely to have been connected with the weather, perhaps a north or northwest wind which would bar the passage of the Straits of Messina. It was easier at this stage to make short runs if necessary between good harbours than, for instance, on the southern coast of Crete.

28:13 The mention of Rhegium functions correctly as a refuge to await a southerly wind to carry them through the strait. In this case the desired wind came quickly, and enabled them to make a rapid passage to Puteoli.

28:13 Puteoli was the port where passengers were set ashore, though the cargo of grain was taken up to Portus, the new harbour

[153] See *EBr* (1945) 14.744.

[154] See p. 138, n. 109 for some discussion of the important contribution of W.P. Workman in *ExpT* 11 (1899-1900), pp. 316-19. The pressure of the fleet's schedule helps to explain a little further the reasons for the perilously early start in the spring, which is still required, even on Workman's late chronology of AD 59-60.

built by Claudius at Ostia, by the mouth of the Tiber (cf. Sen. *Ep. Mor.* 77.1).[155]

28:14 We have no means of verifying that there were Christians in Puteoli at this date. There was however an early attested Jewish community (Jos. *BJ*, 2.7.1.104; *Ant.* 17.12.1.328, both relating an incident under Augustus, and giving the city its Greek name Dicaearchia; see Jos. *Vita*, 3.16). It was also a cosmopolitan port, whose inscriptions show abundant evidence of resident aliens from the East, notably an important community of Tyrians (*IG* 14.830). It has been supposed that evidence exists for the presence of Christianity in neighbouring Pompeii and Herculaneum before their destruction a few years later. While the suggested indications are at best doubtful, it seems probable enough that there were Christians in them, though none of the supposed evidence has been substantiated.[156]

---

[155] See the evidence cited in *TB* 36 (1985), pp. 92-93. Before Claudius, cargo as well as passengers had been landed at Puteoli. See J. Crook, 'Working Notes on Some of the New Pompeii Tablets', *ZPE* 29 (1978), pp. 229-39, citing letters dated 28 June and 2 July AD 37, which refer to Alexandrian wheat as stored *in horreis Bassianis publicis Puteolanorum* (p. 235); cf. the text of AD 40, p. 236. Perhaps the most interesting testimony to the significance of Portus is on the remarkable series of *sestertii* of Nero, of AD 64-66 (H. Mattingly, *Coins of the Roman Empire in the British Museum* [London: British Museum, rev. edn, 1976-] Vol 1. pp. clxxvi-clxxvii, and Nos. 131-35, of Nero, inscribed AVGVSTI POR. OST. S.C.), depicting the curving moles and attached slipways, entrance island and lighthouse, and recumbent Neptune, with varying numbers of ships shown in the basin. Mattingly notes that several other variants of the type exist which are not held in the Museum. The harbour is described in Suet. *Claud.* 20.3; Dio 60.11.4-5; cf. *CIL* 14.85, of AD 46. For Puteoli as the port for passengers (and mail) cf. Sen. *Ep. Mor.* 77.1-3; Jos. *Vita* 3.16; *BJ* 2.7.1.104; *Ant.* 17.12.1.328; Suet. *Titus* 5.3.

[156] For Herculaneum, see A. Maiuri, 'La Croce di Ercolano', *Rendiconti della Pontificia Accademia romana di Archeologia* 15 (1939), pp. 193-218. Maiuri describes and illustrates extensively a cross-impression in a wall above a 'cupboard-altar' (*armadio-ara*) in a room of the Casa del Bicentenario. The evidence however appears indecisive, and the wall-impression is likely to have been made not by a Christian cross but by a bracket supporting a shelf or the like. Among Pompeian graffiti which have been supposed to have a Christian (or perhaps Jewish) origin, the most significant and interesting is the occurrence of two examples of the ROTAS-SATOR word-square, far earlier than any other known instances. Their discovery posed serious doubt against the traditional view of the Christian origin of the square, and various alternative explanations have been offered. There is no reason to doubt that Christians used the square and developed a Christian symbolism related to it, but the question remains open whether Christian meaning attaches to its invention at so early a date rather than to its secondary use. I am inclined to think, in the face of much modern opinion, that the balance of probability favours a Christian origin, and also that the spread and development of Christianity happened more rapidly than our fragmentary sources are likely to

28:14 This passage reads surprisingly as though the prisoner is free to be invited to spend time with his friends. Perhaps the element of pressure and desperation had been taken out of the journey with the safe arrival on Italian soil, and the soldiers were given some leave ashore in the intervals of their duties. Julius had treated Paul with courtesy throughout, for he was in any case a man of some social standing, whose Roman rights were not to be abused. No doubt suitable arrangements were made to guard Paul, even while granting him considerable freedom of movement, and his guards would still have been answerable with their lives for his safety. We may compare the case of Ignatius, who was able to visit some churches on the route of his journey, and leaves first-person evidence in letters generally received as authentic.

28:15 Appii Forum and Tres Tabernae are correctly placed as stopping-places on the Appian Way, respectively 43 and 33 Roman miles southeast of Rome.[157]

show or than some scholars would accept. But I should lay no weight on this tentative supposition about the origins of the square. See further F.V. Filson, 'Were there Christians at Pompeii?' *BA*2 (1939), pp. 13-16; D. Atkinson, 'The Sator-Formula and the Beginnings of Christianity', *BJRL* 22 (1938), pp. 419-34 and 'The Origin and Date of the "Sator" Word-Square', *JEH* 2 (1951), pp. 1-18 (for Christian view); D. Fishwick, 'On the Origin of the Rotas-Sator Square', *HTR* 57 (1964), pp. 39-53 (Jewish). There is now a vast literature and an extraordinary variety of interpretations. The fullest survey is in H. Hofmann, *PW* Supp. 15 (1978) col. 477-565. W.O. Moeller, *The Mithraic Origin and Meanings of the Rotas-Sator Square* (Leiden: Brill, 1973) is an example of the improbable over-elaboration of many theories; the author depends on the supposition of cryptic multi-lingual word-plays. This work however contains a most useful bibliography (pp. 44-52). For the most recent discovery see C.J. Hemer, 'The Manchester Rotas-Sator Square', *FTh* 105 (1978-79), pp. 36-40 (of late 2nd AD). Some of the most recent discussion returns to the fruitless task of trying to interpret it through forcing a meaning from AREPO (M. Marcovich, *ZPE* 50 [1983], pp. 155-71; G.M. Browne, *ZPE* 52 [1983], p. 60, both arguing that AREPO stands for Harpocrates, as god of good luck). ([Ed.] Cf. now W. Baines, 'The Rotas-Sator Square: a New Investigation, *NTS* 33 (1987), pp. 469-76.)

The Pompeian samples of the square were published as *CIL* 4 Supp. 8623 and 8123 (fragmentary). There is another Pompeian graffito, fragmentary and barely legible, which contains a word doubtfully read as CHRISTIRAII(?), and often supposed to refer to Christians (*CIL* 4.679).

[157] This was the route traversed by Horace on his way from Rome to Brundisium (*Sat.* 1.5.1-3) before continuing by canal-barge at night through the Pomptine marshes (cf. Strabo 5.3.6 = 233; milestone *CIL* 10.6825). Three Taverns, situated at the crossing of the road from Norba to Autium, is several times mentioned in the letters of Cicero (*ad Att.* 1.13.1; 2.10; 2.12.2; 2.13.1), one of which (2.10) was written from Appii Forum. See further *PW* 2.4.2.1875 and K. Miller, *Itineraria Romana*, col. 336.

28:16 Paul had a soldier to guard him. Bruce cites Mommsen for the distinction in the Digest between two types of custody, *militi tradere*, as here, and *carceri* (or *vinculis*) *tradere*.[158] In this case he would be lightly chained by the wrist (cf. ἅλυσις in 28.20).

28:21 It is surprising that the Jews in Jerusalem had apparently not communicated with the Jews in Rome about Paul. Bruce (*Acts*, p. 477) suggests that they were likely to have been content to let the case go by default, realizing that they had less hope of a conviction before the imperial court than before a provincial magistrate. Roman law was severe on unsuccessful prosecutors. The ignorance of the Roman Jews about Paul still invites explanation. They knew of Christianity (v. 22) and of opposition to it. If the leaders had returned to Rome since the death of Claudius in 54 they may have come from diverse areas of the Diaspora, and the particular identity of one such Christian preacher whose posthumous importance was not then apparent was not necessarily of moment. As an educated Rabbi of impeccable Jewish credentials he rated a hearing which might not have been accorded to others.[159]

---

[158] Bruce, *Acts*, p. 476 citing Mommsen, *Römisches Strafrecht*, p. 317.

[159] This difficulty is discussed by most of the commentators, and the more traditional seem not to be too troubled by it. Rackham (p. 501) makes the point that there may have been little contact between the newly returned Jewish community and a predominantly Gentile church whose Gentile members alone presumably kept a Christian presence alive in Rome during the time of the expulsion. Munck (p. 258), points out that Paul's ship must have been among the first to arrive in Italy that spring; unless word from Palestine had arrived before the winter closure, it might still be on the way. The difficulty is not stressed in BC 4 or in Edmundson (p. 100). The matter is considered readily explicable by Marshall (p. 423) following Bruce.

Haenchen, however, is strongly critical of the whole passage, stressing not only the Jews' alleged ignorance of Paul and of Christianity generally, but the disappearance of the Roman church from notice upon Paul's arrival in the city (*Acts*, pp. 726-32). He explains it all as an unhistorical creation by Luke, where his determination to present Paul as a pioneer missionary to the Jews of Rome leads him into impossible and contradictory statements. This is too facile. Such difficulties challenge more direct explanation, within a recognition of the unexpected complexities of events and motivations in real life.

The possibility that Paul's accusers never intended to pursue their prosecution requires much thought. Roman justice at this period was also severe on default, and A.N. Sherwin-White (*RSRL*, pp. 112-19) shows that the thrust of contemporary legislation was rather to enforce prosecution than to favour release of the unindicted. See further pp. 390-91. If Paul was released upon default this would have been attributable, in Sherwin-White's view, to an act of clemency under the Emperor's *imperium* rather than to a statutory limit for the date of trial. Long delay was likely in any case, perhaps through congestion of court business if not delay in accusation. I am inclined to believe that Paul *was* brought to trial,

28:30-31 The conditions of Paul's captivity, living 'at his own expense' (so rightly ἰδίῳ μισθώματι) in *libera custodia* offered opportunity for the freedom of access implied here.

---

and that he wrote Philippians when the crisis was near.

Chapter 5
Evidence from Historical Details in Acts

D. Correlations of Date with Ostensible Chronology

The ramifications of this problem make necessary a brief preliminary retrospective excursion into the Third Gospel.

Lk. 3:1-2 The ministry of John the Baptist began in the fifteenth year of Tiberius (AD 28-29), when Jesus was about thirty years of age (Lk. 3:23). This is the only formally stated date in the New Testament. The other correlations here are correct so far as they are verifiable (which is perhaps itself noteworthy in a work written at some distance in time), but uninformative as they cover relatively broad spans: Pilate was procurator 26-36; Herod (Antipas) tetrarch of Galilee 4 BC-AD 39; Philip, his brother, tetrarch of Ituraea and Trachonitis 4 BC-AD 34; Annas, technically high priest 6-15, continued to exercise powerful influence after his deposition during the tenure of five of his sons and especially his son-in-law Caiaphas, c. 18-36. For Lysanias, surviving evidence does not suffice for firm conclusions.[1]

---

1 S. Sandmel (*IDB* 1.481-82 *ad* Caiaphas) is too sceptical about Annas, whose continuing influence is apparent in his unique dynastic succession (cf. Jos. *Ant.* 20.9.1.198), reasserted after his deposition by Valerius Gratus (Jos. *Ant.* 18.2.2.34-35; cf. 18.4.3.95). Annas' power behind the scenes is reflected in Jn 18:13, 24, independently of the Synoptics, though Caiaphas is there called 'high priest'. In Lk. 3:2, ἐπὶ ἀρχιερέως (rightly singular) should not be taken exclusively with Annas (though some probably continued to recognize him as high priest throughout the period) but with both names, to denote the current *de iure/de facto* arrangement. καί may serve as the counterpart of a hyphen, oblique stroke or bracket in modern type, or render 'or', 'also', 'otherwise' or the like. For the use of the title ἀρχιερεύς of a *former* holder of the office cf. Jos. *BJ* 2.12.6.243, of Jonathan, high priest c. 36-37, so called in association with Ananias in c. 52.

Sandmel's treatment of Lysanias is also lacking (*IDB* 3.193). He works from a transcription of one inscription in *CIG* and does not observe the factor of date in the only other he uses (*CIG* 4523 = *IGRR* 3.1085 and *CIG* 4521 = *IGRR* 3.1086 = *OGIS* 606). The restoration of the latter is further to be modified in the light of the later discovery of a complete copy of what appear to be the identical words, subject only to stonecutters' errors (R. Savignac, 'Texte complet de l'inscription d'Abila relative à Lysanias', *RB* n.s. 9 [1912], pp. 533-40). Boeckh in *CIG* offered a misleading reconstruction of the first. Thus he did not recognize the dynastic reference in the phrase Ζηνοδώρῳ Λυσα[νίου τ]ετράρχου in his truncated Ζηνο- δώρῳ Λυσ[ιμ]άχου. Sandmel treats this text as alluding only to one Lysanias,

Lk. 23:54 Jesus died, and the first arrangements were made for his burial, on the day of παρασκευή, just before the Sabbath began in the evening.[2] While the Synoptics and John are beset here with well-known chronological problems about the day of the Passover, our point here is simple, that the Feast approximated to the full moon, whether Thursday or Friday, and on the evidence of Luke (or of John) 30 or 33 are more or less probable options for the year of the Crucifixion, where neighbouring years are excluded.[3]

corresponding to a dynast of the Ituraeans executed by Antony in 36 BC (Jos. *Ant.* 15.4.1.92; cf. Dio 49.32.5). But later restorations in *IGRR* give probable ground for finding the name in three generations of the family, the two latter subsequent to Lysanias I on what may have been his family tomb: ...]ου γυν[ἡ, ?Λυσανίου] θυγάτηρ, Ζηνοδώρῳ Λυσ[ανίου τ]ετράρχου καὶ Λυσ[ανίᾳ Λυσανίου ? καὶ τ]οῖς υἱοῖς | [καὶ] Λυσαν[ίᾳ ... καὶ τοῖ]ς υἱοῖς κτλ. In the second text a freedman Λυσανίου τετράρχου makes a dedication ὑπὲρ τῆς τῶν κυρίων Σεβαστῶν σωτηρίας. In the period of the tetrarchy, which was absorbed into the rule of Herod Agrippa I in AD 37, the 'Augusti' (Σεβαστοί, plural) can refer only to Tiberius and his mother Livia, who received the title 'Augusta' in AD 14 and died in AD 29. Thus we have evidence for a tetrarch Lysanias contemporary with an inscription dated somewhere between those limits. It is however possible that the inscription might refer to a much later period of the freedman's life, when the 'Augusti' could be Nero and his mother Agrippina. In either case, Lysanias was tetrarch at some date before 37, but contemporary with a dependent who was still active after 54. Although we have the grounds for no more than a rough approximation about Lysanias, those approximations are fully consonant with the probability that he was tetrarch in AD 28-29. A different, and perhaps more difficult, question is why Luke chooses to mention this obscure dynast rather than the legate of Syria, unless perhaps Jesus' ministry had at some point known to Luke touched places within the borders of Lysanias. Cf. Schürer, Vermes and Millar, I.567-69.

2   Luke 23:54, and in particular the words σάββατον ἐπέφωσκεν, are not precisely paralleled in the other Gospels, though cf. Mark's slightly different placing of a similar note of time (ἤδη ὀψίας γενομένης, 'for it was the παρασκευή', 15:42). A difficulty attaches to the use of the word ἐπιφώσκειν, further complicated by the crux in Mt. 28:1. It will suffice here to say that this verb must be taken to denote the evening onset of the Sabbath in Luke, and not necessarily bear its etymological sense of daylight 'dawning'. See C.H. Turner, 'Note on ἐπιφώσκειν', *JTS* 14 (1913), pp. 188-90; F.C. Burkitt, 'ΕΠΙΦΩΣΚΕΙΝ', *ibid.*, 538-46; cf. P. Gardner-Smith, 'ΕΠΙΦΩΣΚΕΙΝ', *JTS* 27 (1926), pp. 179-81.

3   The options are clearly set out by J.K. Fotheringham, 'The Evidence of Astronomy and Technical Chronology for the Date of the Crucifixion', *JTS* 35 (1934), pp. 146-62. In AD 30, Nisan 14 should have fallen on Friday 7 April, suiting the Johannine chronology, in AD 33, on Friday 3 April. These dates are not certain, in view of the observational base which in theory still governed the reckoning of the lunar months, and so the dates might occasionally diverge by a day from retrospective modern calculations, possibly accommodating the Synoptic implication that Nisan 14 fell that year on a Thursday. The same end might first possibly be reached with AD 31, but only by supposing that Nisan fell a month late,

Acts 4:6 The joint naming of Annas and Caiaphas again sets a terminus prior to the deposition of Caiaphas in AD 36 for this scene. The John and Alexander mentioned here cannot be identified, but were presumably known without further specification to the original readers (see H, pp. 193f. below for the impinging of the identification

on Wednesday 25 April, and was delayed a day further by late observation of the crescent at Nisan 1. But when the dates of festivals must have been fixed far in advance to accommodate a far-flung Diaspora, the incidence of days and months could scarcely be left at the mercy of a cloudy evening (even if the observational tradition were maintained). Even so, ancient reckonings did not necessarily exactly duplicate the modern. In any case other neighbouring years are clearly excluded. Fotheringham's own preference for AD 33, on the basis of supposing a confused reference in Luke's use of ἐκλείπειν (Lk. 23:45) to the briefly visible partial *lunar* eclipse of 3 April 33 as confounded with the Crucifixion darkness, is tenuous and unwarranted on that ground. G. Ogg, *The Chronology of the Public Ministry of Jesus* (CUP, 1940), esp. pp. 276-77, gives other and stronger reasons for preferring 33. More recently H.W. Hoehner, *Chronological Aspects of the Life of Christ* (Grand Rapids: Zondervan, 1977) argues strongly for 33. While parts of his argument are impressive, I am not convinced by his rejection of 30, where his interpretation of John 2:20, for instance, fails to explain the pointed antithesis between three days and forty-six years (pp. 38-43, 103-104). Conversely, he rejects objections to 33 which seem to touch the heart of the problem. He writes (p. 104), 'In the end one does not determine the chronology of the Gospels on the basis of the chronology of the apostolic age or vice versa'. But in the last analysis the issue at stake is precisely that: can the chronological data, specifically in Luke-Acts, be integrated into an overall framework which does justice to the evidence about both Jesus and Paul? The more diversified Pauline evidence and tighter sequence may actually be the easier approach to the composite problem. I know of no such attempt to integrate the whole of Lukan chronology. The problems posed are in fact probably insoluble in the current state of our knowledge, because variables, uncertainties, approximations and clashes with Josephus are so compounded with variant calendar reckonings as to forbid any approach to precision on many of the key points. The issue between 30 and 33 remains open, in default of a compelling reconstruction of all the relevant terms of the complex. If I continue to incline towards 30, it is because it may give more latitude for the tight Pauline sequence, though this could be reconciled with 33 if Pauline timespaces are shortened elsewhere (cf. *Pauline Studies Bruce*, pp. 13-14). While we are not concerned here to pursue the question, the date of the Crucifixion is a factor which cannot be disregarded in assessing either the chronological correlations of Paul or Luke's claim to accuracy overall. Among the many who adhere, at least tentatively, to the traditional date of AD 30, we may mention Bruce, *Acts*, p. 55; Caird, *IDB* 1.603; J. Blinzler, *The Trial of Jesus*, tr. I. and F. McHugh (Cork: Mercier Press, 1959), pp. 72-73, in addition to the long list cited by Blinzler. The older tradition in favour of 29, held by C.H. Turner, *HDB* 1.410-15; Ramsay, *Was Christ Born at Bethlehem?* (London: Hodder, 2nd edn, 1898), p. 203; Lake, *BC* 5.467, seems now excluded by the astronomical argument. See also C.J. Humphreys and W.G. Waddington, 'The Date of the Crucifixion', *JASA* 37 (1985), pp. 2-10, and chapter 6, pp. 261-67.

problem on a different topic).

5:34 The activity of Gamaliel cannot be precisely dated, but it is sufficiently clear that he flourished through the middle years of the first century. He was the grandson of Hillel, who was active under Herod the Great, and the king and queen with whom he is associated in Pesaḥim 88b are alternatively identified as Agrippa I and Cypris (Derenbourg, Bacher) or Agrippa II and Berenice (Büchler).[4] The moral strength and revival of Pharisaism in the period following 70 are attributed largely to his influence in the time before. Paul's claim to have studied under him (22:3) must be placed before c. AD 32.

5:36 The reference to Theudas is a famous crux, and is generally considered to be one of the major difficulties for the historicity of Acts. Theudas is said to precede Judas (5:37), whose revolt was directed against the census of Quirinius in AD 6, and therefore *a fortiori* he must precede the dramatic date of the Gamaliel scene. But this sequence clashes with Josephus' dating of a revolt by a Theudas under the procurator Fadus (AD 44-46; *Ant.* 20.5.1.97-98), a time *after* Judas and more than ten years too late for the ostensible chronology of this scene in Acts. Krenkel and others have explained the discrepancy by supposing Luke miscopied Josephus in his consecutive mention of Theudas and the *sons* of Judas (*Ant.* 20.5.2.102), but it is generally agreed that Luke did not use Josephus as a source. It is possible that Josephus rather than Luke is wrong. It is not altogether impossible that there was an earlier Theudas.[5] Yet even if Luke has

---

4   See H. Freedman in the Soncino edition of the Babylonian Talmud *ad loc.* (I have not seen the works of J. Derenbourg and A. Büchler to which he refers); W. Bacher, *The Jewish Encyclopedia* 5.559.

5   The relatively infrequent attestation of the name 'Theudas' is misleading here, for it leaves out of account the evident abundance in informal usage both of alternative names and of hypocoristics. 'Theudas' seems to serve as the hypocoristic of many such forms as 'Theodotus', 'Theodorus', 'Theodotion' etc., all Greek theophoric names popular among Jews. On 'Theudas' and orthographically similar forms see *New Docs* 4.183-85, No. 101. Further, in view of the great prevalence of Greek-Hebrew alternative names of corresponding meaning, names of this type may often have served to render 'Jonathan', 'Nathanael', 'Mattathias', or even 'Hananias', 'Jehohanan' (John) and the like. A glance at the onomastics of the Jerusalem ossuaries, which offer an unusually close comparison for time and place, reveals a remarkable frequency of names of these groups, whether written in Hebrew or Greek, e.g. Theodorus (*CIJ* 1237, Gk.), Matthiah (1240, Heb.), Jehohanan (1244, 1245, 1248, 1257, all Heb.), Matt(at)iah (1246, Heb.), Theudas (1255, Heb.), Hananiah (1262, Heb.), Theudion (1265, Heb.), Theodotion (1266, Heb., 1270 Gk.), Mattathias (1276, Gk). The ruler of the synagogue in the famous Ophel synagogue inscription (*CIJ* 1404) is also 'Theodotus'. And in the ossuaries of the first-century 'Goliath' family at Jericho,

committed an anachronism by placing these words on Gamaliel's lips and has reversed the order of the two uprisings, one such slip on his part would not entitle us to argue for his general unreliability. The fact that Luke's background information can so often be corroborated may suggest that it is wiser to leave this particular matter open rather than to condemn Luke of a blunder.

5:37 The mention of Judas, taken apart from its involvement in the Theudas problem, presents no difficulty, and accords with Josephus in its allusion to the census (AD 6; cf. *Ant.* 18.1.1.4-10; 20.5.2.102; *BJ* 2.8.1.118; 2.17.8.433; 7.8.1.253). It is clear from Josephus that Judas was a notorious figure, to whom was ascribed the origin of 'the fourth philosophy' (presumably that of the Zealots, *Ant.* 18.1.6.23), apt to Gamaliel's point, but too early to be of more than formal chronological significance in our quest.

8.27 The reference to Candace is not chronologically informative as this appears to have been a hereditary title of the Ethiopian queens, not a personal name. An inscription of Pselcis on the Ethiopian border, which mentions τὴν κυρίαν βασίλισσαν, is dated 13 BC, but there is no ground for U. Wilcken's identification of this queen with that of Acts, ostensibly nearly fifty years later.[6]

9:24-25 If this escape from Damascus is identified with the occasion mentioned by Paul himself in 2 Cor. 11:32-33 (cf. F, p. 182), it is

---

the only pure Greek name is again 'Theodotus', and seems to be an alternative for 'Nath(an)el' of the same man (R. Hachlili, 'The Goliath Family in Jericho: Funerary Inscriptions from a First Century AD Jewish Monumental Tomb', *BASOR* 235 [1979], pp. 31-65 inscrs. nos. 3a, b, 7a, b). (For the colloquial pronunciation -ευ- for -εο- cf. Λαυδικια and variants *passim* for Λαοδικεια in the inscriptions.) There were many tumults in Judaea after the death of Herod the Great (Jos. *Ant.* 17.10.4.269-8.285), and Origen refers to Theudas as active before the birth of Jesus, though there is no reason for seeing more in his words than an inference from the present passage (*contr. Cels.* 1.57).

None of this justifies the glib assumption of a second Theudas. Yet the possibility is not so unlikely as it can be made to seem. Nor is it unknown for a revolutionary to trade on his identity of name with a previous popular hero, or indeed to adapt a cognate name to the same evocative familiar form. We must not press what may yet read like special pleading to save Luke's credit— though possibly it is rather Josephus' credit at stake here.

([Ed.] R.J. Knowling [*Expositor's Greek Testament* II.158] mentions the suggestion of Wiesler that 'Theudas' is the equivalent of 'Matthias', the name of an insurgent at the time of Herod the Great [Jos. *Ant.* 17.6.2.149-4.167]; this hypothesis has been revived by D.J. Williams, *Acts*, San Francisco: Harper & Row, 1985, pp. 99f., but it must be said that the account in Acts shows closer resemblances to Josephus' account of Theudas than to his account of Matthias.)

6   *IGRR* 1.1359; Wilcken, *Hermes* 28 (1893), p. 154. Cf. a tombstone of Egyptian Thebes (*IGRR* 1.1232, of 15 July AD 109) for the use of 'Candace' as an (alternative) personal name: 'Cleopatra, also called Candace'.

brought into conjunction with the activity of Aretas IV. The apparent difficulty here is in Paul's own evidence, not in Acts, for it is surprising if Aretas actually controlled Damascus; perhaps his ethnarch's presence may be explained otherwise. The only firm terminus here is that the scene must be placed before Aretas' death in 40.[7] No Roman coinage is known to have been minted in Damascus between 34 and 62. This gap may or may not be significant. If it is, it may point to an occupation by Aretas at some time after 34. R. Jewett, *Dating Paul's Life*, pp. 30-33, is insistent that Aretas could not have held Damascus under Tiberius, but was likely to have been given it under the policy of Caligula which was designed to favour client-kings. He presses this to the point of making a basic *terminus a quo* in the accession of Caligula in 37. The argument is not persuasive enough to make this a solid datum, where many terms of the equation remain uncertain.[8]

10:1 Reference to the 'Italic cohort' might be helpful if we had evidence for the identity of the military units in Palestine at the appropriate dates. Bruce notes the attestation of a *cohors II Italic(a) c(iuium) R(omanorum)* in Syria in AD 69 (*ILS* 9168), and it may have been in the area earlier.[9] According to Josephus (*Ant.* 19.9.2.365), Agrippa I's forces consisted of an *ala* of men from Caesarea and Sebaste (Samaria), with five cohorts. Claudius intended to transfer these troops, in view of their conduct on Agrippa's death, but yielded to their plea to stay, and they remained until deported from the province by Vespasian (*Ant.* 19.9.2.366).

11:28 The Famine under Claudius: there is abundant evidence for recurring famines in the period 41-54, attributed by Suetonius (*Claud.* 18.2) to persistent droughts. Two crises in Rome itself are dated explicitly, one in 42 (Dio 60.11), the other in 51 (Tac. *Ann.* 12.43).

---

7   I adopt here the classic chronology of R. Dussaud, 'Numismatique des rois de Nabatène', *Journal asiatique* 10th ser. 3 (1904), pp. 189-238, based on the combined evidence of coins and inscriptions. Thus too Y. Meshorer, *Nabataean Coins*, Qedem Monographs (Jerusalem: Hebrew University, 1975), p. 8; cf. Meshorer's full discussion of the coinage of Aretas IV (pp. 41-63), citing *CIS* 2.1.214, which refers to the month Nisan in the 48th year of Aretas, beside coinage dated to that year (p. 47). For the beginning of Aretas' reign see Jos. *Ant.* 16.9.4.294; this is usually placed in 9 BC. Jewett (p. 30) draws attention to the possible flexibility in the ancient reckoning of regnal years, and prefers 39 (possibly even 38) for Aretas' death. While this would perhaps help to narrow our chronology further, we are not justified in claiming more than the later option as a *terminus ad quem*.

8   See further *Pauline Studies Bruce*, pp. 4-5, 15.

9   Bruce, *Acts*, p. 215. Cf. the inscription from Forum Sempronii in Umbria which honours a *trib. coh. mil. Italic. volunt(ariorum) quae est in Syria* (*CIL* 11.6117), unfortunately not dated.

Famine, however, was not a matter of widespread harvest failure and sudden crisis so much as an accumulation of local failures and difficulties which progressively priced the available supplies out of the reach of the poor before the rich were affected. The dating of a famine is a matter of tracing its origins and its complex economic and geographical outworkings. K.S. Gapp has used the records of Egyptian prices to confirm the occurrence of famine there c. 45-46, consequent upon either a deficient or an excessive seasonal inundation of the Nile.[10] As Egypt was an important source of grain, this concurs with the famine in Syria-Palestine attested independently by Josephus as the occasion of Queen Helena of Adiabene's relief mission (*Ant.* 20.2.5. 51-53) and dated by him to the procuratorship of Tiberius (Julius) Alexander (46-48), though it may have begun under his predecessor Fadus (*Ant.* 20.5.2.101).[11] It is likely that it was the cumulative effect of these Eastern famines which led to the Roman crisis of AD 51. If Agabus' prophecy here may be placed early in the complex of events, perhaps when the signs of trouble were first apparent in Egypt, then the love of God and of his church in Antioch for the poor in Jerusalem was seen in the promptness of the succour. This incident cannot be precisely placed, nor is it necessarily in rigid sequence of time in the unfolding of the narrative, but it is reasonable to suggest a date c. 45-46 for the mission of Barnabas and Saul consequent upon this intimation, probably earlier than Helena's response to the actual famine. We have here at least an approximation to a fixed date.

12:1 The Herod mentioned here is Herod Agrippa I (41-44). This unit of narrative culminates in the account of his death in 44.[12]

---

10 K.S. Gapp, 'The Universal Famine under Claudius', *HTR* 28 (1935), pp. 258-65. His case is based on the record-office documents in *Papyri from Tebtunis*, Part 1 (*Michigan Papyri*, Vol. 2) ed. A.E.R. Boak (Ann Arbor: University of Michigan Press, 1933) Nos. 123, 127; cf. later *Papyri from Tebtunis*, Part 2 (*Michigan Papyri*, Vol. 5) ed. E.M. Husselman *et al.* (1944) Nos. 238-40. Pliny assigns to the reign of Claudius the highest Nile inundation ever recorded, but does not date it more precisely (*NH* 5.10.58).

11 If we read ἐπὶ τούτου here ('in his time'), the reference is explicitly to Ti. Alexander; if the plural ἐπὶ τούτων, we may include Fadus, unless we then render the phrase 'in these circumstances'. J. Dupont has used Josephus in an able advocacy of a later dating of this famine in Jerusalem, following Jeremias in linking its climax with the sabbatical year of 47-48 (J. Jeremias, 'Sabbathjahr und neutestamentliche Chronologie', *ZNW* 27 [1928], pp. 98-103; Dupont, 'La Famine sous Claude (Actes, XI, 28)', *RB* 62 [1955], pp. 52-55). Dupont however does not take account of Gapp's specific arguments, which should be preferred to a hypothesis that depends on a circumstance of doubtful relevance. See my discussion in *Pauline Studies Bruce*, pp. 5-6.

12 The two sections 11:27-30 and 12:1-24 are both episodic, both introduced by

12:20-23 There is substantial agreement between Luke and Josephus as to the manner of Herod's death, though their independence of detail seems to rule out any possibility of literary relationship (see Jos. *Ant.* 19.8.2.343-52). Josephus characteristically embroiders and dramatizes a scene which must have been sufficiently dramatic. Both writers stress that Agrippa allowed himself to be flattered as a god. In ¶ 351 Josephus dates his death explicitly three years after the accession of Claudius (cf. 343; *BJ* 2.11.6.219). Josephus' authority is more secure for a well-known event within his own experience, and his dating here is confirmed by the dated sequence of Agrippa's coins, the latest belonging to year 8 of his reign, or 44.[13] If the occasion in honour of Caesar was Claudius' birthday, it is possible that the actual day was 1st August 44 (cf. Suet. *Claud.* 2.1).

13:1 Manaen (Menahem) who was presumably an elderly teacher in the church in Antioch, had been brought up as a contemporary with Herod Antipas. The date of the tetrarch's birth is unknown, but he was evidently of adult age in 4 BC at his accession and had reigned 42 years at his exile in AD 39. Hoehner suggests he was not born earlier than 20 BC.[14] Manaen may then have been in his mid-sixties at the ostensible date of the sending of Barnabas and Saul.

13:7 If the year of office of the proconsul Sergius Paulus could be identified, we should have another fixed point. But none of the attempts to identify this man are more than speculative possibilities (cf. C, p. 109).[15] Cyprus was a senatorial province from 22 BC. The title proconsul is thus correct for the period, but the fact is not chronologically informative (cf. B, p. 108).[16]

---

approximate statements of time: ἐν ταύταις δὲ ταῖς ἡμέραις (11:27), κατ' ἐκεῖνον δὲ τὸν καιρόν (12:1) and there is no need to find chronological difficulty. Both recount events extended in time, and perhaps actually overlapping. If Agabus' prophecy is placed so early as 44, both may even focus on that year.

13 See J. Meyshan, 'The Coinage of Agrippa the First', *IEJ* 4 (1954), pp. 186-200.

14 H.W. Hoehner, *Herod Antipas* (CUP, 1972), p. 12.

15 See Van Elderen in *Apostolic History*, ed. Gasque and Martin, pp. 151-56. If Mitford is right in restoring 'Gaius', not 'Claudius' in *SEG* 20 (1964) 302.9-11, this disposes of the most promising possibility: see *ANRW* 2.7.2 (1980), p. 1300 n. 54 and p. 1330, n. 195. It is possible that the Lucius Sergius Paullus mentioned as one of five *curatores riparum et alvei Tiberis* under Claudius was the same man: one of his colleagues there is known as consul in AD 34 (*CIL* 6.31545, of Rome), but there is nothing to corroborate this possibility beyond the coincidence of name and time, and nothing to connect this man with Cyprus, still less to justify Ramsay's construction of the history of a Christian family of Sergii Paulli. Wikenhauser (p. 338) thinks this official was identical with our man.

16 The names of a number of proconsuls of Cyprus are known from the inscriptions, but few of these can be dated exactly. Apart from the 'Sergius' now

17:7 The 'decrees of Caesar', against which Paul was accused of offending at Thessalonica, have not been securely and specifically identified. If E.A. Judge is right in seeing reference to edicts against predictions, especially of the death or change of rulers, first promulgated by the aged Augustus in AD 11 (Dio 56.25.5-6) and enforced through the local administration of oaths of loyalty,[17] the scene is placed in the general legal framework appropriate to the Julio-Claudian period, and may, in fact, be meant to cover Jewish Messianic agitation in particular, but we cannot be more specific.

18:2 Claudius' expulsion of Jews from Rome has usually been placed in AD 49, following Orosius, *Hist. adv. Paganos* 7.6.15, who attributes this date to Josephus, where it cannot now be traced. His actual source may have been Julius Africanus. Dio 60.6.6 places in AD 41 an embargo on Jewish meetings in Rome, but there is no hint there of an actual expulsion. G. Lüdemann has recently argued strongly in favour of 41 for the expulsion,[18] but the argument from supposition

probably assigned to Caligula, there is an inscription of Curium (*IGRR* 3.971) which appears to name and date two proconsuls under Claudius, L. Annius Bassus in the 12th year (AD 52) and Julius Cordus as his (presumably immediate) predecessor. Even allowing for some uncertainty in the years of office between 51/2 and 52/3, that would be tantalizingly near the time of Paul's visit, which must have been about five years earlier on the ostensible chronology. But Ritterling in *PW* 12.1701 (followed by Groag in *PIR* 1.108 No. 637) restores the *praenomen* Νέρωνι before Κλαυδίῳ Καίσαρι etc. in the inscription, and moves this proconsulship to the 12th year of Nero (AD 66). This would accord with the fact that both men (or their namesakes) are otherwise known only from a slightly later date (*PIR loc. cit.* and *PIR* 4.201 No. 272). For Q. Julius Cordus see also *IGRR* 3.978, of Citium, and Tacitus *Hist.* 1.76 (AD 69). Bassus was *consul suffectus* in AD 70. And an improved transcription (including a date) of the ἐπὶ Παύλου reference (*IGRR* 3.930) led Lake to suggest the thirteenth year of the provincial era, giving 14 BC, or if assigned to Claudius' regnal years, to AD 53, which is too late. But most recently T.B. Mitford restores δεκαπρωτε [ύ]σ[ας], an office not known before Hadrian, and dates the inscription tentatively to AD 126 (*ANRW* 2.7.2 (1980), pp. 1303-1304 n. 62).

[17] Judge, 'The Decrees of Caesar at Thessalonica', *RTR* 30 (1971), pp. 1-7.

[18] G. Lüdemann, *Paul: Apostle to the Gentiles. Studies in Chronology*, pp. 164-71 (*Paulus* I.183-95), and 'A Chronology of Paul', in *Colloquy*, ed. Corley pp. 289-307, esp. pp. 302-303. I find great difficulty in the chronological scheme he offers (*Paul*, pp. 262-63 = *Paulus* I.272-73 = *Colloquy*, pp. 303-304), which proceeds from an uncertain base-date (the Crucifixion, given as 27 or 30), reorganizes the ostensible evidence to bring Paul to Corinth in 41 to give the only absolute correlation for Paul with a date from which many differ, and gives no explicit correlation with the Gallio proconsulship, except that on the early reckoning of the Crucifixion Paul could have been in Corinth about that time. This seems to reflect a principle which proceeds from the selective use of evidence and compounds arguments *obscurum per obscurius* and *incertum per incertius*. Jewett, who aligns

which is involved there gives cause for caution. Dio says expressly that Claudius did not expel the Jews on the occasion of which he speaks. It is entirely probable that he was impelled to a more drastic measure by the recurrence of trouble, and arbitrary to suppose that Dio is correcting Suetonius while giving a different (and later) account of what is assumed to be the same event. The explicit testimony concurs with Acts. If it appears that we are choosing the explicit testimony *because* it favours Acts, we can only reply that the concurrence of ostensible evidence and the possibility of extending this interlocking warrants taking the evidence seriously.

If Aquila and Priscilla had left Italy in 49, this sets a terminus for the present incident. The presumption is that they were recently settled in Corinth at Paul's arrival. The plausibilities of the case would thus suit a date within a year or two of the expulsion. Bruce has suggested that Paul's hopes of proceeding from Macedonia to Rome had been frustrated by news of the expulsion and had occasioned his own journey southward to Athens and Corinth (*Paul*, p. 235).

18:12 Gallio proconsul of Achaia: while the restoration of the fragmented inscription of Delphi remains open to some debate, and may affect slightly the chronological inference, it is sufficiently clear that it

himself with Lüdemann in acknowledging a debt to Knox, is firm in his adherence to a dating of the expulsion in AD 49 (*Dating*, pp. 36-38), insisting that it is erroneous to suppose that Suetonius refers to the edict of 41 mentioned by Dio (126n). See further E.M. Smallwood, *The Jews under Roman Rule* (Leiden: Brill, 1981 [orig. 1976]), pp. 212-16, though I doubt her acceptance of the Nazareth Decree; cf. also other literature cited by Jewett, pp. 126-27. ([Ed.] More recently, F.F. Bruce has replied to some aspects of Lüdemann's chronology in 'Chronological Questions in the Acts of the Apostles', *BJRL* 68 (1986), pp. 273-95, esp. pp. 280-82.)

A different objection may be raised to the view suggested by Knox (*Chapters*, pp. 81-82) that Paul appeared before an earlier governor whom Luke confused with Gallio. Achaia and Macedonia had been made imperial provinces attached to Moesia from AD 15 to 44, when they were restored to senatorial rule (Tac. *Ann.* 1.76; 1.80; Suet. *Claud.* 25.3; Dio 60.24.1). Luke uses correctly the title ἀνθύπατος, applicable only since 44 (Acts 18:12), itself another correlation with the ostensible chronological sequence, but adaptable to Knox's system only on the gratuitous assumption that errors are compounded in our source. An apparent fixed date ought to be assessed at the outset, rather than being rejected parenthetically after a hypothesis has been elaborated without reference to it. On the changes of provincial status, see further J. Wiseman in *ANRW* 2.7.1 (1979), p. 503. It is unnecessary to list separately this *terminus a quo* in 44 when we have the precise date of Gallio. Knox's speculation that Gallio's period of office may have been two years and that its limits may have been anywhere from 50 to 54 is belied not only by the annual appointment of senatorial governors, but by the specific evidence for his leaving his province before the expiry of his year (see next note).

must be assigned to the spring or summer of 52 and is addressed either to the Delphians at the close of Gallio's tenure or to his successor immediately after his arrival. In either case the implication is that Gallio was proconsul in 51-52. See the more complete discussion in *Pauline Studies Bruce*, pp. 6-9. The precise relationship of Gallio's year of office to Paul's sojourn will be discussed in ch. 6, pp. 251-56. Gallio's proconsulship of Achaia is otherwise attested in the writings of his brother.[19]

19:38 ἀνθύπατοι may be a generalizing plural, but its use is odd, and might naturally reflect the time of confused interregnum following the murder of Julius Silanus, proconsul of Asia, after Nero's accession in October 54 when two men held office simultaneously (cf. C, p. 123 above).

20:6-7 While these verses give no explicit correlation with persons or events known to history, they have provided a base for a plausible calculation of the year of the events. The sequence of 20:1-21:16 gives a fairly full conspectus of the travel diary of a seven-week period between Passover and Pentecost. If the early part is detailed without unrecorded gaps, it becomes possible tentatively to reckon back from the gathering at Troas ἐν τῇ μιᾷ σαββάτων (= Sunday night: cf. Lk. 24:1) to a placing of the Passover that year on a Thursday. The relative fullness of the record of days, and the tightness and haste of its early stages in particular, supports the feasibility of this attempted reconstruction, which might otherwise seem speculative and suspect. The Passover of 57, as calculated from the full moon, fell probably on Thursday 7 April, and the Passovers of neighbouring years could not have fallen on that day of the week. While this coincidence is both tentative and unspectacular, it is unforced, and suits that year rather than adjacent possibilities.[20]

---

[19] 'Illud mihi ore erat domini mei Gallionis, qui cum in Achaia febrem habere coepisset, protinus navem ascendit clamitans non corporis esse, sed loci morbum' (Sen. *Ep. Mor.* 104.1). The health-cruise of Gallio to which Pliny refers (*NH* 31.33.62) followed his subsequent consulship (cf. E.M. Smallwood, 'Consules Suffecti of AD 55', *Historia* 17 [1968], p. 384).

[20] See the fuller discussion in *Pauline Studies Bruce*, pp. 9-12. This idea has been canvassed (with some variations in calculation) by W.M. Ramsay, D. Plooij, O. Gerhardt and others. See especially Ramsay, 'A Fixed Date in the Life of St. Paul', *Expos* 5th ser. 3 (1896), pp. 336-45. The cautions expressed by C.H. Turner in *HDB* 1.415-25 are still salutary, though he wrote before the discovery of the Gallio inscription, which now effectively excludes, on a natural reading of the texts, any option so early as that which allowed consideration of the Passover of 55. See further the criticism of these approaches in Ogg (*Paul*, pp. 140-45). I have not seen the works of Plooij and Gerhardt. In any case it is important to stress the tightness of the timing, especially in the early part of this voyage, which

21:16 Mnason is described as an ἀρχαῖος μαθητής, that is, from the beginning of the church. The point is trivial, but it is not unnatural to distinguish thus a man whose Christian experience was of 25-30 years' standing at the date of the narrative, when many must have died, moved, or grown cold. There is no plausible redactional explanation of this unstudied designation.

21:38 This reference to the Egyptian is paralleled in Jos. *BJ* 2.13.5.261-63 and *Ant.* 20.8.6.169-72. The insurrection begun by this man had been suppressed by Felix, but the ringleader had escaped. Josephus portrays the period as one of constant violence and brigandage. While the Egyptian's revolt cannot be closely dated from Josephus, and the length of Felix's governorship remains in some dispute, the two writers concur in connecting this incident or its aftermath with the time of Felix, and Luke's reference suits the nervous reaction to a revolutionary still at large in the latter years of Felix (cf. C, pp. 126f.). It seems wisest to refrain from dating his outbreak to Nisan 56, according to the ingenious suggestion of B.Z. Wacholder, although this would admirably suit the picture here presented.[21]

22:28 The χιλίαρχος had bought his citizenship at great cost. The sale of citizenship was notoriously a feature of life under Claudius (Dio 60.17.5-7). Dio's statement is placed annalistically in A D 43 (60.17.1), and he says that the privilege, first sold at great cost, became cheapened later under Claudius, an interesting parallel with our present passage. This man, whose name Claudius Lysias (23:26) sufficiently confirms his enfranchisement by Claudius, had presumably gained his rights early in the reign, and had seen his pride reduced by Claudius' later practice, and his remark reflects this. There is in fact circumstantial support at least for a dramatic date plausibly reflecting the aftermath of Claudius' later citizenship policy in the lifetime of a man still in his prime after living in adulthood through the period (cf. C, p. 127).

23:2 The high priest Ananias, son of Nedebaeus: this man's career can be partly reconstructed. He was appointed by Herod of Chalcis c. 47 (Jos. *Ant.* 20.5.2.103), sent to Rome to face trial with the procurator Cumanus before Claudius (Jos. *BJ* 2.12.6.243; *Ant.* 20.6.2.131) after the Samaritan troubles dated by Tacitus (*Ann.* 12.54) to A D 52, but was evidently acquitted, for he continued to wield great influence under Albinus (61-65), long after his replacement c. 58-59 (Jos *Ant.* 20.8.8.179; 20.9.2.205; 20.9.3.213). He was murdered in 66 (*BJ* 2.17.9.441). His brutal and rapacious character is reflected in the

minimizes the uncertainties of the reckoning. Ramsay and Plooij concur with the view tentatively maintained here.

21 B.Z. Wacholder, *HUCA* 46 (1975), p. 216.

sources (e.g. *Ant.* 20.9.2.206-207; TB Pesahim 57a). If his high priest-
hood ran c. 47-58 and he exercised an unrestrained arrogance of
power under Felix, as our sources indicate, this suits well our estimated dating of Paul's trial before him in 57. No significance should
be attached to the fact that Paul did not recognize Ananias: Paul's
previous, briefly noted visit to Palestine (18:22) was ostensibly in
summer 52, likely to have been the very time when Ananias had been
sent in chains to Rome.

23:24 Both the beginning and the end of Felix's governorship pose
chronological problems. For the beginning see on 24:10 below. A
combination of reasons may now be given for preferring a later date
(c. 59) rather than an earlier (c. 56) for Festus's succession. The early
date is based on the statement in Eusebius *Chron.* that Festus became
procurator in the second year of Nero, and Albinus in the sixth or
seventh. Josephus' account presupposes a short tenure by Festus before his untimely death (*Ant.* 20.8.9.182-20.9.1.197; 20.9.1.200; *BJ*
2.14.1.271-72), for which Eusebius' date (61 or 62) is more likely to be
correct. H.J. Cadbury points to a change of coinage in AD 59, which
may be associated with the arrival of the new procurator.[22] If this interpretation is correct, it points specifically to 59 as the year of Felix's
departure, and Festus may be placed 59-c. 61. If Felix was in office at
least c. 52-59, this precisely suits our emerging pattern, and Paul's
two years' captivity in Caesarea falls into place as summer 57 to
summer 59.[23]

---

[22] H.J. Cadbury, *The Book of Acts in History* (London: A. & C. Black, 1955), pp. 9-
10. *BMC Palestine*, Procurators under Nero, Nos. 1-28: see C, p. 130, n. 90.

[23] The antedated chronology is defended by Lake (*BC* 5.466-67) and fully discussed by Ogg (*Paul*, pp. 146-59). The strongest argument for this position is that
which stresses the fall of Pallas in 55 as setting a terminus for his influence in
protecting his brother Felix from condemnation. If however this preceded the
death of Britannicus, as in Tac. *Ann.* 13.14-17, ostensibly before that prince's
fourteenth birthday in Feb. 55, there is little time for the recall of Felix by Nero,
for new governors were not sent out in the winter season. Nero had succeeded
on 13th October 54, and the narrative of Josephus clearly implies that Felix was
active in Judaea for a considerable period after the accession of Nero (*Ant.*
20.8.2.152) and is integrated with the appointment of Ishmael son of Phabi as
high priest, an event usually dated c. 58 (*Ant.* 20.8.8.179). Ogg however doubts
the common assumption that Pallas continued to exercise considerable influence
after his dismissal in 55 (*Paul*, pp. 158-59), for Nero was already disgusted by his
arrogance, according to Tac. *Ann.* 13.2, and Ogg believes that Josephus' account
of his standing with Nero (*Ant.* 20.8.9.182) is misrepresentation rather than mere
exaggeration. But there is no reason to doubt Josephus here. Pallas, even on
Tacitus' view, had the arrogance to make terms with Nero for his resignation
(*Ann.* 13.14), and retained the power conferred by immense wealth to his death
in 62 (*Ann.* 14.65).

23:34 Felix's question and his acceptance of Paul's case on learning he was a Cilician is both interesting and difficult, and may have chronological implications. The basic point is well made by E.M.B. Green that Cilicia Pedias, which included Tarsus, was subject to the governor of Syria as part of the double province Syria-Cilicia before Vespasian's creation of a separate, enlarged Cilician province in 72. Felix then was a responsible official within the same complex of jurisdiction, and at the least his action suits the pre-Flavian period.[24]

24:10 Paul's statement that Felix had judged the nation 'for many years' (ἐκ πολλῶν ἐτῶν): the context is rhetorical, and the force of πολλῶν flexible, comparative rather than absolute. Felix was a governor of long standing, not an inexperienced new arrival. In any case Felix had been a governor since 52, but in reckoning beyond that we encounter a well-known clash of evidence between Josephus and Tacitus. While many scholars prefer Josephus, who first introduces Felix as the successor of Cumanus (*Ant.* 20.7.1.137; *BJ* 2.12.8.247), there are good reasons for taking serious account of Tacitus' narrative of a previous history of conflict between the two as rulers of different sections of the country (*Ann.* 12.54), Felix having been *iam pridem Iudaeae inpositus*. If Josephus' evidence may be supplemented by a modified acceptance of Tacitus, as seems in principle the most likely solution, the words of our text are the more pointed, when viewed from a dramatic date late in Felix's sole tenure.[25]

24:24 Drusilla as the wife of Felix: according to Josephus, *Ant.* 19.9.1.354, she was six years old at the death of her father Agrippa I in

---

24 E.M.B. Green, 'Syria and Cilicia— A Note', *ExpT* 71 (1959-60), pp. 52-53. Sherwin-White's discussion (*RSRL*, pp. 55-57) is unclear; his implication of a change in the early years of Nero might greatly refine our chronological perspective, but the status of Cossutianus Capito in Tac. *Ann.* 13.33 (of AD 57) is not recorded. After a nuanced account of an intricate question, Sherwin-White concludes that the narrative 'shows remarkable familiarity with the provincial and juridical situation in the last years of Claudius' (*RSRL*, p. 57). But it belongs ostensibly to the early years of Nero (see further *CAH* 11.603).

25 See especially M. Aberbach, 'The Conflicting Accounts of Josephus and Tacitus concerning Cumanus' and Felix' Terms of Office', *JQR* 40 (1949-50), pp. 1-14. Aberbach argues that Tacitus' essential error lies in his mistaken assignment of territories to the rivals, that Cumanus undeniably held Jerusalem and had jurisdiction in Samaria, and that Felix then probably held Galilee, not Samaria, as Tacitus wrongly supposes. This reconstruction is plausible, and offers a neat explanation of the difficulty, but must remain conjectural in the current state of our knowledge. Momigliano in *CAH* 10.853 essentially accepts Tacitus' account, but without any specific treatment of the problem of reconciling it with the evidence of Josephus. The whole Cumanus affair, as well as the following misgovernment of Felix's sole governorship, was disastrous for Roman prestige in Judaea (cf. Aberbach, p. 14), and probably contributed much to the drift into final conflict.

44, and so born c. 38. After the end of Claudius' twelfth year (53), according to *Ant.* 20.7.1.138-39, Agrippa II gave Drusilla in marriage to Azizus king of Emesa, but not long afterwards she deserted her husband to marry Felix (μετ' οὐ πολὺν χρόνον, *Ant.* 20.7.2.141-43). This incident is placed in Felix's procuratorship, and as she was only about fifteen at the time of her first marriage, she was evidently married to Felix while still in her teens, and only about nineteen at the ostensible time of our narrative. Felix is said to have been married to three queens (Suet. *Claud.* 28). This ex-slave owed his success to the favour of Claudius, and perhaps all his distinguished alliances were initiated in that reign, or at least before the dismissal in 55 (Tac. *Ann.* 13.14) or death in 62 (Tac. *Ann.* 14.65) of his powerful brother Pallas, but the chronology of his other marriages is otherwise unknown.[26]

24:27 The two years are naturally taken to refer to the duration of Paul's custody in the remaining period of Felix's tenure of office and certainly do not imply that this was the whole duration of Felix's term, which would be a bald contradiction of 24:10, quite apart from the implication of conflicting evidence in Tacitus and Josephus. The view of Lake which places Felix c. 53-55 (*BC* 5.464-67) is simply unacceptable. The two years appear to run from the early summer of Paul's Jerusalem Pentecost to the early summer of Festus's arrival. This suits the accumulation of pointers to 57-59.

25:13 Bernice as consort of Agrippa II: enough is known of the course of the lives of brother and sister to illustrate the general chronological suitability of the reference, though the notes of time are not otherwise sufficiently precise to set close and exclusive criteria. Bernice was aged sixteen at the death of her father Agrippa I, and so born c. 28 (Jos. *Ant.* 19.9.1.354; cf. on Drusilla). She was already then married to Herod of Chalcis, who died in the eighth year of Claudius (48-49; Jos. *Ant.* 20.5.2.104; cf. *BJ* 2.11.6.221; 2.12.1.223). She then lived for a long time as a widow, but when rumours arose of an incestuous relationship with her brother Agrippa, she was married to Polemo king of Cilicia, though she soon deserted him (Jos. *Ant.* 20.7.3.145; cf. Juv. *Sat.* 6.156-60). Later references to Bernice, in incidents under Florus (AD 65-66; Jos. *BJ* 2.15.1.310ff.) and at the outbreak of war (Jos. *Vita* 11.48) clearly assert her presence with Agrippa at that period. This visit to Festus at his assumption of office belongs ostensibly on our reckoning to summer 59.[27]

---

26 For Felix see further A. Stein in *PIR* 1.157-58, No. 828; P. von Rohden, 'Antonius Felix [54]', *PW* 1.2616-2618; for Drusilla, Stein in *PW* 5.2.1741. Felix's two known wives were both called Drusilla. Cf. Tac. *Hist.* 5.9.

27 On Ber(e)nice see further G.H. Macurdy, 'Julia Berenice' *AJP* 56 (1935), pp. 246-53; J.A. Crook, 'Titus and Berenice' *AJP* 72 (1951), pp. 162-75; D.C. Braund,

27:1 The reference to the σπεῖρα Σεβαστή might be more helpful chronologically if we were better informed about the movements of units in Syria-Palestine in the Julio-Claudian period. If we accept the tentative identification of Julius' unit offered above, we may have some slight corroboration, but as the matter stands, the chronological data are too tenuous to help (cf. C, pp. 132-33, n. 96 where we also list reasons for rejecting alternative identifications).

27:9 The implication of the reference to the Fast, taken with the chronological sequence of the winter following, is that the Fast was particularly late that year, a detail open to verification by the lunar phases, and suiting the autumn of 59 better than neighbouring years (see C, p. 138, n. 109 on H.P. Workman).

28:30 The chronology of this διετία presents complex problems and depends on a reconstruction across a broader canvas. We may anticipate later argument to the extent of claiming a probability that this captivity began before news came of the Lycus valley earthquake dated by Tacitus (*Ann.* 14.27) to AD 60 and concluded before the Neronian persecution of AD 64 (Tac. *Ann.* 15.44), a position consonant with our assignment of it to 60-62[28] (cf. p. 255; see F, p. 190).

'Berenice in Rome', *Historia* 33 (1984), pp. 120-23. Macurdy offers some rehabilitation of the traditional view of her character. An inscription of Athens (*CIG* 361 = *IG* 3.1.556) designates her βασίλισσα, a term usually reserved for queens regnant, and she is also called *regina* in Latin (*CRAI* [1927], pp. 243-44). Macurdy points out the favourable view Josephus takes of her in *BJ* and *Vita*, and argues that the imputations in the *Antiquities* were vindictive falsification after the deaths of Agrippa and Berenice. Only Josephus and the contemptuously anti-Jewish Juvenal are ultimate authorities for the unfavourable tradition. Macurdy sees her as fully co-ruler with her brother, but not in the Hellenistic sister-wife tradition, until her ambitions led her into association with Titus. Juvenal's manner however is highly allusive to that which is purported to have been common knowledge. This is an apt instance of the difficulty of historical reconstruction through redaction-critical method. Josephus' partialities are blatant, but it is not clear that we are justified in setting aside his explicit statements because they are explainable as hostile invention. It is certainly a possible option, but not a provable one. Even calculated malice might either have embroidered falsehood or have repeated scandal or have publicized truth. We ought to take textual evidence seriously and exhibit its alternative possibilities even where it may be suspect. In other contexts scholars are prone to take Josephus simplistically at face-value in places where they reconstruct Luke with little control. Conversely, in this section they have often been found to be consonant. That is in some degree a corroboration of both, and an encouragement in the careful use of Josephus, whose demonstrable inaccuracies and contradictions in areas unconnected with Luke's veracity I have had previous occasion to note (*JTS* n.s. 26 [1975], p. 107n; *BJRL* 60 [1977-78], p. 50).

[28] The fire of Rome and the persecution evidently set a tacit *terminus ad quem*, and it is sometimes supposed that Paul is likely to have perished in 64. It might

This brief outline of areas of possible correlation permits interim conclusions. Many of the indications are too slight and uncertain to be of more than marginal value (though even such clues help to illustrate that we are not dealing with radical anachronisms); one reference, that to Theudas, is quite intractable, but otherwise they tend to fit, however tentatively, an approximate ostensible outline of the internal chronology, and this fit becomes unexpectedly specific and precise for the period 57-62. The arguments for several of the correlations in this period are of circumstantial probabilities which may be disputed, and their combination may be supposed to combine uncertainties. But indications seem to point here to the converse phenomenon, the indications of a correctly integrated reconstruction which tends rather to corroborate that its components are rightly built into the structure. If this is so, it is an historical platform of considerable significance. We concur here with Jewett, from whose methods and results we differ substantially elsewhere.[29]

The attempt to reconstruct a more detailed chronology and its bearing on the veracity of the Acts account must await assessment of the interplay of other categories of evidence.

E. Details broadly suggestive of date

This is a difficult category, not rigidly separated from the preceding, which dealt with the more specific dates of kings, governors, etc. Included here are only examples, to illustrate in principle where practices or terminology are suggestive of a first rather than a second century setting, or of one earlier or later in the first century.

4:1 etc. The prominence of the Sadducees accords with a pre-70 setting, for the Jewish revolt destroyed their political ascendancy.[30]

6:1 The 'Hellenists' pose a notoriously difficult problem. It seems

then be argued that the early church knew the διετία terminated in Paul's death in the pogrom. But the weight of evidence points to an expected, judicial termination, whatever its outcome, at a date prior to that terminus.

29 Cf. Jewett, *Dating*, pp. 100-102, which with his supporting discussions (pp. 40-44) concurs largely with our arguments, though I should be more cautious about several of his absolute dates and termini. I differ here somewhat from Ogg, *Paul*, who places the accession of Festus in 61 and ties Paul's trial to the Neronian persecution, while reading differently several of the indicators which impress me by their interlocking. The differences from Knox and Lüdemann are more fundamental, and will be discussed in Chapter 6.

30 For their demise after 70 see e.g. K. Kohler in *Jewish Encyclopedia* 10.632; A.C. Sundberg in *IDB* 4.161-62; and for the bearing of this factor on the setting of Acts cf. I.H. Marshall in *Apostolic History and the Gospel*, ed. Gasque and Martin, pp. 97-98.

likely that as a group, however precisely defined, they belong distinctively to the earliest period of the church.[31]

6:9 Synagogue of the libertines, etc.: it seems most likely that only one synagogue is meant, and possibly it is to be identified with that of Theodotus in the Ophel inscription, certainly pre-70 (*CIJ* 1404).

7:2-53 Stephen's views seem best explained as involving a very radical critique of Jewish religion in a setting when the temple yet stood. The arguments for a specially Semitic background or for the use of sources for this speech are consonant with indications of an early setting.[32]

7:57ff. The irregularity and illegality of Stephen's stoning presents its own problems, but there is no reason to question its historicity, for it is perhaps the crucial incident presupposed in Paul's own sense of his special previous guilt as persecutor (1 Cor. 15:9; Gal. 1:13, 23; Phil. 3:6; cf. Acts 22:20). It is at least suitable to the period, ostensibly the troubled last years of Pilate, when the continuance of Caiaphas until Pilate's recall in 36 again suggests political accommodation between the two.[33]

---

[31] See especially H.J. Cadbury in *BC* 5.59-74 for the view that they were equivalent to Ἕλληνες, Gentiles; E.C. Blackman, 'The Hellenists of Acts vi.1', *ExpT* 48 (1936-37), pp. 524-25, that they were converted Jewish proselytes; M. Simon, *St. Stephen and the Hellenists in the Primitive Church* (London: Longmans, Green, 1958), pp. 10ff, partly following G.P. Wetter, A.D. Nock and others, that they were a radical, even 'paganizing', party in the Judaism of the earliest Christian period; C.F.D. Moule, 'Once More, Who Were the Hellenists?' *ExpT* 70 (1958-59), pp. 100-102, that they were Jews unable to speak Hebrew. The commonest view is probably still that which sees them as Greek-speaking Jews. It may be in any case that the terminology is not used with a rigid and technical consistency of application. Moule and Bruce (*Acts*, p. 151) allow for flexibility according to context. While Cadbury's view is not necessarily tied to an early setting, and even allows for reworking of sources, the other views generally feel constrained to explain the Hellenists as a primitive phenomenon. The occurrence of Ἕλληνες as a variant in some places (though not here) for Ἑλληνισταί complicates, but does not obviate, the basic problem of explaining the term.

[32] The views of C.C. Torrey, *The Composition and Date of Acts* (Cambridge Mass: Harvard University Press, 1916) were speculative and are now dated. See further H.F.D. Sparks, 'The Semitisms of the Acts', *JTS* n.s. 1 (1950), pp. 16-28; M. Wilcox, *The Semitisms of Acts*,(Oxford: Clarendon Press, 1965); D.F. Payne, 'Semitisms in the Book of Acts', *Apostolic History*, ed. Gasque and Martin, pp. 134-50. Along with salutary cautions, these writers tend to reinforce, at least tentatively, the bearing of residual Semitisms upon early setting or sources. For Stephen's speech in particular see Wilcox, pp. 159-61; Bruce, 'Stephen's Apologia', in *Scripture, Meaning and Method: Essays Presented to A.T. Hanson*, ed. B.P. Thompson (Hull University Press, 1987), pp. 37-50.

[33] It is difficult to be sure whether we should understand the case as an instance

8:1 The violence of the reaction against Stephen again seems to fit his implied radical attack on the Temple and priestly religion at the time of their special ascendancy.

8:9 This incident may be broadly linked to date, if the details given by Justin, a native of Neapolis (Nablus) in Samaria, preserve authentic traditions of the historical Simon Magus. He is dated by Justin firmly to the reign of Claudius (*Apol.* 1.26.2; 1.56.2; cf. *Dial.* 120.6).[34]

10:1 The use of the simple *nomen* Cornelius reflects an older Roman practice which persisted into the Julio-Claudian period among older and more conservatively minded men in the army.[35]

11:26 The date of the coining of the term 'Christian' might be of interest here. I am not persuaded by the interesting suggestion of H.B. Mattingly that it was modelled on the Augustiani of the young Nero, a body whose formation is assigned by Tacitus (*Ann.* 14.15) to AD 59.[36] The term was in any case presumably in use in Rome before the outbreak of the fire in 64 (Tac. *Ann.* 15.44). Luke's aside does not imply the word was in use at the date of which he writes; it will suffice if it was widespread at the date *at* which he writes. The formulation in -*ianus* is common, however, as in adoptive *cognomina* like Octavianus, and an earlier origin needs no special justification.

13:16 The problem of the 'God-fearers': the existence of a class of Gentile adherents attracted to the synagogues has often been assumed, but recently challenged afresh.[37] This verse and v. 43 below

---

of lynch-law or as an excess of the Sanhedrin's authority (Bruce, *Acts*, p. 179). It is not necessarily to be decided by differences from the procedures laid down in the Mishnah (Sanh. 6.3-4) as Haenchen argues (pp. 292-93), nor by the fact that he was mourned and reverently buried (8:2).

34 On Simon Magus see D. Flusser, 'The Great Goddess of Samaria', *IEJ* 25 (1975), pp. 13-20, esp. pp. 18-20; cf. *New Docs* 1.107, No. 68, and the literature there cited.

35 *RSRL*, pp. 160-61; cf. 27:1.

36 H.B. Mattingly, 'The Origin of the Name *Christiani*', *JTS* n.s. 9 (1958), pp. 26-37. See *MM* for καισαριανός as 'imperial slave' from *P Lond* 256 *recto*, (καίσαρος) and Epictetus 1.19.19 which uses the form καισαριανοί. Ἡρωδιανοί are named not only in Mk 3:6; 12:13 = Mt. 22:16, but paralleled in Jos. *Ant.* 14.15.10.450: οἱ τὰ Ἡρώδου φρονοῦντες.

37 Many older writers have cautioned about reading a technical sense too readily into such terms as θεοσεβής where they mean simply 'pious'. So e.g. Lake in *BC* 5.77. The usual understanding of 'God-fearers' has however recently been challenged by M. Wilcox, 'The "God-Fearers" in Acts— A Reconsideration', *JSNT* 13 (1981), pp. 102-22, and more radically by A.T. Kraabel, 'The Disappearance of the "God-Fearers"', *Numen* 28 (1981), pp. 113-26; cf. 'The Roman Diaspora: Six Questionable Assumptions', *JJS* 33 (1982), pp. 445-64; T.M. Finn,

give apparent reference to distinct groups, where some references to σεβόμενοι or φοβούμενοι in Acts are less clear. It is right to be cautious towards the tendency to see a technical term here; similar words are widely used to mean no more than 'pious worshippers'. But the context in several places in Acts points to the phenomenon of Gentile adhesion to the synagogues, even if the terminology is less formal than sometimes supposed. And on this view, illustrated further by some evidence outside Acts, we can see the phenomenon as characteristically pre-70, likely to have been radically changed or curtailed by the traumatic effects of the fall of Jerusalem on Jewish-Christian relations. The presence of Gentiles in the synagogue (cf. 13:44, 48) and their response to Paul's words in that context belong ostensibly to the earlier setting.

14:6 The implication is that Iconium was not in Lycaonia. It was ethnically Phrygian, but political borders were subject to change. Beyond affirming the city's Phrygian character in the Roman period and its later political re-attachment to Lycaonia, we must allow that the chronological net is too broad here to help much, save as fitting the prominence of regional divisions in the province of Galatia, which is characteristic of first century terminology (cf. excursus, pp. 228-30).

14:11 The indigenous languages of Asia Minor yielded rapidly to the presence of Hellenization. While we have no means of knowing the chronology of the persistence of Lycaonian, for all surviving monuments of that country are in Greek or colonial Latin, this interesting reference to its vernacular prevalence may naturally suit an earlier rather than a later setting (cf. C, pp. 110f.).

14:19, 21 Pisidian Antioch, Iconium and Lystra, here associated together, were all Phrygian cities, linked in the early Imperial road and defence system, and in adjacent southern districts of the province of Galatia. This is appropriate to the first century setting, especially when seen in the context of provincial awareness in this period. We cannot claim that such things are specific or exclusive, but they contribute subtly to a flavour which may be illustrated and in some degree appraised elsewhere.

'The God-Fearers Reconsidered', *CBQ* 47 (1985), pp. 75-84. ([Ed.] See now also J.A. Overman, 'The God-Fearers: Some Neglected Features', *JSNT* 32 [1988], pp. 17-26.) See Appendix 2 on the 'God-fearers'.

There seems no reason to doubt that Acts intends to present the phenomenon (whatever the interpretation of some of the words) of pious Gentiles attracted to the synagogues and ripe for the Christian message, the classic instance being Cornelius. The criticism of the idea that the Acts references reflect technical terminology is justified: cf. R.W. Cowley's 1985 Tyndale Lecture 'Technical Terms in Biblical Hebrew?' (*TB* 37 [1986], pp. 21-28) for a salutary analysis in a related field, showing the lack of criteria by which such alleged terms may be identified.

15:23 The characteristically Lukan manner of reference to a capital city and province (cf. Acts 1:8) reflects here the time when Syria-Cilicia was still a double province, an arrangement changed when Vespasian made all Cilicia into a separate province.[38]

16:6 The use of the term 'Asia' has engendered much unnecessary debate. It should be taken in the provincial sense, and this accords with the strong sense of provincial identity fostered by Julio-Claudian policy and abundantly illustrated in the formulations of contemporary documents. Cf. 19:10.

16:8 The use of the name Troas, formerly Alexandria, is characteristic of first century usage, after Augustus made the city a colony formally designated 'Colonia Augusta Troadensium' or 'Colonia Augusta Troas'.[39] This usage serves, of course, only to demarcate the appropriateness of Acts with regard to an earlier, not a later, period.

18:15 The character of Gallio's response (and indeed that of the accusation, v. 13) suits the early period when the Christian movement could be seen by Roman authority as a theological schism within Judaism of which it need not take official cognizance. This does not of course mean that the Romans were unaware of Christianity, only that it appeared as one more difficult problem in the explosive task of handling Judaism. This pattern of controversy would not suit a situation post-70, or even post-64, when the separation of the faiths was manifest. This represents a crucial challenge to the Judaistic legitimacy of the Christian way, and Gallio's decision evidently set a precedent eroded by the rapid march of events at a still early date.

20:4 The designation of these men by their province as Ἀσιανοί is again characteristic of first-century usage, though not exclusive to it. Trophimus is identified specifically as an Ephesian in 21:29, and both men by the Western text here (cf. H, p. 198). Much needless scepticism over the propriety of calling people 'Galatians' could have been avoided by closer attention to first-century documentary usage.

21:23-24 Paul's practice of acts of characteristically Jewish piety (cf. also 18:18) may seem problematic from some perspectives on his theology, and so a difficulty in Acts. But we may also make a converse point that the difficulty is one which belongs to an early period when Christianity had not yet become separated from the practice of Judaism. It is not naturally explained as redactional invention or as archaeologizing. Haenchen (*Acts*, pp. 612-13) recognizes Luke's use here of an itinerary source.

21:28 Again the sensitive question is Temple defilement. It would be

---

38 *CAH* 11.603; cf. 15:41; 23:34; see E.M.B. Green in *ExpT* 71 (1959-60), pp. 52-53.
39 *CIL* 3.39; *BMC Troas, Aeolis and Lesbos*, Alex. Troas *passim*; *TB* 26 (1975), p. 90.

disingenuous to doubt the essentially early character of this material.

21:38 Reference to the *sicarii* suits the period from the time of Felix to the fall of Jerusalem. As a party they were apparently distinct from the Zealots, and also arose earlier (Jos. *BJ* 7.8.1.262, 3.268), being the group deriving ultimately from Judas of Galilee in the time of the census.[40] Their rise as a party, however, is assigned by Josephus specifically to the time of Felix (*BJ* 2.13.3.254-57), shortly before his account of the Egyptian (*BJ* 2.13.5.261-63), and so closely consonant with the present allusion.

22:25, 29 The protection of a Roman citizen from certain abuses by persons in authority may be referred to the *lex Julia de vi publica*, which derived from the time of Augustus.[41]

22:28 This verse can be read as a reference to the purchase, and subsequent cheapening, of citizenship under Claudius (cf. D, p. 170).

23:29 Again, as in 18:15, the attitude attributed to Claudius Lysias reflects the early perspective that Christianity lay within the protection accorded to Judaism. Cf. also 25:19.

23:34 Felix's acceptance of a case involving a man from Cilicia may be explained as reflecting a time when Cilicia, like Judaea, lay within the provincial complex subordinate to Syria, and therefore within the same ultimate jurisdiction (cf 15:23).[42] This is at least a pointer to a setting earlier than Vespasian's re-creation of a separate province comprising all Cilicia in AD 72 (cf. D, p. 172).

24:14 Paul's defence again emphasizes his Judaism, as a correct worshipper of the 'ancestral' God of his people.

25:11 According to Sherwin-White, Paul's appeal fits the practice of *provocatio* current in his period: Acts study 'provides a useful chronological countercheck in more ways than one'.[43]

25:26 Reference to the reigning emperor simply as ὁ κύριος was a common practice in Egypt and the East, as attested *passim* in the papyri since Ptolemaic times, but this form becomes much more frequent and widespread under Nero and later.[44]

27:1 The use of the simple *nomen* 'Julius' again reflects older practice (see 19:1 and *RSRL*, pp. 160-61), appropriate only to an older man in the Julio-Claudian setting.

27:6-28:14 The voyage, successively on two ships of the Alexandrian fleet, reflects, and is illustrated by, available documentation of

---

[40] Cf. Morton Smith, 'Zealots and Sicarii, their Origins and Relation', *HTR* 64 (1971), pp. 1-19.

[41] See *RSRL*, pp. 57ff.

[42] *RSRL*, pp. 55-57.

[43] *RSRL*, pp. 63-70 (citation from p. 69).

[44] See Deissmann, *LAE*, pp. 353-55; Bruce, *Acts*, p. 438.

the organization of the corn-supply, especially as developed to its peak of efficiency by Claudius in response to the recurrent famines of his reign and publicized in the numismatic propaganda of Claudius and Nero. A later period would not of course be excluded by these considerations, but the narrative admirably suits the classic period of public interest in the venture (cf. e.g. Seneca *Ep. Mor.* 77.1).[45]

28:17-20 Paul's first interview with the Roman Jews again emphasizes the Jewish perspective in terms superseded by the break of the two faiths after 70. This could be explained by the use of older sources, if not by archaeologizing, but points ostensibly to the earlier setting.

It is recognized that these examples are of differing value and application, and that some are capable of diverse explanation. It suffices here to indicate the general case for seeing in principle that there are kinds of material available for discriminating between an earlier or a later setting of many details of the text, whatever the explanation of these phenomena.

F. Correlations between Acts and Epistles

This section will present situational links with Acts in the whole Pauline corpus, including epistles whose authenticity is widely questioned. Before we attempt to draw conclusions on such matters we shall have complex critical questions to consider, at least parenthetically. But at the present stage of tabulating evidence, it seems important to present the whole range of the ostensible material without prejudging its validity. The marker '(W)' has been added to instances noted in Wikenhauser's tabulation of parallels (p. 59). Some of his, however, are not used here, where they are parallels only of thought or expression rather than substantive situational correlations.[46] And as many of the apparent correlations are keenly contested, I shall try to acknowledge in the notes where we are on debated ground, even if I am personally convinced that the foothold is secure.

Acts 7:58, 60 matches Paul's own references to himself as

---

45 See also C.J. Hemer, 'First Person Narrative in Acts 27-28', *TB* 36 [1985], pp. 79-109, esp. pp. 87-94.

46 Such parallels might be used to make a point at a different level from the present. In any case they require careful selection and analysis. A parallel like Acts 2:21 with Rom. 10:13, for instance, consists in the common use of Joel 2:32, once in a speech attributed to Peter, the other by Paul himself. There may be some ground for saying that Joel 2 was a *testimonium* widely used in primitive preaching, but not for furthering the search for specific situational contact between Acts and Epistles. Among striking parallels of thought in Wikenhauser, cf. Acts 10:34f. with Rom. 2:10f.; 10:36 with Eph. 2:17; 10:43 with Rom. 3:22; 13:34 with Rom. 6:9.

persecutor and 'chief of sinners' (Gal. 1:13, 23; Phil. 3:6; 1 Tim. 1:13-15). Cf. also the similar language placed in Paul's mouth in Acts (22:3-4; 26:9-11).

Acts 9:2ff. with Gal. 1:17 imply that Paul's conversion was associated with Damascus, to which he 'returns again' from Arabia. Again cf. the Pauline speeches at Acts 22:5-6; 26:12.

Acts 9:3-8 with 1 Cor. 15:8-9; Gal. 1:12, 16 speak of Paul's conversion through a revelation of Christ, subsequent to the appearances to the first disciples. Cf. Acts 22:6-11; 26:13-18.[47]

Acts 9:15 with e.g. Rom. 1:5 Ananias receives intimation of Paul's calling to the Gentiles. Cf. again Acts 22:21; 26:17-18, 20, 23. See G, p. 191.

Acts 9:21 with Gal. 1:13, 23 speak of Paul as persecutor again (W).

Acts 9:20, 22, of an initial ministry in Damascus, fits the implication of Gal. 1:17 that he was first in Damascus before going to Arabia and then returning, while 2 Cor. 11:32-33 indicates that he had already incurred hostility and persecution by activities in Damascus.

Acts 9:24-25 with 2 Cor. 11:33 Paul escaped by being lowered from the wall of Damascus in a basket,[48] a striking connection in view of the widely recognized independence of Acts and Epistles. In Acts however the opposition is ascribed to the Jews, and in 2 Cor. to the ethnarch of Aretas. It should be unnecessary to point out the possibility that different opponents may make common cause. It is much harder to believe the redactional speculations and psychologizings in Haenchen, *Acts*, pp. 333-36. (W).

Acts 9:26-29 with Gal. 1:18-19 speak of the first visit to Jerusalem. This identification may be regarded as problematic on various grounds. Here it will suffice to stress the common factor of tardy and limited contact with the Jerusalem church. In Acts all were afraid until Barnabas brought him to the apostles; in Galatians he met only Peter and James. There is nothing in Acts 9:26 to require immediate sequence of travel from the escape of v. 25.

Acts 9:30 with Gal. 1:21 The departure to Tarsus corresponds with

---

[47] I do not accept the view of John Knox which identifies the ecstatic vision of 2 Cor. 12:1-4 with the occasion of Paul's conversion, nor the equivalence of the fourteen year periods of 2 Cor. 12:2 and Gal. 2:1. It seems more likely that 2 Cor. refers to an experience which might have seemed a ground for boasting, heavenly visions not vouchsafed to lesser Christians, whereas Paul's references to his conversion reflect the arrest and reversal of a bitter adversary and persecutor, an occasion of great thanksgiving, but also of bitter shame and repentance, far from the temptation to boast.

[48] σπυρίς, σαργάνη, both terms apparently applicable to a very large, flexible basket; see F.J.A. Hort in *JTS* 10 (1909), pp. 567-71.

the reference in Galatians to the double province Syria-Cilicia.

Acts 11:3 is a first intimation of controversy over table-fellowship with Gentiles, appearing first in the eirenical tendency of Acts. Cf. Gal. 2:11-14 for a subsequent occasion, where Peter yields to pressure on the point for which he faced criticism here.

Acts 11:28-30 with Gal. 2:1 The second visit to Jerusalem: in this identification we touch a major crux (see chapter 7, pp. 261-65). It will suffice here to claim this identification proleptically while pointing out that we are following the natural sequence of correspondence in the ostensible texts, second visit in Acts with second visit in Galatians, where Paul is at pains to point out he is omitting nothing, for that would give his opponents a handle. This equivalence concurs with the view of the chronology here presented (see D, p. 165).

Acts 11:28 with Gal. 2:2 Paul went by revelation, though Galatians does not say that the impulse was famine-relief. That may however be just the point of Gal. 2:10, if we render ἐσπούδασα as a pluper-fect.[49] See above pp.164-65 on famines under Claudius.

Acts 11:30 with Gal. 2:1 Paul went with Barnabas on this journey, in Acts apparently as the junior partner.

Acts 13:1 with Gal. 2:11 Barnabas and Saul were again in Antioch after this visit to Jerusalem. Their return is stated in 12:25 if we are permitted to read the easy ἐξ or ἀπό for the better attested and difficult εἰς (cf. Metzger, *Textual Comm.*, pp. 398-400). Peter's visit to Antioch is placed at this juncture.

Acts 13:14 with Gal. 4:13 On the 'South Galatian' view, the arrival in Pisidian Antioch corresponds with the occasion of Paul's first coming to Galatia. This is an 'equation' rather than a 'correlation' of any probative value, and we refrain from pressing speculations about the illness of Paul as providing occasion for the journey.

Acts 13:21 with Phil. 3:5 Paul's Hebrew name is known only from Acts and his tribe only from Philippians. It is seen from the combination of these independent notices that he was named after the most famous Old Testament member of his tribe. This is a classic instance of an 'undesigned coincidence'.

Acts 13:26 (cf. 13:16) matches Paul's calling to the Gentiles in e.g. Rom. 1:5. Without necessarily wishing to make a technical term of οἱ φοβούμενοι τὸν θεόν, it does seem this phrase is used here in Acts of a separate category or sub-category of persons. The inclusion of Gentiles among the audience is apparent in the response triggered, according to 13:44, in a thoroughly Gentile Roman colony.[50]

---

[49] Cf. D.R. Hall, 'St. Paul and Famine Relief: A Study in Galatians 2:10', *ExpT* 82 (1970-71), pp. 309-11.

[50] On the term and concept of 'God-fearers', see Appendix 2 below.

Acts 13:39 with Gal. 1:6; 2:16, etc. Justification is by faith where men cannot be made free under the law of Moses. A close parallel of thought is reinforced here by a situational correlation, for the Galatians have so quickly 'deserted this gospel for another'. The specific terms of Paul's first preaching to the Galatians here are at stake in the controversy following their desertion of it. We may note subsidiary nuances: the cross as a 'tree' (ξύλον) in Acts 13:29 reflects the use of Deut. 21:22-23 in primitive Christian preaching, and this thought and citation are developed explicitly by Paul in Gal. 3:13 with reference to the Gospel first preached to the Galatians on the occasion of Acts 13.[51]

Acts 13:50; 14:5, 19 with 2 Tim. 3:11 Persecutions and sufferings specifically in the three cities of (Pisidian) Antioch, Lystra and Derbe were known to Timothy, who was a native of the area. While Acts is on almost any view independent of 2 Timothy, it would be disingenuous to suppose that a pseudepigraphist contrived the 2 Timothy note from Acts.[52]

Acts 14:15-17 with Rom. 1:19-23 The speech to a pagan audience uses a 'natural theology' akin to Paul's own words in Romans (W).[53]

Acts 14:19 with 2 Cor. 11:25 Paul had been stoned once before the date of writing 2 Corinthians. In this case the epistolary reference is certainly the earlier written, but Acts is generally acknowledged to be independent of it. Conversely, Paul tells us of *more* sufferings than we know from the restrained and selective account in Acts: natural perils and banditry were generally outside its scope, and it tends rather to play down spiritual conflict than otherwise. Cf. on Acts 16:22-23 below.

Acts 15:1 (cf. 15:24) with Gal. 1:7 This probably concerns the visit of Judaizers to Antioch and to Galatia, at a time when Paul and Barnabas were spending an extended time in Antioch (14:28), providing the occasion for the writing of Galatians on the eve of Paul's third Jerusalem visit, also prompted by the same crisis. This is the most natural and sequential restoration, which may be defended in detail, though much disputed. This involves setting aside the commonly

---

[51] It is unnecessary at this point to make specific defence of the South Galatian view on which some of our other points depend, for Gal. 4:13 speaks of Paul's first coming to Galatia (see on Acts 13:14 above), and Acts 13 ostensibly corresponds with the first occasion when Paul reached territory so designated in what is normal, documented usage.

[52] Harrison, *The Problem of the Pastorals*, pp. 124-25 and App. IV, accepts this as genuinely Pauline, *contra* e.g. A.T. Hanson, *The Pastoral Letters*, pp. 94-95, who sees other difficulties.

[53] See especially B. Gärtner, *The Areopagus Speech and Natural Revelation* (Lund: C.W.K. Gleerup and Copenhagen: Ejnar Munksgaard, 1955).

assumed equivalence Acts 15 = Gal. 2 (thus W). The point is so crucial as to require a separate chapter, but the usual identification will not figure in the resultant reconstruction to be argued in this book.[54] (Cf. Acts 15:24 with Gal. 1:7; 5:10, W).

Acts 15:1, 5 with Gal. 2:12; 5:2-6; 6:12-15 The circumcision of Gentile converts is the central issue here, whereas in Rom. 2:4 circumcision is treated in a more detached way, as the mark of the Jew and of the Jewish Law. Galatians seems to reflect the sharp initial conflict, and Romans a later stage of the controversy, when the focus had shifted. In our view, the delivery of the Apostolic Decree marked the closure of this first phase, but the controversy persisted on slightly different grounds. Therefore this passage of Acts can be seen to connect specifically with the situation reflected in Galatians.

Acts 15:13 ff. with Gal. 1:19; 2:12; 1 Cor. 15:7 all reflect the special influence of James in the Jerusalem church, though not the same immediate occasion. James seems to have been the recognized chairman and the object of deference. There is no reason to polarize relations between Paul and James, to whom Paul refers favourably, but there were no doubt tensions between different perspectives, and an essentially eirenical work like Acts does not deny the sharpness of the present issue.

Acts 15:20, 29 The injunctions against εἰδωλόθυτα and πορνεία may be compared with Paul's treatment of these problems at Corinth, in 1 Cor. 8:1-13; 10:18-30 and 1 Cor. 5:1; 6:12-20; etc. respectively. These things, conjoined in the preferred reading of Acts with ritual matters, are basic stumbling-blocks to a *modus vivendi* of Jew with Gentile in the primitive situation, only later adapted to a more abstractly moral and spiritual rule. Paul met two of these issues acutely at Corinth. The fact that he chose to handle them differently, without reiterating the Jerusalem Decree in a new situation, is not the present point. It is simply that these issues are paralleled in Acts and Paul as crucial to the primitive context.

Acts 16:1 with 2 Tim. 3:11 Timothy was apparently from Lystra. The appeal in 2 Timothy is apparently not so much to shared experiences as to Timothy's first acquaintance with Paul's sufferings, observed in his own home district.

Acts 16:1 also with 2 Tim. 1:5 which names Timothy's believing mother and grandmother.

Acts 16:3 The circumcision of Timothy, at first sight startling after

---

54 For this view see generally F.F. Bruce, 'Galatian Problems', esp '1. Autobiographical Data', *BJRL* 51 (1968-69), pp. 292-309; '2. North or South Galatians?', 52 (1969-70), pp. 243-66; '4. The Date of the Epistle', 54 (1971-72), pp. 250-67; C.J. Hemer, 'Acts and Galatians Reconsidered', *Themelios* n.s. 2 (1976-77), pp. 81-88.

the controversy preceding, is consistent with Paul's remarkable flexibility in conciliation where the truth of the Gospel was not at stake. Cf. 1 Cor. 9:19-22.

Acts 16:6 with Gal. 1:1 The expression τὴν Φρυγίαν καὶ Γαλατικὴν χώραν corresponds to the primary destination of the Galatian epistle, the district of Pisidian Antioch and Iconium (Acts 13-14), which together with Lycaonia constituted the churches of (South) Galatia. See chapter 7. The delivery of the Apostolic Decree in the Galatian churches (cf. 16:4) is then seen as the agreed response to the challenge on which Paul had had to argue his case and authority in Galatians.

Acts 16:12-40 with Philippians, which reflects Paul's long association and care for this church (cf. e.g. Phil. 1:5).

Acts 16:22-23 with 2 Cor. 11:25 Paul is beaten with rods (ῥαβδίζειν), a characteristically Roman form of chastisement, presumably administered at Philippi by the lictors (ῥαβδοῦχοι) attendant on the colonial *duoviri*. This is the only flogging we can place of the three to which Paul himself refers at the date of his writing.

Acts 16:22-23 also with 1 Thess. 2:2, which relates the shameful treatment at Philippi immediately before coming to Thessalonica, in a letter ostensibly written within a few weeks or months of the events at Philippi (W).

Acts 17:1-9 with 1, 2 Thess. The two Thessalonian epistles, both sent in the names of Paul, Silvanus (Silas) and Timothy, belong ostensibly to the immediate aftermath of this first visit, and deal with misunderstandings consequent upon the incompleteness of Paul's teaching at his premature and enforced departure.

Acts 17:5-9 with 1 Thess. 2:14 The sufferings of the Thessalonian Christians occurs in so short a space at the hands of their fellow-citizens, just as the churches of Judaea had suffered at the hands of their fellow-Jews (cf. also Acts 17:5).

Acts 17:9 with 1 Thess. 2:18 Paul's reference to the hindrance of Satan may be connected with the binding over of Jason, apparently forced to be guarantor that Paul would not return, a point bearing on his use of an emissary and letters to supplement his work.

Acts 17:14-15 with 1 Thess. 3:1-6 Silas and Timothy were left behind in Macedonia, Timothy in particular being sent back to Thessalonica (1 Thess. 3:2), while Paul himself was alone in Athens. According to Acts 18:5 they rejoined him at Corinth.

Acts 17:28 with Tit. 1:12 The first citation in Acts belongs to the same traditional passage as that cited in Titus, which Clement of Alexandria (*Strom.* 1.14) attributes to Epimenides the Cretan. The common use of a pagan tag as a proof-text in the two writings might be taken on some recent views of the Pastorals to show a common

Lukan tendency. But by as good a right the correspondence may be claimed as Pauline. Paul quotes Greek verse in undisputed writings (1 Cor. 15:33), and an Epimenides background is otherwise embedded in the context of the Areopagus address. Cf. C, p. 118.

Acts 18:2 Paul's meeting at Corinth with Aquila and Priscilla may be compared with the references to this couple in the Epistles, especially the earliest instance, in 1 Cor. 16:19 where their special greetings are conveyed, as from people well known to the Corinthians.

Acts 18:5 and 1 Thess. 3:6 concern the return of Timothy to Paul at Corinth.

Acts 18:5 with 2 Cor. 1:19 Silas and Timothy are Paul's associates in his first preaching in Corinth.

Acts 18:18 with Rom. 16:1 The incidental reference to Paul's action at Cenchreae may be set beside his commendation of Phoebe, who had been his valued helper.

Acts 18:19 with 1 Cor. 16:19 Paul leaves Aquila and Priscilla at Ephesus, where they are still located as hosts of a church at the next chronological reference to them.

Acts 18:27 with 1 Cor. 1:12; 3:6; 4:6 After the first meeting of Apollos with Aquila and Priscilla in Ephesus and their fuller instruction of him, he goes to Achaia, and specifically to Corinth (Acts 19:1). Paul, writing to Corinth two or three years after the events of Acts, can speak of Apollos as his colleague and successor in Corinth. Apollos' learning and eloquence is highlighted in both writings. He evidently did not countenance the factionalism which misused his name at Corinth, and Paul presses him to revisit Corinth (1 Cor. 16:12).

Acts 19:1 τὰ ἀνωτερικὰ μέρη may refer to the hilly, overland direct route from the interior to Ephesus, thus explaining why Paul had apparently not set foot in the Lycus-valley cities (Col. 2:1).

Acts 19:10 with Colossians and Philemon The spread of the gospel through associates of Paul beyond the apparent limits of his own travel is illustrated by the ministry of Tychicus and Epaphras to Colossae and its neighbours, where Paul seems not to have been in person (Col. 2:1) at the ostensible date of writing (AD 60 on my view).

Acts 19:21 with the plans of Paul in 1 Cor. 16:3-8, developed later in 2 Cor. 8, 9. The 'collection' is never explicitly mentioned in Acts, but the occasion certainly is, and the intentions expressed in these two verses correspond. The planned visit to Achaia/Corinth served then both to organize the contribution there and to deal with the recurring problems of the Corinthian church, factors which we know from the fuller evidence of the acknowledged epistles. This point stands in essence despite differing reconstructions of preceding visits and letters of Paul and his associates to Corinth. The 'collection' receives implicit notice in Acts 24:17.

Acts 19:22 Paul's sending of Timothy and Erastus into Macedonia is to be placed near the end of his Ephesian residence (c. 52-55). The Corinthian correspondence gives evidence for a previous visit of Timothy to Corinth from Ephesus (1 Cor. 4:17; 16:10) and also of Titus (2 Cor. 8:6; 12:18) as well as the 'painful' visit of Paul himself (2 Cor. 2:1). The present mission to Macedonia is in advance of Paul's progress there to meet Titus (2 Cor. 2:13), from whom he anxiously awaited news of Corinth.

Acts 19:23-41 with 1 Cor. 15:32; 2 Cor. 1:8-10 The Ephesian riot of Acts is to be aligned with the period of the allusions written at the end of Paul's Ephesian residence and its immediate aftermath. The incident recounted in Acts probably does not exhaust the violence of this period, nor its traumatic personal and spiritual effects on Paul. Where Acts is perhaps selective and restrained, Paul himself is reservedly allusive to events of which we presume the Corinthians were already informed.

Acts 19:29 Aristarchus, a Macedonian, identified specifically in 20:4 as a Thessalonian, and a companion of Paul on his voyage to Rome (27:2), is also mentioned in Col. 4:10 and Phlm. 24, both of which I take to have been written soon after arrival in Rome.

Acts 20:1 with 2 Cor. 2:12-13 At least the first nine chapters of 2 Corinthians seem to have been written from Macedonia at this stage, as the travel-plans outlined both in Acts 19:21 and 1 Cor. 16:5 begin to be fulfilled.

Acts 20:2 with 1 Cor. 16:3 concern Paul's coming to Greece from Macedonia.

Acts 20:3 with 1 Cor. 16:5 Paul's intention of staying, perhaps wintering, in Corinth corresponds with the three months' stay indicated in Acts, probably extending through the winter of 56-57.

Acts 20:3 with Rom. 15:25 Romans appears to have been written at this point, on the eve of Paul's last departure for Jerusalem.

Acts 20:4 presents a list of representatives of the churches of Greece and the Aegean area to accompany Paul in the delivery of the 'collection'. Cf. 1 Cor. 16:1-2; 2 Cor. 8, 9.

Acts 20:4 with Rom. 16:21 Luke's Sopater of Beroea is probably the same as the more formally named Sosipater in Paul. He was one of the Macedonian representatives, presumably one of those whom Paul expected to bring with him to Corinth (2 Cor. 9:4) at the time of the writing of Romans.

Acts 20:4 with Eph. 6:21 and Col. 4:7, etc. Tychicus was evidently a faithful companion and emissary of Paul present with him in Rome some three years later, and mentioned again, ostensibly yet later, in the Pastorals. The correlation here is only in the name, evidently denoting the same person, an Asian in Acts, whose detailed movements at this time are known only from Acts.

Acts 20:6-12 with 2 Cor. 2:12-13 Troas, at a focal point of communication, was a strategic place where Paul had found an 'open door' a few months previously, and had not then felt able to stay. On his return in Acts he seizes all available time, even beyond the scheduled sailing of the ship, in this city.

Acts 20:19 with 1 Cor. 15:32 etc. and with Rom. 9-11 There is a hint in the Miletus speech of Paul's sufferings at Ephesus shortly before. Bruce (*Acts*, p. 378) suggests that the Jewish plots there had brought him face to face with the acuteness of the problem of Israel's unbelief, which he had recently dealt with in Rom. 9-11.

Acts 21:20 A note in the eirenical account in Acts of the great number of believers in Jerusalem who were ardent for the Jewish law, a fresh indication of the continuing problem to whose earlier phase the Galatian epistle had been addressed.

Acts 21:23-24 with 1 Cor. 9:19-23 Paul is 'all things to all men'. In particular he is seen in both passages as a practising Jew, who personally keeps the Law, and is not properly open to criticism in the Jewish milieu. An over-simplified, antinomian view of Paul's views on justification may overlook his continuing devout Jewish piety.

Acts 22:4, 7-8, 20 Paul is pictured as the former persecutor; see parallels under Acts 7:58, 60. Cf. 26:9-11.

Acts 22:21 with Gal. 2:2, 7 Paul's calling is to the Gentiles.

Acts 23:6 with Phil. 3:5 Paul was a Pharisee. Cf. Acts 26:5.

Acts 24:17 with the references to the 'collection' (1 Cor. 16:1-4; 2 Cor. 8, 9; Rom. 15:25-28) Paul here is represented as motivated by bringing offerings to his people in Jerusalem, as the occasion of his visit. Haenchen's comment here seems disingenuously hypercritical. It will suffice to quote his words: 'It is only because we know about Paul's great collection from his letters that we recognize an allusion to it here; for Luke's readers that was not possible. That the collection was intended only for the Christian community and not for "his people" is likewise an obstacle which cannot be removed if we are looking here for absolutely reliable historical statements'.[55]

Acts 28:17 matches the implication in Romans of the presence of a Jewish (including Jewish-Christian) community in Rome before this date. It is not a matter of inconsistency with Acts 18:2; Claudius' decree was evidently a dead letter upon the accession of Nero. The

---

55 Haenchen, *Acts*, p. 655.

implication of Jews in Rome is to be taken from Romans (cf. e.g. Rom. 9-11).

Acts 28:30-31 Paul's Roman imprisonment can be correlated with the occasions of writing of the captivity epistles, Philippians being separated at some distance in time after the others, and reflecting the approach to a crisis which might result in death or life, presumably the trial terminating the διετία.

It will be evident how much in the foregoing correlations depends on views which might be widely disputed, and so may be thought to savour of special pleading. It should be noted, however, (1) that I have consistently used what seems the most probable reconstruction based on a straightforward, rather than a drastically reinterpreted, reading of the evidence, and (2) that these reconstructions cohere with the trend of a synthesis argued cumulatively through the book. They must of course still be justified on their merits; they are not necessarily interdependent with that synthesis, nor are they authenticated simplistically by it.

G. *Latent internal correlations within Acts*

The examples we will present in this section are selective and unsystematic. They are of particular interest where they link incidentals in different sections of the book, which seem to derive from different categories of source material but point to a situational substratum to which both categories relate.

2:29-30 with 13:22-23 The preaching about Jesus as descendant of David to a Jewish audience appears to be characteristic of the primitive Jewish period, while set here in significantly different sections of the book.

3:11 with 5:12 It is implicit that Solomon's porch was a meeting-place of the Christians in the Temple, as according to John 10:23, Jesus had walked there with his disciples (cf. Acts 2:46). See also the Excursus.

5:34 with 22:3 The great Gamaliel I is mentioned in Paul's defence as having been his mentor (cf. Phil. 3:5).

7:48 with 17:24 Stephen's critique of conceiving God as dwelling in 'temples made with hands' is reflected in words ascribed to Paul, on whom Stephen's words ostensibly made great impact.

8:40 with 21:8 (cf. 6:5) Philip, designated clearly as one of the seven 'deacons' of 6:5, is left at Caesarea and reappears at the same city, where he had his home. The case is an interesting latent connection between a 'we-passage' and material of presumably different origin, across an ostensible time-span, c. AD 32-57.

9:15 with 22:21 Ananias receives intimation of Paul's calling to the Gentiles. The first Jerusalem visit, to which 22:21 evidently refers, was quickly followed by the Tarsus residence (9:30), which gave opportunity to preach to the Gentiles. Cf. Gal. 1:21 with Gal. 2:2, 7-9.

9:29-30 with 22:18 Paul's hasty departure from Jerusalem and rejection by Jews at the time of his calling to the Gentiles.

11:19 with 15:3 The preaching to Jews in Phoenicia is reflected in the existence of a (Jewish) church there in 15:3, and later in Paul's visit to the church in Tyre (21:4), the last again in a 'we-passage'.

11:28 with 21:10 Agabus is another link between the 'we-passages' and earlier events. Bruce cites Lake and Cadbury on this prophet's sudden appearances and disappearances: 'That is not fiction, but real life'.[56]

13:27 with 15:21 The stress is on regular Jewish preaching on the Sabbath in different kinds of context.

15:1 with 21:21 We find recurrence of the circumcision controversy first apparent in Acts at 11:2 (cf. 10:45). The point is the more notable as Acts is often treated as an artificially eirenic document. Although settled in principle among the apostles at the Council, the issue was not then closed in the eyes of a large sector of Jewish believers.

16:17 with 20:5 The first 'we-passage' ends at Philippi and the second begins with a resumption at the same place. The ostensible inference is that the narrator spent the interval in that city.[57]

18:22 with 24:17 Paul's defence in the latter passage speaks of an interval of several years since visiting Jerusalem. Ostensibly this denotes an interval between c. 52 and 57. For the implicit reference here to the collection cf. F, p. 189 and see on 20:4 below.

---

56 Bruce, *Acts*, p. 388, citing Lake and Cadbury (*BC* 4.268). Harnack, *Acts*, p. 204, objects to the fact that Agabus is introduced in 21:10 as though mentioned for the first time, and others have conjectured that Luke has taken over without change a first mention of Agabus in a 'we-source' (see Haenchen, p. 601). It seems hypercritical to find undue difficulty or significance in such verbal points. Haenchen (p. 602n) repeats Overbeck's difficulty that Paul acted against the guidance of the Spirit when he continued his journey, and that this consideration explodes not only v. 46 but also the entire Agabus scene. But Haenchen notes that Luke sees the warning only as prophetic announcement of coming events, not as directive guidance. To Overbeck's objection that Paul's journey is unmotivated anyhow, Haenchen responds that Luke makes it seem enigmatic by his silence about the 'collection'. The circumstances of the collection are, however, implicit in Acts, though it is no part of Luke's purpose to stress it. Conversely, Haenchen's comments implicitly recognize the Acts framework as conveying a variant account of the same events.

57 The ends of the 'we-sections' are marked only by a formulaic disjunction between 'Paul' and 'us' (16:17; 21:18; cf. *TB* 36 [1985], p. 81n.).

20:4 with 24:17 The persons mentioned in 20:4 may be understood as the delegates of various churches bearing the collection, and this again compares with the implicit reference of 24:17.[58] Cf. F, p. 188.

20:6 with 20:16 and 27:9 Paul's observance of Jewish feasts is implicit in all these passages (as in the variant reading of 18:18). 21:24-25 reaffirms the Jerusalem apostles' recognition of the freedom of Gentile converts from bondage to the law while attesting again Paul's personal care to observe it.

21:18 with 27:1 The concluding formula of the second 'we-passage' (cf. 16:17) leaves the narrator in Jerusalem, and he reappears as a companion in Palestine when Paul sails as a prisoner from Caesarea.

21:24 with 24:26 These and later references such as Paul's hiring of lodging in Rome, and indeed his standing and entourage as a prisoner, indicate unexpectedly that Paul's financial state was more comfortable at this period than we might have supposed. This apparent change of circumstances is implicit and not easily explained.[59]

21:27 with 24:11 The note of time (12 days in the latter passage) seems to refer to the total period which Paul had spent in Jerusalem. Haenchen (following Schlatter) reckons the sequence of days on this basis, in accord with Luke's careful notes throughout.[60]

23:5-6 Paul's failure to recognize the high priest or indeed the division of parties represented in the Sanhedrin has often occasioned difficulty for the commentators. The implicit correlation here is negative rather than positive, that Paul had not been physically present in

---

[58] We must refrain from pursuing here the correlations of the movements of members of the group, like Aristarchus and Timothy, for these lie more obviously on the surface of the narrative than the implicit allusions, which lock into underlying circumstances. The case of Timothy could be complicated by textual variants (cf. H, p. 198), but ostensibly he was sent to Macedonia in 19:22 and is found there at Philippi in 20:4. As a Lystran he is then paired here with Gaius of Derbe.

[59] We cannot discount the possibility, raised by Haenchen (pp. 612-14), that the Jerusalem church, for whatever reason, actually refused the 'collection'. But in such a case Paul, as we know him from his own letters, would have been scrupulous not to use on himself, even in the Lord's service, funds contributed for the Jerusalem church.

[60] Haenchen (p. 654); cf. Schlatter (*Apostelgeschichte*, p. 285n). Bruce's earlier opinion (*Acts*, p. 394 *ad* 21:27; cf. 424 *ad* 24:11) was that ἔμελλον in the former passage referred to the beginning of the seven-day period, so that the subsequent events were partly concurrent with that intended span. But Bruce changes his mind in *Book of the Acts*, p. 468n., preferring the option that Paul was arrested near the end of the week. This view, as presented by Haenchen, is followed also by Marshall (pp. 347, 376). It does clearer justice to the precise notes of time throughout, and concludes the period with Paul's departure from Jerusalem, not as in Bruce with his appearance before Felix.

Jerusalem for some five years, and that his preceding visits as a Christian had probably been discreet and private, even if he participated unobtrusively in the crowded festivals. He had been effectively a stranger for twenty-five years to the religious leadership among whom he had been raised.

23:6 with 24:15 The resurrection as a doctrine at the heart of Paul's message as presented in Acts may be widely paralleled. Here Paul's defence before Felix carries implicit reference to the Sanhedrin incident and the common ground he shared with some of his hearers, a point made explicit in 24:20-21. This motif recurs through the book in different categories of material (2:24, 31; 3:15 etc. *passim*). It is interesting to note that this characterization of Paul's gospel as about the living Jesus is also put in the mouth of the outsider Festus (25:19).

This selection will suffice to contribute a simple point to the argument, that the book shows latent correlations across different classes of material which invite the explanation that their links are rooted in the situation rather than in a redactional stage. This point stands apart from the obvious and superficial observations that Luke is broadly self-consistent, and conversely that unresolved anomalies may be found by the diligent critic.

H. *Details involving differences between Alexandrian and Western texts*

1:23 ἔστησαν: the Western ἔστησεν (D it^gig Augustine) makes Peter alone the subject, emphasizing his role in the appointment and reflecting a later perspective.

2:17-21 The text of the quotation from Joel agrees in B almost exactly with the LXX, where D has it in a form apparently adapted to its present occasion. Luke generally displays great faithfulness to the LXX text, but the problem here is complex, and has been variously resolved.[61]

3:11 The differences of text in this verse touch on the problem of the location of Solomon's porch. D makes it explicit that the apostles came out of the ἱερόν again before the gathering of the crowd in the portico. This expansion clarifies the topographical sequence unspecified in the elliptical brevity of ℵ A B C 81 *al.* Cf. G, p. 190 and Excursus, p. 224.[62]

4:6 Ἰωάννης: D reads Ἰωνάθας. 'John' and Alexander here are unknown. Jonathan, however, was the son of Annas who succeeded Caiaphas in 36 (Jos. *Ant.* 18.4.3. 95), and it is arguable that D gives

---

61 See Metzger, *Textual Comm.*, p. 295; Ropes, BC 3.16-19.
62 The syntactical solecism in D does nothing to favour its originality.

either the original reading or an accurate correction. Yet the external evidence strongly favours Ἰωάννης.[63]

5:18, 21 These are examples of a widespread type of Western expansion, giving details which may be lively and picturesque, but are unnecessary to the bald narrative, that the high priests' party went each to his own house, and that they got up early in the morning. These details may be seen as part of a tendency to smooth and expand a narrative. Cf. e.g. 5:38-39; 11:2, 25-26; 12:23; 14:2, 7.

7:43 A small point of substance appears in the Bezan harmonization of ἐπέκεινα to ἐπὶ [τὰ μέ]ρη before Βαβυλῶνος where the LXX of Amos 5:2 reads ἐπέκεινα Δαμάσκου. The rare word is evidently original, and the correction is apparently made to adapt the words to a factual equivalence, for the Babylon area was certainly 'beyond' Damascus.[64]

11:20 The reference to 'Hellenists' in this verse poses complex problems highlighted in the contrast between Ἑλληνιστάς in B and Ἕλληνας in D. This is not in fact a simple case of assessing a 'Western' reading, for the great uncials show much confusion and the versions render the word as 'Greeks'. The difficult Ἑλληνιστάς is probably original, but is not to be given the same sense here as in 6:1 or 9:29. If here 'Greek-speakers', they are apparently Gentiles, in contrast with Jews, not, as before, 'Greek-speaking Jews'. As the term 'Hellenist' seems to have been current only in the primitive period of the church (cf. E, pp. 175-76 and note 31), all the occurrences of Ἕλληνας seem to represent a secondary stage of interpretation.

11:28 This Western expansion, otherwise unremarkable, is notable for the introduction of the first person plural (συνεστραμμένων δὲ ἡμῶν). This probably reflects the reviser's knowledge of the tradition that Luke was a native of Antioch.[65]

---

63 Thus the UBS Committee: Metzger reports a probability grade (C) for 'John'. It is possible that Bezae corrected Luke's original Ἰωάννης, or, conversely, that the more familiar name was substituted for an original Ἰωνάθας. But it is most probable that 'John' (or even 'Jonathan') and Alexander were persons unknown to history but either well-known in their day or to the early church in particular. Both are of course common names. If they became Christian converts or sympathizers, this may give point to their mention, and perhaps indicate that they were the ultimate source of the account of the closed session of the Sanhedrin. The mention of such persons without further identification is consonant with the supposition that writer and readers stand relatively close in time to the event, when the reference was still meaningful.

64 The reading cited is the original reading of Bezae, where the facsimile has ἐπέκεινα over a blurred deletion. The Latin has not been altered, and reads '*in illas partes Babylonis*'.

65 Metzger, *Textual Comm.*, p. 381, points out that 'in Acts Codex Bezae is fond

12:10 The addition 'seven steps' reads like the kind of self-conscious local colour generally absent from Luke's concise narrative. The description may, for all we know, be true of the actual or supposed place and so embody a tradition resting on pre-70 memory. But it is not to be taken as original (cf. Chap. 2, pp. 53-57).

12:25 εἰς ᾽Ιερουσαλήμ: this difficult textual puzzle involves a difference between ℵ B and D, which reads ἀπό, but this is not a characteristically 'Western' reading. εἰς is both strongly attested and difficult, for it seems to give the wrong sense. The correction to ἀπό or ἐξ (A) is found in other textual traditions. There may have been a primitive textual corruption here.[66]

13:8 Ἐλύμας: this difficult name should be preferred to the Bezan reading Ἐτ(.)μας (Latin 'Etoemas'). It is possible that the latter shows knowledge of, and influence from, the name of the Jewish Cypriot magician Atomos in Jos. *Ant.* 20.7.2.142, who was active at the same period. There is no ground for identifying the two. While we should argue strongly that Acts in its original form was not influenced by, and indeed antedates, Josephus, this possibility does arise here in the case of what we take to be a secondary revision. Even if there is such a link, it may of course be from another source independent of, or earlier than, Josephus.

13:14 τὴν Πισιδίαν must be preferred to τῆς Πισιδίας. See the excursus, pp. 228f. below. The better attested reading is surely original and the Western a revision due either to false assumption or reflecting much later arrangements.

13:33 'The Second Psalm': D stands apart here from all the other uncials in ascribing the reference to the first psalm, and patristic evidence for the reading πρώτῳ is also very impressive. The choice is complicated by the fact that the oldest available reading, that of p[45], is τοῖς ψαλμοῖς, and there are variations in the word order with both numerals. The reading πρώτῳ appears to reflect rabbinical exegesis that counted the first two psalms of our reckoning as one.[67] The decision here is difficult, but UBS (with probability {D}), Bruce and Haenchen accept δευτέρῳ. The possibility that D offers a reworked revision in the light of a different reckoning is consonant with its extended continuation of the LXX citation.

14:13 The 'priest' of Zeus: the Bezan text has 'priests'. This reading,

---

of the verb συστρέφειν, which it introduces in 10:41; 11:28; 16:39; 17:5.'

66 See the discussions in Metzger, pp. 398-400, Bruce, pp. 251-52. The UBS text retains εἰς, after long deliberation, and with probability {D}. Ropes (*BC* 3.114) and Haenchen (p. 387) treat εἰς as a Hellenistic equivalent for ἐν and offer renderings based on that.

67 See Metzger, *Textual Comm.*, pp. 412-14.

especially when taken in conjunction with other Western variants in the immediate context, is very attractive. Ramsay argued for it, noting four such nuances, that great temples in Asia Minor did possess colleges of priests, that the idiomatic phrase τοῦ ὄντος Διὸς πρὸ πόλεως is a characteristic formulation, that ἐπιθύειν denotes a special, additional sacrifice, and that ὁ θεός (cf. τὸν θεόν in v. 15) was the regular phrase in allusion to the god of a local temple.[68] Calder further published an inscription from Sedasa, near Lystra, which mentions together three priests of Zeus.[69] Ramsay's two latter points are suspect: his special sense of ἐπιθύειν is dubious, and the insertion of τὸν θεόν is natural in reference to 'God' (not the local Zeus). The Western reading is still attractive, if only on the two former considerations. But its attractiveness is not tantamount to an argument for originality. In this case the plausible details might as easily be the work of a reviser.[70]

14:25 D adds a note of preaching undertaken in Attalia before returning to Antioch. But this is likely to be pious addition, for Attalia was the coastal port, where a coastal vessel could give a passage, and its mention serves only as point of departure.

15:20, 29 The textual problems of the Apostolic Decree are complex and cannot be treated here. The best kind of solution seems to be that which abides by the fourfold prohibition with its ambivalence between ritual and ethical regulations, and interprets this as a necessary basis for a *modus vivendi* of Jew with Gentile, in which the ethical and cultural spheres were intertwined.[71] The insertion of the

---

68 Ramsay, *SPTR*, p. 118.

69 'A Cult of the Homonades', *CR* 24 (1910), pp. 76-81 (p. 77), cited by Wikenhauser, p. 363; 'The "Priest" of Zeus at Lystra', *Expos* 7th ser. 10 (1910), pp. 148-55. Calder argues further that this inscription refers to the same cult as that implied in another dedication of Sedasa, cf. C, p. 111 above.

70 Several arguments on this point are suspect. Blass, often a champion of D, protests against the idea of a college of priests (Metzger, *Textual Comm.*, p. 423). Ropes defends B on the ground that the 'unhellenic' phrase τοῦ Διὸς τοῦ ὄντος πρὸ τῆς πόλεως may reflect a Semitic original. But there is no probability that this narrative in a Gentile setting ever had a Semitic original, and others have explained it as derived from the D-form. Haenchen's objection (p. 427n) that the inscriptions associating Zeus and Hermes are of the third century is in any case hypercritical: the continuity of religious cults in Anatolia is a point on which we can usually be confident, whatever later accretions they may assimilate. A different argument for ἐπιθύειν is raised by G.D. Kilpatrick's interesting suggestion that the compound denotes 'pagan sacrifice' (*ZNW* 74 [1983], pp. 151-53), a development in Biblical Greek. But even if this sense be accepted, it would be quite in the manner of a reviser to spell out the obvious.

71 This generalized type of solution will stand, however we interpret πορνεία, where both ethical and ritual and cultural causes of offence were conjoined even

negative Golden Rule then betrays a secondary development, of ethical teaching abstracted from the specific situation which called forth the particular grouping of provisions.

15:34 This verse is rightly omitted by modern critical texts, and is explained as an interpolation to explain the presence of Silas in Antioch in v. 40. The Bezan version is further expanded with a reference to Judas travelling alone. But its intrusive character is evident, and while smoothing the elliptical narrative it conflicts with the statement of v. 33.

16:12 The famous crux in the text and interpretation of πρώτη (τῆς) μερίδος (or πρώτης μερίδος) touches only indirectly on the Western text question. D reads κεφαλή (Lat. *caput*). This reading is certainly secondary, and factually incorrect; Philippi was certainly not the 'capital' of Macedonia. Cf. C, pp. 113-14, esp. n. 31.

18:7 ἐκεῖθεν: the D reading ἀπὸ τοῦ ᾽Ακύλα appears to be an erroneous attempt at interpretation. Paul moved from the synagogue, not from Aquila's house. This case tells heavily against the attribution of the D revision to Luke himself.

18:21 Mention of the Feast as the occasion of Paul's haste to leave Ephesus may well be correct as an inference, but seems to have originated as an addition by the Western reviser.

19:9 Paul's teaching in the school of Tyrannus (D 'Tyrannius') is the occasion of the interesting addition 'from the fifth hour to the tenth', a probable enough reflection of Paul's using the premises during the midday siesta, but not likely to be original.

19:14, 16 A problem is often felt in the switch from ἑπτά to ἀμφο-τέρων, unless the latter word is taken as equivalent to πάντων. Interesting, but not persuasive is the suggestion of G.M. Lee[72] that ἀμ-φοτέρων denotes 'both categories' of exorcists, using the wording of the Bezan text to distinguish the (there unnumbered) sons of Sceva from a separate grouping in v. 13. Lee however holds a view akin to that of Blass that the Western version was a Lukan first draft. This mention of ἀμφοτέρων is by no means clear even in the D text, and the context, here as elsewhere, bears marks of secondary expansion or smoothing, not of first draft prolixity.

19:28 Bezae adds δραμόντες εἰς τὸ ἄμφοδον, a vivid detail which may be topographically accurate if the word be taken to refer to the great harbour-avenue represented in the present ruins by the reconstruction under Arcadius (late 4th AD). This however was a familiar piece of local colour, which may have been well known to a reviser.

in varying technical or non-technical senses of the word.

72 'The Seven Sons of Sceva (Acts 19, 13-16)', *Biblica* 51 (1970), p. 237.

20:4 Γαῖος Δερβαῖος: D reads Γαῖος Δουβ(έ)ριος. Doberus was a Macedonian city not far from Philippi. This case has been variously evaluated. It seems probable that the Western reading was a change made under influence of the reference in 19:29 to a Macedonian Gaius. But the name is exceedingly common, and it may be just the point to distinguish this man from the bearer of the same name mentioned previously. And as this Gaius is coupled with Timothy, probably of Lystra, the sequence fits the assembling of those who represented various groups of Gentile churches.[73]

20:15 The mention of a stop at Trogyllium is geographically appropriate and entirely plausible. It could have been insertion by one familiar with the route, to heighten the local colour, or it could be an original phrase which was dropped, perhaps accidentally, in early copies. While widely attested, and passing into the Byzantine text, it is absent from the great uncials, and the weight of evidence may be deemed against it. It has however the best claim of any Western reading to transmit independently a significant factual detail.[74]

21:1 It seems most probable that the reference to Myra, again geographically appropriate, has been added in assimilation to 27:5. If a swift passage were secured at the port first mentioned, and a direct crossing made (διαπερῶν) without coasting stops, and with regular favouring winds, a stop at Myra would be unnecessary.

21:16 The Western text-type locates the lodging with Mnason (Νάσωνι D) in 'a certain village' *en route* for Jerusalem. This reading is strongly defended by Blass but rejected by Ropes as 'inherently highly improbable'.[75] A reviser aware of the distance from Caesarea to Jerusalem may have seen the need of an overnight stop and have adapted the mention of Paul's host to the assumption that he fulfilled this service.[76]

---

[73] Cf. Haenchen, pp. 52-53. Metzger (*Textual Comm.*, pp. 475-76) gives {C} probability for Δερβαῖος. The Western reading here is however widely accepted, the names of Clark, Streeter, Lagrange, Williams, Zuntz and Bruce being mentioned. But Δοβήριος (or variants) was not such a 'difficult' reading in the early church, when the name was more familiar than it is to us, and would be suggested as the specific city of a 'Macedonian' by a reviser thinking to amend Δερβαῖος. The same kind of inferential specification appears immediately afterwards in the Western designation of 'Eutychus' (Tychicus) and Trophimus as Ἐφέσιοι, not merely Ἀσιανοί, a change explainable in the latter case from 21:29. It is an attractive possibility, if currently unfashionable, to suggest that Luke himself, the tacit 'first person', represented the Philippian church.

[74] UBS prefers the shorter reading, with probability rating {C}. See Metzger, p. 478.

[75] Blass, *Philology of the Gospels*, pp. 128-31, Ropes BC 3.204.

[76] Interesting circumstantial arguments of opposite tendency have been urged: by Blass that it would be odd for Paul to be dependent on a stranger's hospitality

27:5 The Western text adds δι' ἡμερῶν δεκάπεντε. This could well be a realistic estimate of the time taken by a ship battling with adverse winds. Ropes defends its originality, supposing it to have been an accidental omission from the B-text.[77] But the great weight of textual evidence is against it, and it is the type of information added by the kind of reviser who tried to leave nothing to the reader's imagination. It may be a well-informed guess.[78]

28:16 Western witnesses add the significant statement that the centurion delivered the prisoners to the 'stratopedarch', and the expansion passed into the Byzantine text. The point merits note, as any information to be gleaned about the circumstances of Paul's Roman captivity may prove important to the historical puzzles surrounding the end of Acts. If accepted, at least as a secondary vehicle of authentic information, a problem remains over the technical Roman identification of the officer designated 'stratopedarch', whether the *princeps peregrinorum* (Mommsen, Harnack, Ramsay) or the praetorian prefect, at this time the famous Afranius Burrus (Zahn, Haenchen) or his subordinate the *princeps castrorum* (Sherwin-White).[79] But the

at Jerusalem, and by Ropes that this emphasis on a village-stay would be futile and insignificant when the whole focus was on their destination. It is not necessary to infer that Mnason was a stranger to Paul, only that Luke needed to introduce him to his readers. Wherever located, he may have been significant to Luke as an informant, though Ramsay's attribution of the stories of Aeneas and Dorcas to his authority (*BRD* p. 309n) is an unwarranted speculation, perhaps coloured by building on ideas of the origins of churches in the country west of Jerusalem as derived from Western readings here and in 11:2. See Bruce, *Acts*, pp. 389-90.

77 Ropes, *BC* 3.241; cf. Lake and Cadbury, *BC* 4.326-27.

78 'Western' attestation is generally weakened in these latter chapters by the deficiency of Bezae, and I am limiting my choice of examples. Omission might possibly be explained here by parablepsis, from the homoioarkton of δια-. Metzger (*Textual Comm.*, p. 497) gives probability {B} for the shorter text.

79 See especially Bruce, *Acts*, p. 476; Haenchen, p. 718; Sherwin-White, *RSRL*, pp. 108-11. Cf. Mason, *Greek Terms*, pp. 13, 86. According to Sherwin-White the office of *princeps peregrinorum* is known in the time of Trajan, but not apparently earlier, and the *frumentarii* under his command are not known to have assumed police-duties until later. The *princeps castrorum*, as head administrator in the Praetorian Guard, is also not known at Rome before Trajan (*ILS* 9189), but a corresponding office existed in the organization of a legion from the time of Claudius (*princeps praetorii legionis*). There are inscriptions which appear to support a similar identification. Thus a bilingual text of Amastius in Pontus (*IGRR* 3.1432, 2nd-3rd AD) refers to a centurion *primipilaris* and *praef(ectrus) kastro(rum) leg(ionis) XIII gem(inae)*, rendered in Greek as πρειμιπειλαρίῳ, | [σ]τρατοπ[ε]δάρχη λεγ(εῶνος) ιγ' (lines 3-4, 15-16). This man was also *trecenarius*, that is centurion in command of the 300 *speculatores* distributed among the *praetorian* cohorts. Reference to 'stratopedarchs' are preserved

longer version, and the peculiarly 'Western' addition ἔξω τῆς παρεμ-
βολῆς, bear the marks of a smoothing of the narrative apparent so
often before as a revision technique, and the word may be imprecise.
Metzger gives rating {B} in favour of the shorter version.[80] It is still a
real question where exactly in Rome responsibility lay for Paul's custody and trial, but we should avoid attempting a premature short cut
through extrapolation from the terminology of what may be an inferential and unspecific statement. Identifications in the Latin versions
may be of real, if secondary, interest, as representing ancient inferential solutions, which may have had the advantage of residual knowledge of the practices of Paul's day.[81]

In the foregoing samples we have focused specifically on cases
where Western readings involve additional or discrepant factual
details. The generalized conclusion from these gleanings must be that
in no case can we with confidence take a Western reading as a basic
datum. In some places a secondary text may preserve correct traditions or inferences, but they cannot be given higher status, nor be
used as a convenience to suit an argument. Yet the type has an early
pedigree as a revision; its antecedents can be traced to the second
century.[82] The reviser had some knowledge of Asia Minor, as passages touching Lystra, Ephesus, Trogyllium and elsewhere can show.[83]

---

elsewhere. The man in *SEG* 17 (1960) 584, of Attalia in Pamphylia (2nd AD) had
also been *primipilaris* in one legion and stratopedarch in another. Cf. also *PLond*
2.196.5 (AD 138-161), with F.G. Kenyon's note; *MAMA* 6.97 (Heraclea ad
Salbacum). Sherwin-White, however, cautions against the identification of the
praefectus castrorum, here equated with στρατοπεδάρχης, with the *princeps prae-
torii legionis* (=*princeps castrorum*), which he accepts here (p. 110 n.3). There is
much need for caution in identifying officials, especially in literature, where
Atticistic fashion sometimes favoured the stylistically acceptable, rather than the
formally accurate, term (Jos. *BJ* 6.4.3.238 and Lucian, *de Hist. Conscrib.* 22 are not
informative). The term στρατοπεδάρχης also underwent change of application in
later imperial times (see Mason, *Greek Terms*, p. 13), and in *OGIS* 605 it
designates a man of consular, not centurial, rank (Heliopolis [Baalbek], AD 440).

80 Metzger, *Textual Comm.*, p. 501.

81 Thus the 13th century Codex Gigas, representing the Old Latin, gives the rendering *princeps peregrinorum*, a version going back to an identification presumably current in the early church, if later than the first century.

82 Metzger, *Textual Comm.*, p. xviii.

83 It might be expressed in terms of our present categorization by saying that the
Western text seems to offer some details of B or C-type classification, such as
suggest local knowledge, at least of parts of Asia Minor. But isolated cases of this
kind, mingled with much gratuitous expansion and some erroneous or un-
focused changes do not suffice to give the variants the status of widely integrated
and unstudied accuracy, such as impresses me progressively as characterizing
the uninterpolated text.

A residual danger lies in the converse possibility that we have too simplistically narrowed the options in favour of a preference for the Alexandrian text, thereby ignoring the inherent complexity of the textual question to circumscribe the field of action where some eclectic fluidity is inevitable. That may be so, but the study of detail persuades me inductively that the truth lies generally on the side of what is here taken to be the more usual representative of the original text. It is the way of caution, and it is a gain to have been able to clarify our stance on this facet of this complex task. The revision is still significant. While itself so early, its existence, if rightly explained, presupposes an even earlier version which its editor used with a surprising freedom.

There remain cross-currents where the D-text omits rather than adds. Such cases as the naming of Damaris (17:34) or the prominence of the Beroean women (17:12) may have been the subject of deliberate omission.[84] Elsewhere the Western type concurs in its testimony to an early reading like Εὐρακύλων (27.14) against Byzantine witnesses.

J. Unstudied Allusions

By 'unstudied allusions', we have in mind matters that are mentioned by the author in such an informal or allusive way as to make it highly unlikely that they have been consciously included. Where these details of geographic knowledge etc. are accurate, they imply a familiarity with the places and perhaps time period. The cases which might be included in this category have often been treated previously, and the few samples following are chosen simply to illustrate how they (and many other materials) might be regarded from this perspective.

13:14 'The Pisidian Antioch' is an informal manner of allusion to a city of Phrygia on the Pisidian border. See the excursus, p. 228 below.

13:28 Pilate is presented as known by reputation to a Jewish audience in the Diaspora.

---

84 It might be argued further that redaction-criticism is more easily applied to the D-text than to the B-text, for the very reason that it represents the revision of an archetype more nearly reproduced by B. Judgement that Codex Bezae is unfavourable to women or shows other theologically-motivated tendencies is then amenable to comparative assessment. See generally Epp, *Theological Tendency*.

The virtue of brevity in an original text may also be related to the practical constraints placed on a writer by the length of a papyrus roll. Acts as it stands is the longest writing in the New Testament and the tightest fit for a roll. It is easier to explain a longer edition as arising in the context of the codex-form, which was an early introduction in the history of the New Testament text, the earliest surviving fragment, p[52] (=*PRyl* 3.457), being from a codex leaf.

14:6, 8, 21; 16:1-2 These verses show the heteroclitic declension of 'Lystra'.

15:23 Antioch is grouped under a common article with Syria and Cilicia, the double province whose capital it was.

16:6 The notorious phrase 'Phrygian and Galatian country' is to be taken as an informal allusion to a definite entity, and the difficult resumptive phrase 'the Galatian country and Phrygia' in 18:23 is probably to be taken as partly repeating the allusion.

17:19, 22 Ἄρειος πάγος is used informally of the council, and there is a natural shift into the one-word derivative form Ἀρεοπαγίτης in 17:34, an interesting and distinctive example paralleled in many uses of names and ethnic-type adjectives.

17:28 The citation of Greek poetry displays a latent appropriateness to the occasion, first the lines attributed to Epimenides, the Cretan seer associated by tradition with altars to 'unknown gods' at Athens, and then of Aratus of Soli, a Stoic poet born close to Paul's native Tarsus. The links here are significantly Pauline and situational, not Lukan and redactional, and others are embedded in the scene.

19:1 The 'upper country' is a likely allusion to travel to Ephesus by a direct hill-road across the hinterland.

19:27, 34, 35, 37 Titles and designations of Artemis are placed in the mouths of her Ephesian devotees, and illustrated from the inscriptions. Note the characteristic ἡ θεός.

21:3, as contrasted with 27:4 Luke comments on sailing south of Cyprus on the direct eastward journey, and under its lee in the face of the adverse winds on the return. This must have been quite normal, but the manner of reference may be taken to reflect the record of one who had experienced the difference for the first time.

27:5 The sea of 'Cilicia and Pamphylia': a natural grouping for a unitary stage of the journey along the south coast of Asia Minor.

27-28 The voyage and shipwreck *passim*, in which many references savour of direct experience or hearsay information about terminology or about a regular port unvisited on this occasion (Phoenix, 27:12), or of nautical procedures perhaps imperfectly appreciated by the careful reporter (27:17, 40 etc.). See C, pp. 108-58 *passim*.

K. Differences of formulation within Acts

Our aim in this section is to note any differences of terminology which may provide clues for different types of sources. This is a rather specialized category where judgment may be difficult. I can do no more than indicate the existence of the problem. In some cases the differences may be due to different sources, but elsewhere differences of contextual nuance may offer a sufficient explanation. Pauline usage is occasionally important as offering comparative and illustrative material. It will be convenient here to list examples under names rather than passages.

Achaia, Macedonia, Greece: 'Achaia' appears always to denote the Roman province both in Acts and Paul; the older Greek geographical application to a territory on the southern shore of the Corinthian Gulf is unused. Gallio was specifically proconsul of the province (18:12). In 18:27, as commonly in Paul (1 Cor. 16:15; 2 Cor. 9:2; 11:10), Achaia is named where its capital Corinth is primarily in view. In 19:21, as in Rom. 15:26 and 1 Thess. 1:7,8, Macedonia and Achaia are coupled as a pair of provinces together comprising approximately the entity known then and now as 'Hellas'. This latter name occurs in the New Testament only at Acts 20:2, apparently as an informal territorial description of (southern) Greece, again perhaps primarily Corinth. The term 'Macedonia' is less easily categorized, for the provincial and geographical senses fall nearly together, but allusion to a μερίς (or possibly to 'the first μερίς') in 16:12 is to a specifically provincial subdivision, and the same nuance is in view in the coupling with Achaia. Nothing in this complex suggests different sources. Semantic variations are contextual, with some fluctuation between the formal and informal.

Asia: twelve out of eighteen New Testament occurrences of this name are in Acts, if we exclude two cases confined to Western expansions. Many contradictory things have been written about its meaning.[85] There is no case, either in Acts or elsewhere, where it

---

85 In three different contexts and when making different points Haenchen argues for or assumes three different understandings of 'Asia': (1) 'Asia Minor' in *JTC* 1 (1965), p. 82 = 'Kleinasien' in the corresponding *ZTK* 58 (1961), p. 347; (2) the continent of Asia in *JTC* 1 (1965), p. 82n, a footnote on the same page; and (3) an apparently smaller area focused on the west coast (wrongly equated with the 'Asia' of Rev. 1) in *Acts*, p. 484n. Only in arguing against Dupont for the continental view does he cite evidence. This evidence might in fact be greatly extended, but is almost always restricted to geographical contexts where continents are specifically indicated, in contradistinction with ordinary usage. See my discussion and evidence cited in *TB* 26 (1975), pp. 99-100. An interesting epigraphical example of the continental sense is in *I. Smyrna*, 1.536 (= *IGRR* 4.1445 = *CIG* 3311, of Smyrna, 1st AD), in the personal bibliography of a medical, historical and geographical writer. Inscriptions referring to provincial Asia or its officials, or of outlying parts of Phrygia and Mysia designated as of 'Asia' may be numbered in hundreds. It will be ample to cite a few interesting specimens of comparable date: *IGRR* 4.144, of Cyzicus (time of Tiberius), 188, of Poemanenum in Mysia (1st BC), 644, of Acmonia in Phrygia (1st AD), 779-80, of Apamea in Phrygia (early 2nd AD). At Sardis οἱ ἐπὶ τῆς Ἀσίας Ἕλληνες honour one of

may not be taken of the province Asia, though some examples in Acts are not explicit, or 'Asia' may be used informally where the great cosmopolitan centre of Ephesus was mainly in view. This essentially 'provincial' view is confirmed by the whole thrust of first century epigraphical usage. A test case is Acts 16:6, which may be explained as of the province. The point is that Mysia, and also Troas, were in 'Asia' in this sense. Paul was not forbidden to travel in it, indeed his westward progress entailed that, but was forbidden to preach there. They were 'passing by' Mysia (παρελθόντες). Further, the ethnic Ἀσιανός, occurring only at Acts 20:4, groups two men, one later designated an Ephesian (21:29). This might of course apply to 'Asia' in a narrower sense, and Ephesus was 'Asia' *par excellence*, but the ethnic is common in the inscriptions, and is used habitually of the current provincial sense. The real question here is more about the earlier references in 2:9 and 6:9. While there is nothing to exclude pressing the provincial sense here too, the passages rest on earlier information, and Luke may have lacked the contextual knowledge to place the persons more exactly.

Jerusalem (Ἱεροσόλυμα / Ἱερουσαλήμ): this is an interesting case of diverse forms of the same name in Acts, but the indications are sufficient that the difference is contextual, and in a degree theological, and spans the ostensible division between the early and later chapters and the 'we passages' (Cf. Excursus, pp. 239-40).

Hellenist: we have argued above (p. 194) that this term of the primitive church bears a different meaning in 11:20 from that in 6:1 and 9:29, but the difference is contextual and gives no base for further conclusions. Otherwise the word Ἕλλην is characteristically opposed, explicitly or implicitly, to 'Jew' alike in Acts, John and Paul (opposed to 'barbarian' in Rom. 1:14).

Jew, Hebrew, Israelite: Moulton and Geden list 79 entries for 'Jew' in Acts, the large majority in a neutral sense of members of an ethnic/religious community, but sometimes of Paul's opponents among them (9:22-23; 13:45, 50 etc.), qualified as οἱ ἀπειθήσαντες Ἰουδαῖοι in 14:2 (cf. 14:4). This difference of application is probably purely contextual, the adverse uses being far fewer than in John, where controversy with Jesus' opponents among the Jewish leaders is more prominent. Ἑβραῖος occurs only at 6:1, for Hebrew-speaker, and 'Israelite' five times as a complimentary form of address, throughout the book.

Phrygia: forms or derivatives of the name occur at 2:10; 16:6; 18:23.

their body designated Ἀσιανόν (*IGRR* 4.1756.113-16, of 5 BC), and at Apamea again the people of Apollonia and Rhyndacum, on Paul's route across Mysia, make a dedication in which the two areas are linked under the aegis of 'Asia' (*IGRR* 4.787, early 2nd AD).

The two latter are specific designations: 16:6 as embedded in a phrase denoting 'Phrygia Galatica', a territory including Pisidian Antioch and Iconium; 18:23 more obscure because of its resumptive brevity, perhaps denoting the areas of Lycaonia and of Phrygia comprised within the province of Galatia. But most of Phrygia was in provincial Asia, and the term 'Phrygia Asiane' is attested.[86] These phrases, however, seem to use the term in a different sense from 2:10, where Phrygia is mentioned as an item separate from Asia. This difference may be taken as having a significant bearing on the source question. Luke had information about a person or persons from Phrygia present at the day of Pentecost, but lacked access to a context by which to assimilate the geographical list to a common pattern or to know which part of Phrygia. 'Phrygia' is then a territorial name without political status at this date, but grouped with provincial names and provincial ethnics.

The list of nations at Pentecost: most of these names offer no comparative material within the book. They should however be understood of Diaspora Jews resident in the areas mentioned and speaking indigenous languages or divergent dialects, whether of Greek or Semitic or other. It may be noteworthy, for instance, within the predominantly Greek-speaking regions, that aberrant Greek dialects persisted in Pamphylia and in Crete, and a distinct language in Phrygia.[87] The selection and formulation here seems to have been controlled by the availability of information.

Familiar personal names: there seems to be a fairly general

---

86 Whereas the term 'Phrygia Galatica' is inferential, and nowhere extant, its viability is indicated by comparison with 'Pontus Galaticus' as distinct on one hand from 'Pontus Polemoniacus' outside the original extent of this province and the Pontus which was coupled with Bithynia as a double-province in its own right. All these are attested on many inscriptions (e.g. *CIL* 3.6818.5-6, of Pisidian Antioch, for Pontus Galaticus and Polemonianus [undated]; *CIL* 5.2.8660, of Concordia in Venetia, for Lycaonia An[tioch]iana, as distinct from Lycaonia Galatica [AD 166]).

87 For Pamphylian dialect see originally W.M. Ramsay, 'On Some Pamphylian Inscriptions', *JHS* 1 (1880) 242-57; now C. Brixhe, *Le dialecte grec de Pamphylie. Documents et grammaire* (Paris: Adrien-Maisouneuve, 1976). The city of Side in Pamphylia had its own script and language until the 2nd century BC, still essentially undeciphered. The Doric of Crete had many strange forms, and marked variations between different cities. See *I. Cret., passim*, and some samples cited in ch. 4 above. Neo-Phrygian is extensively attested in imprecations appended to Greek epitaphs of about the 3rd century AD, when it was clearly a living language, and the repetitive formulae can be fairly well understood. See O. Haas, *Die phrygischen Sprachdenkmäler* (Sofia: Académie bulgare des sciences, 1966). The Greek inscriptions of the same area are characterized by many bizarre solecisms which testify clearly to the living influence of a Phrygian substratum.

difference of practice between Luke and Paul in rendering the names of the same persons. This is of interest as it is generally agreed that Acts is independent of the epistles. Luke has Silas for Paul's Silvanus, Priscilla for Prisca, and speaks much of Peter (Συμεών in James's mouth in 15:14) whereas Paul usually has 'Cephas' (8 times; Πέτρος twice). Another hypocoristic, 'Apollos', is common to both writers, and perhaps he was universally known in the primitive church by this distinctively Egyptian form (see the excursus, p. 233 below), which at once set him apart from other bearers of the very common name 'Apollonius'. The tendency in these cases is for Luke to prefer the familiar, Paul the more formal (or the Hebraic) version, but there is some variation according to context. (The most striking case within Acts is of course the group Σαούλ, Σαῦλος, Παῦλος, but the distinction between these three is probably to be seen as wholly contextual. There is no light here on sources.) The general conclusion from the variations seems rather to be this, that Luke refers independently to persons also mentioned by Paul, and often uses more familiar forms of their names. Unless that be explained as elaborately contrived by Luke to match Pauline references, it is a point of some note. The thrust of current scholarship is in any case to emphasize the disjunction between Luke and Paul, and so Luke's independence. But that entails not only his theological distinctiveness, but the independence of his historical testimony.

The source question in Acts is notoriously difficult, as we shall see below. And the consideration of variations of formulation within Acts serves in the main only to reinforce this sense that Luke has made his material his own. But there are some grounds for believing that for some events at the beginning of the book Luke had less contextual control of the form of his material.

L. *Peculiar Selection of Detail*

In this section, we will look at seemingly unnecessary detail given in the book of Acts, the inclusion of which does not lend itself to theological explanation. Alternate explanations may affect the historical question. A passing note is justified here on the prominence given to lengthy repetitive narratives and minor episodes which are given space in what is elsewhere an extremely terse account. The following examples are listed under separate headings for longer passages and minutiae. While some of the former may lend themselves variously to theological explanation, the cases chosen for the latter will not.

(a) Longer passages

7:2-47 Stephen's retrospect over Old Testament history is integral to the build-up of the argument of the speech, but lengthy for modern taste, and the thrust of the passage is unclear and open to debate.[88]

10:1-11:18 The long and repetitive telling of the Cornelius incident may be taken to show that Luke thinks it a crucial turning-point.

9:1-19; 22:4-16; 26:9-18 The three accounts of Paul's conversion involve considerable repetition, but are explainable as differently angled to different contexts, and as a motif of central significance for Luke's narrative, to be displayed in its different relations.

23:26-30; 24:2-8 Space is found for the letter of Lysias and the speech of Tertullus. While these passages bring before us in dramatic form the attitudes of authority and of opponents to Paul, and provide rich scope for Luke's ironical humour, their prominence in this brief narrative might be questioned. They might be explained in terms of Luke's artistry, a point which does not foreclose the different question of their historicity. The letter was presumably read in court, and Paul himself is the ostensible claimant to have been Luke's informant on both passages. The richly entertaining irony belongs to the situation. Luke's serious purpose did not exclude vitality and actuality. It might be quite unconventional, but completely plausible, to see the genesis of this passage in the hilarious and memorable manner of Paul's telling the story.[89]

27:1-28:16 The voyage to Rome is told with a fullness of circumstantial detail which is not naturally explained by theological motifs. Theological significance is by no means absent in the narrative, but its extent and specificity goes far beyond anything sufficiently explained in theological terms.

(b) Small details

4:6 Mention is made of the unspecified John and Alexander among the high priest's party.

12:13-17 We note the part played by Rhoda, and the departure of Peter. Efforts to identify the 'place' to which Peter went are misconceived attempts to find an unintended significance.[90]

---

88 It would be premature to attempt to resolve this question here. One is struck with a parallel with the oriental mode of argument today, where a narrative or expository format presents the facts and themes from which the questioner is expected to extract the relevant matter.

89 Cf. J. Jónsson, *Humour and Irony in the New Testament Illuminated by Parallels in Talmud and Midrash* (Leiden: Brill, 1985), who notes that the humour of Acts is largely that of situation (p. 222; cf. p. 208), though, surprisingly, he cites no examples after the incident consequent on the plot of Acts 23:12, and doubts humour in the speeches.

90 The story is rounded off with the statement, in effect, that he went into

12:20 There is named one Blastus, a servant of the king.

17:34 Dionysius and Damaris are named.

18:7-8 Paul's shift to teaching at the house of Titius Justus is mentioned along with the naming of the ἀρχισυνάγωγος who believed. These points however have their significance for his relation with Judaism and Jewish response to the Gospel, matters apposite to his case before Gallio that he was preaching the fulfilment of Judaism within definitions acceptable to Roman authority.

19:29 The naming of Paul's companions, Gaius and Aristarchus, is perhaps natural to the extent that he would have been anxious for their safety, and so a vivid touch belonging to the situation but not lending itself to theological explanation.

20:4-5 Several companions of Paul are here named; most of them play no overt part in the story, their function is explicable as representatives of the churches with the 'collection'. Here Acts receives its explanation from the Epistles, as Haenchen implicitly acknowledges.[91] Cf. F, pp. 188f. above.

21:8, 16 Philip the evangelist and Mnason, Paul's hosts at successive stages of the journey to Jerusalem, are mentioned by name.

hiding. The location is immaterial. Haenchen (p. 386n) cites Wellhausen for the view that Peter's destination was Antioch. Others, like Jacquier (p. 369) accept this as probable, though Jacquier also raises the possibility of Rome at this stage. S.G.F. Brandon, *The Fall of Jerusalem and the Christian Church* (London: SPCK, 1951), p. 211, argued that Luke's 'vagueness' was due to a desire to suppress the fact of Peter's destination, and chose Alexandria as the nearest above Rome and Corinth on this ground. J.W. Wenham, 'Did Peter Go to Rome in AD 42?', *TB* 23 (1972), pp. 94-102, maintains an early visit of Peter to Rome as indicated here (p. 99), and like Edmundson (*Church in Rome*, p. 50) he follows Jerome's statement that Peter went to Rome in the second year of Claudius. ([Ed.] See now also C.P. Thiede, *Simon Peter: From Galilee to Rome* [Exeter: Paternoster, 1986], pp. 153-58). But these views build much too much on the phrase εἰς ἕτερον τόπον. τόπος is not commonly used of a 'city' as 'place' is in English. It may be a settlement or locality, a position or station, in the plural an extended district, as in Acts 16:3; 27:2, and it is freely used in figurative senses, but it is hard to parallel in the sense where πόλις would be appropriate. On checking a number of instances cited in *BAGD* from Josephus and Diodorus, I find they all refer to a locality or at most to the site of a city or a settlement without civic standing, but not to a city as such. This common word merits further investigation on this score. The point, however, lies neither in Luke's motivated vagueness, nor in dismissing the relevance of a 'Peter-legend' (Dibelius, *Studies*, p. 96n, Haenchen, p. 386n), but in recognizing where not to over-interpret an unspecific statement. Whether Peter went to Rome in the aftermath of his release is a different question, not to be settled from this phrase.

91 Haenchen, pp. 581ff. ([Ed.] Cf. W.-H. Ollrog, *Paulus und seine Mitarbeiter* [Neukirchener Verlag, 1979], pp. 52-58).

28:11-13 The second Alexandrian ship is said to be called the 'Dioscuri', and the detailed account of its prosperously uneventful voyage is given.

These few passages will serve to illustrate the range of the phenomena. To devote greater space to examples would entail excessive repetition on our own part. We have focused especially on names, and suggest that the recording of personal names may have diverse kinds of significance. They are not to be explained from theological motivation, and the idea that they are developed and inserted progressively in line with 'laws of tradition' is highly suspect. Sometimes they rate a mention because the persons were known in the primitive church and were thus meaningful to the first readers. It was almost a case of 'name-dropping'. An interesting case was the ship. Paul completed his voyage on a famous 'clipper', perhaps the first that year to have braved the earliest spring seas. The narrative can be taken to display something of the warm human interest of a good modern autobiography whose author recounts in passing encounters with persons of interest to the reader. Perhaps on other occasions, people were mentioned just because they played their part in a memorable scene or engaged the emotions of Paul or Luke (Gaius and Aristarchus, Tertullus). Sometimes, perhaps, they were actually Luke's informants, whether or not another explanation also partly applies.

M. *Immediacy in details*

Many details in the 'we-passages' and more particularly in the final 'we-passage', which narrates the voyage and shipwreck, are characterized by an 'immediacy' of narrative interest, not easily explained from the perspective of selective hindsight. Most of these items have already been discussed, but the point here is that such details cannot to be explained by theological purpose, and are not conveniently amenable to the insights of redaction criticism. A few examples taken *passim* from Acts 27-28 will suffice.

27:2 The name of the ship's home port and destination are given.

27:4 The route north of Cyprus and the adverse winds, a normal feature of Eastern Mediterranean climate and currents, are mentioned by a writer who had travelled eastward with favouring winds, and notes a difference in the experience of the return.

27:8 Again, Luke draws attention to the (normal) westward route south of Crete.

27:11 We note the composition of the centurion's *consilium*, where Paul was out-voted.

27:12 The hearsay account of the harbour at Phoenix, and its bearing to the winds is related.

27:16-17 We have description of the manoeuvre at Cauda and the fear of the Syrtis.

27:19 The casting the σκεύη overboard on the third day is mentioned.

27:27-28 The passage contains the unexplained perception that land was near and the taking of soundings twice.

27:29 Anchors are cast from the stern to hold the ship pointing shorewards.

27:30-32 The panic escape attempt of the sailors and the likely explosion of tension between sailors, soldiers, passengers and prisoners are related.

27:40 The technical manoeuvres are made in preparation for running the ship to shore.

28:2 We are told of the exceptional kindness of the local people.

28:11-14 The author presents details about the ship 'Dioscuri', the timing of its voyage to Puteoli, and the stay there.

28:15 Christians come from Rome to meet Paul at Appii Forum and Three Taverns.

I have carefully excluded from this list statements which might be taken as significant for Paul's fate or which might show the providential working of God, as in the cold and rain on Malta which led to the fire and snake incident. Yet some of these details which are thus locked into the occasions of more evidently 'theological' material, are themselves marked by the same circumstantiality and 'immediacy'. The cases chosen seem to be told for the sake of the telling, as what actually happened. If they do not recount actual experience, and experience little filtered through the selective processes of memory, they are hard to explain, unless as creative verisimilitude, and that option is progressively excluded as we explore their integration with an implicit context. Deeper study promotes the integration of these chapters with the situation of Paul (see chapter 6). The concept of 'immediacy' raised here is one to which we shall return.

N. *Idioms or cultural features suggestive of date of composition*

Here we propose to deal with characteristics of the language and cultural understandings assumed rather than *portrayed* by the author. This category is easier to propose in principle than to establish clearly. But it will be worthy of mention, if only to indicate possible directions for further research. It includes both general features of the book, and individual nuances, subject to the possibility of our being able to demarcate stylistic and cultural developments on a sufficiently clear time-scale.

Atticism and fashions in terminology: Hellenistic literature is marked by a trend towards a self-conscious classicizing which reached its peak in the 2nd century AD, when it is best exemplified in the work of Lucian. It has in fact been suggested that the paucity of surviving first century Greek literature (other than in factual and scientific genres) is due to the neglect of it by the stylistic fastidiousness of the succeeding period. The application of these factors to an assessment of the language of Acts is a very complex and elusive matter.[92] We can only hope to illustrate the principle as a proposition for further study. One factor is the use of Latinisms. In various contexts Latin terms were transliterated, translated (often as 'calques'[93]), or replaced by conventional equivalents. Some transliterated borrowings became well established early, but then fell foul of literary purism, and were replaced in literature by more respectably classical, if sometimes inexact and misleading, substitutes.[94] The position is complicated by the difference between literary and official usage, though the latter became increasingly affected by the fashion,

---

[92]   P.N. Harrison's note on classical words in the Pastorals (*The Problem of the Pastoral Epistles* [OUP, 1921], p. 66) and his lengthier comparison of their language with that of second-century writers seem unsuccessful for the lack of clear and sufficient criteria. It is not our aim to attempt a similar exercise. If however a firm terminus may be set for a semantic change, or the introduction of a new name for a new institution, this might be suggestive. The position is greatly complicated by the evident differences between popular speech, official formulation and the progress of literary purism.

[93]   That is, the literal semantic rendering of the etymological components of a word into another language, like modern Greek σιδηρόδρομος for the French *chemin de fer* or Πλατεία τῆς Ὁμονοίας ('Homonia Square') in Athens for 'Place de la Concorde' in Paris. The principle is well illustrated in our period by πρεσβευτής (και) ἀντιστράτηγος as the habitual rendering of *legatus pro praetore*.

[94]   See H.J. Mason, 'The Roman Government in Greek Sources. The Effect of Literary Theory on the Translation of Official Titles', *Phoenix* 24 (1970), pp. 150-59, and *Greek Terms for Roman Institutions* (Toronto: Hakkert, 1974) esp. pp. 11-13. In his article Mason cites Athenaeus *Deipn*. 3.121e as an example of the strong feeling against Latin loan-words in 2nd-3rd centuries AD (p. 151). He further observes that Galen, in referring to a patient who was a *cubicularius*, says that Greeks now commonly use κοιτωνίτης, but οἱ περιέργως ἀττικίζοντες prefer σωματοφύλαξ (p. 152). Cf. also A. Cameron, 'Latin Words in the Greek Inscriptions of Asia Minor', *AJP* 52 (1931), pp. 232-62. Cameron gives another interesting example, where Lucian (*Amores* 12) paraphrases to avoid using the verb σκουτλοῦν, then well naturalized in Greek, because of its connection with Latin *scutula* (Cameron, 'Latin Words', p. 257). For linguistic strictures of the period cf. Lucian, *Soloecista* and Phrynichus, *Ecloga* (*Die Ekloge des Phrynichos*, ed. E. Fischer [Berlin and New York: W. de Gruyter, 1974]).

until a great new influx of Latin loan-words entered official and documentary usage in the third century.[95]

Acts shows no sign of self-conscious Atticism, and indeed uses forms on which Atticism frowned, including such Latinisms as κολωνία and πραιτώριον for Roman institutions, and conventional equivalents elsewhere (ἀνθύπατος, ἑκατοντάρχης, ῥαβδοῦχος, σπεῖρα, etc.). But this may amount to no more than saying that Acts does not aspire to literary fashions, whether early or late. Certainly we may be glad that Luke prefers the standard rendering of an exact term to classicizing fancy. It is not clear that we can take this topic much further, unless through very specialized study which might still be rendered uncertain by the number of unknown or uncontrollable variables. The shifts of terminology noted by Mason may be pointers, but the *termini a quo* are often too uncertain to build upon.[96]

Aramaisms: the proposition that Acts contains Semitisms, in particular Aramaisms, might be held to suggest an early origin of its material in the Aramaic-speaking church. In this case the focus of the problem lies in the early chapters of the book, and the Jerusalem setting, rather than the Graeco-Roman ambiance of the latter part. It now seems clear that C.C. Torrey's Aramaic theories were highly conjectural, and have not stood up to subsequent criticism.[97] But the

---

[95] See Mason, *Greek Terms*, pp. 3, 11. This proliferation of Latin was characteristic of the post-Constantinian Empire, but the trend began under the Severi.

[96] Mason says (*Greek Terms*, p. 12) that στρατηγός for 'governor' (*praeses*) gave way to ἡγεμών by the end of the first century AD, that ἔθνος became more acceptable for 'province' during the 2nd century, and that κύριος (and κυριακός) for the emperor became acceptable in Egypt from the mid 1st century, but is elsewhere first recorded later, about AD 100. His fuller study of ἡγεμών (pp. 148-49) however gives a different and more complex picture, with a variety of applications. It is commonly used of the *praefectus* of Egypt, and for 'governor' in the New Testament writers and Josephus (and, we may add, earlier in Strabo 17.3.25 = 840), and he suggests that in Judaea the term possibly had the same semi-official status as in Egypt. He also cites this usage of the governor of Achaia from *IG* 7.2.2711.6 (AD 37, of Acraephiae in Boeotia). The same text (line 108) also has ἔθνος of 'province'. And it is well known that the title κύριος was applied to Nero, and this usage can scarcely have been restricted to Egypt, even if the restricted provenance of the papyri serves to focus the attestations there.

[97] Torrey, *The Composition and Date of Acts* (Cambridge, Mass: Harvard University Press, 1916), pp. 1-41; with criticisms in H.F.D. Sparks, 'The Semitisms of the Acts', *JTS* n.s. 1 (1950), pp. 16-28 (though Sparks in turn tends to reduce the variety of phenomena to Septuagintalisms); M. Black, *An Aramaic Approach to the Gospels and Acts* (Oxford: Clarendon Press, 3rd edn, 1967), esp. pp. 4-14; M. Wilcox, *The Semitisms of Acts* (Oxford: Clarendon Press, 1965). There is a valuable survey by D.F. Payne, 'Semitisms in the Book of Acts', in *Apostolic History and the Gospel*, ed. Gasque and Martin, pp. 134-50.

residual problem remains exceedingly complex. Diverse kinds of Semitisms may be involved. And while specially prominent in the early chapters, the likely Semitisms are not confined to them. Several writers have drawn attention to their special prominence in the speeches, though in some cases this tendency is accentuated in the D-text.[98] Wilcox also draws attention to the fact that Semitisms in narrative are concentrated in passages connected with Antioch.[99]

This group of observations has its relevance for our prospective study both of sources and of speeches, but the present point is simpler, that Aramaisms suggest nearness to an Aramaic substratum in the earliest church. Yet the possible difficulty caused to this view by the Semitizing tendency in D ought to be recognized.[100]

---

[98] Black, p. 36, cf. 51; Wilcox, *Semitisms*, pp. 158-64; Bruce, *The Speeches in the Acts of the Apostles*, pp. 8-9; Dodd, *The Apostolic Preaching and its Developments* (London: Hodder, 1936), pp. 34-36.

[99] Wilcox, *Semitisms*, pp. 178-79.

[100] This might be held by the same reasoning to imply a primitive origin for the Western variants, where it would be facile to suppose them all 'secondary Semitisms'. The difficulty of the matter is illustrated by the crux at Acts 3:14, where D substitutes ἐβαρύνατε for the B reading ἠρνήσασθε, and the difference has been variously explained as due to a misreading or mistranslation of a Hebrew, Aramaic or Syriac substratum, or even to the influence of a misreading rendered into Latin (Rendel Harris). Epp, *Theological Tendency*, pp. 51-53, notes the inadequacy and incompatibility of all these attempts, and sees here the expression of the anti-Judaic tendency of D. A different, and apparently unobserved, reason for seeing D as secondary here touches the theme of our present section more closely, that βαρύνω is an Atticistic form otherwise unexampled in the New Testament, where βαρέω is used, always in the passive. See Lucian *Soloec.* 7. Cf. G.R. Stanton in *ZPE* 54 (1984), p. 53n.

Much could be said in detail of Luke's language in its possible bearing on the question of date. Like other New Testament writers, he uses forms which are condemned by the Atticists: passive for middle in ἀπεκρίθη, ἀποκριθείς etc. (except ἀπεκρίνατο in Acts 3:12), forms condemned by Phrynichus *Ecl.* 78 (86); weak aorist endings on strong aorist stems (Acts 4:20; 6:15; etc.). Other words in Acts similarly condemned include κράβαττος (Acts 5:15; 9:33; Phrynichus *Ecl.* 41 [44]); ἤμην (Acts 10:30; 11:5, 17; *Ecl.* 123 [130]); λόγιος in the sense 'eloquent', 'articulate' (Acts 18:24; *Ecl.* 171 [176]); βασίλισσα (Acts 8:27; *Ecl.* 197 [202]); παρεμβολή (Acts 21:34; etc.; *Ecl.* 354 [353]). One could list similarly rejected words which occur in the Third Gospel but not in Acts: such include βουνός, βρέχει, κλίβανος, πάντοτε, σκορπίζω, φάγομαι (future). Other such words are found in Matthew and Mark, but not in Luke: γενέσια, κοράσιον, οἰκοδομή. An interesting case is in Lk. 18:25, where the UBS text reads the approved βελόνη against the condemned ῥαφίς (*Ecl.* 63 [72]) of the other Synoptics. Such samplings cannot of course take us far, and in this space there can be no question of making an analysis of the instances. The language of Luke in the Third Gospel

Legal Practices: this is a difficult and technical subject, but it is worth drawing attention to places where Sherwin-White in *RSRL* sees Acts as reflecting first-century, as opposed to later, practice. See for example the governor's option to refuse jurisdiction over a prisoner of a different province (pp. 31, 55; cf. Acts 23:34-35); the discussion of the judicial powers of the Sanhedrin before 70 (pp. 40-43; cf. the case of Stephen); the whole conduct of Paul's hearing before Felix as an example of the procedure *extra ordinem* as applicable at that period (pp. 48-55); Paul's citizenship and appeal to Caesar (pp. 57-70; a difficult matter, where after lengthy discussion Sherwin-White stresses appropriateness to early practice, pp. 68-70).

P. Interrelated complexes leading to larger areas of historical reconstruction

In the following examples, two or more categories of correlation are involved. Related details of the same issue will sometimes show separate correlations with external evidence, or the same details may be linked with several kinds of categories. If there are such complexes of data, their interlocking unity may be more suggestive than any number of individual correlations, as they are much harder for an author to fabricate convincingly.

1. Paul's arrival at Corinth, according to Acts 18:1-2, brought him into association with Aquila, who had recently come from Italy upon Claudius' expulsion of the Jews from Rome. The explicit evidence places this (*pace* Lüdemann) in 49, and this fits well with the chronology fixed by Gallio's proconsulship in Achaia, which probably began in the early summer of the year following Paul's arrival. It also sets the background for Paul's subsequent series of Corinthian letters from a residence in Ephesus and its aftermath, leading to the occasion of the 'collection' and the gathering described in Acts 20:4. Further light is shed on Gallio's proconsulship by the writings of his brother Seneca. Independent pieces of this complex may be gathered from literature, epigraphy and the relation of Acts with Epistles.[101]

is evidently influenced by his sources in a way inapplicable to the freer compositional style of much of Acts. There are sufficient indications that he often modifies Mark in the direction of a more literary Greek, and elsewhere that particular usages are from the Septuagint. And the Atticistic structures are not all of a piece; some of the recommended forms were evidently good current literary usage while others were attempts at reviving archaic and obsolete classicisms. One may suggest that Luke writes Greek of higher level, especially in some passages of Acts, than most other parts of the New Testament, but that he shows no trace of the self-conscious Atticistic trend. The absence of an influence does not prove contrary conclusions, but is fully consistent with them.

[101] In the present climate of opinion it may seem temerarious to make claims for

2. Some aspects of the Galatian question: this topic will require fuller treatment in its own right (See Chapter 7) Gal. 4:13-14 refers to Paul's first preaching to the Galatians as occasioned by a 'bodily ailment', and this should be aligned with Paul's first entry in Acts to territory comprised within 'Galatia' in contemporary usage, his coming to Pisidian Antioch in Acts 13, an occasion closely subsequent to a crisis in Pamphylia which precipitated the defection of Mark. This sequence of events is open to diverse explanation, and it may be safer not to speculate. But one is impressed with the possibility that Paul's 'thorn', if a physical condition, was a factor in the unhealthy coastal plain of Pamphylia on the very eve of his coming to Galatia. The application of this geographic term is open to evaluation from a variety of perspectives when the evidence of the inscriptions is taken into account.

3. Paul's escape from Damascus in a basket (Acts 9:25) links with 2 Cor. 11:32-33; the difficult historical problem in this case is located in Paul's own undoubted testimony, not in Acts. Yet the terminology of 2 Cor. may be linked with that of some inscriptions of the area, notably the memorial of Ἀδριανοῦ τοῦ καὶ Σοαίδου Ι Μαλέχου ἐθνάρ-χου στρα Ι τηγοῦ Νομάδων (*IGRR* 3.1247 = *OGIS* 616, lines 1-3, of El Malka, Arabia). The man was an Arab called 'Saïd bin Melek'. Cf. *IGRR* 3.1254, of Tharba in Syria; *IGRR* 3.1136 = *OGIS* 421, of Eitha in Batanea (Transjordan), in each case apparently referring to native chieftains dignified also with Roman names and appointments.

4. The Areopagus address and its setting: in this case there are several latent motifs which are not explicable as redactional. The topographical unity of the scene, for which I have argued in *NTS* 20 (1974), pp. 341-50, is focused in Pauline Athens, and embedded in literary and archaeological backgrounds which are never made explicit by Luke. There is the further point that the speech appears to use implicitly arguments directed at the thinking of Stoics, Epicureans and the traditional religion of Athens, and that a catena of

such a reconstruction. Historical reconstruction is in any case a matter of probabilities. But the point here is that the ostensible reading of the text and of other evidences contributes to a fragment of an interlocking picture, where alternatives resort to an unjustified reinterpretation of evidence and may then aspire to an undue confidence and dogmatism in asserting what is less controlled by the evidence and may savour of special pleading.

The present suggestions might be extended. If for instance Paul had intended to go from Macedonia by the Via Egnatia towards Rome, and was deflected south to Athens by news of the expulsion of Jews, this would be another link, but it depends more heavily on the assumption that we have correctly divined Paul's strategic thinking at this stage. Cf. Bruce, *Paul*, p. 235; Bowers, *JTS* n.s. 30 (1979), p. 511; *NovT* 22 (1980), pp. 316-23.

citations from Aratus, Epimenides and Aeschylus underlies the debate.

5. The incidental notes of time in Acts 20 permit a fairly full reconstruction of the passing of time in the ostensible seven-week period between Passover and Pentecost in the year of Paul's voyage to Jerusalem. In the early part, the travellers were apparently anxious over time, and the computation of days can scarcely be less than complete. I have argued elsewhere that the evidence of Acts 20:7 points to the year 57 for this journey.[102]

6. The voyage to Rome and the shipwreck on Malta display a remarkable integration, where many details of geography, nautical terminology and Roman organization are open to scrutiny. Many of these details have been considered in chapter 4 above. But this passage is a crucial one because of its importance for the interpretation of the 'we-passages'. It is thus a test case for discriminating between radically alternative views of Acts.[103]

These instances are far from exhaustive. They are chosen simply to illustrate a possible manner of combining perceptions outlined in the last two chapters into larger integrated groupings supported by different kinds of evidence together.

Q. New Background Information: Unfinished Tasks

It would be relevant at this point to give indications of areas of literature which bear significantly on the period and places of our study.[104] But it must suffice to mention detailed passages and topics. The point is that background is not an instant springboard for apologetic, nor for proof of any kind, but does have an essential contribution to make to understanding.

Some of the themes are obvious: Roman legal practice and administration, the gradual piecing together of the network of Roman roads, the indigenous religious character of Asia Minor and the cults of individual cities, and its ethnic and linguistic boundaries in their bearing on geographical nomenclature and administrative arrangements. Many of the questions raised by these topics have no direct

---

[102] *Pauline Studies Bruce*, pp. 9-12.

[103] See my study 'First Person Narrative in Acts 27-28', *TB* 36 (1985), pp. 79-109, and Chapter 8 for further discussion.

[104] Among recent major epigraphical publications it may be especially relevant to mention the appearance of major *repertoria* in the series *Inschriften griechischer Städte aus Kleinasien* (*IGSK*), including the eight volumes on Ephesus and the first volumes available of Smyrna, as well as to the first fascicle of *TAM* 5, covering north and east Lydia, in the hinterland of Sardis and Philadelphia.

application to the historical criticism of Acts in the narrow sense. But there must be a wider framework, a larger matrix within which the points of contact between Acts and Epistles may be viewed. If the more direct illumination is perhaps cast sometimes on the Epistles rather than Acts, that is still valuable, for it all serves to enlarge and diversify the picture. We need a framework within which to study relationships, not necessarily as a setting for harmonization.

It will suffice to list sample passages where the larger study of background is of prospective importance.

2:7-11 The demography of the Jewish Diaspora.

6:1, 5, 9 etc. The problem of the Hellenists and the investigation of the use of names and languages in first century Jerusalem, and the organization of synagogues (cf. the ossuaries and the Theodotus inscription).

11:28 The detailed chronology of the recurring famines under Claudius.

14:6, 11; 16:6 etc. The linguistic map of Asia Minor and the identities of Anatolian ethnic divisions and their effect on the pattern of Paul's work.

27:6ff. The organization of the Roman corn fleet from Alexandria under Claudius and Nero.

R. Uncheckable details

Our final category is one of loose ends. They are interesting because they give hostages to criticism. To that extent they make Acts a much more interesting book than it would be on the view which is uninterested in history and would exempt religious truths from the realm of verification. Of course, to say that a detail is uncheckable is to say it occurs only once. It is not necessarily suspect on that account, but it is open to the possibility that illustrative, confirmatory or contradictory detail will come along as new texts are discovered. Meanwhile it must be held as a statement in isolation, and our opinion of it must be guided by our general evaluation of Luke's trustworthiness on matters of fact. There must in the nature of things be statements made only once, and there is no call to hasten to emend out unique statements, so that their occurrence can be blandly denied. It is probably inevitable that in most cases they will remain isolated, but the possibility of correlative discovery remains.

There is a sense in which this category comprises much of the content of Acts, and so leads into the focus of our larger problem, for Acts is our only source for much that concerns the growth and inner life of the primitive church and the activities of persons who otherwise make no mark on recorded history of any kind. And it is the essence of our problem to know how reliable a source Luke is on such matters. But the examples presented here are chosen for their more 'public' nature, for only in such cases, barring a freak coincidence, are we likely to gain further light from external sources. And these cases cannot be rigidly separated from those which must remain debatable in the face of inconclusive evidence, such as the 'Italian Cohort' (10:1).

12:10 The topography of Peter's prison escape.

12:20 The background of Herod Agrippa I's quarrel with Tyre and Sidon, which is not specified in Josephus. The court official Blastus, too, otherwise unknown, was evidently a man of some influence, for whom epigraphical mention might conceivably appear.

13:7 The proconsul Sergius Paulus, for whom the supposed attestations are not acceptable (cf. C, p. 109; D, pp. 166f.).

16:13 The existence of a riverside place of Jewish worship by the Gangites at Philippi.

16:26 The occurrence of an earthquake at Philippi at this date, ostensibly c. AD 50.

17:4, 12 The prominence and responsiveness of leading women in the social life of Thessalonica and of Beroea.

20:35 A different class of example, a saying attributed to Jesus but unparalleled in our Gospel traditions.

23:16 Reference to members of Paul's family of whom we have no intimation from anything in epistles ascribed to him.

23:23 The word δεξιολάβοι (RSV 'spearmen') clearly denotes a type of soldier, but the term is unparalleled, and of uncertain meaning. Thus far it cannot be related with confidence to any Latin equivalent.

27:37 The number of persons forming the ship's complement, relatable broadly only to the known size of the vessel described by Lucian, and complicated by textual divergence, and by the much larger figure for Josephus' ship. See also pp. 149-50.

28:7 The identity of Publius, the πρῶτος of the island of Malta.

Examples of this type are not different in essence from details of similar kinds for which it has been possible to offer illustration in previous sections. There is indeed a wide spectrum of cases where fresh attestation would be illustrative, from matters as secure already as the title 'politarch' to the present kind. The most urgent needs are in controverted areas. Inscriptional light on the date of the accession of Festus would be invaluable, and that at least is the kind of datum we might reasonably hope to obtain.

Implications

Several possibilities must be noticed. (1) It will be obvious that we are far removed from a simplistic attempt to *prove* the historicity of Acts. There is no simple correspondence between the confirmation of individual details and the overall historicity of a book. If there is a pattern of unobtrusive correlations, this is at most suggestive. It is perfectly possible to have a fictional narrative with accuracies of locality and background included, where for instance a writer intimately acquainted with the localities has used actual names and factual details and reproduced a setting transcribed from life, rather as a picture could be composed of an incongruous mixture of painting and photography. This may not be the right explanation of Acts, but the possibility cannot be excluded *a priori*.

(2) We can exclude certain options as not viable. Strangely incautious statements are sometimes made that Luke was not interested in details, and that he either adapted them recklessly to the dictates of theological point or was vague and careless when he had no point to make. If we can show that he was actually careful of detail in many places amenable to checking, that suffices to put some theories out of court as serious options. It does not of course automatically exclude more subtle syntheses like that of Haenchen which take this factor into account.

(3) We may establish in general terms something further of the character of Luke as a writer, an objective highly relevant to the focus of interest in these days of redaction criticism. The body of data suggests that, in their treatments of similar types of detail, the work of Luke is marked by carefulness but that of Josephus by carelessness. Again, this is not a simplistic judgment on their relative value, for Josephus is without doubt a writer with contemporary inside knowledge of his subject, the very point which stands at issue in the case of Luke. The assertion here is about a temper of mind, one which makes us use Josephus' personal knowledge with appropriate critical reserve when questions of numerical exaggeration or of self-justification may be involved.

(4) The character of Luke as a writer is in turn a factor in the interrelated problem-complexes of date and authorship. These issues have in part to be settled on the character of the writing. Our decisions about the treatment of detail pose restraints on the options viable in other critical issues.

All these suggestions have their implications, however indirect, upon the central question of historicity, and the matter needs closer exploration. Could Acts be explained, for instance, by what might be called a 'parabolic model'? It could be argued that the admitted accuracies of detail in Acts no more support historicity than do accuracies of setting in a parable. The story of the Good Samaritan, for instance, is set on a real road between real places, and, whatever we make of traditional sites, it is clear that there would have been an inn at a suitable point *en route* which possessed a rare supply of water, and that Jesus referred to realities familiar to his hearers. But none of us would want to argue for the 'historicity' of this story. It would be an error of genre criticism even to try. That remains the case even if we sharpen the question. Let us grant (with many scholars) for the sake of argument the essential authenticity to Jesus of the parables in question. They are true to first-century Palestinian life. We could even suppose that Jesus' words were close to actual events, that his audience was shocked by sudden news of just such a case of banditry on that very road. None of this would induce us to think in terms of 'historicity': the operative term would be 'topicality', and topicality is a valuable factor in teaching technique. May not this be the case with Acts also, that local colour, and vivid gleams of real life, may be embedded in a matrix of different texture, like currants in a cake?

But there is no convincing analogy. Acts still purports to be a narrative of what happened. Even if we take it to be teaching couched somehow in a narrative form, the character of the mixture is still very different from that of parable or *mašal*. To suggest for instance that the historical components are there to give topicality or verisimilitude to Paul as a lay-figure of Lukan theology seems forced beyond all probability. Even to treat Acts as a theological treatise or polemical document which incorporates historical traditions from a diary or itinerary-source seems to risk making a difficult mixture of a book which appears to have a more integrated unity of character. Such a view is at odds with the 'immediacy' of the very sections which it has to reinterpret as unassimilated blocks of older material. A more satisfactory view must be one which brings the history and theology together. Where a polarized separation of these aspects is made, the tendency seems to be to downplay the historical component of the narrative in such a way that the accuracies of detail become nothing more than an embarrassing complication. It poses a problem why Lukan theology should have been incarnated in an ostensibly historical narrative in the first place. Perhaps all these difficulties can be explained by those who wish to do so, but the exercise seems unnecessary. The evidence of details is strongly aligned with the trend of the answers suggested by kindred questions, while also providing a foundation for much of the discussion in following chapters.

Names and Titles in Acts

Local Names and Titles Illustrative of the Text[1]

The occurrence in Acts of personal names and inconsequential details of no probative value in themselves, but paralleled in local documents from the same cities. This is illustration in its most trivial sense, and of interest for that very reason, because of its manifestly undesigned character. Yet cumulatively such cases may point to local and contemporary fashions in nomenclature, and their fortuitous preservation may provide suggestive coincidences. The accumulation of insignificant parallels may point beyond the intrinsic evidential value of the individual items.

1:13 James the son of Alphaeus is mentioned in all the lists of the twelve (Mk. 3:18 = Mt. 10:3 = Lk. 6:15) among those called by Jesus in Galilee. An Aramaic Jewish inscription (*CIJ* 982) displayed *in situ* in Capernaum bears the name 'Halphai' in association with the names 'Zebidah' and 'John'. These names are not rare, but their grouping in the focal place of Jesus' ministry is interesting. The text has been dated variously from the 1st to the 4th centuries. It is even possible that the same names remained in use among descendants of the same families in this small place.

1:23 Joseph Barsabbas surnamed Justus: 'Justus' is a characteristic Latin name used by Jews as a Gentile alternative to a Jewish name. Examples are numerous.[2] A Jewish ossuary in Jerusalem names one Justus of Chalcis (*CIJ* 1233). Josephus (*Vita* 35.175) refers to the rival

---

1 I shall not address here the question of the identity or standing of Theophilus, nor whether this name is symbolic only. It will suffice to note that the name is fairly common in the Hellenistic and Roman periods, and there is no necessary reason to connect it specially with a Jewish provenance. A casual check quickly revealed the following examples: *IG* 2^2 11663-11670 (Athens, dates from 4th BC to 1st AD); *IGRR* 3.243 (Lycaonia, of an imperial freedman); *IGRR* 4.184 (Troad), 297.24 (Pergamum, the father of an emissary of Sardis), 1653 (Asia, all of Roman period). An explicitly Jewish Theophilus occurs in *CIJ* 119 (Rome). Nearly two-thirds of the 66 examples known from Rome are ascribed to the 1st cent. AD, and nearly all of those determinable are men of servile or freedman status (see *New Docs* 3.38, No. 9).

2 E.g. *CIJ* 3, 13, 125, 357, 358, 359, 502 (all of Rome, in Greek); *CIJ* 224, 245, 252 (Rome), 533 (near Ostia), 629a (Tarentum), 670 (Narbonne, all in Latin).

Jewish historian Justus of Tiberias. The pattern of alternative names is abundantly attested, especially where a person operates under alternative linguistic or cultural identities. It may be a common phenomenon among Jews in particular, perhaps to a larger extent than our sources reveal.[3]

2:9-11 The range of Jewish presence in the Diaspora may be broadly illustrated from the incidence of Jewish inscriptions. While the collection in *CIJ* is incomplete, and cannot admit of close chronological analysis, its range will suffice to make the point clear in general terms.[4] Though Frey's work offers no documentation of some other areas mentioned here, most of the gaps may be filled. A new collection of the Jewish inscriptions of Roman Africa contains 124 items,[5] where Frey has none. The area of Cyrenaica, not covered there, has references to a Jewish πολίτευμα at Berenice (Benghazi) in G. Lüderitz, *Corpus jüdischer Zeugnisse aus der Cyrenaika* (Wiesbaden: Ludwig Reichart Verlag, 1983) No. 70 (= *CIG* 5362 = *IGRR* 1.1024, 1st BC / 1st AD) and 71 (= *CIG* 5361, October 24/25 AD). The independent evidence for Cyrene as a considerable centre of the Diaspora is strong.[6] As for Crete, I have found a tombstone of Joseph for his

---

3   On double-names see esp. *New Docs* 1.89-96, No. 55; G.H.R. Horsley, 'Name Change as an Indication of Religious Conversion in Antiquity', *Numen* 34 (1987), pp. 1-17.

4   See *CIJ* 1-529 (Rome), 738-55 (Ionia and Lydia, comprising Asia in a narrow sense), 760-80 (Phrygia), 781 (Pamphylia), 801-802 (Pontus), 1415-19 (Mesopotamia), 1420-23 (Arabia), 1424-1539 (Egypt). ([Ed.] These last have been reproduced, with minor improvements, as an appendix in *CPJ* III.)

5   Yann Le Bohec, 'Inscriptions juives et judaïsantes de l'Afrique romaine', *Antiquités africaines* 17 (1981), pp. 165-207; cf. *id*., 'Juifs et Judaïsants dans l'Afrique romaine', *ibid*. pp. 209-29, and see *SEG* 30 (1980) 1235. His collection includes 81 stone inscriptions, mostly sepulchral, the remainder being made up of inscribed lamps, amulets and *defixionum tabellae*, from Mauretania, Numidia and proconsular Africa. Though many are not explicitly Jewish, and some are placed only by context, not content, they constitute *in toto* a formidable body of evidence. The eastern lands of Parthia, Media and Elam are in any case outside the main range of Greek (or Semitic) epigraphy. In view of the unpredictable, and sometimes very localized, pattern of the survival of evidence, the spread of illustrative material is the more interesting. Other classes of material, like the excavated synagogue at Dura-Europus, could greatly extend the evidence for even the more out-lying regions. For different approaches to the present selection of geographical regions see Chapter 5 above. Note here the characteristic usage fluctuating between territorial name and ethnic when speaking in either case primarily of Jews. These visitors to the Feast have come from every ἔθνος (2:5).

6   See S. Applebaum, *Jews and Greeks in Ancient Cyrene*, Studies in Judaism in Late Antiquity 28 (Leiden: Brill, 1979). Jos. *Ap*. 2.4.44; *Ant*. 14.7.2.114-16, 118, cites Strabo for the account of four regular classes of inhabitants of Cyrene,

son Judas (*I. Cret.* 1.5.17, of Arcadia, central Crete, dated 3rd/4th cent. AD). Frey himself provides the attestation of a Cappadocian Jew buried at Joppa (*CIJ* 910), and of a Cappadocian synagogue or community there (*CIJ* 931).[7]

2:10 The mention of proselytes in the Pentecost crowd is illustrated by the ossuary of a man so designated, named Judas, but with a father bearing a Greek name: (ossuary of) Ἰούδατος Λαγανίωνος προσηλύτου (*CIJ* 1385), from Jerusalem and probably of similar date.[8]

3:2 If the 'Beautiful Gate' is correctly identified with the Nicanor Gate named in the Mishna (Middoth 1.4; cf. Yoma 38a) and described by Josephus as distinguished by remarkable doors of Corinthian bronze (*BJ* 5.5.3.201-203), there is a remarkable illustration in the preservation of the ossuary of its maker, inscribed Ὀστᾶ τῶν τοῦ Νεικά Ινορος Ἀλεξανδρέως, Ι ποιήσαντος τὰς θύρας (*CIJ* 1256 = OGIS 599). It seems to have been that which led from the Women's Court to the sanctuary, though Josephus' words are not clear.[9] Nicanor and

---

citizens, farmers, metics and Jews. Josephus records an appeal of the Cyrenian Jews to Augustus against abuses (*Ant.* 16.6.1.160-61) and cites a subsequent letter of M. Agrippa to the Cyrenians to reinforce the emperor's response (*Ant.* 16.6.5.169-70). Jews of Cyrene are elsewhere prominent in the New Testament itself: Mk 15:21 = Mt. 27:32 (cf. Rom. 16:13); Acts 6:9; 13:1. Josephus further attests an insurrection under Vespasian leading to the deaths of 2000 Jews resident in Cyrene (*Vita* 76.424); 3000 in the longer account in *BJ* 7.11.1-3.437-50), and according to Dio, a Jewish revolt under Trajan involved a savage massacre of the Cyrenian Greeks (Dio 68.32), in which 220,000 are said to have perished. One inscription of Jaffa (*CIJ* 950) records the burial of a Jew of the Pentapolis, probably that of Cyrenaica.

The lack of epigraphical material from Cyrene illustrates the fragmentary and unpredictable state of our evidence, which may depend not only on accidents of survival but on imponderables of local custom or circumstance. A glance through some inscriptions of Cyrene reveals a surprising frequency in the area of several unremarkable Greek or Latin names otherwise popular among Jews (Theodorus, Dositheus, Theodotion, Rufus, etc.), sometimes in association in the same families or groups (e.g. *CIG* 5316). Judaism may often be hidden under Hellenized nomenclature.

7 On 'Judaea' see above ch. 4, pp. 126-28, and below p. 243 where it is argued that this name is freely used without the articles.

8 (Ed.) The term is also found in the Aphrodisias inscription; see Appendix 2 and the literature there cited.

9 Luke's narrative is not explicit about the topography, though if the D reading of 3:11 preserves an accurately inferential expansion of the sequence of events, it would well fit the alternative supposition that the gate lay between the Court of the Women and the Court of the Gentiles. The difficulty is complicated by the evidently erroneous topography of the Mishnah. See Haenchen, p. 198; Marshall, pp. 87-88 *ad loc.* for discussion of the problem. Haenchen is not however justified in his gratuitous doubt reserved exclusively for Luke's evidence (p. 199n).

his gate are apparently to be dated no later than early 1st cent. AD.

3:11 Solomon's colonnade: according to John 10:23 this was the place where Jesus had walked at the Feast of Dedication, ostensibly only a year or so before. Acts elsewhere represents this as a place of meeting of the Christian community (5:12; also perhaps 2:46, where the location in the Temple is not specified). Cf. G, p. 190 above.[10]

5:1 Ananias: for this name cf. *CIJ* 944 (Jaffa), 967 (Gaza; an Aramaic-Greek bilingual, where the Aramaic preserves the original guttural ח, better rendered in Greek with a rough breathing), 1086 (Beth She'arim), 1262a, 1307 (all Hebrew or Aramaic ossuaries of Jerusalem). These are all examples of (H)ananias/Hananiah ('Yah is gracious'), itself fairly common and with other cognates and variants.[11]

5:1 Sapphira: a name well attested in contemporary Jerusalem. J. Klausner went so far as to claim the actual identification of this woman's remains in a beautifully decorated bilingual ossuary discovered in Jerusalem in 1923, apparently *CIJ* 1378.[12] This is mere wishful thinking.[13] But the name occurs also on *CIJ* 1272a in Greek and on 1282c in Semitic, also Jerusalem ossuaries. It is taken to be Aramaic *shappira* ('beautiful') and seems not to be easily paralleled in more western or Hellenized Judaism.

5:36 Theudas: The problem has been noted above and some discussion of the name is offered on pp. 162f., n. 5 in Chapter 5. The

---

[10] This reference, according to Haenchen (p. 204 *ad loc.*), 'is intended to heighten the local colour'. His strictures on Luke here are based on a literalistic hypercriticism, and claim that Luke's topography is incompatible with that of Josephus and the Mishnah, which are on Haenchen's own showing unclear or erroneous, and probably contradictory. One need say no more than that Luke is not concerned to detail sequentially all the movements of the apostles, where these are immaterial to the thrust of his narrative. Whether or not Luke was familiar with the Temple is scarcely answerable either way from this passage. If any local reference may be dismissed as contrived 'local colour', it becomes hard to know how *any* narrative could be authenticated. Where such reference is unstudied and parenthetic, and correlates with other implicit evidence, the pattern may point rather to authenticity. Instances must be judged on their merits rather than prejudged.

[11] In an interesting note C.G. Tuland, 'Hanani-Hananiah', *JBL* 77 (1958), pp. 157-61, gives telling reasons for the actual identification of a man of this name in the Elephantine papyri with Hanani the brother of Nehemiah (Neh. 1:2; 7:2). Both texts fluctuate between the short and long forms of the name, though in the book of Nehemiah different persons may be denoted.

[12] J. Klausner, *From Jesus to Paul*, pp. 289-90n.

[13] We are not often in the case of Acts in the position to claim reference to an actual person independently attested, except where dealing with rulers and governors otherwise known to recorded history. Cf. p. 235 *ad* Erastus (19:22), below.

point to stress is that it was probably a great deal more common than is suggested by the number of formal attestations, and is often, but not necessarily, Jewish.[14] Apart from the Jewish examples previously noted, cf. *I. Eph.* 1001.2 (Ephesian Curetes-list of time of Tiberius); 1015.7; 1016.12 (both of same man, late 1st AD); *IGRR* 4.841 (Hierapolis; Flavius Theudas, brother of Flavius Theodorus). Other minor variants are found: Theoda[s] in *IGRR* 1.1438, of Tyra, Moesia; AD 181); Theudes (*I. Eph.* 3312, of Teira [Tire], Lydia). The evidence could be much extended.

5:37 The designation ὁ Γαλιλαῖος is paralleled by the Hebrew designation הגלילי on several ossuary texts from the group from Bethphage (pre-AD 70): *CIJ* 1285 Nos. 5, 14; 1286 Nos. 4, 10.

6:1 For the 'Hellenist' problem see pp. 175f., esp. n. 31. If the terminology, at least here, reflects a tension between Greek and Hebrew speakers in the Jewish (and Jewish-Christian) communities in Jerusalem, the situation is abundantly illustrated *passim* by the mixture of languages and transliterations in the contemporary Jerusalem ossuaries. The seven deacons (6:5) all have Greek names, some rare.

7:58 Saul: the name seems fairly rare in the inscriptions, and I have not found instances outside the Semitic East. Josephus mentions a prominent Jewish activist Σαῦλος or Σαοῦλος in the events in Jerusalem in AD 66 (*Ant.* 20.9.4.214; *BJ* 2.17.4.418; 2.20.1.556, 558) and a different namesake in *BJ* 2.18.4.469. In the inscriptions cf. Σαοῦλος in *IGLS* 4.1319 (=*CIJ* 803, Apamea, Syria); Σαούλ, *CIJ* 953 (Jaffa); שאול, *CIJ* 1208 (Touba, AD 433, in Aramaic). There are also two references to Jews of Tarsus resident in Jaffa (*CIJ* 925, 931). The variants Σαούλ and Σαῦλος are both found in Acts (cf. 9:4; 22:7; 26:14 for the uninflected Hebraic form). The former is used in solemn address and Hebraic contexts.

8:5 'The city of Samaria' has caused difficulty, for the Old Testament city of this name had been renamed Sebaste at its refoundation by Herod the Great, and many scholars have been tempted to adopt the textual variant with anarthrous πόλιν, and then to identify 'a city' with Shechem or Gitta, the birthplace of Simon Magus (Justin Martyr, *Apol.* 1.26.2; cf. v. 9), rather than with Samaria-Sebaste.[15] It is not however clear that the new name invariably superseded the old. There are several passages in Josephus where the contexts require us

---

14 Thus in English the name 'Bert' is probably rare in documents, but may represent colloquially several distinct formal names.

15 Alternatively, some understand Sebaste by rendering 'the [main] city of Samaria'. Metzger, *Textual Comm.*, pp. 355-56 *ad loc.*, reflects the dilemma. The committee was convinced of the need to print the article by the external evidence, though internal considerations favoured its absence; it is placed in square brackets.

to understand 'Samaria' of the city, and while some of these have historic reference to Herodian or earlier dates (*BJ* 1.7.7.156; 1.8.4.166; 1.11.6.229; 1.15.6.299; etc.), others, like *Ant.* 17.10.9.289, have a post-Herodian setting. Indeed the city is once designated Σαμαρείᾳ τῇ κληθείσῃ Σεβαστῇ (*Ant.* 15.7.7.246), a common variant of the formula introducing alternative names, a phenomenon attested thousands of times for persons and many times also for places. There is also much fluctuation in the ethnic between Σαμαρείτης and Σαμαρεύς. Both are found in Josephus, and it is not clear whether there is any consistent distinction between them, though in some cases Σαμαρεύς is better understood of an inhabitant of the city (*BJ* 1.3.7.65). Similar variation can be found in the inscriptions: Σαμαρίτας (*IG* 12.8.439, Thasos); Σαμαριτανός (*IG* 14.633, Vibo/Valentia = Montelione, Italy); Σαμαρ(ε)ῖτις, fem. (*IG* 3.2.2891, 2892, both Athens), beside Σαμαρεύς (*IGRR* 1.506, Himera, Sicily, Roman period). The New Testament always has Σαμαρ(ε)ίτης, but always in contexts best taken of an inhabitant of the territory or member of a religious community.[16]

8.25 The name, or rather title, 'Candace' is attested elsewhere (e.g. Strabo 17.1.54 = 820-21; Pliny, *NH* 6.35.186; Dio 54.5.4; all cited by Bruce, *Acts*, p. 191). Cf. D, p. 163 *ad* 8:27.

9:11 The 'addresses' given here and in 10:6 may be compared with the σημασίαι attached to some papyrus letters (e.g. *POxy* 14.1678.28-31; 1773.40; and most interestingly the lengthy directions preserved separately in *POxy* 34.2719; all of 3rd AD).[17]

9:36 There is an interesting parallel in Josephus (*BJ* 4.3.5.145) for the equivalence Tabitha = Dorcas, where an assassin John is designated as son of Dorcas in his native tongue, presumably Bar Tabitha (son of 'Gazelle').[18] While this, as in Acts, is a translation of an Aramaic name or title, 'Dorcas' is recorded, somewhat rarely, as a Greek name in its own right, and the point of mentioning it here may be that Tabitha used it as an alternative name. There are also at least three examples from Athens (*IG* 2².11214, 4th BC; 11215, 2nd BC; 9128, of a woman of Cyrene, 2nd-1st BC).

10:1 Cornelius (cf. E, p. 177 above): for the Greek formulation of a Roman name of earlier date without *cognomen* see e.g. Λεύκιος Κορνήλιος | Λευκίου Ῥωμαῖος (*IG* 2² 10153, of Athens, 2nd-1st BC);

---

16 Σεβαστηνός is also, quite naturally, attested as the city ethnic (e.g. Jos. *Ant.* 19.9.1.356; 20.8.7.176). *Samarita* is also found as the Latin ethnic (Tac. *Ann.* 12.54).

17 See further R.W. Daniel, 'Through Straying Streets: A Note on ΣΗΜΑΣΙΑ-Texts', *ZPE* 54 (1984), pp. 85-86. He argues that σημασία should be rendered 'directions' rather than 'address'.

18 Was his mother another Jewish Tabitha = Dorcas, or is his *soubriquet* merely an allusion to his elusiveness?

with the inclusion of *cognomen* in closely similar later formulations see *IG* 2² 10148, of 1st-2nd AD ; 10160, 1st AD.

12:13 Rhoda: the name is well attested. See for example *IG* 2² 12570 (Athens, Roman period), 12571 (Athens, 4th BC), and several examples of burials far from home: *IG* 2² 9864 (n.d.) and 9865 (2nd AD) are both of Milesian women at Athens; *SB* 1.392, a Mysian in Egyptian Alexandria (3rd BC), *IG* 2² 8274, an Antiochene at Athens (1st BC) and Maiuri, *Nuova Silloge Epigrafica di Rodi e Cos*, 159, another Antiochene in Rhodes (n.d.).[19]

13:1 Manaen: this belongs to that group of Hebrew Jewish names which are rarely found outside the Semitic East, often no doubt being replaced elsewhere by Greek or Latin alternative names. The usual sources do not cite documentary instances, but these are easily found, though spellings and Hellenizations of the name vary greatly: Μανάημος (*CIJ* 883, near Haifa, the form which is usually printed in texts of Josephus), Μεναμός (*CIJ* 965, Ascalon), Μεναή(ς) (*CIJ* 1137, Beth She‘arim), beside the Aramaic מנחם [*sic*] (*CIJ* 988, Nazareth), and a bilingual ossuary inscription with Greek Μαναήμ (*CIJ* 1344, Jerusalem). For the term σύντροφος, in this technical sense of a client-companion, see *New Docs* 3.37-38, No. 9, and documents there cited.

13:7 Sergius Paulus (see C, p. 109; and D, pp. 166f.): While recognizing that we cannot identify this man among the possibilities offered, the existence of a prominent Roman family bearing these names and active in the period of Acts is sufficiently established.

13:8 Elymas: some commentators seem to have made an unnecessary problem for themselves (and then exercised unnecessary ingenuity in trying to solve it) by explaining 'Elymas' (or some variant) as a translation or explanation of 'Bar-Jesus' (or a variant) for Greek readers.[20] The point is rather that the obscure 'Elymas' is rendered μάγος, as deriving from a Semitic root cognate with the Arabic *'alim* (wise, learned).[21] Alternatively, L. Yaure offers a derivation from the

---

19 Cf. also Ramsay's chapter 'Rhoda the Slave-Girl' in *BRD*, pp. 209-21. The name, 'Rose', seems less common than might have been supposed. Its occurrence in Greek Comedy has often been noticed, e.g. Menander, *Hiereia* frag. 245.6, 546.5, and it was the name of the mistress of the slave Hermas (Herm. *Vis.* 1.1.1). I have here added several references to those contained in *MM* and *BAGD*.

20 Zahn, *Apostelgeschichte*, 2.417-18; Lake and Cadbury, *BC* 4.143-44.

21 Thus Bruce, *Acts*, pp. 256-57, Haenchen, pp. 398-99. It is to Haenchen's credit that he does not use the apparent difficulty and incongruity of the passage to criticize Luke where the text points here to a different explanation. I am not persuaded by Lake and Cadbury's alternative suggestion that μεθερμηνεύεται has become so weakened in sense as to amount to little more than a formula for a *supernomen*. Such formulae are abundantly attested (see esp. *New Docs* 1.89-96,

228 *The Book of Acts in the Setting of Hellenistic History*

Aramaic *haloma* (dreamer), seeing this narrative as recalling closely Jeremiah's struggle with the 'dream-prophets', oniromancy being of the essence of his art.[22] There is no more essential difficulty here than the occurrence of a rare and obscure name, presumably in any case a Semitic name in transliteration.

13:9 Paul: for further discussion and documentary illustration of the name see my article 'The Name of Paul', *TB* 36 (1985), pp. 179-83.

13:14 Pisidian Antioch: the preferred reading is Ἀντιόχειαν τὴν Πισιδίαν ℵ A B C p⁴⁵ where Western and Byzantine texts have τῆς Πισιδίας. The city belonged to Phrygia, not Pisidia, but was called 'Pisidian Antioch', or more fully 'Antioch near Pisidia' (τὴν ... Ἀ ... τὴν πρὸς τῇ Πισιδίᾳ, Strabo 12.6.4 = 569; 12.8.14 = 577) as it guarded against the turbulent tribes of that area.[23] Metzger, *Textual Comm.*, pp. 404-405 gives {B} probability to this reading. The objection has occasionally been made that the adjective 'Pisidian' ought to be Πισιδική, not Πισιδία, but Ptolemy (*Geog.* 5.5.4) ascribed the city to Φρυγία Πισιδία; one of those terms must be taken adjectivally.[24]

13.20 Saul: the uninflected Hebraic form in speaking of the OT king. Cf. 7:58.[25]

14:6 The implication is that the crossing from Iconium to Lystra involved a passage across a linguistic and administrative boundary from Phrygia to Lycaonia, a fact reflected in onomastics of the district. Thus, to take a rare example of a Phrygian name in the New Testament, Apphia of Colossae, in Phrygia (Phlm. 2). This name, in variant spellings Ἀπφία, Ἀφφία, rarely Ἀφία etc., is common in

No. 55) and no evidence is cited for the postulated sense of the verb. There is nothing to be gained from the Western reading Ἐτυμᾶς or Ἐτοιμᾶς, or from the possible influence on this form of the name of the Jewish magician Atomos in Jos. *Ant.* 20.7.2.142, also a Cypriot. There is no ground for identifying him with Elymas.

22 Yaure, 'Elymas-Nehelamite-Pethor', *JBL* 79 (1960), pp. 297-314. His case looks impressive, though in dismissing the idea of an 'Arabic' derivation (pp. 302, 303) he may be too facile. The point is that the Arabic is taken to represent a Semitic root which may have been represented also in Aramaic. That may still be hypothetical, and indeed wrong, but it need not be presented as an absurdity.

23 See further W.M. Calder, 'The Boundary of Galatic Phrygia', *MAMA* 7.ix-xvi; C.J. Hemer, 'The Pisidian Texts', *Kadmos* 19 (1980), pp. 54-64, esp. pp. 62-64.

24 The later manuscripts reflect a much later situation, when Antioch had become metropolis of a new province of Pisidia under Diocletian. The formulations however vary, even in the first two centuries, when Antioch was assigned to Pisidia by Pliny (*N H* 5.24.94), and Ptolemy (*Geog.* 5.4.9) calls the city Ἀντιόχεια Πισιδίας.

25 Cf. the problem of the two forms of 'Jerusalem' in Acts (Ἰερουσαλήμ, Ἱεροσόλυμα). See further I. de la Potterie, 'Les deux noms de Jérusalem dans les Actes des Apôtres, *Biblica* 63 (1982), pp. 153-87.

inscriptions of Phrygia and rare elsewhere, even allowing for possible confusions with feminines of the *nomen* 'Appius' of Rome.[26] The examples are drawn from every part of Phrygia, including the west and southwest from which the language is unrecorded, and include examples partly written in Phrygian proper (*MAMA* 4.122) or in a corrupt Phrygian-Greek patois (*MAMA* 4.310). Systematic search might well reveal examples specifically from Antioch and Iconium. Conversely, the native names recorded from Iconium, such as (masc.) Tatas, Manos, Nesis, Indakos, Papas (fem.), Babeis, Doudous, Ba, Tatis, Kakka, are of types paralleled all over the area, but not southward (*MAMA* 8.300-16). The long lists of male names in the Tecmorean documents of Pisidian Antioch provide such recurring forms as Menneas, Papas, Papias, Appas, Iman, Dadés, Manos, which would also lend themselves to further study. The Christian Papias (c. 60-130) was bishop of Hierapolis in Phrygia. S. Mitchell (*ANRW* 2.7.2 [1980], p. 1061 n. 38) makes a similar point about Phrygian names: 'The commonest forms become tiresomely familiar: Αμμια, Αππα, Ατταϛ, Δουδα, Κουσοϛ, Μανηϛ, Μειροϛ, Μουνα, Νοννα, Πρειειϛ, Σουσουϛ', but stresses also that the population cf Iconium was 'demonstrably mixed'. After citing some Phrygian names, including several in this list, he notes also the occurrence in Iconium of Thouthous, Ouddous, Ouadous, Ourandis and Trokondas, all paralleled in the mountains of S. Anatolia.[27]

The varied testimonies of the literary texts must be understood in this context of a well-defined ethnic identity which occupied a territory including both Antioch and Iconium over many centuries. Xenophon's ειϛ ᾽Ικόνιον, τῆϛ Φρυγίαϛ πόλιν ἐσχάτην (*Anab.* 1.2.19, 394 BC) correctly describes the position in the 1st cent. AD. Pliny *NH* 5.41.145 ascribes 'Conium' to Phrygia, though his unclear expression in *NH* 5.25.95 appears to contradict this, associating Iconium with

26 Note the inscriptions: *IGRR* 4.868 (Colossae); *MAMA* 1.4, 117 (both Laodicea Combusta); 4.17 (mod. Afyon Karahisa), 122 (Metropolis), 276A, 304 (Dionysopolis, the former alluding to a woman of Hierapolis), 310 (Motella), 318, 320 (Pepouza); 5.256 (Nacolea); 6.133, 141a (Heraclea and Salbacum), 191, 206 (Apamea Cibotus), 307 (Acmonia), 353, 357 (Dioclea), 362 (mod. Olucak, Tembris valley); 7.153, 155 (Hadrianopolis), 237 (? Claneos), 356 (? Vetissus); 8.253 (Savatra). Of these, all locations except Heraclea are in Phrygia; Heraclea is just in Caria, but in the two texts there the name 'Applina' is associated with characteristically Phrygian names (Tatias, Midas, Nanas).

27 The standard works on indigenous names of Asia Minor are L. Zgusta, *Kleinasiatische Personennamen* (Prag: Tschechoslowakische Akademie der Wissenschaften, 1964), and L. Robert, *Noms indigènes dans l'Asie Mineure gréco-romaine* (Paris: Librarie Adrien Maisonneuve, 1963).

Lycaonia but then drawing an implicit antithesis with 'Lycaonia proper'. He also assigns Antioch to Pisidia (*NH* 5.24.94). The explanation of these anomalies may lie in his undigested juxtaposition of sources of different periods, as where again he shifts from a Celtic view of Galatia to an enumeration of places on the borders of Pamphylia in one paragraph (5.42.146-47). Cicero reckons Iconium to Lycaonia (*ad Fam.* 15.4.2); Strabo (12.6.1 = 568) is not explicit; Hierax, a native of the city, assigns it explicitly to Phrygia (*Acta Justin Martyr,* 4, 2nd cent. AD).[28] It must be noted that Roman administrative boundaries were imposed for historical or strategic reasons which took no account of older national identities, and that rearrangements of this kind subsequently did attach Antioch and Iconium to Pisidia and Lycaonia respectively. The association of Iconium with Lycaonia is plausible as a level plain extends eastward from Iconium with no apparent geographical boundary, such as might appear in the mountains to the west. When I visited the area in April 1969, there was extensive flooding from the spring overflow of the Çarşamba Su, and the floods and swamps of this imperceptible depression must have created a seasonal barrier in antiquity and helps to account for the continued separation of the Phrygian and Lycaonian peoples in this neighbourhood.[29]

14:11f. For the grouping of Zeus with Hermes in the local religion of the Lystra district, as attested by inscriptions, see C, p. 111.

15:22 Judas called Barsabbas: cf. Joseph Barsabbas in 1:23, a *cognomen* meaning 'son of the Sabbath'.[30]

15:22 Silas in Acts is clearly identical with Paul's 'Silvanus' (1 Thess. 1:1; 2 Thess. 1:1; 2 Cor. 1:19; cf. 1 Pet. 5:12), and the latter Latin name serves as his *cognomen* as a Roman citizen (cf. Acts 16:37). The name Silas is relatively rare, but parallels for it as a Semitic name have been noted in Palmyrene inscriptions, and it has been explained as a Hellenization of the Aramaic form of 'Saul' (*BAGD*). *MM* and others have cited *IGRR* 3.817, from Cilicia. Note also *OGIS* 604, of Emesa (Syria). Both examples are interesting cases of alternative names joined by ὁ καί. There is also a Jewish instance from the later synagogue at Dura-Europos (*CIJ* 830, 3rd cent. AD); another from Antibes (Antipolis) has been reported in *New Docs* 1.120, No. 78.[31]

---

28 See Ramsay, *BRD*, p. 56; Wikenhauser, p. 336-37; S. Mitchell, *ANRW* 2.7.2 (1980), p. 1061.

29 See further Ramsay, *Cities of St. Paul*, pp. 324-25.

30 Bruce, *Acts*, p. 79.

31 This text, discovered in 1884, is unknown to all the usual publications, and may be cited fully here from its publication by B. Blumenkranz, 'Premiers témoignages épigraphiques sur les juifs en France', *Salo Wittmayer Baron Jubilee Volume*, ed. S. Lieberman and A. Hayman (Jerusalem: American Academy for

16:14 Lydia: for the name cf. L. Robert, *BCH*, 102 (1978), p. 405 (Sardis, 1st AD), *SEG* 28 (1978) 869 (= *I. Eph.* 424a; Ephesus, 1st—2nd AD), both of women of social standing; *TAM* 3.661, of Termessus, as a *supernomen* (Cf. C, pp. 114f.). For the social status of this Lydia see *New Docs* 2.26-28, No. 3; 3.54, No. 17. There is an interesting illustration of the Thyatiran purple trade and its continuing links as a Macedonian colony with the homeland in a 2nd cent. inscription of Thessalonica (*IG* 10.2.1.291). The guild of πορφυροβάφοι in 'Eighteenth Street' of that city (cf. L. Robert, *Études Anatoliennes*, p. 535 n. 3) set up a memorial to a colleague from Thyatira.[32]

16:17 The classic study by Nock, Roberts and Skeat,[33] discusses *Theos Hypsistos* as well as the more explicitly pagan *Zeus Hypsistos*. Nock sees both Jewish and pagan henotheistic trends as possible strands in the background of cults so called. The term 'Hypsistos' is not necessarily an indicator of Jewish influence. He notes however a characteristically Macedonian background of the epithet, and that many of the places where Hypsistos cults are attested were Macedonian colonies, and include Thyatira (p. 62). Two new dedications to Zeus Hypsistos are reported from near Serrae, close to Philippi itself (*SEG* 30 [1980] 591, of c. AD 154; 592, n.d.). The concept of 'salvation' may be illustrated in pagan contexts, especially in Asia Minor.

Jewish Research, 1974) I. 229-35: ['Io]ῦστος Σείλου ἔζησε ἔτεσι οβ' (pp. 234-35). While unremarkable in itself, this text, ascribed to the late 2nd cent. AD, is an important addition to the scanty evidence for Judaism in Roman Gaul. Its Jewish character depends wholly on the personal names, and Blumenkranz, strangely, stresses the common Jewish use of 'Justus' (= Zadok) without mentioning its collocation here with 'Silas'. The stone is said to be lost, but the article carries a photograph from a mould in the Antikes Museum. Blumenkranz *et al.*, *Histoire des Juifs en France* (Toulouse: Édouard Privat, 1972), p. 14, also refers to this inscription, but adds nothing to the fuller account.

32 συνήθεια, the term used here for 'guild', is not cited in this sense in *LSJ*, but the Supplement notes it from Thessalonica and Beroea, but not apparently from this inscription. The text was noticed in Wikenhauser, pp. 410-11, and hence mentioned in Haenchen, p. 494. For Philippi cf. also the epigraphic fragment ... pu]rpurari[... (*CIL* 3.664).

33 A.D. Nock, C. Roberts and T.C. Skeat, 'The Gild of Zeus Hypsistos' *HTR* 29 (1936), pp. 39-88. The actual inscriptions of Philippi are not very informative about local cults, as they are mostly in Latin, and reflect the Roman interests of the colonial settlement rather than the indigenous culture which predominates in this scene. Many colonies display this sharp cultural dichotomy, even where there is no ground for believing they were formally constituted as 'double communities', a suggestion rejected for the case of Philippi by S. Mitchell, *Historia* 28 (1979), p. 438. Note however a Latin dedication to *I O M* (*Iuppiter Optimus Maximus*; Dimitsas 941) and a Greek dedication to the Mother of the gods (Dimitsas 931; cf. 997).

17:34 Damaris: the suggestion that this apparently unparalleled name is a variant of 'Damalis' (heifer) goes back to Renan, *Saint Paul*, p. 209n. The latter form is indeed attested in Macedonia, but not, to the best of my knowledge, in Athens: Dimitsas 438 (= *IG* 10.2.1.452, Thessalonica, early imperial), 1050 (Latin fragment, Doxaton, near Philippi, n.d.). It also appears in Horace, *Odes* 1.36.13, 17-18. A form nearer to that in Acts is a man's name appearing in the genitive as Δαμάριος in a fragmentary dialectal context (*I. Cret.* 4.235, of Gortyn). Perhaps this, and some other similar or derivative forms, are Doric variants incorporating the element δᾶμος (δῆμος). Cf. Δαμαρίων (*POxy* 4.706.11, of c. AD 115; *POxy* 14.1734.2, of late 2nd-3rd AD); Δημαρίων (*SB* 1.4206.78, of Hermoupolis Magna, 80-69 BC); Δημάριον (fem.) (*IG* 2².8618, of Athens, 1st AD: a woman of Heraclea, presumably in Pontus; *BGU* 702.5-6, from the Fayum, AD 151); also shortened to Δημάριν (fem.; *PRyl* 2.243.1, provenance unknown, 2nd AD. Cf. ll. 13, 16 of the same papyrus, which have the longer form).[34] There is also a Spartan ephor P. Memmius Damares (*CIG* 1241.18, Hadrianic).

18:2 Aquila is a frequent Roman name, regularly Hellenized in the

---

[34] The statement of *BAGD* that 'Damalis' was a 'rather common' name needs to be taken with the fact that it is unexampled in Preisigke's *Namenbuch* and among the thousands of personal names in the epigraphic index to Athens in *IG* 3.2. Nor have I succeeded in finding it in the (unindexed) expanded replacement of *IG* 3 in *IG* 2², where I have noted several other attestations of names mentioned in this study. *BAGD* refer to *MM*; *MM* refer to Renan, who cites W. Pape, *Wörterbuch der griechischen Eigennamen* (Braunschweig: Biewig, 3rd edn, 1863), p. 266. Pape notes the reference in Horace, and otherwise cites only a fragment of the 6th cent. Byzantine historian Hesychius of Miletus. His work (ed. K. Mueller, *Fragmenta Historicorum Graecorum*, Vol. 4 [Paris: Firmin-Didot, 1885], pp. 151-52, frag. 4.29-30) tells an anecdote of a memorial built in Byzantium by the Athenian commander Chares to his wife, embodying a visual play on the meaning of her name 'Damalis'. That seems to be the sum total of primary evidence for *BAGD*'s claim; it is notable that successive writers quote preceding authors rather than attestations. Solin, *GPR* 2.1046 gives 22 examples from Rome, but there the Greek nomenclature is aberrant, and seems heavily weighted by Greek names conventionally given to slaves. 'Damalis' certainly occurred as a name, and I have added here to the instances, but it remains an open question whether or not it is connected with the present name. The L/R change is certainly possible in Greek of different periods, but many examples exist also in Roman Athens of Doric α for η. Names based on the stems 'Damal-' and 'Damar-' both occur, but both may fairly be considered rather rare. In Acts h reads 'Damalis', but we should hesitate to build on the occurrence of an isolated variant. The omission of the woman's name altogether in most witnesses to the Western text seems to reflect a tendency apparent elsewhere in that text-form (Bruce, *Acts*, p. 341; Epp, *Theological Tendency*, pp. 75n, 168n.). The masculine Δαμάλης also occurs (*SIG*³ 153.62, Athens, 337-373 BC, a man of Andros [and his father]).

inscriptions as Ἀκύλας or Ἀκυΐλας. It merits a brief note as being interestingly attested in contemporary Pontus, the stated origin of our character. A Roman official of some note, one C. Julius Aquila, whose career can be in part reconstructed, was apparently a native of Amastris in Pontus. *IGRR* 3.83 (= *CIL* 3 *Suppl.*6983, of near Amastris, AD 45), Tac. *Ann.* 12.15 (events of AD 49) and *IGRR* 3.15 = *CIL* 3.346 (Bithynia, AD 58-59) all appear to refer to the activities of the same man. Aquila the Bible translator also came from Pontus, but was of Gentile birth, and does not substantiate specifically Jewish use of the name (2nd AD). The name occurs in *CIJ* 797, of near Pessinus, North Galatia, but the Jewish ascription of this text is not certain.

18:3 Tentmaking: we have previously dealt with the reasons for taking σκηνοποιός in the traditional sense as 'tentmaker' rather than 'leatherworker', cf. C. *Ann. épig.* (1967), 528 reports a Jewish inscription of Caesarea, reading: [θήκη?] Ἰωσῆ | [υἱο]ῦ Λεον | [τίου] τεντ | [ορί]ου.[35] τεντόριος is unattested in the lexica, but the restoration is claimed as certain and seems a plausible enough Latinism.[36]

18:24 Apollos: the name is evidently a familiar abbreviation of the common 'Apollonius' or cognates. It is however of unusual interest as it seems to be almost unexampled outside Egypt, but is conspicuously common there. There are some thirty examples in the index to Preisigke's *Sammelbuch*, Vol. 2, alone. While some of these are late, the name is frequent throughout the Roman period, and several examples are contained in one list (*SB* 1.4206, of Hermoupolis Magna, 80-69 BC).[37]

---

35 This was first published by B. Lifshitz, 'La nécropole juive de Césarée', *RB* 71 (1964), pp. 384-87 (p. 385, No. 2).

36 *Tentorium* is frequent in Latin for 'tent', but 'tentmaker' is *tabernac(u)larius*, from *tabernac(u)lum* (*CIL* 6.9053, 9053a). The arguments for σκηνοποιός = 'leatherworker' are inconclusive at best. Meaning is not necessarily be inferred from etymology where usage is paramount, but here there is no sufficient ground for supposing that usage had strayed from the etymological sense, which certainly fits cognate words. I cannot however follow the interesting, but ultimately unconvincing, suggestion of O. Broneer, 'Paul and the Pagan Cults at Isthmia', *HTR* 64 (1971), pp. 169-87, that providing tents for the biennial Isthmian Games in April-May 51 was a major factor in Paul's choice of Corinth as a place of work. In view of Paul's own teaching in his Corinthian letters, and his scrupulous care not to be a cause of stumbling in so sensitive a cultural mix, it seems doubtful that he would, at least by such conscious choice, have laid himself open to the imputation of profiting from servicing a festival with inescapably pagan connotations. The idea would fit precisely the chronology I favour, but that is no reason for accepting the convenient. Perhaps a special outlet in Corinth was a market in sailcloth.

37 This strikingly Egyptian provenance may be in some degree fortuitous, in the

19:9 Tyrannus (cf. C, p. 120, n. 53): the name is not rare in Western Asia Minor, and is frequent in Ephesus. Its recurrence in the 1st-2nd cent. Curetes lists may suggest its use as a *cognomen* in successive generations of a small group of perhaps interrelated leading families from whom these functionaries were drawn. To those previously cited may be added from the same series of documents M. Pacuvius Tyrannus of the time of Tiberius (*I. Eph.* 1001.5).

19:14 Sceva: this name presents greater uncertainty. It is evidently not Greek. It may be a Greek rendering of the Latin *cognomen* 'Scaeva' rather than a Hebrew name. But that probability throws no clear light on the social standing of the man. In some cases a Roman *cognomen* may have marked a Roman citizen, but unless we have a *nomen* the case is doubtful.[38] MM cites an instance of Σκευᾶς as a 'Thracian' gladiator of Miletus, the slave of a woman owner (*CIG* 2889). To this can be added the epitaph of another gladiator, originating from Thessalonica (*IGRR* 1.701, of Bessapara, Thrace). A gladiator might naturally on occasion bear a name 'left-handed',[39] indeed the word is recorded as a gladiatorial term: cf. *mur(millo) scaev(a)* (*CIL* 6.10180). Such parallels may be held to confirm the probability of a significant Latin origin. Possibly the man in Acts was left-handed, or his name expressed a secondary, metaphorical sense of the word as 'favourable omen'.

---

preservation of more informal contexts in the papyri. But this qualification will not suffice to explain the pattern of distribution, as formal epigraphical documents, like that cited, are prominent among the Egyptian materials, whereas the name is not represented, for instance, in the innumerable rustic Greek inscriptions of Asia Minor, where hypocoristics are otherwise common. The evidence at least suggests that 'Apollos' was a peculiarly Egyptian abbreviation of 'Apollonius', whereas other forms prevail elsewhere, most commonly Ἀπελλᾶς (e.g. *IG* 2² 10710, Athens, 1st BC-1st AD; *IGRR* 3.513, Cadyanda, Lycia), but also Ἀπελλῆς (e.g. *TAM* 2.1011, Olympus, Lycia), Ἀπολλᾶ (e.g. *MAMA* 5.218, Nacolea), and Ἀπολλοῦς (*IG* 2² 9401, Athens, 2nd AD , of a Milesian). All these forms are relatively much rarer than 'Apollos' in the Egyptian indexes. On this name see also *New Docs* 1.88, No. 50. In an interesting note Kilpatrick, 'Apollos-Apelles', *JBL* 89 (1970), p. 77, argues for the originality of 'Apelles' in Acts, as appearing in ℵ* and elsewhere. He questions why 'Apollos' should have been altered to 'Apelles'. The answer may be simply that it was the form more familiar outside Egypt.

[38] See E.A. Judge in *New Docs* 2.106-108, No. 84.

[39] I have not found any different Hellenization of 'Scaeva', though the cognate 'Scaevola' appears as Σκαιόλας in the restoration of *IGRR* 4.297.2 = *OGIS* 437 (Pergamum, early 1st BC). In any case it is likely that he possessed alternative names. There is no need for the supposition that the 'seven' sons arose from a gloss explaining the name as equivalent to Heb. *sheba*. Greek –ευ– for Latin –aev– is natural enough as soon as itacistic tendencies affected Greek pronunciation and spelling.

19:22 Erastus: this name is perhaps less common than sometimes suggested, but is attested in Ephesus, whence Paul sends this man. The best example is the Ti. Claudius Erastus from a Curetes list dated to AD 54-59, referring to the son of the *prytanis* named at the head of this list (*I. Eph.* 1008.8). The example in *MM* (*SIG*³ 838, cited by them from *SIG*² 388) is also about a leading Ephesian, but is later (= *I. Eph.* 1487, Ephesus, A D 128-29). A further question is raised whether this Erastus is the same as that associated with Paul in Rom. 16:23 or in 2 Tim. 4:20, passages connected with Corinth, and whether the latter are further to be equated with the Corinthian magistrate of this name mentioned in a well-known inscription. There is no sufficient reason to affirm either of these identifications, and the illustrative value of the case is rather that Paul's helper(s) associated with Ephesus and Corinth bear a name otherwise attested among prominent persons in those cities.[40]

19:24 The word ἀργυροκόπος is well attested in the lexica, and *MM* and *BAGD* refer to an inscription of Smyrna: *SIG*³ 1263.1 (*SIG*² 873.1), but it seems not to have been linked more closely with Ephesus. Attestations of the 'silversmiths' of Ephesus can be found in no fewer than seven inscriptions of the city. The guild is formally entitled τὸ ἱερὸν συνέδριον τῶν ἀργυροκόπων (*I. Eph.* 636.9-10; cf. *I. Eph.* 2212.17). The other examples are *I. Eph.* 547 (1); 547 (2); 586; 2441; and the acclamation *I. Eph.* 585, which uses the word ἀργυ- ροχόος. Its president is designated προστάτης (*I. Eph.* 636.11), and the epitaph of one member calls him ἀργυροκόπος νεοποιός (*I. Eph.* 2212.a6-7). That is, he combined with his trade the office of νεωποιός,

---

40 See H.J. Cadbury, 'Erastus of Corinth', *JBL* 50 (1931), pp. 42-58. The focus of Cadbury's discussion is of the possibility of equating the Erastus who is οἰκονόμος τῆς πόλεως (evidently Corinth) in Rom. 16:23 with the colonial 'aedile' of the inscription. He inclines to doubt the identification, as (1) the two functions were of differing importance, and their holders were likely to have been drawn from different social strata, so that an οἰκονόμος was unlikely to graduate to the aedileship; (2) the inscription is undated, but is likely to be somewhat later than Paul's time. Cadbury's doubts are probably justified. Our present concern is more immediately whether Paul's circle included an Ephesian Erastus distinct from the Corinthian, or whether the same person is denoted throughout, and had connections with both cities. From the brief references we cannot answer that question confidently. The prospects of identifying actual persons in Acts from epigraphic sources are generally remote, except where we are dealing with a famous person known to secular history. It is apparent in this section that coincidences of name, even of the same place and date, may often be substantiated, and illustrate the provenance of names and local popularity even of groups of names represented in Acts. But, as mentioned above *ad* Sapphira (p. 224) there is no case outside the handful of kings, queens and governors where we should claim actual identifications.

one of the board of wardens of the temple of Artemis. This office is attested *passim* in the inscriptions, and should not be taken to reflect ποιῶν ναούς in our text. See C, p. 121.

19:29 Aristarchus: this Macedonian is identified more specifically as being from Thessalonica in 20:4, and appears in the letters of Colossians and Philemon (cf. F, p. 188). While the name is itself unremarkable, it is interestingly attested from Thessalonica, notably in a text where an Aristarchus son of Aristarchus heads a list of politarchs (Dimitsas 368, ascribed to the first or second century of Roman rule).

20:4 Sopater son of Pyrrhus:[41] this man is probably identical with the Sosipater of Rom. 16:21, where Luke characteristically uses the shorter and more familiar form of the name. Both versions are again characteristic of Macedonia. For 'Sosipater' cf. Dimitsas 671.55 (= *IG* 10.2.1.1028, Thessalonica, late 3rd BC), *IG* 2² 12726 (Athens, 1st-2nd AD); for 'Sopater' cf. Dimitsas 677.17 (Thessalonica, perhaps pre-Roman), *IG* 2² 12712 (Athens, 2nd BC), 12713 (Athens, 2nd-3rd AD) and 9265 (a Macedonian at Athens, 2nd-1st BC). The patronymic 'Pyrrhus' is likewise characteristic of Macedonian nomenclature. Cf. Dimitsas 410 (= *IG* 10.2.1.524, AD 119) and 411 (= *IG* 10.2.1.564, early 3rd AD), both again of Thessalonica. Other parallels could be pursued in the corresponding feminines. Thus among aliens in Athens: Pyrrha in *IG* 2² 9268 (2nd-1st BC) and Sopatra in *IG* 2² 9271 (3rd BC) are both explicitly Macedonian women.

20:4 Tychicus: this name is not very common and according to Horsley in *New Docs* 2.109, No. 86, the majority of attestations come from Rome, and often concern men of servile origin. Solin in *GPR* 1.446-47 lists 29 examples from Rome, all within the 1st-3rd AD.

20:4 Trophimus: in 21:29 it is specified that he was an Ephesian. The name is listed as the twelfth commonest Greek *cognomen* in Rome in *GPR* 2.990-95; 3.1439), with no fewer than 297 occurrences. Horsley points out (*New Docs* 3.91-93, No. 80) that its popularity peaks markedly in the first century A D. Some of the Roman frequencies are very surprising, and may reflect peculiarities of social sampling, in particular a high percentage of possible slaves or freedmen.[42] As a slave-name this probably denoted a house-born slave,

---

[41] Metzger, *Textual Comm.*, p. 475, gives rating (B) in favour of acceptance of the father's name as original.

[42] The commonest names in *GPR* include some surprising items at the top. In order we find: Hermes, Eros, Alexander, Onesimus, Elpis, Nice, Tyche, Eutyches, Eutychus, Irene, Antiochus, Trophimus, Epaphroditus, Apollonius, Dionysius. This may be contrasted with the order in a (much smaller) sample in the index of *IGRR* 4 (covering proconsular Asia in the Roman period): Apollonius, Alexander, Dionysius, Artemidorus, Julianus, Asclepiades, Glycon, Rufus, Demetrius,

reared in the family. But in Ephesus it is another of those names attested in the families which provided the Curetes and associated officers. In *I. Eph.* 1005.9-10 it is an *agnomen* of a man formally designated as a citizen by his *chiliastys* (time of Claudius or Nero). A different man, a Roman citizen, appears in *I. Eph.* 20A.43, again of AD 54-59 and, in a long series of Curetes lists from the Flavian period past the turn of the century, one Trophimus regularly serves as σπονδαύλης (*I. Eph.* 1011-1029).[43] One of the earlier of these mentions another Trophimus (*I. Eph.* 1011.3), and a dynastic connection with the cult seems to be maintained in Trophimus son of Trophimus into the mid 2nd century (*I. Eph.* 1045.14). In fact the name is frequent and indigenous in western Asia Minor, and among Ephesian officials in particular, apart from its apparent proliferation as a slave-name in Rome.

20:9 Eutychus: this is a common name, on which comment may be brief. Again it proliferates in Rome, where this and 'Eutyches' rank respectively 9th and 8th among the most common Greek names (337 and 360 times: *GPR* 2.796-801; 2:801-806; 3.1439), but the variant 'Eutychus' is more popular earlier, with a very strong dominance of occurrences in or near the first century, whereas 'Eutyches' predominates later.

21:16 Mnason: this form seems relatively rare, and attestations are scattered, though cognate names are more frequent. Cf. *SEG* 31 (1981) 507, from Thebes in Boeotia (c. 400 BC); *IG* 2².8070, of Athens (2nd-1st BC), of a man from Amisus in Pontus; and several instances from Delphi (*SIG*³ 585.47, 78, 238; *SIG*³ 602; both early 2nd BC; *SIG*³ 826.H.6.30, 117-116 BC).

Metrodorus, Trypho. (This is on a simple count of entries. It will be noted that all these names are masculine, and that Greek renderings of two Latin names have rated mention). Such a comparison will give some idea of the factors of social and local diversity in the incidence even of the commonest names. 'Hermes' appears 841 times in the one list and three times in the other. Probably the first contains a disproportionately high percentage of tombstones of oriental house-slaves in Roman households, and the second a disproportion of local civic officials. Contrast again a sample of over 3000 names from Termessus in Pisidia (*TAM* 3 Index), where the order of abundance is heavily influenced by indigenous forms: Hermaeus, Artemeis (f), Trokondas, Moles, Armasta (f), Arteimas, Diotimus, Apollonius, Artemon, Nan(n)elis (f), Thoas, Plato, Oa (f). 'Apollonius' is the only name at all numerous in all three lists.

[43] I was first interested in this group of names on reading the names 'Tyrannius' and 'Trophimus' *in situ* (together with the common 'Alexander') on a Curetes list inscribed on the left-hand front column of the Prytaneum, of which I possess a clear photograph (cf. C, pp. 120f. *ad* Tyrannus). The text in question is *I. Eph.* 1012, of AD 92-93, in the prytany of the priestess Claudia Trophime.

25:13 Bernice: this queen is of course well known to history (cf. D, pp. 173f. above), but the form in which her name is transmitted merits some comment. It has been pointed out that 'Berenice', as a Macedonian royal name, was a Macedonian version of Attic Φερενίκη. Later the short unstressed vowel after 'r' was dropped in accordance with Kretschmer's Law.[44] The present form of the queen's name is supported by the usual readings of Josephus (e.g. *BJ* 2.16.3.344), but the name is given formally in epigraphy as Βερεν(ε)ίκη (*IG* 2².3449 = *OGIS* 428, of Athens). In formal documents the fuller form seems usually to be retained until about the 2nd cent. AD. Contrast e.g. the similar tombstone formulations of *IG* 2² 9464: Βερενίκη (1st AD) and *IG* 2².9465: Βερνίκη (2nd AD), both women of Miletus. It is likely that the vowel was commonly dropped in pronunciation before it was omitted in formal spelling, and the short form appears in a Jerusalem ossuary (*CIJ* 1366; presumably pre-70). The earliest case of Βερνίκη I have noted in a formal document is in *PTebt* 2.316.56, of AD 99.[45]

These samples will suffice to illustrate the main point in this section. Most of the names treated are either relatively rare or show distinctive patterns of popularity in time and place. The onomastics of Acts are spread across a variety of types, from the unobtrusively and ubiquitously common (Alexander, Dionysius, Demetrius), the less common which are of familiar type and derivation and wide-spread occurrence (Aeneas, Lysias, Tertullus), the common Greek names much affected by Jews (Jason, Justus), the names which, while probably widespread, were characteristic of the very cities where Acts locates them or of the first century (Tyrannus, Trophimus, Aristarchus, Erastus), hypocoristic variants highly characteristic of a geographical region (Apollos), rare and obscure names (Damaris) in particular those of Jewish background which may be Hellenizations of uncertain Semitic roots (Agabus, Elymas, and *cognomina* like Barnabas). Along with this spectrum of distribution is the balance of Greek, Latin and Semitic names, in appropriate contexts, but reflecting the strange mixture of cultures apparent, with infinite gradations, in the index of almost any regional collection of documents of the imperial period.[46] Perhaps any conclusion here must in its very nature be

---

[44] See Bruce, *Acts*, p. 434.

[45] Latin versions of the name seem to have been uninfluenced by the Hellenistic change, and to have rendered it as 'Beronice' with surprising consistency at all periods, with only a slight late tendency to 'Veronice'. See H. Solin, *GPR* 1.211-12, for 31 instances; also *CIL* 4.2198, 2256 (Pompeii; 1st AD : the error in the latter is not a significant variant). Another Jewish example, also Latinized as 'Beronice', comes from Sulcis in Sardinia (*CIJ* 658, of 4th or 5th AD).

[46] The names on the Jerusalem ossuaries will give a startling impression of the

impressionistic. But the way in which the names of Acts, and indeed of the interlocking epistles, fit into the nomenclature of their times is impressive. It is not that they obtrude striking parallels all the way, in the manner of a skilled novelist creating local colour. It is rather the balance of the significant with the common, the obscurely rare and the unremarkable which speaks of real life. See now too the valuable discussion by E.A. Judge in *New Docs* 2.106-108 No. 84, on the proportion and significance of Roman names in the Pauline literature, and their incidence in Romanized colonies or Hellenic cities.[47]

'Jerusalem' and 'Luke'

Two other names should be mentioned briefly, one which does not appear in the text and one which recurs *passim*, those of Jerusalem and of Luke himself. The possible significance of the use of the alternative forms Ἰερουσαλήμ and Ἱεροσόλυμα is a standing puzzle. The problem is not confined to Acts, the alternation occurs in all the Synoptics and in Paul, both forms being contained in Galatians. Both versions are, however, found much more often in Acts than in any other New Testament book. Ἰερουσαλήμ is found 28 times in Luke and 41 in Acts of a New Testament total of 83, Ἱεροσόλυμα, respectively 5 and 19 out of 59. Josephus seems to use Ἱεροσόλυμα exclusively, if we may trust the manuscripts, save in one place where he cites Clearchus, who puts Ἰερουσαλήμ(η) in the mouth of Aristotle (*Ap.* 1.22.179).

The above statistics may be uncertain on account of textual variants,[48] but the problem is apparent. While the usage of names was sometimes much more fluid in antiquity than modern practice allows, it is difficult in the present case not to read significance in the alternation.[49] This may be supplemented with the observation that we have in effect an alternative name analogous with Σαῦλος ὁ καὶ Παῦλος, coexisting further in the same work with the pure Semitic

confusion of Greek and Semitic in nomenclature, language, script and spelling.

47 Thus in Paul, 'Corinth supplies a ratio of Latin to Greek names of 10:7, compared with 6:5 for the list in Romans 16, and 0:19 for the eastern Aegean seaboard' (Judge, *New Docs.*, 2.107). Again the ratio of Roman *praenomina: nomina: cognomina* on Latin names in a catalogue of the signatures of Corinthian lamp-manufacturers is 4:3:11, compared with 7:5:18 in Paul's allusions to Corinthians. Parallels for many of the names not discussed here could be readily supplied.

48 These have been drawn from J.B. Smith's *Greek-English Concordance*; Moulton and Geden give 39 and 25 for the two forms in Acts, de la Potterie 36 and 23.

49 See I. de la Potterie, 'Les deux noms de Jérusalem', pp. 153-87.

transliteration Σαούλ, all of the same man, where proper names are subject to the kind of stylistic and semantic variation we accord to the lexical choice between synonyms. The Greek ethnic is regularly Ἱεροσολυμίτης (fem. -ῖτις).[50] City names and their ethnics are also freely designated by the ὁ καί formula: in literature Πομπηϊούπολις ἡ καὶ Σόλοι (Ptol. *Geog.* 5.7.4), and even in the confined space of a coin legend ΝΥϹΑΙΕⲰΝ ΤⲰΝ ΚΑΙ ϹΚΥΘΟΠΟΛΙΤⲰΝ (*BMC Palestine,* Nysa-Scythopolis No. 4, of Nero, the city otherwise also Biblical Bethshan).

The name Λουκᾶς, occurring in the NT text only at Col. 4:14; 2 Tim. 4:11; Phlm. 24 presents other points of interest. This is another hypocoristic, which has sometimes been connected with the Latin *cognomen* 'Lucanus'. It is however preferable to relate it to the Latin *praenomen* 'Lucius', commonly adapted into Greek from an early date as Λούκιος (in early examples sometimes Λεύκιος), and then giving the short form Λουκᾶς in familiar Greek. This equivalence has been established by Ramsay (*BRD,* pp. 370-84) on the basis of three dedications to the god Men from Pisidian Antioch. The first (p. 374) is of a man Λουκᾶς Τίλλιος Κρίτων, who bears the Roman *tria nomina,* but renders the *praenomen* by a form which can only stand for 'Lucius'. In Nos. 2-3 (pp. 376-77) two dedications are made by the same family, the same collocation of four names and relationships recurring in both, except that the eldest son is in one case Λούκιος, in the other more familiarly Λουκᾶς. Here the two variants appear as alternative designations of the same person.[51]

The evidence may now be variously extended. Λουκᾶς is well attested elsewhere in inscriptions, and occurs also in the papyri. See e.g. Lüderitz, *Corpus jüdischer Zeugnisse,*pp. 5-6, No. 3 (= *SB* 1.224.3) ('Λουκᾶ', Apollonia in Cyrenaica); *CIG* 4759 (Egyptian Thebes); *POxy* 12.1446.17 (genitive Λουκᾶτος, AD 161-210); cases which show no probability of Christian influence. In Asia Minor Λούκιος was often shortened in pronunciation to Λούκις, and this variant too is well attested: *MAMA* 1.103 (Laodicea Combusta). The name restored as Λούκ[ι]ς [Ο]ὐαλέ[ρ]ιος Π[ο]ὐλ|χερ (*MAMA* 5.40.1-2, of Dorylaeum) might equally have been Λουκ[ᾶ]ς. But the larger number of both variants is in identifiably Christian texts, which if nothing else indicate that Λουκᾶς = Λοῦκις = Λούκιος was then taken to have been

---

[50] Thus e.g. W. Blümel, *Die Inschriften von Iasos* (Inschriften griechischer Städte aus Kleinasien 28.1), I.193 (= *CIJ* 749, Iasos, mid 2nd BC), *IG* 2² 8934 (fem., Athens, 1st AD).

[51] These texts are now republished as *CMRDM* 1, Nos. 248a, 195b, 195a respectively. Cf. also No. 221 (Λοκᾶς), and 4, No. 9. The use of Latin *praenomina,* absolutely or as *cognomina,* is habitual throughout the corpus.

the evangelist's name. A marble lintel with medallion busts of four saints has one inscribed ὁ ἅ(γιος) Λουκᾶς (*MAMA* 4.40, at Afyon Karahisar), and the name proliferates among Christians (*MAMA* 3.80, 87-89, all of Diocaesarea [Uzuncaburç] in Cilicia; 250, 567, 472, all of Corycus, the two former with genitive Λουκᾶτος; *MAMA* 6.59, of Tripolis in Lydia). Λοῦκις too abounds in a Christian setting. One Loukis of the Axylon valley in E. Phrygia has brothers named Peter and Paul in a text dated before 400, *MAMA* 1.312). Other examples are *MAMA* 1.242, of Laodicea Combusta, and 'Aur(elius) Loukis' of Tyriaeum (*MAMA* 7.124), this last illustrating the liberty taken by Hellenized Anatolians with Roman names, in making *praenomen* into *cognomen* at will. *POxy* 8.1122.6 has Λουκᾶς as the alternative name of one Aurelius Phoebammon (AD 407).

None of this excludes the possibility that Λουκανός might on occasion have been shortened to Λουκᾶς, but I have found no evidence to substantiate the possibility, and all the signs point to the equivalence with 'Lucius'. There is no hint that Λουκανός is even more than an occasional Latin *cognomen*, whereas the 'Lucius' group becomes common among Christians outside its traditional incidence as an abundant Roman *praenomen*.

Place-Names and Ethnic Titles In Acts and the Inscriptions

So many confusions and sceptical shibboleths have been festooned around Luke's usage of toponyms that it seems desirable to make a separate summary statement of some features of ancient nomenclature, to set some of the detailed points in various sections of this book in a clearer context. The following general propositions might be abundantly illustrated from acquaintance with the epigraphy. They concern matters which are sometimes the subject of unsupported generalizations about what is improbable or impossible.

(1) The usage of place-names and ethnics is patterned and flexible, and their interpretation must be studied in relation to documents of the appropriate date, with due recognition that the patterns of usage may be remarkably complex.

(2) It is an oversimplification to distinguish 'Greek' from 'Roman' usages, and to ask whether Luke (or Paul) follows 'Greek' or 'Roman' practices.

(3) The *LSJ* entries for ethnics and adjectives of nationality are haphazard, fragmentary, and badly misleading. The lexica are in fact of little service in this study. It is essential to search the documents at first hand.

(4) Ethnics and their adjectives are used freely in Greek, where for

instance 'the city of the Ephesians' is a much commoner formulation than our preferred 'city of Ephesus'.

(5) At various levels of the pattern the name of a city or country and its ethnic correspond closely to each other across the flexible range of application of both. The common dogma that you cannot call civilized people in (South) Galatia 'Galatians' reflects this misconception. The term does not carry the implication 'wild Celtic barbarians', but is a simple reflection of the fact that a territory or province was (honourably and officially) called 'Galatia'. There are partial and localized exceptions to this, as where in early sources Σικελιώτης was a Sicilian Greek as opposed to a native Σικελός, but this distinction too fell into disuse later. One need only note at this point the innumerable cases of apparent Greeks, with Greek names, who are honourably designated on their tombstones by such 'barbarian' ethnics as Ἄραψ, Ἀσσύριος, Θρᾷξ, Λιβύς, Μῆδος, Σύρος or Φρύξ, or for that matter Γαλάτης, all instances I have found in the epigraphy of Athens alone. Occasionally the person's city is spelled out, and a 'Syrian' may turn out to be a citizen of Antioch, the third city of the Roman world.

(6) There are considerable trivial variations in the formations of ethnics, local eccentricities and alternative forms. Amid this confused welter, the self-designation of a city and its people on its own inscriptions and coins merits special attention as giving the basic form. If, as very commonly, Luke gives this form, the fact is of some positive interest, though the point may be slight; literary sources are often unpredictably variable. But in any case little weight can be attached to the existence of variations and aberrations.

(7) Fluctuations between different forms of an ancient name may be akin to the variation between synonyms. The co-existence of Ἱεροσόλυμα and Ἱερουσαλήμ in the same writings (cf. also Jos. *Ap.* 1.22.179) is not *per se* so odd as it may seem to us. There is a real semantic/theological problem posed by it, but that problem is perhaps rather like that of discriminating between synonyms which may not cover quite the same semantic fields. Variations in language, formulation, literature or application may in fact permit important historical or chronological inferences, and the study of the documents is again important from this perspective.

(8) Due allowance must be made for the variable and irregular spellings in the documents, and for miscopyings and false corrections in the Biblical and other manuscripts, so that trivial variations are separated clearly from substantive ones. Phonetic spellings and stonecutters' errors are quite prevalent and confusing in the private

and less elevated epigraphy, and less known place-names often appear in corrupt forms in manuscripts of even such sources as Pliny.

(9) The attempt to make theoretical distinctions between supposedly separate 'substantial' and 'adjectival' territorial names, as being anarthrous or articular (but ἡ 'Ιουδαία sc. γῆ) is misconceived. The section in Blass-Debrunner on articles with names can be shown in the light of representative examples to be fundamentally flawed. It is based on extrapolation from a few New Testament examples to an erroneous theory. There is much greater fluidity than they allow, and the New Testament examples must be explained within a larger framework of usage.

(10) Where real semantic conclusions are to be drawn, those conclusions must be based on the broadest possible description of usage and the application of clearly relevant examples.

Chapter 6
Acts and Epistles

Introduction

There is no simple and automatic route from the confirmation of details in Acts to a general defence of its historicity, but there is at least
a *prima facie* argument for taking their evidence seriously in addressing the larger question. A major part of the case against historicity is made up not of problems of systematically contradictory
evidence, but of a theoretical objection: that Acts is a 'secondary'
source. This theoretical objection may be immediately countered by a
theoretical retort, that there is a logical *non sequitur* in the objector's
argument. There is a step missing from the reasoning, in which the
objector imports the tacit presupposition of the conclusion, that the
'primary' and 'secondary' sources *are* in conflict. It may be that they
are, and it is crucial to our task to examine whether that is so. But
then the 'primary'/'secondary' distinction is not a helpful formulation to that end, for it is used in a manner which *presumes* the conflict. There is of course a perfectly valid category-distinction between
the two types, but that does not carry an automatic value-distinction.
A writer's own self-revelation may well be tendentious; another's
account of him may actually be more objective. That may be considered wildly improbable in this case, but the range of possibilities is
not on that account to be limited *a priori*. Once again, we must know
what kind of source Acts is, quite apart from the matter of its 'secondary' status. And one focus of that decision turns on the question
whether its evidence for Paul is in fact consonant with that of his own
epistles.[1] It is crucial to our inquiry that we have these two distinct

---

1 We must defer the question of which epistles are to be regarded as genuinely
Pauline. The main argument will in fact be concerned with epistles which are
generally accepted as genuine, though sometimes of disputed date and
provenance within Paul's life (e.g. Galatians). But we must attempt to wrestle
critically with the whole Pauline corpus in so far as all the ostensible epistles
purport to give evidence for Paul. Only by considering the range of relevant
material can we evaluate accurately the disputed portions of it.
   The 'primary'/'secondary' distinction is posed in its acutest form by Knox.
Cf. his three principles in Corley (ed.), *Colloquy*: '(a) that the merest hint in the
letters is to be deemed worth more than the most explicit statement of Acts; (b)

categories of source material.

We start from the widely accepted point that Luke shows no knowledge of the Pauline Epistles. There are diverse explanations of that phenomenon. It has been used to argue a very early or a very late date for Acts.[2] It could mean that the Epistles were not seen as a matter of special note during Paul's life. But our present point is a simple one, that Acts is agreed to be essentially independent of the Epistles, whatever the explanation for the fact.[3] It is clear for instance that Acts is not a narrative composed around the real or supposed occasions of the Pauline writings. It is not conceived as an introduction to the Pauline Corpus, or anything of that kind. Indeed, the tendency of scholarship has been rather to stress the disjunction, to see radical problems in the value of Acts, not in any contrived harmonization, but in the conflict of independent 'primary' and 'secondary' evidences. The central planks in this argument from clashing evidence are in the areas of theological disparity and of conflicting biographical data. It has become the trend to extrapolate from these areas of difficulty to read related questions through sceptical spectacles.

The 'Theological Disparity' between Paul and Luke

The question of disparity is not easily settled, but it is a less decisive matter than it is often made to appear. To put it for the moment in general terms: (1) a memoir of Paul by a friend and admirer (if that is how we are to read Acts) will not necessarily display profound understanding of Pauline thought. The purpose of the book is otherwise delimited, and it remains possible that even a companion did not

---

that a statement in Acts about Paul is to be regarded as incredible if it conflicts directly with the letters (as many statements do) and is to be seriously questioned even if a conflict is only suggested; and (c) that statements about Paul in Acts are to be accepted with confidence only if such statements are fully and explicitly confirmed in the letters.' Knox goes on to speak of Luke's 'palpable and gross errors', which 'raise doubts about his credibility in general' (pp. 342-43). Our previous chapter should suffice at least as a caution against such generalized condemnation.

2   For the early date on this ground see e.g. Guthrie, *Introduction*, p. 345, and for the later see Goodspeed, *Introduction*, p. 195. Goodspeed's argument, however, seems idiosyncratic and subjective, and is tied to his view that the Pauline Epistles were ignored until a revival of interest prompted by the relatively late publication of Acts led to their collection as a corpus. The essential point may be seen in the contention of Vielhauer that Luke's 'material distance' from Paul implied 'temporal distance' (*SLA*, p. 48).

3   [Ed.] *pace* now L. Aejmelaeus, *Die Rezeption der Paulusbriefe in der Miletrede (Apg. 20:18-35)* (Helsinki, 1987), who argues that the author of Acts knew and used some of Paul's epistles.

understand the depths of Paul. (2) Paul's epistles are themselves occasional documents, and do not represent the straightforward exposition of Paul's 'gospel', which they rather presuppose. If Romans stands nearest to a reasoned presentation of its essence, and if Galatians contains a polemic of recall to fundamentals, they may be our best prospects. (3) The concept of a Lukan theology distinct from that of Paul is overplayed. There is no need to doubt the validity of looking for Lukan motifs and characteristics, but the prospects of locating a focused and systematic scheme of thought in the narratives and speeches of Luke-Acts are not as good. The speeches of Acts, on any view, may be taken to illustrate approaches to different audiences rather than to labour the content of Luke's 'gospel', with which we presume Theophilus (or a larger Christian readership) to have been familiar. In fact neither Luke or Paul are offering direct theological exposition in a form lending itself easily to direct comparison or antithesis. (4) The attempts to make such comparisons lead to extraordinarily diverse results. Some for instance find a close (and essentially Pauline) kinship between the Areopagus address (Acts 17) and Romans 1, which others as strenuously deny.[4] This is not to discount the prospect of resolving such disagreements, but to note that there is as yet no agreed platform from which to extrapolate when talking about theological differences. Conversely, if the evidence is strong for Luke as eyewitness participant, this will require reassessment of the framework in which we measure theological differences. They may be differences of emphasis, perspective, audience or function, rather than constituting the fundamental problem.

In fact the theological difficulty, however acute it seems, is often a matter of impression, which might indeed serve as a makeweight to confirm a disjunction securely grounded in established clashes of evidence elsewhere, but does not suffice of itself to move the scales. If we are to confirm a pattern of contradiction between Acts and the Epistles, the foundation must lie in exposing basic ignorance and error in Luke's purported knowledge of Paul's life and circumstances.

The problem cannot be adequately treated today without at least some preliminary consideration of Philipp Vielhauer's essay on the 'Paulinism' of Acts.[5] The strong implication of that essay is that the Lukan Paul is not only a creation of Lukan theology, but also betrays both ignorance of, and distance from, the historical Paul. The four

---

4   For the kinship cf. F.F. Bruce, *BJRL* 58 (1975-76), pp. 301-303; *Paul*, pp. 243-46; for the conflict, Vielhauer, *SLA*, p. 36. See also the discussion in B. Gärtner, *The Areopagus Speech and Natural Revelation*,(Uppsala, Lund: Gleerup and Copenhagen: Munksgaard, 1955), pp. 73ff.

5   P. Vielhauer, 'On the "Paulinism" of Acts', *SLA*, pp. 33-50.

pillars of Vielhauer's case are that Luke differs from Paul in (1) his more positive attitudes to paganism and (2) to the Jewish Law, (3) that his Christology is actually pre-Pauline but (4) his eschatology post-Pauline, indeed largely replaced by a historicizing scheme belonging to the perspective of 'Early Catholicism'. Haenchen[6] highlights other aspects of the differences between the Paul of Acts and of the Epistles: for both Luke and Paul, the overriding problem was that of the admission of Gentiles without the Law, but Luke is 'unaware' of Paul's solution; Luke's Paul is a miracle-worker, whereas Paul himself must plumb the depths of suffering rather than overcome them miraculously; Luke's Paul is an outstanding orator, whereas Paul himself pleads the feebleness of his speech (2 Cor. 10:10); Acts, while glorifying Paul, denies him the title 'apostle', which it restricts strictly to the Twelve, whereas Paul himself is at pains to uphold his apostleship; and finally, Acts draws a picture of the relations between Christianity and Judaism which contradicts that of the Epistles.

These summarized objections must for the moment be met with a generalized response, pending the fuller discussion of details on the historical front. (1) These apparent conflicts are all matters open to explanation as deriving from different perspectives and contexts. It would be facile to try to dismiss their real difficulty on such grounds without detailed examination in due course, but it is equally facile to harden them absolutely into contradictions. (2) The essential unity of the New Testament witness must be seen as capable of comprising a considerable degree of internal diversity without this diversity being seen as necessarily problematic as it seems to some. In fact our reply to these contentions is of a piece with the four points listed above in response to a kindred, if broader, line of objection.

The Heart of the Historical Question

A focal problem is the relation of the Jerusalem visits in Acts with those described by Paul himself in Gal. 1-2. It is commonly regarded as a decisive condemnation of Luke that the two versions cannot be reconciled, and a great deal may be built out of extrapolation from this one point. But it is possible to identify the visit of Acts 9 with that of Gal. 1, and the visit of Acts 11 with that of Gal. 2, the Council visit of Acts 15 not being mentioned because it had not taken place by the time of the writing of Galatians (which on this hypothesis is the earliest of Paul's epistles). This view is now fairly widespread among

---

6 Haenchen, *Acts*, pp. 112-16.

British scholars, and has recently been advocated afresh in Germany also.[7] Its persuasiveness is tied to the acceptance of the 'South Galatian' view of the destination of the epistle, identifying Paul's first coming to 'Galatia' (Gal. 4:13) with the narrative of his 'first journey' in Acts 13-14. This aspect of the question may ultimately be resolved into one of geography and terminology, a more objective sphere in which firmer answers about usage may be obtainable.[8]

Each of the elements in this solution has been argued at length by others,[9] but we here stress the implications of the synthesis between them, reserving for a separate excursus further consideration of the crucial matter of first century usage of the term 'Galatia' (see chapter 7). The visits as reported in Acts and Galatians are clearly different, but then, so are the apparent purposes and perspectives of the two writers. The second visit is probably the easier of the two: In Galatians 2, Paul is concerned only with his relations with the Jerusalem apostles. His account centres upon his discussion with them on a point of basic importance for the justification of his apostleship for the Galatians. This discussion was doubtless an important outcome of the visit, but there is no need to think that a conference with the apostles was the only original or even principal object of the journey. Paul went 'by revelation', by divine command, not because summoned by authorities in Jerusalem to account for his actions. Luke tells us only of the occasion. The 'revelation' may plausibly be identified with the prophecy of Agabus. The occasion was the impending famine. The divine prediction and the response in love of Gentile to needy Jew were a testimony to the transforming presence of God in this Christian movement, and so properly belonged to the story of the primitive church. Granted the occasion, it was natural that Paul should take the opportunity of conference with the Jerusalem leaders. And their injunction to remember the poor, as Paul phrases it, fits the supposition that this had been the very occasion of the visit.

The first visit involves sharper differences. In Galatians 1, Paul went to see Peter, and saw no other apostle except James; in Acts 9 Barnabas brought him to 'the apostles'. Here it seems that the intention of the two accounts differs. Luke is giving a generalized account of this visit. Only in Paul do we sense the underlying tension in

[7] H. Stadelmann, 'Die Vorgeschichte des Galaterbriefes. Ein Testfall für die geschichtliche Zuverlässigkeit des Paulus und Lukas', *Bibel und Gemeinde* 2 (1982), pp. 153-65.

[8] See further my article 'Acts and Galatians Reconsidered', *Themelios* n.s. 2 (1976-77), pp. 81-88.

[9] See especially Guthrie, *Introduction*, pp. 452-65; Bruce, *BJRL* 51 (1968-69), pp. 292-309; 52 (1969-70), pp. 243-66; 54 (1971-72), pp. 250-67.

his personal relations with the Jerusalem apostles. And here he is at pains to specify the precise limits of his contact with them at this time. Peter and James were representative of 'the apostles'. It is, I think, needless to quarrel with Luke's vaguer expression, or to ask how many constituted a quorum of the whole body. Luke says Paul had apostolic contact: Paul tells us whom he saw. The other matter goes deeper. In Galatians 1 he remained unknown by face to the churches of Judea, but in Acts 11 he apparently moved openly among the apostles, preached and debated boldly, and was finally conducted by Christians to Caesarea. Here we find at least one suggestive implication common to both accounts, that Paul's introduction to the church was oddly limited and difficult. In one case he met few individuals and was unknown to the church at large, in the other the church feared him and disbelieved his conversion. It seems very likely those two things go together.[10] Paul first came to Jerusalem not to a welcome as a mighty evangelist of the future, but as a virtual outcast, rejected by both communities. Barnabas broke the ice, and representatives of the apostles responded, perhaps fearfully. Paul declared Christ in the synagogues, but the bulk of the church shunned contact with him.

Our solution affects the understanding both of the Epistle to the Galatians and of Acts, but principally of Acts. In the case of the epistle the obvious consequences of accepting it are to imply that the Galatian defection to Paul's opponents had happened rapidly, in response to teachers who must have followed hard upon his heels, and conversely that the epistle is to be separated by several years from the Roman and Corinthian epistles with which it appears to show the closest affinity. Both of these implications may be thought difficulties, and the latter touches upon central issues of the development of Paul's thought and the core of his theology. If in fact the common threads in this group of letters are close to the heart of Paul's Gospel, and he was clear in his stand and perspective on law and grace before he ever engaged in extensive mission and controversy, it is not difficult to believe that such fundamental themes recur at different stages of his epistolary ministry as occasion called afresh for the restatement of basics. The pastoral needs of other churches did not require him to repeat again in writing what was integral to his initial teaching and preaching in situations bridging the gap from Galatians to Romans and extending before and after them. Such a view fits the evidence of Galatians itself: the Galatians have

10 One of the tragedies of Christian missions in the Middle East today is that established Christians will reject converts from Islam whose sincerity is suspected though they may have lost everything through their conversion.

abandoned the essence of Paul's Gospel for another so-called 'gospel', and he must recall them to the basics he might elsewhere have pre-supposed (Gal. 1:6-9; 2:14-16; 3:1-5; etc.). The theological affinities are not of the weight they seem to carry for some who use them to place Galatians necessarily close to Romans in the development of Paul's thought.[11] In fact the implications of our view for the actual interpretation of Galatians seem to be largely limited to the two points made above. Thus Beker, who presents the epistle as his principal test case for the tension of the 'coherence' and 'contingency' of Paul's thought,[12] gives a reconstruction of its 'contingent' setting which differs considerably from the view here stated, yet his actual interpretation is not essentially different. Perhaps that only means he has not chosen the most persuasive example for contingency; the present author agrees with the principle that contingent background is important. Conversely, Galatians abounds in interpretative problems, but they do not seem to centre largely on the synthesis with Acts, save partly on the geographical placing of the Galatian churches, and the chronology of the visits.[13]

It is in the case of Acts that the consequences are much more far-reaching. If our solution is accepted, a key objection to the basic historicity of the Acts outline is at once eased, and the question of the evidential base for our knowledge of Paul is reopened. This is of course far short of a compelling argument for the historicity of Acts. It is however crucial in meeting exaggerated claims to the contrary, where the assumption of conflict has been used incautiously to

---

[11] If we accept that these two epistles are likely in any case to bring us nearest the exposition of 'Paul's gospel', and that he had thought through the concept of justification by faith before the preaching and controversy even of his early public ministry, there is nothing against the likelihood that Paul repeated similar themes throughout his career as occasion required. In separating Galatians from Romans by about seven years, as I do, I open the question of development in Paul's thought, but also doubt whether the themes of these particular two epistles give clear indications for tracing it. Differences between them probably turn more on differences of setting, between urgent controversy and deliberative exposition, than on developments in Paul. We must question the arguments of J.B. Lightfoot, who seems to have exercised much greater influence on the study of Galatians, where his views are seriously dated, than elsewhere, where his continuing importance is often neglected. For example, we should not attach much weight to the kind of argument by which Lightfoot (*Galatians*, pp. 45-49), places Galatians close *before* Romans.

[12] Beker, *Paul*, pp. 37-58.

[13] [Ed.] On this dating, Galatians is chronologically prior to Paul's correspondence with the church at Thessalonica. For discussion of the possible difficulties raised by this aspect of the hypthesis, see F.F. Bruce, *Galatians*, pp. 53-55.

extrapolate to a wholesale condemnation of Acts, which has then found a presuppositional context within which to discount or over-rule any ostensible evidence. The question must at least be held open. Then we may find that there are the elements present of a natural correlation, a usefully interlocking fragment of a larger jigsaw, and a piece capable of extension to illuminate in fresh ways the careful consideration of the larger picture. To posit such possibilities is not proof, but it is at least suggestive, and exhibits the character we should expect of an essentially true solution.

If it be objected that the historicity of Acts is here too tightly and narrowly bound to one solution of the highly controverted Galatian question, alternative lines of response are possible. (1) This view is in fact on much stronger ground than its debated status might lead us to suppose. (2) The case is not positively and exclusively dependent on this view, for we have adduced already many details which make out a *prima facie* case for Luke's accuracy. All these phenomena need a sufficient explanation, and we ought to recognize some presumption in favour of Luke. (3) Some, like J.B. Lightfoot, have combined a high view of the historicity of Acts with a different resolution of the Galatian question. An argument might be mounted on that basis.[14] (4) The simple and integrated solution has its own attraction. It may be another mark of correctness. It touches the recurring need to choose between the 'ostensible' and the 'reinterpreted' along the whole length of the debate. We ultimately seek an integrated position, not merely a congeries of opportunistically convenient salients. It may still of course be acknowledged that there are many unsolved issues.

Chronology

Lightfoot and Harnack in their day both sought a fixed point, but none of the correlations could then be determined with sufficient precision.[15] Since that time the discovery of the Gallio inscription, and subsequent refinements in our reading of it, enable us to place Paul's presence in Corinth with a high probability of accuracy.

14 But I am not persuaded of the need to do so, and think the attempt today might savour of a masochistic desire to make our own problems, for we should now be better informed by new knowledge than Lightfoot was, and unfettered by misconceptions then inevitable. The history of the 'North Galatian' view since Lightfoot is revealing, and standard later treatments contradict at key points the grounds on which he held it, or where he and Ramsay agreed against those who are content to cite his authority for their conclusions. Cf. pp. 3-4, 282-84.

15 Cf. Lightfoot, *Essays on Supernatural Religion*, pp. 291-302, where he has to confess his inability to place Sergius Paulus exactly; Harnack, *Acts*, pp. 1-6.

The reading of this inscription of Delphi has been discussed else-where,[16] but it is desirable to repeat here at least a brief statement of the problems involved, and to reaffirm that the date of Gallio's actual proconsulship is fixed beyond cavil, even though differing restorations of the text may shift slightly the basis of the inference. There is in any case the somewhat intricate, but clear, inference from the imperial titulature of Claudius which places the inscription itself in the spring or summer of 52, for the emperor is still *imp. xxvi*, and so the text is placed before 1st August in that year, the occasion of his 27th imperial salutation.[17] A question remains about the precise relation between the dating of this text and the year of Gallio's proconsulship. On the traditional reading this might have been 51/52 or, less probably, 52/53. But the traditional reading has commonly been content to follow the old text of Deissmann and Pomtow, based on the piecing together of four fragments, whereas nine are now known.[18] The assumption that the letter of Claudius, referring to Gallio in the third person, was addressed to the citizens of Delphi is open to Plassart's contention that it was addressed to his successor in office, though Plassart's second person singular (σε) is in turn dependent on doubtful word-division.[19] The choice then lies between two options which concur in placing Gallio's tenure in 51/52. Either the letter addresses the Delphians about Gallio's activities during the year

[16] *Pauline Studies Bruce*, pp. 6-8.

[17] Cf. Frontinus, *de Aquaeductis*, 1.13; *CIL* 6.1256 = *ILS* 218, and see the discussion in *Pauline Studies Bruce*, p. 17n.

[18] The fragments were first published in E. Bourguet, *De Rebus Delphicis imperatoriae aetatis capita duo* (Paris, 1905) and popularized in their bearing on Pauline chronology by W.M. Ramsay in *Expos* 7th ser. 7 (1909), pp. 467-69. Although three further fragments were published shortly afterwards by A. Brassac, 'Une inscription de Delphes et la chronologie de saint Paul', *RB* 10 (1913), pp. 37-53 and pp. 207-17, the influence of Deissmann, *Paul*, pp. 235-60 (*Paulus*, pp. 159-77) and H. Pomtow in *SIG*³ 801D has led to their exclusion from consideration in much of the subsequent literature. The interpretation made familiar by Deissmann has held the field for half a century, but must now be reconsidered. For the best reading see now A. Plassart, *Fouilles de Delphes*, Part III, 'Épigraphie', fasc. 4.3 (Paris: Boccard, 1970) No. 286; and 'L'inscription de Delphes mentionnant le proconsul Gallion', *REG* 80 (1967), pp. 372-78.

[19] See the discussion of Plassart's *REG* article by J.H. Oliver, 'The Epistle of Claudius which mentions the Proconsul Junius Gallio', *Hesperia* 40 (1971), pp. 239-40. Note that the gaps are inaccurately placed in the publications both of Plassart and of Oliver. The placings and the length of line are now partly controlled by the observation that two of the original four fragments fit at the back of the stone. In *Pauline Studies Bruce*, p. 7, I have illustrated *exempli gratia* the possibility of offering a reconstruction on Oliver's lines. There is then no ground for seeing a second person singular addressee.

preceding or his successor close upon his assuming office. In either case a text of spring or summer 52 refers to Gallio's preceding actions in 51/52.

The date is crucial, for it links the ostensible account of Paul with an externally documented date. There is still the question how precisely we correlate it, but it must be given its due weight. This is a place where we find a fundamental methodological problem in Knox's approach. In his preference for 'primary' evidence he elevates a hypothetical (and probably wrong) synchronism in the epistles (Gal. 2:1 with 2 Cor. 12:2), mounted on a conjectured date for Paul's conversion, above this specific ostensible date, whose relevance he dismisses.[20] It is a proceeding so odd that it is difficult to understand the continuing influence of a reconstruction rooted in so curious an aberration. We make no apology for using the Gallio inscription as an external anchor for the following sequence. It is in some degree inevitable that there is need to justify this procedure against the most radical alternative, but the real problems are of a more intricate kind, within the acceptance of the need for critical study to establish a broader evidential base.

Let us then summarize, from the items discussed at the beginning of Chapter 5, a tabulation of the points in Acts which are amenable to an approximate dating.

4:6 The reference to Annas and Caiaphas implies a date before the deposition of Caiaphas in AD 36 (cf. B in ch. 4, pp. 159-62).

9:24-25 (with 2 Cor. 11:32-33) Assuming the correspondence of these incidents, we must place the event before the death of Aretas in 40. Narrower termini are not justified, and the apparent historical problem involves Paul's writings, not Acts.

---

20 Knox made the identification of the two periods of fourteen years the starting point of his earlier articles, yet in his book (*Chapters*, p. 78n.) he virtually abandons it in the face of critical objections (cf. e.g. Haenchen, p. 67) while elaborating the chronology it prompted. For his subsequent treatment of the Gallio question see *Chapters*, pp. 81-82; *JBL* 58 (1939), p. 20. A proconsul held office for only one year, and the circumstances of the close of Gallio's year are otherwise known from the allusion by his brother (Sen. *Ep. Mor.* 104), and Knox's estimate of the proconsulship as somewhere in the range 50-54 is inadequate. Knox brings Paul to Corinth 'hardly later than AD 45', concedes that 'this [Gallio] datum is incompatible with the chronological scheme developed here' (p. 81), and offers two alternative solutions to alternative Lukan errors, without raising the third possibility that his own scheme could be mistaken. His case is not saved by a facile invocation of an equation of Suet. *Claud.* 25.4 with Dio 60.6.6, which make ostensibly contradictory statements about apparently separate occasions. Even if some would identify them after close study, it will not do simplistically to invoke 'errors of historians' when Dio says the opposite of what Knox wants him to say.

11:28 Intricate and overlapping synchronisms of reference to famine with the evidence of Josephus and of the papyri point to the period c. 45-47 for a famine extending from Egypt to Syria-Palestine. If the Agabus incident is placed at the outset of this period, it may have preceded a prompt relief-mission in c. 45-46.

12:1 This mentions Herod Agrippa I (41-44) in narrative leading to climax of his death in 44 (12:20-23). Time-notes here are approximations, and it is unnecessary to press rigid chronological sequence in Acts 11-12 in the recounting of complexes of events ordered separately and perhaps even overlapping chronologically.

18:2 Claudius' expulsion of Jews from Rome in 49 (*pace* Lüdemann) sets a recent *terminus a quo* for the coming of Aquila and Priscilla to Corinth.

18:12 Gallio was proconsul of Achaia in 51-52. This suggests a reconstruction where Paul arrived in Corinth in autumn 50 and departed in spring 52, possibly about the time of Gallio's own premature departure from his province.

19:38 The time of disorder in Ephesus might plausibly be placed in the interregnum following the murder of the proconsul Silanus after Nero's accession in October 54.

20:6-7 Reasons have been given for the tentative correlation of the detailed travel diary of this chapter with the period of seven weeks following the Passover of Thursday 7 April 57.

23:2 The high priest Ananias son of Nebedaeus was in office c. 47-58, and he exercised power with unrestrained arrogance in the last years of that tenure under Felix.

24:24 Drusilla's first marriage was after the end of 53 (Jos. *Ant.* 20.7.1.138-39), but she quickly deserted her husband to marry Felix. These events are wholly appropriate to a trial of Paul before Felix about 57, when Drusilla would have been about nineteen.

24:27 A combination of factors now seems to favour 59 as the year of Festus' succession to Felix. See also Sherwin-White's discussion of 23:34 (*RSRL* pp. 55-57; p. 171 above).

27:9 The implication of a later incidence of the Fast that year suits 59 and the short chronology of the following winter better than would any neighbouring year.

28:30 The Roman διετία is amenable at least to two significant arguments *ex silentio*. It probably began before news came of the Lycus valley earthquake of 60 and probably ended before the Neronian persecution of 64.

Integration: 57-62

It will be observed that these chosen points make an entirely credible sequence as far as they go. There is one minor dislocation at 11:28/12:1, and we must not forget the intractable Theudas problem. Further, there are several more generalized time-spans, like those at 21:38, 22:28, 24:10, 25:13, which offer no actual dates, but are fully consonant with the emerging picture. In fact the events at least of the last nine chapters may be placed in the five-year period 57-62 by interlocking correlations.

Voyage to Jerusalem (20:6-21:16)	April - May 57
Caesarean Imprisonment (διετία of 24:27)	Summer 57 - Summer 59
Voyage to Rome (27:1-28:16)	Late Summer 59 - Spring 60
Roman imprisonment (διετία of 28:30)	Spring 60 - Spring 62

This table calls only for two interim comments: (1) that διετία denotes a full two-year period, as opposed to the usual reckoning of numerals inclusively;[21] (2) that the terminal event of the latter διετία is unspecified and unclear.

Jewett and Ogg, who differ widely in their overall treatment of the evidence, are essentially at one on this sequence, though Ogg, who is usually preferable, places the whole sequence two years later from a later dating of the succession of Festus. By this arrangement he brings the conclusion of Acts neatly to the date of the Neronian persecution of 64, but at the cost of neglecting the combination of circumstantial indications which seem telling.

Integration: 50-52

Another fragment of what seems a firmly integrated piece of reconstruction concerns the period from Autumn 50 to Spring 52:

Arrival in Corinth (18:2)	Autumn 50
Arrival of Gallio at Corinth (18:12)	Early Summer 51
Paul's departure after a year and six months (18:11,18)	Spring 52

Comments: (1) Opposition builds up to a crisis point with the arrival of a new and untried proconsul. Gallio's response then affords Paul's work *de facto* protection. The ἡμέραι ἱκαναί of v. 18 are then included in the eighteen months and amount to Gallio's tenure of office.[22] (2) Gallio's premature departure (Sen. *Ep. Mor.* 104.1) may

---

21 The lexica are brief and unhelpful on διετία and διέτης, words well attested in the inscriptions as well as the papyri, and frequently used of the ages of children on their tombstones. A curiously explicit one is the Roman inscription of the boy Critias (*IGUR* 2.727) whose age is given in verse as διέτη ... μησὶν ἐπ᾽ ὀκτώ beside the prosaic precision of 2 years, 8 months, 15 days and 5 1/2 hours.

22 See my discussion in *Pauline Studies Bruce*, p. 8, in response to Haacker, 'Die Gallio-Episode und die paulinische Chronologie', *BZ* n.s. 16 (1972), pp. 252-55.

have faced Paul with the prospect of a disturbed interregnum and have occasioned his leaving Corinth.[23]

Reconstruction: 52-57

Between these two reconstructed fragments is a five-year period which can be approximately filled from the data of Acts alone, though the internal notes of time are neither precise nor exhaustive. Its main feature is the Ephesian residence, reckoned inclusively at three years (20:31), and comprising three months' teaching in the synagogue (19:8), two years based on the hall of Tyrannus (19:10), and an unspecified continuance in Asia after sending Timothy and Erastus ahead into Macedonia (19:22). Before this central episode Paul is represented as having made a rapid journey from Corinth via Ephesus to Caesarea (for Jerusalem), down to Antioch, and by Galatia and Phrygia (in whatever sense) to his residence in Ephesus. That is a lengthy itinerary, and an obvious question is whether it occupied more than one summer travelling season. But let us move first to the end of the Ephesian residence. Paul lingers in Asia, eventually crossing to Macedonia (20:1). After an unspecified time of travel in those parts (20:2) he went to Greece, and spent three months there before changing his mind about sailing to Syria (20:3), and travelled to Macedonia, where we pick up at Philippi our postulated date in April 57.

To put the same data differently, we have accounted for four of the five winters in the period 52-57, three at Ephesus and the last in Greece (20:3). So far as this evidence takes us the Acts narrative *might* be structured on a four-year lapse here. But there are two opposite cautions to be offered at this point. (1) We cannot be sure that the notes of time in Acts are chronologically exhaustive, apart from what Luke selects to recount in detail. (2) We cannot assume a licence to expand the chronology without careful discrimination. It is tempting to suppose for instance that particular travels or events took a long time, and to assign them blocks of time consecutively.[24] But

---

[23] I would not press this possibility, nor exclude the likelihood that Paul's decision to visit Jerusalem at this point was a concurrent, if not a decisive, motive. If such a reason was operative, it was not necessarily that he feared for his personal safety, but that irregularities or violence during an interregnum, or pressure on the incoming governor, might imperil also the delicate legal precedent established under Gallio.

[24] There is reason to be concerned about the reckoning in Jewett (pp. 59-61) and in his statement that the so-called 'second missionary journey' involved a journey of 3497 km and a time span of three or four years (p. 92). While I essentially concur with Jewett, at least in his placing of events between 57 and 62, I am

time could vary enormously with circumstances and conditions. A voyage eastward may have taken ten days and the return two or three months.[25] Furthermore, it is likely that Paul sometimes laboured long and uneventfully in one strategic place, and sometimes sacrificed settled opportunities ruthlessly to an overriding purpose or distinction. The problem with which Luke's terse narrative often leaves us is that of understanding those aspects of Paul's motivation which he has not been concerned to tell us. It sometimes happens that the epistles give us the Pauline rationale of Luke's balder reports—the 'Collection' is the classic instance.

In the present case we simply draw attention to Paul's apparently unmotivated journey to Jerusalem at 18:18-22 and suggest it be seen in Pauline terms. Paul was deeply concerned with preserving the unity of Jewish and Gentile congregations and keenly sensitive to the Pharisaic and legalistic influences operative in the Jerusalem church. He made it a priority on occasion to be present at one of the great Jewish feasts at Jerusalem, to let it be seen he was a law-abiding, pious Jew (cf. 18:18), and also no doubt to keep his finger on the pulse of the delicate situation in Jerusalem. Jewett and Lüdemann are critical of the traditional 'five-visit' framework of Acts.[26] But this recurring pattern is significant, and the rationale for it comes from Paul rather than Acts. The Acts 18 visit does not apparently figure largely in the perspective either of Acts or epistles, yet it was in the period following it that Paul develops his 'Collection' as a strategic initiative towards the continuing Jerusalem problem.

We suggest that Paul left Corinth in spring 52 as soon as the seas were safe, early enough to reach Jerusalem for Passover,[27] declining

---

bewildered by the mathematical character of his claim that for the period 53-64 the chances against his correlations being accidental are 14,170 to 1 (p. 102; 151n.). It may be noted incidentally that his measurements on p. 92 includes gratuitous travels by improbable routes across Galatia (North as well as South).

25 Cf. L. Casson, 'Speed under Sail of Ancient Ships', *TAPA* 82 (1951), pp. 136-48. See also pp. 134-36 above.

26 Jewett (p. 67) criticizes even Haenchen for his subservience to the essence of the Acts framework, though Haenchen also criticizes Knox for ascribing too high a degree of historical credibility to Acts (p. 544-45n.). See Haenchen's treatment of the chronology on pp. 60-71. The phrase 'five-visit framework' may be seen as a central focus of Jewett's criticism of traditional chronologies (e.g. pp. 60, 84, 92; *Colloquy*, ed. Corley, pp. 273-74, 281). He and Lüdemann concur in reducing the ostensible sequence of visits by accepting Knox's equation of the visit of Acts 18:22 with that of Gal. 2:1-10 (cf. Lüdemann, *Paul*, pp. 147-57 = *Paulus*, 1.165-73).

27 Such may have been his first intention also in 57 before the plot against him in his intended voyage diverted and delayed him northward overland to Macedonia.

en route a pressing invitation to stay in Ephesus (18:20-21) because of his prior commitment to Jerusalem. After his visit to Jerusalem he used the remaining summer season travelling westward overland in pastoral visitation to Antioch and across Asia Minor, making Ephesus his chosen objective for the winter of 52-53.[28] The two winters 55-56 and 56-57 may be seen as following Paul's Ephesian residence, the former being that unspecified in Acts, the latter spent in Greece (20:3). The need to fill out this time appears the more plainly when we turn to Paul's epistles. To establish the point requires at least a tentative outline of the complex series of events involved in Paul's relations with the Corinthians during his Ephesian residence and especially its immediate aftermath. This permits some enlargement of the picture so briefly summarized in 20:1-3, which covers the period 55-57.

There is an immediate problem here on the Pauline front, over the number and sequence of Paul's Corinthian letters. Let us try to begin by piecing together the most secure ground. In 1 Cor. 16:8 Paul expresses his intention to stay in Ephesus until Pentecost: he is planning his future movements with relation to Macedonia and Corinth, and we are ostensibly near the end of an Ephesian residence, during which he has had stormy relations with Corinth. The writing of 1 Corinthians is then placed in c. 54-55. The case of 2 Corinthians is immediately complicated by the debate over the relation of 2 Cor. 1-9 with 2 Cor. 10-13. But the first indications seem clear enough that the early chapters refer to some of the same events as 1 Corinthians, but from a later perspective. 2 Cor. 1:8 probably corresponds with 1 Cor. 15:32 (though both are allusive to events which the Corinthians must have known); the frustrated plan of 2 Cor. 1:15 corresponds with the intention expressed in 1 Cor. 16:5-6; the repentance and discipline of 2 Cor. 7 with the immorality preceding in 1 Cor. 5 (esp. 2 Cor. 7:12 with 1 Cor. 5:1); the progress of the collection in 2 Cor. 8 with the instructions in 1 Cor. 16:1-2. Then the movements of Paul indicated in these chapters of 2 Corinthians fall into place as subsequent to the same Ephesian residence, when he had finally moved to Troas (2 Cor. 2:12-13), found himself unable to settle there because he could not find Titus, and went on to Macedonia. There too he had no rest until comforted by the coming of Titus with the good news of reconciliation

---

[28] The ideas that Paul's ministry in Galatia had been unsuccessful and that Luke may have wanted to minimize the prominence of this period (Ogg, *Paul*, p. 134) is not the point here. Rather the new (and long-awaited) commitment to Ephesus was the controlling factor, and Paul merely took as much opportunity as possible of ministry *en route*, in places indicated here only by the briefest summary reference.

with the Corinthians (2 Cor. 7:5-7, cf. 13-15).

Now this whole sequence of events corresponds with the stage marked by Luke's simple statement that Paul 'departed to go into Macedonia' (Acts 20:1). There is nothing in Acts to suggest the motivations in this time of controversy and emotional tension over Corinth combined with the organization of the Collection. There is only the barest correspondence, but that is a correspondence of sequence.[29] The probabilities of Paul's dealings with Corinth may be tentatively reconstructed here from his own correspondence, and suggest that Paul's anxiety to see Titus was further tied to the realities of travel. His restless progress to Troas, and then to Macedonia, indicates perhaps a realization that Titus was returning late in the year overland, in autumn 55 on our reckoning.[30] Paul apparently wrote 2 Cor. 1:9 from Macedonia soon after the reunion, and presumably wintered there.[31]

Romans was ostensibly written in the period immediately after the time when we lose the link with the Corinthian letters. In Rom. 15:25-27 Paul refers to the Collection, but from a later perspective, where

---

[29] The brevity of Acts is not necessarily significant here. The difference serves only to emphasize afresh the variation of perspective and selection between Acts and Paul. There is no necessity that a record essentially correct in the statements it makes should be judged by a criterion of exhaustive completeness of information. That Luke omits internal controversies and Paul's sufferings and emotions is an evident feature of his work. It does not automatically imply that he is suppressing the truth. It is not the part of the truth pertinent to his story of the progress of Christianity towards Rome, and unless omission involves falsification of relevant facts, a further stage in the argument requiring independent demonstration, it is not necessarily problematic *per se.*

[30] Cf. W.L. Knox, *St. Paul and the Church of the Gentiles*, p. 144n, cited in Bruce, *Acts*, p. 369.

[31] It is not necessary at this point to enter into the controversy over the unity of 2 Corinthians, for the events noted are all drawn from 1-9, and the theories which further dissect those chapters are not convincing. The classic statement of the division of the letter is in J.H. Kennedy, *The Second and Third Epistles of St. Paul to the Corinthians*(London: Methuen, 1900), which relies heavily on equating the past tenses of 2 Cor. 1:23; 2:3, 9 with the futures of 13:2, 10; 10:6 respectively, and placing 10-13 earlier than 1-9. See however A.M.G. Stephenson, 'Partition Theories on II Corinthians', *SE* 2 (1964), pp. 639-46, who argues forcibly that 2 Cor. 12:18 refers back to 2 Cor. 8:16-24. I accept the essential unity of the letter, though without rejecting the possibility that a delay in the process of composition might help to explain the apparent shift of tone and perspective after chapter 9. This reading of 2 Cor. 12:18 would permit the inclusion of the evidence of that verse, without the need to multiply visits of Titus in the period preceding the movements of Paul in which we are here mainly interested. Again, the real problems here lie in Paul, not in Acts.

Macedonia and Achaia have made their contributions and he is about to start for Jerusalem with them, and is looking ahead to the possibility of visiting Rome on his way to Spain (15:24). The apparent implication is that this letter was written from Corinth on the eve of the Jerusalem journey, on our reckoning c. early 57. This location receives some support from the commendation of Phoebe of Cenchrea (Rom. 16:1), and the man Erastus (Rom. 16:23) may also be linked with Corinth.[32] These personalia cannot be pressed, and of course it is questioned whether the greetings of this chapter were originally part of the Roman letter.[33] Of more particular significance is the reference to preaching as far as Illyricum in Rom. 15:19, especially if linked with Rom. 15:23 to suggest that Paul saw this as representing the completion of his pioneer mission in the Greek East.[34] There is no point in the narrative of Acts before 20:2 where we could easily place such a mission, for his original mission in Macedonia was marked by harassment and haste, and enforced departure for Athens. But here in Acts 20:2 we have the implication of a mission tour (διελθὼν δὲ τὰ μέρη ἐκεῖνα). If 'those parts' may reasonably be taken in a broad sense, of territories adjoining and beyond Macedonia proper, we have a placing for a mission including Illyricum, which newly completed the geographical range at the date of Romans. Then we may assign this work in Macedonia and Illyricum to the year 56 before wintering in Corinth.

---

32 Men of this name are mentioned also in Acts 19:21 and in 2 Tim. 4:20 in contexts variously associated with Corinth or Ephesus. It is not certain that they all refer to the same man, and doubtful whether the city official of Rom. 16:13 is further identifiable with the Erastus of a Corinthian inscription. See p. 235-36; Cadbury, 'Erastus of Corinth', *JBL* 50 (1931), pp. 42-58. Broneer, however, inclines to accept this identification (*BA* 14 [1951], p. 94).

33 For the view that Rom. 16 was part of a separate letter addressed to Ephesus see Moffatt, *Introduction*, pp. 134-39. The plausible arguments for this case may however be answered, and there is a problem of 'bibliographical probability', how the detached greetings of a lost letter were likely to have been combined with Rom. 1-15. The further difficulty of the textual and redactional history of Rom. 15-16 is also raised. The least problematic solution seems to be that which ascribes the attempt at a shorter recension to Marcion. See also H. Gamble, *The Textual History of the Letter to the Romans* (Grand Rapids: Eerdmans, 1977).

34 The geographical range of such a mission is not immediately clear, but would naturally be based on a continued traverse of the westward section of the *Via Egnatia*, perhaps to its coastal limit at Dyrrhachium (Durazzo), whence it was not far north on the coast to the major Illyrian city of Salonae (near Split). I am inclined to link Paul's terminus with the limit of Greek as the first language of the Eastern Empire. The Dalmatian coast had its quota of Greek cities, though Salonae itself was a Roman colony, and the bulk of its rich epigraphical harvest is in Latin (see relevant sections in *CIL* 3 and Supps.).

We may then summarize an inferential outline of the five years intervening between the limits of our firmer date-ranges in 52 and 57.

Visit to Jerusalem from Corinth; return overland	
to Ephesus (18:18-23; 19:1)	Spring - Autumn 52
Ephesian residence; Corinthian troubles	Autumn 52 - c. Summer 55
Paul at Troas; crosses to Macedonia	Autumn 55
Paul winters in Macedonia	55-56
Mission in Macedonia and Illyricum	? Spring - Autumn 56
Winter in Corinth	56-57

The writing of the Corinthian letters and of Romans, but probably not Galatians, may also be placed in this period. Suffice it to say here that the autobiographical notes of Galatians appear not to relate at all to the sequences of events in which we have linked Acts with Romans and 1 and 2 Corinthians. The fourteen-year period of Gal. 2:1 is not the same as that of 2 Cor. 12:2, and the attempt to calculate back from the date of the latter leads us to place Paul's ecstatic experience about AD 42.[35] On Paul's own evidence that cannot be equated with his conversion, which must have antedated the death of Aretas in AD 40.

Reconstruction pre-50

This leads us naturally to consideration of the more difficult earlier period of Paul's ministry. The central problem here is posed by Paul's own evidence in Galatians. Is there enough time to accommodate the periods of three and fourteen years of Gal. 1:18, 2:1, or will the attempt to place them force Paul's conversion back to an impossibly early date? On our suggested equivalence in the Jerusalem visits (Gal. 2 = Acts 11), the fourteen years will terminate at the time of the 'famine-relief' visit, about 46. Many scholars have insisted that the chronology is impossibly tight to permit this scheme.

There are several uncertain factors in the case. (1) It is debated whether the date of the Crucifixion was 30 or 33.[36] (2) The lapse of

---

35 This is then to be placed ostensibly in the 'hidden years' of Paul's life, possibly when he was resident in Tarsus (between 9:30 and 11:25, cf. Gal. 1:2), and is otherwise apparently unattested in Acts or epistles. It seems clear that this experience of spiritual ecstasy and exultation was different from the occasion of Paul's conversion, which involved the bitter regret and repentance of a persecutor. The present reckoning assumes only the essential correctness of dating 2 Cor. 12 about 55-56, and even if this passage is assigned to a preceding 'severe letter', the experience can scarcely be brought into the lifetime of Aretas. Knox himself places 2 Corinthians in 51-53 (*Chapters*, pp. 85-86), but only upon evidence internal to his own scheme. The only requirement on which he insists is that Galatians shall have been written *after* the Conference and not earlier than, say, 51. But we may differ from him even on this. Otherwise he offers rather an order of letters than absolute dates.

36 This is a difficult question, complicated further by the differences between

time between the Crucifixion and the conversion of Paul is never specified. The complex development of events in Acts 1-8 gives the impression of requiring considerable time. But this may be no more than
an impression: the dynamic vigour of the early Christian movement
was such that the whole story may conceivably have been contained
within the first few months. On the other hand, it may have extended
into years. While guarding against assumptions which might seem to
close the question prematurely, we must remain open to conviction
either way. (3) It is debatable whether the three and fourteen years
are to be reckoned concurrently from Paul's conversion, or consecutively. The former, despite Jewett, is natural to Paul's wording, if also
easier in keeping the period short.[37] (4) It may be argued whether or

the Synoptics and John in the chronology of Passion week itself. The following
variables are involved: (1) the date of Jesus' birth, a major crux in its own right
involving the Quirinius and census problems; (2) the reckoning of the fifteenth
year of Tiberius (Luke 3:1) as the starting point of John's ministry; (3) the
duration of Jesus' ministry in the face of the differing numbers of Passovers
mentioned by the Synoptics and by John; (4) the statement of Luke 3:23 that Jesus
began his ministry when about thirty years of age; (5) the possible years when
either 14 or 15 Nisan might have fallen on a Friday— a probable choice between
30 and 33 unless the system of intercalation had produced an unusually early or
late option in a different year; (6) the reckoning of 46 years in John 2:20, another
datum beset with problems of interpretation and calculation, but if counted from
late in 20 BC (Jos. *BJ*, 1.21.1.401 [15th year? from 34 BC] = Jos. *Ant.* 15.11.1.380
[18th year from 37 BC]) to the first Passover of Jesus' ministry, it might point to
that of AD 27 or 28.

[37] The question cannot be solved simply by reference to the lexica. While it is
certain that ἔπειτα denotes sequence of time, the point at issue in Gal. 1:18-2:1 is
whether we have here *consecutive* rather than *concurrent* sequence of time. Thus
Jewett's conclusions (pp. 52-53, 135-36 notes), which make the finer semantic
discrimination, would not follow from the evidence he cites, even had *M M*
made the statement which he attributed to them. The lexica show us no more
than that ἔπειτα *per se* is as ambiguous as the English word 'afterwards'. The
question we want to ask is 'after what?'; a question which must be settled on
contextual rather than lexical grounds.

It is precisely at this point also that the analogies from the other epistles break
down. Lüdemann argues that Paul almost always uses the particle in a temporal
sense (*Paul*, pp. 63f. = *Paulus*, 1.85-86), which, of course, is not disputed. None
of the analogies (1 Thess. 4:17 and 1 Cor. 12:28, or indeed 1 Cor. 15:5-7, 23, 46)
provides a rigorous parallel for this context of measuring periods of time from
one or more *termini*.

We may place the passage in context by recalling 1:15-17. The central theme is
that Paul did not receive his calling from any man (let alone the Jerusalem
pillars), he is here stressing his independence of them. Were the thrust of the
passage concerned with Paul defending his practices over the years, we should
be obliged to take the ἔπειτα constructions consecutively: 'first I did this, 3 years
later that, and something else 14 years after that'. But here his argument is best

not these periods are to be reckoned inclusively. Ancient practice seems essentially clear here, but the inclusive reckoning should not be overplayed on dubious analogies from regnal years. To argue for a value below thirteen would be special pleading, but we may accept thirteen plus rather than fourteen plus.[38]

If then we start from 30 and combine the shortest likely options throughout, we *might* compress the whole period from the Crucifixion to the second Jerusalem visit into about fourteen calendar years, allowing only months before Paul's conversion to offset the possibility

understood 'I was converted by God, and did not meet the apostles at that time. I did however visit them 3 years after and again 14 years after'. Either interpretation is a legitimate use of the word, and only context can help us decide. Were it not for the extra and less contextually clear ἔπειτα in 1:21 (which is not situated in the grammatical construct common to 1:18 and 2:1), it is doubtful that there would be any serious problem.

Jewett's reading would make a significant point of the change from μετά in Gal. 1:18 to διά in Gal. 2:1 (Jewett, p. 53, so similarly Lightfoot, *Galatians*, p. 102 *ad loc.*), as implying that Paul had had no contact with Jerusalem in the interval. Preferable is the view of Bruce (*Galatians*, p. 106) that the variation is stylistic, and cannot in itself decide the reckoning of the fourteen years.

Jewett uses the claim that other scholars have impossibly compressed this sequence as a basis for rejecting a long series of alternative views (Jewett, pp. 69-74), which include some of those among the best grounded. This and his Aretas datum (both indeed from Paul, not Acts) are treated as fundamental, whereas a more cautious and critical approach shows that both are beset by such difficulties of interpretation and application as to be very insecure ground in themselves. The tightness of the time-scale is a datum of the problem, and tends to impose the converse question whether a shorter reckoning is not to be examined sympathetically if we are to hope to do justice to the overall evidence. It is clear that many scholars of otherwise divergent viewpoints have agreed on the concurrent view. It will not do to argue as though they have all been 'forced to reduce' a plainly attested time-span to accommodate their own hypotheses.

38 C.J. Cadoux, 'A Tentative Synthetic Chronology of the Apostolic Age', *JBL* 56 (1937), pp. 177-91 reduces the period to twelve years in offering a dating scheme broadly consonant with the present view. Cadoux however is driven to strain the limits of probability by an unnecessary and unwarranted attempt to force the events of Acts into an artificial annalistic pattern in five-year sequences. The tightness of the chronology in any case poses an acute problem for such a view as that of D.R. de Lacey, 'Paul in Jerusalem', *NTS* 20 (1974), pp. 82-86, who argues for a dating of Galatians even *before* the famine-relief visit. The difficulty has been further highlighted by J. van Bruggen, *Na Veertien Jaren* (Kampen: J.H. Kok, 1973), accessible through an English summary, pp. 233-39, who contends that the South Galatian view is tenable *only* in the synthesis accepted here, but that the chronology is fatal even to that, and he is therefore driven perforce to a later occasion and a North Galatian destination. He feels obliged, however, to date the Crucifixion in 33, and defends the reliability of Acts while identifying the visit of Gal. 2 with that of Acts 18.

of months involved in the inclusive reckoning. We should then have time to spare: any date after 44 would be possible for the visit. The questions surrounding the famine are still complex and imperfectly resolved, and its progress extended in time. Even if Paul's visit may be placed substantially earlier within the sequence than Helena's relief mission, it is not likely to have been earlier than c. 46.

But that combination of the extreme options is unlikely. There might be a lead from some readings of the Aretas episode, but there are grounds for caution here. If there were secure reasons for placing it after 34 or after 37 and then linking it with the first Jerusalem visit of Gal. 1, we could find a *terminus a quo* for Paul's conversion in about 32 or 35, and the latter would be near fatal to the early chronology. But the political background of the ethnarch's presence remains unknown, and the question cannot be decided upon the unproved assumption of Nabataean control at a date we could only guess. It is a major query against Jewett's work that he uses a specific reading of this problem as a firm datum.[39]

There are still several ways of combining the variables. If we start in 33 with the later and longer reckoning of other points, that would definitely exclude the view proposed. But various intermediate positions are at least possible. Even 33 for the Crucifixion, with a lapse of fourteen years all told, would yield a possible 47 for the famine visit; a consecutive reckoning from an early dating of the conversion following 30 for the Crucifixion could produce a similar result. Again, if the period before Paul's conversion were more extended, or if the fourteen years were near to full calendar years and the reckoning virtually non-inclusive, there is still ample time if these possibilities are combined with other shorter options. In fact, each of the longer or later options in (1) to (4) might be included in a conceivable reconstruction. It seems likely that the actual truth lies in one of them or in an adjustment between two or more of them. My estimate would be somewhere in the range: Crucifixion in 30; conversion c. 32-34; visit c. 46-47; with perhaps a preference for the earliest limits of the two latter.

It still remains difficult to offer an overall chronology of the earlier chapters of Acts which can make any pretence to precision. But this is not because the framework can be shown to involve contradictions or impossibilities, but simply because there are too many variables still

---

[39] Again, Jewett lays great weight on this, and uses it absolutely to exclude diverse alternatives (Jewett, pp. 64, 68, 70-72, 74, 81). He uses this, like the fourteen-years reckoning, against both Acts-based and Epistle-based chronologies. It remains debatable whether Aretas ever held Damascus, and there is no secure terminus other than Aretas' death in 40. See most recently E.A. Knauf, 'Zum *Ethnarchen* des Aretas 2 *Kor. 11:32*', ZNW 74 (1983), pp. 145-47.

unknown for us to have the means of being more specific. All that can really be done here is to show in principle that there is enough time to accommodate the events. In so far as that gives a fairly tight fit, that circumstance gives some prospect of coming a little nearer exact dates than might otherwise have been possible.

A residual problem is that of integrating a possible outline chronology of the whole sequence of Jesus and Paul, especially as the Crucifixion is a pivotal date for both, the evidence of Luke is involved in both, and his credibility is the crucial issue at stake. This problem could not be satisfactorily resolved without going beyond our present brief, but something needs to be said in passing, at least as it bears on the character of Luke as a source. The various chronologies of the life of Jesus and of Paul seem to leave something of a hiatus at the key point of their meeting.[40] The work of G. Ogg stands out here for its painstaking critical study of both halves of the problem.[41] But he places the Crucifixion in 33, and reckons the fourteen years from Paul's conversion, placed c. 34-35, to the Jerusalem Conference, placed in 48, accepting the separate historicity of the famine-relief visit but arguing that Paul omitted this from Galatians: 'indeed it seems that no room for it can be found there' (*Paul*, p. 43).

This solution is implausible. Paul's argument in Galatians hinges upon his frankness in confessing the total extent of his visits to Jerusalem. The omission of a visit, even if it were unimportant, would arouse suspicion. Despite some impressive, if inconclusive, recent arguments for a Crucifixion in 33, the earlier option (30) still seems to do the most justice to the evidence bearing on the whole period.[42]

---

40 For the chronology of the whole life of Jesus cf. e.g. H.W. Hoehner, *Chronological Aspects of the Life Of Christ* (Grand Rapids: Zondervan, 1977). Many studies however are articles or monographs devoted to areas of special difficulty, the Nativity, the length of the Ministry, the day of the Crucifixion Passover and the year of the Crucifixion, all considered in isolation from the evidence for Paul. See e.g. E.F. Sutcliffe, *A Two-Year Public Ministry Defended* (London: Burns Oates and Washbourne, 1938); A. Jaubert, *La Date de la Cène* (Paris: Gabalda, 1957). The many studies of the Crucifixion itself focus on specialized questions, whether calendrical or astronomical.

41 G. Ogg, *The Chronology of the Public Ministry of Jesus* (CUP, 1940); *The Chronology of the Life of Paul* (London: Epworth, 1968).

42 Among those who have favoured 33 are Ogg, Jewett, and Hoehner. There have also been important astronomical arguments in J.K. Fotheringham, 'The Evidence of Astronomy and Technical Chronology for the Date of the Crucifixion', *JTS* 35 (1934), pp. 146-62; C.J. Humphreys and W.G. Waddington, 'The Date of the Crucifixion', *JASA* 37 (1985), pp. 2-10. Fotheringham provides an authoritative statement of the reasons for offering the option of 30 or 33, but his supposition about a confused reference to the *lunar* eclipse of 3 April 33 is unwarranted as a ground for preferring that year, which Ogg (see esp. *Public*

The tendency of the Acts/Paul part of the question is to push back the Crucifixion. This is not to be made a piece of special pleading to overrule plainly contrary evidence in the Gospels. But such is not the situation. Almost every chronological datum for the life of Jesus in the Gospels is subject to interpretative problems more elusive in their combinations of variables than in the case of Paul. Ogg has in effect made his view of the Gospel evidence determinative for Paul. But the Pauline evidence may possibly provide a better retrospective control. On the reconstruction of the Gospel sequence our conclusions must remain tentative, but we may suggest some such synthesis as the following: that a Jewish reckoning of the years of Tiberius points to 27-28, a date fitting well with the 46 years of John as pointing to Passover 27 or 28 for the beginning of the ministry; then a two or three year duration of ministry leading to 30 for the Crucifixion. Such a scheme, taken with the statement that Jesus was about thirty years of age in 27-28, is more easily consonant than a later date with likely dates for the Nativity, if that may be presumed to precede the death of Herod in March 4 BC.[43] Further, most of the specific chronological details are from Luke, and it may be apposite to our central theme to observe that Luke may be interpreted as broadly self-consistent and capable of such calculations from a point much nearer events whose precise synchronisms are now obscure to us.

But it must be emphasized that such a solution is tentative, designed only in principle to confirm some preference for 30 as the date of the Crucifixion, without excluding 33. Neither this date nor any date for the conversion of Paul may be lightly assumed as *termini a quo* for the Acts chronology. Rather we have to work back to them from the more secure later events, while attempting to correlate the resultant options with those deriving from the Gospel accounts of the ministry of Jesus. We then submit the following summary as

Ministry, pp. 276-77) holds for other reasons derived from the Lukan evidence.
[43] Whatever the resolution of the notorious census problem, Matthew (2:1-19) and Luke (1:5) are agreed in placing at least the antecedents of the Nativity story within the lifetime of Herod. Recent attempts to solve the puzzle by redating Herod's death as following a different eclipse in 1 BC (cf. Jos. *Ant*. 17.6.4.167) are not conclusive. The arguments of W.E. Filmer, 'The Chronology of the Reign of Herod the Great', *JTS* n.s. 17 (1966), pp. 283-98, are trenchantly answered by T.D. Barnes, 'The Date of Herod's Death', *JTS* n.s. 19 (1968), pp. 204-209. The work of E.L. Martin (*The Birth of Christ Recalculated* [Pasadena and Newcastle-upon-Tyne: Foundation for Biblical Research, 1978] with Supplements), is a piece of vigorous and ingenious advocacy, but lacks rigour in meeting objections. Cf. my review of Martin in *Faith and Thought*, 107 (1980), pp. 128-31. The traditional 4 BC date still holds the field as a *terminus ad quem* for the Nativity. It remains unclear how much earlier it should be placed.

representing at least the balance of probability:

Crucifixion	7 April 30 (or poss. 3 Apr. 33)
Conversion of Paul	c. 32-33 (c. 34)
First visit to Jerusalem (Gal. 1 = Acts 9), 2-3 years later	c. 35 (c. 36)
Second visit to Jerusalem (Gal. 2 = Acts 11), 13-14 years later	c. 46 (c. 47)

There remains of Paul's activity only the period of roughly 46-50 to be filled in, at least in tentative outline, the former figure an approximate construct, the latter relatively firm if our account of Paul at Corinth be accepted.[44] There are ostensibly the Pauline activities from Acts 12:25 to 17:34 to be fitted into this time, that is the sending of Barnabas and Saul from Antioch, the 'first missionary journey', the return to Antioch and the Jerusalem Conference, and the 'second journey' as far as the arrival at Corinth. That is an extremely rich and crowded programme, which gives an impression of occupying a lengthy period. This appearance is reinforced by such a computation as that contained in the tabulation in Jewett (pp. 59-61), which implies that the relevant segment of the 'second journey' alone took a minimum of about 21 months and at a more 'normal' pace nearly four years. But this scheme does not relate to the realities of the case. It involves a ('normal') reckoning of a year's mission in North Galatia, a supposition fuelled only by what is arguably a fundamental misunderstanding, and is in itself both gratuitous and highly improbable. With the removal of this year there fall away also several hundred kilometres of gratuitous travel and the weeks they are made to occupy. In fact many of the other time-spans are guesses, with no textual foundation. Thus the 'normal' version for the sojourn at Philippi is another year, whereas the evidence of the text is that Paul's departure was prematurely forced, and there is nothing which seems to require more than a truncated stay of a few weeks. An odd case is the mission in Troas (8 weeks 'normal'), for as Troas was situated in 'Asia' in the current provincial sense of that term, it was presumably comprehended in the ban on preaching in Asia. Whatever delay or indecision *was* involved at Troas, this is not warranted, and to bring a reference to Acts 20:6-12 in at this point only compounds the problem.[45]

---

[44] I cannot accept the view of Knox (*Chapters*, pp. 79, 82-83) which places Pauline travels to Macedonia and Achaia soon after 41, long before the Gallio correlation, while conceding probable accuracy to Acts in its geographical sequence (p. 79). M.J. Suggs, 'Concerning the Date of Paul's Macedonian Ministry', *NovT* 4 (1960), pp. 60-68, goes further in arguing from the wording of Phil. 1:5; 4:15-16; 2 Thess. 2:13 that Macedonia was the earliest scene of Paul's missionary endeavour. Suggs himself seems to admit the tenuousness of this 'possibility' (p. 68), while proceeding with considerable confidence to the rejection of other views.

[45] Jewett, pp. 58, 60. Apparently the references to Acts 20 here are meant to

In fact much of this lengthy scheme melts away under analysis.

There is a more basic objection. Jewett proceeds upon theoretical spans for the measurement of distances and the establishment of churches. But the text itself implies that some sections of these travels were in fact excessively hurried and that the harassment by opponents made the leisured teaching of converts impossible for Paul to attain. The occasion of the Thessalonian correspondence is to remedy deficiencies and misunderstandings consequent upon inadequate opportunity of initial teaching. The following visits of Paul's associates to Macedonia, and perhaps the leaving of the writer of the 'we-passages' at Philippi, are to be seen as a necessary pastoral follow-up where Paul himself had become prematurely *persona non grata*. There is also the impression of breathless haste, for whatever reason, in the rapid narrative of Acts 16:6-8. In fact this intensely interesting, dynamic account is not open to the kind of mechanical, theoretical calculation that Jewett offers, save as it follows textual specifics or cautions against reducing actual travel-times below a reasonable minimum.[46] It is likely for that matter that there are unspecified lengthenings of the time-scale latent elsewhere, a relatively immobile writer, for instance, alternating with an unexpectedly rapid long-distance transit by post-vehicle. Even on Jewett's own figures, the deletion of items like 6 months 'minimum' in North Galatia brings the total 'minimum' reckonings far below the traditional eighteen months.

While certainty here is not attainable, it is probable that this

indicate that a church already existed in Troas and must have been founded by Paul at this point. But Paul himself speaks of preaching in Troas, where he found an open door c. AD 55 (2 Cor. 2:12), perhaps following up the work of evangelists travelling there from his Ephesian residence. A key point here is the sense of the term 'Asia'. Epigraphical testimony to first century usage is abundant. The provincial sense seems to exclude mission there at the time of the ban in Acts 16, but to include it in the range of outreach in Acts 19:10. I should place the evangelization of Troas in the Ephesian period and its aftermath, on the concurrent evidence of 2 Corinthians and a different reading of Acts.

46 See generally Ramsay, 'Roads and Travel (in NT)', *HDB*, Extra Vol. (1904), pp. 375-402; L. Casson, *Travel in the Ancient World* (London: Allen and Unwin, 1974); for the speed of travel by sea, Casson, 'Speed under Sail of Ancient Ships', *TAPA* 82 (1951), pp. 136-48, and on land, Casson, *Travel*, p. 189. It is possible that on some occasions Paul had the advantage of horseback or of a vehicle. Such is probable at Acts 20:13, where πεζεύειν is not to be pressed in an etymological sense, and at 21:15-16, a possible implication of ἐπισκευάζεσθαι. High speeds were possible over shorter distances, and the imperial post was capable of fifty miles a day over many weeks (A.M. Ramsay, 'The Speed of the Roman Imperial Post', *JRS* 15 [1925], pp. 60-74), but emergency or record-breaking journeys which are occasionally recorded were not the norm, and the private traveller lacked the organized facilities of the official courier.

journey (15:36-17:34) occupied from the spring of one year to the autumn of the next: from spring 49 to arrival in Corinth in autumn 50. A new departure is generally made in spring, and a longer-term residence (with tentmaking) initiated by a wintering at the objective of a summer's travels, with shorter pastoral visits *en route*.[47]

By similar processes of reasoning, we suggest that the 'first journey' occupied the period from spring 47 to late summer or autumn 48 and that the Jerusalem Council took place in winter or early spring 48-49. A significant, if controversial, point is then the placing of the Epistle to the Galatians c. late 48. The circumcision controversy in Galatia followed hard upon Paul's first visit to South Galatia in 47-48. He had to write defending his apostleship and independent divine commissioning in radical terms, without yet being equipped with the Jerusalem agreement. The occasion of the letter occasioned also the Conference, and the latter enabled Paul to return to Galatia in 49 with evidence of the agreement and blessing of the Jerusalem leaders.[48]

We then have the summary, in this case tentative:

First Journey	c. 47-48
Epistle to the Galatians	c. late 48
Jerusalem Council	c. early 49
Second journey to Corinthian residence	Spring 49— Autumn 50

Thus it is possible to construct in outline a consistent Acts-based chronology as far as its abrupt conclusion in AD 62, with some prospect of fitting the occasions of at least some Pauline letters to its sequence. Some events cannot be closely placed. Some can be approximately or inferentially aligned with fixed points of greater or less certainty. Some references to Jewish feasts may even be linked to the

---

47 Again, the concept of assigning 'minimum' and 'normal' spans to such visits, which are not amenable to a mechanical reckoning, is questionable. Where Paul had a more distant objective, he was prepared to use whatever time he could afford *en route* however brief or extended.

48 It was his immediate task (at Acts 15:40-16:5) to encourage the churches and deliver the Jerusalem letter to the churches of (South) Galatia (16:4). This effectively closed a phase of the Judaistic controversy rather than the whole. There is no further indication in the NT of continuing controversy in Galatia, and the point over circumcision of Gentile converts may have been cleared up at this stage. But Paul himself evidently never applied the Jerusalem Decree to churches beyond Galatia, preferring at Corinth to base his case on loving consideration in the use of liberty rather than repeating prohibitions which might be applied legalistically, and a strong element in the Jerusalem church clearly remained wedded to the Law and suspected Paul personally of having betrayed his Jewish heritage. That appears clearly in the notably eirenic narrative of Acts (21:20-24). On such a view the Galatian phase, as recorded for us, was concluded by AD 50, for Galatians and the events of Acts 15 are placed before that date. If there were later difficulties in Galatia, the record of them is not preserved.

known phases of the moon in actual years, so that we might venture the computation that the Eutychus incident took place on the night of Sunday 24th April AD 57 and that Paul celebrated the 'Fast' (Yom Kippur) at Fair Havens on 5th October AD 59.[49] Such computations are in one sense trivial curiosities, and the grounds for them may of course be disputed, but they also illustrate the occasional possibilities of chronological reasoning, and are not without value in stressing the inherent 'reality' of our inquiry, as an argument irreducibly concerned with detailed factuality.

Dates of the Epistles

The foregoing outline essentially establishes a point of principle, that the Acts framework is deserving of respect, is at least internally self-consistent and opens the possibility of closer correlation with the epistles. It is no more than a framework, for it has omitted any account of many sections of Acts which are not directly material to questions of the lapse of time. In the process, the placings of some, but not of all, of the epistles have been indicated as they became involved in the piecing together of the chronological argument. This section contains first a summary of the views of the letters already discussed, and then an exploration of the prospects for enlarging the resultant picture to include the other epistles.

Galatians is placed as the earliest epistle, c. late 48.

The *Thessalonian* letters are placed in the immediate aftermath of Paul's first visit to Macedonia (Acts 16), and were apparently written from Corinth, soon after Paul's arrival there. It is an open question which was written first. The two may be dated c. 50-51.[50]

---

49   For Eutychus see originally W.M. Ramsay, 'A Fixed Date in the Life of St. Paul', *Expos* 5th ser. 3 (1896), pp. 336-45, a reckoning accepted in essentials by D. Plooij, *De Chronologie van het Leven van Paulus,* (which I have not seen), cited by Ogg, *Paul*, pp. 140-43, and tentatively accepted by Jewett, pp. 49-50. I have cited the calculation for the first day of the week at Troas rather than the departure from Philippi. Cf. also *Pauline Studies Bruce*, pp. 10-11. For the Fast see W.P. Workman, 'A New Date-Indication in Acts', *ExpT* 11 (1899-1900), pp. 316-19; cf. *TB* 36 (1985), pp. 106-107.

50   The authenticity of 2 Thessalonians has often been questioned, notably by C. Masson, *Les Deux Épitres de Saint Paul aux Thessaloniciens* (Neuchâtel and Paris: Delachaux et Niestlé, 1957), and frequently since. The central problem is the nature of the relation between the two Thessalonian Epistles, which has been variously addressed by positing a difference of destination or recipients, inversion of order, the inauthenticity of 2 Thessalonians, or the composite character of one or both letters. The canonical order rests on no more than length, and plausible reasons have been advanced for the priority of 2 Thessalonians. See the discussion in Bruce, *1 and 2 Thessalonians*, Word Bible Commentaries (Waco,

The *Corinthian* controversy and the letters it generated are to be located in the Ephesian residence or directly afterward, broadly in the span 52-56. More precise placings lie beyond the needs of our present case, as involving the critical problems of the number and sequence of letters. I incline to a four-letter sequence: a 'previous letter', 1 Corinthians, the 'severe letter', and an essentially unitary 2 Corinthians.[51] 1 Corinthians was written from Ephesus no later than early 55 and 2 Corinthians from Macedonia in 55-56.

Finally, in this group, *Romans* may be assigned to the period in Corinth before the last Jerusalem voyage, in about early 57.

The first question immediately raised about the epistles yet unplaced is the provenance of the four imprisonment epistles. Again the problems are complex. While Philippians and Philemon are widely accepted as authentic, Colossians is debated, and there is a strong body of opinion against Ephesians.[52] There is an open question whether some or all of these letters are from the same imprisonment or from the same stage even within the same imprisonment. The ostensible signs are indeed that Philippians fits a different situation from that which at least appears to unite Colossians, Ephesians and

---

Texas: Word Books, 1982), pp. xxxix-xliv, and, for a firmer advocacy of the priority of 1 Thessalonians, E. Best, *A Commentary on the First and Second Epistles to the Thessalonians* (London: A. & C. Black, 1972), pp. 42-45, who makes the interesting point that nobody who had then actually written a commentary on 2 Thessalonians had maintained its priority.

51 The marked difference of atmosphere between 2 Cor. 1-9 and 10-13 may well be explained by Paul's hesitancy to write in the personal terms of the latter chapters. This was not an easily or rapidly written letter. If there were delay and heart-searching over the adequacy of 1-9 and the possible effects of a more radical self-exposure, there may actually have been a time-lapse in the composition of the letter. The arguments for a later rather than an earlier 10-13 (cf. C.K. Barrett, *A Commentary on the Second Epistle to the Corinthians* [London: A. & C. Black, 1973], p. 21 and *passim*, e.g. p. 325 *ad* 12:18) may come near to falling together with the argument for essential unity. See also A.M.G. Stephenson, 'Partition Theories on II Corinthians', *SE* 2 (1964), pp. 639-46; W.H. Bates, 'The Integrity of II Corinthians', *NTS* 12 (1965-66), pp. 56-69. We cannot however endorse Bates's argument where he uses parallels with Galatians and Philippians which presuppose for them a nearness of date and setting to 2 Corinthians.

52 For arguments against authenticity see especially C.L. Mitton, *Ephesians*, New Century Bible (London: Marshall, Morgan and Scott, 1976), pp. 2-10; following his fuller investigation in *The Epistle to the Ephesians. Its Authorship, Origin and Purpose* (Oxford: Clarendon Press, 1951), pp. 7-44; for defence of Pauline authorship see E. Percy, *Die Probleme der Kolosser- und Epheserbriefe* (Lund: C.W.K. Gleerup, 1946); A. van Roon, *The Authenticity of Ephesians*, NovT Supp. 39 (Leiden: Brill, 1974). Mitton seems to influence strongly the trend of opinion despite the thorough response by van Roon.

Philemon. There are also three possible imprisonments to which these epistles have been variously assigned, a hypothetical captivity at Ephesus (c. 54-55),[53] and those at Caesarea (57-59)[54] and Rome (60-62).[55] Perhaps none of these epistles contributes significantly to the basic interlocking of a viable chronology, but there remains a question whether they can add to the resultant picture.

An Ephesian or a Caesarean provenance for any of the group does not seem feasible. The difficulty with Ephesus is that of positing, not an imprisonment as such, but the exceptional, prolonged detention required for the writing of these letters from a developing captivity situation. Imprisonment was commonly used either for the overnight lock-up of a trouble-maker (*coercitio*, cf. Acts 16:23, 35, at Philippi), or for those awaiting trial or execution.[56] Only in exceptional or irregular circumstances might one expect a prolonged captivity pending trial, as at Caesarea and Rome. Both were apparently forms of open arrest imposed by Roman authority, where the victim or his friends, not the state, bore the costs of his support. If at Ephesus Paul had fallen foul of civic authorities, they are unlikely to have had the occasion or facility to hold a prisoner for long. Exile, not imprisonment, was the likely penal sentence, and that would be the prerogative of the Roman governor. Paul evidently suffered some traumatic danger at Ephesus near the end of his residence, as he

---

53 See G.S. Duncan, *St. Paul's Ephesian Ministry* (London: Hodder, 1929); *id.*, 'Some Outstanding New Testament Problems: VI. The Epistles of the Imprisonment in Recent Discussion', *ExpT* 46 (1934-35), pp. 293-98; 'Important Hypotheses Reconsidered: VI. Were Paul's Imprisonment Epistles Written from Ephesus?' *ExpT* 67 (1955-56), pp. 163-66. Philippians is more usually attributed to Ephesus than the other Captivity letters. Thus notably W. Michaelis, *Der Brief des Paulus an die Philipper* (Leipzig: Diechert, 1935), and elsewhere. Cf. Guthrie *Introduction*, p. 531.

54 See B. Reicke, 'Caesarea, Rome, and the Captivity Epistles', *Apostolic History and the Gospel*, ed. Gasque and Martin, pp. 277-86, arguing for a Roman origin of Philippians and a Caesarean for the rest. L. Johnson, 'The Pauline Letters from Caesarea', *ExpT* 68 (1956-57), pp. 24-26 assigns all four (plus 2 Timothy) to the Caesarean imprisonment, but presupposes a dislocation in Acts, placing 28:30-31 after 24:26 and discounting the Roman διετία. J.A.T. Robinson, *Redating*, pp. 57-67, espouses a similar view, without following this dubious treatment of Acts. He also follows Johnson (*op cit.*) and Reicke, 'The Historical Setting of Colossians', *RevExp*, 70 (1973), pp. 429-38, in attributing 2 Timothy to Caesarea also.

55 This traditional view remains widely current. It may be argued that there are no decisive arguments for it, but it is relatively free of serious objections involved in the alternatives. Some who hold to a Roman origin of the other epistles incline to Ephesus in the case of Philippians.

56 Cf. P. Treves, 'Coercitio', *OCD*, p. 258; A. Berger, 'Prison', *OCD*, p. 879; T. Mayer-Maly, 'Carcer', *Kleine Pauly*, 1.1053-1054, citing Ulpian *Dig.* 48, 19.8.9: *carcer ad continendos homines, non ad puniendos haberi debet.*

plainly hints himself (1 Cor. 15:32; 2 Cor. 1:8-9), but if these events involved imprisonment, it was presumably a brief episode in a violent and dangerous context.[57] In the case of Caesarea the problem is rather one of psychological probability and travel conditions. The slave Onesimus might have run away from Colossae to the distant metropolis, or indeed to Ephesus as the nearest cosmopolitan port. But why should he have chosen Caesarea, unless actually to appeal to Paul against his master? That is not how the story is most naturally read. The state of a runaway slave was precarious and vulnerable, and he would surely have chosen anonymity rather than fall in the hands of a known associate of his master's. Only after a radical repentance in Onesimus did the basis exist for Paul to act as conciliator.[58] But there is a more positive consideration for Rome over Caesarea. The lines of communication developed in the imperial service linked the East with Rome, and Philippi, in particular, stood on the great land-route. The sequences of journeys implied by Philippians are more easily explained within the facilities offered by the presence of Christian couriers in the imperial service to and from Rome (cf. Phil. 4:22).[59] Routes and opportunity, rather than mere distance, are

---

57 There is nothing in any of these letters which suggests reference to Paul's trouble with the Corinthian church or to preparations for the Collection, concerns which might have been supposed prominent in the Ephesian period. Not much weight should be laid on such an *argumentum ex silentio*, though such silence is appropriate if the setting is actually different and later. The theological arguments from the development of Pauline thought, which are often given prominence in the discussion, are ambivalent. There is a constant danger of circularity if they are used in the attempt to establish a sequence from which development is then inferred.

58 I picture rather a fortuitous meeting in Rome with friends of Paul, with Onesimus initially unwilling and fearful. Aristarchus (Acts 20:4) and ostensibly Luke (ἡμᾶς, Acts 20:5) accompanied Paul to Jerusalem, and could have been in Caesarea, but they also accompanied him later to Rome (Acts 27:1-2). Demas was with Paul (Col. 4:14; Phlm. 24), but had deserted him at the writing of 2 Tim. 4:10, where a later Roman provenance is at least a plausible hypothesis. Mark was with Paul at Col. 4:10 and Phlm. 24; Timothy at Col. 1:1, Phlm. 1 and Phil. 1:1; but at 2 Tim. 4:11 they are urged to come together to Paul. There are many uncertainties and unknown movements of persons involved, but the balance of probabilities favour Rome, while differences suggest at least some distance in time from the widely accepted personal notes in 2 Timothy. For the seriousness of harboring a runaway slave cf. *P Oxy* 12.1422. The case in Pliny *Ep.* 9.21, 24 is that of a freedman.

59 This is the implication of the 'Saints of Caesar's household'. For the imperial post see A.M. Ramsay, *JRS* 15 (1925), pp. 60-74; O. Seeck, 'Cursus Publicus', *PW*, 4.1846-1863; E. Badian, 'Postal Service', *OCD*, p. 869. It is a point of special importance to observe that Augustus changed the system from relays of couriers

crucial factors, and they point to Rome. Travel elsewhere was more likely to depend on long delays in chartering a passage.

Personal details ostensibly link the occasions of Colossians, Philemon and Ephesians as against Philippians. The case of Colossians is of special chronological importance, for the city of Colossae was probably destroyed by earthquake in AD 60. This is the date given by Tacitus (*Ann.* 14.27) for the great earthquake at Laodicea, and later sources explicitly include mention of Colossae (Euseb. *Chron.* Olymp. 210; Orosius 7.7.12), though they also shift the date to AD 64. If this evidence is correctly understood, it provides a powerful argument for 60 as a *terminus ad quem* for the epistle, unless it be explained as inauthentic and perhaps only then if the attribution to Colossae can be accounted for.[60] If we accept a Pauline setting for it

---

to relays of horses so that a single emissary could travel this whole way in post-chaises (*vehicula*). See Suet. *Aug.* 49.3: *Commodius id visum est, ut qui a loco idem perferunt litteras, interrogari quoque, si quid res exigant, possint.* While conscientious officials might be sensitive about issuing licences (*diplomata*) for private use of the service (cf. Pliny *Ep.* 10.120), the persons employed were ideally placed to bear news to places on their route. Individuals in this employ covered some fifty miles a day with great regularity overland at most seasons to distant parts of the Empire. The journeys implied between Rome and Philippi were probably not all private and sequential, but part of a continuous passage of Christian intelligence by frequent travellers along the whole route. The argument for a dating late in the Roman imprisonment is actually not so strong on this score. *Enough* time is certainly needed, but the lengthy reckoning of consecutive journeys by Christian volunteers on foot is beside the point. This actually becomes a point in favour of Rome.

For *diplomata* in this sense cf. also Pliny *Ep.* 10.64; Suet. *Aug.* 50; Tac. *Hist.* 2.54, *CIL* 8.1027. Imperial freedmen *a diplomatibus* are mentioned in *CIL* 6.8622, 10.1727.

60 For discussion of the implications of this earthquake cf. J.B. Lightfoot, *Colossians and Philemon*, pp. 38-40. Lightfoot however reads the case rather differently, placing it in Paul's Roman captivity, but either before Eusebius' date in 64 or a sufficient distance after Tacitus' date. But he places the Roman διετία in 61-63 (*Philippians*, pp. 2-3), and later evidence calls for some adjustment of his chronology. It seems likely that the dating of the earthquake in Christian writers is coloured by a tradition making it one of a series of judgments on the pagan world for the Neronian persecution of 64. Tacitus' date is surely to be preferred, and thus fixes the actual year of the epistle. The involvement of neighbouring cities (Hierapolis, Tripolis) is independently indicated by *Or. Sib.* 5.317, 320 with 290-91. This important chronological datum has been unwarrantably neglected, or else invoked only to confirm in retrospect a critical evaluation of the epistle reached on different grounds (Lohse, *Colossians and Philemon*, p. 181). In denying authenticity Lohse makes no attempt to account for the address to a city meanwhile destroyed. There are indications of suffering throughout the district, followed by grandiose rebuilding at least at Laodicea. Evidence for Colossae however is so sparse generally that no special significance can be attached to the

on the lines suggested and assign it to Rome, however, it also can be no earlier than 60. Most likely, the group Colossians, Ephesians and Philemon belong to the first year of Paul's imprisonment, at least before news of the earthquake at an unknown date in that year had reached Rome. This suggestion may be checked against the personalia of these letters.[61] Philippians should be placed late in the same imprisonment, for the following reasons: (1) there are indications that a situation has had time to develop in the place of Paul's detention while he has been personally confined (Phil. 1:12-18); (2) the characteristic 'joy' of this epistle is set against a sense of impending crisis (Phil. 1:19-26), which could well fit a trial climax to the διετία of Acts 18:30; (3) the future plans are here conditional on the resolution of that crisis (Phil. 1:23-25, 27; 2:23-24), whereas in Phlm. 22 he seems to anticipate the prospect of a release; (4) if our contention is correct that Colossians is early in the Roman imprisonment and Philippians separated from it in the same imprisonment, this is at least consonant with a later placing of Philippians; (5) references to the πραιτώριον (Phil. 1:13) and the 'saints of Caesar's household' (Phil. 4:22), while arguably not peculiar even to a Roman provenance, lend themselves to more pointed explanation on this reconstruction;[62] (6) it is easier to accommodate the implication of multiple preceding journeys to and from Philippi if at least sufficient time is allowed.

Now if this tentative structure is correct, the implications are interesting, negatively and positively. There are no detailed correlations between these epistles and Acts beyond their simple placing in the period 60-62 marked by Acts 28:30. But that very placing is of importance for the further questions raised by the abrupt ending of Acts which will be pursued in a later chapter (pp. 381-87). In particular, if we are right in supposing that Philippians marks an approaching final crisis, it may hold clues at least to the options and expectations implicit in Paul's Roman trial.

There is in any case an authentic problem of Paul after Acts, even if it involves no more than the attempt to understand the implications of the last two verses of that book. If they imply only trial, condemnation and execution, the point still needs to be spelled out. But Paul had a sound case, and his expectations in Philippians are positive, if

absence of coins or inscriptions datable to the Flavian period.

61 Cf. n. 57 above. The clearest note of sequence is in the companionship and subsequent apostasy of Demas. Paul has with him in these early days of his captivity his ostensible voyage-companions Aristarchus and Luke, and his trusted associates Timothy and Mark are already with him, as later they are summoned again hard upon his arrest (2 Tim. 4:11).

62 See note number 58 above.

also coloured by uncertainty in the imminence of a life or death decision. The possibility that the Pastorals contain notes of Pauline activities subsequent to an acquittal and release is not to be discounted. It is ironical that a major historical objection to the Pastorals is that they cannot be fitted into the narrative of Acts while Acts itself is so often rejected where it does overlap with the 'primary' evidence of accepted epistles. Either contention of course poses a real question open to detailed critical appraisal, but it is clearly unsatisfactory to urge both simplistically together as part of an armoury of common assumptions. But if in fact the Pastorals belong to a period of Paul's life subsequent to the end of Acts, that is a sufficient reason for the silence of Acts. Recent renewed attempts to place the Pastorals, or some of their material, within the framework of Acts, are not successful. The question of the Pastorals is important in its place, but these letters (whether genuine or not) cannot contribute to our first chronological correlation of Acts with epistles because they lie beyond the limits of Acts. Whether they contribute to the further understanding of Paul in a different and later situation is another important question. But it is a different question, which lies beyond our immediate concern (see however chapter 9 below).

There are evident questions raised by this outline. A significant issue is that it involves a radical change of plan and perspective on Paul's part. His determination at the time of writing Romans had been not to build on another man's foundation, and in that spirit he had looked on Rome as a prospective stage on his way to a virgin territory in Spain (Rom. 15:20, 22-24). But in the Captivity Epistles his concerns are turned back to the prospect of revisiting his former scenes of labour in the East, and the personal notes contained in the Pastorals, if we may admit their evidence, show him again travelling there. This problem however also lies beyond Acts, and the change is present even in epistles generally accepted as authentic (Romans, Philippians, Philemon). It is in any case easier to suppose that Paul's strategy shifted in the longer perspective demanded by the Roman setting than in the Caesarean imprisonment. But we must defer the attempt to answer this question more specifically until the complex of questions surrounding the ending of Acts has been treated. The present sketch of the placing of the texts will serve as background for that discussion.

Chapter 7
Galatia and the Galatians

It is no part of the purpose of this study to offer any new reconstruction of the setting and destination of Paul's Epistle to the Galatians. The views presented here are not novel. We propose only to engage in a humbler task, a piecemeal testing of foundations. We shall be mainly concerned to present and discuss the evidence for the contemporary usage of the terms 'Galatia' and 'Galatians'. This is work that needs to be done, and progress will not be made until it is attempted. But the whole subject is far more complex and difficult than usually appears. We must work from the careful assessment of the debated interpretations of fragmentary data.

To illustrate the difficulty, we may picture the problems for scholars of the future posed by inconvenient fragments from our own world. Consider the case of the Latin inscription dated 1670 on the gate of the Royal Citadel in Plymouth, which reads simply: *Carolus Secundus, Dei Gratia Magnae Britanniae, Franciae et Hiberniae Rex.* What is this 'Great Britain?' Does the text point to the use of the term 'Britain' in a double sense, of a larger and a smaller territory? Is it for instance like 'Galatia' in having a wider political and a narrower ethnic sense? Or is the phrase like 'Great Phrygia', an inner area of Britain proper, as distinguished from a secondary or appended territory? Then there is an acute problem over 'France'. Other contemporary documents contradict this stone absolutely, and represent one Louis XIV as king of France throughout this period.

The older Latin name for that land was *Gallia*, and the first-century Greek was Γαλατία. It is extraordinary that the Augustan Empire contained two important territories whose names were identical in the Greek of the day. In the temple of Rome and Augustus at Ancyra (Ankara), the official capital of the eastern 'Galatia' (and in 'Galatia' in its strictest and narrowest 'Northern' sense) is still preserved the *Monumentum Ancyranum*, the most perfect copy of the *Res Gestae* of Augustus.[1] In that text the word 'Galatia' appears five times, and four times without any qualifying

1 IGRR 3.159. The text is also conveniently accessible in V. Ehrenberg and A.H.M. Jones, *Documents Illustrating the Reigns of Augustus and Tiberius* (OUP, 2nd edn, 1955), pp. 2-31.

epithet. Does it refer to North Galatia only, or does it include the whole provincial entity? Neither. Either the context or the Latin version *Gallia* makes it clear that it means 'Gaul' every time, yet only once is it thought necessary to add τῇ περὶ Ναρβῶνα.[2] We should never have known that an eastern Galatia existed at all from this classic document remaining *in situ* in its provincial capital. A Roman document was simply reproduced mechanically, without regard for the different perspective of its local readers.

This matter of usage must then be approached cautiously, with a careful effort to assess the available pattern of evidence in its representative context. There is no place for far-reaching arguments from silence.

As has been stated in Chapter 6 above, we maintain a view of the Galatian problem which embodies a synthesis of three elements: (1) a South Galatian destination of the epistle; (2) an early, pre-Jerusalem Council dating of the epistle; (3) a straightforward identification of the visits to Jerusalem, Acts 9 with Gal. 1, Acts 11 with Gal. 2, Acts 15 being later than the epistle. These three elements have been maintained in conjunction by F.F. Bruce and D. Guthrie,[3] among others. We presuppose here the essentials of their argument, but also to go a little beyond them in emphasizing the connection between the three elements. Together they give a simple interlocking picture, into which the data of Acts and Galatians alike contribute. Certainly this simple picture bristles with difficulties. This ground is chosen, not because it is without difficulties, but because it gives the most probable and economical reconstruction. On other views we may find ourselves confronted by other problems, perhaps of our own making, while missing those which are ostensibly present.

As we have shown, the integration of the journey accounts is not the crucial embarrassment it might be thought.[4] Nor is there a crucial difficulty in the dating from the theological affinities of Galatians with the Corinthian and Roman epistles, if only because Paul's thinking on the central issues involved is likely to have matured before his earliest epistles, and similar formulations are likely to have recurred throughout his ministry as occasion

---

[2] Without qualification in chaps. 12, 25, 26, 29; with the qualification in 28, a passage listing the areas where Augustus had established military colonies. The location of the colonies on the Southern frontier of the Asiatic Galatia is here termed 'Pisidia'.

[3] Cf. Bruce, 'Galatian Problems' published in *BJRL* 51-55, especially the second 'North or South Galatians?', 52 (1969-70), pp. 243-66; Guthrie, *Introduction*, (3rd edn, 1970), pp. 450-66.

[4] I have proposed some of these ideas in the previous chapter, pp. 248-49. See also my 'Acts and Galatians Reconsidered', *Themelios* n.s. 2 (1976-77), pp. 81-88.

required.5 If there is an acute difficulty here, it is not so much in problems of harmonization or of theological development, but in the previous chronology of Paul's hidden years. The early date gives just enough time for a plausible sequence of events, but there are several problems which would bear close scrutiny.6

This brief statement will serve to clarify my position. The early dating is at once a strength and a focus of problems, but the Southern destination is the real key, on whose acceptance the feasibility of the simple synthesis really hinges. This is just where we confront the complex questions of ancient usage. The present study will attempt to formulate the evidence and to answer a few common confusions and misunderstandings. We shall argue for a firm acceptance of the South Galatian view, but not without great caution in treating the fragmentary data on which such a view must in the last resort be based. There is no justification for giving evidence more weight than it will bear or for discounting difficulties.

The question is one of finding the balance of the argument. The North Galatian view often maintains its status by denial. On that view, it becomes necessary to insist upon particular interpretations of controverted verses, where the 'Southern' alternative permits greater flexibility, whether or not one wishes to press a particular narrower option. Again, there are North Galatian arguments whose force derives from their integration with views about date or occasion which conflict with the synthesis outlined here. There is then a danger of non-communication between polarities. The debate tends to resolve itself again into one about the viability of alternative syntheses.

We shall conduct our argument in two stages. First we shall clear the ground by answering a number of particular objections, and second, we shall review various aspects of the evidence for the usage of the terms 'Galatia' and 'Galatian'.

---

5   Cf. J.W. Drane, 'Theological Diversity in the Letters of St. Paul', *TB* 27 (1976), pp. 3-26; *contra* J.B. Lightfoot, *Galatians* (10th edn, 1896), pp. 42-50, and C. Buck, *et al.*, *Saint Paul: A Study of the Development of His Thought* (New York: Scribner, 1969), who have argued strongly for a date close to the Roman and Corinthian epistles from theological affinity. See also F.F. Bruce in his fourth Rylands lecture, 'The Date of the Epistle', *BJRL* 54 (1971-72), pp. 250-67.

6   Such are the calculation of the periods of three and fourteen years (Gal. 1:18; 2:1) with relation to the likely date of Paul's conversion and the lapse of time available after the likely date of the Crucifixion. See above, pp. 262-63 where we have discussed the problem and and mentioned the works of J. van Bruggen (*Na Veertien Jaren* [Kampen: J.H. Kok, 1973]), my 'Observations on Pauline Chronology' (*Pauline Studies Bruce*, pp. 3-18), and D.R. de Lacey, 'Paul in Jerusalem' (*NTS* 20 [1974], pp. 82-86).

1. Objections Considered

We shall here meet the objections largely as presented by Moffatt.[7] While P.W. Schmiedel's treatment is more rigorous, it is largely a detailed criticism of positions other than the one proposed here, and furthermore is approached from the assumption of a systematically different synthesis.[8] Moffatt states his objections plainly in a form amenable to reply.

(1) The first objection is from an earlier writer, S. Cheetham, who goes to the fundamentals of the case. He questions whether the province as a whole was ever called 'Galatia', rather than 'the Galatic province', or being designated by the listing of component territories of a jurisdiction which came under the primacy of Galatia.[9]

There are problems of real substance here to which the latter part of this study will be addressed, but Cheetham's forms of the objection may be more easily disposed of. He complains that Ramsay never tells us the Latin or Greek title of the governor of the whole entity. In Latin it was *Legatus (Augusti) pro praetore provinciae Galatiae*.[10] In Greek this appears as πρεσβευτὴς (καὶ) ἀντιστράτηγος ἐπαρχείας Γαλατίας, but the names of the other component territories of the locality are commonly added.[11] This constitutes the particular difficulty to which we must return.

Cheetham further objects that if inscriptions with such titles were found in the extremities of the territories additional to Galatia, they would actually 'afford ... a slight presumption' that these territories 'were not included in a province called Galatia'; we should expect reference merely to 'governor "of this province" or "of our province"'.

In fact this kind of reference is also easily supplied. One could cite a list of examples which incorporate dating in the form ἐπὶ τῆς ἡγεμονίας (τοῦ δεῖνος) or ἐπὶ (τοῦ δεῖνος) πρεσβευτοῦ, or which refer to a governor as *Leg. Aug. pr. pr.* or πρεσβευτὴς (καὶ) ἀντιστράτηγος

---

7 J. Moffatt, *An Introduction to the Literature of the New Testament* (Edinburgh: T. & T. Clark, 3rd edn, 1918) esp. pp. 90-101.

8 *EB* 2, cols. 1596-1616.

9 'The Province of Galatia', *CR* 8 (1894), p. 396.

10 E.g. *CIL* 3.254, of Ancyra, undated.

11 E.g. *IGRR* 3.316, of Pisidian Apollonia, where 'Pisidia' and 'Paphlagonia' are added to 'Galatia'. It has been said that Greek sources only and exclusively describe the province by a listing of its component parts. See however *IGRR* 3.181, of Ancyra, undated, and of the phrase 'Galatic province' (*IGRR* 3.263, of Iconium, AD 54), on which see further below. A good example of the enumeration in Latin is in *CIL* 3 Supp. 1.6818.2-7), of Pisidian Antioch: *leg. Aug. pro pr. provinc. Gal. Pisid. Phryg. Luc. Isaur. Paphlag. Ponti Galat(ici) ponti Polemoniani Arm(eniae)*: *Luc. sic* for L(y)c(aoniae).

without provincial name expressed. These are drawn from Canna, Salarama and Psibela, all in Lycaonia, and from Iconium, Pappa, and the Isaurian country, a list of places all belonging to South Galatia, and in texts referring in most cases to men independently known to have held office in the province of Galatia.[12]

Finally Cheetham comments on the lengthy territorial lists that 'it is not ... usual in the "lapidary" style to use needless amplification'.[13] In fact, however, that is *precisely* the nature of this style. The accumulation of titles and verbiage is highly characteristic. Thus the objection is not well taken, but there is a real question of usage here which will claim attention later. Why should the inscriptions resort so often to listing 'Galatia, Phrygia, Paphlagonia, etc.', if everybody knew that mere 'Galatia' was the name of the whole province?

(2) Moffatt's first pair of objections concerns the sequence of narrative in Acts 16:6, and may be considered briefly (Moffatt, *Introduction*, pp. 92-93). (a) He argues that Acts 16:6 marks a fresh departure, and is not a recapitulation of 16:1-4, as Ramsay would make it. But Ramsay changed his mind and contradicted himself on this point (as Schmiedel noticed), and Ramsay's second view in fact meets the objection.[14] Verse 1 brought the narrative to Derbe and Lystra, and verse 6 continues the progress into the district denoted by the notorious phrase τὴν Φρυγίαν καὶ Γαλατικὴν χώραν, which on Ramsay's view includes Iconium and Pisidian Antioch, and constitutes a perfectly natural sequence. (b) Moffatt objects that κωλυθέντες cannot be a participle of subsequent action. Here, in F.H. Chase's phrase, 'The South Galatian theory ... is shipwrecked on the rock of Greek grammar'.[15] But recent studies of the Greek aorist, especially by K.L.

---

12 T. Callander in *Studies in the History and Art of the Eastern Provinces of the Roman Empire* (ed. W.M. Ramsay), p. 162, No. 18 (Canna, AD 106-107); pp. 172-75, Nos. 56, 58 (milestones of Salarama and of Psibela, both AD 198); *IGRR* 3.262 (Iconium, Augustan); 3.1469 (Pappa, Trajanic); *CIL* 3.288 (Isauria, under Claudius). Cf. also *IGRR* 3.125, of Comana in Cappadocia, which refers to a πρεσβευτὴς καὶ ἀντιστράτηγος, without provincial name, the man being known from coins both of Ancyra in Galatia and of Caesarea in Cappadocia to have been governor of the double province in 78-80, shortly after the amalgamation of these two territories by Vespasian. The formulation 'our province' seems not to be used, though *noster* is sometimes found in the phrase '*legatus* of our emperor'.

13 'The Province of Galatia', *CR* 8 (1894), p. 396, although he admits to only having done a 'small observation'.

14 Schmiedel, *EB* 2, cols. 1597-1598. Ramsay changed his wording on this point in later editions of *CRE*. Contrast e.g. *CRE*, 1st edn, 1893, p. 77 with the 7th edn, 1903, p. 77.

15 F.H. Chase, 'The Galatia of the Acts', *Expos* 4th ser. 8 (1893), p. 411. But there are alternative views on the South Galatian side here as well: some would

McKay, have challenged the traditional Latin-based formulations of its use.[16] The element of time-sequence is less rigid and less prominent than has been supposed. Indeed, the prevalence of 'aspect' over 'time' in the use of the aorist, and its participle in particular, may be illustrated from examples in Luke's own usage in Acts.[17] In a sequence so ordered as this one, we may *most naturally* take κωλυθέντες as a natural contraction for καὶ ἐκωλύθησαν. McKay does not discuss this verse, but cites several New Testament passages which illustrate the like principle in the treatment of aorist participles.[18]

(3) Moffatt brings a threefold objection against the South Galatian reading of the geographical phrase in Acts 16:6 (*Introduction*, p. 93). The three points are nearly variant statements of the same contention, but will take answering in all three guises. He maintains that τὴν Φρυγίαν καὶ Γαλατικὴν χώραν cannot denote 'Phrygia Galatica' because (a) Φρυγίαν is not an adjective, (b) καί does not mean 'or', and (c) the phrase 'denotes not one district but two'. He does not offer any

understand from the aorist participle that the prohibition had been received previously, and include this possibility in their reconstruction of events. So e.g. F.F. Bruce, *BJRL* 52 (1969-70), p. 257, suggesting that the prohibition was communicated at Lystra.

[16] K.L. McKay, 'Syntax in Exegesis', *TB* 23 (1972), pp. 39-57, and in later studies focusing on aspect in the Greek verb, e.g. 'Aspect in Imperatival Constructions in New Testament Greek', *NovT* 27 (1985), pp. 201-26; cf. F. Stagg, 'The Abused Aorist', *JBL* 91 (1972), pp. 222-31. On the aorist participle in particular cf. W.F. Howard, 'On the Futuristic Use of the Aorist Participle in Hellenistic', *JTS* 24 (1923), pp. 403-406; A.T. Robertson, 'The Aorist Participle for Purpose in the Κοινή', *JTS* 25 (1924), pp. 286-89; C.R. Harding, 'Subsequent Action Expressed by the Aorist Participle', *TAPA* 57 (1926), proceedings, p. xxxix [with valuable examples]; G.M. Lee, 'The Aorist Participle of Subsequent Action (Acts 16, 6)?' *Biblica* 51 (1970), pp. 235-37. Two points here seem worth particular note: (1) that aspect is of cardinal importance in the present/aorist distinction; (2) that the aorist should be treated as aspectually neutral rather than 'punctiliar' so that care is needed not to overtranslate its implications. Similar considerations apply conversely to the usage of the present participle of antecedent but linear action (e.g. Acts 14:21); see further H.G. Meecham, 'The Present Participle of Antecedent Action—Some New Testament Instances', *ExpT* 64 (1952-53), pp. 285-86.

[17] The instances merit extensive study and may be classified in several distinct categories, though many examples are indecisive. Thus some aorist participles are best taken as defining the action of the main verb (e.g. Acts 7:24; 10:33, 39), others as concurrent, like διακρίναντα in Acts 11:12, and the participles in 11:13, or else time sequence may simply not be in point (7:27, 39, etc.). A striking case of the participle of subsequent action is κατήντησαν εἰς Καισάρειαν ἀσπασάμενοι τὸν Φῆστον (25:13), where the early evidence is overwhelming against the variant –όμενοι (cf. Metzger, *Textual Comm.*, p. 492).

[18] A striking, if perhaps anomalous, example (of an adjectival instance) is ὁ καὶ παραδοὺς αὐτόν in Mt. 10:4, which refers to Judas's *subsequent* act of betrayal.

argument for these three denials, though he cites some assumed, though debatable, parallels for the views he prefers.

On (a), the adjectival use of 'Phrygia', Kirsopp Lake wrote: 'Φρύγιος ... was "of three terminations" in earlier Greek, but Lucian uses it as of only two, and I know of no instance of the nominative with the feminine termination in Greek contemporary with the New Testament'.[19] Haenchen proceeds from this denial syllogistically: 'ἡ Φρυγία *therefore* is a noun ... Γαλατικὴ χώρα is *therefore* a second country named beside Phrygia' [my italics].[20] This second country he interprets without further ado as 'North' Galatia.

But there are examples of Φρυγία as a feminine adjective or ethnic, from Pseudo-Aristotle, Apollodorus, Strabo, Dio Chrysostom, Pollux, Alciphron, Arrian, Aelian, Athenaeus, Diogenes Laertius, Pseudo-Lucian and the Sibylline Oracles, and in inscriptions from Athens, Delphi, Ephesus, Erythrae, Rhodes, Lindos and Camirus, and from Panticapaeum in the Crimea, dating from almost every period from Alexander to the 4th century AD, and the published list might now be extended.[21] Might the misleading entry in *LSJ* be responsible for the 'inability' of these scholars to find such examples?

On (b), the contention that καί does not mean 'or', we may refer simply to a note containing examples of such a usage, and entitled 'Καί Meaning "Or"', published twenty years *before* Moffatt's work and dealing with this very passage; this was written by Ramsay in anticipation of this possible criticism, long before the unhappy controversy between the two men.[22] One may understand Ramsay's later frustration at having to face the recurrence of criticisms which took no account of answers already offered. In fact, it seems unnecessary to insist on the rendering 'or' here, as discussion of the next point will attempt to show.

(c) is really the crux of the matter. Here Moffatt is too rigid. The whole formulation of the case is questionable, although we must also be careful not to fall into a converse fallacy which interprets too mechanically a pair of items bound by a common article. There are varied examples to suggest that the relationship in such pairs may be of more than one kind. The items may be synonymous or alternative

---

19 BC 5.231.

20 *Acts*, p. 483.

21 'The Adjective "Phrygia"', *JTS* n.s. 27 (1976), pp. 122-26 and 'Phrygia: A Further Note', *JTS* n.s. 28 (1977), pp. 99-101.

22 'Καί Meaning "Or"', *CR* 12 (1898), pp. 337-41. The controversy between the two men stemmed from Ramsay's unfortunate publication *The First Christian Century: Notes on Dr Moffatt's Introduction to the Literature of the New Testament* (London: Hodder, 1911).

designations, or the names of the component or overlapping parts of an entity, or simply a pair which are for some reason being considered together. The usage is no more rigid than is the relationship between items compounded or hyphenated. This καί may well be nearer an English hyphen than an English 'or'. It is enough to say that the phrase naturally denotes something conceived as one rather than two units. Here Moffatt's examples actually confirm this against him. He cites κατὰ τὴν Κιλικίαν καὶ Παμφυλίαν (Acts 27:5), but without the context which shows that the phrase qualifies adjectivally the *singular* articular noun πέλαγος (τὸ πέλαγος τὸ κατά...). It is *one* sea bordering the continuous shore of what we should now term 'the south coast of Turkey'. Likewise 'Macedonia and Achaia' (Acts 19:21) comprise the unity which we (and the ancients) recognize as 'Greece'. This point might be extensively illustrated.[23] It is noteworthy that Lightfoot agreed with Ramsay on the adjectives and the common article, but Lightfoot's difficulty lay in the geographical interpretation, which in his day was not yet clarified.[24]

(4) Moffatt says that 'the terminology ... really supports the North Galatian interpretation' (*Introduction*, p. 93). He derives this judgment directly from the simple assertion that Luke's phrase 'the Galatic region' (as distinct from Φρυγίαν) emphasizes a new departure and denotes 'the district inhabited by the Galatians proper', whereas 'Galatia' was ambiguous and might have referred to the province.

That, of course, is just the question, and will lead to our final section. It is a matter which can only be settled by the appeal to actual usage, and of this Moffatt says nothing. A phrase from Arrian is sometimes cited as a parallel: ἐπ' Ἀγκύρας τῆς Γαλατικῆς (*Anab.* 2.4.1). But the force of the epithet here is to distinguish 'the Galatic Ancyra' from the other Ancyra in Asian Phrygia (cf. Strabo 12.5.2 = 567). It functions like the use of the epithet in the well attested phrase 'Pontus Galaticus'. Compare conversely the phrase in Galen

---

23 There is an interesting instance where Josephus is describing the war between Herod Antipas and Aretas IV: τὰ ... περὶ τὴν Ἰουδαίαν καὶ Ἀραβίαν (*Ant.* 16.9.4.297), which might be freely rendered 'the Arab-Israeli conflict'. Cf. also Gal. 1:4. For the use of καί between the elements of a pair note also the random variation in the Greek renderings of Roman double-barrelled titles: πρεσβευτὴς (καὶ) ἀντιστράτηγος Πόντος (καὶ) Βιθυνία. For the dangers implicit in too absolute an interpretation of the pair with common article (the so-called 'Granville Sharp rule') see further Carson, *Exegetical Fallacies*, pp. 84-86 and examples cited there.

24 Lightfoot, *Galatians* (10th edn, 1890), p. 22n.; *Colossians and Philemon* (3rd edn, 1879), p. 23n. Schmiedel, *EB* 2, col. 1594 concurs that Φρυγίαν is an adjective, though he differs from both Lightfoot and Ramsay in his interpretation of the phrase.

describing Dorylaeum as ἐσχάτῃ τῆς Ἀσιανῆς Φρυγίας.[25]

(5) A group of Moffatt's objections is directed towards problems of the historical reconstruction.[26] Thus he notes that the Galatians seem to have been unaware of the controversy and decree in Jerusalem, and this would suit the supposed new converts of North Galatia rather than the more established churches of the South. But if we date the letter before the events in Jerusalem had happened, the Galatians could not have heard of them. This and similar objections are not in fact communicating with the effective alternative. They presuppose a reconstruction which the alternative does not share.

(6) The compromise suggestion is occasionally made that Paul might have touched the western edge of North Galatia in a substantially South Galatian mission in Acts 16:6. Such a 'pan-Galatian' view is less than convincing. It seems a gratuitous attempt to combine two different interpretations of the phrase. Moffatt's commendation of it as an attempt 'to do justice to the plain sense of Acts 16:6' (p. 92) is somewhat surprising, for that sense is highly debatable, and Moffatt has simply passed over the geographical problems of its interpretation. This view would need a convincing working out in terms of geography and of chronology. There is no special merit in combining, or in splitting the difference between, two readings of the evidence if the resulting picture does not integrate convincingly with either. We are dealing with essentially exclusive alternatives.

F.F. Bruce has correctly questioned the geographical reconstruction of Paul's route by Lake, who made of the phrase a territory 'in which sometimes Phrygian and sometimes Gaelic was the language

---

25 Galen, *de Aliment. Facult.* 1.13.10 = 515, ed. K. Koch *et al.* in the series *Corpus Medicorum Graecorum*, Volume 5.4.2 (Berlin: Teubner, 1923). For 'Pontus Galaticus' see Ptol. *Geog.* 5.2, 5.4 (though the region was in Ptolemy's day known as Cappadocia). He lists the Asian Ancyra as Ἄγκυρα Φρυγίας, and includes it among the cities of 'Phrygia Magna'. Ramsay however, in *CRE*, 7th edn (1903), pp. 79, 81, goes beyond evidential support in supposing that the adjective Γαλατικός was not applicable at all to North Galatia and that this involves in Acts 16:6 an assertion that Paul did not traverse North Galatia. There is in this an element of the dogmatically negative against which Ramsay himself more often protests. The adjective simply corresponds to the noun Γαλατία, and may presumably be used of any appropriate application of that name.

26 See the authorities cited by Moffatt, *Introduction*, p. 92. For a comparable view held at one stage by Kirsopp Lake cf. the next note. Moffatt's specific criticism is that the 'pan-Galatian' view fails to bring out 'the evident homogeneity' of Paul's Galatian churches. But the real difficulties are more fundamental, and while they certainly seem likely to have been a group subjected to similar legalistic influences on Paul's departure, it is not clear that their 'homogeneity' is to be a rigid critical axiom.

of the villagers'.[27] There is an incidental point of terminology: the Celtic of Galatia was 'P-Celtic', and certainly not Gaelic. More to the point— the surviving indications suggest quite a different language distribution, with a precise territorial limit of Phrygian.[28] Lake suggests a route through Laodicea Combusta, Amorium and Orcistus ('surely a Gaelic place') to Nacolea and perhaps Dorylaeum. But the roads, so far as we may know them, do not align these places, and the focal part of this progress, where he presumably locates the 'Gaelic' speakers, through Amorium and 'Gaelic' Orcistus, does not help his case at all. Both places, and the viable routes to and through them, lie in proconsular Asia, and not in Galatia in any sense whatever of that term.[29] It will suffice to follow Bruce in quoting Sir W.M. Calder: why should Paul have made a detour to visit such a district 'unless he had a prophetic vision of what Lake was going to say in the fullness of time, and some interest in proving him right?'[30]

(7) Many of Moffatt's arguments are couched in the form of answers to South Galatian counter-objections. Some of them are arguments from silence, in particular the silence of Acts. There is no evidence that circumcision was a major issue before Acts 15. Again, if Luke had regarded Derbe, Lystra and the rest as 'belonging to Γαλατία proper, it is inexplicable why the name should not occur in Ac 13-14' (Moffatt, *Introduction*, p. 93). There is no mention in Acts of the illness of Gal. 4:13, and no mention in Galatians of such persecution or suffering as implied by Acts 13-14 (Moffatt, *Introduction*, p. 99). But, of course, there is no compelling reason why any of these things should have been mentioned. There is certainly no unnecessary emphasis in either writer on Paul's personal sufferings.

Moffatt actually regards what he calls 'one of the most plausible

---

27 Bruce in *BJRL* 52 (1969-70), pp. 256-58, citing Lake in *BC* 5.236.

28 See W.M. Calder, 'The Boundary of Galatic Phrygia', *MAMA* 7 pp. ix-xvi, and his sketch-map of the extent of the language remains (p. xlvi). The total area of ethnic Phrygia includes districts west and south-west of the limits of the Neo-Phrygian texts, notably the cosmopolitan Lycus valley, and is defined by a characteristic style of art, by the typical house-tombs or door-tombs, and by a characteristic epichoric nomenclature, which all divide this territory sharply, especially on the south and east from the styles and onomastics of adjacent Pisidia and Lycaonia, both of which show rather South Anatolian affinities. See generally L. Zgusta, *Kleinasiatische Personennamen*. The division of this Phrygian area between the provinces of Asia and Galatia is now likewise becoming progressively better defined.

29 See W.M. Calder and G.E. Bean, *A Classical Map of Asia Minor* (London: British Institute of Archaeology at Ankara, 1957). On Orcistus, cf. p. 291, n. 41 below.

30 Bruce, *BJRL* 52 (1969-70), p. 258, citing a personal letter from Calder, dated 18 February 1953.

pleas' for South Galatia (*Introduction*, p. 96), the greater prominence in Acts of the South Galatian mission, as itself another argument from silence, which he counters by the assumed North Galatian references of Acts 16:6 and 18:23, 1 Cor. 16:1 and 1 Pet. 1:1. But this begs the question so far as these passages are concerned: I have argued elsewhere for a primarily 'East Galatian' view of 1 Peter.[31] We must insist that the alternative in our present discussion is a positive one, involving the positive correlation of Galatians with Acts 13-14.

(8) Moffatt directs his own reply largely towards a group of South Galatian arguments which are not at issue here. References to Barnabas, the implication of Gal. 2:5 for the early existence of the Galatian churches, the absence of North Galatians from the presumed delegate-list of Acts 20:4, the arguments about the backward character of North Galatia and its lack of Greek culture, all these and their like are questionable, and Moffatt is justified in pointing out their indecisiveness. But they do not touch the heart of the debate in any case. Arguments about 'fickle Gauls' or 'pitiless Phrygians' are valueless, as Moffatt rightly says (*Introduction*, p. 99). Yet he sees local colour himself in a supposed allusion in Gal. 6:17 to the custom of marking slaves by scars and cuts, 'which was notoriously a practice of the North Galatians'. He refers here to Ramsay, but Ramsay in fact argues that the practice was specifically Asiatic, and not Gaulish;[32] no weight can really be attached to the point.

(9) The South Galatian argument from Paul's evangelistic strategy is of some value. It is an oversimplification to argue merely that Paul sought out important centres, for Lystra and Derbe were not. But Moffatt is too quick to discount the argument, presenting it in a caricatured, absolutized form.[33] This matter underlines the need for a

---

31 'The Address of 1 Peter', *ExpT* 89 (1977-78), pp. 239-43, esp. p. 241. There is in my view no specific evidence in the NT for the evangelization of North Galatia, and indeed in 1 Peter, while the early position of Galatia in the list may be due to Silvanus' prospective arrival in the eastern extension Pontus Galaticus, the churches primarily addressed may actually have been those otherwise known in South Galatia. This is not to say that North Galatia was untouched by the earliest Christian mission, only that we are not compelled to apply any of our NT allusions specifically to it, even if any existing churches there may be implicitly included in the 1 Peter reference.

32 Moffatt, *Introduction*, p. 99, citing Ramsay, *Hist. Comm. Galatians*, pp. 82-84.

33 Moffatt, *Introduction*, p. 99, builds excessively on the relative unimportance of Derbe and Lystra, which 'were quite second-rate cities, with very little in common between them and the Roman world' (that is oddly and incautiously put, for Lystra was, in fact, a Roman colony). Ramsay himself registers surprise at Paul's going to Lystra (*Cities of St Paul*, p. 408). Moffatt continues however: 'Since he did evangelise such places, we may perhaps be spared the argument

careful and critical reconstruction of the journeys, their sequences, routes and purposes. The whole narrative merits realistic explanation in detail. Reasons may be offered for Paul's exceptional visits to lesser centres without thereby invalidating the assumption that he followed an intelligible strategy whose direction we may hope to unravel.

(10) Moffatt offers an application of his view to the complex problem of the relationship between Acts and Galatians. On the subject of the Jerusalem visits he is brief, maintaining that certain forms of the South Galatian hypothesis succeed in evading the difficulties, but only by conjectural alteration of the order of narratives in Gal. 2:1-10 and 11-16. He then moves directly to the question of the Council of Jerusalem, where he offers his reconstruction on the basis of the assumed identification of Gal. 2:1-10 with Acts 15. He does not argue for this in detail, indeed he accepts it, despite differences of a kind which he thinks fatal to the identification with Acts 11.[34] And there is no need for any transposition of Gal. 2 on the South Galatian side; indeed, the occasion for it only arises on the Acts 15 identification which we have argued should be rejected. This was another point on which Ramsay changed his mind: the criticism is not applicable to the

---

that North Galatia would have been beneath his notice'; he was an evangelist with 'a passion for the regions beyond'. But this is not the argument. Nobody is suggesting that Paul despised North Galatia, only that we have no warrant for supposing he ever went there. Moffatt omits to observe that his coming to Lystra was enforced (Acts 14:5-6) or to note Ramsay's explanation of this move as to a 'refuge'. The immediate motive may have been no more than seeking the nearest different jurisdiction, pending perhaps no more than a change of annual magistrates in Iconium. If Lystra and Derbe were on a major road, a stop there becomes perfectly understandable. It seems clear not only that Paul saw reaching 'the regions beyond' in strategic terms, working out from major centres, subject to the necessities of travel and the closures and changes engendered by opponents, but also that he fulfilled this mission with flexibility and with an eye to the needs of the churches and of those among whom unpremeditated moves brought him.

34 'This hypothesis is not wrecked by the patent difference of motive noticed in the two narratives', whereas 'the object of the two visits in Ac 11:27-30 and Gal. 2:1-10 is different' (Moffatt, *Introduction*, p. 100). Nor do I wish to change the order of Gal. 2:1-10 and 11-16. Moffatt's allusion to the identification with Acts 11 as 'a view which has found favour with several South Galatian advocates in their *manipulation* of the Lucan narratives' (*Introduction*, p. 102, my italics) is an unworthy and inappropriate charge. It is precisely the point that this identification, whatever its difficulties, is born of the attempt to take the integration of the evidence straightforwardly. Nor is the prior position of Galatians in Marcion's list of the Pauline letters a matter of any relevance whatever. If Moffatt (*Introduction*, pp. 102-103) means to imply that it is a bad reason for dating Galatians early, he is of course correct, but the advocate would neither wish nor need to use it.

matured form of the South Galatian view.[35]

A word of summing up on Moffatt's argument: we have tried to give him his own say before offering any general evaluation of his contribution. There seem to be many places where his work is vitiated by a looseness of statement. This applies particularly to his countering of South Galatian arguments. It leads him to speak of 'the province of Northern Galatia' and of 'the northern province', and to treat Corinth and Achaia as independent entities (*Introduction*, pp. 97, 98, 96 respectively). The occurrence of numerous slips of this kind is a serious matter where the argument turns on fine points of usage. He also writes: 'On both sides, but especially on the S. Galatian, there is too great a tendency to tamper with the text of Acts in order to bring it into line with the requirements of a theory' (*Introduction*, p. 99). I should neither wish nor need to adopt any such expedient, nor do I accept any of the inferior readings he cites as examples of this tendency. On the central topic of our next section he writes: 'The title *Galatians* (Gal. 3:1) is alleged to be more suitable to the inhabitants of Southern Galatia than to those of N. Galatia' (*Introduction*, p. 95). But no one would want to say that it was '*more* suitable'. No doubt a northern Celtic-speaking aristocrat of impeccably Gaulish descent was a 'Galatian of the Galatians', and it was only in a secondary sense that the term was extended southward or to people of different origins. But Moffatt chooses to reject a misleading and hyperbolic formulation. The question is whether the title 'Galatian' was suitable *at all*, and this question we may answer affirmatively. There is no suggestion from any quarter that it was '*more* suitable'.[36]

35 After long uncertainty since dating the epistle in AD 53 in *SPTR* (1896), pp. 189-92, Ramsay moved to favour the early date in *Teaching of St. Paul* (1913), pp. 372-92; cf. 'The Date of the Galatian Letter', *Expos* 8th ser. 5 (1913), pp. 127-45. It is noteworthy that Ramsay did not seize quickly upon this view as an open door to an apologetic synthesis, but as an explanation of such difficulties as the case of Titus in Gal. 2:3. At that point in time, he seems not even to have observed further implications of this change of mind.

36 It is difficult to avoid seeming overly harsh with Moffatt, and somewhat of a relief to be able to cite Moffatt against Moffatt without too much comment. The matter is unhappily sensitive, especially in view of Ramsay's unfortunate and ill-judged book *The First Christian Century*. While Ramsay's polemics rebounded disastrously on himself, his essential case, at least in those aspects of the Asia Minor background of the NT where he was a master and Moffatt was not, has not received due justice. Moffatt is actually open to a more systematic and devastating refutation than I have the wish or space to attempt. The problems in his work have tended to perpetuate confusion and darken counsel. It is particularly worrying that he repeatedly uses such phrases as 'arbitrary', 'incredible', 'inexplicable', 'tamper with the text', 'avoid difficulties', 'manipulation', in every case of positions where these charges are either inapplicable or may readily be

2. 'Galatia' and 'Galatians'

The objections do not reach the real difficulty of the matter. It is good at least that the attempt at positive statement should be set off against a clarification of the doubts raised by them. This chapter concludes with the attempt to answer positively two questions: (1) What evidence have we for the concept of 'Galatia' as an enlarged provincial unit? (2) What kinds of people might be addressed as 'Galatians'? The latter is a crucial question.

(1) The province of Galatia had an extremely complex history. Its status and extent were changed several times within the first century AD.[37] These changes are reflected in the inscriptions, but the variability of formulation is such that synthesis is sometimes precarious.[38]

The Roman concept of *provincia* was properly of a 'sphere of duty', and only secondarily did this concept find territorial expression. So in Republican times the 'province' Cilicia was almost equated with the responsibility for the communications of Rome with the East, the safeguarding of the land and sea routes from brigands

---

answered. Apart from such, the inapplicable argument is especially prominent in those sections which I forbear to answer in detail. Thus he writes: 'If Paul had evangelised S. Galatia prior to the Council, it is not easy to understand why he did not say so in Gal. 1:21' (*Introduction*, p. 99). It is easy enough: if the Council had not yet taken place, it might have required unusual prophetic powers to have said so at this point. Moffatt however goes on to say of a group of objections which include that just mentioned: 'None of these objections is satisfactorily met by the S. Galatian theory, *in any of its forms*' [my italics]. I submit that the answer provided by the early-date form of the theory, *is* sufficient, to say no more. Moffatt has not communicated with the effective alternative.

[37] For the province generally see most recently A.D. Macro, 'The Cities of Asia Minor under the Roman Imperium', *ANRW* 2.7.2.658-97, esp. p. 666; R.K. Sherk, 'Roman Galatia: The Governors from 25 BC to AD 114', *ibid.*, pp. 954-1052; S. Mitchell, 'Population and the Land in Roman Galatia', *ibid.*, pp. 1053-1081. Galatia received successive additions on the north and east: Paphlagonia in 6-5 BC, Pontus Galaticus in 3-2 BC, Pontus Polemoniacus in AD 64, Armenia Minor in AD 72, when also the whole was amalgamated into the huge double province of Galatia-Cappadocia (see esp. Sherk, pp. 960-63). There were other changes on the southern border, but not such as materially affect our present question. The status of Pamphylia under Augustus was uncertain, but R. Syme seems to have shown conclusively that it then belonged to Galatia ('Galatia and Pamphylia under Augustus: the Governorships of Piso, Quirinius and Silvanus', *Klio* 27 [1934], pp. 122-48). In AD 43 Claudius formed a separate province of Lycia-Pamphylia. After the brief reattachment of Pamphylia to Galatia by Galba, Vespasian restored Lycia-Pamphylia (see A.H.M. Jones, *OCD*, 2nd edn, p. 773).

[38] The attempt to argue from the listings of component territories in inscriptions is thus fraught with pitfalls, and Ramsay (*Hist. Geog.*, pp. 253-54) is not now acceptable.

and pirates. Its territorial aspect was fluid as the focus of the need changed. It even came at one stage to exclude Cilicia proper in our pedantic geographical sense.[39] Now the province 'Galatia' was largely the functional inheritor of the older 'Cilicia'. It was however an arbitrary unit organized from the territories held by the client-king Amyntas at the time of his death. His northern power-base resulted in the formation of a territory whose axis ran anomalously from northeast to southwest. What follows is a tabulation of some of the strands of evidence for the provincial entity. Some of these are individually slight, but contribute to the total picture.

(a) Officials who are honoured as benefactors in the cities of South Galatia are designated as officials in Galatia, or, among cases where the provincial name is omitted, some of the persons concerned are independently known to have held the office in Galatia.[40] Moreover, the boundary of Asia with provincial Galatia is increasingly defined by the contrast between the senatorial title *proconsul* (ἀνθύπατος) and the imperial title *legatus Augusti pro praetore* on inscriptions relating to the respective governors.[41]

(b) There are private documents from South Galatia whose dating is based on the 'Galatian' provincial era of 25 BC.[42]

---

[39] Thus in Cicero's time the territory was defined as *Lyciam, Pamphyliam, Pisidiam Phrygiamque totam* (Cicero, 2 *Verr.* 1.38.95), cited by G.E. Bean in *OCD*, 2nd edn, p. 239.

[40] Cf. examples on p. 281, n. 12 above.

[41] See W.M. Calder, 'The Eastern Boundary of the Province Asia', *CR* 22 (1908), pp. 213-15. In a subsequent note, however, 'Corrigenda et Addenda', *CR* 27 (1913), p. 11, he corrected and withdrew a mistaken reading which wrongly found reference to a proconsul of Asia in one of the texts discussed in his previous note. More important now is a lengthy Latin inscription of Orcistus, comprising the citation of texts and decrees of c. AD 323-31 and which refers to that city as of ancient standing as a border-city of Phrygia and Galatia, while itself belonging to Asia: *[Patri]a nostra Orcistos vetusti[s | sim]um oppidum fuit et ex antiquis[si | m]is temporibus ab origine etiam | [civ]itatis dignitatem obtinuit | [e]t in medio confinio Gal[a]tiae P(h)ri[g] | iae situm est* ... (*MAMA* 7.305, Panel II, lines 22-27). Panel III reproduces an imperial rescript, dated precisely 30th June AD 331, addressed to the *ordo* of the Orcistani through the provincial official, the *rationalis Asianae dioeceseos* (III, lines 24-25).

[42] Thus e.g. *MAMA* 4.140, of Uluborlu (Apollonia ad Pisidiam), where the year 247 (= AD 222) is restored from an earlier copy; 4:189, of Ilegöp, year 301 = AD 276, also from Apollonia. *MAMA* 4.248, of Yazdi Viran (Tymandos), year 335, is less certain, for the lettering suggests an earlier date, and the man was a Synnadan, who may have used his native Asian era rather than the Galatian. It is possible that the Galatian era was still in use in a very late Christian inscription, also of Uluborlu, where year 670 is AD 645 on the Galatian reckoning, but might be AD 639 [not 651] on the Actian. *MAMA* 7.486, of Beskavak, near Vetissus in E.

(c) Ancyra figures as the principal road-head of a systematic development of the road-system under the Flavians throughout the provincial complex Galatia-Cappadocia.[43] There is also evidence for a road, maintained officially by the legate of Galatia, to link Ancyra with Pisidian Antioch, the southern capital, even though a large part of its course ran through proconsular Asia.[44]

(d) Boundary stones set up under imperial authority at places in the extreme south or west of South Galatia evidently mark not only the bounds of city territories but also of the provinces of Galatia and Asia.[45] One such, dated AD 135 and dedicated to the 'gods of the boundary' (θεοῖς ἐνορίοις) mentions Apollonia, in South Galatia, and divides its territory from that of Apamea in Asia. Another example, erected under the personal supervision of a legate of Galatia, separates by name the territory of Sagalassus, in Galatian Pisidia, from that of Tymbrianassus in Asia. The date is Neronian.[46]

Phrygia, west of Lake Tatta, is an example from the central plateau, but south of the Celtic settlement (year 114 = AD 89). Ramsay argued at the end of his life that the Galatian era should not be dated from 25 BC, as in Dio 53.26.3, but 20 BC, on the strength of a coin of Tavium which poses a dilemma of anachronism for the earlier date (*Anatolian Studies Buckler* [ed. Calder], p. 203). More recent scholarship however attributes the reckoning on the coin to a local city-era peculiar to Tavium, and probably dated from some local benefaction of Augustus (see B.M. Levick, *Roman Colonies in Southern Asia Minor*, pp. 193-94; so R.K. Sherk now in *ANRW* 2.7.2.959). It is an interesting reversal to find that where a dating system united the province and persisted for centuries, an anomaly affected only one of the original Celtic tribal capitals. The dating of the era in M. Grant, 'The Official Coinage of Tiberius in Galatia', *Numismatic Chronicle* 6th ser. 10 (1950), pp. 43-48 must also now be queried.

43 This was a logical extension of Vespasian's reorganization of the Eastern frontier. Milestones, previously few, begin to proliferate, and inscriptions testify to the systematic road-paving enterprise of the legate of Galatia, A. Caesennius Gallus (see D.H. French in *ANRW* 2.7.2.711 and R.K. Sherk, *ibid.*, pp. 1004-1006), in AD 80-82. The texts are drawn from places as diverse as the Ancyra district (*CIL* 3.312), Mülk, on the road to Dorylaeum in Asia, 71m from Ancyra (*CIL* 3.318, of AD 81) and Apa in Konya *vilayet* (*CIL* 3 Supp. 2.12218, of AD 81). Another later milestone from Lycaonia, published by T. Callander (*SERP*, p. 173, No. 58 of AD 198) appears to give the distance of Psibela (Zivarik) from Ancyra (105 Roman miles). There are however problems in this mileage: see *MAMA* 1.372 and p. 193n, M.H. Ballance, *AS* 8 (1958), pp. 230, 232 n. 17.

44 See the milestone of Philomelium (*MAMA* 7.193, Trajanic), which presents the legate of Galatia, P. Calvisius Ruso [not 'Rusticus'] Julius Frontinus, of AD 106-109?, as directing building of a new road across Asian territory. Cf. Sherk, *ANRW* 2.7.2.1020.

45 Ramsay, *Hist. Geog.*, p. 172. Cf. the brief text '*finis Caesaris N*' found nearby.

46 *OGIS* 538, from a village on the south side of Lake Burdur. The date, here specifically Neronian, is confirmed by reference to the same procurator L. Pupius

(e) A metrical dedication to Zeus, from the same Apollonia, dated by the Galatian era to AD 222, seems to refer to the district as 'the land of the Galatae', and to the local people as 'the godly Trocmi'. This may be poetic metonymy, but has been taken to suggest that this southern city was actually incorporated into a structure based on that of the old Celtic tribes of the north.[47]

(f) There are many incidental hints of the prevalence of the provincial idea even in Greek sources, and in some of the first century in particular.[48] There are 'Galatarchs', corresponding to the better-known Asiarchs, and there is a κοινὸν Γαλατῶν or τῆς Γαλατίας.[49]

Praeseno as 'procurator of Claudius and Nero' and therefore in office at the time of the succession, in the famous inscription of Iconium (*CIG* 3991) which names ἡ Γαλατικὴ ἐπαρχεία.

[47] *MAMA* 4.140. This stone has suffered damage, and much of its text, including the date (Galatian era year 247) has been restored from early copies. For the suggestion that southern cities were assigned to Celtic tribal divisions, cf. the inscription of Yalvaç (Pisidian Antioch) published by W.M. Calder in *JRS* 2 (1912), pp. 84-86, No. 3, where the city Sebaste Tavia of the Trocmi honours with a statue of Concord her 'sister' Antioch (undated).

[48] For the habitually provincial concept of 'Asia' cf. my remarks in *TB* 26 (1975), pp. 100-101, *contra* Haenchen's views (cf. *TB* 26 [1975], pp. 99-100). The point is particularly abundantly and diversely illustrated in the case of (proconsular) Asia. Thus, in the *Monumentum Ancyranum* (*IGRR* 3.159), par. 24, the Latin *omnium civitatium provinciae Asiae* is rendered simply πασῶν πόλεων τῆς Ἀσίας. Inhabitants of Asia in the broader provincial sense were quite normally designated Ἀσιανοί: thus Ἀσιανὴ πόλεως Λαοδιαείας (*IGRR* 1.322), Λαοδικεὺς τῆς Ἀσίας (*IGRR* 1.191, 198), all inscriptions of Rome referring to persons from a city of Phrygia Asiana. With the characteristic titles 'Asiarch' and 'Galatarch' cf. also the paired Βειθυνιάρχες καὶ Ποντάρχης corresponding to a double provincial title, where the pairing is attested from both parts of the double province, e.g. *IGRR* 3.69.10, of Prusias in Bithynia and *IGRR* 3.90, of near Amastris, Pontus. 'Galatarchs' are abundantly attested (*IGRR* 3.179, of 3rd AD; 194, perhaps Hadrianic; 195, undated; 196, 197, 198, 201, all undated; 204, mid- 2nd AD; all of Ancyra; 231, undated, of Pessinus). Other provincial titles of interest are also found, often in combination with that of Galatarch. The function of the 'Helladarch' is disputed (*IGRR* 3.202, undated; 211, Hadrianic, both of Ancyra), but he may have been president of the *Koinon*, and the same title is found in other provinces in similar collocations, e.g. of a Bithyniarch and Helladarch and Sebastrophant at Prusias in Bithynia (*IGRR* 3.63). Another significant provincial title was πρῶτος/πρώτη τῆς ἐπαρχείας (*IGRR* 3.179, 3rd cent.; 191, undated, both of Ancyra), apparently equivalent to πρῶτος (τῶν) Ἑλλήνων (*IGRR* 3.173.13-14; 190, both 2nd cent. AD, of Ancyra), where these Greek terms are used in each case of persons descended from Gallic royalty. Such details, which might doubtless be greatly enlarged, offer illustration of the close parallels between the provincial terminology of Galatia and that of neighbouring provinces, and of the integration of Hellenization into the provincial idea.

[49] The usual formulation in the inscriptions actually uses the ethnic τὸ κοινὸν

The terminology is like that of Asia, where the provincial idea was strong. But there are also difficulties, to which we must return presently.

Let us next focus more closely on the evidence for the status of the smaller district which included Pisidian Antioch, Iconium, and the Apollonia to which we have just referred. Ramsay argued that the official name of this entity was 'Phrygia Galatica', on the precise analogy of 'Pontus Galaticus' and 'Phrygia Asiana', both of which are attested.[50] The 'Phrygo-Galatic country' (Acts 16:6) is simply a variant of the standard phrase.

(a) First, there are literary sources. Strabo describes Galatia essentially as a Celtic country (12.5.1-3 = 566-68), but goes on to say that the Romans have united all the territory of Amyntas into one province. He refers in particular to Phrygia Parorea and the part towards Pisidia, and indicates that the Antioch towards Pisidia came under the successors of Amyntas (12.8.14 = 577), that is, that a section of Phrygia belonged to the province of Galatia. Pliny gives a different perspective. He speaks of Galatia as 'superimposed' (*superposita*) on the original Phrygia (*NH* 5.42.147); he lists such southern peoples as those of Lystra and Neapolis in an alphabetical list of some of its main component states, with no regard for geographical or racial distinctions, and he locates the boundary of Galatia at places in Pisidia, Pamphylia and Lycaonia, taking an exclusively provincial view.

Most important and explicit of the literary sources is Ptolemy, writing in the second century AD. He too gives an exclusively provincial view, defining Galatia by its border with Pamphylia, and listing Olgassys in Paphlagonia first among its mountains. He arranges its cities under seven headings, each occupying one section, and proceeds from north to south: Pontus, Paphlagonia, the cities of the Tolistobogii, of the Tectosages, of the Trocmi, and then to the Proseilemmene, and finally Pisidia, Isauria and their neighbourhood, the group in which he includes Pisidian Antioch. He does not name Phrygia here (Ptol. *Geog.* 5.4), but his arrangement is purely

τῶν Γαλατῶν, whereas in Asia the form τὸ κοινὸν τῆς 'Ασίας is customary. Thus *IGRR* 3.157 (of AD 14, the dedication of the Temple of Rome and Augustus); 195, 204, 205, all referring to high priests of the *Koinon*, and all of Ancyra; 225, 230, 232, also of high priests, all of Pessinus. While all these instances are located in the North they relate to a provincial body which controlled the Imperial cult in the province and to the attempt to Romanize the whole entity whose capital was there. For the formulation κοινὸν Γαλατίας cf. *BMC Galatia, Cappadocia and Syria*, ed. W. Wroth (1899), *Koinon* of Galatia, pp. 5-7, Nos 1-15.

50 Pontus Galaticus in innumerable inscriptions of the type which list this among component territories; 'Phrygia Asiana' in Galen, cf. pp. 284-85

geographical; he gives no pride of place to the ethnic Galatia.

(b) The Phrygian character of this district is further established by a great variety of indirect epigraphical evidences. In particular the co-incidental occurrence of a Phrygian style of tomb and of fragments of the Phrygian language extends over the area, and the style is demarcated from that immediately southward in Pisidia. The Phrygian area reaches east to include Iconium, which may actually have had a somewhat mixed population, and at one point the linguistic remains extend to within a few miles of the location of the uninterpreted 'Pisidian' inscriptions of Sofular.[51]

(c) A third century inscription of Pisidian Antioch honours a 're-gionary centurion' (if the restoration is correct) for keeping the peace.[52] On the reverse of the same stone another dedication was subsequently found, alluding to the same man and occasion, expressed in what purports to be metre, and naming the district as 'Mygdonia'. This term is known as an occasional poetic name for Phrygia, but is listed by Pliny specifically as a district along the southern edge of Phrygia, toward Pisidia (Pliny NH 5.41.145).[53]

There is then a series of pointers to indicate that the country in question was in contemporary thought and usage both 'Galatian' and 'Phrygian'. But again we must stress the difficulty of the matter, the

---

51 See W. Brandenstein, 'Die Sprache der Pisider', Archiv für Orientforschung 9 (1933-34), pp. 52-54 and in PW 20.2 cols. 1793-97; R. Shafer, '"Pisidian"', AJP 71 (1950), pp. 239-70; J. Friedrich, Kleinasiatische Sprachdenkmäler, pp. 142-43; L. Zgusta, 'Die pisidischen Inschriften', Archiv orientální 25 (1957), pp. 570-610 and 'Die epichorische pisidische Anthroponymie und Sprache', Archiv orientální 31 (1963), pp. 470-82; P. Metri, 'Le iscrizioni pisidiche di Sofoular', Archivio glottologico italiano 43 (1958), pp. 42-54; J. Boschhardt, G. Neumann and K. Schulz, 'Vier pisidische Grabstelen aus Sofular', Kadmos 14 (1975), pp. 68-72; C.J. Hemer, 'The Pisidian Texts: A Problem of Language and History', Kadmos 19 (1980), pp. 54-64; C. Brixhe and E. Gibson, 'Monuments from Pisidia in the Rahmi Koç Collection', Kadmos 21 (1982), pp. 130-69.

52 J.R.S. Sterrett, Epigraphical Journey, No. 92, cited by W.M. Calder in JRS 2 (1912), p. 81, with the explicit statement that reexamination of the stone proves ρεγεωνάριον correct, despite the reversion to [λ]εγεωνάριον in IGRR 3. The word is omitted from LSJ, but noted in the Supplement. The Latin term regio in Greek transliteration as ρεγιών or ρεγεών is paralleled in the epigraphy of Asia Minor: thus ρεγιών (CIG 3436, of Lydian Philadelphia: Βοηθὸς ἐπιτρόπων ρεγιῶνος Φιλαδελφηνῆς); ρεγεών (BCH, 24 [1900], p. 337, from Ceria). Both texts are probably of the 3rd century AD, to judge from their onomastic evidence.

53 Calder, JRS 2 (1912), p. 80 (No. 1): τόνδε σε Μυ|γδονίη Διονύ|σιον ἀντὶ Β(ί)βου |πολλῶν | καὶ τῆς εἰρήνης | στέμμα, of probably c. AD 250. The implication is that 'Mygdonia' is the regio where Dionysius held office. See further Calder's discussion on pp. 81-84. This may have been an extensive area equivalent to 'Phrygia Galatica' and perhaps indeed still so called, though that designation is necessarily replaced here by a traditional name amenable to verse.

unsolved problems, the anomalies:

(a) There is the custom, found both in Latin and Greek formulations, of designating the governor of Galatia by a listing of the component territories of his province, among which Galatia is merely one item: e.g. *Leg. Aug. pr. pr. provinciae Cappadociae et Galatiae Ponti Pisidiae Paphlagoniae Armeniae Minoris*. The lists vary remarkably, and Phrygia is sometimes included as a separate item. It is difficult, on the face of it, to resist the feeling that 'Galatia' is used here in a narrow sense, a doubt is strengthened by other complicating phenomena. What for instance is the force of the phrase ἐπίτροπον ... ἐπα[ρ]χείας Γαλατίας καὶ τ[ῶν] σύνεγγυς ἐθνῶν (*IGRR* 3.70, of Dusae in Bithynia)?

The last point may perhaps be answered first. There is some evidence that certain procuratorships were held over a wide area comprising several distinct provinces. Perhaps the procurator of the inscription cited held an office parallel with one attested of another procurator on an inscription of Ancyra itself: *Procurator familiae gladiatoriae per Asiam, Bithyniam, Galatiam, Cappadociam, Lyciam, Pamphiliam, Ciliciam, Cyrum, Pontum, Paphlagoniam*.[54]

The practice of a similar listing of separate territories within the single provincial complex remains a difficulty, especially as there are instances where these territories are designated *provincial*, plural: (*A. Caesennius Gallus*) *leg pr. pr. vias provinciarum Galatiae Cappadociae Ponti Pisidiae Paphlagoniae Lycaoniae Armeniae Minoris stravit* (*CIL* 3.312, 318, both of Ancyra; cf. *CIL* 3 Supp. 2.14184.48, of near Ancyra, all of AD 80-82). These lists seem to be related to the constant shifts of provincial boundaries. The phenomenon seems to occur first and mainly, if not exclusively, in the Flavian period and its aftermath, the time when Galatia and Cappadocia and their various appendages were united in a larger entity, and then to a brief period of undecided and shifting combinations when they were again separated, in texts of c. AD 112-14. In each case appendages like Armenia Minor and Pisidia are named where they were currently included in the double (or later single) provincial entity. Phrygia is often not named, but is more likely to be taken for granted, or included implicitly in Galatia proper. But the variability of the lists is such that we cannot press the point, certainly not to mount on it an argument that the Phrygian area was so basically 'Galatia' as not to merit separate designation. One should be cautious in arguing in any direction from variations

---

54 *CIL* 3.6753; cf. 3.6994; 10.7583, 7584 add., cited by D. Vaglieri in E. de Ruggiero, *Dizionario epigrafico di antichità romane*, Vol. III (F-H) (Rome: Pasqualucci, 1922), p. 363 *ad* Galatia. For this interpretation see Calder in *JRS* 2 (1912), p. 83 n. 17 as against Brandis (*PW* 7.1. cols. 555-56) and *CIL* 10, Index. Brandis argues for a reference to the other two Celtic tribes.

and omissions in such formulations.[55]

(b) Another problem involves the history and interpretation of the *Koinon* of Galatia. Reference to the *Koinon* and to the Galatarchs seems to be confined to Ancyra and the north, whereas a κοινὸν Λυκαόνων is now known from the coins of several southern cities.[56] This pattern seems to differ from the usage of the parallel terms in proconsular Asia.

The essential problem here may be answered in the light of a later study by Ramsay, which attempts to trace the history of Roman dealings with the *Koinon*.[57] He maintains that the *Koinon* was used here as an instrument of Hellenization: Ancyra was the tribal centre of the Tectosages and capital of the province, but it was not yet a Greek *polis*. Coinage was struck there in the name of the governor, or of the *Koinon*, or of the tribe, but never in that of the city. He repeats his suggestion that the tribal structure was widened to comprehend all the peoples of the province, and thereby overwhelm the Celtic element. The *Koinon* met in Ancyra, but was the assembly representing the whole province. Ramsay reconstructs an acephalous inscription and finds there a record of its meeting in AD 101. The personal names listed include rare or characteristic forms associated with leading families otherwise known from Pisidian Antioch, Iconium, Apollonia and other southern cities.[58]

---

55 It now seems clear that the practice of naming the double province from the enumeration of its parts dates from Vespasian's reorganization. It arose, according to Ramsay, 'partly because of mere pride of power, but probably more because of real differences in administration between the different parts' (*JRS* 12 [1922], p. 153). But this system was cumbrous and the enumerations never complete. His earlier attempt in *Hist. Geog.*, pp. 253-54 to deduce variations in the limits of the province from variations in the lists proved to be incorrect and gave no useful results.

56 See the evidence cited in n. 49 (pp. 293-94) above for the Galatian *Koinon*. For the Lycaonian see the coins in *BMC Lycaonia, Isauria, Cilicia*, ed. G.F. Hill (1900), of Barata (Nos. 1-5), Dalisandus (Nos. 1-2), Ilistra (Nos. 1-3), Derbe (p. xx), Hyde (p. xx), Savatra (p. xxii). Most are late: only Savatra shows a change of formulation, where reference to the *Koinon* first appears after Antoninus Pius. No other city shows an example earlier than the younger Faustina.

57 'Studies in the Roman Province Galatia', *JRS* 12 (1922), pp. 147-86 [given wrongly in the bibliography in *Anatolian Studies Ramsay*, p. xxxvii], esp. p. 156ff. 'Ancyra must hellenize itself before it could be permitted to develop any individuality' (p. 163). Its importance with regard to the eastern frontier was a measure of the importance attached to Hellenizing it (p. 164).

58 This important but neglected inscription was first published by A. von Domaszewski in *Archaeologisch-epigraphische Mittheilungen aus Oesterreich-Ungarn* 9 (1885), pp. 119-22, No. 81, with a conjecturally restored heading which misses the true character of the document and attributes it to Antoninus Pius.

Such is the first century picture. Later there were changes of policy and of territorial disposition. The *Koinon* of the Lycaones seems not to be attested before Marcus Aurelius.[59] Diachronic study is needed here. Quite possibly the provincial idea was at its strongest in the first flowering of the *pax Romana*. The actual designation ἐπαρχεία

The version in *IGRR* 3.162 reproduces this but elects to omit the catalogue of 92 personal names which is integral to the special interest of the text. In an extended discussion in *JRS* 12 (1922), pp. 165-76, Ramsay argues for a dating under Trajan, 23rd September AD 101, on the ground of relatively early lettering and nomenclature, and reference to the 4th consulship of the unnamed emperor, a title excluding other possibilities such as Hadrian. Ramsay was however unaware of a problem caused by the naming of the governor P. Alfius Maximus, whose date remains unknown, but whom Ramsay took to have succeeded [T.] Pomponius Bassus, who held office c. 95-100 (p. 170). One Aufidius Umber is now placed in 100-101 (Sherk, *ANRW* 2.7.2.1016, 1045), and while this might not exclude absolutely the unplaced Alfius Maximus from late 101, it poses a likely problem. Sherk (p. 1017 n. 167), following R. Syme in *Gnomon*, 29 (1957), p. 522, favours the Antonine date. While the dating problem touches some of the more speculative developments of Ramsay's reconstruction, it does not touch the basic strength of his case for finding reference here to a meeting of the *Koinon*, otherwise paralleled in a text like *IGRR* 3.223 (of Pessinus, AD 79). He infers the day of the meeting from the assumption that the *Koinon* met on Augustus' birthday. In any case this is a most important document of the Imperial cult in the province.

In this context the names are important, as likely to represent delegates from leading families in cities of the province, South as well as North. Most are of Greek or Roman types, whether or not formal Roman *tria nomina*, but Celtic and native forms are sparsely represented among them. Interesting examples are 'Caristanius', a rare *nomen* apparently unique to Pisidian Antioch, but borne by a leading family of that city throughout the 1st cent. AD. 'Ebourianos', which appears twice is not otherwise known except in Iconium, and may be Lycaono-Pisidian in origin. 'Anthestius' is a rare Anatolian name (perhaps a rendering of Latin 'Antistius', found in Lycaonia. 'Boiorix' (thus better than Domaszewski's form) is evidently Celtic (see Ramsay, *JRS* 12 [1922], p. 172ff.). These are interesting signs of the 'provincial' character of the text, and more refined study of the prosopography of individual cities might extend the range of the evidence. It is notable that, if usual formulations may be restored in the lost heading, these persons constitute the *Koinon* of the *Galatians*, and are so designated.

Other facts of the document deserve brief mention. The record of names is important, as of persons dedicated to the imperial cultus (ἀνέθηκαν Ι [τὴν σ]τήλην καὶ τὰ ὀνόματα, Domaszewski, pp. 119-22, lines 2-3), and there is a concluding reference (lines 61-62) to the γραφαί, apparently here a regular written liturgy of emperor worship.

59 Cf. p. 297, n. 56 above. The various cities exhibit this designation on coins of the same limited range of imperial persons, among whom the younger Faustina, Lucius Verus and Philip Senior recur. The only instance I have noted from Marcus Aurelius is Ilistra, No. 1 (*BMC Lycaonia, Isauria, Cilicia*, p. 8), where the reference to the *Koinon* is restored.

Γαλατική or *provincia Galatica* seems to belong specifically to the time contemporary with Paul (thus in Greek *CIG* 3991, of Iconium, AD 54; in Latin *ILS* 9499.6-7 of Ephesus, c. AD 56-64, cited by R.K. Sherk in *ANRW* 2.7.2.988). The verbal parallel with τὴν Φρυγίαν καὶ Γαλατικὴν χώραν may not be insignificant. And other early evidence including specific territorial designations is scanty. Vespasian's reorganization seems to have occasioned marked changes of terminology.[60] It is no wonder if the provincial idea lost its vitality under the constant administrative adjustments which followed.

We need not prove here that 'Galatia' *necessarily* means 'South Galatia'. We can, however clear the ground in the face of the objection that it cannot include 'South Galatia'. The evidence of Acts with Galatians (if we are allowed to read them together) points convincingly in practice to a 'South Galatian' background on the lines suggested, with room for flexibility of interpretation. But there remains a strong residual objection over the suitability of addressing recipients in the south as 'Galatians'.

(2) What kinds of people could be addressed as 'Galatians'? The ethnic occurs in the New Testament only at Gal. 3:1, but the 'Galatians' of that verse are evidently equivalent to 'the churches of Galatia' in Gal. 1:2 and 1 Cor. 16:1, in Paul's own usage. On this ground alone we should not expect to have to drive a wedge between the identity of 'Galatia' and of the 'Galatians'. But the question is still a challenge in Gal. 3:1, and merits consideration in its own right. It has become a crucial question whether people in the Pauline churches in the South might be acceptably called by this title, or whether it would carry some pejorative connotation inappropriate to them, like 'wild Celtic barbarians'. Some scholars have been insistent that the term could only be aptly used of ethnic Celts in the North.[61]

---

60 Cf. p. 297, n. 55 above. The reorganization seems to have been dictated by strategic needs. The pre-existing Galatia was based on a historical accident, a group of heterogeneous territories acquired at the same date. The eastern frontier problems now necessitated an integrated army command uniting the front line with a systematic development of communications and supply in the Galatian hinterland. Corbulo's special command in the East under Nero had doubtless pinpointed the need. The Flavian road-works in Galatia and Cappadocia were a crucial part of working out the policy (cf. Sherk, *ANRW* 2.7.2.991-95, etc.). On a point of terminology— Ramsay suggests elsewhere that after this time Galatic Pisidia became more easily mixed with Galatic Phrygia, as a great part of the former had been transferred to Pamphylia (*JRS* 7 [1917], p. 255).

61 Thus quite dogmatically Moffatt, Kümmel (*Introduction*, p. 298), W. Bauer in *BAGD* (for which see next paragraph) among others. It is well to reiterate strongly the fact of the habitual fluctuation between 'Galatia' and 'Galatians', typically seen in that between τὸ κοινὸν τῶν Γαλατῶν in the inscriptions and

(a) *LSJ* gives us no help whatever here. Many of the important territorial ethnics of Asia Minor are absent from its pages, and others are given fragmentary or misleading attestation. Γαλάτης is actually a surprisingly common word, yet its masculine singular is unrecorded in the lexicon, though its plural and its feminine Γαλάτισσα are both mentioned. No interpretation is offered for any of the word-group except a simple equation of Γαλάται with Κέλτοι and its corresponding derivatives, with no hint under the entries for either root that these word-groups were used of peoples in two totally diverse parts of the Roman world, in France and in Turkey. The entry in *BAGD* is much fuller, but also misleading. Apart from such odd errors as a definition of the province which includes Cilicia in Galatia (p. 149), it is claimed that 'impressive support' is given to the North Galatian view by the historian Memnon (c. 1st cent. AD). It must be noted that Memnon, whether in fact an older or a younger contemporary of Paul (W. Bauer in *BAGD* p. xxvii *contra BAGD* p. 150), is dealing with the Gaulish invasions of Asia Minor in a historical context 300 years earlier, when nobody doubts the application of the term Γαλάται to the Celtic invaders. It is anachronistic to wrench the references out of context as an improperly emphatic and repeated argument for contemporary usage, selected to the exclusion of other kinds of evidence. It does not follow that Memnon 'would certainly never address Lycaonians as Γαλάται' (*BAGD* p. xxvii, repeated p. 150), nor are Lycaonians even the people primarily in view. It is a pity that the editors of *BAGD* were not more critically alert to errors in Bauer's work.

(b) One instance from the literature is of particular interest for our present inquiry. Pausanias writes Γαλατῶν ... οἱ Πεσσινοῦντα ἔχοντες, ὑῶν οὐχ ἁπτόμενοι (7.17.10). The reference here is to the specifically Phrygian religion and to a practice whose origin is placed long before the coming of the Celts. Pessinus is, of course, in North Galatia, but the cultural context is *not* Celtic, yet the people are called 'Galatians'.

(c) Linked with this is an epigraphical reference which perhaps only complicates the issue. Certain inscriptions of Pessinus refer to priests of the cult by their position in order of precedence. There was a college of ten under the high priest, of whom the first five were designated Φρύγες and the latter five Γαλάται. This presumably points to an accommodation in religion, in which traditional titles commemorate the adhesion of the newcomers to the older cult. One Ti.

κοινὸν Γαλατίας in the coins, at least of Trajan (pp. 293-94, n. 49). I have not seen coins of the *Koinon* of Augustus and Nero, which according to Ramsay (*JRS* 12 [1922], p. 171), use the ethnic form κοινὸν Γαλατῶν. We have seen that the ethnic designation specifically includes individuals believed to be delegates of Southern cities and of native Lycaonian or similar origin.

Claudius Attis was 'ninth after the high priest and fourth of the Galatae, and twice high priest of the Augusti and of the *Koinon* of the Galatae'.[62] 'Attis' is of course itself a Phrygian, perhaps here a cultic, name.[63] The priests may have been chosen from the distinct native and Celtic elements in the population, or perhaps the ethnic names merely preserved the tradition of a time when this had been so. It is hazardous to argue from traditional religious terminology.

(d) A small point may serve to illustrate a distinctive use of the title 'Phrygian' within the province. References to the military units on the southern border include mention of the seven *alae Phrygum*. Auxiliary troops were recruited from among non-citizens and their units bore distinctively alien names.[64]

(e) An inscription of Pednelissus, on the southern edge of Pisidia, ascribed to the first century, appears to designate that city unequivocally as ἡ πόλις Γαλατῶν.[65] The text is of cultic interest, and is expressed in a peculiar Greek with many dialect forms suggestive of the aberrant Greek of neighbouring Pamphylia. The priestess who figures centrally in it is herself named 'Galato'. Its first editor, D. Comparetti, made a curious attempt to explain the content from the supposed religious fanaticism of the Celtic temperament, on the assumption that Pednelissus contained an isolated pocket of Celts.[66] But the phenomena of cult and language are to be seen in Hellenized Anatolian terms. The Greek *polis* concept is specifically linked with the term 'Galatian' in a manner alien to the usage of the specifically Celtic Ancyra itself in this early period. The date here is presumably before Vespasian transferred most of Pisidia to an enlarged Pamphylia, and the inscription therefore belongs to that period when the provincial concept of Galatia seems to have been in its initial vigour.

---

62 *IGRR* 3.225; cf. *IGRR* 3.230, designating a man, probably father of the same Attis, tenth after the high priest and fifth of the Galatae. If this text is rightly assigned to the later 1st cent AD, No. 225 will be placed a generation later.

63 [Ed.] I am indebted to Mr Michael Howe for bringing to my attention Catullus *Carmina*, 63 which links the story of Attis specifically with both Phrygia and with cultic activities; cf. Pausanias 7.17.9 (citing the poet Hermesianax).

64 *IGRR* 3.487; 500, I. line 55, refer to an ἔπαρχος of the 7th εἴλη of Phryges (both Trajanic, after AD 102, of Oenoanda in Lycia). Cf. *IGRR* 3.670-72, all of Patara in Lycia, undated; Ramsay *JRS* 12 (1922), p. 153. It is not clear from the texts that the units were actually stationed in these regions, and their location is in one case attributed to Syria. The significance of the onomastic point is not affected by this.

65 D. Comparetti, 'Iscrizione di Pednelissos (Pisidia)', *Annuario della regia Scuola Archeologica di Atene* 3 (1916-20), pp. 143-48. For the site, at Çozan, see R. Paribeni and G. Moretti in *Annuario* 3 (1916-20), pp. 73-133.

66 Comparetti, p. 148. He argues from the letter-forms to an early imperial dating of the text.

(f) Ten of the slaves who figure in a group of sacral manumission inscriptions of Delphi are designated Γαλάτης or Γαλάτισσα.[67] Not one of them has a Celtic name. Most are Greek. One can be paralleled as indigenous Phrygian, and the Greek ones include Sosus, Sosias and Sosander, a collocation which recalls the 'saviour-god' (Sozon) cults so characteristic of the native religion of northern Phrygia. And the date of the whole group is relatively early, the mid-second century BC. These 'Galatians' were hardly likely to have come from the Gaulish aristocracy. They bear every sign of being native Phrygians, the typical slaves. This instance of the ethnic does not then show us the term as an honourable title— that, I suggest, was a characteristic development of the Roman period— but at least as applicable to non-Celts from the territory currently called 'Galatia'.

This type of observation can be paralleled from a number of other categories of persons whose names may be sampled from the epigraphy. One must stress that we have no means of telling how far these names are representative, or to what extent they reflect actual ethnic differences. It is common enough, for instance, to find records of families where Greek, Roman and Anatolian names are used indiscriminately, and the occurrence of an isolated Celtic name in an otherwise Graeco-Roman or Anatolian environment is not unknown.

(g) The personal names which occur in the inscriptions of Ancyra and the north are largely Greek, but soon become very Romanized in the Roman period to which they almost all belong. There are relatively few clearly Celtic names, and these usually refer to prominent persons in the tribal royal families, usually dignified with a Roman *praenomen* and *nomen*. See especially IGRR 3.155-218.

(h) The names in the epigraphy of South Galatia are mostly Greek or Roman in the cities (the Roman mostly in the colonies and the innumerable late epitaphs), but there are numerous native Anatolian names, Phrygian and other, especially in the more rural areas, and many native-style abbreviations and corruptions of Greek names. Many names in both parts of Galatia and elsewhere in Asia Minor show a markedly Anatolian, especially Phrygian, background of culture and religion.

(j) S. Mitchell reports on a specific survey he has made of the incidence of Celtic names in the rural areas of specifically Gaulish settlement (*ANRW* 2.7.2.1058-1059). He finds only twenty Celtic names, amounting to 4.6% of the total of personal names in the epigraphical indices he has made for Central Anatolia, usually in families also

---

[67] The corpus of over four hundred inscriptions of this class is published in C. Wescher and P. Foucart, *Inscriptions recueillies à Delphes* (Paris: Firmin Didot, 1863), 3ème sér., 'Actes d'Affranchissement'.

using Greek, Roman and Phrygian name-types. In two of the three major North Galatian cities, Ancyra and Pessinus together, he finds 23 recorded Celtic names, or 1.5% in Ancyra and 2.7% in Pessinus. Outside the original area of Celtic settlement, though still well north of the Pauline churches of South Galatia, he finds in isolated pockets 19 names (1.1%) around Haymana, 5 names (0.3%) in Laodicea Combusta, and 4 names (1.3%) in the district of Perta, Savatra and Cana, all heavily outnumbered by Phrygian forms. *MAMA* 7.314 is a unique instance of a Celtic name (Βωδορις) occurring in a text with a curse-formula in the Phrygian language. Mitchell suggests tentatively that the outliers point to some Celtic colonization of the central plateau in the Hellenistic period. It is still notable how extremely low the Celtic percentages are even in the Celtic homeland.

(k) There are many cases of individuals resident as aliens in such cosmopolitan centres as Athens and Rhodes who are designated on their tombstones Γαλάτης or Γαλάτισσα.[68] Such names are found virtually throughout the Hellenistic and Roman periods. They are almost uniformly Greek, though a few show Anatolian, especially Phrygian, variants or background.

(l) A surprisingly large number of such tombstones from Athens bear the single city ethnic Ἀγκυρανός (Ἀνκυρανός).[69] These range from about 300 BC to the late Roman period. They are uniformly Greek throughout the whole time-span, but certain recurring names with the 'Men-', 'Meter-' and 'Soter-' elements suggest a Phrygian background.

(m) Other resident aliens in cosmopolitan cities bear the ethnic Φρύξ or its feminine Φρυγία. Here again we have the same kind of pattern, Greek names with occasional Phrygian background.[70]

(n) It is difficult to find in significant quantity parallel ethnics of persons from the individual cities of South Galatia. There are occasional persons designated Πισίδης, and Λυκαών or Λυκαόνισσα, and their names too are usually Greek.[71]

---

68 Evidence will be most conveniently found in *IG* 2² 3.8451-8457/8 for Athens, and in A. Maiuri, *Nuova silloge epigrafica di Rodi e Cos* (Firenze: Felice le Monnier, 1925) 213-16.

69 See *IG* 2² 3.7883-7937.

70 These will be found in the same cities and publications. For the occurrence of the feminine Φρυγία beside the masculine Φρύξ cf. *JTS* n.s. 27 (1976), pp. 122-26; 28 (1977), pp. 99-101.

71 I have collected scattered examples of these and similar categories. The only significant sequence is of examples of Πισίδης in *IG* 2² 3.10079-10085 (πείσιδης in 10080), all of Athens, ranging from the 3rd cent. BC to the Roman period. The feminine Πισίδισσα occurs in *SB* 1.2041, of Alexandria, 3rd cent. BC. Both forms are unrecorded in *LSJ* and Supp.

(o) Almost ninety personal names are preserved of the list already mentioned, which Ramsay took to be a list of the delegates of all the cities to the assembly of the *Koinon* in AD 101 (n. 58 above). These names and the patronymics attached to most of them are nearly all Greek or Latin, with a handful which might be Celtic. A score or so have full Roman names, mostly of types which would denote enfranchisement by the Julio-Claudians or the Flavians. One bears the personal name 'Galates'.[72] If then these names are indeed representative of civic leaders of all the province, and include some which are characteristic of particular southern cities, they may be regarded as a useful sample. And this sample accords pretty closely with the others.

Where does all this leave us? There is no prospect of using the chance occurrences of names as the basis for some sociological survey, for the various samplings are of their nature limited and arbitrary, and they might be wholly unrepresentative. It is in fact a fair guess that our materials are misleadingly biased towards the Graeco-Roman elements in the various cities and regions: city-officials, expatriates, and slaves emancipated in a Greek environment. But then we should also expect that the central thrust of Paul's mission was towards the same kind of Graeco-Roman elements in Gentile society. Such people may have been of native blood: their names really tell us nothing of their racial origin, if perhaps something of their aspirations. Their culture was Hellenized or Romanized, however superficially; their blood was probably most often Phrygian, both in North and South Galatia. The truly surprising thing is the lack of traceable development, in the early prevalence, for instance, of use of the term Γαλάτης of Hellenized Anatolians even before the Roman period.

If we suppose, for the sake of argument, that Paul went to North Galatia, what kind of people was he likely to have met there? Perhaps a Hellenized stratum of the population, of mixed, largely Phrygian, blood, perhaps largely similar to the people in the Phrygian parts of the South. Would it then have been correct to call such Northerners 'Galatians' at all except in the rather extended 'courtesy' sense also applicable in the south? Could the terms in fact be applied at all outside a circumscribed Celtic aristocracy and an unknown remnant of pure-blooded Celts?

There is sometimes a danger that critical rigour may be used to carry its own *reductio ad absurdum*. It is clear enough in principle that Γαλάτης was a widely used and honourable self-designation, that it was applicable to persons of Phrygian rather than Celtic origin, and that it corresponded rather generally to 'Galatia' in the shifting senses

---

72 Γαλάτης Ἀλεξάνδρου col. 2, line 19; cf. Ramsay, *JRS* 12 (1922), pp. 147-86.

of that term. Ancient geography often deals in people rather than places: 'the city of the Ephesians', 'the land of the Phrygians'. Ethnic and territory are closely identified (cf. Excursus, pp. 241-43). We pass easily from one to the other. The inscriptions and coins here fluctuate between '*Koinon* of Galatia' and '*Koinon* of the Galatae'. So 'the churches of Galatia' (Gal. 1:2) pass into the 'Galatians' of Gal. 3:1. The difficulty and the fluctuation of usage tends to affect both alike, but the combination of circumstantial details points to the viability, and even the temporary prevalence, of the wider interpretation of both. This kind of usage may be abundantly paralleled by the 'provincial' uses of 'Asia' and its derivatives in the same period. There are even some hints, contrary to views often repeated, that the term 'Galatian' was a correct and honourable title especially acceptable to the more Hellenized or Romanized people in the province.

We will not deal further with the questions of geography here. Our general conclusion is that any Pauline churches in provincial Galatia are eligible to be regarded as the 'Galatians' of the epistle. If we accept the essential correctness of the Acts account which names Pauline churches of the south, we should naturally expect them to meet the case adequately. When Paul speaks of coming to 'you' (the Galatians) τὸ πρότερον (Gal. 4:13), we may naturally link this with the first visit in Acts to people who might be fairly described as Galatians, and that takes us to Acts 13 and Pisidian Antioch.[73] If indeed the South Galatian view is viable at all, a natural reading of the texts tends to impose it, and all geographical probability supports this.

Concluding Remarks

It has not been possible to discuss all the facets of the Galatian problem. Many of these have been admirably treated elsewhere, and I have been content to assume the results of others in many cases. Our central concern here has been with usage.

Here we return to our original paradox: the evidence is exceedingly complex, difficult, fragmentary, elusive and circumstantial, yet it is possible to hold to our synthesis with some firmness. The integration of the texts, Acts with Galatians, gives a convincing and economical historical reconstruction. This hypothesis is actually

---

73 Some have been over-insistent in treating τὸ πρότερον as referring to the 'former' of two visits, as in a different argument Ramsay and others have made of τὸ πρῶτον λόγον (Acts 1:1) the 'first' of three books. But the usage of this period is more fluid (cf. *BAGD*). τὸ πρότερον here should be rendered 'originally', 'at the first' (so e.g. Betz, *Galatians*, p. 224 n. 52). It is unnecessary even to invoke the notion of first visit and return journey to Pisidian Antioch or Iconium (Acts 14:21-22).

supported by the varied intricacies of such considerations as the detailed topography and the existence of likely routes. The present study has been directed to the attempt to answer a crucial objection to the viability of the whole enterprise. But if viable at all, everything goes to suggest it is right. The successful objection requires particular interpretations of Acts 16:6 and 18:23. The required interpretation of the former has been supported by denials, which we have counteracted by positive evidences on each point. We interpret the phrase in 16:6 as denoting one geographical unit, following Lightfoot, but giving that interpretation the geographical context we owe to Ramsay. Acts 18:23 remains difficult and debatable; but does not restrict our options, though in fact the North Galatian option seems unnecessary and improbable. We then have some latitude, and can rest willing to see the matter decided by considerations of usage and probability.

The total impression of usage is in some respects an unexpected one. The idea that Paul uses Roman and Luke Greek nomenclature is itself an oversimplification. The tendency is explainable enough. Paul's vision involved the strategy of mission and the problems of dealing with authority. His aim could perhaps be formulated as the establishment of local city churches grouped in indigenous provincial units. Luke caught and transmits to us many of the anomalous complexities of popular usage as he heard them used by Paul or on occasions when he was present. Some of these have caused the commentators a lot of trouble. In the first century in particular Greek sentiment in Asia expressed itself in a Roman mould. Pliny, Ptolemy and Dio Cassius testify to the vigour of such geographical terms as 'Phrygia', 'Pisidia' and 'Lycaonia' in contemporary usage. They coexisted with the provincial names. But 'Phrygia or 'Phrygia Magna' seems to be largely equated in practice with Asian Phrygia, unless otherwise qualified. 'Galatia' however seems to be used by the same writers of a provincial entity within which the Phrygian-speaking parts are not conceptually separated unless it is necessary to specify a district. In fact geographical usage, then as now, was a more complex and fluid, yet also a more intelligible and patterned, thing than our simplified and rigid criteria tend to allow. The usages both of Paul and of Luke seem to fall representatively into the natural variations of the pattern, so far as it can be understood today.

The crucial difficulty in all this subject is in fact the matter of usage, and its difficulty puts a weapon into the hand of the objector. He can never be decisively refuted. The evidence, by the nature of the case, is only circumstantial, but we are then under some obligation to make the best possible assessment of its trend. We have offered what seems the best reading of the case. The question is whether the objector can provide an alternative synthesis which is more convincing and less open to objection in its turn.

This may seem a somewhat esoteric inquiry, but it is the ground on which a far-reaching debate happens to hinge. The synthesis I have offered is one in which the evidence of Acts and Epistles may be naturally integrated, and that speaks for the essential integrity of the Acts account. Differing assessments of Acts may be combined with many other syntheses, but most other options are more complex and involve difficulties and improbabilities more intractable than are found here. The North Galatian view in particular seems wholly unconvincing, despite the undeserved axiomatic status it holds for many scholars. Some ostensibly important recent studies are radically flawed by dogmatic and unexamined presuppositions on a question amenable to the assessment of evidence which is left unconsidered.[74] If the debate is to be fruitfully pursued, a prerequisite is the restatement of the North Galatian view in a form which attempts to make a balanced and representative use of epigraphical evidence and which will stand up to detailed criticism. That is quite an important challenge. It seems doubtful that it can now be adequately achieved. But let us have no more argument from sceptical dogma.

---

[74] Apart from such influential Acts commentaries as that of Haenchen, one may instance R. Jewett, *Dating Paul's Life* (London: SCM, 1979) = *A Chronology of Paul's Life* (Philadelphia: Fortress 1979). The problem with the persistence of unexamined North Galatian assumptions is that either far-reaching conclusions are drawn deductively from them, or that they are implicit in what I take to be faulty historical reconstruction. In either case suspect conclusions are often popularized, with the frequent unproved implication that the Acts account is radically erroneous.

Chapter 8
The Authorship and Sources of Acts

Introduction

Enough has now been said to establish a background, to maintain that the writer has given an independent account of Paul into which the evidence of Paul's letters can be extensively dove-tailed. This raises the question of the sources of his knowledge. It suggests a *prima facie* judgment that he either stood close to Paul's time or at least depended on sources close to Paul. Such an assumption would present no difficulty to a traditional view of the case. Tradition assigns the book to the physician Luke. We have followed convention thus far in using the name 'Luke' as a convenient shorthand designation for the author, whom we have agreed to be the writer both of the Third Gospel and of Acts (see Chapter 2, pp. 30-33). The time has now come for some evaluation of the tradition. And the question of authorship is intimately interwoven with that of the passages of first-person narrative in Acts, and their bearing on the author's sources of information.

The man Luke is named in the New Testament at Col. 4:14; Phlm. 24; and 2 Tim. 4:11. Only Colossians characterizes him as the 'beloved physician', and its context (vv. 10-11) implies also that he was a Gentile. There is no apparent reason why the early church should have chosen to ascribe the two longest books in the New Testament, together some two-sevenths of its total bulk, to so relatively obscure a person unless it preserved sound tradition. The ascription was almost universally accepted until 19th century criticism began to question more radically the supposed authorship by a companion (or contemporary) of Paul. The late dating of Acts in the Tübingen School's reconstruction of early Christian history necessarily involved discarding the tradition. But F.C. Baur's work was centred upon a broad conception of the dialectic of history, and he produced an unwarranted oversimplification of its actualities, as Haenchen (*Acts*, p. 17) observes. While attributing the book of Acts to a much later eirenic writer, Baur thought it not impossible that it may have been founded on genuine sketches and narratives from the hand of the historical Luke, especially for the Apostle's last journey. Acts thus remained, within limits, 'a highly important source of the history of the Apostolic Age'.[1] Baur's followers Albert Schwegler and Eduard Zeller went further than Baur himself in dismantling the tradition. They systematized the Tübingen viewpoint, Schwegler across the range of early Christian literature, Zeller on Acts in particular.[2] For Schwegler, Acts was a tendentious document of reconciliation in the form of a history, belonging to the period 110-50. Zeller, who made the only thorough study of Acts by a member of the Tübingen School, stressed the Peter-Paul parallelism as a creation of the writer. This writer aims to justify the existence of a Gentile Christianity in the period 110-30, and therefore compromises the distinctiveness of Paul in order to conciliate the Jewish Christians. There is no room in these writers for any connection with authentic traditions deriving from a companion of Paul. But their views did not carry the day without dispute even among their German contemporaries. M. Schneckenburger, while treating Acts as a *Tendenzschrift*, defended its essential historicity, and maintained both an early date (66-70) and Lukan authorship.[3] Outside Germany criticism of the tradition was much slower to take hold. E. Renan retained the concept of Lukan authorship in his relatively sceptical treatment of Acts as bordering on edificatory legend.[4] And in Britain the tradition persisted, and was in due course given a new lease of life in the work of W.K. Hobart and of W.M. Ramsay.[5]

The question of the tradition arises at several levels:

(1) Whether material in Acts goes back to a companion of Paul, perhaps especially in the 'we-passages';

(2) whether the author of the book (or at least of these passages) was himself a companion of Paul, and an eyewitness of the events of the first-person sections;

(3) whether such a companion and partial eyewitness is further to

---

1   F.C. Baur, *Paul the Apostle*, pp. 12-13, quoting from p. 13.

2   A. Schwegler, *Das nachapostolische Zeitalter in den Hauptmomenten seiner Entwicklung*, 2 vols. (Tübingen, 1846); E. Zeller, *Die Apostelgeschichte nach ihrem Inhalt und Ursprung kritisch untersucht* (Stuttgart, 1854); ET *The Contents and Origin of the Acts of the Apostles, Critically Investigated*, 2 vols., tr. Joseph Dare (London: Williams & Norgate, 1875-76). See further the discussions in Haenchen, *Acts*, pp. 17-18; Gasque, *History of Criticism*, pp. 40-50.

3   M. Schneckenburger, *Über den Zweck der Apostelgeschichte* (Bern: Fischer, 1841). See Gasque, *History of Criticism*, pp. 32-39; Haenchen, *Acts*, pp. 18-19 treats him somewhat dismissively.

4   E. Renan, *Les Apôtres* (Paris: Lévy, 1866); *passim*, esp. the introduction.

5   W.K. Hobart, *The Medical Language of St. Luke* (Dublin: Hodges, Figgis and Co., 1882); W.M. Ramsay, *Luke the Physician and Other Studies in the History of Religion* (London: Hodder and Stoughton, 1908), pp. 1-68.

be identified with the traditional 'Luke the physician'.

The question of historicity is not necessarily to be tied to positive answers to all these questions. It might be at least a start to establish the
essential relation of the eventual author to traditions emanating from
a companion of Paul, but that would still be insufficient without subsidiary arguments for the integrity of the material and his relative
forbearance in editorial alteration. On the other side, the particular
identity of the author with the physician of Col. 4:14 is inessential to
the fundamental question. It would be possible to argue for authorship by a companion of Paul without specifying his traditional identity, and certainly without weighting the case with remarks about his
use of medical language or the like. It emerges that position (2) is the
fundamental one. If it can be established, it offers an *a fortiori* argument which includes and extends all that would be established by
position (1) without insisting on more than is necessary, relevant or
provable. No such view can of course be established without careful
consideration of all the terms of the problem and all the steps of the
argument, the book's unity, method and possible sources of information. Only if position (2) can be upheld, is it possible to ask
whether position (3) is defensible; even if it is inessential, some
secondary considerations arise in this context which are at least
worthy of mention.

In 1882 W.K. Hobart published a classic study, *The Medical Language of St. Luke*, which argued with impressive documentation that
the medical vocabulary of Luke-Acts, as paralleled with the language
of the Greek medical writers, showed the author's medical background. This long seemed a powerful corroboration of the tradition,
until Hobart's work was trenchantly criticized by H.J. Cadbury, who
exposed the perils of arguing from uncontrolled parallels.[6] Many of
Hobart's examples are indecisive or inappropriate. Where a word
might seem distinctively medical it is not necessarily Lukan: αἱμορ-
ροεῖν, for instance, is found only at Mt. 9:20 in the New Testament. In
any case, Greek medicine, which had its roots in philosophy, seems to
have been slow to develop a technical vocabulary, at least until Galen
a century later. Most of the words in Hobart had a much wider currency. So his case can no longer be accepted, though his work

---

6   H.J. Cadbury, *The Style and Literary Method of Luke* ,Harvard Theological
Studies, VI (Cambridge Mass: Harvard University Press, 1920), pp. 39-72, a book
based on Cadbury's doctoral thesis. It has been said that Cadbury won his doc-
torate by taking away Luke's (cf. R.N. Longenecker, 'The Acts of the Apostles',
The Expositor's Bible Commentary, ed. F.E. Gaebelein, Vol. 9 [Grand Rapids: Zondervan, 1981], p. 240). Cf. also Cadbury, 'Lexical Notes on Luke-Acts. II. Recent
Arguments for Medical Language', *JBL* 45 (1926), pp. 190-209.

remains valuable as a compendium of lexical evidence. It also remains true that the failure of a hypothesis does not amount to disproof of its essential contention. Hobart reveals 'Luke' as a man of considerable Greek culture, which is consistent with the tradition.

The tradition of 'Luke the physician' continued to find strong advocates in W.M. Ramsay and A. von Harnack[7] before Cadbury's strictures and the shift of interest in Germany induced by Dibelius changed the focus of this aspect of debate. Cadbury himself stressed that arguments for or against the tradition are essentially unaffected by the medical argument. 'Superficially, however, the traditional view, which at first seemed so brilliantly confirmed by the medical argument is in danger of suffering undeserved discrediting by reason of the continued effort to support it by fallacious and specious arguments.'[8] Thereafter the traditional view carried little weight in Germany, not so much because it was ever refuted as because the developments of form-criticism and style-criticism by-passed the question with an implicit answer.[9] Many British scholars and commentators have continued to adhere to a more traditional view of authorship, without necessarily stressing the medical aspect of the writer's identity.[10] The recent article by W.G. Marx does not really

---

7   A. von Harnack, *Luke the Physician* (London: Williams & Norgate, 1911) tr. J. Wilkinson.

8   Cadbury, 'Recent Arguments', p. 209.

9   Dibelius held firmly to Lukan authorship while also regarding the pronoun 'we' as secondary, and as literary in Acts 27-28, where it did not represent an 'itinerary' source. His reasons for defending traditional authorship were anomalous (and dubious), and hence vulnerable to successors who carried further the logic of his approach. See esp. Dibelius, *Studies*, pp. 146-48 for his view of the work being distributed through Theophilus as patron and requiring a known author's name (cf. also pp. 89-90). A.D. Nock points out Dibelius' misunderstanding of the nature of ancient publication (*Gnomon* 25 [1953], pp. 501-502 = *Essays*, ed Z. Stewart, 2.825-26), while himself inclining to shift for other reasons to a traditional view of authorship (*Gnomon*, p. 502 = *Essays* 2.827). Haenchen firmly rejects Dibelius argument, without thereby meeting different reasons for adhering to the tradition '"We" in Acts and Itinerary', *JTC* 1 [1965], p. 71 = *ZTK* 58 [1961], pp. 335-36).

10 Thus among post-Dibelius writers W.L. Knox, *Acts* (CUP, 1948), pp. 1-15; A. Ehrhardt, *Acts* (Manchester University Press, 1969), pp. 3-4; Bruce, *Acts* (London: Tyndale, 1951), pp. 1-8; Williams, *Acts* (London: A. & C. Black, 1957), pp. 5-7; W. Neil, *Acts* (London: Oliphants, 1973), pp. 22-25 (cautiously); Marshall, *Acts* (Leicester: InterVarsity, 1980), pp. 44-46; among non-British writers also J. Munck, *Acts* (Anchor Bible, 1967), pp. xxix-xxxv; W. Michaelis, *Einleitung in das Neuen Testament* (Bern: Graf-Lehmann, 1946), pp. 61-63; Dibelius, *Studies*, p. 192; B. Reicke, *The Gospel of Luke*, tr. by R. MacKenzie from *Lukasevangeliet*, 1962 (London: SPCK, 1965), pp. 10-24.

rehabilitate Hobart against Cadbury.[11] His account of the diversity of contemporary Greek medicine is valuable as a caution against simplistic assumptions, but his arguments for placing Luke in a specific medical context are in their turn essentially illustrations and parallels for his own assumption, and lack rigour to respond to the objections of those not already convinced.

The 'We-Passages'

The evaluation of the 'we-passages' is a crucial issue for the dual problem of authorship and source. These are the passages which lend themselves to the *prima facie* judgment that the writer is claiming to have been present on the occasions described.

The first-person sections may be demarcated as Acts 16:10-17; 20:5-21:17; and chs. 27-28.[12] In each case the passage begins with an unheralded shift from third person to first person narrative, and in the two former cases ends with an unobtrusive transitional shift separating Paul from 'us' (16:17; 21:18), and continuing the account of him where the first person simply fades out.[13] In the final passage there is no first person after 28:16, but also no need for a transition, as the climactic scene in Rome extends to the end of the book. All the three 'we-passages' are essentially travel-narratives, and all focus strongly on a sea-voyage.

Explanations of these passages may be classified under four headings in their possible bearing on the authorship/source question:

(1) that they indicate directly the author's presence as eyewitness;[14]

---

11 W.G. Marx, 'Luke the Physician, Re-examined', *ExpT* 91 (1979-80), pp. 168-72. Marx's article contains a number of interesting speculations based on parallels with contemporary ancient medicine, as that Luke was influenced by the Pneumatist School, and that his interest in the Spirit reflected his earlier concern with πνεῦμα in its different, medical usage. These are perhaps possibilities worth airing, but their status is no higher than that: speculative parallels are without probative force. ([Ed.] See now also 'Doctors in the Graeco-Roman World', *New Docs* 2.10-25, No. 2, which gives various inscriptions.)

12 The first-person plural in the Western variant of Acts 11:28, a passage located in the church in Antioch, is not included in this enumeration. It is possible that this reading reflects the early tradition which connected Luke with that city, but it not to be seen as original. See Metzger, *Textual Comm.*, p. 391.

13 There is no occasion for finding a difficulty in the shifting application of 'we' between inclusive and exclusive senses. It may be applied to any group of persons among whom the speaker is included, even though its composition otherwise changes. Cf. C.J. Hemer, 'First Person Narrative in Acts 27-28', *TB* 36 (1985), p. 81.

14 Thus, for example, Reicke, *Gospel*, p. 20. See throughout this section the

(2) that they reproduce the author's own diary or itinerary notes of events where he was present;[15]

(3) that they reproduce the diary or notes of a person other than the eventual author, who may or may not have redacted them drastically;[16]

(4) that they rest upon no distinctive tradition or source, or are the creation of the author or at most an elaboration of materials without independent integrity the pronouns being explained by some literary device appropriate to a fictional or edificatory genre.[17] These

valuable survey by Vittorio Fusco, 'Le sezioni-noi degli Atti nella discussione recente', *Bibbia e Oriente* 25 (1983), pp. 73-86. The traditional view was first formulated in Irenaeus, *adv. Haer*, 3.14.1: 'Lucas inseparabilis fuit a Paulo, et co-operarius eius in evangelio'.

15   Thus e.g. Barrett, *Luke the Historian*, p. 22; Neil, *Acts*, p. 24.

16   Thus e.g. Kümmel, *Introduction*, pp. 125ff. Kümmel's manner of treatment is problematic. After reaching indirectly the question of authorship, Kümmel rejects the possibility that the 'we-passages' indicate authorial participation on the ground of a misinformation about Paul inconceivable in a companion. He cites three such instances. But two of these are wholly, and the other partly, dependent on what we have argued to be a misidentification of Gal. 2 with Acts 15. He compares unlike with unlike, and stresses the conclusion that they are unlike. But if the identification is wrong, this is a tautology which does not address the problem at all. It is a tangle which pulls out into a single strand of rope, and disguises the fact that there is really a different knot to be untied. The question against Luke needs to be taken more seriously than this would require, and that is at the heart of our theme. Yet Kümmel has created a presumption against Luke by questionable arguments *before* proceeding to discuss the substantial issues, which *follow* his negative judgment. We have said that rejection of a bad argument does not disprove its thesis. It is equally relevant to insist here that Kümmel's problematic choice of examples does not invalidate the case he might have made, and also to recognize that he will often go unchallenged because many scholars would concur with his assumptions and identifications. Our point is simply that he has not interacted with the effective alternative explanation of those who do not share that partial consensus.

17   Haenchen is a prime exponent of this type of view, though it assumes varying forms in his writings (cf. Fusco, p. 77), to express the vividness or importance of an incident (Haenchen, '"We" in Acts', p. 83), or to indicate a source in a personal record (pp. 84-85). Cf. Conzelmann, *Apostelgeschichte*, pp. 5-6; Marxsen, *Introduction*, p. 168. Conzelmann cites Lucian's satirical fantasy *A True Story*. Writers of this school are sometimes confusingly unclear in their statements, seeming to shift their ground and implying in 'Luke' a (false) claim to authorial participation (so Haenchen, *Acts*, p. 85), while elsewhere speaking of literary devices by which nobody was presumably deceived. Fusco (p. 78) points out however that none of the presumed literary practices are effectively attested from Luke's day. It is perhaps the essence of this category that the first person pronoun is explained as secondary, as a device of the eventual author/redactor and therefore potentially separate from the source-question.

categories are not rigidly separate, but represent a spectrum including opposite extremes. We may for instance place Dibelius' view conceptually under (4), not because it represents an extreme of scepticism as such, but because he declines to view the 'we-passages' as a separate entity, and isolates an 'itinerary' by criteria which cut across their distinctiveness, which he explains as a literary figure. Thus his view tells against the use of these passages for our present investigation, though Dibelius actually held to Lukan authorship.

A point of general relevance to the discussion is the widely accepted stylistic unity of Acts. There are certainly diversities within it, the formal literary style of the preface, or the rhetorical opening of the Tertullus speech, beside the Semitic flavour of the Jerusalem scenes, but these are widely accepted as instances of the flexible skills of a writer who knew how to imprint his viewpoint on his work. In fact in a climate sensitive to the distinctives of Lukan theology one need hardly argue closely for the unity of the eventual work, even if this is seen as a wholly redactional phenomenon.[18] Within this larger postulated unity one cannot separate by style or method the actual 'we-passages' from the third-person narratives in which they are embedded. They are certainly among the most vivid and detailed narratives in the book, but so are the Ephesus riot or the Jerusalem arrest, both of which retain the third person.

It is apparent that the 'Lukan' unity of Acts will relate differently to different explanations of the 'we-passages'. It will suit in principle either the assumption that the unity derives from the experience and inquiry of a participant, or that it is redactional, in the former case explanations (1) or (2), in the latter (4). Of course the choice is not so simple as this, and (3) may stand here as representing the possible range of complexity where independent sources may be subject to redaction. Also the factors of source and redaction are relevant across the spectrum, for the participant's experience is filtered and selected through his own individuality and purpose, and the freest composition has its antecedent stimuli.

We may use classification as a starting-point for evaluating the different kinds of explanation. Here (1) and (2) fall close together. They are separated only by the postulation of a two-stage process of composition in the later case. (2) might allow for lapse of time in the writing, for hypotheses which see shifts in Luke's perspective or plurality of editions of his work.[19] Apart from such special

---

18 This final unity of Luke-Acts has become virtually a datum of the problem rarely doubted since the older studies of Harnack and Hawkins. For the attempt by Clark to attribute Luke and Acts to different writers see Chap. 2, pp. 30-32.

19 Those who hold a view of this type include some who for various reasons feel

considerations, it is not clear that a more complex argument is saying anything which may not be included in (1), if we allow for uncertainty in the processes of composition. And there is a stronger point against the (2) formulation. If it is really saying anything distinctive it is that there is a shift in focus from the essence of the case to the reproduction of a putative personal source without altering the pronouns. How is a reader to understand the pronouns? Surely rather as saying 'I was there' than as 'I am using my diary'. The former is more natural and pointed. If the latter is true, the former is being implicitly claimed. Thus (2) tends to collapse into (1), and the use of 'we' involves the claim to personal participation.[20]

The case (3) may include a variety of opinions, but in its simple form poses a similar difficulty. Why should the writer have preserved mechanically the inappropriate pronouns from a narrative by a different, unidentified person? It is a phenomenon oddly out of step with the smooth 'Lukan' unity we have observed, and is hard to square with arguments for redaction. And how could the reader understand it, if not as a claim, true or false, to authorial participation? As an indicator of the limits of a distinctive source it is otherwise rather a mystification, for there is no clue by which the reader may take the point. In fact a sophisticated view of this kind requires a special literary explanation of the pronoun. In this respect (3) and (4) fall together, differing essentially over the issue whether or not a special explanation of the pronoun serves to demarcate a discrete source-unit. This part of our inquiry in fact resolves itself into the question whether the first person is to be understood literally or as a special literary device. The answer to that is not simplistically

---

obliged to date Acts at some distance from the events of its last chapters. The use of a diary is then an understandable *aide-mémoire*. There have also been the questions posed by the 'proto-Luke' hypothesis of the Gospel, and the two editions of Acts, if we may so consider the different versions presented by the Alexandrian and Western texts. In the latter case the arguments of Blass and Zahn for two *Lukan* recensions of Acts have persuaded few. There may in fact be some advantage in looking for a more complex hypothesis if it is necessary to account for a lapse of time. If this is not considered a crucial factor, it may prove gratuitous.

20 Some have sought a Biblical antecedent in Ezra (7:28; etc.), but the use of the first person in this section is part of a complex series of literary, critical and historical problems. It will not suffice to cite so difficult a case as a parallel when clearer parallels are lacking. In any case the use of the pronoun in Ezra functions differently and belongs to a date and literary setting considerably different from that of Acts. If it be argued that the reminiscence is a deliberate following of a Biblical model, one can only repeat the ostensible difference of context and function as rendering an imitation hypothesis implausible.

aligned with the answer to the fundamental question of historicity, but it is a focal point of approach to one of the avenues leading into the heart of that problem. Authorial participation would actually bring sections of Acts into the 'primary' evidence category, in the Knoxian sense, but does not simplistically close in their favour the question of historical value. Conversely, if the first two options are rejected, it is not thereby proved that the passages, being 'secondary', are without historical value. Knox's kind of analysis is too simplistic and dogmatic. But when careful qualifications are made, the 'we-passages' are likely to prove a very helpful guiding thread in the recurring task of discriminating between the ostensible and the reinterpreted. It is another case of choice between straightforward and special interpretations.

Our first task will be to consider the viability of various literary explanations. These seem to be classifiable under four headings, of which the second in particular, may comprehend a variety of hypotheses of a related type.

(a) The 'we-passages' should be explained as the writer's device for indicating an ultimate eyewitness source.

(b) The device is to be understood as a secondary or redactional signal to draw special attention to the passage, as vivid, or important, or 'typical'.

(c) This device is a literary convention applied specially to a sea-voyage narrative genre, without any suggestion of the writer's personal participation in the voyage.

(d) The 'we-passages' are used in order to (falsely) claim personal participation.

(a) represents a more sophisticated explanation of the second option above, suggesting that the unassimilated 'we' of a source was not merely left anomalously unedited, but deliberately retained as an indicator to the reader. It seems open to the same type of objection, perhaps even in greater degree. It is not clear how the reader is expected to get the message. The reader will naturally take the point in its direct sense, that the writer himself is claiming to have been there, by-passing this refinement. The case is not saved by parallels purporting to prove the existence of a literary convention of this more elaborate kind. Nock, a writer sceptical towards Dibelius' defence of Lukan authorship, if himself a hesitant convert to that position, and a formidable authority on the ancient literature, knew 'only one possible parallel for the emphatic use of a questionable "we" in consecutive narrative outside literature which is palpably fictional'.[21]

---

[21] Nock, *Essays* 2.827-28.

Even that one case is keenly debated, and in other suggested instances the 'we' is almost certainly that of an eyewitness. In fact this option tends again to resolve itself into a simpler and more direct recognition of an eyewitness claim, however mediated through diary or notes.

(b) Views of this kind are characteristic of the Dibelius School. Dibelius himself, in isolating the 'itinerary' source from any organic link with the 'we-passages', regards the latter as secondary and redactional. Some of them happen to overlap with parts of the 'itinerary', but in Acts 27-28 the whole passage is a secular literary structure, with inserted references to Paul, the 'we' indicating that Luke was there, without apparently inhibiting his freedom of literary composition.[22] The problem with this approach is again in the difficulty of finding satisfactory parallels for the supposed literary practices. Unless something specific can be shown, it is hard to overcome the ostensible difficulty that the reader is given no clue to what the critic supposes to have been in the author's mind.

(c) The most elaborately expounded and defended view of a literary explanation of the 'we-passages' is contained in the recent articles of V.K. Robbins.[23] Robbins seeks to isolate a narrative genre for sea-voyages, as being conventionally rendered in the first person plural, and cites extensive examples from ancient literature alleged to be in support of his contention. I have discussed Robbins' views extensively in a recent article, and need not repeat here more than the gist of that argument.[24] His examples are not necessarily representative, nor are they always taken correctly in context, nor are they subject to control, nor do they prove the conclusions he draws from them. These criticisms are especially applicable to the instances he offers as the most precise parallels with Acts. (i) In the *Voyage of Hanno* 1-3 the two opening sentences are in the third person, and the remainder of the document in the first plural.[25] But the opening is a

---

22 Dibelius, *Studies*, pp. 107, 136, 205-206; cf. Haenchen, '"We" in Acts'. See further p. 313, n. 17.

23 V.K. Robbins, 'The We-Passages in Acts and Ancient Sea-Voyages', *BibRes* 20 (1975), pp. 5-18; 'By Land and By Sea: The We-Passages and Ancient Sea Voyages', *Perspectives on Luke-Acts*, ed. C.H. Talbert (Edinburgh: T. & T. Clark, 1978), pp. 215-42.

24 C.J. Hemer, 'First Person Narrative in Acts 27-28', *TB* 36 (1985), pp. 79-109. I am grateful to Professor C.K. Barrett for his kindness in letting me see the typescript of his paper on 'Paul Shipwrecked' in the *Festschrift* for A.T. Hanson which includes a valuable critical discussion of Robbins' view. ([Ed.] B.P. Thompson, ed., *Scripture and Meaning– Essays presented to Anthony Tyrrell Hanson* [Hull University Press, 1987], pp. 51-64.)

25 The text will be found in *GGM*, 1.1-14.

formal heading which gives the explorer's commissioning, and it should be printed as a prefatory paragraph, as it is by its editor, and not as part of a continuous undifferentiated narrative, as it is in Robbins' rendering.[26] In any case the narrative *is* presented as the report on an actual voyage under the command of the author. (ii) In the case of the fragmentary papyrus narration of some incidents in the Third Syrian War, Robbins takes his citation out of its (mutilated) context.[27] Enough is preserved to show that the text contains a narrative of conflict between 'us' and 'them', the Ptolemies and the Seleucids, narrated by a participant on the Ptolemaic side. Robbins contrasts what 'they' do on land and 'we' by sea, but, in fact, the sentence preceding tells what 'they' (the enemy) did by sea. Clearly, the use of 'we' has to do with the identity of the actors and not with the nautical setting. (iii) *The Antiochene Acts of Ignatius* is the most difficult case, and does certainly contain an abrupt and unmarked shift to the first person plural in mid-course (as it were).[28] J.B. Lightfoot is severe on this document, which seems to be both composite and late. The 'we-passage' comes in *during* a sea-voyage, and extends *beyond* it. Awkward as it is, it seems to mark out Ignatius from companions who include the narrator. And it is precisely the 'we-section', allied to an eyewitness profession and to its intrinsic plausibility and lack of the demonstrable blunders apparent elsewhere, which leads Lightfoot to entertain the possibility that this part contains authentic tradition. In any case the document as a whole does not further Robbins' thesis. As it is probably both late and composite, it is at best uncertain material for arguing literary intention. And, as it stands, the preceding part of the voyage is rendered in the third person, and the change of pronoun comes in the wrong place. Robbins' many other examples are open to criticism on various similar grounds, and it is unnecessary to repeat the discussion of them.[29]

---

26 The text begins ἔδοξε Καρχηδονίοις "Αννωνα πλεῖν ἔξω Στηλῶν Ἡρακλείων ... καὶ ἔπλευσε. The first sentence of the actual narrative has the verb ἐπλεύσαμεν. This document, whose authenticity seems not to be disputed, is evidently a rendering of a Punic original.

27 First published by J.P. Mahaffy, *The Flinders Petrie Papyri* (Dublin: Academy House, 1893), 2, No. 45, pp. 145-49. There is an improved text in L. Mitteis and U. Wilcken, *Grundzüge und Chrestomathie der Papyruskunde*, Vol. 2, Part 1 (Leipzig: Teubner, 1912), No. 1, pp. 1-7. The account deals with the events of 246 BC.

28 J.B. Lightfoot, *The Apostolic Fathers* Part 2, Vol. 2 (London: Macmillan, 2nd edn, 1889), pp. 477-95 (text and commentary), pp. 575-79 (translation), pp. 383-91 (critical discussion).

29 See Hemer, 'First Person Narrative', pp. 81-86. The examples are of widely diverse kinds. The first person narratives of the *Odyssey* and the *Aeneid* are part

Nothing said here disposes of the fact that voyage-narratives are often couched in the 'we-form', but this is a natural tendency dictated by the situation. Such accounts are indeed often in the first person, because they recall personal experience, and plural because they recall communal experience. That tendency is as true of colloquial English as of literary Greek (or Latin), but it is no proof of the existence of a literary style appropriate to what was *not* personal experience. If the narrative is fiction anyhow (as in Lucian, Achilles Tatius or Heliodorus) the 'we' still functions naturally within the dramatic dimension of the fiction. Indeed, the examples discussed by Robbins are drawn from widely differing genres (in a more usual sense of that word), and the notion that an exclusively defined *Gattung* can be isolated by simple or composite verbal or syntactical criteria across a wide variety of prose and poetry of different types and languages is inherently suspect. Robbins' paradigm does not work, and cannot be used to draw larger conclusions about the narrative of Acts 27-28.

(d) The suggestion that the 'we-passages' embody a false claim to personal participation seems a stronger alternative than any of the preceding. It involves no special explanation. Where others postulate literary practices which we cannot satisfactorily parallel but by which nobody then, it seems, was deceived, this requires only a straight reading of the ostensible significance of the pronoun, subject to a realization that its implied claim is false, and that its intention was to deceive. The whole question, of course, cannot be reduced to a simplistic, monolithic choice between truthfulness and deceit. We

of a 'flashback' technique in the larger structure of the poems, not limited specifically to sea-voyages. Similar techniques are employed in the fictional narratives of the first person in Hellenistic romance (Achilles Tatius, Heliodorus), in satirical fantasy (Lucian's *True Story*) or in personal anecdote in oratory (Dio Chrysostom). In each case the pronouns fulfill their natural function, and the first person plural sections are coterminous not with a voyage, but with the narrator's inclusion in a group. In Ovid's lament in exile (*Tristia* 1.2) first persons singular and plural are mingled *metri gratia* in maritime and none-maritime contexts alike, but the meaning in every case is 'I'. The geographical compilers in *GGM* on whom Robbins also relies relapse on occasion into an 'authorial' first person, or refer to 'our time' (the present) or 'our sea' (the Mediterranean) in otherwise impersonal catalogues of places and distances. These phenomena are trivial, natural and unpretentious, and do not suffice as parallels for a supposedly significant usage in Acts. They grade rather into the cases where a less literate writer (or stone cutter) may be unable to sustain a formal self-reference in the third person, and slips incongruously into the first. Thus in confession texts: (ὁ θεὸς) ἐκολάσετο αὐτήν ... καὶ ἐκέλευσεν ... καταγράψαι ἐμαυτὸν [sic] ἰς ὑπηρεσίαν τοῖς θεοῖς (*CMRDM* 1, pp. 30-31, No. 47, of Ayazviran, Lydia, AD 118-19).

must have a sense of caution and respect for those who for chronological or redactional reasons feel obliged to remove the final Lukan redaction from the 'we-source' and to make the best of the literary difficulty this causes. But this difficulty is not a necessary one, and if in fact Acts is to be dated earlier than they might require, the objections to a simpler hypothesis tend to evaporate. This last alternative highlights the real clash of opinion, whether 'we' really represents a participant writer or source, at however many removes you will, or a pseudo-authentication of an unaccredited document. The argument that the latter could have been produced by acceptable literary practices seems to have worn exceedingly threadbare. You may insist at least that there was no intention to deceive, and I take your word for it. But when we are asking the question of historicity, which we must ask, we have to ask not only of the literary morality of our author but about the credentials of the evidence he purports to provide. And the discussion of the literary questions has often been allowed to blur or foreclose that issue, the more so in scholars whose positions seem to shift confusingly between literary explanations and an implicit, unargued historical scepticism.[30] In fact option (d) is not often put so bluntly as an option at all. Yet Fusco (p. 80) goes so far as to suggest that it is the only real alternative to the tradition. It is certainly the point which opens the sharpest dichotomy of opinion for our own question of historicity, and diverse literary explanations tend to be subsumed as qualifications to one side or other of the dichotomy.

There is a widespread academic tradition which justifies pseudonymity but ours is not even a case of pseudonymity, but of anonymity. The writer does not claim an identity, but implies a participation, and in the most restrained terms. The conventional defence of pseudepigraphy, itself questionable, is not exactly applicable here. If our author is implying an unjustified claim, the very fact has far-reaching implications for our estimate of him as a writer, and a precarious defence of him as using supposedly acceptable practices of his day will not suffice to rehabilitate him when we ask the crucial question how we may value him from our own perspective.

Option (d) has however been defended by some. Overbeck, accepting that the first person indicated that the writer was using a source, though very freely, explains its retention as due to a deliberate attempt to pass himself off as a companion of Paul, probably the traditional Luke.[31] Conzelmann and Lindemann see the

---

30 Cf. p. 313, n. 17.

31 *Introduction*, pp. 43, 52-53 in Zeller, *Contents and Origin*, Vol. 1. Note

'we-passages' as heavily reworked, and not at all close to the events.[32]

The difficulties in this view are evident. (i) If the writer were attempting to carry conviction by inserting an implicit eyewitness claim, why did he do this sporadically? If the claim was true, this is natural enough, for his presence was sporadic. But it would have been remarkably disingenuous in a redactor.[33] (ii) Why did he make his claim so inconspicuously? The pseudepigrapher might be expected to make his point much more emphatically, to ensure that his reader could not miss it.[34] (iii) This issue leads us back into the crucial centre of the debate, the question what kind of writer Luke was, and whether or not his claims are likely to be justified by the larger evaluation of the evidence he provides. This matter again seems too often to be prejudged negatively on strongly held assumptions about Luke's distance from Paul. But this is once more the very point of debate. We must at least give weight to complementary aspects of the evidence.

We may conclude by stressing afresh the choice posed by the ostensible claim of the author to have been a participant. Alternatives to admitting that claim involve their own difficulties. It may be thought that the necessities of the case entail accepting those difficulties, but it remains a crucial question whether or not (in principle, with whatever qualification is thought to be required) the 'we-passages' have an eyewitness origin. That issue must be judged from the evidence.

The Meaning of the 'We-Passages': Internal Evidence

It will be the purpose of this section to begin addressing the evidence for Luke's purpose and practice. This will involve in part the drawing together and application of several strands of evidence discussed in earlier chapters, together with some discussion of Luke's stated principles in his own Preface. It is with the terminology of the Preface that we must begin.

The word αὐτόπτης (Lk. 1:2) is commonly rendered 'eyewitness'.

however the difficulty of sorting out the conflicting contributions of de Wette and Overbeck to this work (see Gasque, *History of Criticism*, p. 81n). There is no question that this more sceptical view belongs to Overbeck.

[32] H. Conzelmann and A. Lindemann, *Arbeitsbuch zum Neuen Testament* (Tübingen: J.C.B. Mohr, 2nd edn, 1976), pp. 272-73. Cf. also G. Lüdemann, *Paul*, pp. 25-29 = *Paulus* 1.52-53.

[33] Cf. Kümmel, *Introduction*, p. 184.

[34] Cf. van Unnik in Kremer, p. 42.

The question is raised whether this and other expressions in the Preface throw any light on the 'we-passages'. The immediate response here is negative, for Luke makes no claim here to have been himself αὐτόπτης, but says he received material from 'αὐτόπται and ministers of the word'. We may allow that he is referring here principally, if not entirely, to his sources for the Gospel, for which in any case the question of eyewitness participation does not arise. Another question is however raised by the verb παρακολουθεῖν in Lk. 1:3. Cadbury has repeatedly stressed the importance of this word, as implying a strong claim, more to participation than to mere inquiry.[35] But this interpretation too is indecisive. It attempts to prove too much, for it involves the supposition that Luke is making a claim, primarily for the Gospel, which is appropriate only to the latter half of the sequel. It is of interest that the actual usage of the verb tends to support Cadbury.[36] But the implication is not to be pressed here. The verb may rightly be taken at least as a claim to have undertaken close and careful research, itself a point of importance.

There is now a most important study of the word αὐτόπτης in the work of Loveday Alexander on Luke's Preface.[37] Alexander distinguishes generalized uses of the word from those places where it carries a methodological force, and shows how its literary usage developed. In some cases, she suggests, it may be less strictly 'eyewitness' (μάρτυς) than 'inspector on the scene of the crime'. Its background is often geographical, and allied to a Herodotean concept of history written by the travelling investigator, an idea taken up especially in Polybius. She lists all available occurrences of the word in surviving Greek, literary and non-literary, and this permits a careful determination of the exact force of the word in terms of its specific semantic oppositions. In many contexts it is precisely 'eyewitness'. Yet you cannot necessarily prearrange to witness unexpected events or to choose to be present at those whose

---

[35] H.J. Cadbury, 'The Knowledge Claimed in Luke's Preface', *Expos* 8th ser. 24 (1922), pp. 401-20; *BC* 2.501-502; '"We" and "I" Passages in Luke-Acts', *NTS* 3 (1956-57), pp. 128-32.

[36] See *MM* pp. 485-86, referring *inter alia* to Cadbury's two earlier statements of his case. The strength of his point here must be acknowledged; he is emphatic against the conventional 'investigative' view: 'It is nearly as difficult to find any modern protest against it as to find any ancient evidence to support it' (Cadbury, 'Knowledge Claimed', p. 408).

[37] Originally in her Oxford D.Phil. thesis L.C.A. Alexander, *Luke-Acts in its Contemporary Setting with Special Reference to the Prefaces (Luke 1:1-4 and Acts 1:1)* (Oxford, 1977). See now her article 'Luke's Preface in the Context of Greek Preface-Writing', *NovT* 28 (1986), pp. 48-74. Her work is due to be published in the *SNTS Monograph* series.

significance only appears in retrospect. Alexander emphasizes the very close connection of thought between empiricist medicine and some types of historiography: the bulk of all occurrences of αὐτόπτης and its cognates are in a historian, Polybius, and a medical writer, Galen. In fact she tends to find the closest parallels for Luke's Preface in the Greek scientific writers rather than the historians.

Conclusions cannot be pressed at this stage, but some interim observations may be offered. The conjunction between medicine and some types of historiography is an interesting one, capable of wider illustration. Thus a classic description of the symptoms of the plague in classical Athens is given by a historian who practised an exacting standard of critical observation (Thuc. 2.48-50), and a tombstone of Smyrna records a select bibliography of the deceased, an otherwise forgotten doctor, medical writer and historian Hermogenes, with 77 medical works to his credit, as well as books on Roman and local history (CIG 2.3311 = IGRR 4.1445). In fact medicine might have some link with history just where αὐτοψία is a concept significant for both, as medicine was otherwise seen as cognate with philosophy. But these cultural connections are merely illustrative, and *prove* nothing. Luke's language just gives a *prima facie* impression of claiming to offer rigorous standards of research analogous with those professed by avowedly scientific disciplines. But its similarities with the language of such as Josephus need to be acknowledged, and we may doubt whether the preface amounts to much more than a literary convention.[38] Arguments of the significance of literary parallels in the forms or content of prefaces are interesting, but we must evaluate Luke and Josephus differently on other grounds. After all these cautions, we must repeat that Luke does not claim in his preface to be αὐτόπτης, but only to have received material from αὐτόπται.[39]

There is a vast literature on the Lukan preface, and our present concern is narrowly defined by our investigation of the author's implied claim to have been an eyewitness participant in parts of Acts. There are two points where the debate impinges, in the suggestion that the preface is akin to those of eyewitness historians or technical

---

38 Cf. Lk. 1:1-4 with the very similar language of Jos. *Ap.* 1.10.53-55, where ἀκριβῶς, παρηκολουθηκότα τοῖς γεγονόσιν and αὐτόπτης are conjoined, and with 1.23.218. The prefaces are less evidently parallel, but cf. the allusion to τὸ ἀκριβές in Jos. *BJ* 1.1.1.2. While Josephus is indispensable when used critically, I am not disposed to value his claims highly at face value. It would be ironical if doubts over Josephus appeared unjustly to impugn Luke's use of the same phraseology.

39 [Ed.] Cf. J.W. Scott, 'Luke's Preface and the Synoptic Problem', unpublished Ph.D. thesis, St. Andrews, 1986, who argues from a detailed study of the preface that Luke used no written sources.

writers, and in other items of the preface's language (ἀσφάλεια, παρακολουθεῖν, etc.).

Most of the arguments from literary parallels are of doubtful importance. They are apt to measure by mechanical criteria, whether of form or content, within too narrow a field of comparison to establish effective controls. This is precisely the difficulty with the arguments of V.K. Robbins[40] for a biographical model and those of T. Callan[41] for comparison with a new style of historiography reviving Thucydides, to note but two recent studies of this kind. There is better ground for studies which have combined a broader range of evidence with more cautious conclusions, as, for instance, W.C. van Unnik[42] and L. Alexander. There is much to be said for Alexander's contention that Luke's opening was dictated by an 'unconscious' or 'fairly instinctive' adherence to the kind of technical manuals with which he was probably familiar, that this was no self-conscious signal to his readers about the kind of book his Gospel was to be, but exhibits rather 'a *nexus* of parallels which add up to a family resemblance' (with scientific prefaces).[43] He is a natural exponent of a '"Zwischenprosa", literate but not literary' (Alexander, 'Luke's Preface', p. 61), designed primarily for conveying factual information. None of this is to be treated as a back-door way back to 'Luke the physician', nor does Alexander present it as such. Nor does it support self-conscious literary affinity with any of the diverse schools of Greek historiography. In the opposite direction, it should also be noted that even if Luke's cultural presuppositions were absorbed more informally, diverse cultural ideals of history were current, and it still makes sense to ask at what he was aiming and how well he succeeded.

Extensive debate has focused on other key words in the Preface, especially παρηκολουθηκότι ἄνωθεν, κατηχήθης and ἀσφάλειαν. Van Unnik makes the interesting point that there seems to have been no great dispute in antiquity about their meaning, and no suggestion

---

40 V.K. Robbins, 'Prefaces in Greco-Roman Biography and Luke-Acts', *SBL Seminar Papers 1978*, Vol. 2, ed. P. Achtemeier (Missoula, Montana: Scholars Press, 1978), pp. 193-207. Cf. discussion of Talbert in Chapter 2, pp. 37-39.

41 Terrance Callan, 'The Preface of Luke-Acts and Historiography', *NTS* 31 (1985), pp. 576-81. A further problem here is that Callan finds his examples for a new concern with historical truth in writers whose practice is diverse. The deficiencies of Sallust and of Josephus have already been remarked. The group as a whole is a mixed bag, not simply comparable with Thucydides or Polybius.

42 W.C. van Unnik, 'Remarks on the Purpose of Luke's Historical Writing (Luke i 1-4)', *Sparsa Collecta* (*NovT* Supp 29 [1973]), pp. 6-15; 'Once More St. Luke's Prologue', *Neotestamentica* 7 (1973), pp. 7-26.

43 Alexander, 'Luke's Preface', pp. 64-65.

then that they were felt to be ambiguous.[44] Rather, he suggests, modern interpreters are inclined to forget Lk. 1:1-4 as soon as they proceed to Lk. 1:5ff.[45] The trend of these remarks is to deter the attitude of scepticism which battens on over-subtlety in denying that Luke means what he appears to say. Of παρακολουθεῖν we have written above (see pp. 322; 98-99), declining to press it as far as the evidence of usage might perhaps permit. The starting-point for consideration of the other terms must be Cadbury's commentary on the Preface in *BC* 2.489-510. His cautions against reading too precise an implication into the passage are salutary, yet his own word-by-word analysis seems to accumulate variants rather than limiting them by their semantic context. If after all the author's lofty pretensions are no more than a literary convention, the effort to categorize them might seem wasted. Some selective comment is called for, to give Luke's statements their reasonable weight, without overplaying the hand. It sometimes appears, for instance, that modern writers are inclined to read in over-subtle theological implications which make Luke answer questions belonging to our time, not his.[46] For example, Cadbury's contention that κατηχήθης implies hostile misinformation, and that Theophilus was an influential non-Christian to be disabused of misunderstandings is an nuance that is due more to modern arguments about the purpose of Acts than to first century usage of the term.[47] When extraneous considerations are excluded, we are still left with a claim involving ἀσφάλεια and ἀκριβῶς, which it seems best to take with παρηκολουθηκότι.[48] A further point is the association of

---

44 Van Unnik, 'Once More', p. 9. The problem, if problem there is, lies not in Luke's ambiguity of expression, but in his different cultural presuppositions.

45 Van Unnik, 'Once More', p. 9.

46 Thus perhaps I.J. du Plessis, 'Once More: The Purpose of Luke's Prologue (Lk. 1 1-4)', *NovT* 16 (1974), pp. 259-71. In rendering ἀσφάλεια as 'certainty' or 'reliability' on the basis of New Testament usage, he insists that not only 'the historical veracity' but also Luke's 'theological reflection' is important to this ἀσφάλεια: 'Luke fits historical facts into his theological schema to suit his purpose and does so without having any objections to claim his narrative as a true report' (p. 270). I have no problem with this conjunction of history with theology, though I should formulate it rather differently. Yet one cannot escape the feeling that these are du Plessis's reflections rather than Luke's.

47 Cadbury is non-committal in his first discussion of the word in *BC* 2.508-509, but inclines to the negative view, and a more apologetic thrust for Luke's work in view of (unspecified) passages in Acts (*BC* 2.510). But usage seems not to favour this nuance, and the question of context here is projected into the larger arena of the purpose of Acts. Cf. Jos. *Vita* 65.366 ('inform you of much not generally known'). See further note 49 below.

48 So J.M. Creed, *The Gospel according to St. Luke* (London: Macmillan, 1942), p.

the term ἄνωθεν with the same participle, though again we shall not press as an equivalence the apparent parallelism with ἀπ' ἀρχῆς in the preceding clause. Even a restrained interpretation of the whole sentence implies a claim at least to personal investigation of events going back to the ministry of Jesus. ἀσφάλεια is a focus of debate here. Cadbury argues again from the associations of words in Lukan usage,[49] to link this word with the accusation context of τὸ ἀσφαλές in Acts 21:34; 22:30; 25:26 to mean 'the facts' (as opposed to misinformation and slander) rather than the 'trustworthiness' of a message received, a view consonant with seeing a strongly apologetic thrust in the double work.[50] But this sharply antithetical background is doubtful, and it seems wiser to follow van Unnik in understanding the term as 'certainty',[51] the guarantee of the truth Theophilus had heard from preceding, but not contrary, sources.

Differing judgments on these intricate exegetical points are equally supportive, if on slightly shifting ground, of the general contention that the preface embodies an important claim to reliable reporting. And here its first person pronouns are in point. The question may be raised whether these in any sense anticipate the 'we-passages' or otherwise bear on the question of authorship. In the preface, however, the first person plurals (ἡμῖν in Lk. 1:1, 2) are of unspecific reference, and the author designates himself by the singular (κἀμοί, Lk. 1:3), a natural usage resumed in ἐποιησάμην in Acts 1:1. ἡμῖν in Lk. 1:1 presumably denotes the Christian community generally, with which the author identifies himself. The question is then whether ἡμῖν in v. 2 must be refined to apply to Christians 'of our generation', as recipients of a tradition of earlier origin. Such a view might serve as *prima facie* cause to move Luke from participation at an early date. There is no need to argue for a rigid consistency in the application of such inclusive pronouns. Equally, they do not mark a contrast here. Both are generalized, and indeed we should not press other aspects of the wording of this sentence into rigid antitheses where these seem not to have been intended.[52]

5, *ad loc.*

[49] See here Cadbury, 'The Purpose Expressed in Luke's Preface', *Expos* 8th ser. 21 (1921), pp. 431-41.

[50] This view was challenged by F.H. Colson, 'Notes on St. Luke's Preface', *JTS* 24 (1923), pp. 300-309, who criticizes Cadbury's understanding of κατηχήθης and makes a distinction between ἡ ἀσφάλεια as abstract and τὸ ἀσφαλές as concrete. J.H. Ropes, 'St Luke's Preface: ἀσφάλεια and παρακολουθεῖν', *JTS* 25 (1924), pp. 67-71 supports Cadbury on these words, and concurs with his stress on the significance of the preface with regard to the *double* work, including Acts.

[51] Van Unnik, *Sparsa Collecta*, pp. 13-14.

[52] So rightly Cadbury, 'The Knowledge Claimed in Luke's Preface', pp. 412-14:

Cadbury and Ropes both stress the applicability of the Preface to the double Lukan work, and its importance as a background to the otherwise abrupt 'we-passages'.[53] Luke is acknowledging both literary predecessors and oral tradition, while stressing his own qualification to write because of his close contact with events (if πᾶσιν is neuter) from an early stage.[54] He is thus enabled to provide 'confirmation' of the truth in which Theophilus has been instructed. He is not criticizing his predecessors, but rather focusing on his own opportunities to provide fresh corroboration. He is not pointedly separating himself from the αὐτόπται, but affirming the church's debt to them, perhaps with the climactic events of Jesus' ministry particularly in mind. The thrust of the clauses in this carefully structured sentence is cumulative rather than antithetical (cf. καθώς ... ἔδοξε κἀμοί), and Luke's slight ambivalence about his own qualifications (cf. the uncertainty of application in παρηκολουθηκότι ἄνωθεν πᾶσιν) is in keeping with his generally self-effacing character elsewhere. He will not highlight the claim 'I was αὐτόπτης', when this applied in any case only to events late in the sequel and not the bedrock facts about Jesus which were foundational to the tradition, but his use of παρακολουθεῖν (even if we still hesitate to follow Cadbury closely on this) may rather hint at this connotation than exclude it. Most interpreters seem to approach this preface with the idea that Luke is making a large claim which may not be true, as it was a frequent literary convention to make boastful professions sometimes belied in the practice. But careful rereading of the passage imparts a different feeling, that his self-reference is limited to a parenthetical, four-word, participial phrase in an oblique case, as no more than the briefest justification of his purpose in writing.[55] The extant literary parallels are not characterized by this extreme personal reserve. He is drawn into his unobtrusively worded claim only by the need to assure his reader of his credentials. And yet the implications of that claim are still large, even if, in Luke's own spirit, we interpret

'not ... exclusive contrasts but inclusive comparisons', p. 414.

53 Cadbury, 'Knowledge Claimed', p. 414; Ropes, 'St Luke's Preface', pp. 70-71.

54 Our paraphrase intentionally leaves the force of παρακολουθεῖν somewhat open, without necessarily affirming or denying an 'eyewitness' interpretation of it, and certainly not building an argument on any such assumption in either direction. While taking Cadbury's emphatic point that the word does not mean 'investigate', the fact of investigation cannot be excluded from the possible connotation of what may be taken as a more inclusive and less specific term.

55 In the general desire to do justice to all the debatable terms of the statement, the narrow limits and parenthetical character of the actual self-reference are easily overlooked. This personal phrase stands out in clearer isolation when we recognize the generalized reference of the repeated ἡμῖν.

them cautiously. There are two obvious confirmatory arguments for this view. (1) psychologically, a writer making conventional boasts to advertise his wares will make the most of his personal claims. It would be too improbable to posit a writer so disingenuous as to insinuate false credentials through his reluctance to press them.[56] (2) This understanding of Luke provides a natural background for the unobtrusiveness of the 'we-passages', as the work of the same self-effacing reporter, and makes their abruptness the more easily understandable. It may of course be precisely the mark of a careful writer that he does not overstate, and sometimes that involves a generalized, restrained or nuanced assertion of what a less cautious man would claim baldly. Luke was not an eyewitness of the focal events, and he covers his more complex pattern of access to written sources, oral tradition, research, and later personal involvement with a less specifically analysed claim.

To offer such an impression as an appropriate reading of the case does not prove its truth, and an objector may differ, especially if he is already persuaded that Luke-Acts cannot be the work of an author so close to the events. But in that case he must interpret the Preface otherwise, as well as doing justice to the external evidence. I should not in fact press the nuances of my interpretation, but other variant exegeses offer approximations to similar (or stronger) claims for Luke. We turn next to the external evidence to help judge whether these claims are viable.

---

56 Cf. 2 Cor. 10-12. Paul was despised by the Corinthians for not indulging in boasting. There is an interesting and important background in the contemporary practice of rhetoric, and it is an intriguing question how Paul (or Luke) related to it. See E.A. Judge, 'Paul's Boasting in Relation to Contemporary Professional Practice', *ABR* 16 (1968), pp. 37-50; C. Forbes, 'Comparison, Self-Praise and Irony: Paul's Boasting and the Conventions of Hellenistic Rhetoric', *NTS* 32 (1986), pp. 1-30. There is an interesting cultural diversity observable today in the contrast between the remarkable modesty of the opening words of such a British writer as G.B. Caird, *The Language and Imagery of the Bible* (London: Duckworth, 1980) and the bold claims of many American writers. The quality of the work in either case bears almost no relation to the self-projection, and reviewers misread the difference in presentation at their peril. For the idea that Paul actually rejected cultural conventions espoused by some other Christians see Judge, 'The Reaction against Classical Education in the New Testament', *Journal of Christian Education* 77 (1983), pp. 7-14, esp. p. 11 ff. Cf. also Judge, 'Cultural Conformity and Innovation in Paul: Some Clues from Contemporary Documents', *TB* 35 (1984), pp. 12-15. To stress Paul's self-effacement as a rejection of contemporary values by no means proves that the like was true of Luke, but at least this provides an explanation worthy of consideration.

The Meaning of the 'We-Passages': External Evidence

It may seem anomalous to turn to the text of Acts itself, and especially Acts 27-28, in order to discuss the external evidence. We begin therefore with a brief explanation of the sense in which the term is intended. Hitherto we have been concerned with the possible interpretations of Luke's own claims. Here we turn to his practice, and it is at this point that various categories of external evidence impinge upon our understanding of the text and help us further to discriminate between alternatives. It is in that sense that 'external' evidence becomes crucial to what is still essentially the study of Luke's own writing.

Acts 27-28 is a key passage. It may be felt on general grounds that this narrative is vivid and circumstantial, and carries conviction. Such an impression is no doubt widely shared, and is not to be despised. But it will not of itself resolve the objections which have been made against the idea of Luke's participation in the event. Redactional objections on this plane may hold either that the whole narrative is a literary creation incorporating typical themes of voyage and ship-wreck,[57] or, if its individual circumstantiality is acknowledged, that the references to Paul (if not also the implicit ones to Luke) have been interpolated with it.[58]

The former version of the objection is hard to sustain, and the detailed evidence must be deemed fatal to it. It seems apparent even at first sight that the detailed accounts of winds and weather, the correct placing of ports, and the natural association of the voyage with the ships and conditions of the Alexandrian corn-fleet, are too specific and circumstantial to be a mere assemblage of typical literary themes. Invention is not a serious option, apart at least from the experience of an actual voyage to serve as model. The evidence presented below will serve *a fortiori* to argue against sheer invention. The urging of literary genre and the like will do nothing to save this view. We have already observed the failure of Robbins' hypothesis on these lines.[59]

---

[57] Thus e.g. P. Pokorný, 'Die Romfahrt des Paulus und der antike Roman', *ZNW* 64 (1973), pp. 233-44, seeing in the passage a polemic response adopting the form of the 'mystery romance'. Cf. S.P. and M.J. Schierling, 'The Influence of the Ancient Romances on *Acts of the Apostles*', *The Classical Bulletin* 54 (1977-78), pp. 81-88.

[58] Thus e.g. W. Marxsen, *Introduction*, p. 168; H. Conzelmann, *Apostelgeschichte*, p. 6.

[59] I am disquieted by the difficulty of laying to rest hypotheses which never had substantial foundation in the first place. A negative is hard to prove, but it is unfortunate when the landscape becomes littered with demonstrably mistaken

The more serious form of the objection is that which concedes the reality of such a voyage but argues that Luke and Paul are extraneous to it and might be removed from it without damage to the narrative. The implied presence of Luke is intended on this view to lend verisimilitude to a glorification of Paul upon a stage he never really trod. It is of course almost impossible formally to disprove such a negation as Conzelmann offers. But R.P.C. Hanson, in a characteristically fresh and provocative essay,[60] shows that Conzelmann's methods, if applied to Thucydides, could on precisely similar grounds dismiss as improbable, tendentious and legendary a sea-voyage narrative 'which every historian of the ancient world admits to be reliable, not only in substance but in detail' (namely, Thuc. 6.1-61, Hanson, 'Journey', p. 318). In particular, 'it is perfectly possible to detach all the incidents in which Nikias figures and still to leave the account of the expedition quite intact' (p. 317). How could any mention of Paul have been made without such mention being detachable? He was a passenger, 'and passengers are by definition detachable' (p. 318). Yet even the story of Nikias' voyage does not, according to Hanson, give 'as vivid and authentic an impression of historical truth' as that of Paul (p. 318).

Formal proof or disproof is not possible. But, conversely, when there are many progressive indications of the need to integrate the narrative with its ostensible historical situation and to link Luke with Paul at the times and places of the events, it may be claimed that the onus lies rather on the doubter to establish his case for breaking this integration. The essential evidence is contained in my surveys of detail in Chapters 4 and 5, and it remains here only to assess the bearing of such contextual materials on the criticism of our passage. The naming and placing of such rather obscure places as Lasaea and Cauda ought to be verified against contemporary epigraphical documents of those places rather than only against literary sources

---

views which are nevertheless perpetuated and given fresh currency. I find my own words abstracted in a form which suggests I dispute that the Acts narrative was 'characteristic of *the* ancient sea-voyage genre' (*NTA* 30 [1986], p. 38 [my italics]) while implicitly conceding the existence of that entity. But my article disputes fundamentally the supposed evidence for talking at all in such terms, and I think no service is done by the gratuitous perpetuation of a concept whose only function, if it is indeed misconceived, is to confuse and darken counsel. That is what I was saying, however gently I should wish to do so. I have no wish for polemics, nor to criticize a scholar's hypothesis or an abstractor's precision. But there are times when progress depends on clearing mistaken cross-currents from the field of debate.

[60] R.P.C. Hanson, 'The Journey of Paul and the Journey of Nikias. An Experiment in Comparative Historiography', *SE* 4 (1968), pp. 315-18.

which may be inaccurate, or corrupted in transmission. We have offered documentary attestations of both, which, if not *in situ* (apart perhaps from the one fragment to Caudian Zeus), concern the external relations of both places, and evidently preserve the local, perhaps dialectal, forms.[61] The sequence of Luke's narrative places both accurately. Cauda, for instance, is precisely where a ship driven helpless before an east-northeast wind from beyond the shelter of Cape Matala might gain brief respite for necessary manoeuvres and to set a more northward line of drift on the starboard tack. As the implications of such details are further explored, it becomes increasingly difficult to believe that they could have been derived from any contemporary reference work. In the places where we can compare, Luke fares much better than the encyclopaedist Pliny, who might be regarded as the foremost first-century example of such a source. Pliny places Cauda (Gaudos) opposite Hierapytna, some ninety miles too far east (*NH* 4.12.61). Even Ptolemy, who offers a reckoning of latitude and longitude, makes a serious dislocation to the northwest, putting Cauda too near the western end of Crete, in a position which would not suit the unstudied narrative of our text (Ptol. *Geog.* 3.15.8).

Other examples of this kind could readily be assembled from the preceding material. The concurrence of epigraphic testimony to identified places with the topographical requirements of the incidental events of Acts is a bond not easily broken. Theological intention will not explain these details. As the accumulation and compounding of similar indications make alternative explanations progressively more difficult, it becomes exceedingly hard not to believe at least that the author had travelled this way himself.

We can go a little further. Some of our indications reflect, in the same unobtrusive and unstudied way, the pressures, perils and climatic conditions of the end of the sailing season. Observations about the general organization of the corn-supply service are in point here no less than the specifics of winds and harbours on which our documents throw new light. The incidentals are too integrated to have suffered a shift of context, a double *Sitz-im-Leben*. We should have expected either a more self-conscious correctness, or an unconscious shift into vagueness, distortion or error. In fact those who make much of faults in this narrative do so on the grounds of what they consider to be inherent improbabilities, not upon specific and verifiable errors in a passage which lays itself peculiarly open to

---

61 See above, p. 142 and cf. my full discussion in my 'First Person Narrative', *TB* 36 (1985), pp. 79-109 throughout this section.

verification on a number of relatively obscure details.[62]

Further, it would seem Luke's experience was not that of expert nautical knowledge. The documents confirm the impression of a careful observer recording what happened, describing in layman's terms the measures taken by the crew for the ship's safety, without necessarily understanding the rationale of their actions, except as he made it his business to ask for information. He appreciated their obsessive fear of the Syrtes, the obvious peril of being driven on a rocky lee-shore. He is not explicit about the peril of the ship breaking up at sea before they could reach the neighbourhood of land at all, but this fear is evident in the undergirding at the earliest possibility at Cauda and probably implicit in the unspecified desperation of Acts 27:20, when their ignorance of their position combined with the realization that the ship was at the point of breaking and foundering at sea. They were probably well enough able to estimate their likely line of drift, to conclude that they had already missed their only likely salvation in a landfall on Sicily. But matters like these are not stressed interpretatively by Luke. They are implicit in his account of the scene, and yet also fruitful in the light they shed on the explanation of other details. In a similar way, the cumulative indications of the use of Latin or hybrid nautical terms corroborate the likelihood, at first unexpected in a ship of Greek Alexandria, that the seamen's speech was mainly Latin, and that Luke had a Latin-speaking informant or informants. Yet this in turn is the more easily explicable in a ship of the imperial service which may have numbered many Italians, and some Romans on official business, among its ship's company. The actual soundings, too, of the course of a ship approaching St. Paul's Bay in Malta from the east suit the precise locations where, according to Smith, they must first have become aware of the coastal surf and then of the rocks ahead.[63]

Considerations of this kind cannot take us formally beyond the belief that the writer had experienced just such a voyage as he describes. But the crucial question is whether he was the companion of Paul on an actual occasion in Paul's life. May not Paul's part in this narrative still be extraneous? There may be indications to help in

---

[62] Haenchen, for instance, transmits tacitly the acceptance of enough documented detail to suggest a different interpretation from that which his more theoretical scepticism leads him to impose. It is part of our case that that kind of detail needs to be greatly reworked, extended and reapplied.

[63] See above, pp. 146ff. The location on Malta has been debated, but Smith's arguments for the traditional site are most impressive (*Voyage*, chap. 4), and this placing is tacitly accepted by Haenchen, *Acts*, pp. 707-708. For the harbour of Malta and its neighbour, cf. Diod. Sic. 5.12.1, 3; J. Busuttil, 'Maltese Harbours in Antiquity', *Melita Historica* 5 (1968-71), pp. 305-307.

taking our integration of the context yet further. The 'Fast' of Acts 27:9 was the Day of Atonement on 10th Tishri.[64] It must be presumed that this occasion is marked because Paul, a Jew, rather than Luke himself, traditionally a Gentile, celebrated it at Fair Havens. Its date depended on the lunar calendar, and the reference gathers added force from the implication that it fell late that year. Apart from the fact that this again indicates the more forcefully the perilous lateness of the voyage, it eases the chronology of the winter following. For even on a late dating of the Fast they presumably sailed before the Feast of Tabernacles five days later, which is not mentioned, and they could scarcely have reached Malta before the end of October. Even if we allow three days with Publius on Malta and some further days to settle there outside the reckoning of three full months on the island, it is difficult to place the departure on board the 'Dioscuri' later than the beginning of February, a time when Pliny says the west winds mark the onset of spring (*NH* 2.47.122), but still perilously early for men under less pressure of duty or profit (2.47.126). As we have argued above, the chronological data point to the further integration of the first person narrative with the requirements of ostensible Pauline chronology.

None of this, I repeat, serves as formal 'proof', but the piecing together of these details and their like tends progressively to the integration of Luke with Paul at a particular date and occasion appropriate, even exclusively appropriate, to the ostensible chronology of Paul's life. In such a case the onus is scarcely upon me to prove my point. Rather it is the objector's task to break the integration *which is latent in the narrative*, and merely brought to the surface in the present discussion.

The question might be pursued whether the previous 'we-passages' exhibit similar phenomena. A good case of a similar kind may in fact be argued for Acts 20:5 - 21:17, where we have time-sequence in a narrative covering in a diary-like form the seven weeks between Passover and Pentecost.[65] Acts 16 is further in the past. In character it differs somewhat from the very detailed, vivid and circumstantial narratives of Acts 20-21 and 27-28. It remains a singularly interesting pericope, consistent at least with the possibility

---

64 See above pp.137-38, n. 109. The chronological point discussed in this para-graph comes essentially from W.P. Workman, 'A New Date-Indication in Acts' *ExpT* 11 (1899-1900), pp. 316-19, and is often mentioned by later writers (e.g. Bruce, *Acts*, pp. 455-56; Haenchen, *Acts*, p. 700). I have slightly modified the presentation of his argument.

65 Which has been linked to the calendrical requirements of AD 59 after two years' captivity in Caesarea.

that its reserved brevity covers Luke's diffident self-introduction, leading to a very vivid scene in Philippi, where the author was ostensibly then present, and from where the first-person narrative is resumed at 20:5.

Enough has been said to indicate the prospects of integrating the common participation of Luke and Paul in specific occasions further integrated into the ostensible course of the latter years of Paul's ministry. This view inevitably conflicts with the far-reaching scepticism of those who have denied the possibility of Luke's presence upon extrapolation from his supposed errors (cf. p. 313, n. 17 above). If our reading of the Galatian crux can be accepted, the main basis for that sweeping judgment is removed. No adequate argument for or against Luke can reasonably be mounted upon the fragmentary (and even interdependent) grounds on which some have been content to build. In the present study we have sought at least to provide an extensive survey of the evidence bearing on Luke's knowledge of detail, and that excludes the kind of scepticism which damns a writer who is at odds with his critic on a cluster of related issues which the critic himself may have misapprehended. To say that is not to prove Luke reliable, nor to prove him a participant, but to suggest that the grounds on which this option has been confidently denied are so trivial and superficial as to be unworthy of serious attention. The presumption, at least, ought to be in Luke's favour unless his work is subjected to a far more searching and detailed criticism. If he is suspect, the challenge to him ought to be a far more serious one. As the evidence stands, we are constrained to see him as present in the 'we-passages', for this option gives the most reasonable explanation. A structure built on a debated point is usually to be avoided, but in this case there are good reasons for supposing our position is a strong one. And the task is not exactly to build on it, so much as to argue that the trend of this study is aligned with that of complementary approaches to the character of Luke's work.66

66 It will be useful to cite some of the (often emphatic) judgments of scholars in favour of a view of authorship by a companion of Paul:

A. Plummer, 'It is perhaps no exaggeration to say that nothing in biblical criticism is more certain than this statement' ['The Author of Acts was a companion of S. Paul'], *A Critical and Exegetical Commentary on the Gospel according to St. Luke,* ICC (Edinburgh: T. & T. Clark, 4th edn, 1901), p. xii.

G. Edmundson, 'The case for the Lukan authorship of the Third Gospel and Acts I consider however to have been so thoroughly established [by Ramsay and Harnack] ... as to have been placed ... on a solid bedrock of reasoned and exhaustive argument against which the waves of controversy will beat in vain' (*Church in Rome*, pp. 31-32).

Id., 'There are few passages in ancient historical literatures more clearly the

Sources

Any judgment on the vexed question of authorship would be a watershed also for the intimately linked question of sources. Yet this problem retains its independent difficulty. It is widely agreed, on any view of authorship, that Luke has made his material his own. His double-work is a compositional unity, and its sources are correspondingly harder to detect and demarcate. The classic work of J. Dupont[67] shows the difficulty clearly, and we make no pretension to attempt to duplicate with a superficial study what he has undertaken so meticulously and comprehensively. He concludes with a pessimistic impression: 'Despite the most careful and detailed research, it has not been possible to define any of the sources used by the author of Acts in a way which will meet with widespread agreement among the critics' (*Sources*, p. 166). To this he adds a positive note that these efforts are not lost, but that they uncover special features of the book's composition which both promote and frustrate the search, and also reveal the author's individual turn of mind. 'The information is not only reported in his own style, in its very substance it generally reflects his personality. Everything is done as if Luke were at the origin not only of the edited version, but even of the sources on which that version is based' (p. 167). His final comments concern the crucial matter of the 'we-sections', in which he insists on careful literary method, and maintains that the author wishes it to be known that he had personally taken part in some of the events he narrates.

My purpose here is much more modest, to focus on the question of how Luke is likely to have gained access to the material contained in his double work. In this limited sense, the question of sources is directly ancillary to that of authorship. If the author was indeed a companion of Paul, his opportunities were of a different kind from those likely to have been available to a theological advocate of a later generation. If our understanding of his access to material proves consistent with one judgment about authorship, this will afford some support for our position.

The present section will develop remarks adumbrated in *BJRL* 60 (1977-78) pp. 48-49. I offered there four 'putative categories' in the

work not merely of a contemporary writer but of an observant eye-witness than is the narrative contained in the last seven chapters of the Acts' (p. 87).

[67] J. Dupont, *The Sources of Acts. The Present Position*, tr. K. Pond (London: Darton, Longman and Todd, 1964) from *Les sources du livre des Actes. État de la question* (Bruges: Desclée de Brouwer, 1960).

source-material of Acts: (1) passages based on Luke's personal recollection of events at which he was present (the 'we-passages'; (2) those based on personal communication with Paul of Tarsus, a person with whom he was in constant and intimate association before and perhaps during the period of the writing— to these two categories belong kinds of material which may be taken to be vivid, rich and subtle in their circumstantiality, often selected and summarized from a fuller context of knowledge; (3) isolated fragments of vivid eyewitness material from other persons, often embedded in a vaguer summarized context;[68] and (4) material hitherto unclassified, for which the whole source-question is wide open. There may or may not have been documentary sources in this category. Luke was not the earliest evangelist, but he may have been the earliest church historian. There may well be here too summary material which came from personal inquiry. The catalogue of nations at Pentecost does not require elaborate explanation from astrological geography,[69] but may be simply a summary of cases Luke heard about when pursuing inquiries in Jerusalem. It would have taken a much larger context of knowledge to have assimilated the geographical nomenclature to his usual forms, so he has to reproduce it in the forms in which it reached him. So in these categories of material which were more remote Luke was probably limited by the patchier availability of sources.

There is no suggestion that these 'putative categories' correspond to actual source documents which may be demarcated. The classification is intended only as a conceptual tool to denote kinds of material. And here our study must take account of the double work Luke-Acts, and raise also the question of how our categories relate to the sources and literary method of the Third Gospel. In terms of this analysis the essential Synoptic source-problem might be subsumed under (4), as comprising whatever written sources or oral traditions were available to Luke, in this case including Mark and Q (whatever status we may choose to give the material so designated). Categories (1) and (2) will not apply at all, for there is no serious suggestion that Luke was an eyewitness of events in Jesus' life, nor any probability

---

[68] An example is the incident of Peter's release from prison in Acts 12, which could be explained as drawn from personal interviews with Peter and with Rhoda. Here are the vivid perspectives of two witnesses combined in a setting of loose ends.

[69] Thus Stefan Weinstock, 'The Geographical Catalogue in Acts II, 9-11', *JRS* 38 (1948), pp. 43-46. See the response by B.M. Metzger, 'Ancient Astrological Geography and Acts 2:9-11', *Apostolic History and the Gospel* (*Festschrift* F.F. Bruce), ed. Gasque and Martin (Exeter: Paternoster, 1970), pp. 123-33.

that he was in prolonged intimacy with any who were. His information there does not have the contextual control and completeness that we have in parts of Acts. Category (3) is of particular interest here, and it is worth pursuing the question whether there are significant parallels between the Acts examples and the 'L-passages' and Lukan nuances in the Gospel. The existence of similar types of matter in the two works is most likely to appear in this category, which may thus be the most valuable indicator of Lukan method. It will not be surprising if its quantity is sparser in Luke's Gospel, in view of the greater lapse of time. Yet the two works are united by common characters in the narrative, the most notable being Peter.

It is no part of our theme to pursue the Synoptic source problem, but it is at least desirable to consider whether the common authorship of Luke-Acts has imprinted some continuity of method in the handling of sources in the two writings. The quest is made more difficult by the evident difference in type between them, and the diverse kinds of source problems involved. The Third Gospel depends mainly on sources preserved or inferable, whereas Acts seems to lack written precursors. The source problem in the Gospel can at least be posed in a very tangible form, whereas in Acts the difficulty of isolating the prehistory of our text is in tension with the abundance of collateral evidence in literature and epigraphy for evaluating the finished product. It is then just in the third category that our prospects reside of furthering the inquiry into continuity of method, overlaid elsewhere by the diversity of access to material.

We are reduced then first to the consideration of a single relatively limited category. At this point we observe two phenomena which repeatedly fall together. One is the recurring mention by Luke, in both parts of his work, of persons incidental to the narrative, especially women. The other, concurrent with it at least in the Third Gospel, where alone we have the necessary comparative material, is that these are the same passages which contain other details, nuances or editing of content peculiar to Luke, what we may term, without prejudice to further consideration of their states, 'L-passages' or 'L-nuances'. Further, the sort of additional detail in all these passages is amenable to a similar kind of analysis. The following tabulation offers first a group of passages from the Third Gospel, with a note of a person mentioned in each, and of details peculiar to them which separate them from preceding Synoptic tradition as represented by Mark or Q (a term which is used here simply as a useful classification for an inferred type of sayings material). This brief has however been interpreted broadly, to bring together a full statement of the possible evidence even if some instances may prove to exemplify related or different phenomena. Secondly, there is listed a number of passages from Acts, mainly from the earlier chapters, which also mention an otherwise unimportant person, and appear to exhibit similar phenomena which suggest the possibility of a similar source analysis, though in Acts we lack the comparative material for isolating them with the same precision.

We shall not press here what might appear as the first and longest passage which might be placed in this Lukan category, the whole Nativity complex of Lk. 1:5-2:40, which may be considered *sui generis*. It might indeed at face value be thought to corroborate the same approach, and Luke 2:19 might be deemed just the type of personal note which belongs to this form. But there are special difficulties in using this passage, and those difficulties ought at least to be recognized before making any simplistic appropriation of it for the support it might be claimed to provide for our case. (1) The whole complex is unparalleled in the other Synoptics, and poses its own source-problem on a larger scale, where the comparative base is lacking. (2) The passage contains a number of acute and unsolved historical problems, for which at best we lack the necessary context of knowledge to attempt a solution in any direction. In such circumstances we should at least not rush to claim singly what might suit a case, apart from a deeper study. (3) Even if 2:19 be pressed, the pattern of this passage differs in form from that which we have noted as characteristic of a recurring type, for Mary (and her cousin Elizabeth) are central figures in the scene, whose presence has not to be explained apart from their relevance to the action. (4) Other features of the scene, like the extended hymns of praise, are distinct from anything elsewhere in the Third Gospel. These four points together counsel caution. It might indeed prove that there is nothing in them inconsistent with what we propose to argue from clearer instances, but the passage is at most consonant rather than probative.[70]

Here are tabulated the instances which follow the Nativity passage:

Luke 2:41-52 The incident in the Temple when Jesus was twelve years of age: His mother 'kept all these things in her heart' (2:51; cf. closely 2:19).

---

[70] It may indeed be argued forcibly that the whole section derives in essence from the perspective of Mary herself and constitutes a striking and extended example of the phenomenon under consideration, and this possibility will be taken up again below. But I will not begin to build a case by invoking a passage beset with so many special problems.

Luke 5:1-11 The call of Peter and the draught of fishes: This may be contrasted with the differently placed Mt. 4:18-22— Mk 1:16-20, and contains unique material focused strongly upon Peter and re-counting his reactions and those of James and John (5:10), who do not otherwise figure in Luke's version.

Luke 7:18-23 The mission of John's two disciples to Jesus is de-scribed with details of their questions absent from Mt. 11:2-6, which gives no indication either of the number of emissaries.

Luke 8:1-3 An interesting but brief pericope, peculiar to Luke con-tains the names of several women who ministered to Jesus and to his disciples.

Luke 8:29 A brief addition to the story of the Gadarene (Gerge-sene) demoniac, describes unsuccessful attempts to restrain him, ostensibly derived from the crowd of local people (cf. 8:37).

Luke 9:37-43 The healing of the epileptic boy: A more marginal case, where the Lukan version displays some different focusing and the omission of much of the long Markan account, but includes a specific note of time (9:37) and some significant additions from the father's perspective in 9:38-39. This boy, for instance, was his father's only child (μονογενής).

Luke 9:51-56 The Samaritans refuse to receive Jesus: This pericope initiates the long Lukan 'travel-section', which again poses special larger-scale problems. Let us note however at this stage simply that this is an L-passage which includes the particular reactions of the disciples James and John.

Luke 10:1 The sending out of the seventy: The succeeding peri-cope is largely paralleled in Matthew in the different setting of the sending of the twelve. The return and report of the seventy is again peculiar to Luke (10:17-20).

Luke 10:23-24 Words uttered in private to the disciples: The differently placed Matthean parallel (Mt. 13:16-17) does not specify the audience.

Luke 10:25-37 The uniquely Lukan parable of the good Samaritan (10:29-37) is given a setting which itself differs from the Synoptic parallels in its designation of the man as νομικός τις (10:25) and in specifics of his dialogue with Jesus. The parable is set specifically in the course of the dialogue with this individual.

Luke 10:38-42 Mary and Martha: This is another uniquely Lukan pericope appearing to embody Martha's perspective on a family tension.[71]

Luke 11:1-4 The Lukan version of the Lord's Prayer is given in

---

71 Cf. however the light on the character of the two women in John 12:2-3.

response to an individual disciple's request for teaching, again an unparalleled setting.

Luke 11:27-28 A woman in the crowd acclaims the mother of Jesus.

Luke 11:37-12:1 Discourse against the Pharisees: This is differently placed from the parallel in Mt. 23:23ff., and here set specifically in the home of an individual Pharisee and presented in response to his dialogue with Jesus in 11:53-12:1. The story presumably came from disciples present.

Luke 12:13-21 The parable of the rich man's barn is provoked by the demand of a man in the crowd for his share in an inheritance. While this story has an individual and personalized setting, the man in this case is not a plausible candidate for being the source of the pericope, which looks more likely to derive from disciples present.

Luke 12:41-46 The discourse on faithful stewardship is placed in response to a question specifically from Peter. Lk. 12:42-46 is differently placed from the parallel Mt. 24:45-51, and the peculiarly Lukan passage in 12:35-38 may also be explained as a part of the same discourse pericope with its Petrine setting. Similar phenomena, of L-passages mingled with Matthean (Q) parallels from different settings extend to Lk. 12:59, and raise a question about the limits of what might be read as a single sequence.

Luke 13:1-5 The report of Pilate's violence against Galilean worshippers is attributed to persons unnamed, who provide the occasion for Jesus' response.

Luke 13:10-17 The healing of the deformed woman is objected to by the ruler of the synagogue.

Luke 13:22-30 The discourse about entering in at the narrow gate is again introduced by the question of an individual, absent from the corresponding sayings in four different places in Matthew.

Luke 13:31-33 Some Pharisees bring the news of Herod's wish to kill Jesus: The brief responding pericope is again unique to Luke.

Luke 14:1-6 The man suffering from dropsy in the house of a leader of the Pharisees: The following pericope (14:7-14), also peculiar to Luke, is addressed to the guests (v. 7) and then the host (v. 12), ostensibly on the same occasion.

Luke 14:15-24 The parable of the wedding-feast is again in a different setting from the Matthean parallel, and delivered in response to the words of one of those present.

Luke 15 Most of this chapter is peculiar to Luke. Cf. only Mt. 18:12-13. It is a marginal case for our purpose. The setting is given, and an audience of tax-collectors and sinners specified, as well as criticism by the Pharisees and Scribes, all peculiar to Luke.

Luke 16:1-13 The unique parable of the unjust steward is addressed to the disciples.

Luke 16:14-15 This is another unique passage in response to the Pharisees.

Luke 17:1-2 The seriousness of causing offence to 'one of these little ones', is given in a slightly different form from Mk and Mt. and in a setting addressed to the disciples.

Luke 17:5-6 The power of faith like a mustard-seed is a response to a specific request of the disciples, again distinct from the partial parallel in Matthew.

Luke 17:11-19 The healing of ten lepers: Again unique to Luke, and placed in a specific journey setting, focusing on one of the number who was a Samaritan.

Luke 17:20-21 A unique saying about the coming of the kingdom is presented as an answer to the Pharisees.

Luke 17:22-37 The discourse on the day of the Son of Man, largely unique, with a mixture of contexts in partial Matthean parallels, is another response to the disciples.

Luke 18:1-8 The parable of the unjust judge is addressed to 'them' (18:8), again the disciples, and again a unique pericope.

Luke 18:9-14 The parable of the Pharisee and the Publican, peculiar to Luke, is a response to some who were confident in their own righteousness.

Luke 18:34 A peculiarly Lukan addition to a common tradition notes the reaction and lack of understanding in the disciples.

Luke 18:35-43 The blind man, Mark's Bartimaeus, in which Luke gives different (and in 18:35, contradictory) details, presenting the blind man's own perspective. An interesting, though difficult and rather atypical case, where Luke shortens parts and omits the name. This is a case worthy of special study.

Luke 19:1-10 The story of Zacchaeus is a unique personal incident in a specific setting and locality.

Luke 19:11-27 The parable of the pounds, as distinct from that of the talents in Mt. 25:14-30, is addressed to 'them' (the disciples) in a specified geographical setting as they were nearing Jerusalem.

Luke 19:39-44 Some Pharisees in the crowd call on Jesus to rebuke his disciples, and call forth another unique saying about the destruction of Jerusalem.

Luke 21:20-28 The first section of this paragraph is the subject of much debate but verses 25-26, 28 are particular to Luke, and in 28 the second person plural exhortation indicates address to the disciples.

Luke 21:34-36 The final warning, again an exhortation to the disciples, is peculiar to Luke.

Luke 22:15-18 Distinctive words of Jesus to the disciples at the beginning of the account of the Last Supper are recorded.

Luke 22:31-34 The passage addressed to Peter about Satan's desire to 'sift' him is peculiar to Luke.

Luke 22:35-38 The dialogue with the disciples over the taking of sword and purse is again unparalleled in the other Synoptics.

Luke 22:43-45 The angel strengthening Jesus and the bloody sweat is a unique passage of events enacted in the presence of the disciples.

Luke 22:61 The most remarkable Lukan addition to the common tradition of Peter's denial is this statement that Jesus looked at Peter, and Peter's response is linked to this.

Luke 23:2 The specified charges against Jesus before Pilate are peculiar to Luke. Cf. also Pilate's response to the 'high priests' and the crowds in 23:4-5.

Luke 23:6-16 The trial before Herod is again peculiar to Luke, and includes the remarkable comment in v. 12 on the relationship of Herod with Pilate. This pericope may be seen in the context of Luke's special interest in the Herod family.

Luke 23:27-32 This L-passage recounts the lament of women in the crowd following Jesus and his response to them.

Luke 23:47-48 The words of the centurion are presented differently from the parallels in Mk 15:39 = Mt. 27:54; he sees Jesus as a 'just man' not as 'son of God', and the saying is followed by an additional note of crowd-reaction.

Luke 23:55-56 The women who had followed Jesus from Galilee observed the tomb and made preparations for the burial; again a peculiarly Lukan passage with an emphasis on the women.

Luke 24:10-11 The story of the named women and the sceptical reaction of the disciples are again peculiar to this gospel.

Luke 24:13-35 The meeting of Jesus with two disciples on the road to Emmaus is a classic example, wholly peculiar to Luke and involving an otherwise unknown Cleopas, and including a lot of interesting circumstantial detail.

Luke 24:36-49 Appearance of Jesus to the disciples in Jerusalem: Here there is an interesting parallel of 24:36-43 with John 20:19-23.

Luke 24:50-53 The Ascension is paralleled only (and problematically) in Acts 1.

In the preceding tabulation we have cast the net rather wide. Further analysis of these instances will be deferred until we have listed the other category from Acts, which cannot be isolated with the same comparative precision, but which seems to represent a parallel of historical method.

Acts 1 The Ascension, and the first activities of the disciples: The group of disciples involved is listed by name in 1:13.

Acts 2 Peter's sermon: While this, like the preceding, is less than a clear example of the explicit phenomenon, it raises the observation that ostensibly (if we might be so bold as to draw an inference from reading at face value) Luke could only have gained (and presumably did gain) information on these events from traditions deriving from Peter himself or other disciples present. The same may be said of the material in e.g. 4:32-5:32 *passim*.

Acts 3:1-12 The healing of a lame man at the Beautiful Gate by Peter gives occasion for another Petrine speech. Here John is also mentioned, though he plays no active part in the event.

Acts 4:1-22 The appearance of Peter and John before the Sanhedrin: This passage includes a very interesting instance related to an obvious difficulty. How could Luke claim to know the substance of the debate in the closed session (4:15-17)? The options might appear to be invention or inference, were it not for the personalia of 4:6. This 'John' is not identified, and the name is uncertain in the text; Alexander is also unidentified. Both were then presumably known to Luke's readership, or else some further specification, or reason for mentioning them, would have surely been necessary. They seem not to have been brought in as prominent figures, like Annas and Caiaphas. It is attractive to suppose they were mentioned as known to the early church as (perhaps subsequent) converts or sympathizers, and implicitly as Luke's sources here.

Acts 5:33-39 Again a closed session of the Sanhedrin is attached to the mention of the great Gamaliel: the question is raised how Luke could have known his advice.[72]

Acts 6:1-7:53 The Stephen narrative: It is at least worth noting that the names of the seven deacons are all given, though only Stephen plays any immediate part in the subsequent narrative. Otherwise only Philip figures elsewhere, but he is of further significance for our present discussion (see below on Acts 8:4ff., 21:8). The material here could ostensibly have come from the disciples, or from any of the

---

[72] If again we may be bold to accept and answer this question at face value, there seem to be two possibilities: either from the persons mentioned in 4:6 or from Saul/Paul. It may be doubted whether Paul was of age to be a member of the Sanhedrin, but likely enough in any case that he received an account from Gamaliel himself at a time when his mind was much exercised over the new teaching. He had apparently been close to Gamaliel, and his teacher's reaction would have made its mark. And Luke, we suppose, was later close to Paul. Such a reconstruction can only be inferential and speculative, but it is plausible. It might be Paul's first latent imprint on the narrative.

Seven, among whom the prior position of Philip's name (after Stephen himself) may be noted.

Acts 7:54-8:1 The stoning of Stephen is linked explicitly with the first actual mention of Saul. The implication that Saul was profoundly shaken by his connivance is almost palpable. On a traditional understanding of Luke's association with Paul this looks an almost paradigmatic case of a pericope derived from Paul, on whom the occasion must have made an unforgettable impact.

Acts 8:4-25 Philip's mission in Samaria and its aftermath: This narrative centres upon Philip, but includes the visit of Peter and John. While the former deals directly with Simon Magus, John is not otherwise further mentioned specifically, though the statement of their preaching in a Samaritan village *en retour* is only ostensibly derivable from themselves.

Acts 8:26-40 Philip and the eunuch: it would appear that this meeting of a man alone with a departing stranger could only have derived from the participant Philip, unless the whole passage be explained as invention.

Acts 9:1-19 The whole narrative of Saul's conversion embodies the perspectives of Saul himself and of Ananias. The same may be true also of 9:19b-30, part of which shows an evident perspective of Saul, but the notes of the results and reactions seem to reflect rather a Damascene origin. Note also the naming of Saul's host at 9:11.[73]

Acts 9:32-35 Peter's healing of the paralytic Aeneas: The details and the memory of Peter's words suggest the reminiscence of Aeneas himself.

Acts 9:36-43 The raising of Tabitha: A vivid and interesting pericope, especially in the grief of the widows and their display of Tabitha's work, suggesting an account derived from eyewitnesses among the Christians of Joppa. In 9:43 the mention of Peter's host, Simon the tanner, looks inconsequential. It may be that Luke was interested in lodging,[74] or was at pains to note Peter's willingness to stay with a man who followed an unclean occupation. More particularly, this note anticipates the direction to Cornelius in 10:6 (cf. 10:17-18, 32). While this Simon may have been a significant local Christian, there is nothing to suggest he was a specific source for this or the following Cornelius story.

Acts 10:1-11:18 The whole Cornelius story seems to combine the two perspectives of Peter and of Cornelius, and could be wholly

---

[73] Cf. also the two later accounts of Saul's conversion, differing in purpose and detail, but all ostensibly deriving from the same Pauline source.

[74] Cf. Bruce, *Acts* pp. 201, 214.

explained by the joining of their narratives. This does not exclude the possibility of traditions from others in the Jerusalem church for the debate in Jerusalem in the latter chapter.

Acts 11:19-30 Events in Antioch: An interesting and important passage, largely summary, suggesting an Antiochian source and information derived from Saul and perhaps Barnabas. The passage seems however to belong to rather a different category from most of the preceding, as nearer to a brief resumé of complex happenings extended in time. It may perhaps be seen as presupposing in Luke a more extensive knowledge of this church, appropriate to his link with Saul, though he has not chosen to enlarge on particular events, save as the visit of Agabus provides an important link in the developing role of Saul.[75]

Acts 12:1-17 Peter's escape from prison: The essence of this story gives the perspectives of Peter and of Rhoda, and matters outside their ostensible experience are vaguely sketched.[76]

Acts 12:18-23 Two separate traditions about Herod Agrippa are here combined, the former actually concluding the preceding pericope, because both raise a question about Luke's sources of information about the Herods. In any case Herod's savagery here, followed so closely by his spectacularly public arrogance, collapse and death, were likely to have been public knowledge, and a spur to popular moral reflection. The impact of the final scene is also reflected in Josephus (Jos. *Ant.* 19.8.2.343-50). Neither of these observations excludes the possibility that Luke's actual version of these public events owed something to the tradition of the Jerusalem church or other sources for the Herods which inform his narrative elsewhere (cf. e.g. Luke 8:3; 23:6-16; Acts 13:1). The mention of the otherwise unknown Blastus is interesting, and may testify to the specific nature of Luke's information, though there is nothing here to suggest he was the actual source of it.

Acts 12:25-13:3 The call of Barnabas and Saul: This brief section includes the mention of three prominent leaders in the Antioch church otherwise unknown to us. The name of Manaen is of

---

75 It is relevant to note here the tradition linking Luke the Physician with Antioch, which I should not press (see Euseb. *HE* 3.4.6; Anti-Marcionite Prologue, cited in Bruce, *Acts*, p. 6). The 'we' in the Western reading of Acts 11:28 may reflect the early currency of this tradition. There is also the occasional identification in Acts of an Antioch-source (thus originally Harnack; see full discussion in Dupont, *Sources*, ET, pp. 36, 62-72).

76 Thus notably the much-debated phrase εἰς ἕτερον τόπον (Acts 12:17). Peter went 'into hiding'. The place is immaterial and beyond the knowledge or interest of the writer. The various far-reaching theories based on assumptions of Lukan suppression or euphemism are beside the point. See pp. 207-208, n. 90 below.

particular interest, in view of his specified connection with the tetrarch Antipas. The mention of this man immediately suggests a route by which Luke, through Paul, could have had access to the special information about the Herods which we have already observed (cf. also on Lk. 8:3 above for another possible source). It is worth considering whether Luke could have had direct contact with Manaen. But if he were a contemporary of Antipas he would have been a very old man if still alive at a viable date for Luke's collection of materials for Luke-Acts.

Acts 13ff. Throughout the latter half of Acts the narrative centres upon the activities of Paul, and we pass essentially into a more direct category of source-material. My remarks here will accordingly be very selective, focusing on isolated places where a different perspective seems to be incorporated or where some other hint is given which might throw independent light on the source question.

Acts 14:11-13 An interesting converse point: The missionaries are in trouble through their unawareness of a contrary perspective across a linguistic and cultural barrier. This vivid narrative is not idealized, and there is no attempt to pretend to a comprehensive knowledge on the part of writer or participants. Their enlightenment comes only with hindsight.

Acts 15 The account of the Jerusalem Council shows in the main a Pauline perspective throughout, but the inclusion of traditions derived from Jerusalem is wholly likely, and the specific mention of Judas Barsabbas and of Silas in the sequel is noteworthy (15:22, 27, 32). If we are right elsewhere in seeing a Petrine origin for material in Luke-Acts, we may hardly suppose that Luke was uninterested in the Petrine version of this crucial meeting, and the ostensible reading of 21:18 recounts an actual meeting of the 'first-person' writer with James.

Acts 16:9-10 The beginning of the first 'we-passage' is associated with the mention of the vision of an unnamed Macedonian (Μακεδών τις). It can be no more than a speculation that Luke was himself the individual of the vision.[77] In view of the close conjunction of the first person with the anonymous reference, the identification seems at least possible, but is not to be pressed. The travel detail and description of the status of Philippi (16:11-12) may be taken to reflect

---

[77] Thus Ramsay, *SPTR*, pp. 201-205. There is no implication that the man of the vision was a stereotype Macedonian, to be identified by a conventional peculiarity of dress or speech. Rather he was a person who could have been named. Luke himself seems at least to have had a special connection with Philippi, such as appears in the sequel, whatever the truth of the tradition which says he came from Antioch.

the directly Lukan perspective in a manner not seen previously in Acts.

Acts 18:24-28 The instruction of Apollos at Ephesus: This short pericope stands apart as non-Pauline and not easily categorized. Functionally, it anticipates the account of Paul's meeting with the group of Ephesian disciples in 19:1-17. The material could have derived from Priscilla and Aquila and/or Apollos himself. All were important figures in the Pauline literature, but Apollos himself not otherwise in Acts. There is no material difficulty here for our approach, and the sources were ostensibly available, if more difficult to crystallize in the perspective of an original informant. In any case the incident would have been familiar in the tradition of the Ephesian church.

Acts 19:23-41 The riot in Ephesus: This vivid scene presents one unobtrusive difficulty in the often overlooked statement that Paul was not himself present (19:30). He was however close to the situation, and two of his associates were dangerously involved (19:29), and at least the latter, Aristarchus, was present also, ostensibly with the author, during the events of the following 'we-passages' (20:4; 27:2). Aristarchus and perhaps Gaius are the likely sources for events within the theatre.

Acts 20:1-21:6 While the voyage is a 'we-passage' and calls for no special comment here, it is noteworthy that it contains 'Lukan perspectives' of first-person travel briefly apart from Paul (20:13-14), of routes and times, including specific travel observations (e.g. 21:3; contrast 27:4).

Acts 21:7-15 The journey up to Jerusalem: This section is marked by the lodging at the homes of Philip (21:8) and Mnason (21:16), and the meeting with Agabus. The ostensible meeting of Luke with these three men is interesting, for we have already noted the possible significance of Philip traditions (8:4-40). The references to Philip and to Agabus are cases of the integration of the 'we-passages' with the earlier chapters, and that to Mnason specifies his having been a disciple since the beginnings of the church (ἀρχαίῳ μαθητῇ). Mnason, we may suppose, was thus a suitable informant, a bearer of the tradition of the Jerusalem church. A companion of Paul, enjoying the hospitality of two such hosts in perhaps his first personal contact with the Palestinian church, was presumably not uninterested in what they had to tell. His mention of them is suitable to this implication.

Acts 23:26-30 The letter of Lysias to Felix: An obvious question is raised about the origin of this document, but the commentaries often pass over the issue. Hanson (*Acts*, p. 224) regards it as a Lukan composition; Marshall (*Acts*, p. 370) points to the introductory words (ἔχουσαν τὸν τύπον τοῦτον), interpreting them as a disclaimer, that these were not the *ipsissima verba* (cf. 3 Macc. 3:30). The final answer is unclear. I am inclined to speculate that the original letter was actually read in court in Paul's presence, and that the humorous irony in the juxtaposition of this with the speech of Tertullus (24:2-8) belonged to the situation.[78] Luke has of course placed the latter in the logical sequence of narrative, without thereby losing the effect of juxtaposition. Perhaps both passages are resolvable as regular instances of Paul as source.

Acts 25:13-22 Festus' conference with Agrippa: This passage is difficult. There is no hint here of a source by which Luke could have known the substance of any such conversation. The sentiments are appropriate to what we may suppose to have been Festus' view of the case, but it looks as though Luke's form of composition is inferential rather than based on sources. This need not be seen as a serious qualification of a claim to historicity, for this concept must be judged by realistically flexible criteria. What is worrying, on a different ground, is that it differs from our concept of Luke's actual practice elsewhere. The element of composition here looks to be significant, but is not marked by disclaimer or qualification.[79] It may be relevant to note the references to the motives of opponents in 25:3,9; these are of course inferential, but the inferences are plain from the

---

78 I trust it is no irreverence to the solemnity of critical scholarship to suppose that Paul told the story with vivid relish. Luke's humour, sometimes as reflecting Paul's humour, is a topic which may be illustrated elsewhere in Acts. Cf. J. Jónsson, *Humour and Irony in the New Testament Illuminated by Parallels in Talmud and Midrash* (Leiden: Brill, 1985). Jónsson, however, surprisingly gives no examples from Acts after 23:12-33, and considers that humour is lacking in the speeches and belongs rather to the situation, a feature different from the Gospels, including Luke (pp. 221-22).

79 The question is not easy to resolve. To offer a facile harmonization would savour of special pleading, that Luke's access to inside information about the Herods extended here also into an apparently closed conversation which had been then discussed more widely, or, less improbably, that Festus, in rather prosy chairman's remarks, had repeated in open court his difficulties with the case, his self-conscious stand for Roman justice, and his request to Agrippa. The scene is by no means lacking in the subtle humour we have noted above as a reflection of actuality. It is perhaps really not improbable that the circumstances were capable of such a simple explanation, but it would be improper to invoke such speculative ideas as more than possibilities. The essential difficulty consists merely in the apparent divergence from Luke's usual practice of signposting the credentials of his evidence, but that is a point of some consequence for an argument from Lukan practice.

actions. Paul was ruthlessly realistic and perceptive about human nature.

Acts 26:31-32 Again, there is no apparent source for the private consultation of Festus with Agrippa. Here the difficulty is not nearly as great in view of the brevity of the comments, and presumably a verdict in some such terms must in any case have been made known to Paul after the *consilium* of the judges.

Acts 28:30-31 A concluding Lukan summary, which, whatever its problems, is an intended conclusion, and implies a larger knowledge, tantalizing the reader with the unspecified end of the two-year term.

Let us then attempt to make a closer assessment of the types of material cited.

(1) *The Third Gospel.* Something should be said first about the general authenticity of the passages. Some might be adjudged to fall into doubted categories by the criteria commonly in use. The 'criterion of dissimilarity' is not helpful, for there is little reason to see anything of a suitable discreteness in these nuances, and the parables peculiar to Luke are widely accepted anyhow, irrespective of this criterion. The test of multiple attestation fails here, for by definition we have selected items to which it does not apply. A subsequent use of coherence with established passages does not get off the ground for the failure of the preceding tests. Yet none of these failures is at all consequential. They only indicate that we have been trying to use a sieve with large holes for admittedly refined material. Such methods, properly applicable only to the teaching material, and hardly to refinements of narrative, are at best directed to establish firmly a few, often untypical, sayings, and cannot substantiate a negative elsewhere. They only appear to do so when built into a structure that is presuppositionally sceptical.

The passages listed exemplify a wider range of possibilities than unambiguous instances of the simple phenomenon. Variant possibilities must be acknowledged. Where Luke specifies Jesus' hearers, he may be hinting at sources of information, or he may just be offering a setting, and it may be argued, rightly or wrongly, that that setting is a theologically motivated construct. This, however, is less easy to argue where the naming of persons is stubbornly inconsequential. Moreover, there are cases where different categories fall together, and the hearer seems cast also for the part of informant. Further, the implicit presence of disciples on the occasion of a pericope addressed, say, to the Pharisees repeatedly gives a tacit indicator of ostensible source even outside our more articulate examples. Elsewhere again, a major participant in an L-pericope is also the ostensibly likely source, and such is the case, if I may dare for a moment to essay comment on the hardest crux of all, with Mary in the whole Nativity sequence.

One feature of our material is that it repeatedly highlights Luke's introduction of specific settings to Gospel pericopes which appear in the common tradition as floating incidents, amenable to differing schemes of arrangement. It is of course easy to argue that Luke has simply created his settings and audience dialogues. But on the baldest formulation of the question there are at least two options, with whatever intermediate positions. Either Luke was free in his creation of settings, or he was not. In the latter case it is reasonable to ask whether he found his settings in a source, or whether he took special pains to discover what was absent in a formal source, and whether he included them only when he had some warrant.

An answer to these questions is not to be offered glibly. It will suffice for the present to formulate them in these terms before examining the corresponding material in Acts. We conclude with some interim observations. It is notable that some of the distinctive L-traditions embody the perspectives of some of the same recurring persons, notably Mary, Peter, James and John, beside such as Martha, Zacchaeus and Cleopas in isolated instances. There are many, less explicit, references also to the disciples, to unnamed persons, and to women in particular. Many of the less explicitly marked incidents are seen from the viewpoint of the disciples, including those already named. Another feature of Luke's account is that he alone gives certain details which the thoughtful modern reader wants to ask, in many points of sequence and context, and in matters such as the actual charges against Jesus before Pilate (Lk. 23:2). A fresh reading of the text reveals that Luke himself wanted to know the springs and motives of the action, and where these were not apparent in the formal traditions, he seems to have made it his business to elicit them by deliberate inquiry.

(2) *Acts*. Nearly all the material in the first twelve chapters is open to consideration from our present approach, though the incidence of striking examples of personal traditions is of course more limited. It is good to exhibit briefly the range of evidence, and its limitations, and to suggest that the plausibility of the best examples justifies the exercise. In any case the network of ostensible personal traditions is more extensive here than in the Gospel. There are the recurring perspectives of Peter, John, Philip and perhaps James (here however a different James, the brother of Jesus, not the son of Zebedee), and the occasional traditions which may be linked with the names of such as Ananias, Aeneas, Cornelius, Rhoda and later Aristarchus. Then

there are the interesting figures of Manaen and Mnason, neither presented as the ostensible source of a pericope, but both introduced in terms which highlight their possible function as bearers of tradition. Much of the remaining, less focused material presumes tradition in the churches of Jerusalem and Antioch, though in either case we could name individuals eligible to be the actual bearers of those traditions. Finally, we must not forget that the other, more direct categories of Acts material, beyond the segment we have chosen here for discussion, may be described as embodying the personal perspectives derived from Paul and from Luke himself.

There is a *prima facie* conformity here between the Gospel and Acts, especially in the traditions which we have attributed to Peter in both parts of the work. But a fundamental question is raised about Luke's access to the persons involved, and this is difficult to answer precisely in the case of Peter, whose movements after departure into hiding in Acts 12:17 are unclear. Where and when could Luke have met him? Was it for instance in Palestine in 57-59 or in Rome in 60-62? Is there any significance in the silence of Acts 21-26 to suggest that Peter was not in Palestine in this period? Most of the other persons in the two lists were located in Palestine, though the point is of slight weight, for the material involved concerns the church in Palestine. Exceptions, like Ananias and Aristarchus, occur in passages which overlap with Pauline or Lukan perspectives anyhow, but Aristarchus in particular was a companion of the two principals on the voyages to and from Palestine. And the contribution of Ananias was already included in the ostensible conversion narrative of Paul (cf. Acts 22:12-16), quite apart from any implication of direct contact between him and Luke.

(3) *Implications and Conclusions.* We have hitherto been fairly reserved about stating the possible implications of observation, referring to 'Petrine perspectives' or 'traditions' rather than trying to build prematurely on any assumption that Luke had interviewed Peter. But the thrust of our studies and comments has pointed increasingly to the confirmation of this hypothesis, and it is good to state the position frankly before we go further. I propose to argue that it is an important feature of Lukan criticism to recognize that Luke obtained parts of his material by interviewing participants, and that he sometimes edited older traditions by re-interviewing such surviving participants as may have been accessible to him, and that this process accounts for some of the significant 'L-nuances' in the Third Gospel.

There are three important preliminary remarks necessary to guard against misunderstanding before we venture to enlarge upon this proposition.

(a) The legitimacy of this stance today. This approach is out of fashion, and to propose it may provoke a reaction which has nothing to do with the merit or demerit of the idea or with rigorously argued reasons for rejecting it.[80] I am well aware of the proper importance of redactional study, but if modern techniques are applied mechanically, and exempted from the interplay of other disciplines and differing perspectives, the options become artificially narrowed. It seems rather a mark of insecurity than otherwise to insist on closing the debate. Any particular formulation of a special 'critical orthodoxy' will almost certainly be wrong in some areas where opinion is apt to change, and this is such an area. Scholarly orthodoxy can, in its way, exercise a conformist pressure as real as that of the most conservative religious orthodoxy. I count myself fortunate to be able to work in an ambience of perhaps unusual openness.

(b) I make no pretence to originality in my basic contention. A surprisingly large number of scholars of distinction have held similar positions, though often as judgments expressed in an *arbiter dictum* and never followed up.[81] It might even be claimed that in the longer perspective this is a normative kind of position, and that its modern rejection depends on a complex of reinterpretations. But in saying this I repeat my caution against the argument from counting heads and reputations when matters of evidence are at stake.

[80] I find myself condemned as *'outdated'* in a recent survey of *Actaforschung* for having previously suggested an idea on these lines, but condemned in such distinguished company as to feel highly flattered. But the question is not whether one is out of step with the latest thinking, a fault to which I must freely confess, but what is the most probable reading of the evidence.

[81] See esp. the discussion in Wikenhauser pp. 76-79. Among many other references may be mentioned: Knowling, 'Acts' (1900), pp. 16-18; Rackham, *Acts* (1901), pp. xli-xliii; Zahn, *Einleitung* 2 (1900), pp. 415-16 (= *Introduction* 3 [1909], pp. 127-28); J. Vernon Bartlet, *Acts* (1901), pp. 22-23; Harnack, *Luke the Physician* (1911), p. 157 (stressing information from Philip's daughters, but placing the link later at Hierapolis [if the same Philip]); Edmundson, *Church in Rome* (1913), p. 61 (Philip as authority for Simon Magus story); F.H. Chase, *Credibility* (1902), pp. 19-25; R.H. Connolly in *JTS* 37 (1936), pp. 375-76 (on Syriacisms and Luke's traditional Antioch background); Bruce, *Acts* (1951), pp. 22, 387; A. Hastings, *Prophet and Witness in Jerusalem* (London, New York and Toronto: Longmans, Green and Co., 1958), pp. 30, 33-35 (noting esp. Simon of Cyrene = Simon Niger); V. Taylor *IDB* 3 (1962), p. 185; D. Guthrie, *Introduction* (1970), pp. 369-70, 377; J.W. Wenham, *TB* 23 (1972), p. 95 (arguing further that the Gospel was written in 57-59 before the shipwreck destroyed Luke's notes from his informants). While these sources reflect a strong predominance of older British scholars, the strength of the case and the breadth of opinion represented in this selection is not to be discounted for that reason.

(c) There is need for a careful working out of this position, to offer a tentative reconstruction of the possible processes of composition, at least to show its *feasibility in principle*. Such a reconstruction cannot in the nature of the case be much more than conjectural, *exempli gratia*. It is a matter of plausibility, not of proof. But if at least it shows the possibility that something on these lines could be near the truth and accounts for different dimensions of the problem, it constitutes a challenge to the objector to explain so much of the setting better otherwise.

If then our view of the 'we-passages' and so of authorship is correct, we may assert provisionally the likelihood of a relatively early date for the gathering of material. We shall not press any view of dating at this stage, prior to fuller discussion. It will suffice to admit here the possibility that Luke was engaged fairly early in collecting traditions, even if the redaction or finalization of the double work in its present form was considerably later.

If Luke was a companion of Paul, when did he begin to understand the career of Paul as so significant in the earliest church? When and how did he first conceive the importance of writing the larger story, to join narratives of Jesus and the primitive church with his memoir of Paul? There are no means of answering such questions definitively. The Pauline part of his work need be conceived no later than the voyage to Jerusalem. It seems impossible to specify whether it might have been earlier. The grounds for this suggestion are simply the very specific account of the day-to-day details of the voyage, which probably imply the purposive keeping of a careful record at that stage. The earlier 'we-passage' of Acts 16 certainly exhibits similarly vivid reminiscence, and includes a statement of the stages of a short voyage (16:11-12), but nothing to suggest in comparable degree the conscious and concurrent keeping of a dated record.

In this discussion we have been preoccupied with Acts, but this is only part of the much larger question of Luke-Acts. When did Luke conceive the idea of writing the Gospel, or the double work? The answer is unclear. If our suggestion about the Pauline part of Acts can stand, his first literary plans appear to antedate the production of Mark on any date usually considered viable for that earliest Gospel. Moreover, Luke refers in his Preface to 'many' previous writers (Lk. 1:1), and purports to stand at the apex of a literary development. Even if we postulate a spate of pre-Markan compilations, we are still left with the apparent fact that Mark was itself a source. It may be that Luke's prefaces were written last, in the light of his progressive assimilation of sources even in the process of composition and that his fitting of Markan material into a Q + L complex may reflect the sequence of accession and composition, apart from the supposition of an actual 'Proto-Luke'.[82]

It is also worth asking whether the concept or the execution of Acts *preceded* that of the Third Gospel. There is a tendency to reject this option prematurely because it may be held for an unnecessary and inappropriate reason, i.e. the dating of Acts before 70 and of Luke after. But Acts *might* precede Luke, at least in concept, even if both were pre-70, or both post-70. Could Acts, or a first draft of Acts, follow a pre-Markan Proto-Luke, whatever their dates? These are merely ideas, but they illustrate further the complexity of the variables. In fact the options are disconcertingly open, though less so in the case of Acts than for the Third Gospel. It seems possible that the idea of writing a Gospel was subsequent to the first promptings to the novelty of writing about the early church, or that the idea of a two-volume work was not original to Luke's first concept, even if the logic of the situation quickly impressed on him the need and opportunity. Was a companion of Paul, already recording material for a narrative in ostensibly historical form, likely to be uninterested in information about the earliest Jerusalem church which became newly accessible to him on arrival in Palestine? Are the references to Philip and Mnason, for a start, not plausibly explicable as reflections of a new dimension of facility to fulfill a formulated or developing purpose?

The picture may tentatively be reconstructed in this way: Already having kept a purposeful record as early as the spring of 57, Luke found access in Palestine to traditions both of Jesus and of the earliest church, and he appreciated the possibility of eliciting better-focused

---

[82] The classic formulation of the 'Proto-Luke' theory is that of B.H. Streeter, *The Four Gospels. A Study of Origins* (London: Macmillan, 1936), pp. 199-222: cf. V. Taylor, *Behind the Third Gospels. A Study of the Proto-Luke Hypothesis* (Oxford: Clarendon Press, 1926). See for later discussion S. MacLean Gilmour, 'A Critical Examination of Proto-Luke', *JBL* 67 (1948), pp. 143-52; V. Taylor, 'Important Hypotheses Reconsidered. 1. The Proto-Luke Hypothesis', *ExpT* 67 (1955-56), pp. 12-16. Some of those who reject the full hypothesis would accept the observations made here (e.g. J.M. Creed in *ExpT* 46 [1934-35], p. 103), which need not require recognition of an actual draft document amenable to identification and analysis as a stage in composition. Others, such as C.S.C. Williams, 'The Date of Luke-Acts', *ExpT* 64 (1952-53), pp. 283-84; H.G. Russell, 'Which was written first, Luke or Acts?' *HTR* 48 (1955), pp. 167-74 have invoked Proto-Luke as an element in a more elaborate dating theory, where Proto-Luke precedes Acts before 70 and our present Third Gospel is seen as a post-70 redaction incorporating the Markan material.

information by questioning the surviving eyewitnesses. Keenly sensitive to the imperfections and incompletenesses of the then-current written memoirs of Jesus, he conceived the larger plan of bringing together a narrative spanning those parts of the whole story of Jesus and the church to which he was able to obtain sufficient access. For the lifetime of Jesus he was much controlled by existing written tradition, within which he made a conservative treatment of the actual words attributed to Jesus, but edited the settings in the light of his investigative inquiry (perhaps this is the real force of καθεξῆς in Lk. 1:3) and added many additional traditions, chiefly those placed in the long 'travel-section' (Lk. 9:51-19:27). At this conceptual stage, we might guess that Q existed in written form, but that Mark did not.

There are obvious issues raised by this sort of suggestion which deserve an airing. We are postulating in Luke a treatment of evidence reminiscent of Polybius' claims (chapter 3 above), personal participation supplemented by the critical questioning of eyewitnesses, and even a view of editorial selection as controlled by the accessibility and credentials of evidence. Such a position may seem to be cavalier towards Luke's theological purpose, while also arguing illegitimately from a parallel of dubious validity. But I am arguing the latter point only in a lower key against a denial: Luke was not necessarily or even probably a conscious follower of a particular tradition of historiography, and he is not to be measured by the argument from parallels. But it is relevant to insist that serious standards of historical truth existed even before his day. If then he took it upon him to write a careful account and to improve on his predecessors, it seems natural enough to suppose that he applied what seemed to an educated man of his time the methods and standards most appropriate to his expressed desire to make a reliable record. And with regard to his purpose— it is enough to repeat here that his demonstrable care for accuracy of detail is at least a factor in his writing, and must be included in our assessment of him. The picture of the late theologian making free with the facts is one-sided and untenably simplistic. Apart from a more broadly balanced view of the qualities of Acts it is hard to explain the book even theologically.

Another important, and often unconsidered, question is that of Luke's access to Peter. Again the unknown variables here seem to make it impossible to offer definite answers. There are two crucial points: (1) Do the Petrine traditions which form an important unifying element in Luke-Acts require us to believe that Luke had direct personal access to Peter rather than mediated traditions? (2) If so, can Peter's likely movements be reconstructed in any sufficient degree to indicate where or when Luke might have met him?

(1) This problem merits consideration with more rigour than often appears in advocates of the present approach. It has been suggested that Luke could have derived Petrine traditions from John Mark,[83] and this is both plausible and chronologically feasible, for Mark was apparently in Rome at the time of Paul's imprisonment there (Col. 4:10; Phlm. 24). Or the Petrine traditions could have been mediated through Paul, whose first interview with Peter was presumably devoted in considerable degree to an extensive briefing (cf. ἱστορῆσαι, Gal. 1:18).[84] That, however, was already years in the past.

No doubt we could try to make our point at such a fairly low level, developing plausible possibilities on these lines, and answering our first question negatively, and perhaps that is correct. But my reading of the texts inclines me increasingly to suppose personal contact with Peter. This makes the problem the more acute, though if the supposition is correct, it brings us yet nearer a major participant in both halves of the work.

The basic grounds for this impression take us back to the examination of Huck's *Synopsis* which underlies the tabulation above, and it will have to suffice here to confine my remarks on the Third Gospel to a representative pericope illustrating Luke's handling of a Petrine tradition largely paralleled in the other Synoptics, the Transfiguration narrative (Lk. 9:28-36; cf. Mk 9:2-8; Mt. 17:1-8). The following Lukan nuances call for comment:

9:28 Luke has 'about eight days after' where Mk and Mt. both say 'after six days'. It should be noted that 'eight days' is the normal inclusive rendering of a 'week', and that Luke's version is accordingly a round-figure approximation, less precise than the others.

9:28-29 Only Luke mentions the purpose of Jesus' going as to pray, and that the following scene occurred in the context of Jesus'

---

[83] Some of the writers mentioned in n. 81 above (Harnack, Knowling, etc.) take this view, without apparently raising the question of Luke's possible access to Peter himself. Chase (*Credibility*, p. 20), however, while also noting Mark among the likely sources, thought that Luke also probably talked with Peter in Rome. There have been other suggestions of a special link between Mark and Luke. Zahn, accepting a traditional view of the authorship of Mark's Gospel, argued that the author intended a continuation, and that Luke inherited his notes as a source for the early chapters of Acts. A somewhat similar view is propounded in A.E. Haefner, 'The Bridge between Mark and Acts', *JBL* 77 (1958), pp. 67-71, but is tied to a dubious analysis of the sources of Acts, following Harnack. Cf. also L. Dieu, 'Marc Source des Actes?', *RB* 29 = n.s. 16 (1920), pp. 555-69 and 30 = n.s. 17 (1921), pp. 86-96.

[84] Cf. G.D. Kilpatrick, 'Galatians 1:18 ΙΣΤΟΡΗΣΑΙ ΚΗΦΑΝ', *New Testament Essays. Studies in Memory of Thomas Walter Manson 1893-1958*, ed. A.J.B. Higgins (Manchester University Press, 1959), pp. 144-49.

praying.

9:30 The visual detail of two men speaking with Jesus is given before their identity is specified.

9:31 The subject of the conversation is described. This is quite unparalleled.

9:32 An additional passage describes the sleepiness of Peter and his companions, but insists afresh that they were awake to witness Jesus' glory and the two men standing with him.

9:33 Peter's bewildered outburst is set in the unique context of the statement that the two men were parting from Jesus.

9:33b While the emotions of the group (Mk 9:6) are omitted, the note of Peter's own bewilderment is retained in brief, parenthetical form. Matthew has no parallel.

9:34 The version ends with the coming of a cloud while Peter is still speaking (cf. Mt. 17:5), but the disciples' fear at entering the cloud is peculiar to Luke.

9:36 Only Luke associates their awareness of Jesus alone with the divine voice. (Only Matthew specifies Jesus' return to comfort them, Mt. 17:6-7).

9:36b The concluding statement of the disciples' awed silence is peculiar to Luke.

These details raise interesting questions of interpretation. It is easy to note, for instance, that 9:31 makes a theological point, looking forward to Jesus' destined death. But most or all of them are very natural if seen as elicited by an interlocutor working from a tradition similar to that of Mark, going over the story with a participant to clarify significant points in his testimony. Each item could be recast, in a sort of form-critical exercise, as an answer to a specific interviewer's question: How long after? What was the first thing you saw? There was actual conversation— did you hear what was said? How did you feel? If so sleepy, are you really sure about what you thought you saw? What prompted you to cry out like that? How exactly did the vision end? How did you react when the cloud came? Did you tell anyone else at the time?

All this gives us no more than one sample of a phenomenon which might be studied elsewhere in Luke wherever a suitable comparative basis exists. My case rests in this point on the *plausibility and not the factuality* of my suggested line of interpretation. The fact that the chosen incident concerns supernatural or ecstatic experience perhaps only points the issue the more sharply: the interviewer wants to be quite clear about points in the testimony to purported personal experience of such unusual character.

Some other interim observations are in order here. (1) The approximation in Lk. 9:28 is particularly interesting. It may be the mark of a careful writer to be *imprecise* where definiteness is not warranted: he is unwilling to press the current hesitancy of an informant into the convenient mould of other tradition. (2) The tradition first known to Luke was not necessarily identical with our written Mark, and the relationship with Mark may not be simple, and needs further study.[85] (3) The 'Petrine' passages are not necessarily derived exclusively from Peter, but the versions of companion disciples may sometimes be included. It is still relevant to stress the specially Petrine perspectives in the passage before us and elsewhere.

The methodological approach to Acts must be a little different for want of the like comparative material. The case here must rest largely on incidents like the release from prison and the Cornelius episode, which show strongly Petrine perspectives, that could not easily have been derived otherwise than from Peter, and where the picture loses focus outside the experience of Peter or other identified participants.

We may claim that, at one level of analysis, there are two types of tradition in Luke-Acts, that which comes from *inaccessible* sources which redaction cannot assimilate to Lukan formulations, and that from *accessible* sources to which Luke can apply a more investigative method and achieve a more selective control in presentation. If this is justified, the Petrine passages seem at least to include some in the latter category, an observation not inconsistent with the recognition that Luke inherited much tradition about Peter in the former category from the primitive church. The Petrine traditions are a test-case of special difficulty. Our study of the Transfiguration is offered as representative of an approach applicable to other personal sources also. And if the case of Peter is pressed, we must assume that Luke had access to him. Our second question must then be taken into account.

---

[85] I am reckoning throughout with the probability that Mark is not earlier than c. 60, aware that most scholars today would want to put it somewhat later, often in the lead-up to the destruction of Jerusalem. It seems however that its dating is open, and the prospects of fixing Mark through Luke-Acts may be better than the converse. I should not exclude a date earlier than 60, nor advocate it. An unnecessarily (and perhaps improbably) early date is no more warranted than excluded. It seems likely on such assumptions that Luke was already gathering materials before the appearance of Mark and that the processes of composition were not then tied neatly to questioning witnesses with Mark's text already in his hand. A difficulty has been felt in any notion that the two Gospels could have been produced close together in time and milieu. But even this seems explicable, should our inquiry point in this direction, if Mark preceded a larger double work already in gestation before the inclusion of Mark as a major source.

(2) We lose sight of Peter for most of Acts after he departed 'to another place' after release from prison at Acts 12:17, an incident apparently placed just before the death of Herod Agrippa I in 44. He was however in Jerusalem at the time of Paul's second visit there (Gal. 2:9), probably c. 46, and he subsequently travelled to Antioch (Gal. 2:11), if only for a short visit as a delegate of the Jerusalem church. He reappears in Jerusalem in Acts 15:7 at the Apostolic Council in 49.[86] Next, the invocation of his name by some of Paul's critics at Corinth (1 Cor. 1:12; cf. 3:22) is most probably understood to imply that he had visited that city between Paul's departure in 52 and the writing of the letter c. 54-55, perhaps in the company of Barnabas, who seems by then to have been known personally to the Corinthians (1 Cor. 9:6).[87] We have two epistles bearing Peter's name, of which only the first purports to give details which might prove relevant, being addressed to recipients in five provinces of Asia Minor (1 Pet. 1:1) from 'Babylon' (1 Pet. 5:13), a name here generally taken as a symbol for Rome, where Mark is with him and whence he sends Silvanus (Silas) as his emissary.[88]

Such is the extent of the ostensible New Testament evidence, but we have to reckon also with the early and persistent tradition which connects Peter with Rome. It is beyond all serious doubt that Peter ended his life in Rome, though the dates of his presence there are wide open to debate. The earliest reference to his martyrdom, and that of Paul, is in *1 Clem.* 5.4-5, written from Rome before the end of the century, and the two apostles together are seen as joint-founders of the Roman church by Irenaeus (*Adv. Haer.* 3.3.1, Latin).

---

[86] *Pace* the view of D.F. Robinson, 'Where and When Did Peter Die?' *JBL* 64 (1945), pp. 255-67 and Warren M. Smaltz, 'Did Peter Die in Jerusalem?' *JBL* 71 (1952), pp. 211-16. These writers maintain that Peter died in c. 44, and the 'other place' of Acts 12:17 is a euphemistic or allegorical allusion to his death. Robinson has to resort not only to rejection or alteration of Acts 15 but has also to see inter-polation or textual alteration in Gal. 2.

[87] I am not however sure of the suggestion that this was a stop in transit to Rome. The evidence points strongly to the route south of Crete as the normal way from the Levant to Rome by ship (cf. chapter 4, pp. 134f.), and if Peter went by Corinth it seems more likely that his visit was deliberate and prearranged, and to that extent a more significant treading of Pauline territory. A visit by Peter to Corinth remains plausible, as does the possibility that Barnabas accompanied him, though the inevitably conjectural nature of both propositions must be acknowledged.

[88] The point of the early association of Peter with Rome would hold even if it be taken that 1 Peter is pseudonymous. It may be noted, however, that the provincial terminology of 1 Pet. 1:1 is suitable to the situation before Vespasian's reorganization in 72, though that point is not to be pressed (cf. C.J. Hemer, 'The Address of 1 Peter', *ExpT* 89 [1978], pp. 239-43).

Other traditions are much less compelling. Eusebius records that Peter followed the heresiarch Simon Magus to Rome in the reign of Claudius and opposed him there as he had in Samaria (*HE* 2.13-14; cf. Acts 8:9-24).[89] The supposed twenty-five year bishopric of Peter in Rome has then sometimes been linked with this and with Peter's departure in Acts 12:17 to suggest he was in Rome in the early forties, and that the twenty-five years reflect an association with Rome extending intermittently from then to his martyrdom, a period boldly dated c. 42-67.[90] In fact we know so little of his movements that an early visit to Rome cannot be excluded, though not even the better arguments for this are persuasive. Thus some scholars have made much of identifying the 'other place' of Acts 12:17, J.W. Wenham making it Rome, S.G.F. Brandon Alexandria, but both seeing Luke's imprecision as a cover to avoid an embarrassing admission.[91] But the phrase εἰς ἕτερον τόπον is most likely simply to signify 'into hiding'. The place was not embarrassing for Luke; it was just immaterial.[92]

It is also suggested that Peter may have gone to Rome about 55, and his inferred presence at Corinth near this time provides a useful circumstantial link, to suggest he visited that city on his way to Rome. The edict of Claudius against the Jews, which we have dated to 49, probably lapsed on his death, and a new door was opened. There is certainly a flourishing Roman church with a strong Jewish base as early as the writing of Romans in 57.[93] It has been

---

89 It is not clear from Eusebius' wording whether Justin or Irenaeus, both of whom he has previously cited, is his authority for this part of his account. For argument in defence of this early visit of Peter to Rome see Edmundson, *Church in Rome*, pp. 59-65.

90 Thus J.W. Wenham, 'Did Peter Go to Rome in AD 42?' *TB* 23 (1972), pp. 94-102.

91 Wenham, pp. 95, 99, suggesting that it would not have been tactful to draw attention in Acts to the foundation of the Roman church by a fugitive from justice; cf. Brandon, *The Fall of Jerusalem and the Christian Church* (London: SPCK, 1951), pp. 210-12, who makes much of an argument from Luke's silence about Alexandrian Christianity.

92 Cf. generally *MM*, *BAGD*. For the recurring tendency to read far-reaching (and incompatibly diverse) hypotheses into supposed reticences underlying this generalized form of expression cf. n. 86 above.

93 This point does not depend on the personalia of Romans 16, which are often taken to have belonged originally to a letter to Ephesus or elsewhere. The difficulty over the closing chapters of Romans has a base in the textual problem of the diverse placing of the doxology printed by UBS³ in square brackets as Rom. 16:25-27 (cf. T.W. Manson, 'St. Paul's Letter to the Romans— and Others', *BJRL* 31 [1948], pp. 224-40). There is however no necessary difficulty in the idea that Paul had many previous acquaintances then in Rome, in view of the remarkable new mobility of people under the Roman peace and the fact that Rome itself was

conjectured that in Rom. 15:20 Paul is indicating a scrupulous care not to trespass on territory already occupied by Peter.[94] T.W. Manson argued that Peter had visited Rome some time in the period 55-60, and that Mark had been his ἑρμηνευτής there (Euseb. HE 3.39.15) before his departure from that visit (cf. Anti-Marconite Prologue [post excessionem ipsius Petri]; Irenaeus adv. Haer. 3.1.1 [μετὰ δὲ τὴν τούτων (Peter and Paul) ἔξοδον]).[95] Mark himself was apparently in Rome at least in the subsequent period of Paul's imprisonment there, if we may accept the relevance to that period of Col. 4:10 and Phlm. 24.

We are left with a persisting uncertainty over Peter's movements. The whole question is largely a matter of conjecture from doubtful allusions and ambiguous and occasionally contradictory traditions. There is almost certainly much tradition of real value, but beset by such uncertainties of contextual interpretation that we cannot synthesize a firm base from which to attempt to fill the crucial gaps. It may best sum up my impression of the range of probabilities to suggest that it seems doubtful that Peter visited Rome in the forties, so far as our information goes, very possible that he did so about the mid-fifties, and almost certain that he ended his life there, presumably at some time in the sixties. The last period is really the one of crucial interest. It appears that he was associated with Paul at this stage, though again the chronology of such an association is unclear. It cannot for instance be inferred from Clement's words that they were martyred at the same time. The basic choice may perhaps be reformulated into two likely options: either Peter was based in Jerusalem until a fairly advanced date, subject to visits elsewhere and

the focus of their aspirations.

94 Edmundson, Church in Rome, pp. 27-29.

95 Manson, BJRL 28 (1944), pp. 130-31. It is not clear that there are good grounds for reading ἔξοδος and excessio as euphemisms for 'death' rather than straightforwardly of 'departure'. The citation from Papias in Euseb. HE 3.39.15 does not necessarily support the assumption that Mark wrote after Peter's death. Manson's alternative inferences are of course equally uncertain, but the openness of the question must be recognized, and his conjecture is attractive. One might speculate that in any case the Christian presence in Rome was so crucially strategic that as soon as the death of Claudius re-opened the way for Jews to flood back, the Jerusalem church would see the importance of sending an emissary of the highest standing to help establish the renewed community. Peter, as apostle and eyewitness, and a veteran of Jewish-Gentile meeting and controversy, was at the least pre-eminently fitted for the task.

Edmundson argues that Peter was in Rome c. 42-45, in Antioch c. 47-54 and in Rome again c. 54-56 (Church in Rome, pp. 75-85). Wenham does not refer to this fuller statement of a view essentially similar to his own.

perhaps to Rome, or else his association with Rome was earlier and more nearly consecutive than we should gather from the New Testament evidence alone. In the former case it is likely enough that he was in Palestine as late as 57-59, in the latter that he was involved with Rome by 60-62. But this still leaves us with a problem of silence. The silence of Acts is readily explained. The self-effacing Luke had no occasion to specify 'I talked with Peter', when such interviews did not belong to his actual story and presumably took place in one of the captivity interludes in Paul's career. He did not need to mention his access to Peter, for that was presumably known to his first audience. It sufficed to hint occasionally in such passages as we have tabulated where in particular he was drawing on Peter's knowledge. We must however recognize the absence of any greetings from Peter in those epistles which we take Paul to have written from his Roman captivity, a point partly offset by the ostensible association of Peter with Mark and Silvanus (Silas) in 1 Pet. 5:12-13. Paul's fate in 62 is a crux yet to be considered more fully; Peter was surely in Rome in the period following.

That is perhaps as far as we can take the question here. We turn back finally to the person of Luke himself. His personality and movements so far may be briefly summarized in conclusion. He first appears at Acts 16:10 at Troas, is lost to view at Philippi and reappears there at 20:5. He then accompanies Paul to Jerusalem, keeping a close record of the voyage, and is keenly stimulated by the new facility of access to sources for Jesus and the primitive church opened even by his first contacts in Palestine. It is in some such setting, we conjecture, that the concept developed for what grew into Luke-Acts, and that he occupied himself collecting materials in the period of Paul's Caesarean imprisonment in 57-59. The desire to give a reliable account was included in his purpose, and he adopted procedures of verifying sources which seemed appropriate to this facet of his intention. Comparison with the best ideals of existing historiography is suggestive in this context. Upon Paul's release, Luke accompanied him to shipwreck and to Rome, and was again presumably resident there through the period of Paul's captivity and aware of its conclusion. If we take the further step of identifying him with the traditional 'Luke the physician', this presence is attested in Col. 4:14 and Phlm. 24, which we assign to that time.

We have noted the indecisiveness of the traditional arguments from medical language and the like, and decline to build any arguments on this assumption. The fact remains, however, that the traditional ascription is strongly attested and there is no serious alternative contender in the field. I am content to accept the identification of the author with Luke the physician but not to build on it.[96]

The source question is a vast problem on which we have touched only briefly. It does seem that there is a positive point to be made through the attempt to trace a common method of treating sources in Luke-Acts, and to find such a link in the notion of a redaction involving the questioning of eyewitnesses. I submit for consideration the pilot study of the Transfiguration pericope, where the Lukan peculiarities may be explained form-critically as deriving from replies of an eyewitness to questions of the author/redactor and directed to clarify the tradition known to him.

In all the foregoing a distinction should be drawn between Luke's gathering of material and his finished work. This discussion is not of the dating of Acts, but lays a necessary foundation for that further topic. So far as this stage of the study takes us, it is still open whether the actual composition of the book was delayed beyond the assemblage of sources. The suspicion of successive drafts of the Gospel and the different textual editions of Acts add ostensible force to the contention that the processes were complex and so presumably

---

[96] Other identifications of the author from within the Pauline circle have been suggested in modern times, but are ingenious rather than convincing. Such is James A. Blaisdell, 'The Authorship of the "We" Sections of the Book of Acts', *HTR* 13 (1920) 136-58, who identifies the 'Diarist' with Epaphras = Epaphroditus. While making some acute points, like the absence of mention of Luke in the greetings of Philippians, itself however an *argumentum ex silentio*, he strains probability elsewhere, as in the supposition that Epaphras came conveniently from an existing ministry in Colossæ to meet Paul at his arrival in Troas. The cities are well over 200 miles apart, and our only knowledge of this Epaphras ostensibly years later. There have been similar theories propounded about Timothy, Silas and Titus (see M. Goguel, *Introduction au Nouveau Testament, Tome III: Le Livre des Actes* [Paris: Leroux, 1922]).

The question has given occasion to many more curious conjectures. Such is the article of P.-L. Couchoud and R. Stahl, 'Les deux auteurs des Actes des Apôtres', *RHR* 97 (1928), pp. 6-52, which attributes the book to Marcion and Clement of Rome (using the alternative forms of Jerusalem, Lystra [but see p. 110 above for heteroclitic declension], and other expressions to posit diversity of authorship, and drawing inferential portraits of the characters of the persons to fit the supposed authors). For good measure Couchoud and Stahl conjecturally invoke Clement also as corrector of the Pauline epistles, author or corrector of the Pastorals, and redactor of John's Gospel.

The ancient references to Luke imply knowledgeable tradition rather than mere inference. We are not however concerned to pursue too far a question of marginal significance. The central point is that the writer was a companion of Paul: his particular identity with Luke is secondary, unless we insist on involving arguments from medical language or practice.

extended in time. We have focused here mainly on the Palestine period 57-59. In the next chapter we must wrestle with the implications of the ending of Acts and its aftermath. Our next focus will be upon Rome and beyond.

Chapter 9
The Date of Acts

Although the historicity of Acts is not directly at stake in a decision about its date, yet that decision has a significant bearing on the way we formulate many other questions. The topic overlaps with other facets like authorship, and is at least an important tributary in establishing an overall view of Acts and a touchstone of alternative theories.

Some hypotheses postulate, for instance, a 'Lukan' theological perspective belonging to a decisively later period, or require a long lapse of time for the necessary processes of tradition-history. In view of the prevalence of such positions, it may be temerarious to suggest that most of the arguments offered for a later (or indeed for an earlier) date are curiously indecisive. A *prima facie* consideration of Robinson's *Redating* shows how open the question really is, and how tenuous the arguments by which it has often been prematurely closed. The arguments used on both sides of the debate are often of the kind which may confirm an opinion in one already convinced, rather than meeting the objections of an opponent with a different reconstruction of the situation. The argument for early date drawn from the abrupt ending of Acts is an inadequate basis, though it offers a neat reconstruction and may be a valuable confirmatory consideration for one who is convinced of the early date upon a different and broader base.

Our study of detail has uncovered much material which is not easily explained as the product of reflective editing. It seems that some considerable weight should be given to this 'immediacy' factor. One would expect a voyage-narrative to become reduced and schematized even in the mind of a participant when it had lain untapped for an extended time. An important factor in the study of detail in Acts is the marked variation in its presentation, in the varying extent to which it has been shaped by tradition or hearsay. We can find among the stones on a beach a significant mingling of those which have been wave-worn and smoothed with those which have been freshly broken from the primeval rock. That is an image apt to redaction-critical study: the rough pieces stand closest to the final state of the book, and have been least shaped. It is this valid perception that underlies the ultimately unconvincing evaluation of Acts which attributes these unshaped pieces to a diary-source deriving from far back which then a later author incorporated unadjusted. Is it not more convincing to suppose that these are among the latest pieces, newly quarried from the rock and only briefly removed from the events? The 'immediacy' of the whole of the later chapters, and not of the 'we-passages' alone, is to be contrasted with the indications of a more distant and 'secondary', still carefully reported, treatment of the Jerusalem church at the beginning of the book.[1] If the dating of the book is removed further from its later events, the pattern of differences seems progressively more difficult to explain without resorting to unnecessary hypotheses which in turn only complicate the situation to be explained.

The early dating of Acts has a lengthy and worthy pedigree, and has only been discounted in recent scholarship under the influence of strong recent trends. One can only be dubious about the kind of scholarship which argues from counting heads. Here it might be diversely used. If we are principally concerned to indicate agreement with the leaders of the present fashion, any form of dissent may easily be rejected as improper and dated. The different convergence of older scholars may then be rationalized as work superannuated by new developments. What is worrying about that is that the same new developers have not addressed themselves with sufficient rigour to the necessary historical elements of the problem. On grounds of evidence one finds people such as J.B. Lightfoot still holding the field, save in areas (like the Galatian question) where they have been decisively rendered out of date by newly discovered evidence. But the new approaches to Acts are not impelled by new discovery; as we have shown, they have rather held surprisingly aloof from new discovery, so that the basic literary and epigraphic groundwork of testing the details of Acts has been neglected, in favour of techniques of internalistic analysis. This is rather a shift of approach and opinion than an advance, and this shift sometimes consciously and explicitly sits loose to any concern with the evidential base.

The State of the Question

It would be a lengthy and unnecessary task to attempt an exhaustive collection of diverse opinions about the date of Acts, but it will perhaps help to clarify the profile of the spectrum to tabulate a fairly representative range assembled in the course of reading. The placings of Acts are here set in rough chronological order, and have included

---

1   Cf. the language of Eusebius, *HE* 3.4.6, in writing of Acts (as contrasted with this Gospel): ὃς οὐκέτι δι' ἀκοῆς ὀφθαλμοῖς δὲ παραλαβὼν συνετάξατο.

in the text the dates of the publications by way of showing at a glance the persistence of the same essential dichotomies of approach. The list is inevitably somewhat arbitrary, for many writers whose views are material to the discussion are not explicit on this point, or tacitly subsume their working assumptions under the answers to different questions.

F. Blass	57-59. *Evangelium secundum Lucam* (Leipzig: Teubner, 1897), p. lxxix; cf. *Philology of the Gospels* (London: Macmillan, 1898), pp. 33-34.[2]
R.B. Rackham	During Paul's Roman imprisonment; completed by 64. *JTS* 1 (1899-1900), pp. 76-87; *Acts* (5th edn, 1910), pp. l-lv.
A. von Harnack	early 60's. *The Date of Acts and of the Synoptic Gospels* (1911), pp. 92-93, 114-16.[3]
G. Edmundson	Before 62. *Church in Rome* (1913), p. 32.
C.C. Torrey	64. *The Composition and Date of Acts* (1916), p. 67; *AJT* 23 (1919), p. 193.[4]
P.S. Bihel	Immediately after 62. *Antonianum* 5 (1930), pp. 293-300.
A.T. Robertson	63. *ISBE* (1939) 1.42.
E.M. Blaiklock	Early sixties. *Acts* (1959), p. 17.
P. Parker	62-63. *JBL* 84 (1965), pp. 52-58.
R.R. Williams	Before about 64. *Acts* (1953), p. 21.
E.R. Goodenough	Early sixties. *SLA* (1966), p. 58.[5]
J. Munck	Early sixties. *Acts* (1967), p. liv.
F.V. Filson	Early (before Peter's arrival in Rome). *Apostolic History* (*Festschrift* Bruce), ed. Gasque and Martin

2   A dating so early may now be treated as little more than a curiosity dependent on the antedated chronology of the succession of Festus to Felix. But the fixed date from the Gallio inscription now suffices to push the events in the last chapters of the book beyond this date for its writing. Blass however placed it in Paul's Roman imprisonment, and so in principle agrees completely with the considerable list following.

3   Harnack changed his mind progresively in favour of earlier datings. Originally he favoured a date between 78 and 93, but already inclined to the early date when writing his *Acts* (pp. 290ff.), while then deferring to contrary opinion. His *Date of Acts* represents his final and considered position.

4   Torrey dates the Roman imprisonment in 62-64. He places the former half of Acts (his *I Acts*) as early as 50 to precede the Gospel c. 60.

5   Goodenough's view must be noted as an example of the complex diversity of judgments, as he combines the early date with the claim that Acts is fictional. There is no logical necessity that those who uphold a high degree of historical reliability will also advocate an early date of composition, although it is obvious that the earlier the date of composition the greater the likelihood of historical accuracy. It is noteworthy, however, that some of the strongest defenders of Luke have *not* been among the advocates of the earliest date-stratum.

	(1970), pp. 76-77.6
D. Guthrie	(Implicitly) before 64. *Introduction* (3rd edn, 1970), pp. 340-48.7
A.J. Mattill	Before the end of Paul's imprisonment. *Apostolic History* (1970), p. 122; cf. *CBQ* 40 (1978), pp. 335-50.
B. Reicke	62. *Studies in New Testament and Early Christian Literature* (*Festschrift* Wikgren) ed. D.E. Aune (*NovT* Supp 33 [1972]), p. 134.
E.F. Harrison	About 62. *Acts* (1975), p. 20.
J.A.T. Robinson	Completed 62+. *Redating* (1976), pp. 116, 352.8
R.E. Longenecker	c. 64. *Acts* (1981), p. 238.
J. Finegan	Near the end of Paul's imprisonment. *The Archaeology of the New Testament. The Mediterranean World of the Early Christian Apostles* (Boulder, Colorado: Westview and London: Croom Helm, 1981), p. 6.
V.E. Vine	c. 62-64. *ExpT* 96 (1984-85), pp. 45-48.
A. Wikenhauser	End of Paul's imprisonment; later— after Paul's death. *Geschichtswert*, pp. 45-46; *Introduction* (1958), p. 343.9
F.F. Bruce	c. 62; later 'towards 70'. *Acts* (2nd edn, 1952), pp. 10-14; *NBC* (revised, 1970), p. 969.
H.G. Russell	pre-70. *HTR* 48 (1955), pp. 167-74.
C.S.C. Williams	Prefers c. 66-70. *Acts* (1957), p. 15.
M. Schneckenburger	Between 66 and 70. *Uber den Zweck der Apostelgeschichte* (Bern: Fischer, 1841), reported by Gasque. *History of Criticism*, p. 39.10
J. Dupont	After Paul's death. *FTL* 26 (1953), p. 306, n. 32.
E.E. Ellis	Early; in Paul's generation; perhaps Luke-Acts around 70. *NTS* 26 (1980), p. 500, cf. p. 488; cf. *Luke* (1966), pp. 50-52, 56-57.
I.H. Marshall	Perhaps towards 70. *Acts* (1980), p. 48. Cf. *Apostolic History* (1970), pp. 97-98, where he argues against a post-70 date.
T.W. Manson.	Published 64-70 or the years immediately following. *BJRL* 28 (1944), p. 392; cf. pp. 400, 403.11

6   This depends on a late coming of Peter to Rome, strongly at variance with the opinions considered above.

7   Guthrie gives an admirable discussion for and against the principal alternatives without offering a formal conclusion, but from the balance of his argument it is clear that he favours this option.

8   Robinson maintains that the process of composition for Acts, as yet more in the case of Gospels, was under way well before this. He mentions the date 57, which accords with our remarks on the collection of material.

9   This evidently represents a significant change of judgment, though the span of years is relatively short.

10   Schneckenburger first raised the interpretation of Acts 8:26 as a proposed *terminus post quem* in 66.

11   Manson elsewhere makes the significant point that the date of Mark may be 'a

J.B. Lightfoot	Probably early seventies, after fall of Jerusalem. *A Dictionary of the Bible*, ed. Sir William Smith and J.M. Fuller (London: John Murray, 2nd edn, 1893), p. 40.[12]
A.C. Headlam	Shortly after 70. 'Acts of the Apostles', *HDB* 1 (1900), p. 30.
J.V. Bartlet	Perhaps 72-74. *Acts* (1901), p. 19.
R.J. Knowling	To be determined by date of Luke, citing views of Lightfoot and Headlam with approval, but himself noncommittal. *Acts* (1900), p. 36.
T. Zahn	75. *Einleitung* (2nd edn, 1900) 2.436 and 440-41 n. = *Introduction*, 3.159, 164-65n.
T.E. Page	Post-70. *Acts* (1900), pp. xvii-xviii.
D.J. Williams	About 75. *Acts* (1985), p. xxvi.
R.P.C. Hanson	After 70. *Acts* (1967), p. 29.
W. Neil	Doubts early date. *Acts* (1973), p. 29.
W.K. Lowther Clarke	No objection to a date before Paul's death, but c. 80 more satisfactory. *Theology* 4 (1922), p. 320.
A. Plummer	Not later than c. 80. *St. Luke* (4th ed, 1901), p. xxxi.
H.A.W. Meyer	c. 80. *Acts* (1877) 1.15.
W.G. Kümmel	70-90. *Introduction* (1973), p. 151.
W.M. Ramsay	Immediately after 81. *SPTR* (1896), p. 387.[13]
A.A.T. Ehrhardt	75-90. *Acts* (1965), p. 4.
E. Trocmé	Last quarter of 1st century. *Livre des Actes* (1957), p. 71.
G.H.C. Macgregor	c. 85. *Interpreter's Bible* (1954) 'Acts', p. 22.
M.-E. Boismard	Not before 80. *RB* 61 (1954), p. 275.
G. Schneider	80-90. *Apostelgeschichte* (1980) 1.121.
A. Weiser	80-90. *Apostelgeschichte* (1981) 1.40.
D. Juel	80-90. *Luke-Acts. The Promise of History* (Atlanta: John Knox Press, 1983), p. 7.
R. Maddox	Eighties or early nineties. *The Purpose of Luke-Acts* (Edinburgh: T. & T. Clark, 1982), p. 9.
M. Goguel	85-90. *Les premiers temps de l'église* (Neuchatel and Paris: Delachaux et Niestlé, 1949), p. 32.

few years earlier than is usually thought likely. A date before 60 would be quite possible' (*BJRL* 28 [1944], p. 131n.).

[12] Lightfoot rejects both the interpretations given to Acts 8:26 and to Lk. 21:20-24 as setting a terminus, but he also doubts the argument from the ending of the book to an early date (p. 27).

[13] It is surprising that a writer so commonly regarded as an archetypal apologist should hold a date relatively later than many less conservative writers. It may indeed be that Ramsay changed his mind, especially in view of Harnack's early dating, and there are indications at least that he regarded c. 80 as the *latest* suitable date. But in any case he was by no means a traditionalist, as he has been portrayed, and rather attained his final opinions by hard-won advances from a Tübingen position. I cannot find that he devoted explicit discussion to the question in his later writings.

F.J. Foakes Jackson	Before c. 90. *Acts* (1931), p. ix.
H. Windisch	Eighties or nineties; possibly 100-110. *BC* (1922) 2.309.
A.H. McNeile	c. 90. *Introduction* (1st edn, 1927), p. 36 = (2nd edn, 1953), p. 37.14
M. Dibelius	c. 90. *Studies* (1956) from German (1951), pp. 72, 135.
E.J. Goodspeed	c. 90. *New Solutions of New Testament Problems* (University of Chicago Press, 1927), pp. 94-103; *Introduction* (1937), pp. 191-97.
J. Roloff	c. 90. *Apostelgeschichte* (1981), pp. 5-6.
B.H. Streeter	c. 90-95. *The Four Gospels* (London: Macmillan, 1936), pp. 529, 535.
H. Conzelmann	After 93. *Apostelgeschichte* (1963), p. 2.15
G. Bornkamm	Towards end of the first century, at earliest. *Paul* (London: Hodder, 1971), p. xv, from German (1969).
J. Moffatt	c. 100. *Introduction* (3rd edn, 1918), p. 312.
W. Schmithals	90-110. *Das Evangelium nach Lukas* (1980), p. 9.
A. Jülicher	100-105. *Introduction* (1904), p. 434.
P.W. Schmiedel	105-130. *EB* 1 (1899), p. 50.
J.C. O'Neill	115-130. *Theology of Acts* (1961), pp. 21, 25.
J. Knox	125. *SLA* (1966), p. 286.
H. Köster	135. Reported by F. Neirynck, *ETL* 59 (1983), p. 365 from *Introduction* (1980) 2.310.

This range of opinion overlies a huge variety of divergent and often contradictory criteria and arguments. The task of assembling this list has often seemed frustrating, for some of the most significant scholars have not committed themselves to an easily tabulated figure, and many others have argued for a specific inferential redactional setting without appearing to make any attempt to relate it to a convincing reconstruction supported by hard evidence of appropriate date. It is disturbing to see how many of the incompatibilities rest on tenuous approximations or *obiter dicta* based on the mechanical application of one or two debatable termini.

It might indeed be argued that the question of date is of secondary importance partly subsumed under such fundamental overlapping questions as those of authorship and sources. There is some truth in this, and certainly a decision about the date does not itself prove any-thing for our larger theme. It does however provide another avenue into the same complex of questions, and a conclusion may serve as another straw in the wind, another pointer to discrimination between

---

14 The second edition was revised by C.S.C. Williams, but this passage, which remains unchanged, represents McNeile's opinion, and not that of Williams, who held to a much earlier date.

15 On this influential work cf. the perceptive review by R.P.C. Hanson in *JTS* n.s. 15 (1964), pp. 371-75, esp. 373 on Conzelmann's dating.

essential alternatives.

Among the criteria and termini which receive recurring mention are the following: (1) the end of Paul's imprisonment, perhaps AD 62; (2) the fire of Rome and the Neronian persecution, AD 64-65; (3) the outbreak of the Jewish War, AD 66; (4) the destruction of Gaza, AD 66 (Jos. *BJ* 2.18.1.460); (5) the traditional death of Paul, perhaps c. AD 67; (6) the fall of Jerusalem, AD 70; (7) the date of Mark, much debated, and itself argued upon a similarly diverse group of proposed termini;[16] (8) the date of the Third Gospel, commonly placed at various dates after AD 70, or of a hypothetical 'proto-Luke', often placed well before 70; (9) the likely active life-span of a companion of Paul, often placed ±80, but wholly uncertain; (10) the insertion of the Curse of the Minim into the Eighteen Benedictions, c. 85-90; (11) the appearance of Josephus' *Antiquities*, AD 93, or even the completion of all Josephus' known works, c. 100; (12) the publication of a Pauline Corpus, ?± AD 90. In addition to all these essentially specific points (however uncertain), most of which are presented as *termini post quem*, there is a great variety of postulated kinships with such settings or writings as Gnosticism, the Domitianic persecution, the Pastorals, Plutarch or Justin Martyr, or with cultural phenomena exclusively characteristic of a chosen date almost anywhere along the spectrum.

We find a welter of wildly incompatible arguments, where contradictory opinions obtain alike of the importance and bearing of most of the items on the list. This need not however be a matter for total agnosticism. The incongruities between the suggested criteria are so extreme that most of them simply cannot be relevant together, and on any particular view, which chooses any particular path through the maze, most of the other claimants must appear irrelevant.

Some of the supposed criteria may be discarded fairly easily. Thus the words αὕτη ἐστὶν ἔρημος in Acts 8:26 are open to alternative interpretations, but on neither main option is there a clear case for seeing editorial allusion to the destruction of Gaza in 66.[17] Or

---

16 Such criteria include (a) the death of Peter, itself an uncertain date; (b) the 'departure' (not 'death', ἔξοδος, *excessio*) of Peter from a Roman visit of indeterminate date (cf. pp. 355-62 above); (c) the outbreak of the Jewish War in 66; (d) the fall of Jerusalem (so Brandon). These and the like criteria are more uncertain or less tangible than the possibilities offered for Acts.

17 It is an open question whether the antecedent of αὕτη is ὁδόν or Γάζαν. It may well be argued that the point is to stress the loneliness of the road (for the usage of Arrian, *Anab.* 3.3.3 ἐρήμη τε ἡ ὁδός; so *BAGD*), even to distinguish the hill-route via Hebron from the busy coastal highway (thus Jacquier, *Actes*, pp. 268-69; etc.). Even if the epithet be applied to the city, it may appropriately have been used of the former site of the city razed by Alexander, rather than that since restored on a different site. This 'Old Gaza' is designated ἔρημος by Strabo 16.2.30

contradictory use is made of a connection which may be deemed immaterial anyhow: thus Schneider (*Apostelgeschichte*, p. 120) argues against a persecution setting and Schmithals (*Apostelgeschichte*, p. 11) for it, and so place the book respectively before and after the outbreak of a Domitianic persecution, itself an occurrence which many scholars deny.[18] But a case of much more far-reaching import is the recurring claim that Luke depends on Josephus. The best refutation of this position may actually be to look at Krenkel's classic defence of it.[19] He finds Lukan dependence in 92 passages of Luke-Acts, long and short, as well as linguistic dependence as shown, *inter alia*, in the extensive listings of individual words, especially those common to Luke and Josephus, but absent from the Septuagint.[20] Krenkel's case is argued from a huge assemblage of tenuous parallels, of common words apart from context, a huge overkill of the insignificant. If the question be reduced, as it is by most of those who have invoked Krenkel, to the few places where the *content* of Luke and Josephus overlaps, the two are apt to contradict.[21] If either used the other, he

---

= 759, writing half a century or more earlier. But I doubt reference to the city: there is no point in Luke's making an immaterial distinction between the two sites (any more than in supposedly adding gratuitously a gloss on the later fate of the existing city, whose mention serves only to locate the road).

[18] It remains most likely that there was a persecution under Domitian, though the criteria for recognizing the evidence for it are not of the explicit kind often desired. See the suggested reconstruction in my book *The Letters to the Seven Churches of Asia in their Local Setting* (Sheffield: JSOT Press, 1986), pp. 7-12.

[19] M. Krenkel, *Josephus und Lucas. Der schriftstellerische Einfluss des jüdischen Geschichtschreibers auf der christlichen nachgewiesen* (Leipzig: Haessel, 1894).

[20] Among words in this group may be mentioned terms characteristic of Roman and first century times, like ἀνθύπατος, κολωνία, Σεβαστός, σικάριος, τετραρχέω, with other common words, whose occurence in a particular writing may depend on subject matter, like ἀποπλέω, ἐκεῖσε, εὔθυμος, λόγιος, πλοῦς, ῥήτωρ. There is scarcely significance to be found in the absence of such from the Septuagint, or indeed in the thirteen-page list of mostly common words which the two writers share with the Septuagint.

[21] The classic case is the Theudas crux in Acts 5:36, and in the Gospel the multiple problems centring upon the Quirinius census. On a smaller point, the Egyptian Messianic pretender in the time of Felix is given 4,000 followers in Acts 21:38 and 30,000 in Jos. *BJ* 2.13.5.261. We might be inclined to prefer the smaller figure. See the refutation of the notion of Luke's dependence in Ehrhardt, *Framework*, pp. 85-86, accepted also by Kümmel, *Introduction*, p. 132. He offers two reasons as decisive: (1) that Paul's epistles were widely read before 100, as evidenced, for instance, in the Greek of Ignatius; (2) that Jos. *Ant.* 20, which contains the Theudas references, is a compilation from Nicolaus of Damascus, to which Luke also could have had access from a much earlier date. I am less sure of these reasons. The former, while suggestive, is still an argument from the silence

misused him. They are surely independent, and follow independent, indeed conflicting, sources. There is no evidence for direct literary relationship between them, and it is unlikely that either knew the other.[22]

For all the complexity of the matter it may be claimed that the spectrum of opinion falls into three main groupings, divided by two main types of issue. In terms of actual dating they divide mainly between those who favour (a) an early, pre-70 date; (b) a date ±80; (c) a date near the end of the first century or in the second. The first essential dichotomy is that which unites (a) and (b) against (c), the second that which divides (a) from (b).

The alliance of (a) with (b) unites in the main those who attach strong value to the arguments for a more traditional view, those who are inclined to see the author (or at least an original diarist) as a companion of Paul and who find a high degree of historical value to Acts. It does not in the least exclude interest in Luke's theological purposes, nor imply that his work is to be given a primarily historical orientation, but it tends to limit the time-span which more thorough-going redactional approaches need to justify the supposition that the tradition has been radically altered. Group (c) consists in the main of those who take this more radical view of Luke as redactional theologian, but link particular datings to diverse and often incompatible specific arguments, dependence on Josephus, relation to Jewish-Christian separation engendered or defined by the curse of the Minim, or to the Domitianic persecution, or cultural or theological kinship to various features of later date. None of the divisions are to be stereotyped. The early date has for instance been combined with a fictional view of Acts (as by Goodenough), a latish date with traditional authorship (Goodspeed) or a moderate acceptance of historical value (Maddox).

The second division, between groups (a) and (b), centres on the relation of Luke-Acts to the fall of Jerusalem. Those who are convinced that the Third Gospel must be post-70 usually feel constrained to place Acts slightly later, though some (e.g. C.S.C. Williams, Russell, Parker) adhere strongly to a pre-70 date of Acts, and make it follow an earlier 'Proto-Luke', while conceding that our present Gospel is post-70.

---

of Acts; the latter is based on a source-critical inference and does not explain the blatant contradictions in the postulated use of a common source. In the face of the dependence theory, it is inevitably difficult to prove a negative, but it may be claimed that the grounds of or the supposition are too tenuous to be plausible.

22 [Ed.] See H. Schreckenberg, 'Flavius Josephus und die lukanischen Schriften', in W. Haubeck and M. Bachmann (ed.), *Wort in der Zeit: Festgabe für K.H. Rengstorf* (Leiden: Brill, 1980), pp. 179-209.

The destruction of Jerusalem was certainly a catastrophe whose outworkings must have transformed the relations of Roman, Jew and Christian, and a fuller study of its implications is urgently needed.[23] New Testament scholars have often tried to use it as a rule-of-thumb criterion of date. By this measure it is argued that Luke 21:20-24 shows a post-70 editing of Mark. But the measure is too crude. Conversely, the admitted silence of Acts on this topic does not prove its early date. Even if Robinson is right that no part of the New Testament shows clear allusion to the fall of Jerusalem as a past event, that silence is no more than suggestive apart from positive arguments.

There are two preliminary points to be made about the use of this criterion. (i) An acceptable theory of date needs to be integrated with a fuller historical study. If, for instance, the book is to be placed after 70, some attempt should be made to wrestle with the outworkings of the event in reconstructing its possible milieu. (ii) The argument over Luke 21 is bedevilled by a latent conflict of presupposition as to whether Jesus could have foreseen or foretold the catastrophe. It is, however, arguable that Mark gives an essentially authentic saying at a pre-70 date, and a doctrinaire scepticism as to what Jesus *could not* have said is unjustified.[24] The Lukan question can however be taken out of this sensitive issue. We may hold that Jesus could have uttered such a saying yet argue that the manner of Luke's allusion shows awareness of the fulfilment of Jesus' prophecy. It may be a case of writing with hindsight rather than of *vaticinium post eventum*.

Despite what may appear a near consensus, the validity of the common argument from the editing of Mark in Luke 21:20-24 seems open to question. C.H. Dodd argued convincingly that the distinctive features of the Lukan version are fully and sufficiently explained from the Old Testament language of the fall of Jerusalem to

---

[23] We do have, of course, S.G.F. Brandon, *The Fall of Jerusalem and the Christian Church* (London: SPCK, 1951). Brandon, however, took some individual views, reviving approaches confessedly indebted to those of the Tübingen School (p. x), and placing Mark in the aftermath of 70. Perhaps it is really questionable whether any of our New Testament books belong to the period immediately after 70, when we might expect to find in them a setting unambiguously amenable to the study of the traumas of that time. Most are probably pre-70, but (*contra* Robinson) a few are so far past 70 as not to reflect the catastrophe or its immediate aftermath. While some date Acts c. 75, it seems more plausible to suppose that if not early it could only well be placed c. 80, when the dust had settled and not earlier, nor much later. There is thus often a dichotomy between the dates advocated by groups (a) and (b), though their views of the book may be similar, apart from the 70-factor, and that as affecting the Gospel more strongly than Acts.

[24] See for example C.S. Mann, *Mark*, Anchor Bible (Garden City: Doubleday, 1986), pp. 75-83 and the literature there cited.

Nebuchadnezzar in 586 BC.[25] Dodd himself adhered to a post-70 date of Luke, for reasons which he does not specify in his article. But he disposes sufficiently of the fundamental argument for making a dogma of that dating. So far as this clue will take us at present, both Luke and Acts might be placed either before or after 70, pending only a more wide-ranging study which might integrate the setting of either or both with a much more specifically argued background on one side or other of the watershed. Further, with regard to the 'hindsight' argument, it should be noted that the theme of prophecy fulfilled was seen as forcefully evidential. Luke might have been expected, here as elsewhere, to have made that point far more explicitly, if that were possible at this time of writing. (This objection would not apply if the reference be seen as a *vaticinium post eventum*: in that event the writer might be expected to conform his wording to the event without hinting that it had happened).

The above tabulation displays the real division of opinion. It is often made to seem that there is now a near-consensus in favour of later dates and redactional theology, and advocates of a different view feel obliged to justify their right to dissent (e.g. Vine). It is probable enough that our survey is weighted in favour of views which are more familiar and accessible. But even so, the combined weight of the (a) and (b) options cannot be gainsaid, even in the context of the most recent discussion. Conversely, the later datings often seem forced to avail themselves of diverse later connections whose relevance may be doubted.[26]

Such is the general profile of opinion. It will be good to pause at this point to stress particularly what seems a central crux, the heart of the objection to an early date among those who tend to the (b) option, namely the literary sequence Mark – Luke-Acts, where Acts is the sequel to Luke and Mark is a source of Luke. There is then the double-pronged objection that Mark is no earlier than c. 65 and Luke

---

25   C.H. Dodd, 'The Fall of Jerusalem and the "Abomination of Desolation"', *JRS* 37 (1947), pp. 47-54, reprinted in his *More New Testament Studies* (Manchester University Press, 1968), pp. 69-83.

26   The weight of opinion for a later date seems to rest on the strong current influence of a particular school of thought rather than on a rigorous treatment of evidence or on the actual spread of opinion over the years. Current works have not superannuated older opinion, which they have often not discused, and which was often more carefully argued than are modern views. In our tabulation we have not in general taken account of the older mainstream British work, like that of H. Alford, for whom the early date was generally received, or the Tübingen School and their followers, among whom late dates were general. We have included 19th Century work only where, as with Schneckenburger, it represents a significant break with the contemporary pattern.

is after 70. The third item in the series must follow this neat sequence. But this dating of Mark is no more assured than that of Luke, and to argue from Mark through Luke to Acts is to argue *ignotum per ignotius*. The criteria for dating Mark are elusive (cf. n. 16 above), and indeed, it may be that there is a better prospect of dating these Synoptics through Acts than the reverse. Acts is more closely integrated with contemporary events than any other New Testament book. It appears antecedently more likely to offer the kind of correlation with hard evidence which might assist our search, and even to help in the yet more difficult task of placing the Synoptics. If this is so, the question assures a yet wider importance than as one avenue into the study of Acts alone. The choice between essentially ostensible and reinterpreted views of the documents affects a wider spectrum of the evidence, and the time-factor is important in that yet wider debate. Pointers to an integration of the related writings about a relatively early group of datings nearer the events have their implications for our total understanding of Christian origins.

In the following pages we will attempt to treat the question first by discussing some possible general indications of date, then by examining the special cruxes of the ending of Acts and the end of Paul's life (for which explanations are needed on any view), and finally by attempting a reconstruction of the relation of the composition of Acts to these factors.

I. *General Indications*

(1) There is no mention in Acts of the fall of Jerusalem. This (like the following points) is relevant only as an argument from silence, and, if Acts is considered as part of 'Luke-Acts', it may be claimed that the point loses its force. Nevertheless, it remains puzzling that no reference is made to the fall of Jerusalem in Acts, and this may have some probative force when combined with other more specific and positive arguments.

(2) There is no hint of the outbreak of the Jewish War in 66, or of any drastic or specific deterioration of relations between Romans and Jews. If unbelieving Jews (and not Romans) are represented as Paul's main opponents, that is natural enough in the early period, where Paul himself appears as a devout Jew (e.g. Acts 18:18; 21:24; 22:3) and operates from within Judaism. There is no such decisive severance between Jew and Christian as we suppose to have been engendered or finalized by the war and its consequences.[27]

---

[27] I express this carefully in view of the standing need for a fuller study of the

(3) There is no hint of the more immediate deterioration of Christian relations with Rome involved in the Neronian persecution in particular (unless, by a converse argument from silence, such is to be read into the puzzle of Paul's fate). While that may of itself have been a relatively isolated outburst rather than the expression of a consistent and continuing policy, the expectations of Rome in Acts, as in Paul himself, are positive and essentially unclouded. The chosen appeal to Roman justice is harder to place when the character of the later Nero was known, or after the conflicts which followed.

(4) The author betrays no knowledge of Paul's letters.[28] This widely recognized factor may be used in contradictory ways. The independence of Acts has become a critical principle, and the disjunction is often used against Acts. But that very disjunction remains easier to explain on the hypothesis of an early date. If Acts were indeed later, the question is raised why Luke, who shows himself so careful of incidental detail, did not take trouble to attempt to conform his narrative to the Epistles artificially, since they must then have been prime sources. While the whole question is beset with uncertainties, the situation is naturally understood of an early date, and only requires special explanation at a later one.[29]

(5) There is no hint of the death of James at the hands of the Sanhedrin in c. 62 (Jos. *Ant.* 20.9.1.200). This may not be significant in a book marked by surprising silences about the fate of individuals,

---

implications. It is not likely in any case that the fall of Jerusalem, however catastrophic in its effects, marked simplistically a dividing line in the relation of Jew with Christian. Divisive tendencies were certainly present long before, and final separation was not established until long afterwards, as appears even in the controversies faced by Ignatius.

[28] [Ed.] As noted above, however, see the recent argument of L. Aejmelaeus in *Die Rezeption der Paulusbriefe in der Miletrede (Apg. 20:18-35)* (Helsinki: Academia Scientiarum Fennicae, 1987).

[29] Such an explanation might be sought in Goodspeed's idea of a collection of the Pauline Corpus about AD 90. A theory tied to his view of the production of Ephesians as a covering letter about that date. See E.J. Goodspeed, *Introduction* (1937), pp. 210-21; *New Solutions* (1927), pp. 1-64; *The Key to Ephesians* (University of Chicago Press, 1956); 'Ephesians and the First Edition of Paul', *JBL* 70 (1951), pp. 285-91. Cf. also J. Knox, *Philemon among the Letters of Paul* (University of Chicago Press, 1935). These views depend on a nexus of hypotheses, such as a supposed posthumous neglect of Paul until the publication of Acts stimulated the collection. To dispute the reasoning does not disprove the contention, but it seems more likely that the process of collecting the letters began directly after Paul's death. Conversely it might be argued that letters were of secondary interest when Paul was alive and might visit in person, but assumed a new significance at his death. This would suit even a supposition that Paul could still have been alive.

though it has been argued that the mention of this case would suit so perfectly Luke's apologetic aim to a Roman audience as to merit inclusion.[30] This point, which depends for its force on a prejudgment of Luke's purpose and setting, should not be pressed.

These five points are, if nothing more, at least consonant with an early date, and their conjunction is suggestive.

(6) The significance of Gallio's judgment at Acts 18:14-17 may be seen as setting a precedent to legitimize Christian teaching under the umbrella of the tolerance extended to Judaism. The apologetic thrust of this reference implies that the precedent had not yet been rendered obsolete and irrelevant by the march of events.

(7) The prominence and authority of the Sadducees in Acts belongs to the pre-70 situation, before the collapse of their political cooperation with Rome. This might be consistent with a later date of composition, but the point of their prominence would be dulled if they were no longer the focus of Jewish opposition.[31]

(8) Conversely, the relatively sympathetic attitude in Acts to Pharisees (unlike that even in Luke's Gospel: cf. Ehrhardt, *Framework*) is a challenge to any interpretation, but would become extremely difficult in the period of Pharisaic revival towards the Council of Jamnia, when a new phase of conflict with Christianity emerged through Pharisaic leadership.

(9) It has been argued that the book antedates the coming of Peter to Rome, and also that it uses language which implies that Peter and John, as well as Paul himself, were still alive at the date of writing.[32] The former point may well be true, but we have already noted the peculiar difficulty of tracing Peter's movements. It is likely enough on differing reconstructions that Peter came (or returned) to Rome after the writing of Acts, but this in itself is no more than another tenuous argument from the silence of Acts, which might well be otherwise explained. Jacquier's point is actually erroneous, for every passage he cites contains a present tense in *oratio obliqua* which is determined not by the author's standpoint in time, but by the internal sequential structure of the sentence.[33] It may be true that these men were all

---

[30] Robinson, *Redating*, pp. 89-90.

[31] Cf. Marshall, *Apostolic History*, pp. 97-98.

[32] Filson, *Apostolic History*, pp. 76-77, cf. Jacquier, *Actes*, p. cxiv.

[33] For Peter and John he cites Acts 4:13; for Paul, 16:38; 20:38; 21:33; 22:29; all are contained in ὅτι clauses. Conversely, he cites 4:13[b]; 5:41; 8:14; 10:45 as past tenses. He does not however draw from the two former, which also refer to Peter and John, an inference that they were dead, nor do any of these refer to persons now dead, and the two latter are perfects. 4:13 in fact has successively εἰσιν ... ἦσαν of the same persons in *oratio obliqua* where the English must be 'were ... had

still alive, but these texts say nothing to support it.

(10) The prominence of 'God-fearers' in the synagogues in Acts may well point to the current relevance of a pre-70 situation. This point is difficult to handle, not least in view of recent attacks on the actual existence of such a category of person.[34] It may be freely granted that such epithets as εὐσεβεῖς on inscriptions have been mis-read as referring to a separate class of persons where they merely denoted 'pious Jews', or again that the informal participles used in Acts, φοβούμενοι or σεβόμενοι, are not to be hardened into the tech-nical designation of a formal status.[35] But the attraction of pious Gentiles to the synagogue and to ethical monotheism is not a pheno-menon confined to Acts and to be deemed unhistorical on that ac-count. There is a larger testimony to the tendency, if not to the termi-nology, and that tendency is easier to focus before rather than after 70, when Judaism became defined more rigidly in national terms against Christian and Gentiles.[36] The attitude to proselytes in the

been' (cf. Vulg. *essent ... fuerant*). None of this says anything about the perspec-tive of Luke's time of writing. Most recently F.F. Bruce, in *BJRL* 68 (1985-86), p. 273, inclines to think that Peter, Paul and James were all dead by the time of writing, and that their passing released Luke from preoccupation with temporary controversies and animosities to stress their respective contributions.

34 Thus especially A.T. Kraabel, 'The Disappearance of the "God-Fearers"', *Numen* 28 (1981), pp. 113-26; 'The Roman Diaspora: Six Questionable Assump-tions', *JJS* 33 (1982), pp. 445-64; more cautiously, M. Wilcox, 'The "God-Fearers" in Acts— A Reconsideration', *JSNT* 13 (1981), pp. 102-22. See also the response to Kraabel in T.M. Finn, 'The God-fearers Reconsidered', *CBQ* 47 (1985), pp. 75-84. See, however, Appendix 2 below.

35 See Chapter 5, pp. 177-78 and below, Appendix 2.

36 Again, the date is not to be made a rigid dividing-line. Here, however, as the change of Roman policy required the Jewish Tax to be paid to Rome from the time of Vespasian, this payment provided a new control on Jewish identity, and worked itself out in a markedly changed way before the time when the Curse of the Minim provided a new mechanism of exclusion. See *Seven Churches*, pp. 7-12; Jos. *BJ* 7.6.6.218; cf. Dio 65.7. See now the important study by W. Horbury, 'The Benediction of the *Minim* and Early Jewish-Christian Controversy', *JTS* n.s. 33 (1982), pp. 19-61, esp e.g. 53, 59, 61. ([Ed.] Though not affecting the central point at issue here, see Reuven Kimelman, '*Birkat Ha-Minim* and the Lack of Evi-dence for an Anti-Christian Jewish Prayer in Late Antiquity', in *Jewish and Chris-tian Self-Definition*, Vol. 2 [ed. E.P. Sanders, *et al.*] [Philadelphia: Fortress Press, 1981]) Apart from the new inscription of Aphrodisias, there may be reference to 'God-fearers' in terms very similar to Luke's if we may read a phrase in a first-century inscription of Panticapaeum in the Crimea as ἐπιτροπευούσης τῆς συν-αγωγῆς τῶν Ἰουδαίων καὶ θεὸ[ν] σεβῶν (*Corpus Inscriptionum Regni Bosporani* 71; cf. B. Lifshitz in *RB* 76 [1969], pp. 95-96; M. Hengel in *Tradition und Glaube* [*Festgabe* K.G. Kuhn] [Gottingen: Vandenhoeck & Ruprecht, 1971], p. 174). The phenomenon was clearly widespread, for circumcision seems to have been a ma-

Rabbis is ambivalent, and there are indications that the pattern of proselytism altered after 70 and was in decline soon afterwards.[37]

(11) The prevalence of insignificant details of a cultural milieu of early, even Julio-Claudian, date is important in principle, though some aspects of it are difficult to quantify or to place with sufficient chronological precision. Whereas preceding points may gain force from their purposive relevance to an early reader, these raise the question whether a later writer could have succeeded in archaizing unobtrusively in incidental features without betraying his hand. Some of these points have been noted in previous chapters. Among examples included in this category may be mentioned: (a) the prominence of the popular assemblies rather than administrative councils in city life (*RSRL*, pp. 85, 175); (b) the importance of Roman citizenship and the status of dual citizenship, when the distinction between *cives* and *peregrini* rather than that of *honestiores* and *humiliores*, as first under Trajan, was paramount (*RSRL*, pp. 173-74); (c) an early phase in the history of Roman provincial administration, exemplified in Paul's trial experiences (*RSRL*, p. 121); (d) a tone and feel of civic life which finds its nearest parallels in the first century writers Strabo, Josephus and Dio Chrysostom (*RSRL*, p. 120); (e) more specifically, the occurrence of personal names of old-fashioned type, suggesting older, conservatively-minded military personnel even in the Julio-Claudian period (*RSRL*, pp. 160-61); (f) references to the 'Hellenists' and to the 'synagogue of the Libertines', etc. (if one synagogue), as features of Judaism contemporary with the earliest church; (g) provincial terminology appropriate to the period

---

jor barrier to the full proselytism of male adherents. For the attraction of Jewish practices to a wider circle of Gentiles in the early period cf. Philo, *Vita Mosis* 2.17-24. In Philo's usage ἐπηλύτος and πάροικος are used in both a literal and religious sense without apparent distinction, in comment on Lev. 25:23 (*de Cherubim* 34.120). Josephus stresses the Jewish welcome to strangers and the multitudes attracted to their faith and practices (Jos. *BJ* 7.3.3.45; *Ap.* 2.28.210; 2.39.282-84), and also indicates, as in the interesting case of Izates of Adiebene, how circumcision might be a barrier to those who were eager, short of this, to adhere to Judaism (*Ant.* 20.2.4.38-48). The literature of this period suggests a more active proselytizing movement than we might have supposed, and this is reflected also in pagan literature (Hor. *Sat.* 1.9.68-72) and in the New Testament (Mt. 23:15).

37 See e.g. M.H. Pope in *IDB* 3.931. The case of Flavius Clemens and Flavia Domitilla (and perhaps that of Acilius Glabrio), condemned for a Jewish-type 'atheism' under Domitian (Dio 67.14) is unclear. It is possible that these persons were actually Christians, or that their cases had political or dynastic dimensions quite apart from their alleged religious practices. While the machinery activated against an irregular association with Judaism may have been invoked against them (cf. Suet. *Dom.* 12.2) they are probably normative neither of Jewish proselytism nor of Christian conversion among people of humbler rank at that time.

preceding Vespasian's reorganization in AD 72;[38] (h) the 'decrees of Caesar', if we accept the interpretation of E.A. Judge as alluding to an edict of the last days of Augustus, applicable in the Julio-Claudian period (Acts 17:7; cf. Dio 56.25.5-6, on AD 11);[39] (j) reference to the sicarii (21:38), as suiting the period between Felix and the fall of Jerusalem.

(12) There are areas of controversy within Acts which presuppose the relevance of an early Jewish setting while the Temple still stood. The whole Stephen episode, and the violent reaction to him, and the trouble over Paul's supposed introduction of a Gentile into the Temple precinct are cases in point. This is in some degree the positive converse of (1), but as an argument for dating is inconclusive. Such things might indeed have been written after 70, but their setting and significance are pre-70, and at least we may claim that a positive case for post-70 redaction is not apparent here.

(13) Harnack (*Date*, p. 103) notes that the prophecy placed in Paul's mouth at Acts 20:25 (cf. 20:38) may have been contradicted by later events, and, if so, must presumably have been penned before that happened. But the force of this argument depends wholly on the assumption that 2 Tim. 4 contains genuine information about Paul subsequent to a hypothetical release from Roman captivity. Most scholars would reject either the authenticity of the Pastorals *in toto* or accept these personal notices as Pauline fragments from a different, perhaps indeterminate, context (cf. Harrison). Discussion of these issues must be held over for the moment, as they belong to the complex of questions consequent upon consideration of the ending of Acts.

(14) Christian terminology is used in Acts which may be taken to represent primitive formulations. Harnack lists a number of Christological titles: Ἰησοῦς and ὁ Κύριος are used freely, whereas ὁ Χριστός always designates 'the Messiah', and never has the feel of a proper name, and Χριστός is otherwise used only in formalized combinations. Titles like ὁ παῖς θεοῦ (αὐτοῦ in Acts 3:13, 26; σου in Acts 4:27,

---

38   This point is a delicate one which cannot easily be reduced to mechanical formulae. See excursus, pp. 241-43. Among relevant factors may be mentioned the apparent strength of the provincial idea, where 'Asia' and 'Galatia' in particular are used of provincial entities, with the corresponding ethnics likewise, whereas after 72 'Galatia', in this larger sense, was further coupled with Cappadocia, and the component territories of this doubled entity often listed separately, as in numerous Flavian inscriptions. Conversely, the compiling of Syria with Cilicia in Acts 15:23, 41, as in Gal. 1:21 (cf. Acts 9:30) reflects the pre-72 situation, before Vespasian separated this pairing. See E.M.B. Green, 'Syria and Cilicia— A Note', *ExpT* 71 (1959-60), pp. 52-53. Throughout this list of examples cf. Chapter 5, pp. 175-81, which documents details suggestive of an early setting.

39   Judge, 'Decrees of Caesar at Thessalonica', *RTR* 30 [1971], p. 7

30) and ὁ ἴδιος (υἱός) in Acts 20:28 are also cited as primitive (*Date*, pp. 104-107). Harnack goes on to argue on a wider front for a primitive Christology in Acts (*Date*, pp. 107-10). Again, Luke uses μαθηταί of the Christians, ὁ λαός of the Jews, and does not use ἐκκλησία as a regular term for Christian community (*Date*, pp. 110-13). This kind of point has been taken up elsewhere,[40] though Haenchen (*Acts*, p. 93) sees it, not as primitive, but as Luke's own 'simple' theology, which he shared with his community at a later date. Some of Harnack's points are impressive, and they tend to corroborate the early setting from yet another angle, and are at least consonant with an early date of composition. Religious terminology, however, may of itself be less telling than the unpremeditated and incidental. Primitive language might be rather a testimony to Luke's conservative and unredacted usage of early material than to his actual date of writing. The fact that some of the most interesting examples are contained in speeches is interesting from more than one point of view.[41]

(15) Rackham draws attention to the optimistic tone of Acts.[42] This overlaps with some of the preceding points and is a positive counterpart to some of the arguments from silence listed at the outset. It might be held to conflict with the suggested premonition of Acts 20:25 (see (13) above), but the significance of that hint in either direction depends on questions yet to be discussed, and does not serve to dispel the impression made throughout the book. If there is arguable hindsight here about the fate of Paul, there is none apparent with regard to the traumas of war and persecution.

These points are of varying weight, and indeed we have seen no probative value in some of them, but they contribute to a cumulative case that Acts reflects the situation and concerns of the church in the pre-AD 70 period and betrays no clear indication of a later period.

---

[40] Thus e.g. Foakes-Jackson, *Acts*, pp. xv-xvi, who regards them as Lukan compositions, and then has to acknowledge a marvelous skill on his part to present such primitive preaching; also J. Jeremias, *TDNT* 5.700, 703. Cf. however O'Neill (1st edn, 1961), pp. 117-45.

[41] The speeches are commonly regarded as the expression of Lukan theology, and the suggestion of such early material at this point poses the choice between alternative explanations in sharper terms. Cf. the case for finding Semitisms particularly in the speeches in the early chapters of Acts. This also raises questions about the possibility of Luke's use of sources for speeches, or leaving early materials with little redactional change where an anachronistic hand might easily have betrayed itself.

[42] R.B. Rackham in *JTS* 1 (1900), pp. 80-81.

II. *The Ending of Acts*

The central problem is why Luke does not tell us what happened to Paul at the end of the διετία of Acts 28:30. The mention of this defined period implies a terminal point, at least impending, but almost certainly past.[43] Many alternative explanations have been offered, perhaps none of them completely satisfactory.

(1) It has been urged that Luke's purpose was fulfilled otherwise than by recounting the fate of Paul, that the real climax was the coming of the Gospel to Rome, the completion of the programme of expansion outlined in Acts 1:8. Beside that great progress of the church, the outcome for Paul was immaterial, and neither he, nor Peter, nor James, receives any personal notice or epitaph at the end.[44] Yet even to state this suggestion confronts us again with its inherent difficulty, for if the structure and thrust of the book be invoked, the climax seems intimately built *around* Paul. The book offers no explanation of the two years. If Paul's fate were immaterial, why tantalize the reader with a cryptic and unnecessary focus on it?

(2) It is of course possible that an ending which seems unsatisfactory to a modern reader was not necessarily seen in the same light by an ancient. There is indeed a considerable debate over the literary character of endings, as affecting many works of ancient literature, and the New Testament itself contains a notable, if different, problem in the case of Mark's Gospel, apart from the textual uncertainties of Romans 15-16.[45] There are however two general comments to be

---

43 'Impending' only on the assumption either that Acts was intended as a document for Paul's trial, which is an inadequate view (see below), or that Luke for some reason chose to issue the book before the verdict, which is hard to justify. The well-attested aorist ἐνέμεινεν may suffice to connote a completed period.

44 This, in its variations, is perhaps the most popular approach among those who adhere to a later date of Acts. We may cite Jülicher, *Introduction*, p. 439, for whom Luke could not seem to draw a parallel between the Passion (and Resurrection) of Jesus and the fate of his followers; Haenchen, *Acts*, p. 732, for whom Luke was unwilling to enhance devotion to a martyr. O'Neill, pp. 66-70 is among those who stress the geographical aspect, that Rome was here more important than Paul (cf. BC 4.350). The cases of Peter and James may be held to illustrate the same phenomenon, though the issues in each are different, and Peter, after leaving the centre of the stage, reappears at Acts 15:7 and apparently survived beyond the dramatic date of the end of Acts. We have noted above a possible explanation of the silence over the death of James c. 62.

45 In both these instances there is a textual component in the problem, and even Mark is only in any degree comparable if it be assured that ἐφοβοῦντο γάρ in Mark 16:8 was the original and intended ending. Even then, its peculiarity is of an entirely different order and seems to have generated attempts to provide a more satisfactory conclusion, a feature unparalleled in Acts.

made: (a) literary endings in antiquity usually differ from ours not in being abrupt, but in the opposite direction, of moving beyond the climax into a gentle resolution and continuity; (b) in exceptional cases, where the ending is abrupt or climactic, the issues at stake are different from those in Acts, and it is not clear that it has any literary parallel at the focus of the problem. A classic problem is Virgil's *Aeneid*, which ends boldly and violently at the moment of Turnus' death. While this anomaly has engendered diversity of opinion, the issues there offer no foothold for a resolution of our present problem.[46] We may grant in principle that ancient literary task sometimes differed from ours, but that observation seems not to help us in our present quest.

(3) It has sometimes been suggested that Paul's fate is left unmentioned because Luke's audience already knew of his condemnation and death (or, if you will, of his release).[47] But, if it is valid at all, it could be saying too much, for an audience which knew the outcome presumably knew much of the situation which produced that outcome, and the idea poses a larger query against the point of other facets of Luke's book. The point cannot perhaps be pursued without

---

[46] See e.g. S. Farron, 'The Abruptness of the End of the *Aeneid*', *Acta Classica* 25 (1982), pp. 136-41; cf. *id.*, 'The *Furor* and *Violentia* of Aeneas', *Acta Classica* 20 (1977), pp. 204-208, with response by M. Scott in 21 (1978), pp. 151-55. The problem here however is that the work concludes at the moment of climax, without the further resolution of consequences and that its final violent twist poses questions over Virgil's conception of the character both of Aeneas and of Turnus. Acts, while not in literary terms aptly paralleled in the *Aeneid* anyhow, seems to end *before* its expected climax. A possible literary parallel of a different kind, applicable only to a different estimate of the Acts ending, is in Xenophon *Hell.* 7.5.27, which concludes with the bold statement that this is as far as his account goes, and perhaps another will continue it. It is unnecessary to discuss other supposed literary parallels in detail. B.W. Bacon, 'More Philological Criticism of Acts', *AJT* 22 (1918), pp. 1-23, made much of Philostratus' *Life of Apollonius*, where the supposed source Damis is said to end with the man's departure (*Vita Ap. Ty.* 8.28-29), and diverse accounts are given of the sage's death or assumption into heaven, and of his posthumous appearances (8.29-31). But this material is prolix and legendary; it gives multiple traditions and explanations rather than stopping short of any.

[47] Thus e.g. R.P.C. Hanson, *Acts*, p. 34, who recognizes that this answer 'does not quite satisfy' (p. 35). Hanson's discussion is helpful, and a useful catalyst of opinion. He argues strongly for Paul's release, and often on lines congenial to those presented here. He feels obliged, however, to take a post-70 date of Acts (p. 29) which generates added difficulties for his views on related matters. The theory that Paul was condemned at the close of the διετία he regards as 'very brittle'. 'There is no single piece of concrete evidence in its favour; it rests upon pure conjecture, and it has against it the strong objection that it would make nonsense of much of Acts if it were true'. (p. 32).

further consideration of purpose and audience, but perhaps neither can be seen in such restricted terms as to explain such an apparently eccentric omission.

(4) This approach may however be built into a specific view of Luke's apologetic or other purpose, that it was unwise, for instance, to draw attention to Roman participation in Paul's condemnation.[48] The picture given elsewhere in the book points to Rome as essentially the upholder of justice against Paul's opponents among the Jews. It must be noted, however, that the plausibility of this idea tends to be tied to the assumption of an early date, when Christianity may still claim to be Judaism *par excellence* and is entitled to Roman protection as included in the scope of a *religio licita*, an argument which would wear thin even before 70. This scenario may indeed deserve consideration, but it does not explain away our difficulty. If the case were so sensitive, Luke could have handled it more smoothly by leaving out his tantalizing conclusion altogether.

(5) The concept of Acts as an apologetic document has been applied in a much more specific way, to suggest that it was in fact intended as a document for the defence at Paul's trial, and that it was produced for that occasion.[49] This would certainly explain the inconclusiveness of the ending neatly, but it gives an inadequate account of Acts. The book is much too diversified to be suitable, relevant or credible for the narrow requirements of a legal brief. If Acts is in any sense apologetic, which seems likely enough, it is only so partially and on broader grounds which do not permit such a conclusion. And it would be difficult to place Acts on the *eve* of the trial, if we may suppose that the force of the aorist ἐνέμεινεν implies the completion of the two-year period.

(6) There is an old view that the ending is merely transitional because Luke intended a third book.[50] Whether or not Luke ever

---

48 Rejected in this form by Harnack, *Date,* p. 96n. If however it be assumed that Paul was released, the focus of the point is changed. It might be argued that it would suit Luke's point to stress an acquittal. See however the concluding suggestion of the present chapter.

49 Cf. Munck, *Acts,* p. liii: 'Would it be possible for Luke's work to influence the verdict ... ?'

50 Thus Spitta, *Die Apostelgeschichte* (Halle: Waisenhaus, 1891), pp. 318-19; Ramsay, *SPTR,* pp. 23, 27-28; Zahn, 'Das dritte Buch des Lukas', *Neue kirchliche Zeitschrift,* 28 (1917), pp. 373-95; W.L. Knox, *Acts,* p. 59n.; also some who date Acts very early are attracted to the supposition that a third volume was intended: thus Edmundson, *Church in Rome,* pp. 32-34; Blaiklock, *Acts,* pp. 12, 16. This view has more recently been renewed in a different form, which regards the Pastorals as supplying the essence of the hypothetical 'third volume'; see J.D. Quinn, 'The Last Volume of Luke: The Relation of Luke-Acts to the Pastoral Epistles', *Per-*

wrote such a sequel is immaterial to the theory. It is claimed that πρῶτον in Acts 1:1 implies that the Gospel was 'first' of a series extending beyond two members. But this idea, despite the redoubtable advocacy of W.M. Ramsay and T. Zahn, has never won wide support. An argument cannot fairly be based on a distinction between πρῶτος and πρότερος. The latter word is never used by Luke, and is rare in the New Testament except in adverbial forms (adjectively only in Eph. 4:22). πρῶτος however is freely used of temporal priority. And, apart from the matter of usage, it may be doubted whether Acts 28:30-31 is any more explicable as an interim ending than as a final conclusion. This hypothesis requires an initial crisis and resolution in the supposed sequel, but it is not clear what events of comparable significance could have been meant to follow.

(7) The possibility should be mentioned that Acts was left unfinished, or that its conclusion was undesigned, if only for some mechanical reason like the filling of a papyrus roll to the limit.[51] But this seems wholly improbable. Luke may indeed have been anxious to make the fullest possible use of the limits of a papyrus roll; certainly his two books are the longest of the comparably long New Testament writings. But there is every reason to suppose that the ending was intended, whatever the motive for it. The copious voyage details and the meeting with the Jewish leaders in Rome are not curtailed, as they could have been, to make room for a final crisis, had that ever been intended. And it would be a counsel of despair to suppose that Luke died or was parted from his manuscript without penning a final sentence or two to resolve the question.[52]

---

spectives on Luke-Acts (ed. Talbert) (Edinburgh: T & T Clark, 1978), pp. 62-75; S.G. Wilson, *Luke and the Pastoral Epistles* (London: SPCK, 1979). These views are related to ideas of kinship or even common authorship between these groups of writings (cf. Moule in *BJRL* 47 [1964-65], pp. 430-52). See the sympathetic discussion by P.W. Walaskay, '*And So We Came to Rome*' (CUP, 1983). But, even apart from the doubts attaching to this view of the Pastorals, they do not fulfil the expectations of a third Lukan volume, nor do they resolve the conclusion of Paul's life, save inferentially, and it must be recalled that the whole structure rests on little more than speculation based on the use of πρῶτος rather than πρότερος.

51 Also rejected by Harnack, *Date*, pp. 96-97n. The converse point might be made that Luke's division of his work in two such copious and equal parts shows a deliberate and calculated use of the available space (cf. Cadbury in *BC* 5.337). Cadbury elsewhere (*Making*, p. 321) raises the possibility that Luke's source had come to an end.

52 Cf. J. de Zwaan, 'Was the Book of Acts a Posthumous Edition?' *HTR* 17 (1924), pp. 95-153; H. Lietzmann, *The Founding of the Church Universal*, tr. B.L. Woolf (London: Lutterworth, 2nd edn, 1950), p. 78, which says the ending 'can only be satisfactorily explained by saying that the author died before the work was completed'. A different ground for arguing an involuntary end to the book is

(8) A strange antithesis of (3) is the idea considered by Bihel that Luke wrote in absence from Rome and did not himself know Paul's fate, although the two had been close until this separation.[53] Such a paradoxical supposition cannot easily be disproved. Nor can it be considered likely.

(9) It may be argued simply that Luke had brought the narrative up to date at the time of writing, the final note being added at the conclusion of the two years.[54] This is more a restatement than a separate alternative, but it poses afresh the question whether a trial had already taken place, and, if so, why Luke does not tell us the outcome. The rationale of this option throws us back on the unsatisfactory suppositions we have considered. We do not know the circumstances, and perhaps we really have no alternative to speculation.

It is thus difficult to explain the ending exactly, regardless of the view one takes about the early or late date of the book. The best way forward is to attempt a fresh consideration of the circumstances of Pauls' captivity and trial, to attempt to reconstruct something of the end of his life. If we can clarify the possibilities, we may be able to offer a more plausible reconstruction.[55]

that which argues that the original ending was somehow removed or altered. Leaving aside the pious Western addition found in Syriac and Latin MSS (cf. Metzger, *Textual Comm.*, p. 503) there is no textual foundation for such a supposition. But F. Pfister, 'Die zweimalige römische Gefangenschaft und die spanische Reise des Apostels Paulus und der Schluß der Apostelgeschichte', *ZNW* 14 (1913), pp. 216-21 argued that the genuine ending was removed to harmonize with contrary traditions preserved in apocryphal Acts. E. Havet, *Le Christianisme et ses Origines* IV (Paris: Lévy, 1884), p. 212 suggested that Paul was released, and that Luke might have continued his story to conclude with his *natural* death, but that all this was later suppressed when a later tradition arose of Paul's martyrdom. If such unsupported speculations are in order, it might be more plausible to air a different possibility that Paul himself died naturally after two years without at that time having come to trial. I do not accept that, nor think it a serious possibility when all the evidence is taken into account, but it is more plausible than options which have commoner advocacy. The problem with all such theories, apart form their hypothetical character, is that our actual ending, however difficult, bears the marks of deliberation.

53 P.S. Bihel, 'Notae de tempore compositionis libri Actuum Apostolorum', *Antonianum* 5 (1930), pp. 293-300. Cf. the suggestions of T.W. Manson in *BJRL* 28 (1944), p. 403 that Luke went to Achaia and did not know what Paul was doing, and of Walaskay that when Luke was writing in the eighties or nineties, 'the apostle has disappeared into the mists of the Spanish moors' ('*And So We Came to Rome*', p. 77n).

54 Thus e.g. Harnack, *Date* , pp. 93-103; Edmundson, *Church in Rome*, pp. 32-33; Bruce, *Acts* 11, 481; and those who place the book *before* Paul's trial: Rackham, *Acts*, p. li; Munck, *Acts*, p. liii.

III. *The 'Immediacy' of Acts*

Any attempt to offer a fuller reconstruction of the events surrounding the end of Paul's life must be prefaced with some consideration of a phenomenon of the book which seems to merit treatment under a separate head, apart from the above grouping of general indications in favour of the early dating option. This is what we have called the 'immediacy' of the latter chapters of the book, which are marked in a special degree by the apparently unreflective reproduction of insignificant details, a feature which reaches its apogee in the voyage narrative of Acts 27-28. It is the extreme converse of the redactional factor. Its presence does not of course conflict with the redactional principle, but requires us to strike a meticulously fair and fresh balance in assessing it.

The final voyage narrative is in fact a key passage from this and related perspectives. It is the place which puts the eyewitness issue in its sharpest form, and is the least amenable to redactional study or to theological reinterpretation. Recent attempts at theological interpretation, to which we have referred previously, do not hold water.[56] They seem to feel a need to justify the inclusion of such a narrative by some special, artificial significance. It is true that Luke admires Paul, that he portrays him as a man of calm faith amid the panic. But this is a natural significance, attached to reminiscence. What then of the vivid details? The supposition that the scene is written up as a literary tableau is untenable today. As we have shown, the integration of the incidentals of time and place around the occasion of Luke's companionship with Paul is hard to break, if only the range of collateral and illustrative evidence is admitted for consideration. No writing up of a 'typical' voyage scene could have embodied this natural integration. Yet it is revealing that the modern scholars who suggest this have no convincing alternative way of handling the details here. They have to assume that Luke included gratuitously the redactionally irrelevant with no apparent motive, beyond a desire for

<hr/>

55 Many other views of the question have been offered, particularly from the ground of literary parallels, but such are less immediately relevant to our historical problem. Thus P. Davies, 'The Ending of Acts', *ExpT* 94 (1982-83), pp. 334-35 argues that Luke has based his ending on that of 2 Kings. J. Dupont, 'La conclusion des Actes et son rapport à l'ensemble de l'ouvrage de Luc', in Kremer, *Actes*, pp. 359-404 argues from the theological purpose of Luke's own structure. Literary and theological approaches are important in their place, but these studies do not help in answering the specific questions with which we are here concerned.

56 See Chapter pp. 317ff.

fine writing. This accords ill in itself with the purposive, 'theological' Luke we are to seek elsewhere.

It is our contention that these inconsequential details are hard to explain except as vivid experiences recalled at no great distance in time. Even an eyewitness writing years later would be likely to shape and smooth his narrative to fit more considered, selective criteria of significance. Examples may be found throughout the narrative. Luke comments on the difference of route between the westward voyage north of Cyprus (Acts 27:4) with his previous experience of crossing south of it (21:3), though both were conditioned by normal wind conditions, and deserved mention only as novel experiences. The locations of insignificant places in Crete, the frustrated plans of the ship's company, the nautical manoeuvres and the topography of the Maltese shore are not only theologically irrelevant, but hard to explain except as vivid experience recalled before the details could blur or be merged in a longer perspective of reflection.

The vivid 'immediacy' of this passage in particular may be strongly contrasted with the 'indirectness' of the earlier part of Acts, where we assume that Luke relied on soures or the reminiscences of others, and could not control the context of his narrative. It also contrasts in lesser degree with the earlier 'we-passages', where the precision is more formalized, less inconsequentially vivid; indeed as we might expect in the comparison of a narrative of the latest period with one of a prosperously uneventful voyage of earlier date. There is also a certain difference between the deliberate 'diary' style of the voyage in Acts 20-21 and the brevity and different focus of the first such passage in Acts 16. The scenes which must have come from Pauls' own vivid description, such as those before the Areopagus and at Ephesus, are again subtly different, vivid but not 'immediate'. These passages are rich in the irony of human behaviour, as they have been shaped by reflective recollection in the teller's mind.[57] Such distinctions may even be illustrated in such tangible ways as the differing usages of proper names, as between the accurate recall of the inconsequentially obscure in Acts 27-28, the general consistency and flexibility of usage where Luke has a command of the context, and the unassimilated character of the more fragmentary information of Acts 2. Again, the interesting nautical *patois* reflected in Acts 27-28, often of mixed Graeco-Latin origin, could most naturally have been acquired on-board ship, and is integrated once more with an immediacy of experience and unparalleled earlier in the book. In

---

[57] They bear the marks of an oft-told story, with the occasional cutting edge of the *raconteur's* comment (cf. e.g. Acts 17:16, 21, 31; 19:32).

general, our suggestions about source-criticism seem to mesh naturally with differences in the scale and precision of narrative, and with gradations both of vividness and immediacy, which can be explained as marking the differences between recent experience and other categories of material.

It may still be objected that the contents of a diary could have been written down later with their vividness and immediacy untarnished. This brings us back to the probabilities considered in the discussion of authorship and sources. Our point here is simply that such suppositions are in conflict with the more natural economy of hypothesis. There *could* have been reasons for delay, but it savours of special pleading to search for them. The needs of the church were urgent, set in what seems to have been a rapidly changing and (in our view) deteriorating situation. There was no likely call for Luke to sit on his work, and the supposition of delay is gratuitous. Even if we insist on some expanse of time, this extension is then to be argued on the ground of a divorce of time-lapse from freedom of redactional change. If then our case for 'immediacy' be accepted, a special explanation for delay does not much assist those who need time to accommodate the growth of tradition and the processes of redaction.

If the insistence on a post-70 dating of Luke-Acts (or even a post-65 dating of Mark) is once questioned as indecisive, the more natural reading of concurrent lines of circumstantial evidence points progressively towards an earlier date. I have not invoked the general considerations or the 'immediacy' of Acts to support each other before discussing each in turn, but it may be claimed that both combine to point in the same direction. Yet the case cannot be fully established apart from an attempt to reconstruct a plausible scenario for the composition of Acts in its relation to Paul's fate. If anthing like our proposed reconstruction is correct, the ending of Acts may be integrated into it and provide evidence for a particular early dating about 62.

IV. *The End of Paul's Life*

How then did the διετία terminate? There are three apparent options: (1) condemnation and death; (2) acquittal; (3) default, deadlock or postponement in some form.[58] Cadbury (*BC* 5.326-38) has argued attractively for a form of the third possibility: that the outcome was indecisive and Paul was then presumably released by default, in circumstances whose recital would add nothing to Luke's indication of

---

[58] This category might include any other hypothetical event which might be invoked to mark the end of the stated period, anything other than the decisive verdict of a trial.

him.[59] If accusers failed to appear, the defendant must presumably have been released. There is, moreover, well-known evidence for the custom of Claudius to give judgment against absent parties (Suet. *Claud.* 15.2; Dio 60.28.6). Claudius' proposals, preserved in a papyrus record of his speech to the Senate,[60] were codified in the provisions embodied in the *SC Turpilianum* of AD 61 under Nero, enacted, on our hypothesis at the precise time when Paul was awaiting trial, and setting a time limit for prosecution on capital cases. This defined the offence of *destitutio*, and enacted penalties for defaulting accusers.[61] Further, Cadbury cites a document (*BGU* 628), attributed to the first century, which sets limits for prosecution, six months for cases from within Italy, nine months for Transalpine overland cases, and eighteen months for cases from across the sea. That last limit in Paul's case would suit the prospect of release when due formalities had been completed, in a period close to two years *in toto*.

There are however two fundamental objections to this attractive picture (for which I am indebted to A.N. Sherwin-White). (1) The latter, apparently clinching, document *BGU* 628 is not of the first century at all, but of the later Imperial period. Cadbury followed an aberration of dating among the Roman lawyers of his day (*RSRL*, p. 115). (2) The central thrust of policy in the period of Claudius and Nero, and indeed later, was to compel prosecutors to prosecute, not to provide for the release of unaccused persons. This is a subtle but important distinction. The focus of concern was to curb *calumnia* (vexatious prosecution) by paralysing both default and unsubstantiated allegations. The passages in Suetonius and Dio are then to be seen from the perspective of changed practices introduced by Trajan, when Claudius' interventions in litigation were made to look absurd (*RSRL*, pp. 112-15).

---

59 I have earlier been strongly inclined to this hypothesis of release by default.

60 *BGU* 611 = Smallwood, *Documents of Gaius, Claudius and Nero*, No. 367. It is worth quoting some of Claudius' words: Hae ne procedant artes male agentibus si I vobis videtur, p(atres) c(onscripti), decernamus ut etiam I prolatis rebus iis iudicibus necessitas iudicandi I imponatur qui intra rerum agendarum dies I incohata iud[i]cia non peregerint ... Nam quidem accu I satorum regnum ferre nullo modo possum, I qui cum apud curiosum consilium inimicos suos I reos fecerunt, relincunt eos in albo pendentes I et ipsi tanquam nihil egerint peregrinantur, I cum rerum magis natura quam leges ta[m] I accus{t}atorem quam reum [co]pulatum constr[ic] I tumque habeat. (*BGU* 611, col. 2, lines 2-6, 11-18.)

61 *RSRL*, p. 113. For the date see Tac. *Ann.* 14.41; cf. the section on this *Senatus Consultum* in Dig. 48.16 (*Corpus Turis Civilis* 1 [Berlin: Weidmann, 1954], pp. 859-61); *Codex Justinianus* 9.45 (*ibid.* II [1959], p. 390; Hitzig, 'Calumnia', P W 3.1414-1421.

All this leaves the argument for default in an uncertain and unsatisfactory state, where the balance of probability is rendered singularly elusive and imponderable. Paul, after all, had a good case. The attack upon him was ostensibly the work of a relatively small group of implacable enemies, if we read the case aright. If the procedure was not then weighted by political influence or the like, he could reasonably expect a successful outcome. Indeed the case looks, on Luke's presentation of it, like a textbook example of *calumnia*.[62] If the prosecution did in the end default, the defendant must presumably have been eventually released, though our sources do not focus on this side of the case. Yet Paul's opponents would not presumably have been satisfied with less than his condemnation. If however they saw no prospect of obtaining a verdict, they may have shrunk from being exposed as *calumniatores* rather than mere defaulters. Yet if Jewish influences, and those of a hostile character, were at work in Nero's court, and this too is highly debatable,[63] pressures might have been brought to bear on the handling of the case. The young Nero was not, like Claudius, addicted to the law-courts, and it is probable enough that Paul's case was a routine matter for a deputed judge. It is an attractive speculation of Edmundson (*Church in Rome*, pp. 113-14) that a favourable climax, whether by acquittal or default, happened under the honest Burrus, just before his death in Spring 62, before the succession of Tigellinus. But we have no reason to be sure that the praetorian prefect of the day presided in person.

The question next arises whether any of the other ostensibly Pauline letters throw light on this period. Here we may draw on the discussion in Chapter 6. There it was argued that Ephesians, Colossians, and Philemon belong together in the first year of Paul's Roman imprisonment, and that Philippians belongs to the last months of that same διετία. Many would deny the authenticity at least of Ephesians, but that epistle is not in any case our primary concern here. The two epistles to Colossae or its neighbourhood appear to belong together, and if indeed from the imprisonment at

---

62 It may of course be objected that Luke's writing is tendentious, and that this is precisely the impression he wanted to create. But there is no logical argument from a judgment of an author's motivation directly to the falsity of his statement.

63 Much has been built on some doubtful hints in Josephus that the empress Poppaea was favourably disposed to the Jews, especially the phrase θεοσεβής γὰρ ἦν (Jos. *Ant.* 20.8.11.195), used in a context where she pleaded for Jewish petitioners. But it is questionable, as we have seen, whether θεοσεβής denotes a 'god-fearer'. It is often a complimentary epithet, 'pious', whether Jewish or pagan, and in this case probably 'religious', i.e. perhaps 'superstitious'. See E.M. Smallwood, 'The Alleged Jewish Tendencies of Poppaea Sabina', *JTS* n.s. 10 (1959), pp. 329-35, who argues against the common assumption.

Rome, may be plausibly dated neither earlier nor later than 60 or possibly the beginning of 61, before the news of earthquakes in the Lycus valley had reached Rome.

Philippians, however, bears clear marks of having been written from a situation where Paul had already been a long time in captivity, for the attempt of rival preachers to embarrass his work bears the marks of a developed local situation (Phil. 1:12-18).[64] Time was also needed for the fairly extensive reference of visits and the interchange of needs between Philippi and Paul's place of imprisonment (Phil. 2:25-30; 4:18) (see further pp. 271ff.). This picture will fit interestingly with the most attractive understanding of the 'saints of Caesar's household' (Phil. 4:22) as imperial slaves or freedmen based in Rome, but known to the Philippians through their employment as couriers between Rome and the East, and so also the informal bearers of Christian intelligence to, from and through Philippi, as a stopping-place on the Via Egnatia section of the great highway. Imperial freedmen, like the *praetorium* (Phil. 1:13), *might* be explained as located elsewhere than Rome, but much more pointedly there. The circumstances of travel may actually favour the Roman provenance over places at lesser distances, and Paul's ready and constant communication with the East from Rome is not without its own relevance to our discussion.

Now a placing of Philippians late in the Roman imprisonment may prove important. It is the letter most likely to shed light on the particular mood and occasion of the closing months of the διετία. It is often characterized as a letter of joy, but that joy is distilled from the response to impending crisis. Paul reflects on alternative possibilities, life or death (Phil. 1:20-26; cf. 2:23), but his expectation is clearly on the side of life and renewed ministry to the churches which still need him (1:24-26; 2:24), whatever his personal desire to depart and be with Christ (1:23).

All this is circumstantial, perhaps tenuously so. But if we must reconstruct, this seems a quite probable line on which to do so. It tends to confirm the impression that Paul was actually brought to trial, and also that it was a reasonable expectation in the circumstances then known to him that he would be released, though that outcome hinged on a critical verdict on which he could not yet presume.

---

64 A question may be raised here about the unity of Philippians, and hence about its unity of date and setting. I am not persuaded by B.D. Rahtjen, 'The Three Letters of Paul to the Philippians', NTS 6 (1959-60), pp. 167-73, and shall treat the letter as having unity of provenance. In fact the present view could be related, *mutatis mutandis*, to Rahtjen's analysis located at different stages of the Roman imprisonment.

At this point attention may profitably be drawn to an apparent difference of perspective between the two groups of letters which we have located in the Roman imprisonment. They share one significant feature to which we shall return shortly, that Paul's concerns and future hopes are directed eastward rather than to Rome and the West (cf. Rom. 15:24). Paul shows an intense emotional concern for the Colossians (Col. 2:1, 5), and expects to visit them soon, as he requests the preparation of a lodging for him there (Phlm. 22). At this time his expectation is to be released following some more or less predictable formalities. But when we turn to Philippians the case is quite different. There is a much deeper wrestling with the issues of life and death, impending crisis, and the same expectation buoyed up by a sense of the needs of the churches in the East. Between these two situations, I suggest, must be placed the enactment of the *SC Turpilianum* which was intended to compel prosecutors to prosecute.

So we come to grasp the nettle of the Pastorals. The question of using their evidence may be raised at two levels. There is the problem of authenticity *per se*, and also that whether, authenticity apart, they contain any evidence which may be firmly related to any particular setting in Paul's life.

Perhaps today the most influential arguments against the Pauline authenticity of the Pastorals are theological ones. The letters are considered to betray a theological situation later than that of the authentic Paulines, in that the writer is concerned to pass on a deposit of traditional faith inherited from the apostolic generation. They present a different Paul from the volcanic controversialist of the agreed Epistles, namely, a 'Paul' mellowed into being a link in the chain of tradition. C.F.D. Moule's 1964 Manson Memorial Lecture serves as a useful catalyst of opinion here.[65] Moule is keenly sensitive to the intractable problems posed by the alternative pseudepigraphical and fragment theories, and comes nearly full circle, advocating (albeit very tentatively) Lukan authorship in a Pauline setting. The real sticking-point for Moule is a difference of atmosphere from the admitted Paulines. In particular, he cannot conceive of Paul speaking of the Law in the terms used in 1 Tim. 1:8.[66]

The hypothesis of Lukan authorship of the Pastorals has had some recent vogue, and if it were established, might give an unexpectedly

[65] C.F.D. Moule, 'The Problem of the Pastoral Epistles: A Reappraisal', *BJRL* 47 (1964-65), pp. 430-52.

[66] But this is indecisive, for Timothy (if he was really the recipient) presumably knew Paul's mind on the Law, and Paul would not have needed to guard against the misunderstanding of those who exalted the Law as the ground of justification.

different turn to our main inquiry.[67] It raises the problem of the style of the Pastorals, a large topic which we can only treat very briefly here, merely to clear the ground. The stylistic argument is suggestive, but indecisive. L.F. Clark, in an unpublished Manchester MA thesis,[68] has exposed statistical flaws in the works of P.N. Harrison,[69] A.Q. Morton[70] and K. Grayston and G. Herdan,[71] all of whom measure statistical diversity by divergence from an inner core of accepted writings, not from within the whole corpus of ostensible writings, a procedure which magnifies differences. It is undeniable that there is relatively a greater lexical richness in the Pastorals than in the accepted Paulines, but it is not clear how much significance can be attached to this difference. It may be heavily influenced by subject-matter, especially by the lists of virtues and vices in the *Haustafel* sections. It is difficult to know whether real statistical significance can be attached to variations in documents of this length.[72] Statistical

---

67 Apart from Moule, cf. Quinn, S.G. Wilson; see p. 385, n. 50 above. The similarity was observed, if differently assessed, as early as Rackham: 'the Acts in itself suggests living intercourse with the apostle. For in the later chapters there is much resemblance in style to the Pastoral Epistles' (*Acts*, p. liii).

68 L.F. Clark, *An Investigation of Some Applications of Quantitative Methods to the Pauline Letters, with a View to the Question of Authorship* (Manchester, 1979).

69 P.N. Harrison, *The Problem of the Pastoral Epistles* (OUP, 1921).

70 A.Q. Morton and J. McLeman, *Paul, the Man and the Myth* (London: Hodder & Stoughton, 1966).

71 K. Grayston and G. Herdan, 'The Authorship of the Pastorals in the Light of Statistical Linguistics', *NTS* 6 (1959-60), pp. 1-15.

72 Cf. the remarkable differences in the frequency and usage of τε in Luke and Acts (see Chapter 2, p. 31). To suggest that this kind of argument is indecisive does not 'prove' the converse. See further the trenchant criticism of Harrison's arguments by B.M. Metzger, 'A Reconsideration of Certain Arguments Against the Pauline Authorship of the Pastoral Epistles', *ExpT* 70 (1958-59), pp. 91-94; cf. J. McRay, 'The Authorship of the Pastoral Epistles: A Consideration of Certain Adverse Arguments To Pauline Authorship', *RQ* 7 (1963), pp. 2-18 (note however his erroneous acceptance of Cadbury's argument from the mis-dated *BGU* 628). In a valuable survey article E.E. Ellis, 'The Authorship of the Pastorals: A Resumé and Assessment of Current Trends', *EQ* 32 (1960), pp. 151-61, gives an impressive and varied list of twentieth century scholars favouring the genuineness of the Pastorals: T. Zahn (1906), F. Torm (1932), G. Thoernell (1933), A. Schlatter (1936), W. Michaelis (1946), C. Spicq (1947), J. Behm (1948), J. de Zwaan (1948), J. Jeremias (1953), E.K. Simpson (1954), and D. Guthrie (1957). See especially Guthrie, *The Pastoral Epistles* (London: Tyndale, 1957), pp. 11-53. For another recent criticism of Grayston and Herdan's methodology see T.A. Robinson, 'Grayston and Herdan's "C" Quantity Formula and the Authorship of the Pastoral Epistles', *NTS* 30 (1984), pp. 282-88. For authenticity cf. also B. Reicke, 'Chronologie der Pastoralbriefe', *TLZ* 101 (1976) cols. 81-94 = 'Les pastorales dans le ministère de Paul', *Hokhma* 19 (1982), pp. 47-61.

quantification of stylistic features may be effective only with large bodies of relatively homogeneous material when examined under strict controls. None of this discounts the difficulty over style, but casts doubt on the assumption that the difficulty can be objectified. The Lukan hypothesis as such seems gratuitous here.

We come back to the indications that the Pastorals are later than Paul as otherwise known. It is important to stress anew the real uncertainty of the criteria by which we measure an atmosphere of lateness. But I am not disposed to question the probability that they are later. Our real contention, to be worked out on a larger canvas, is that the expansion (and also the development and diversification) of Christianity happened more rapidly than often assumed, and not necessarily by a tidy, linear evolution which gives an easy chronological handle. The changes in the Pastorals are probably to be explained by the changes of perspective brought about by circumstances operative within a later ministry of Paul himself. Situational change must have been a very significant factor in the primitive period, however difficult it may be to document its course now.

It may seem excessively bold to renew such a suggestion today, when 'fragment' hypotheses lie to hand and offer the possibility of using evidence of genuine Pauline biographical details. These views yield one crucial point to our contention: that there *are* at least passages which lend themselves to the question whether the Pastorals give us authentic biographical information about Paul. To consider that question is at least to concede the legitimacy of the quest. The serious doubt would then be whether the fragments were so divorced from a clear context in Paul's life that they could not be chronologically placed.

It is ironical that apart from the essentially theological and stylistic arguments, which seem indecisive,[73] the historical objection remains that the Pastorals are suspect because they cannot be fitted into the narrative of Acts. This is an odd reversal of so much held today, when Acts is held suspect wherever *it* cannot be fitted to an (often hypothetical) reconstruction developed form the 'primary' evidence of established epistles. But if in fact the Pastorals belong to a period of Paul's life subsequent to the end of Acts, that is a sufficient reason for the silence of Acts. There is not necessarily a problem here at all.

Let us then begin from the proposition that there is no *intrinsic* improbability in the hypothesis that the personal allusions in the Pastorals refer to Paul's actual ministry, and perhaps a post-Acts

---

[73] I tacitly omit here the separate consideration of points like the late or Gnostic character of the opponents confronted in the Pastorals, for this approach seems less influential today.

ministry. This, it may be claimed, is in line with the expectations in Philippians. If any or all of the Pastorals are treated as unified documents, the question is whether the setting of any or all is (1) in Paul's lifetime as recorded in Acts, (2) in Paul's lifetime beyond the end of Acts, or (3), post-Pauline. (We need not be troubled here with refined questions of who actually wrote them or who acted as *amanuensis*). If however the personal details above are deemed significant, but only as fragments embodied in an alien context, the same options aply, but with much less chance of reaching any satisfactory answer. But these fragment theories seem an unnecessary step, and create harder problems of bibliographical probability than they purport to solve.

We need not linger long over the first option, that the personal allusions are Pauline from within the period of the Acts narrative. J.A.T. Robinson has recently made a valiant attempt to establish this position,[74] but it is difficult to suppose that Paul could have written 2 Tim. 1:17 before he had been to Rome, or that he could have been in Rome before he arrived there as a captive. Nor is Reicke's explanation, which Robinson follows, very persuasive.[75] At most, 1 Timothy or Titus *might* belong within the period of Acts, even if we still feel constrained to place 2 Timothy at the end of Paul's life because of its distinctive captivity references. The specific references in the two former letters are relatively few, and those contained in 1 Timothy seem to contain nothing referring to places or situations which *could* not be accommodated within Acts. But when the allusions in all three letters are isolated and set out together, the subtle links between them are too impressive: Hymenaeus has made a shipwreck of his faith in 1 Tim. 1:19-20, and is upsetting others in 2 Tim. 2:17-18. The name is not common, and it would be difficult to suppose allusion to other than the same man. Again, Tychicus appears as Paul's envoy both in Titus 3:12 and 2 Tim. 4:12. Such connections and their like might in themselves mean little or nothing, but when taken with the many parallelisms in the character and ostensible pupose of the letters, it is difficult to separate them as a group, and the harder again it is to entertain 'fragment' hypotheses as a realistic explanation of the personalia. The crucial issue increasingly takes the form of a decision as to whether the details in 2 Timothy can be located in a Pauline setting. There are distinct signs that this is the latest of the three

---

74 *Redating*, pp. 67-85. Robinson places 1 Timothy tentatively in late 55, at the time of Paul's Corinthian controversies, and Titus in early 57, possibly even as written from Miletus during the voyage to Jerusalem (pp. 81-84). He associates 2 Timothy with the other captivity epistles, and locates them all in Caesarea.

75 *Redating*, pp. 75-76, following the suggestion of Reicke developed in his article 'Chronologie der Pastoralbriefe', *TLZ* 101 (1976), col. 90.

letters, and that the other two concern preceding journeys and activities. So the placing of 2 Timothy seems likely to carry the others with it. We have seen that it is hard to place it before Paul's Roman captivity. Then, too, Titus involves places and movements, to Crete and to Nicopolis (presumably the city of that name in Epirus, near Actium), which are not ostensibly placeable in Acts. The attempt to place the whole group within Acts may actually often stem from an unnecessary desire to tie the essential authenticity of these epistles to an independently documented setting. But if the prospects of Paul's acquittal were good, as seems likely, it need not be a matter of special pleading to entertain the possibility of a career of Paul after Acts. One might even dare to suggest that the Pastorals provide *prima facie* evidence of such a sequel.

There are some specific indications of this outcome. (1) In 2 Tim. 4:16 ἡ πρώτη μου ἀπολογία might be understood either of an indecisive first hearing (*prima actio*) in the present trial, or of a previous situation, where God's deliverance (v. 17) had meant acquittal. The latter option would give us an ostensibly Pauline allusion to previous acquittal. But the case is not so simple, and most recent commentators correctly prefer the former view.[76] This appears to be giving current news, not introducing abrupt reference to the past, and news of crisis more dire than appears in the known Roman imprisonment, when Paul was not apparently so isolated and abandoned by his friends. There is then apparent evidence here for the stages of a legal process different in flavour from that which we have inferred from Acts and the setting of the Captivity Epistles. It remains difficult, if only on account of the stubborn reference to Onesiphorus seeking Paul in Rome (2 Tim. 1:17), to link this process with Caesarea, unless we also resort again to fragment theories to break the integrity of the context. (2) If the view taken here of Philippians be accepted, that epistle registers Paul's reflection on a crisis corresponding to that terminating the διετία of Acts 28:30, but different in flavour and personalia from that encountered in 2 Timothy. These two epistles might

---

[76] Thus e.g. Guthrie, *The Pastoral Epistles*, p. 175; J.N.D. Kelly, *A Commentary on the Pastoral Epistles* (London: Black, 1963), pp. 217-18; C. Spicq, *Les Épîtres Pastorales* (Paris: Gabalda, 4th edn, 1969), p. 818; M. Dibelius and H. Conzelmann, *The Pastoral Epistles*, tr. P. Buttolph and A. Yarbro (Philadelphia: Fortress Press, 1972), p. 124; A.T. Hanson, *The Pastoral Epistles* (Grand Rapids: Eerdmans and London: Marshall, Morgan and Scott, 1982), pp. 160-61; G.D. Fee, *1 and 2 Timothy, Titus* (San Francisco, etc.: Harper and Row, 1984), p. 245. The latter view was traditional in the early church following Eusebius, *HE* 2.22.1-8 and lent itself to the assumption of Paul's release and second imprisonment. It is still accepted in W. Lock in *ICC* (1936), p. 119.

indeed lend themselves to comparison as Pauline responses to successive crises. (3) Conversely, a negative point of method: the process of working out the natural trend of the evidence has often been abandoned in favour of the easy tendency to force together pieces of the jigsaw which may not be adjacent. There is an almost irresistible impulse to find significant links wherever *prima facie* linear inferences may be plausibly drawn, whereas it is in the nature of several New Testament controversies or legal issues that events were liable to be repetitive, perhaps on progressively shifting ground. It may be our hope to be able to document and reconstruct the progressive moves in a controversy rather than to attempt to consolidate into one the references to its successive phases. In the present case there is the prospect of tracing processes of change in the standing of Christians before Roman authority from the provincial precedent set by Gallio, through an imperial indication, to a more dangerous anti-Christian shift leading to the Neronian persecution, and finally to the complex upheaval induced by the fall of Jerusalem, all in the space of 20 years.

If then we may tentatively accept that there are valid indications of a Pauline ministry beyond the διετία, and that the Pastorals might be a legitimate source for at least seeking them, there remain two questions to which answers may be attempted. (1) Were Paul's earlier plans or desires, expressed in his accredited letters, notably his intention of going to Spain (Rom. 15:24, 28), ever fulfilled? (2) Can we reconstruct anything of what did happen to him?

(1) The statement of Paul's intention to go to Spain can be assigned fairly precisely to the eve of his last visit to Jerusalem with the 'Collection' (Rom. 1:13 with 15:23-28). It was his plan to pass through Rome, and be furthered on his way to Spain with the support of the Roman church. There is nothing in the Pastorals to suggest that this intention was ever fulfilled, and it is clear enough elsewhere that Paul's expectations were radically altered. From the ostensible evidence of Acts, we are apparently to understand that Paul was divinely prepared first for the prospect of captivity (Acts 20:22-23; 21:11-14) and then for Rome as an ultimate, rather than an interim, destination (Acts 25:12, 21). Paul's references to Rome in Romans differ from the sequel. He was apparently moved at the time of writing by the determination 'not to build on another man's foundation' (Rom. 15:20), and his plans for Spain were the product of that determination not to trespass on a field already well evangelized. But when Paul came to Rome he had no choice of the circumstances, and demarcation agreements were for the time being inapplicable.

If however he was then released, did this permit him to resume his previous intention? The only possible evidence is in Clement of Rome's phrase ἐπὶ τὸ τέρμα τῆς δύσεως ἐλθών (1 *Clem.* 5:7), taken with a phrase in the Muratorian Fragment, *sed et profectionem Pauli ab urbe ad Spaniam proficiscentis.* Even if the latter is no more than a dubious inference from Romans 15, Clement at least should presumably have been in a position to know. Despite J.B. Lightfoot's argument that τέρμα necessarily implies the *Ultima Thule,* the farthest limit, of the West,[77] its primary reference seems to be to the turning-point at the end of a race-track (Latin *meta*), and in the metaphorical sense either 'pivot' or 'culmination' may be as valid a rendering as 'extremity'. The word would repay some further lexical study. It seems at best indecisive as evidence to corroborate a visit of Paul to Spain. The Corinthians presumably understood Clement's allusion, and probably understood it as of Rome. The point is often made that Paul would have found Jews in Spain, but Paul Bowers has shown that the extant evidence of Spanish Jewry is later and suggests a first considerable colonization after 70, and major expansion no earlier than the third century.[78] Thus the Spanish interpretation of Clement is doubtful, as is the use of Clement to confirm on this score a later ministry of Paul after release from Rome. If Paul was released, if he did travel widely again, and if that later ministry was extended in time, perhaps well beyond the Neronian persecution, as Ramsay believed (*CRE* [7th edn], chart on p. 168; cf. also 346ff., 488ff.), it is *possible* that he went to Spain, but, if so, it has left no unambiguous mark on our sources, and can be no more than a speculation.

There are however intentions expressed by Paul which may be assigned to a later state of his expectations. In Phlm. 22 he requests a lodging to be prepared for him, presumably in Colossae. In Phil. 2:24 he expresses his trust in the Lord that he will himself come to Philippi shortly. If our suggested setting for these two epistles be accepted, we may reconstruct his expectations somewhat on these lines. At the time of writing Philemon (AD 60) he expected rapid and untroubled vindication, perhaps by default. But by the time of Philippians the judicial situation had shifted, and his trust is directed to the outcome of a crisis, and his confidence in God focuses then on the factor that his churches need him (Phil. 1:24-26). In this there is a marked change of perspective since the writing of Romans. There he wrote as though his work as an apostolic pioneer in the East were complete, and he must break new ground. Now his burden is for the continuing needs

---

[77] Lightfoot, *Apostolic Fathers*, Vol. 2, Part 1, pp. 30-31.

[78] Bowers, 'Jewish Communities in Spain in the Time of Paul the Apostle', *JTS* n.s. 26 (1975), pp. 395-402.

of those churches which were the sphere of his previous care.[79] And this may well be significant. It is the Pastorals which reflect the eventual fulfilment of this changed expectation. It was a new phase of Paul's ministry, the organization and preparation of the churches to endure changing and dangerous times when he would personally be taken from them and the first generation passed. It is the kind of change which is reflected in the transition from the argumentative vigour of Paul's earlier epistles to the Pastorals' framework of structured leadership to nurture and preserve tradition. The context of such a change may be plausibly inferred, a shift provoked in part by signs of the deteriorating standing of Christians in the eyes of Roman authority, of the ominous approaching cataclysm of the Jewish War, by recurring division and false teaching in the yet immature Pauline churches, unprepared for the trends of the times. In sum, our point is that Paul accepted a modified role, marked out perhaps by a succession of enforced changes of perspective, ever since his plans for Spain turned to detention and captivity. The evidence, at least for the resultant change of plan upon release, is contained in epistles (Philippians and Philemon) which are widely received as authentic.

(2) The presumption, then, about the remaining course of Paul's life is that it consisted of further travels, apparently in line with his new plan to return to the East, followed by re-arrest and martyrdom in Rome at an uncertain date, either in the Neronian persecution of 64 or its aftermath, or possibly some time later.

The references in the Pastorals permit us to recover some of the places and strategies, but do not suffice to enable us to reconstruct any precise reference of his movements. There is no *a priori* reason for positing whether 1 Timothy or Titus comes first. The lack of any reference in 1 Timothy which, in isolation, *could* not be placed in Paul's known life perhaps testifies in this later setting to his concern to revisit the same places. Evidence of a specifically topographical kind is in fact limited to 1 Tim. 1:3, urging Timothy to stay in Ephesus while Paul himself went to Macedonia. In Titus the specific geographical references lie outside localities where Paul is otherwise known to have worked. Titus 1:5 refers to his having 'left' (κατέλιπον) Titus in Crete, with the implication that Paul himself had been there, and he intended to winter in Nicopolis. The personal allusions associated with these movements lie outside our knowledge of situations elsewhere, in Acts or Epistles. Tychicus, an Asian, had been in Paul's

---

[79] The evidence for this is already apparent in Phlm. 22, a letter generally received as authentic, if this is rightly placed in the earlier part of the Roman imprisonment.

company since the voyage to Jerusalem (Acts 20:4) and was evidently the bearer of the early group of Captivity Epistles (Eph. 6:21; Col. 4:7). He was also Paul's envoy here to Crete (Tit. 3:12) and again to Ephesus in 2 Tim. 4:12. Apollos, too, appears in a new context (Tit. 3:13), while their respective companions, Artemas and Zenos the lawyer, are otherwise unknown to us.

The connection with Crete is intriguing, and not obviously explained. We can only conjecture that Paul returned first to his known churches to encourage them and regulate their affairs with regard to the future. Perhaps that desire is reflected in 1 Timothy. Only then perhaps would he have felt free to accept a new calling, and Crete, on which he had merely touched on his voyage, lay within the general sphere of his responsibility in the Greek East, and was presumably hitherto untouched at least by the ministry of an apostle or major leader. The final stage of his work was to train leaders and establish continuity for the future throughout the area of his labours. It might be a rash speculation to suggest that 1 Peter, an epistle redolent of the threat of impending persecution, is a pastoral letter from a comparable period, complementary with Paul's last pastoral initiative.

2 Timothy seems to be the reflection of sudden arrest, at a time of revisiting the churches of Asia, and interrupting the yet unfinished task. The place of arrest is unclear, but the requests refer to persons and property left in Asia, Trophimus sick at Miletus, and the property with Carpus at Troas (4:20, 13). The need for a cloak, and the exhortation to Timothy to come with it before winter (4:21), suggest a time late in a sailing season. It might be a fair guess that the crisis happened in Ephesus. Alexander the coppersmith did Paul much evil (4:14): Timothy must beware of him. The implication may be that Timothy is currently in the place where this bitter opponent, perhaps the author of Paul's arrest, might threaten him. And in sending Tychicus to Ephesus (4:12) Paul seems to be replacing Timothy with Tychicus as his personal representative there, so that Timothy may be released to come to Paul (4:13). The following reference to Carpus at Troas may imply that Paul's departure thence was abrupt and in haste, even after having had some facility to see a friend there. That may have been due not directly to arrest at that time, but to rapid embarkation after enforced delay at Troas to wait for a suitable wind for the passage to Macedonia *en route* for Rome.[80]

We come then to the question of Paul's martyrdom. The earliest

---

[80] For the function of Troas in the system of communication, and the possible need to embark instantly at short notice when the wind changed cf. C.J. Hemer, 'Alexandria Troas', *TB* 26 (1975), pp. 79-112, esp. p. 102, 106-107, though it now appears more likely that Paul was arrested in Ephesus rather than Troas.

testimony to it is in *1 Clem.* 5:5-7, and that is a vague allusion. Pherigo writes that the tradition of Paul's martyrdom under Nero is first explictly mentioned more than a century later.[81] According to Pherigo, 'The evidence for Paul's martyrdom under Nero, let me repeat, is not nearly as early nor as reliable as that for his release from the imprisonment of Acts, nor is it any more unanimous'.[82] Even so, this remains the most probable outcome, for Clement presumably only alludes to what was well known in his day, though there is no certainty that Peter and Paul suffered in Rome on the same occasion or in comparable circumstances. The coupling of their names in a number of subsequent writers (Ignatius, *Rom.* 4.2; Eusebius, *H E* 2.25.8; etc.) may preserve a genuine tradition of their association in martyrdom, but cannot be pressed for detailed information. The relation of Paul's martyrdom to the Neronian persecution must remain an open question. It may be that Paul suffered then, or that his arrest in Asia resulted from information obtained against him then, or that his later ministry was more prolonged in absence from Rome beyond this date.

Tentatively, then, we may offer the following tabulation, with the bracketed sequel *exempli gratia*:

Roman captivity	60-62
Colossians, Ephesians, Philemon written	60
S.C. *Turpilianum*	61
Philippians written	c. winter 61-62
Trial and acquittal	early 62
Journeys of unknown extent and duration	62 onwards
(possibly: a summer in Asia Minor	62
summer and winter in Crete and Greece	63-64
second arrest in Asia and overland to Rome	64 or later)

The whole preceding discussion offers a scenario to explain the Pauline content of the Pastorals apart from correlation with Acts. The important piece missing from this presentation of this part of the jig-saw is the placing of the composition of Acts itself. We have argued from general and circumstantial grounds for an early dating of Acts, and from the factor of 'immediacy' to a most natural placing close to the events at the end of the book. The function of attempting to reconstruct the actual sequence of events is to suggest the particular place where the book fits into our tabulation. The composition of Luke and Acts in their final form may naturally be placed in the cap-tivity period 60-62, and Acts would thus have been completed and

---

81 L.P. Pherigo, 'Paul's Life After the Close of Acts', *JBL* 70 (1951), pp. 277-84.
82 Pherigo, 'Paul's Life', p. 284.

presumably issued in the immediate aftermath of Paul's release, specifically in 62. The ending of Acts, that is to say, provides *prima facie* evidence of a particular early date confirmed by its relation to the reconstruction of the sequel.

V. *The Composition of Luke-Acts*

We may begin consideration of the second stage with the relationship of Luke to Mark. We have noted the uncertainties in dating both, apart fom the suggestion that both may be fixed by their priority to Acts. In particular, the reasons for placing Mark after 65 are indecisive. If there is value in the tradition which connects this Gospel with Rome, and in the traditional ascription, it may be pertinent to observe Mark's alleged presence in Rome early in Paul's imprisonment (Col. 4:10; Phlm. 24), in both epistles in association with Luke and Aristarchus (Col. 4:10, 14; Phlm. 24), both of whom, according to Acts, had voyaged to Rome with Paul. The traditional ascription of the Gospel to Mark may of course be questioned, though some will use Mark's association with Peter's ἔξοδος in favour of a later date of the Gospel, and the connection of Mark with Peter in Rome is attested elsewhere in the New Testament (1 Pet. 5:13), though the timing of Peter's movements remains uncertain. Let us however stress for the present the simple point of Mark's ostensible association with Luke in Rome in the period of Paul's imprisonment at c. 60.

Although Mark's Gospel need not be later than the early sixties, it would be rash and unnecessary to claim that it is any earlier. Mark's presence in Rome at this period gives a natural placing for its traditional Roman provenance. Now the manner in which Luke uses Mark claims our interest. His work is not structured upon it, but upon the non-Markan material, what we might term, without prejudice to judgments of its status, Q + L. The incorporation in the Third Gospel of blocks of edited Markan material is secondary to a non-Markan structure. To put the implication a different way, Luke's use of Mark is secondary to, and presumably subsequent to, his pre-existing assemblage of material from non-Markan sources. But the case is not simple, for in Palestine he probably had access to material similar to, and overlapping with, Mark, a variant of the same 'Synoptic' tradition, clarified in his case by specific personal inquiry.

It is not necessarily significant whether Q + L ever existed as an actual entity, a draft or first recension, in fact a 'Proto-Luke'. That concept is a logical, if not a literal, precursor of the Gospel, in that it represents conceptually a stage of composition, even if the process was untidy and the stage never demarcated tangibly in an actual draft document. By the 'first stage' we refer to the Palestinian gathering of materials, even if this was not formalized as any more than notes. The 'second stage' is then the Roman stratum. The reading of Mark provided a second stimulus to a writer who was already engaged on a cognate task.

The question seems open whether Luke wrote the substance of Acts before or after his composition of the Gospel, for in either case the Preface, ending of Acts and editorial adjustments between the two are likely to have been the last parts of his work. The material closest to hand from his own notes and experience may even have been treated first, where the Gospel involved a more intricate process of compilation from written sources and perhaps a wait for the availability of the concurrent work of Mark. This possibility may be entertained even apart from the arguments of C.S.C. Williams, Russell, Parker and others for dating Acts before Luke. There is a suggestive point in the two accounts of the Ascension (Luke 24:50-53; Acts 1:6-12). If read consecutively they are awkward, with or without the Western 'non-interpolation' of Luke 24:51, as though the Luke of Acts had obtained new and different traditions in the interval, but left in the Gospel the impression of an immediate parting, while placing it in Acts seven weeks later. If, however, Luke 24 is read as an *appended summary* of Acts 1:6-12 and its aftermath, the difficulty is eased. It is a summary which comprehends also the subsequent practice of the disciples to worship in the Temple (cf. Acts 2:46; 3:1), and the time factor in this longer perspective is unspecified. There might then be some plausibility in the supposition that the Acts version, at least in that pair of pericopes, is compositionally prior. In any case we should build nothing on such a supposition, unless to underline, if such were indeed the case, the closeness of Acts to its latter events. The central point is that Luke-Acts, essentially as a unity, was in process of composition during the διετία, which provides a natural slot for it.

Several difficulties may be explained in the context of this dating. (1) There is perhaps at least some interim light on the ending of Acts. Whatever the explanation, it seems not improbable that Luke did not know the sequel when he was composing the body of the work. Even if the eventual ending was deliberate and carefully judged in the event, it was not, on this assumption, long premeditated as providing a conclusion foreshadowed through a chosen literary and dramatic structure. Acts 20:37-38 may thus have been penned before the sequel was even known, and not then altered with hindsight, a point which we shall discuss further below.

(2) The postulated writing of Mark and Luke, two works of such

similar type, at virtually the same time and place, may be handled on this ground. The two books were functionally different, with different prehistories. If Luke, on arrival in Rome, found Mark with a work in progress or complete, his own prior investigations were not thereby rendered redundant. On the contrary, the limits of the earlier Gospel highlighted the distinctive contribution of his own researches, which derived from his own prior purpose.

(3) This raises afresh the question of Luke's own purpose in writing. We may stress here in provisional terms that it was not simple, nor to be assessed in terms of an exclusively determined audience, but that apologetic and explanatory motifs are present, as well as the desire to instruct and strengthen the churches. I would suggest that Luke-Acts was only part of a sudden spate of Christian writing in this period, and that this development was even related to Paul's own change of perspective. We might conceive his own policy as comprising three such successive stages as the following: (a) In his earlier ministry he was occupied with pioneer evangelism, against a background of expecting an imminent Parousia to which he would survive. (b) A critical experience at Ephesus (2 Cor. 1:8-9) brought home to him his own mortality, and induced a new searching about the state of the believer who has died (2 Cor. 5:1-5), while the problems of the Corinthian church drew out in him a deeper involvement with the continuing situation. (c) At the time of his imprisonment new political and religious tensions were taking shape, and the prospect has unfolded of a second generation Christianity beset by a changing and deteriorating environment, which called for his statesmanship in preparing the churches. This accords with the placing of Luke-Acts shortly before the impending crises about which it seems to be silent, the Neronian persecution, the Jewish War and the more definitive separation of Christian from Jew and the effective withdrawal of official protection.

VI. *The Ending of Luke-Acts: A Suggestion*

The problem of the ending persists whether we have to explain Paul's death or his release. We have argued that it is Paul's release which poses the problem. In the light of our discussion, it appears that there is a reasonable possible scenario for Luke's silence.

The situation is one which lies outside the common experience of people in the modern comfortable West, and may obtrude itself on us only when we have friends living in some politically sensitive part of the world. In Britain today it is hard for people even to comprehend the need for certain kinds of apparently quixotic discretion. If Paul was released, Luke was not at pains to advertise the fact. Paul was returning to scenes of his previous labours. This book, even if primarily directed to a Christian audience, was not likely to be restricted in its circulation to trustworthy insiders. The occasional implacable enemy who might turn to it need not be primed with the advance knowledge that Paul might reappear at any time on his patch.

There is something more to be said here of the likely nature of Paul's last ministry. It may have purposed to avoid any significant entanglement with authority, to be a ministry of encouragement to the churches, as free as possible of public provocation. That is not to say that Paul had 'mellowed', or that he would fear to tackle dangerous issues when the Gospel was at stake. But his ministry was best exercised in quietness, and could be terminated by premature conflict.

How does this relate to Acts 20:38? we have already argued that the argument from apparent *vaticinium ex eventu* to redaction after the event is indecisive, and that perhaps this passage was even written before the sequel was known. The atmosphere of the last chapters of Acts is otherwise optimistic: Paul goes through deep trial and suffering, but the drama issues in a free passage for the Gospel in Rome and an apparently quieter interlude for Paul himself. Even if special significance be attached to 20:38, that significance may be read in contrary ways, either as a foreshadowing of Paul's death, or as a pointer to an early date of Acts, before Paul's renewed travels had falsified the expectation.

The question may be put a different way, about Luke's redaction. How much did he know at the time of composition, and did he in his omission, or in permitting Acts 20:38 to stand unredacted, effectively suppress facts? Was he, on our suggested hypothesis, less than frank, in a manner which touches his character or integrity as a writer? These doubts do not involve serious charges against Luke, and may even be artificially hypercritical, divorced from actualities. So far as Acts 20 is concerned, we may argue that Luke told it as it happened. It really was an emotional farewell scene. And if nothing had happened to nullify the possible finality of that farewell, there was no obligation on him to say, 'Now that Paul is free again, perhaps, after all, he will see them again'. There are diverse explanations to hand for the passage, whether or not we invoke redactional rehandling. There is no occasion to suggest that Luke is suppressing the truth, or even creating a false impression by the truth he tells.[83]

---

[83] This is an ambivalent area, for some scholars will accept with equanimity the supposition that Luke created events and speeches wholesale, while yet as ready to be critical of a defence of him which concedes that he was presenting facts

The operative concept here is that of 'discretion', which need not, and should not, be forced into antithesis with 'truthfulness'. It is one of the simplest facts of human relationships that some things in some contexts are better left unsaid. The unsympathetic reader might be left initially to infer that Paul was condemned. The fact of release would of course become quickly known: the direction of new initiatives need not. If Luke's silence sufficed to see Paul established among trustworthy friends in the East before enemies were alerted to make a systematic search for him, this would serve his purpose.

To argue thus assumes the rapid publication and circulation of Acts and the implacable hostility of opponents. But such hostility is implicit in the reference to Alexander the Coppersmith in 2 Tim. 4:14-15, in a passage widely received as authentic. If this means that Paul suffered damaging accusation or betrayal into arrest at his hand, this would fit the supposition of a violently premature termination of such a ministry as we have inferred. The factor of 'discretion' may also help to explain another *prima facie* objection to the release hypothesis, that Luke looks to the Roman state as the protector of Christianity, and would have been pleased to include the apologetic weight of a Roman acquittal, were that possible for him. The case is rather that he passes lightly over the whole matter of judicial process, noting Paul's captivity in reserved terms, stressing rather the freedom of the Gospel than the delay in bringing an innocent man to trial. Rome does not come so well out of this, even if justice were done in the end. But at a time of deteriorating relations it may have been prudent on this score also to leave Roman favours implicit in generalized optimism rather than to draw attention to a judicial crisis, however favourable its present resolution. It may also be relevant to repeat the suggestion that much of the work was written before the knowledge or problem of the ending was presented to Luke's mind. However deliberate and calculated in the light of the actual sequel, it may not have been premeditated in the writing, and a different issue might have turned the problem of the conclusion into different channels. It is in any case probable that, along with the prefaces, it was written last, of the latest state of play, and on the eve of publication.

Conclusions Summarized

We have argued here for a dating of Acts in 62. The *termini* commonly assumed for the dating of Mark after c. 65 and Luke after 70

selectively. Conversely, his defender may be over-exercised to meet such criticism with an exaggerated and unnecessary attempt to affirm his veracity in an exhaustively literalistic way which exceeds the natural bounds of the relevance of language and context.

are indecisive, and many general indications point to an early setting and compostion of Acts itself. These broadly based general considerations may be taken together with an argument from the 'immediacy' of the latter chapters of Acts. The ending of Acts may then serve as an indication of the particular early date we have suggested.

Such a currently unfashionable view cannot now be established without in some degree accepting the onus of working out its critical implications across a wider field of the evidence, and we have supported it by offering a tentative scenario for evaluating the evidence of the Pastorals as well as the more widely accepted Pauline epistles. The fate of Paul is a crucial question for any such reconstruction, and we have defended the view that he was released, and offered a tentative explanation for Luke's reticence upon that ground.

We conclude with a comment and a note of the possible implications of this section.

(1) This defence of the early date may seem bold to the point of rashness in the present climate. But it is perhaps the climate rather than the evidence which is against it. Some careful scholars appear to be sympathetic to this position, but are unduly influenced by misplaced cautions against challenging prevalent views. The strength of the more traditional position is in the interlocking of the documents upon ostensibly early ground, and its difficulties are engendered by the attempt to sustain inappropriate mediating positions in modified deference to the appearance of a different consensus. I am all for caution, and ready to recognize the need for it in my own attempts at reconstruction, but it should be applied in the appropriate places. The early date of Acts may indeed be offered as firmer ground amid shifting sands, tending to carry with it an earlier placing of Luke and the integrity of the Pastoral evidence rather than being disqualified by prior judgments about them. This is another case where the simple interlocking of ostensible evidence may be the index of truth.

(2) The early dating of Acts is a significant part of our total case. While not *per se* anything like a 'proof' of historicity, it is an important catalyst, which influences the formulation of questions, and excludes inapplicable lines of argument. It is one major avenue into the heart-area of the problem. Theories of tradition-historical reinterpretation by the early church tend to require time, and to become more difficult with early datings. The evidence may be held to exclude absolutely many faulty arguments for alternative views, if not thereby ecluding a better defence of those views.

It is relevant to stress that our opinion places Acts unequivocally in the lifetime of many eyewitnesses and surviving contemporaries of Jesus, Peter and Paul, as prospective readers who could object to the presence of material falsifications. Again, that does not prove the veracity of Luke's account. Indeed, the early date has on occasion been linked with a fictional view of Acts.[84] Yet such a view must immediatly pose another question, whether it is credible that Acts is fiction, credible amid the life-and-death issues which confronted the church under Nero. The seriousness of questions of truth for the community is sufficiently attested in the earnest dialectic of Paul's own epistles.

(3) If Acts is early, there are other considerable, positive implications. Its evidence seems often to have been forced into an artificially and implausibly late synthesis of Christian development, whereas it should be taken as a focal document in the argument for an earlier synthesis, closer to the apparent evidence. It is striking how many unnecessary problems, which may become occasions for an unavoidable compounding of special explanations, are the products of forced and unnecessary hypotheses.

---

[84] Goodenough in *SLA*, pp. 51-59.

Chapter 10
Conclusion[1]

It seems odd and inappropriate that in an era in which our knowledge of the hellenistic world has grown significantly, there was for
so long a pronounced lack of discussion about the relation of the Acts
of the Apostles (the New Testament book which boasts the most ties
to its milieu) to the world and history around it. It is especially unfortunate in that the vacuum seems to have been caused not by a lack of
relevant evidence for consideration or the fruitful consummation of
debate, but rather by exegetical and theological taste and fashion.
Discussions on the subject begun before the First World War and
interrupted by that event were left unfinished as interests turned to
new methods and questions. But the tide is turning again, the discussions are being renewed,[2] and not without good cause. There is a
wealth of new data from inscriptions and papyri from the Graeco-
Roman world which New Testament scholars are unwise to ignore.
Moreover, the questions surrounding the book of Acts are of fundamental importance for our understanding of the historical background of the apostles, especially Paul, and of our understanding of
the genesis of Christianity (Chapter 1).

After a brief preliminary investigation of various questions surrounding Luke-Acts (Chapter 2), we were able to give a cautious
assent to the appropriateness of asking about the relationship between historical method in Acts and that in ancient historiography in
general (Chapter 3). It is not that we have particular literary parallels
which demand such comparisons, but rather there is a common
world of traditions and conventions which the author of Acts seems
to share with other ancient writers of allegedly historical narratives.
In particular, we have stressed that, contrary to modern opinion on
the subject, ancient historians were capable of very rigorous and
critical methods and principles, even if their views on what types of

---

1   (Ed.) This summary chapter has been compiled by the editor.
2   In such works, for instance as M. Hengel's *Acts and the History of Earliest
Christianity* (London: SCM, 1979) and G. Lüdemann's recent *Das frühe
Christentum nach den Traditionen der Apostelgeschichte* (Göttingen: Vandenhoeck
& Ruprecht, 1987). See Stephen Neill and Tom Wright, *Interpretation of the New
Testament 1861-1986* (OUP, 1988), esp. pp. 368-78 for an optimistic survey of the
recent changes in emphases.

sources were most trustworthy were not the same as ours.[3] There was, furthermore, a vast diversity of historical practice, even in the scraps of literature that have survived. We cannot simply assume that, because it was an ancient work, it is therefore impossible that the narrative in Acts (or reported speeches) is historically reliable. As with any historian, ancient or modern, we may expect certain tendencies, but the work must stand or fall in its own right.[4] And although it is often said that ancient standards of historiography differ radically from modern ones, the two are not completely incompatible, and the modern questions of accuracy and the like remain important ones to ask, even if they must be answered negatively. If forced to choose between them, we must in this respect prefer a Haenchen, who at least discusses the historicity of the narrative even if he frequently ends by dismissing it, to a Dibelius, seeking to postpone indefinitely the question of the 'real events' in favour of extended discussion of literary matters. If Luke was a praiseworthy historian by ancient standards, but useless to us in our attempts to reconstruct an accurate picture of the early church, so be it, but we want to know that. The picture may not be so bleak, however.

From the general discussion of historiography and method, we turned to the knowledge displayed and related in the book of Acts (Chapters 4, 5). Here we discovered a wealth of material suggesting an author or sources familiar with the particular locations and at the times in question. Many of these connections have only recently come to light with the publication of new collections of papyri and inscriptions. We considered these details from various, often overlapping, perspectives, risking repetitiveness, since our interest was not primarily in the details themselves, but rather in the way that they supported and confirmed different ways of reading the text— various levels in the relationship of the narrative with the history it purports to describe. By and large, these perspectives all converged to support the general reliability of the narrative, through the details so intricately yet often unintentionally woven into that narrative.[5]

Similarly, the ostensible chronological framework of Paul's life presented in Acts can be seen to mesh well, even if somewhat tightly, with the events and details mentioned in the Epistles (Chapter 6)— if

---

[3] Such as the favouring of eyewitness reports over written evidence, and the stress on interviews, travel and participation.

[4] Acts is, after all, a unique work, unprecedented in its historical interest in chronicling the growth of a religious movement.

[5] The major exception being the 'Theudas problem', see above, pp. 162-63, which, even if a genuine historical error, would not be of sufficient magnitude to call into question the basic credibility of the author.

the best variation of the South Galatian theory is accepted (Chapter 7).[6] This involves a synthesis of three elements: (1) a South Galatian destination for the epistle; (2) an early, pre-Council date for it; and (3) the identification of Gal. 1 with the visit in Acts 9 and Gal. 2 with Acts 11. The straightforward interpretation of Acts along these lines complements very well the time-tables and geography which can be teased from Paul's own writings and we have responded to a number of the objections. We have also shown abundant evidence that 'Galatia' can refer to the larger provincial area and that the ethnic title 'Galatian' would have been applicable to the Pauline churches in the south. The only possible difficulty remaining is the 'concurrent view' of Gal. 1:8-2:1, which is, in any case, a specific understanding of an ambiguous passage, rather than a re-interpretation of an otherwise plain text.[7] We have thus been able to work out a chronology of Paul which contradicts neither the epistles nor Acts, covering the years AD 50-62, and a more tentative reconstruction of the period c. AD 30-50. In terms of the theologies of the two authors, there are, of course, differences of emphases and understanding, but these are expected when dealing with any two writers, especially when their works are of such different genres and purposes as the Acts of the Apostles and the epistles of Paul. If a theory does justice to both sets of evidence, it should be examined carefully; the boat has not been 'shipwrecked' on the rocks of Greek grammar,[8] nor on theologies, nor ethnic titles, nor any of the other navigational hazards, but many have abandoned ship before the sailing.

Only after the chronological and geographical ties between the book and the period about which it tells have been established did we deal with the question of authorship (Chapter 8). Here the we-passages are the most significant pieces of the puzzle. Alternative interpretations having been shown as invalid,[9] we are left only with the possibilities that the author of the final version was a participant in some of the actions or that he was making a false claim to have been. The latter position is shown unlikely by the anonymous nature of the book and the merely sporadic nature of the claims. If, then, the author was an eyewitness and companion of Paul, it is not unlikely

---

6 And we have seen that all too often critics have interacted with less effective alternatives, dismissing the whole enterprise prematurely.

7 The tightness of the chronology cannot be regarded as a serious obstacle, but rather as a datum of the problem, and that can be incorporated in any one of a variety of unremarkable ways; see above pp. 261-67.

8 F.H. Chase, 'The Galatia of the Acts', *Expos* 4th ser. 8 (1893), p. 411: 'The South Galatian theory ... is shipwrecked on the rock of Greek grammar'.

9 Such as that of Robbins, see pp. 317-19.

that the traditional attribution of the book to Luke is correct.[10] On the matter of sources, we have argued that it is most likely that participation and the testimony and interview of eyewitnesses were employed whenever possible, perhaps accounting for some of the distinctive features in Lukan accounts.

We have also argued for a relatively early date for Luke-Acts, AD 62 (Chapter 9). We presented a list of fifteen features which suggest an early setting,[11] and the 'immediacy' of the later chapters in Acts taken together with the peculiar ending to the book make such a date highly probable. We have worked out in some detail how this suggested date would fit in with the *Hauptbriefe* and with the events hinted at in the Pastorals, if those letters are based upon good traditions.[12]

The conclusions that result from all this work may be regarded as unfashionable as, indeed, only a few years ago, would the inquiry itself; clearly the time has come for a change. Much good work has been done in the area of Luke's theological interests, but the historical questions are not thereby answered nor can they be thereby ignored. As our knowledge of hellenistic history continues to grow through the discovery and publication of new inscriptions and other evidence, our picture of early Christianity and the documents it inspired will naturally grow accordingly.

---

[10] Although this external evidence is really all we have to go on; arguments from medical language and the sort are indecisive.

[11] Cf. pp. 376-82.

[12] Even if, however, a later date is accepted, this would in no way affect the arguments advanced in the previous chapters regarding the historical character of the narrative.

Appendix 1
Speeches and Miracles in Acts

Introduction

Two stumbling blocks still remain in the middle of the road that leads to acceptance of the arguments we have here presented. Modern scholars have objected that the ancient author of the book of Acts (1) has coloured the speech material with his non-apostolic (especially non-Pauline) understanding of theology, and (2) has contaminated the narrative with his out-dated supernaturalist world-view. The book therefore can neither be trusted as a record of early events or of apostolic preaching. Both of these are serious objections for the 20th century reader, and are subjects worthy of books in themselves, but a few words here must suffice.[1] Our goal is merely to show that there is insufficient grounds for the closing off of options on the basis of these matters, and to indicate the general direction that a full-scale treatment of these questions might take.

1. The Speeches

The Extent of the Speech Material in Acts

The principal speeches of Acts occupy less than a quarter of its total bulk.[2] In the RSV text, the total of verses occupied by twelve major speeches, five attributed to Peter, one to Stephen, and six to Paul, is 226 out of a total of 1003, or 22.5%. But, somewhat surprisingly, there

---

1 [Ed.] Dr Hemer had projected three additional chapters to have been titled: 'The Speeches', 'The Miracles', and 'Penultimate Problems'. Unfortunately none of the three were completed. Most of the extant general material from the manuscript of the first two has gone into this appendix. The 'Penultimate Problems' chapter was never really begun by the original author. To the best of my knowledge, there is not even an outline of the contents, although it seems certain from earlier chapters that Dr Hemer had planned to tackle the question of the purpose of Luke-Acts, among other matters. It is planned that Dr Hemer's material on specific speeches will be published in forthcoming volumes of the *Tyndale Bulletin*.

2 The verses are: 2:14-36; 3:12-26; 4:8-12; 7:2-53; 10:34-43; 11:5-17; 13:16-41; 17:22-31; 20:18-35; 22:1, 3-21; 24:10-21; 26:2-23.

is as much or more direct speech that does not fall under the heading of 'major speeches'. All together, slightly more than half the book of Acts is taken up with the recording of direct speech.[3]

Further, it is difficult to classify this spoken material. The twelve major speeches cannot easily be differentiated from the others in terms of length or form. Peter's disquisition on Judas and the need to replace him (1:16-22), and the prayer of the disciples (4:24-30) are both longer than Peter's address to the Council (4:8-12);[4] significant speeches of comparable or even greater length are placed in the mouths of pagans, the Ephesian γραμματεύς (19:35-40) and Festus (25:14-21), or Jewish leaders or opponents, like Gamaliel (5:35-39) or Tertullus (24:2-8).[5] There are also speeches contained in dialogue, 15:7-11 (Peter), 13-21 (James), and the purported texts of letters, both Christian (15:23-29) and of the Roman tribune Lysias (23:26-30). There are brief exhortations deeply embedded in context (27:21-26; 33-34) or speeches responding to events of the narrative (25:14-21) or introducing a sequel (25:24-27). These are not rigid categories, but there is a gradation of types through them all into brief narrative dialogue, like 8:19-24, 30-31, to isolated questions and sayings.[6] Even beyond

---

3   The incidence of direct speech is consistent through the book, depending only on the subject matter and a preponderance of longer speeches towards the beginning and end. It is rare to find more than about ten consecutive verses without an interjection of the spoken word. The longest sequences I have noted are at Acts 11:19-12:6 (18 verses) and 13:48-14:9 (14 verses), in each case transitions between incidents with narrative summaries, and not contained in a unified pericope. The long narrative of Acts 27-28 is so far broken up by speech as never to display a comparable sequence. I exclude from the reckoning Old Testament quotation, unless itself contained in direct speech.

4   Peter's words here concern a situation hardly relevant beyond the earliest church. Haenchen (*Acts*, pp. 160-61, 163) builds an unwarranted scepticism on Luke's explanatory note in vv. 18-19, and explains the passage as created to bring into prominence indirectly the Twelve as witnesses and guarantors of the gospel and especially the resurrection. This significance may be valid enough, but is hardly a reason for Luke to have created this rather difficult pericope as his way of stating it. The prayer in contrast is kerygmatic in content, appropriate to theological analysis, but not a speech in the usual sense, nor attributed to an individual.

5   Note however the absence of 24:7 from the best texts of the Tertullus speech (see Metzger, *Textual Comm.*, pp. 490).

6   The arbitrary character of the categories might be variously illustrated. In a recent article, G.H.R. Horsley, 'Speeches and Dialogue in Acts', *NTS* 32 (1986), pp. 609-14 chooses ten Acts speeches beside 8 'dialogues' and 20 'one-liners' as his basis for comparisons. But these categories are much harder to separate for Acts than for the historians and biographers compared, and he combines as one those which form a group in a debate scene in the historians. His tabulation illustrates in general terms the relatively high incidence of direct speech in Acts, but

that there are numerous references to preaching, teaching or arguing or testifying as the very essence of the narrative.

The point may be illuminated by comparison with some of the historians who may be supposed most immediately relevant. The striking thing is the relatively high proportion of direct speech in Acts (and in the Third Gospel[7]), coupled with marked differences in usage. Of 673 short sections in the first book of Josephus' *Jewish War* (itself probably rather unrepresentative as recapitulatory of earlier history), only 59 contain direct speech, 45 in complete or virtually complete sections, the rest often brief sayings within the paragraph-section.[8] The percentage is thus 8.8%, and the actual bulk of direct speech an appreciably smaller proportion. Yet 28 sections are occupied by just four speeches (1.19.4.373-79, 1.23.5.458-65, 1.32.2.622-28, 1.32.3.630-35), all of length comparable with the longest in Acts except the Stephen speech. Further, even among shorter speeches there are paired formal dialogues (e.g. Herod and Augustus, 1.20.1.388-90, 1.20.2.391-92), and the climactic scene of emotional confrontation between Herod and Antipas, where the two final long speeches are the focus of a passage *BJ* 1.32.1-5.620-40, is rhetorically contrived, and the mere evidence for indictment of Antipater is reported briefly and indirectly (1.32.4.637-38).

There is an extreme contrast with this in the first book of Polybius, which contains no oration in direct speech, but only the brief summary of the terms of a treaty (1.62.8-9), a quotation from Euripides (1.35.4), and a single word as the cry of a crowd (1.80.9). The content of two speeches is merely reported in *oratio obliqua* (1.79.11-13; 1.80.1-4).[9] The first book of Dionysius of Halicarnassus is also sparing in its use of speeches, though it includes many citations of literature, the text of an inscription (1.64.5) and of a dated census record (1.74.5), and traditional oracles (1.19.3; 1.68.4). None of the five

not the patterns of its actual content and distribution.

7   In the Gospel no less than 68% of the verses contain direct speech. The amount of brief dialogue within verses is much greater, and the distortion in the percentage correspondingly larger. There are also long tracts of discourse and parable which raise the figure close to 90% in the middle third of the book, corresponding closely to the Lukan 'travel-narrative'.

8   There are also passages, like *BJ* 1.3.3.76, where the spoken word is placed in *oratio obliqua*, even if there shifts to second-person address without losing the optatives of indirect speech.

9   It is of note that the former is interrupted by the arrival of a message (1.79.14), in view of recent discussion of the form of interruption in the Acts speeches (Horsley, 'Speeches and Dialogue in Acts'). Note again in 1.79.12 the shift of personal pronouns to a direct ἡμῶν ... ἡμᾶς.

speeches recorded are long, and there are at least two brief sayings (1.58.2-4, 5; 1.81.5; 1.82.1; 1.83.1; 1.86.4, the harvest of 90 chapters).

Thus the author of Acts displays an interest in direct speech that is not readily paralleled in other ancient literature.[10] The reason for this preoccupation is not difficult to understand, however: the progress of the good news was the very subject of the book of Acts, and preaching of that word (and the words spoken in opposition to it) is therefore the heart of the matter, not mere illustrative material as it might be to authors who write about the history of nations or the causes and effects of a war.[11]

The Speech as Précis

The crucial question of historicity here concerns only the essential content of the speeches. We need not be concerned with any supposition that they are verbatim reports; there is a clear argument against such an extreme position. Paul's first approach to an audience, for instance, required a degree of exposition and explanation of the essence of the kerygma, which is generally not reproduced. He must frequently have spoken at great length, as indeed we are told at Acts 20:7, and the implication is clear enough in other places where he or others 'argued' or 'testified' to their case (Acts 2:40; 9:22; 14:1,3; etc.). The brief summary paragraphs we possess do not purport to reproduce more than perhaps a *précis* of the distinctive highlights. They do not read as transcripts of oral delivery and the responses of the audience to them do not relate realistically to the bald words reported. The real issue is whether they are Lukan summaries or Lukan creations.

There is, of course, still a spectrum of possibilities between the notion of a verbatim report and that of unfounded invention, and the relation of some of the gradations to the consensus of historical

---

10 The comparison with biography falters as well. Cf. the discussion in Chapter 2. Horsley's tabulations ('Speeches and Dialogue in Acts', p. 613) seem to indicate that the numbers of items of direct speech in Suetonius or Plutarch are more nearly comparable with those in Acts, but in Suetonius' *Augustus* they are exclusively 'one-liners', and in Plutarch a mixture of these with 'dialogues', the category of 'speeches' being absent from both writers. It is immediately apparent that the *quantity* of direct speech is again relatively small in both. The character of the speech is also different, consisting of anecdotes or traditional *bons mots*. For Plutarch's attitude to the historical actualities of his famous encounter between Solon and Croesus cf. Plut. *Solon* 27.1.

11 Thus also P. Schubert, 'The Final Cycle of Speeches in the Book of Acts', *JBL* (1968), p. 16: 'The speeches of Luke are an essential part of the story itself, "the story of the proclamation of the Word of God"'.

criticism is complex.[12] But we may subsume the essence of the task under these general issues in hierarchical order, like three sieves of progressively coarser mesh, to sift out three different levels of possible historical value in the speeches. (1) Is the speech historical in its actual substance, in the sense that it represents what was actually said upon the specific occasion? (2) Is it, while 'unhistorical' by the former test, nevertheless acceptable by standards of historiography appropriate to Luke's day, and so deserving of some modified acceptance as fair comment suitable to the tenor of the time, or the like? (3) Is it ultimately 'unhistorical' in both ancient and modern senses, but still usable, whether as evidence of Luke's conception of the primitive kerygma or as evidence at redactional level for the controversies of his own time?

Our primary interest is in question (1). We are drawing the criteria for historicity tightly because that is the central question. If, however, we answer that question negatively, we need not appraise Luke's work as historically useless. He may still be useful on a modified ground, and any evaluation of him may need to be carefully nuanced if (2) or (3) may still be answered positively. These are important as 'fall-back' questions, though it may be noted that (2) seems hard to demonstrate precisely.[13] In any case an evaluation of the speeches, and an analysis of them in such terms will point the way again to a more refined qualification of the virtues of 'Luke the historian'.

---

[12] We may instance such variations as the summary or paraphrase of an actual speech (in varying degrees of fidelity or accuracy); the independent writing up of traditions about what was actually said; the presentation of Luke's conception of what was appropriate to the occasion; Luke's presentation of a piece of authentic primitive kerygma, not necessarily tailored to the occasion; or Luke's presentation of what he mistakenly conceived to have been the primitive kerygma. In any of these cases he could have been in greater or lesser degree concerned with needs of his own time which differed from those of the dramatic date, and such concerns may then have influenced his content or wording, have stimulated him to creative alteration of the tradition, or, for that matter, have merely impressed on him the pointed relevance of Paul's words and the importance of reproducing them as faithfully as possible. The differing members of this series, and their like, and the differing possible degrees of redactional adaptation of any of them are then open to an equally complex variety of judgment from the point of view of their historicity.

[13] Something like (2) is so often a catch-all for mediating positions or tied to simplistic generalizations about the nature of ancient historiography that it needs to be justified as a real option. I am not sure that it is easily definable in terms of ancient practice. Let us categorize it generally as representing the 'appropriate' rather than the rigorously 'true', but as related to the event, not the redactional *Sitz-im-Leben*.

The Case Against

The refusal to credit the speeches in Acts as reliable summaries of actual speeches may be seen as embodying essentially three objections:
(1) The author, writing with ancient standards of historiography, would quite naturally have invented speeches as suited his artistic and ideological purposes;
(2) The unity of the style and vocabulary of the speeches with the style and vocabulary of the rest of the book shows the speeches to be composed by Luke;
(3) There is a continuity of content that stretches from speech to speech, regardless of the alleged speaker, indicating Lukan purpose behind the arguments, an objection which includes the view that the so-called Paulinism of the later speeches are actually *unlike* Paul and betray different perspectives from him.

The first point is generally illustrated by citing the preface of Thucydides' *History*, in which he makes it plain that he has not been able to preserve the orations accurately, and has instead included what he thinks the situation called for. Fruitful appeals for support may also be made to Josephus' works and the writings of Dionysius of Halicarnassus, both of whom have clearly invented material for the speeches they record.

The second item, the matters of vocabulary and style, need not be expounded at any length here, since the point is nearly universally accepted even by those who argue for the reliability of the speeches.

The third point concerns the subject matter of the discourses. Cadbury pointed out that certain arguments in various speeches in Acts actually depend upon each other in a way that could not have occurred in their ostensible setting, but only within the artificial world of a writer and his narrative. The classic example of this is the messianic exegesis of the Old Testament (cf. Acts 2:25-36 [a speech of Peter] and 13:35-37 [a speech of Paul]).[14]

The 'Paulinism' objection is particularly associated with an essay by Philipp Vielhauer, although it does not depart radically from the programme outlined by Dibelius and Cadbury before him.[15] Essentially, it is argued that the passages in Acts which seem to show a connection with the thoughts preserved in the epistles bear only a superficial resemblance which is sustainable neither in terms of actual

---

14 See J.T. Townsend, 'The Speeches in Acts', *Anglican Theological Review* 42 (1960), pp. 151-52; Cadbury, *BC* 5.407-409.
15 P. Vielhauer, 'On the "Paulinism" of Acts', *SLA*, pp. 33-50. Cf. Cadbury, *BC* 5.410-16 and Dibelius, *Studies, passim*.

usage nor statistically in terms of quantity of apparent connections.

Objections Answered

But none of these objections can really stand in the way of the effective alternative, namely that the speeches are Lukan summaries of actual speeches. We have dealt in some measure with objection (1) in chapter 3 above, where it was shown that the ancient historians were not without critical abilities, nor were they uniform in practice or theory.[16] The Thucydidean prologue is especially unfortunate for the objector to bring into the discussion, since (a) it is clear from that passage that Thucydides is warning readers in a way that implies one should expect the speeches to be accurate where such warnings are not placed, and (b) he maintains that even when the actual speech cannot be recalled, he has tried to remain as true as possible to the essence of the words actually spoken.[17] And although it is true that Dionysius and Josephus treated speeches with less than Thucydidean rigour, there is reason to believe that their work, far from representing a 'universal standard', could be considered *substandard* for that reason.[18]

Objection (2) is no real objection at all. It effectively contradicts only a view that the speeches are framed in the very words of the purported speakers, a view which for various reasons no one now holds. Reminiscent of what we have seen in the discussion of the objections to the South Galatian theory, this powerful argument simply does not communicate with the best alternative. If the speeches recorded are summaries, they are certainly to be regarded as *Lukan summaries* and as such will surely bear the mark of his particular language and interests.

It is objections of the type of (3)— objections dealing with theology and content— that alone may decide between the effective options. Here too the critics are in something of a disarray, as they must on the one hand insist that the speeches are later redactions, while at the same time accounting for the evident primitive quality of much of the

---

[16] See also my article 'Luke the Historian', *BJRL* 60 (1977-78), pp. 28-51.

[17] Thuc. 1.22.1. Polybius is, if anything, less open to misinterpretation in his discussions of method. See for example Polybius 2.56.10-13, 12.25b, 36.1.

[18] As is clearly the case with Timaeus' work in the eyes of Polybius: cf. Polybius 12.25i. See also 12.25a where Polybius' comment that Timaeus actually invents speeches is seen as a final argument to answer any who might otherwise be inclined to champion him. Could speech invention have been the universal practice without Polybius knowing it?

material.[19] This is especially evident in the discussions of the speech of Stephen: Dibelius himself comments on the irrelevance of the main section (Acts 7:2-34) as the most striking feature of this speech, and accepts the possibility of an older text underlying the recital of facts (though dismissing any idea of an Aramaic original of the speech). He sees Luke's hand in the polemics which follow (*Studies*, p. 169). Haenchen, too, posits a pre-existing 'history-sermon', even if he seems not to provide a convincing explanation of the difficulties it raises (*Acts*, p. 288). If such are concessions from scholars generally loath to allow sources for speeches, others are much more positive. Among recent advocates of good sources here are (with many variations) R.A. Martin, L.W Barnard, M.H. Scharlemann, C.H.H. Scobie, and among the commentators I.H. Marshall. Others, like M. Wilcox and R.J. Coggins, express themselves with nuanced reserve.[20] Some, like R.P.C. Hanson, who concur in seeing pre-Lukan sources, think it most improbable that the speech really derives from Stephen (*Acts*, pp. 93-95). The survey by Earl Richard[21] stresses that there is little

---

[19] Cf. Conzelmann, *Acts*, p. xliv; Kümmel, *Introduction*, p. 119; Vielhauer, 'Paulinism', *SLA*, p. 48. On the primitive christology, see especially C.F.D. Moule, 'The Christology of Acts', *SLA*, pp. 159-85; J.A.T. Robinson, 'The Most Primitive Christology of All?' *Twelve New Testament Studies*, Studies in Biblical Theology Monograph Series, Vol. 34 (London: SCM Press, 1962). U. Wilckens, *Die Missionsreden der Apostelgeschichte* (Neukirchener Verlag, 1963) argues against the antiquity of the speeches, see especially p. 186.

[20] R.A. Martin, 'Syntactical Evidence of Aramaic Sources in Acts I-XV', *NTS* 11 (1964-65), pp. 38-59; Barnard, *NTS* 7 (1960-61), p. 31; M.H. Scharlemann, *Stephen: A Singular Saint* (Analecta Biblica 34) (Rome: Pontifical Biblical Institute, 1965), pp. 22-30; Scobie, 'The Origins and Development of Samaritan Christianity', *NTS* 19 (1972-73), pp. 390-414 (esp. p. 396: 'the case for the use of a source must surely now be considered proved'). (Scobie cautions that Scharlemann fails to recognize the extent of Luke's editorial activity, and that he is very speculative in his manner of linking Stephen with the historical Jesus [p. 393]); cf. Marshall, *Acts*, p. 133. Wilcox offers several findings of considerable interest. After examination of Semitisms in the text of this speech, he concludes that they 'make it more difficult for us to assert confidently that the speech is a deliberate literary creation by Luke' (*Semitisms*, p. 160). He goes on to argue that this and the speech of Paul at Pisidian Antioch came from an originally independent context with divergent OT traditions (p. 164). More broadly, he finds 'hard-core' Semitisms in a number of places in Acts, almost always in places which have a strong Lukan stamp, and these tend to appear as marks of the ultimate authenticity of the traditions incorporated. The strongest cases appear to be connected in some way with Antioch (pp. 177-78). Coggins, 'The Samaritans and Acts', *NTS* 28 (1982), pp. 423-34, enters a reservation against Scobie's claim that it is established beyond doubt that a distinct source underlies Stephen's speech (p. 428).

[21] Earl Richard, *Acts 6:1-8:4, The Author's Method of Composition* SBL Dissertation

agreement among recent scholars on this matter.

The speeches often contain material that is not just primitive but is specifically tied to its ostensible historical setting. Thus, the Lukan Paul's dialogue with Stoicism is signalled most obviously by the actual citation of the Stoic poet Aratus of Soli (*Phaenomena* 5, in Acts 17:28), Paul's own fellow-Cilician (cf. also Cleanthes, *Hymn to Zeus* 4). The nature of God is thus explained against the backdrop of the Athenians' own terminology, as Paul gently exposes the inconsistency between the transcendent reality to which their thinkers aspired and the man-made images of Athens. Other points take up issues shown by both groups of philosophers or combines common ground which he may share with one or both. In v. 25 he refers successively to the Epicurean doctrine that God needs nothing from men and cannot be served by them, and the Stoic belief that he is the source of all life (Bruce, *Acts*, p. 336). Paul plays off the one group against the other here, for the gods of Epicurus were unconcerned in human affairs, being themselves part of a cosmos engendered by the fortuitous collision of atoms.[22] There are recurring themes which are aptly directed to the Epicurean, God as Creator and Lord of heaven and earth (v. 24), who gives life to all (v. 25), and who has appointed that man seek him, though he is not distant from any of us (v. 27). This God commands repentance (v. 30) and will judge the world.

Similarly, the speech in the Synagogue at Pisidian Antioch is full of quotations more appropriate to the Jewish setting.[23] But behind the text, though never explicitly cited, is 1 Sam. 7:6-16. It has been argued that the speech as recorded is set up as a *proem* style of synagogue sermon, in which the 1 Sam. 7 passage is the *haftarah*, while 1 Sam. 13:14 (cf. Acts 13:22) is the *proem*, and Deut. 4:37f. (cf. Acts 13:17) the *seder* reading. The *proem* text in a *proem* homily was chosen by the exegete as a means of linking the *seder* and *haftarah* readings: this was also done by means of a process called *haruzin*, the 'stringing of beads'. If this interpretation of Acts 13 is correct, the method is exemplified particularly in verses 32-37 of the speech.[24]

Series 41 (Missoula, Mont.: Scholars Press, 1978), pp. 14-26.

[22] For the Epicurean view of the gods, see Lucretius, *De Rerum Natura* 2.165-83; 1090-1104; 5.146-234 and *passim*.

[23] V. 13:17b, Deut. 5:15; v. 18, Deut. 1:31; v. 19, Deut. 7:1; v. 20, Judges 2:16; v. 21, 1 Sam. 8:5; v. 22b, Ps. 89:21/1 Sam. 13:14/Isa. 44:28; v. 26b, Ps. 107:20; v. 33b, Ps. 2:7; v. 34b, Isa. 55:3; v. 35b, Ps. 16:10; v. 36b, 1 Kings 2:10; v. 41, Hab. 1:5.

[24] Thus J.W. Bowker, 'Speeches in Acts: A Study in Proem and Yelammedenu Form', *NTS* 14 (1967-68), pp. 96-104; M. Dumais, *Le Langage de l'Evangélisation. L'annonce missionnaire en milieu juif (Actes 13,16-41)*, Recherches 16 (Montreal: Bellarmin, 1976); J.W. Doeve, *Jewish Hermeneutics in the Synoptic Gospels and Acts*, tr. G. VanBaaren-Pape, Van Gorcum's theologische Bibliotheek, 24 (Assen: Van

Even if the particular form is argued to be undemonstrable in Judaism of this time, the affinities to such structures (or the rudimentary beginnings thereof) is striking.[25] The speech to Christians, Acts 20, and the defence speeches also show touches that mark them as integrated at least with their narrative settings, if not with a real situation behind them.[26]

Apart from those speeches which appear to lend themselves to the argument for Lukan redaction, there are others of little such significance, including the utterances of officials and opponents, which function in the unfolding of narrative, or convey the inner comedy of events, but are opaque to the touchstone of Lukan redaction. At one end of a continuum we have the raw material of theological debate, at the other end interesting examples of the variety and vitality of Luke's narrative technique. It is not easy to draw clear lines of demarcation within the spectrum. The speeches are less like separate 'set-pieces' than they first appear, and much less so than in most of the historians. They represent a virtual continuum of phenomena with narrative which we have found to show detailed correlation with minutiae which can be checked or illustrated from the documents.

Objection (3) relies on homogeneity of form and content across the speeches, which is clearly not the case.[27] Nor are the distinctions always merely matters of arbitrary differences. It seems likely to be more than chance that at the two occasions when Ps. 16 is cited, the simpler argument is ascribed to Peter, while the one that arguably

Gorcum, 1954), pp. 172-76. See however E.E. Ellis, 'Midrashic Features in the Speeches of Acts', *Mélanges Bibliques* (*Festschrift* for B. Rigaux), ed. A. Descamps and R.P. André de Halleux (Gembloux: Duculot, 1970), p. 305 and M. Rese, 'Die Funktion der altestamentlichen Zitate und Ansielungen in den Reden der Apostelgeschichte', in Kremer, *Actes*, pp. 64-66.

25 See G.N. Stanton, *Jesus of Nazareth in New Testament Preaching* (CUP, 1974), pp. 70-85 for a similar analysis of the traditions behind Peter's speech in Acts 10.

26 On the Miletus speech see esp. Barrett, 'Paul's Address to the Ephesian Elders', in *God's Christ and His People* (Festschrift for N.A. Dahl), ed. J. Jervell and W. Meeks (Oslo, Bergen, Tromsö: Universitetsforlaget, 1977), pp. 107-21. On the defence speeches see J. Jervell, 'Paul: the Teacher of Israel', in *Luke and the People of God* (Minneapolis: Augsburg, 1972), pp. 153-83 and J. Neyrey, 'The Forensic Defense Speech and Paul's Trial Speeches in Acts 22-26: Form and Function', in *Luke-Acts: New Perspectives from the Society of Biblical Literature Seminar*, ed. Talbert (New York: Crossroad, 1984), pp. 210-24.

27 Against the attempts of E. Schweizer, 'Concerning the Speeches in Acts', *SLA*, pp. 208-16 and Wilckens, *Missionsreden*, esp. p. 186, see J. Dupont, 'Les Discours Missionnaires Des Actes Des Apôtres', *RB* 69 (1962), pp. 37-60. More positively, see for example Moule, 'The Christology of Acts', *SLA*, pp. 159-85 and M.H. Scharlemann, *Stephen: A Singular Saint*.

reflects Rabbinic training is ascribed to Paul.[28] The Miletus speech is widely conceded to contain Pauline characteristics: (a) *Language* There are some striking parallels of phrase, like δουλεύειν τῷ κυρίῳ (Acts 20:19; cf. Rom. 12:11); τελειοῦν τὸν δρόμον (Acts 20:24; cf. 2 Tim. 4:7); προσέχετε ἑαυτοῖς (Acts 20:28; cf. ἔπεχε σεαυτῷ, 1 Tim. 4:16);[29] and others of sentiment, like Paul's persistent earnestness in cherishing and admonishing his converts (Acts 20:31; cf 1 Thess. 2:7-8). Such instances might probably be extended, but are not to be given undue weight. The argument from parallels is at most illustrative or suggestive, or a counter to a dogmatic denial. (b) *Biography* The speech stresses Paul's pledge to support himself and not be a burden to his converts, or lend colour to any allegation that he was in the business for personal gain (Acts 20:33-34; cf. 1 Cor. 9; 2 Cor. 11:7-11; 1 Thess. 2:9-12; cf. Dibelius, *Studies*, p. 156). Again, the reckoning of the Ephesian residence at three years is specified only here (Acts 20:31), though sectors within it have previously been mentioned, three months (Acts 19:8) and two years (Acts 19:10), the total being probably an inclusive reckoning, and fitting well enough on that ground with the outline chronology we have previously suggested. There are other biographical matters that might also have been brought up, but these will suffice as illustrations of this facet of the speech. (c) *Theology* The most striking point is the reference in Acts 20:28 to the church which God has obtained 'by the blood of his own'.[30] Moule stresses the distinctive significance of this phrase (*SLA*, p. 171). He notes the rarity of the statement of the redemptive interpretation of Christ's death in Luke-Acts generally. Thus Luke omits the λύτρον-saying of Mk 10:45 (= Mt. 20:28),[31] and this theme otherwise occurs in the Third Gospel only at Lk. 22:19-20, and then only in the longer text,[32] and in Acts only here. Otherwise in Acts,

---

28 Doeve, *Jewish Hermeneutics*, p. 176.

29 I recognize that two of these examples are drawn from the disputed Pastorals, though the autobiographical passage in 1 Timothy in particular would be widely accepted as authentic, if only as a disembodied fragment, and in a similar 'farewell' context.

30 Taking τοῦ ἰδίου as a genitive dependent on τοῦ αἵματος and not in agreement with it. The point is unaffected whether we render the phrase 'with his own blood' (RSV) or 'with the blood of his own' (RSV mg).

31 This difference cannot however be simply categorized as a Lukan redactional change, for the pericope in Lk. 22:24-27 is as a whole markedly different from Mk 10:41-45 = Mt. 20:24-28, and its origins and compositional unity are in dispute. Cf. Fitzmyer, *Luke* 2.1411-1416. Both J.M. Creed (*Luke*, p. 267) and V. Taylor (*The Passion Narrative of St Luke* [CUP, 1972], pp. 61-64) derive the whole from a non-Markan source, Taylor specifying it as a 'L'-passage.

32 Metzger, *Textual Comm.*, pp. 173-77. The Committee were divided, but the

according to Moule, the death is simply represented as turned to triumph or vindication by the resurrection, and the stress on salvation is not explicitly connected with a redemptive dimension of the death itself. 'Is it significant, then', writes Moule, 'that the one exception should be on the lips of Paul and in an address to an already Christian community? This is Paul, not some other speaker; and he is not evangelizing but recalling an already evangelized community to its deepest insights. The situation, like the theology, is precisely that of a Pauline epistle, not of preliminary evangelism' (*SLA*, p. 171). It is left to Conzelmann (*Theology*, p. 201) to suggest that Luke adopts a turn of phrase current in the early church to give the speech a Pauline stamp, an 'occasional tendency' in Luke. That is a formula by which the apparently Pauline, no less than the apparently un-Pauline, may be enlisted in an argument about Pauline authenticity.[33]

Vielhauer's specific charges about the 'Paulinism' of the speeches has the same flaw as the second objection— it is only a valid argument against a 'straw man'. The Pauline echoes to be found in the speeches were never meant to exhaust the depths of Paul's thought, and are certainly rephrased and couched in Lukan terms and understanding. Vielhauer's discussion makes no contact with the view that the speeches are a summary made by another individual whose understanding of Paul was tempered (as is our own) by his own context. The 'distance' is not nearly so great as Vielhauer imagines.[34]

majority accepted the longer reading, giving it a (C) probability rating. It is favoured by the overwhelming preponderance of all early text-types except the Western, but relegated to the margin of NEB and RSV.

[33] The failure to *consider* contrary evidence is worrying in view of the self-confident conclusions these scholars draw. According to Haenchen, Dibelius 'finally proved' the speech to be Luke's work (*Acts*, p. 590). If such were the case, our study would be redundant. But this is just the point at issue, and the evidence suffices to mount a strong challenge to the assumption. The best defence these scholars offer here is Conzelmann's 'heads I win, tails you lose'. An interesting comment on the passage is that of Marshall (*Acts*, p. 334), stressing from a contrary perspective that 'we should not underestimate its importance as a statement which represented his [Luke's] own belief as well as Paul's'. In any case it is hard to understand why Haenchen, in so detailed a commentary, should omit any treatment of so important a phrase. His only mention of it seems to be in a concessionary footnote (p. 92n) which qualifies his denial that Acts contains a doctrine of vicarious atonement with the remark that this 'formula' contains an 'echo' of it.

[34] 'The obvious material distance from Paul raises the question whether this distance is not also temporal distance, and whether one may really consider Luke, the physician and travel companion of Paul, as the author of Acts', Vielhauer, 'Paulinism', *SLA*, p. 48. See the discussions by F.F. Bruce, *The Speeches in the Acts of the Apostles*, Tyndale New Testament Lecture, 1942

Summary

We must be content in this brief overview to show that the question of the reliability and source of the material in the speeches is far from settled. There remain good reasons for taking them as abstracts of real addresses rather than fabrications. In Luke's writing the spoken word is not a thing apart, a set-piece embodying a distinct literary technique of commentary. It is embedded in the narrative, in a degree which forces the question whether the sources which can be traced in some parts point to the use of respectable sources elsewhere.

Here the data from the Gospel is of particular relevance. We find there the 'speeches' of Jesus and they derive from sources preserved (Mark) or inferred (Q). To the obvious objection that these 'speeches' are a thing apart, the specially preserved sayings of a Messianic leader, and therefore analogous neither to Acts nor to conventional historiography, there are complementary lines of response. Luke's narrative technique in the inclusion of the spoken word appears consistent across both parts, if we allow for the more complex pattern of traceable sources in the Gospel. Conversely, there is little similarity of method here with the most comparable near-contemporary historians and little more with the biographers.[35] So far as our specific evidence goes, we have to reckon with the demonstrable factor that Luke used sources for the spoken word, and used them rather conservatively, with whatever verbal and selective redaction.

One further note: if we are correct in our previous contentions, that Acts was written by a companion of Paul at a relatively early date, that makes a profound difference to our understanding of Luke's access to sources. But we must be very careful here. This should not be invoked as a cumulative presuppositional thread in any detailed discussion of the speeches, which should be studied as far as possible separately on their own merits. But the force of this motif in reopening the question should be recognized.

(London: Tyndale Press, 1944); and 'The Speeches in Acts— Thirty Years After', in *Reconciliation and Hope* (*Festschrift* for L. Morris), ed. R. Banks (Grand Rapids: Eerdmans, 1974), pp. 53-68.

[35] And, apart from all this, much criticism proceeds on an assumption that the words of Jesus were far from being the object of careful preservation anyhow, that this material was open to radical creation and redaction, and inadequate analogies with the historians are even invoked in defence of this. The objector cannot have it both ways.

2. The Miracles

There is no way to avoid the problem of miracle in Acts.[36] It is true that the subject is treated with reserve by Luke himself. Yet it is so integrated into the narrative that it cannot be prised out without irreparable damage to its context. It may be considered that this factor alone invalidates much that has been said in the chapters above, in which we have been arguing throughout for an 'ostensible' treatment of texts unless there are problems which necessitate reinterpretation. The miraculous may be deemed just such a factor. A narrative which contains it is automatically suspect.

There are several ways of attempting to handle the problem: (1) to deny the miraculous and explain texts containing it theologically, allegorically, as pious creation or the like; (2) to minimize the factor of miracle and refrain from raising the issue too acutely; (3) to adopt a sceptical view of the text generally on this account, and apply the keenest scepticism to accounts of miracle; (4) to admit the generally reliable quality of the narrative, and Luke's own acceptance of the miraculous, and treat his account sympathetically but critically, requiring stricter standards of testimony before taking his miracles too easily at face value. Such are at least examples of possible strategies. They are neither exhaustive nor mutually exclusive, and most scholars probably adopt gradations among them, varying with the instance.

Miracle in the New Testament Context

Miracle has some considerable prominence in many of the Hellenistic and Roman historiographers, especially in the form of bizarre prodigies popularly taken to presage disaster. This aspect of the background has already been sufficiently considered in chapter 3, and

---

[36] See generally C.S. Lewis, *Miracles: A Preliminary Study* (London: Bles, 1947); H. van der Loos, *The Miracles of Jesus* (*NovT* Supp. 9) (Leiden: Brill, 1965); C.F.D. Moule (ed.), *Miracles: Cambridge Studies in their Philosophy and History* (London: Mowbray, 1965); C. Brown, *Miracles and the Critical Mind* (Grand Rapids: Eerdmans and Exeter: Paternoster, 1984); H.C. Kee, *Medicine, Miracle and Magic in New Testament Times* (CUP, 1986). For miracles in early Christianity cf. also G.W.H. Lampe, 'Miracles and Early Christian Apologetic', in Moule, pp. 205-18; Gail Smith, 'Jewish Christian and Pagan Views of Miracle under the Flavian Emperors', *SBL Seminar Papers* 20 (1981), pp. 341-48; H. Remus, 'Does Terminology Distinguish Early Christian from Pagan Miracles?' *JBL* 101 (1982), pp. 531-51. On Acts in particular see J.A. Hardon, 'The Miracle Narratives in the Acts of the Apostles', *CBQ* 16 (1954), pp. 303-18; G.W.H. Lampe, 'Miracles in the Acts of the Apostles', in Moule, pp. 165-78; F. Neirynck, 'The Miracle Stories in the Acts of the Apostles, An Introduction', in Kremer, *Actes*, pp. 169-213.

there is no occasion here to do more than repeat a note of the fluctuation and ambivalence between scepticism and credulity which characterizes many of these writers. In any case the supernatural is little more or less than an anomalous curiosity. If any such pretension is a source of sharp scepticism for a Polybius or a Lucian, it may be admitted by others, without the admission appearing to carry great significance for their overall world-view.

The kind of argument may be curiously illustrated where Christianity came to clash with other world-views. If the question of debate in the time of the Apologists is to be raised at all, it must be with a deliberate caution because of the factor of date. Much water had passed under the bridge, and the focus had shifted to a ground where the Christian claims were already well known. The case of Origen's response to Celsus is of particular interest. As H.C. Kee has recently observed, Celsus, even as a philosopher with Neoplatonist credentials, is not mainly concerned to deny the miracles, nor to regard denial as a viable option, but to impugn the social status and world-view of Jesus and his latter-day exponents (cf. e.g. Celsus *ap.* Origen, *contra Celsum* 1.28).[37] This is an interesting perspective, though its present significance should not be overplayed. It may be a noteworthy reflection of positions inherited from previous debates to stress that opponents of Christianity did not commonly deny the miracles because that option was not open to them.

The New Testament itself is however the most important context for the problem of miracle, and the Synoptics in particular. There is then the significant question whether Luke's treatment differs redactionally from that in the other Gospels.

Some general observations may be made about the character and function of the Gospel miracles, though the degree of emphasis on these elements may prove to vary considerably between the evangelists. (1) Jesus' miracles were the overflow of his love and compassion when confronted by human need, even at times won from him against what might appear the overwhelming claims of his prior purposes in prayer or teaching. Here the injunctions to 'tell no man' find their place. Over against the sceptical assessment of these injunctions by W. Wrede and his followers, it may be urged that Jesus' concern against misunderstanding of his miracles and their detraction from his teaching ministry fortified his determination to do good in secret wherever this were desirable and so far as the enthusiasm of the crowds permitted it.[38] (2) Jesus' miracles were themselves a

---

[37] Kee, *Medicine, Miracle and Magic,* pp. 117-21.
[38] In the classic work of W. Wrede, *The Messianic Secret,* tr. J.C.G. Greig

vehicle of teaching, an emphasis strongest in John, but present in all the Gospels. Sometimes they were the actual occasion of controversy. It is important here to guard against two misunderstandings: (a) Jesus did not set up controversies to serve as a teaching vehicle, and then use miracle as a knock-down demonstration (though cf. the problem case of the withering of the fig-tree); (b) The explanation of miracles as merely symbolic, or as an acted visual aid, seems inadequate. The reports appear to concern real events on real occasions, provoked by authentic antecedent circumstances, where Jesus' response may assume a significance which goes beyond the occasion, but is not lightly to be set in antithesis with it. The idea that the miraculous was readily embroidered into a symbolic piece of teaching is the harder to sustain in the canonical Gospels because of the very reserve with which the miracles tend to be treated. (3) Jesus' miracles are directed to focus on his own person. Part of the essence of their teaching function is in the testimony they bear to him, a point in which the miracles of his followers differ strikingly, for they point *away* from the miracle-worker and again to Jesus himself. The immediate question raised by this observation of the Christocentric character of the miracles is of course whether this was actually Jesus' own self-understanding or only the redactional understanding of the early church. It is not my purpose here to go further than necessary into such debates, merely to observe that the motif of Jesus' Messianic self-understanding is deeply and extensively embedded in the Gospels. (4) The three preceding elements are not separate, but integrated in the presentation of the personality of Jesus. His compassion, brought to expression by circumstance, provides occasion for his further teaching and enlarged testimony to his Messiahship. (5) This concept of 'testimony' seems to be a crucial one, and especially so in Luke and in John. This touches on our preliminary point that the difficulty of miracle calls for an appropriately strong testimony, and this factor of authentication was recognized and developed in the perspective of the evangelists. (6) The whole question needs to be seen in the broader cultural context, in which scepticism and popular credulity were oddly mixed, if perhaps in a subtly different compound from that operative today. As there was widespread belief in the actuality of demonic and magical powers, it was part of the

(Cambridge and London: James Clarke, 1971) = *Das Messiasgeheimnis in den Evangelien* (Göttingen: Vandenhoeck & Ruprecht, 3rd edn., 1963 [1901]), the secrecy motif was a Markan structure to read back Messianic claims unhistorically into the life of Jesus himself. For recent discussion see J.D.G. Dunn, 'The Messianic Secret in Mark', *TB* 21 (1970), pp. 92-117; W.C. Robinson Jr., 'The Quest for Wrede's Secret Messiah', *Interpretation* 27 (1973), pp. 10-30.

evidential force of the miracles to demonstrate the loving and authentic power of God as superior to every rival claim. That was a valid function of the reports, if less apposite to our own case, because our difficulty is not in discriminating between miraculous claims but in accepting any.

Acts cannot be considered in isolation from the Third Gospel, though the pattern of miracle in the two parts appears to be substantially different, because of the personal uniqueness of Jesus as the subject of the one part and the differences in relationship to sources and of critical approach thereby engendered. A brief background discussion will concern Luke's differences from the other Gospels, for the comparison with Acts must await the fuller description of the evidence from that book.[39]

A survey of the Third Gospel to locate its incidence of miracle, and a further comparison of the relevant passages in the Synopsis, permits initially some general observations. The miraculous is rather unevenly distributed through the Gospel, which is notable for relevant incidents peculiar to it. This is especially true of the visions and angelic manifestations which precede and accompany the birth of John and the miraculous birth of Jesus himself. Other unique passages include the draught of fishes as a preliminary to Jesus' calling of the fishermen brothers (Lk. 5:1-11; cf. Mk 1:16-20; Mt. 4:18-22), the raising of the widow's son at Nain (Lk. 7:11-17), the healing of the deformed woman on the sabbath (Lk. 13:10-17) and of the dropsical man, also on the sabbath (Lk. 14:1-6), the cleansing of ten lepers (Lk. 17:11-19), the resurrection appearances on the Emmaus road (Lk. 24:13-35), in Jerusalem (36-49), and the summarized Ascension story (50-53). In basic content Luke thus stands relatively near the mainstream Synoptic tradition except in the special Nativity section and in his final chapter, both areas where the outworking of God's power assumes a prominent and distinctive role. Elsewhere miracles peculiar to this Gospel are relatively few, and the lengthy travel-section, which contains some, is focused more directly on teaching. Apart from these distinctive sections, the Lukan miracles are largely in the common tradition, and the interest focuses on the treatment of that tradition.[40]

---

[39] This subject has been relatively little studied. Cf. P.J. Achtemeier, 'The Lucan Perspective on the Miracles of Jesus: A Preliminary Sketch', *JBL* 94 (1975), pp. 547-62: 'The problem of the way Luke viewed and used the miracles of Jesus is a subject that has remained remarkably innocent of systematic treatment in recent Biblical scholarship' (p. 547).

[40] On Achtemeier's count (pp. 547-48), Mark has 18 miracle stories and 4 summaries of miraculous activity, Luke 20 stories and 3 summaries, Matthew 19 and 4, but Mark is about 57% the length of Luke and 63% of the length of

It is often very conservative, apart from stylistic alteration of Mark and abbreviation or omission of relatively otiose matter, where Luke expects more of his reader. But the phenomena are complex. The healing of the centurion's servant, for instance (Lk. 7:1-10) is longer than the Matthean parallel and differently placed (cf. Mt. 8:5-13), and the relation of both to John 4:46-54 is unclear. An especially important type of case is that which we have argued for earlier, where Luke's investigation has been brought to bear afresh on common tradition, as evidenced in 'L'-type additions and nuances. It is of interest that this critical perspective is particularly applicable to the miracle-stories. We could mention the case of the blind man at Jericho (Lk. 18:35-43) and the transfiguration (Lk. 9:28-36), and other miracles will repay study from a similar angle, to observe in them Luke's concern with testimony, context and audience. It is interesting that Luke sometimes repeats a difficulty embedded in the tradition conservatively, such as the sending of the demons into the pigs (Lk. 8:32-33 cf. Mk 5:11-13), but shortens, and omits a large estimate of their number. Elsewhere he enlarges just the sort of detail which reads as the product of first-hand testimony. It is less easy to present a controlled argument from his omissions, but it is worth observing that he gives a concise version of the feeding of 5,000 (Lk. 9:12-17), but omits the feeding of the 4,000; could it be that he felt a lack of sufficient independent authentication? Several additions clarify the context of a miracle (e.g. Lk. 5:18, 19; 6:6, 7), or give details unmentioned elsewhere, like the casting of 'seven demons' out of Mary Magdalene (Lk. 8:2).

These observations may be brought into clearer focus by the attempt to isolate Luke's distinctive attitudes to the miraculous. We have to look a little further to see how these individual incidents are embedded in a matrix of deeper significance. Luke's presentation of Jesus' self-consciousness, his prayer life, his knowledge of the hearts of others, his foreknowledge of his Passion, are paralleled in the other Synoptics, but specially prominent here. Thus Luke alone specifies Jesus' night of prayer before the calling of the Twelve (Lk. 6:12), the return of the Seventy with remarkable sayings of their power over demons (Lk. 10:17, 19) and the claim of Jesus to have seen Satan fall from heaven (Lk. 10:18), and the appearance of an angel strengthening him in Gethsemane (Lk. 22:43). Yet none of these things argue in Luke a gratuitous interest in miracle. Most of his extra

Matthew, so that proportionately the incidents are less frequent in Luke than in Mark. On this reckoning Luke has omitted 6 from Mark and added 8. Five of the 6 omissions occur in the 'Great Omission' of Mk 6:45-8:26, the sixth is the cursing of the fig tree.

examples are from the first two chapters and the last chapter of the Gospel, places where vision and visitation are intimately linked with the person and work of Christ himself. As in Mark, there is a notable change after Peter's confession, when Jesus is presented as preparing the disciples for the coming Passion.

God at work in providence and in judgment is all part of the irreducible content of the larger matrix within which the miracles operate in Luke. G.W.H. Lampe's essay on the miracles of Acts,[41] which includes preliminary consideration of the Gospel, is helpful here. For Luke the conception of the purpose of miracles is largely determined by the Old Testament. God's power is manifested in 'signs and wonders', but these are also associated closely with the teaching of Jesus and the proclamation of the Kingdom. Lampe distinguishes carefully between Luke's theocentric view and the first impression that he is the initiator of a long (and suspect) Christian tradition of apologetic through the power of miracle. Where God is at work, it is a secondary matter whether he does so through a real or apparent breach of the regularity of nature or through a providential guidance operating in the most mundane sequences of cause and effect. I agree then with Lampe's judgment that it is difficult to pick out the miraculous from the non-miraculous in Luke's story (*Miracles*, p. 171); but I remain sceptical of the thrust of his context, where he sees Luke's work as an 'impressionistic and "supernaturalized" account'.

The Miracles in Acts

The first task is to attempt a descriptive classification or categorization of the miracle material in Acts. There are various classifications on the market, whether form-critical, or arranged by subject-matter, moral or theological significance, or even credibility.[42] I am not

---

[41] Lampe in Moule, *Miracles*, pp. 165-78.

[42] For a helpful survey see F. Neirynck in Kremer, *Actes*, pp. 169-213. For classifications by content see Hardon in *CBQ* 16 (1954), pp. 303-307; Neirynck, pp. 170-71. For form-critical classification see Dibelius, *Studies*, pp. 12-24. The study and classification of motifs in G. Theissen, *The Miracle Stories of the Early Christian Tradition*, tr. F. McDonagh (Philadelphia: Fortress Press, 1983) extends across a much wider field, while focusing on the Gospels. See also G.J. Jordan, 'The Classification of the Miracles', *ExpT* 46 (1934-35), pp. 310-16. The tendency of all these classifications is to isolate narratives of particular types. Our present purpose is different, to illustrate how these specific *pericopae* are embedded in a theocentric world view whose manifestations are displayed in many nuances of thought, argument and reference where the 'apartness' of miracle is less significant.

concerned here with any theoretically based formulation, only with a simple descriptive demarcation of the range of the problem as a preliminary to an attempted analysis. A careful survey of the whole text shows afresh the need to cast the net wide, to pick up all the phenomena conditioned by Luke's theocentric world-view, even if specifically miraculous acts later prove to occupy a surprisingly tiny bulk within this totality. The first survey may thus appear inordinately extensive, but the difficulties which trouble the critical reader relatively few and brief. The miraculous act itself, for instance, is often told as a brief saying or event in a mundanely circumstantial context. Such is the raising of Dorcas/Tabitha, rich in human touches of grief and loving remembrance, although the crisis is treated in two words of Peter and the response, all within one verse (Acts 9:40).

We may observe the following ten categories:

(1) Divine events of fundamental significance for the history of salvation and of the Church and occurring within the limits of Acts, namely the Ascension and Pentecost, together with the divine manifestations recounted on those occasions.

(2) Other references to the great salvation events, including the Incarnation, Crucifixion and Resurrection, whether in narrative, or in the speeches, or proleptically, as in Jesus' foretelling of the Ascension and Pentecost (Acts 1:2, 5, 8).

(3) Acts of power, through Jesus or his disciples, which appear to involve explicit breaking of the regularities of nature, as understood then or now, whether inexplicable healings or 'nature' miracles.

(4) Incidents which may be, or may be implied to be, of the preceding category, but told with such reserve that the question may be left more or less open whether they are to be taken as miracle at all, even if it be granted that the ancient audience reacted with wonderment to them.

(5) General summarized references to unspecified 'signs and wonders'.

(6) Narratives, as of travel or circumstance, which involve nothing strictly miraculous, but where a sense of the overruling Providence of God is implicit: God is at work, even if the chain of events appears mundane.

(7) The explicit recognition of God's hand at work in things like the success of the Christian mission or conversely in the collapse and death of Herod Agrippa I as divine judgment through angelic agency (Acts 12:23).

(8) Ecstatic phenomena— visions, dreams and prophetic revelations, and 'psychological' miracles.

(9) The theme of scripture divinely fulfilled in Christ and in the Church as an argument testifying to God's action in history, a recurring feature of the argument of the speeches.

(10) Claims of magical and demonic opposition to God, and the perspective that God's power is superior to that of any pretended rival.

There is then a generalized difficulty for the modern reader embodied in the whole Christian world-view assumed and expressed in most of these categories, but it becomes specific and acute only perhaps in (1), (3), (8) and (10), and in (4) insofar as that involves discussion of the status of doubtful cases and is not simply subsumed under (3) or dissipated into natural rationalizations. I shall offer brief general comment on some of the principal categories, their extent and significance, and in particular on those of special difficulty.

The first two groups are straightforward (except in the sense that the Ascension and Pentecost pose problems of belief), but it is worth observing the sheer quantity of references in group (2). Thus we have allusion to the Resurrection in Acts 1:3, 22; 2:24, 31, 32; 3:15; 4:2, 10, 33; etc., mostly as the focus of argument in kerygmatic preaching.

The principal examples of (3) are diverse in type, but gathered here for the type of difficulty they present. There is the healing of the lame man at the Beautiful Gate (Acts 3:1-10), Peter's knowledge and judgment over Ananias and Sapphira (5:1-11), the efficacy of Peter's shadow (5:15), the blinding and restoration of Saul (9:8, 18), the healing of the paralytic Aeneas at Lydda (9:33-35) and of Tabitha at Joppa (9:36-42), the temporary blinding of Bar-Jesus/Elymas (13:11-12), the healing of the cripple at Lystra (14:8-10), the casting out of the demon from the girl fortune-teller at Philippi (16:16-18), the efficacy of handkerchiefs and aprons from Paul at Ephesus (19:12), the raising of Eutychus at Troas (20:8-12), and the healing of Publius' father (28:8). That is a remarkably short list, though other incidents might well be considered to belong here. We must certainly add the two releases from prison (5:19-21 and 12:7-10), where the agency might possibly be explained without recourse to the supernatural, the earthquake and opening of the prison at Philippi (16:25-26), Paul's foresight and authority in the storm and shipwreck (e.g. 27:10, 31, 34), and the snake incident in Malta (28:3-6), as possible representatives of the elusive category (4).

Luke shows no such reserve in mentioning in general summaries the occurrence of unspecified miracles as he does in documenting specifics. Type (5) summaries are found at 2:43; 5:12, 16; 6:8; 8:6-7, 13; 19:11; 28:9. It is worth making the point that where similar summaries occur in the Third Gospel they commonly have parallels, and cannot then be automatically dismissed as simplistically redactional: thus Lk. 4:40-41 with Mk 1:32-34 and Mt. 8:16-17; Lk. 6:17-19 with Mk 3:8-10 (where Luke's editing stresses Jesus' δύναμις); Lk. 7:18-22 with Mt. 11:2-5. It is also worth noting that Paul is able to make similar summaries: he mentions signs, wonders and miracles as credentials of an apostle, and includes his own ministry.

Two simple examples of type (6) will suffice. The meeting of Philip with the Ethiopian just at the time when he was puzzled by a scripture apt to Philip's message (Acts 8:30-35), and, much more elaborately, the climatic and geographical factors involved in the voyage to Malta are essentially natural and in the latter case minutely circumstantial throughout, while marked by a timing or direction irreducibly providential. Type (7) is akin. Some examples might be regarded as little more than pious phraseology, save that the language is expressing Luke's fundamental conviction. It is God who opened a door of faith to the Gentiles (14:27); Paul and Barnabas report 'what God had done with them' (15:4); a decision is made under a sense of divine authority: 'it has seemed good to the Holy Spirit and to us' (15:28).

Ecstatic and psychological/spiritual phenomena are perhaps the hardest class to handle, partly because of differences of cultural assumptions, partly through difficulties of demonization and secondary cross-currents. A first point to stress is that the attribution of ecstatic experiences to Paul in Acts concurs in principle with his own testimony in his own undisputed writings. It is enough to cite 1 Cor. 14:18 and especially 2 Cor. 12:1-7. The occurrence of ecstatic phenomena is a matter which will scarcely be denied absolutely, whatever explanation or rationalization be offered for them. Examples in Acts are fairly numerous, and they are present in 'we-passages' and other sections of the book where the source-material seems to be particularly full and direct. An angel, and, again, the Holy Spirit speak to Philip (8:26-29); Ananias converses with the Lord in a vision 9:10-16). In the Cornelius narrative there is a series of visions and divine communications (10:3-6, 10-16, 19-20, and Peter's reports of them in ch. 11). The Spirit calls Barnabas and Saul to mission (13:2), and frustrates Paul's plans (16:6, 7) before the positive vision of 16:9. Paul is strengthened by visions to face need or suffering (18:9-10; 23:11; 27:23-24; cf. Lk. 22:43). Information is conveyed through the prophetic interventions of Agabus (11:28; 21:11), and there is reference to the prophesying daughters of Philip (21:9). Other passages speak in simpler terms of persons 'filled with the Holy Spirit' receiving great grace to testify, or the like (4:31, 33; 7:55-56; etc.). A specific case, which brings us back to category (1), is that of *glossolalia*, apparently associated on each occasion in Acts with a distinctive new break-through of the Gospel message (2:4; 10:46; 19:6) and ostensibly to be distinguished from the xenoglossy of 2:6-11. This last observation leads us to stress, if only as an addendum to (1), that unusual mani-festations, like the men in white at the Ascension (1:10) and the tongues of fire at Pentecost (2:3), are festooned around the events of God's crucial interventions. Again, the problem of *glossolalia* was a practical issue for the Paul of the *Hauptbriefe* (1 Cor. 14).

This welter of phenomena is a strangely mixed bag, and may indeed be open to diverse analysis. One desirable interim remark is to note the tendency in modern thought to explain even in the uncon-genial frame of psychological or spiritual miracle divine events which Christians have traditionally understood as literal and physical miracle, in fact to collapse the ostensible but unthinkable members of categories (1) or (3) into (8).[43]

The fulfilment of scripture is a motif widespread in the New Tes-tament, and most conspicuous in places like the Matthean Nativity story, where the incidents are so constantly linked to the Old Testa-ment as to suggest to some scholars the view that the whole is a 'mid-rashic' creation from the prophecies.[44] The perspective in Acts is slightly different, as this factor is used as providing an explanation or argument, or a guide to action. It will suffice to cite Acts 1:16-20; 2:16-21, 25-28; 3:18, 23-24; 8:32-33; 13:33-35; 15:16-18; 17:11; 18:28; 23:5; 28:23, 26-27. The whole theme may seem distinct from our current focus on miracle, and not sensitive in the same way. The point is that it belongs integrally to Luke's theocentric view, within which miracle is merely one, somewhat arbitrarily isolated, sphere of God's total ini-tiative and activity.

The final category belongs to a different realm of ideas altogether, the notion of superhuman powers wielded by enemies of the Gospel. There are the magic powers of Simon Magus (8:9-11), the girl with the evil spirit at Philippi (16:16-18), depicted as one who possessed de-monic knowledge of the mission of Paul and Silas, the sons of Scaeva at Ephesus (19:13-16), and the consequent overcoming of magicians and the burning of the magic books of new converts (19:19). This group is again troublesome to the modern reader, for the super-natural in any form is a difficulty, whereas Luke lives in a world where different kinds are on the market, and it is sometimes a

---

43 On a point of recent controversy which appears to highlight a similar issue see the discussion of the views of Bishop Jenkins in M.J. Harris, *Easter in Durham* (Exeter: Paternoster, 1985).

44 See however, R.T. France and D. Wenham (eds.), *Gospel Perspectives III*,(1983).

relevant argument to set the power of God over against any inadequate rival claim.

This, of course, has been a mere survey of the ground. It may be granted that there are some marked differences between the phenomena of Acts and of the Gospel, but these are easily explained in principle. (a) The person of Jesus is unique, and the salvific events focused on him have no direct counterpart in the lives of his followers, even though we may claim to trace literary parallels, especially between Jesus and Paul. (b) The Gospel is considerably controlled by its sources, and the base of Luke's portrayal of miracle is strongly conditioned by the common Synoptic tradition, whereas in Acts he had a freer hand to express his concept of historiography through a selection and presentation more independent of fixed tradition or written documents. (c) The perspective is different, being on the other side of the Passion and Resurrection. Apart from the distinct differences of content and treatment engendered by these factors, it may be claimed that there is a notable consistency in Luke's treatment, and this makes occasional comparison fruitful.

Observations

It is specifically the difficulty over miracle which lies at the root of much of our present impasse over Acts. The difficulty for the modern mind of a text embodying miracle has been the first stimulus to reinterpretation, and that reinterpretation of the text has led finally into improbabilities and the rejection of awkward collateral evidence. We must somehow retrace our steps at least to the dividing of the ways where the evidence may come again into its own.

The factor of differing world-views cannot be avoided here. It would be comfortable to suppose that we might settle the matter empirically, and indeed it is important to try so far as possible. But presuppositions are inevitably involved. Post-Enlightenment thought may take an absolute position that miracles do not happen, and that *all* alleged instances must accordingly be either rejected or re-explained. Such a position is, however, dogmatic, not empirical. To say that is not to attack it unfairly, but to insist that we recognize the status of this doctrine. It is rooted in a specific world-view. It is none the worse for that if that world-view happens to be correct, but that is a point at issue.[45] The same argument could equally be turned on a

---

45 Cf. D.E. Nineham, *The Use and Abuse of the Bible* (London: Macmillan, 1976) for a classic recent statement of the post-Enlightenment view arguing for a deep separation of viable world-views before and after the watershed. For a response to Nineham see R.H. Preston, 'Need Dr Nineham Be So Negative?' *ExpT* 90

dogmatically supernaturalist view. Even when we strive to be scrupulously fair, we are operating here in a context of irreducibly conflicting world-views, and the attempt to be scientifically empirical must at least try to wrestle with contrary options.

There is a subtle cultural factor built into differences of presupposition. For some cultures, even today, miracle is regarded as an authenticating feature, whereas for the critical Western mind it is the reverse: an acute difficulty. In Acts itself there are some instances of miracle as authentication (e.g. 2:43; 8:6-7; 19:11-12), coupled with other kinds of evidence more congenial to ourselves. There are complementary points to be made here. We ought not to be arrogant in disdaining the intelligence of those who think differently from ourselves.[46] Conversely, however, we must recognize that our own approach must be critical, in the best sense of that term, and must use different criteria of authentication. If we accept a narrative in Acts, and the miraculous element in it in particular, that will be rather *in spite of* the miracle than because of it.

Against that background we may suggest that there was for Luke a legitimate argument *from* miracle, to be balanced also against his insistence that the unbelieving will not be convinced by miracle any more than by the scriptural evidence otherwise available to them (Lk. 16:27-31). In other words, people were convinced they had witnessed inexplicable healings, and that made them think. The explanation on offer was that these things were done in the name of Jesus, and the power of his Spirit was made manifest in his followers. Luke himself was convinced of such, even in the face of what may have been a natural scepticism. It did convince others, and he duly says it did. The pattern can be seen in Acts 2:12; 3:10, where the amazement of the people in each case provides the setting for an explanatory

(1978-79), pp. 275-80.

[46] There is a danger of what C.S. Lewis (*Surprised by Joy* [London: Collins, 1969], p. 166) has called 'chronological snobbery' in the treatment of cultures of the past. It may be suggested rather that past cultures often differ from our own in the same kinds of ways that diverse modern cultures do. The Japanese, for instance, would appear to have entered the modern technological world through processes of intellectual history so unlike our own that while they have a pervasive sense of the divine in life and nature (*kami*) such as a Westerner might call pantheistic or panentheistic, the notion of a personal God presents acute conceptual difficulty to them. It is likewise unwise to underestimate the ancients merely because they were different. Sometimes we know *more*, because knowledge is cumulative, though particular skills may be forgotten. More often the real difference is simply one of cultural milieu, even in matters where they most strikingly anticipated us. The complexity of the ancient world merits the most careful and detailed study.

address by Peter, and faith responds to the preaching which explains the miracle.

Such a world-view may be condemned by some as untenable today. But this is another dogmatic judgment, and dogmatic in a less innocent way, if it is made to serve as a presuppositional base for illegitimizing not only a contrary, or more open, presupposition, but the debate itself.

The whole preceding point, itself an attempt to state a balance, must itself be balanced in turn from a different angle. I have perhaps implied an underlying separation of modern Western thinking from Biblical culture. But the ancient world was itself extraordinarily complex and diverse. People then were capable of being as hard-headedly sceptical (or as credulous) as we are today. A transcendental Christianity could capture the mind of a Jewish intellectual of the calibre of Paul and not the followers of cults and magical practices and horoscopes who might be deemed among the more credulous elements in that society. (Perhaps such an eccentric comparison is not without its relevance to our own day). But that too could be a misleading oversimplification, for even the scepticism of those times came out of a subtly different soil. The lines between the divine and the mechanistic were differently drawn. Yet when all such necessary qualifications are made, it is reasonable to insist that Luke needed to authenticate his case before educated and sophisticated readers, fully capable, *mutatis mutandis*, of subjecting him to keenly critical assessment. If Acts is in any serious degree intended to be apologetic to outsiders in a religious and not merely a political sense, it must be presumed to address itself seriously to the problems of authentication.[47]

It may be claimed that even if the question of miracle must technically be left open, it is very unlikely, and a specially strict standard of accreditation must be required of alleged instances. This doubt may be held in a stronger or a weaker form. In the former the implication may be that the standard required is so rigorous that no testimony can ever in practice fulfil it. In that case the doubt amounts to a practical assertion of the dogmatic position, merely meeting the previous objection by a formal concession to the appearance of empiricism. In its latter form, however, this doubt may be correct to require testimony as strong as can reasonably be expected before entertaining seriously the possibility of events which are unusual or conceptually

---

[47] I have dealt previously with the assumption that the ancients were not capable of an interest in 'what really happened', see above, ch. 3. This implication is held directly in the face of the concerns of writers like Thucydides, Polybius and Lucian, and may be cited as an example of the 'chronological snobbery' of the preceding note.

difficult. Testimony can only be of a strength appropriate to the case, not of an artificially watertight completeness impervious to doubt or criticism. There can thus be a legitimate type of critical study which accepts some miracles and rejects others. It is possible, in theory, to conceive criteria for acceptance, however difficult in practice to attain agreement about them. The difficulty does not invalidate the principle. It is possible that Luke's reserve in the matter of reporting miracles illustrates that, despite the cultural gap, he was operating on a similar principle.[48]

A further complexity is introduced by a modern issue over the nature of faith. Recent post-Enlightenment thought has been heavily influenced by a disposition to see faith in existential terms. But existential faith and the Biblical argument for faith are significantly different in substance. In the former, faith as trust is stressed to the initial exclusion of faith as assent, but the New Testament argument is for trust which goes beyond (but includes) assent to a practical sufficiency of relevant evidence. It is assent plus trust, not trust apart from assent. Indeed the factor of assent to what is believed true is an essential one, for trust apart from discrimination of objective may be a commitment to the false or unreliable or harmful. There is no virtue in commitment (if that becomes a justifying 'work') apart from the goodness of its object. One sees the problem, for instance, in Dibelius' treatment of the word πίστις in Acts 17:31 (*Studies*, pp. 57, 62-63) as a usage alien to the New Testament. While this sense of this word may be peculiar to this passage, it is frequent in secular Greek, and therefore natural enough in address to a Gentile audience. It expresses an idea of 'proof' or the 'confirmation of truth' which is intimately linked to the concept of 'witness' as testimony to the truth, a motif widespread in Luke and John.[49] The effect of the modern trend is to remove the questions of miracle from the agenda, as unimportant

---

[48] It is clear that ancient writers were not completely naïve or gullible, but accepted or rejected miraculous stories on the basis of their regard for the evidence, albeit differently weighted than modern historians. See for example Herodotus (2.73) on the story of the Phoenix.

[49] The treatment of πίστις and its cognates in the theological dictionaries takes no adequate account of this kind of usage. The work of Bultmann in *TDNT*, Turner in *Christian Words* and the like are are open to the strictures of James Barr (*Semantics*, pp. 275-76). A particular fallacy is that which tries to assimilate diverse usages of a word in different contexts to a regular, theologically technical 'Christian' usage, exclusive of other natural variations of its contemporary semantic field. C. Gilmour, 'The Development of the Language of Faith, A Historical Survey', *Prudentia* 17 (1985), pp. 55-70, is not exempt from this pitfall. For the concept of 'witness', especially in the Lukan and Johannine writings cf. A.A. Trites, *The New Testament Concept of Witness* (CUP, 1977).

from its perspective, thus reinforcing scepticism on this ground by dismissing the problem. But a strong converse point needs to be made. It is the historical facts, and that of the supranatural resurrection in particular, which form the confirmation of Paul's appeal to the Athenians and the base of his argument. A modern approach which rejects the base and the argument as then understood and reinterprets 'faith' must recognize that it is cutting away the object of its own existential appeal. If that object had no reasonable claim to truth in the first place, there never was any substance in Christianity, and the existential appeal is directed to wishful thinking, at odds with reality as interpreted apart from the Christian claims. We might do better in that case to cut our losses than to perpetuate confusion by clinging to the language of an exploded myth become a pretence.

The relationship between miracle and teaching merits further thought. There is an evident difference, relevant to the call above for the establishment of criteria, between the miracles of the New Testament and those of the Apocryphal Gospels and Acts, which indulge wonders for their own sake.[50] It may be claimed, in the broadest terms, that the miracles of the Gospels and Acts are the vehicle of teaching. This factor is sometimes, rather strangely, made the occasion for an exclusive polarization between event and teaching, where the teaching is detached from a context treated with the disbelief or lack of interest. A reversal of this may as readily be argued, that the importance of the teaching prompted the careful record of miracle which had teaching or evidential value, against a background rather reserved than otherwise towards miracle because of the handle it might give to misunderstanding, to superficial curiosity or sensation.[51]

We have presented no easy way out of the problem, but there is equally no *a priori* ground for dismissing Luke's qualities simply because he reports miracle. If he is not radically mistaken in his view of a transcendental God incarnated in man, the factor of miracle may even be accepted in principle as a natural corollary of that *Weltanschauung*. There is a profound difficulty in the assumption that the Enlightenment marks an essential divide in the history of Western

---

[50] See M.R. James, *The Apocryphal New Testament* (Oxford: Clarendon Press, 1924). Thus the contrast between Peter and Simon Magus is introduced by a speaking dog, and Peter wins believers by taking a dead sardine hanging in a window and casting it into a bath, where it proceeds to live and swim (*Acts of Peter* 12-13, James, pp. 315-16; cf. Lampe in Moule, *Miracles*, pp. 165-66).

[51] See the fullest recent discussion in C. Brown, *Miracles and the Critical Mind*, esp. Chapter 10. Cf. *id.*, *That You May Believe. Miracles and Faith Then and Now* (Grand Rapids: Eerdmans and Exeter: Paternoster, 1985).

thought, the more sensitive when many scholars are avowed and professing Christians, whatever the presuppositional framework which they feel obliged to assume as scholars.[52] It is not really a matter of saying that as scholars they cannot import their existential beliefs but must be open-minded and properly sceptical and presuppositionless, for the Enlightenment imposes, not freedom from presupposition, but contrary presuppositions. I am all for open-mindedness, but uneasy when people seem to be compounding their own problems by appearing to work in different contexts from contradictory presuppositions. Yet I am happier not to be entangled with these cross-currents. I am content to operate in a framework where the possibility of miracle is accepted and its appearance is not an automatic cue for reinterpretation or special interpretation.

---

[52] If we hold a supranaturalist world-view, exemplified in the acceptance of a traditional understanding of the resurrection of Jesus, we are immediately in a different ball-game. Within that framework we may still require reasonably rigorous testimony before admitting other miracles, but their possibility may be accepted in principle.

Appendix 2
The God-Fearers[1]

The Aphrodisias Find[2]

At the recent excavations connected with the construction of a new museum at Aphrodisias, a large stele was unearthed bearing legible inscriptions on two of its four faces. Face *a*, it appears, was to inform the reader about a building[3] and a list of the donors who initiated the project, while face *b* presents two lists of names of other people associated with the project. Despite the fact that there is no Hebrew, nor any hint betraying knowledge of that language, the large number of Jewish names and other features[4] make it virtually certain that we are dealing here with a donation by a synagogue. The list on face *a* seems to be made up of a council of some sort, the δεκανία,[5] while side *b* contains two lists of ordinary members of the Jewish community at Aphrodisias, who presumably also contributed to the project initiated by the decany. Although the two faces of the stele have been cut in different hands, it seems most likely that they are contemporary, from the third century AD.[6]

In the list on face *a*, three of the people are specifically called προσήλυτος (ll. 13, 17, 22) and two more are given the title θεοσεβής (ll. 19, 20). The two lists on face *b* probably were each titled, but only the second heading remains: ὅσοι θεοσεβῖς; the upper list presumably originally bore the heading: Ἰουδαῖοι.[7] Aside from the three proselytes, 54 are called *theosebeis*, and about 55 seem simply to be

---

1   By the editor.

2   J. Reynolds and R. Tannenbaum, *Jews and God-fearers at Aphrodisias: Greek Inscriptions with Commentary* Proceedings of the Cambridge Philological Association Supp. 12 (Cambridge Philological Society, 1987).

3   Tannenbaum suggests that what was being dedicated was a charity-food distribution centre, interpreting πατέλλα along the lines of 'soup-kitchen'. See Reynolds and Tannenbaum, *Jews and God-fearers*, p. 27.

4   Such as the phrase οἱ ὑποτεταγμένοι, face *a*, ll. 2-3, paralleled at a synagogue in Cyrenaica; see Reynolds and Tannenbaum, *Jews and God-fearers*, p. 28.

5   Cf. *CIJ* 1.11, where the word is mistaken for a name, if Tannenbaum is correct. Reynolds and Tannenbaum, *Jews and God-fearers*, pp. 28-38.

6   Reynolds and Tannenbaum, *Jews and God-fearers*, pp. 19-22.

7   Thus Tannenbaum, *Jews and God-fearers*, p. 47.

names of Jews.[8]

Several inferences can be drawn from this new evidence:

(1) The heading on face *b* suggests that 'God-fearer' was a title rather than a mere descriptive phrase, although if we had only face *a* either interpretation would be possible.

(2) The title 'God-fearer' seems to have referred to Gentiles. The onomastic data makes plain that the list on face *a* and the upper list on face *b* are made up of Jews, while the names in the list of *theosebeis* are Gentile.[9]

(3) There is a clear distinction made between proselytes and 'God-fearers' as seen in the names on face *a*.

(4) The fact that two 'God-fearers' are listed among the decany suggests that they were regarded to some extent as members of the community, but the separate listing on face *b* would seem to show that they were not incorporated fully into the community without distinctions.[10]

Drawing Conclusions from Evidence

There has, of late, been some discussion about the appropriateness of using the term 'God-fearer' as a technical term for a group of Gentiles hovering around synagogues. In some respects, the questioning started with the essay by Kirsopp Lake in *Beginnings of Christianity*,[11] which argued that the term could be used equally well as a description of a person's piety, whether they were Jew or Gentile, as opposed to specifically referring to non-circumcised adherents. Wilcox has picked up this argument, showing fairly clearly that, although the evidence for the traditional understanding of these

---

[8] The names of the fathers of some of the contributors are present as well, so that we possess more names than actual contributors.

[9] There are, of course, exceptions; see Reynolds and Tannenbaum, *Jews and God-fearers*, pp. 55-56. Of the c. 63 names (as opposed to contributors) in the list of 'God-fearers', there are only two specifically Jewish names, and in both cases, the fathers' names are Gentile. A further two names are Graeco-Roman names known to have been popular with Jews (but also used by non-Jews) and one more is of questionable origin.

[10] It is interesting to note that the 'God-fearers' seem to have been regarded as a somewhat inferior class, to judge from the placement on both lists (the 'God-fearers' were last on the *original* list on face *a* as well, cf. Reynolds and Tannenbaum, *Jews and God-fearers*, p. 4), but only in terms of their status *in the synagogue*, not in terms of their status in society, since there are 9 members of the city council on the list! (face *b*, ll. 34-38, cf. *Jews and God-fearers*, p. 55.)

[11] BC 'Proselytes and God-fearers' 5.74-96.

'God-fearers' has a sort of internal consistency, it is fundamentally a circular kind of proof.[12] The point is a sound one, and, much like Roger Cowley's work on parallel phenomena, a useful caution against taking terms known from a single author as technical terms used by a whole culture.[13] Wilcox does not claim to have established the absence of a technical use of 'God-fearers', but rather is counselling caution in the face of the then insufficient evidence. Thus, he writes, 'the expressions ... in Acts ought not *without further evidence* be interpreted as referring to a class of Gentile synagogue adherents rather than to members of the Jewish community, whether Jewish by birth or by conversion'[emphasis mine].[14]

A.T. Kraabel, on the other hand, has built an argument upon the silence of archaeological evidence.[15] He calls the traditional understanding of 'God-fearers' a 'serious misreading of the evidence',[16] and after listing six Diaspora synagogues that have been excavated without providing unambiguous testimony for the 'God-fearers', and reciting modern 'critical' dogma that 'neither the theology of Paul nor the chronology of his career, as found in Acts, can be made to line up with the Pauline epistles',[17] he concludes that the whole institution is a Lukan invention, made necessary by the evangelist's theological programme.[18] He further concludes from this that 'Luke's freedom to rewrite a part of early Christian history in this fashion surely says something about his distance from the events, that is, about the date of the writing of Acts'.[19]

Kraabel's paper was given on several occasions, the most recent version being the published one, which contains the sentence 'new evidence required to falsify this hypothesis would have to be substantial; one clear inscription ... would be helpful, but not sufficient ...'

---

[12] M. Wilcox, 'The "God-Fearers" in Acts: A Reconsideration', *JSNT* 13 (1981), pp. 102-122.

[13] See R.W. Cowley, 'Technical Terms in Biblical Hebrew?' *TB* 37 (1986), pp. 21-28.

[14] Wilcox, 'God-Fearers', p. 115.

[15] A.T. Kraabel, 'The Disappearance of the "God-fearers"', *Numen* 28 (1981), pp. 113-126; cf. also 'The Roman Diaspora: Six Questionable Assumptions', *JJS* 33 (1982), pp. 445-462.

[16] Kraabel, 'Disappearance', p. 113.

[17] Kraabel, 'Disappearance', p. 118.

[18] 'Acts cannot be used as evidence that there ever were such groups in the synagogues of the Roman Empire. It is a tribute to Luke's dramatic ability that they have become so alive for the later Church, but the evidence ... from archaeology makes their historicity questionable in the extreme,' Kraabel, 'Disappearance', p. 120.

[19] Kraabel, 'Disappearance', p. 125 n. 24.

after which follows a reference to the forthcoming publication of the Aphrodisias inscription.[20] While it is true that Acts and the inscription use slightly different terms to speak of the 'God-fearers', Kraabel's ideas about the non-existence of such a group of people have been shown to be without basis. The inscription confirms the three points about the institution that he has set out to deny: (1) that 'God-fearers' can be a term employed specifically for Gentiles, (2) that they are found in significant numbers, and (3) that they were not full members of the Jewish community, and as such were ripe for Christian conversion.[21]

What remains is to stress the correctness of caution. Showing Kraabel's errors is a long way from demonstrating the accuracy of Acts on this matter; a number of questions remain. The differences in terminology employed by Luke ($\phi o\beta o\acute{u}\mu\epsilon\nu o\varsigma$ $\tau\grave{o}\nu$ $\theta\epsilon\acute{o}\nu$, $\sigma\epsilon\beta\acute{o}\mu\epsilon\nu o\varsigma$ $\tau\grave{o}\nu$ $\theta\epsilon\acute{o}\nu$) and by the inscription ($\theta\epsilon o\sigma\epsilon\beta\acute{\eta}\varsigma$) keep us still from seeing something like a technical term for a category of people in Acts. Similarly, we are not yet in possession of enough evidence to speak confidently about how commonplace such a community of 'God-fearers' might be. Most notably, the inscription has been estimated to have originated in the third century AD, whereas Acts claims to picture the situation before the fall of Jerusalem. All we can say with confidence is that there were in at least some places numbers of Gentiles who were close enough to Judaism to be considered part of the community, albeit a separate part, without becoming full proselytes. The picture presented in Acts may or may not be anachronistic, but it can no longer be thought of as preposterous, or the work of a theologically inspired imagination.[22]

---

[20] Kraabel, 'Disappearance', pp. 121, 125f. n. 26.

[21] These three points are to be found in Kraabel, 'Disappearance', p. 114.

[22] Among the other recent literature about the 'God-fearers', see T.M. Finn, 'The God-fearers Reconsidered', *CBQ* 47 (1985), pp. 75-84; J.G. Gager, 'Jews, Gentiles and Synagogues in the Book of Acts', *HTR* 79 (1986), pp. 91-99 (Gager writes before the publication of the Aphrodisias inscription but with considerable knowledge of it and similar older evidence overlooked by Kraabel); A.T. Kraabel, 'Greeks, Jews and Lutherans in the Middle Half of Acts', *HTR* 79 (1986), pp. 147-57; S.J.D. Cohen, 'Respect for Judaism By Gentiles According to Josephus', *HTR* 80 (1987), pp. 409-30; M.H. Williams, '$\theta\epsilon o\sigma\epsilon\beta\grave{\eta}\varsigma$ $\gamma\grave{\alpha}\rho$ $\mathring{\eta}\nu$— The Jewish Tendencies of Poppæa Sabina', *JTS* 39 (1988), pp. 97-111; and J.A. Overman, 'The God-fearers: Some Neglected Features', *JSNT* 32 (1988), pp. 17-26.

Index of Biblical References

Index of Ancient Non-Literary Sources

Inscriptions

The '=' sign is used in the text of this book to indicate when a different collection is referring to the same piece of stone, although the editors' reconstructions of the text may be different. For the sake of completeness, even such duplicate listings have been entered into this index.

Index of Ancient Literary Sources

Index of Place Names

Index of Modern Authors

Index of Subjects

CPSIA information can be obtained
at www.ICGtesting.com
Printed in the USA
FSHW04n1005060418
46614FS

9 781575 063966